Visual Basic® 6 Database Programming Bible

Visual Basic® 6 Database Programming Bible

Wayne S. Freeze

IDG Books Worldwide, Inc.
An International Data Group Company

Foster City, CA ✦ Chicago, IL ✦ Indianapolis, IN ✦ New York, NY

Visual Basic® 6 Database Programming Bible
Published by
IDG Books Worldwide, Inc.
An International Data Group Company
919 E. Hillsdale Blvd., Suite 400
Foster City, CA 94404
www.idgbooks.com (IDG Books Worldwide Web site)

ISBN: 0-7645-4728-3

Printed in the United States of America

10 9 8 7 6 5 4 3 2 1

1O/TR/QY/QQ/FC

Distributed in the United States by IDG Books Worldwide, Inc.

Distributed by CDG Books Canada Inc. for Canada; by Transworld Publishers Limited in the United Kingdom; by IDG Norge Books for Norway; by IDG Sweden Books for Sweden; by IDG Books Australia Publishing Corporation Pty. Ltd. for Australia and New Zealand; by TransQuest Publishers Pte Ltd. for Singapore, Malaysia, Thailand, Indonesia, and Hong Kong; by Gotop Information Inc. for Taiwan; by ICG Muse, Inc. for Japan; by Intersoft for South Africa; by Eyrolles for France; by International Thomson Publishing for Germany, Austria, and Switzerland; by Distribuidora Cuspide for Argentina; by LR International for Brazil; by Galileo Libros for Chile; by Ediciones ZETA S.C.R. Ltda. for Peru; by WS Computer Publishing Corporation, Inc., for the Philippines; by Contemporanea de Ediciones for Venezuela; by Express Computer Distributors for the Caribbean and West Indies; by Micronesia Media Distributor, Inc. for Micronesia; by Chips Computadoras S.A. de C.V. for Mexico; by Editorial Norma de Panama S.A. for Panama; by American Bookshops for Finland.

For general information on IDG Books Worldwide's books in the U.S., please call our Consumer Customer Service department at 800-762-2974. For reseller information, including discounts and premium sales, please call our Reseller Customer Service department at 800-434-3422.

For information on where to purchase IDG Books Worldwide's books outside the U.S., please contact our International Sales department at 317-596-5530 or fax 317-572-4002.

For consumer information on foreign language translations, please contact our Customer Service department at 800-434-3422, fax 317-572-4002, or e-mail rights@idgbooks.com.

For information on licensing foreign or domestic rights, please phone +1-650-653-7098.

For sales inquiries and special prices for bulk quantities, please contact our Order Services department at 800-434-3422 or write to the address above.

For information on using IDG Books Worldwide's books in the classroom or for ordering examination copies, please contact our Educational Sales department at 800-434-2086 or fax 317-572-4005.

For press review copies, author interviews, or other publicity information, please contact our Public Relations department at 650-653-7000 or fax 650-653-7500.

For authorization to photocopy items for corporate, personal, or educational use, please contact Copyright Clearance Center, 222 Rosewood Drive, Danvers, MA 01923, or fax 978-750-4470.

Library of Congress Cataloging-in-Publication Data

Freeze, Wayne S.
Visual Basic 6 Database programming bible / Wayne S. Freeze.
p. cm.
ISBN 0-7645-4728-3 (alk. paper)
1. Web databases. 2. Client/server computing. 3. Microsoft Visual BASIC. I. Title.
QA76.9.W43 f74 2000
005.75'8--dc21 00-058197

ABOUT IDG BOOKS WORLDWIDE

Welcome to the world of IDG Books Worldwide.

IDG Books Worldwide, Inc., is a subsidiary of International Data Group, the world's largest publisher of computer-related information and the leading global provider of information services on information technology. IDG was founded more than 30 years ago by Patrick J. McGovern and now employs more than 9,000 people worldwide. IDG publishes more than 290 computer publications in over 75 countries. More than 90 million people read one or more IDG publications each month.

Launched in 1990, IDG Books Worldwide is today the #1 publisher of best-selling computer books in the United States. We are proud to have received eight awards from the Computer Press Association in recognition of editorial excellence and three from Computer Currents' First Annual Readers' Choice Awards. Our best-selling *...For Dummies*® series has more than 50 million copies in print with translations in 31 languages. IDG Books Worldwide, through a joint venture with IDG's Hi-Tech Beijing, became the first U.S. publisher to publish a computer book in the People's Republic of China. In record time, IDG Books Worldwide has become the first choice for millions of readers around the world who want to learn how to better manage their businesses.

Our mission is simple: Every one of our books is designed to bring extra value and skill-building instructions to the reader. Our books are written by experts who understand and care about our readers. The knowledge base of our editorial staff comes from years of experience in publishing, education, and journalism — experience we use to produce books to carry us into the new millennium. In short, we care about books, so we attract the best people. We devote special attention to details such as audience, interior design, use of icons, and illustrations. And because we use an efficient process of authoring, editing, and desktop publishing our books electronically, we can spend more time ensuring superior content and less time on the technicalities of making books.

You can count on our commitment to deliver high-quality books at competitive prices on topics you want to read about. At IDG Books Worldwide, we continue in the IDG tradition of delivering quality for more than 30 years. You'll find no better book on a subject than one from IDG Books Worldwide.

John Kilcullen
Chairman and CEO
IDG Books Worldwide, Inc.

Eighth Annual Computer Press Awards 1992

Ninth Annual Computer Press Awards 1993

Tenth Annual Computer Press Awards 1994

Eleventh Annual Computer Press Awards 1995

IDG is the world's leading IT media, research and exposition company. Founded in 1964, IDG had 1997 revenues of $2.05 billion and has more than 9,000 employees worldwide. IDG offers the widest range of media options that reach IT buyers in 75 countries representing 95% of worldwide IT spending. IDG's diverse product and services portfolio spans six key areas including print publishing, online publishing, expositions and conferences, market research, education and training, and global marketing services. More than 90 million people read one or more of IDG's 290 magazines and newspapers, including IDG's leading global brands — Computerworld, PC World, Network World, Macworld and the Channel World family of publications. IDG Books Worldwide is one of the fastest-growing computer book publishers in the world, with more than 700 titles in 36 languages. The "...For Dummies®" series alone has more than 50 million copies in print. IDG offers online users the largest network of technology-specific Web sites around the world through IDG.net (http://www.idg.net), which comprises more than 225 targeted Web sites in 55 countries worldwide. International Data Corporation (IDC) is the world's largest provider of information technology data, analysis and consulting, with research centers in over 41 countries and more than 400 research analysts worldwide. IDG World Expo is a leading producer of more than 168 globally branded conferences and expositions in 35 countries including E3 (Electronic Entertainment Expo), Macworld Expo, ComNet, Windows World Expo, ICE (Internet Commerce Expo), Agenda, DEMO, and Spotlight. IDG's training subsidiary, ExecuTrain, is the world's largest computer training company, with more than 230 locations worldwide and 785 training courses. IDG Marketing Services helps industry-leading IT companies build international brand recognition by developing global integrated marketing programs via IDG's print, online and exposition products worldwide. Further information about the company can be found at www.idg.com.

1/26/00

Credits

Acquisitions Editor
Greg Croy

Project Editors
Brian MacDonald
Valerie Perry

Technical Editor
Allen Wyatt

Copy Editors
Gabrielle Chosney
Kevin Kent

Proof Editor
Neil Romanosky

Project Coordinators
Danette Nurse
Louigene A. Santos

Graphics and Production Specialist
Booklayers.com

Quality Control Technician
Dina F Quan

Media Development Specialist
Travis Silvers

Permissions Editor
Jessica Montgomery

Media Development Coordinator
Marisa Pearman

Permissions Editor
Jessica Montgomery

Media Development Manager
Stephen Noetzel

Proofreading and Indexing
York Production Services

Cover Illustration
Joanne Vuong

About the Author

Wayne S. Freeze is a full-time author and computer technology consultant. He has written nine different books on Visual Basic and SQL Server since he began his career three years ago.

He lives in Beltsville, Maryland, with his lovely wife, Jill, and their wonderful children, Christopher, age six, and Samantha, age five. Jill is a well-respected writer and Microsoft beta tester, specializing in Microsoft Office, Internet Explorer, and Windows. Chris is perhaps the youngest person to beta test software for Microsoft, having tested both Windows 98 and Microsoft Millennium, among other products, in his short career. Sam, on the other hand, loves to sit on Wayne's lap, and one day hopes to write books just like her mom and dad.

Together, they live in a house full of animals, including a golden retriever named Lady Kokomo and four cats named Pixel, Terry, Cali, and Dusty. Wayne also has a pet stingray named Raymond, after his father-in-law. Raymond loves to eat worms from Wayne's hand (the stingray, that is, not his father-in-law).

Wayne maintains a Web site at `www.JustPC.com` that contains information about the various books he and his wife have written. Please take the time to visit their Web site and sign their guest book.

This book is dedicated to the newest member of my family, Dusty.

Preface

With respect to the development of database applications, Visual Basic is the language of choice for programmers all over the world. There are many reasons they choose Visual Basic: one, it is easy to learn how to use; two, you can build complex applications faster in Visual Basic than in any other programming language; and three, Visual Basic programs are easy to debug. In addition, there is a lot of specialized support built into Visual Basic for developing database applications. Not only can you develop traditional, forms-oriented database applications using Visual Basic, you can also use it to develop backend database programs for your Web server that are far more efficient than traditional PERL scripts or Active Server Pages.

Most of the Visual Basic books on the market today, however, downplay these database aspects in favor of all of the other neat features built into the language. While calling API functions from Visual Basic and developing Add-ins for the IDE can be useful topics, I cover far more database-oriented material than you would find in a typical Visual Basic programming book by focusing strictly on database programming aspects. You'll benefit from the more focused coverage, because you'll learn about the database features that you need to know and which will make you a more productive database programmer.

Who Should Read This Book

If you read the back cover, you'll find that this book is aimed at beginning to advanced readers. That's quite a challenge. I don't want to bore advanced programmers, who may want to learn those dirty tricks that would make their applications more efficient, yet I don't want to lose novice database programmers who could benefit from those same tricks.

I'm going to assume that everyone reading this book is familiar with how to create and debug a Visual Basic program — not just the simple "Hello World" variety, but one that had so much code, for instance, it didn't work the first time you tried to compile and run it. I'll introduce you to any other information you'll need beyond this level.

Advanced readers may benefit fromsome of the more introductory material, because I often use nontraditional ways of doing things. (I'm known as The Lazy Programmer, because I try to take advantage of every shortcut available to me, as long as it saves me work in the long run.) After this initial review, advanced readers can then dig into why they should be using both the COM+ Transaction Server and the Microsoft Message Queues with their IIS Application-based application.

What This Book Covers

This book is designed to be the only combination reference and tutorial you will need for building Visual Basic database applications. To accomplish that, this book covers the following database systems:

- Microsoft SQL Server 7
- Microsoft Jet 3.51/4.0
- Oracle 8*i*

Because much of the material you need to know about database programming is common to all three database servers, I have presented it first, in the following list of topics:

- Database Programming Fundamentals
- ActiveX Data Objects (ADO)
- ActiveX Data Object Extensions (ADOX)
- Traditional client/server applications
- IIS Applications
- Bound controls
- Stored procedures
- COM+ Transaction Server
- Microsoft Message Queues
- XML

Once I finish covering the common material, I'll focus on each individual database server to give you the specific knowledge you need to build efficient database applications. For each of the database servers, I'll cover these topics:

- Database server tools and utilities
- Useful SQL language extensions
- ADO considerations
- Unique data types and their Visual Basic equivalents
- Security mechanisms
- Creating stored procedures
- Performance considerations

The accompanying CD-ROM contains all of the sample programs found in this book, plus a sample database that you can use to test these programs. It's my belief that the best way to learn programming is to study as many programs as possible. Since the complete sample programs are on disk, you can load them, try them out, and modify them to see how they work, and hopefully incorporate the same techniques into your own applications.

What This Book Doesn't Cover

This book will not teach you the fundamentals of Visual Basic programming. If you don't know what a `For Next` loop or a `Function` is, run to the nearest bookstore and get a copy of *Visual Basic 6 for Dummies* by Wallace Wang. When you finish that book and understand the material in it, you'll be ready for this book.

While this book includes a primer on relational database concepts and the SQL language, I suggest that you read *SQL for Dummies* by Allen G. Taylor for a more in-depth coverage of SQL and relational databases. You may also want to check out *Microsoft SQL Server 7 for Dummies* by Anthony T. Mann and *Oracle 8i for Dummies* by Carol McCullough for more information about the specific database servers covered in this book.

Another thing to consider is that the emphasis in this book is on database programming. While this is a fairly broad topic, there are many things you might want to include in your programs that I might not cover, such as how to construct help files, how to use resource files to solve localization issues, and how to send e-mail messages using MAPI. You might check out the *Visual Basic 6 Bible* by Eric A. Smith, Valor Whisler, and Hank Marquis, or some of my other Visual Basic books. You can find a complete list of books that I have written at `www.JustPC.com`.

Hardware and Software Requirements

I wrote this book using two computers: one (called Mycroft) for running Visual Basic, and another (known as Athena) to run my database servers plus the COM+ Transaction Server. Mycroft is a Gateway 9100 laptop with a Pentium 200 processor and 64MB of main memory, along with Windows 98 Second Edition, Visual Basic 6 Enterprise Edition, Office 2000, and the SQL Server 7 utilities. I also installed ADO version 2.5 on my development machine from the Platform SDK. You can download the parts of the Platform SDK from `http://msdn.Microsoft.com`. Just go to the Downloads section and follow the directions to download the Platform SDK installation program.

The database server is also Gateway computer with a Pentium 120 processor and 80MB of main memory, running Windows 2000 Server. Obviously, SQL Server 7 and Oracle *8i* were installed, plus the Internet Information Server (IIS), Microsoft Message Queues, and COM+ Transaction Server. Just for fun, I also installed Office 2000 and Visual Basic 6 on this machine. The two computers were connected using a 10 MHz Ethernet LAN. The combination was a lot slower than I would have liked, even after I spent a lot of time retuning the system for optimal performance.

Running a database server isn't a trivial task, especially if you want to run it on Windows 2000 Server. Windows 2000 needs a lot of memory in order to have an acceptable level of performance. I recommend a minimum of 256MB of memory for Windows 2000 Server, though you could get by with 128MB of memory if you wanted to run Windows NT 4 Server. If possible, you should have a minimum of a 400MHz Pentium processor, though you could get by with less if your server isn't heavily loaded.

While it's possible to run your database and Visual Basic on one machine, you'll be happier if you can dedicate one machine to SQL Server and use a second for your programming. If you do choose to use a single machine, you should have a lot of memory, especially if you are running Windows 2000 server. You should also try to invest in a dual processor system with relatively fast SCSI disk drives.

Visit My Web Site

I maintain a Web site at `http://www.JustPC.com` with additional information about the books that my wife and I have written. Each book has its own Web page, on which I answer frequently asked questions and point you to other resources you may find interesting. If you get a chance to stop by, please sign my guest book to let me know you were there.

You're also welcome to send me e-mail at `WFreeze@JustPC.com`. Let me know what you liked about the book and what you didn't. I've made friends with readers from all over the world by doing this. However, please understand that I make my living from writing, so asking me to be your unpaid consultant isn't fair to you or me. I know what it is like to have a critical project and not be able to get the answers I need in a hurry. If I can help, I will. However, my priorities are my family, my current book (though my editors may think it should have a higher priority), my readers, my Web site, and then everyone else. So don't be surprised if you send me a note, and a few weeks (or even months) later you hear from me. Writing a book such as this one takes a considerable amount of time, and many things, like sleeping, eating somewhere other than my desk, and answering e-mail, are often put off until after the book is finished.

Now don't be afraid to send me e-mail. I enjoy reading every note I get and I do read every single note. I've always enjoyed teaching people how to do things, and writing a book allows me to teach more people than I've ever had the opportunity to do before. Unfortunately, I miss the feedback that you get from teaching someone in person. E-mail is my link to you. So while I can't meet everyone in person, hearing from you via e-mail is the next best thing.

Acknowledgments

Sometimes, being a writer can be the pits. The hours are long, the editors are demanding, and you never seem to have time for your family and friends. Everyone believes that you work a few hours each morning if you feel like it, and then have the rest of the day to play. What a laugh! As I write this, my children have been asleep for about eight hours, and they'll be getting up shortly to leave for school. My wife has been asleep for a few hours now, and the only one awake, beside myself, is my cat Pixel, who has walked across my keyboard three times while I've tried to write this paragraph. I wish she would go to sleep, too. On the other hand, writing is sometimes its own reward. I enjoy solving problems and teaching others how to do things. Writing allows me to do both, without the day-to-day headaches that arise as a manager in a large computer center.

So while the rest of the world believes that writing is only a part-time job, I'd like to acknowledge a few other people who believe otherwise.

My agent, Laura Belt, really earns her commissions. She does her best to ensure that I have money for the things that most writers don't have, like electricity to run my computer and a roof over my head. Now if I could only afford something to eat.

My acquisitions editor, John Osborn, challenged me to do this project with an impossibly tight schedule, and in a weak moment, I agreed. However, before I had a chance to really get started on this book, he left for greener pastures. I'm now working with Greg Croy, who has been keeping me both challenged and busy.

Shaun, Elwyn, Rick, Ariane, Dr. Bob, Veronica, Scott, Randy, Vikki, Bob K., and Ian, are but a few of my friends that I haven't seen in months. I promise to call real soon. Really. Okay, maybe after I finish the next book. That is, except for Rick. I may need to stop by and pick your brain and your closet.

Bucky and Goose, my wife's parents. I don't think I could ask for a better set of in-laws. See y'all in a couple of days for the big party.

I want to thank my mom and dad for their support, even though they think I need a haircut. It seems like I never get to see my mother and father as often as I wish. I hope that changes in the future, since they are both very special people to me.

If you read this book carefully, you will find occasional references to Christopher, Samantha, and Jill. Chris, who is six, knows more about computers than some well-paid people I used to work with and has beta tested more software on his computer than most adults I know. While Samantha is only five, she already wants her own laptop computer so she can write books like her mommy and daddy.

My lovely wife, Jill, is a very respected writer and beta tester in her own right, having written books on Microsoft Office, Internet Explorer, and Windows. Jill, if you believe in yourself, anything is possible! I love you!

Contents at a Glance

Contents

Part V: The Impact of XML 431

Part VII: Oracle 8i 579

P A R T

I

Database Programming Fundamentals

Before you can develop relational database applications in Visual Basic, you should have a good understanding of databases and how you can access them from Visual Basic. In this Part, I'll introduce you to the fundamentals of database technology and how they work with Visual Basic.

I'll start with the basic concepts of databases and the relational database model. Then I'll go into detail about how to design a relational database. Next, I'll quickly introduce you to SQL, which is the language of relational databases. I'll conclude by discussing some key issues about Visual Basic and how you can access a database from your Visual Basic application.

✦ ✦ ✦ ✦

In This Part

✦ ✦ ✦ ✦

Basic Concepts

In this chapter, I'm going to introduce you to the concepts behind databases and why databases are important to your application program. I'll also cover different database architectures and follow that up with a brief overview of the database systems to be covered in this book.

✦ ✦ ✦ ✦

In This Chapter

Why use a database?

Database architecture

Common databases

✦ ✦ ✦ ✦

Why Use a Database?

A *database* is simply a general-purpose tool that allows you to store any information you want that can be read and updated by one or more concurrent application programs in a secure and reliable fashion. Note that while this definition describes conventional database systems such as SQL Server and Oracle 8*i*, it can also be used to describe a collection of normal disk files. I want to explore these concepts using conventional disk files to help you better understand why your application needs a database system.

Storing information

There are many ways to store information on a computer, but eventually all of them boil down to placing information in a file somewhere on a disk drive. There are two basic types of files, which are characterized by how they are accessed. *Sequential access* files are accessed as a single unit, while *random access* files allow you to directly access the file in small pieces.

Using conventional file access

In order to process the data in a sequential access file, you must read or write the entire file. This type of access is useful for a word processor where you want to make all of the information in the file available to the user at the same time.

Generally a program will load the entire file into memory, make whatever changes are necessary, and then save the entire file when the user is ready to exit the program.

When dealing with sequential access files, you need not load the entire file into memory. Indeed, many programs merely load enough data from the file to perform a given task and load more data when the task is complete. The main idea is that your program reads the data from the beginning of the file to the end in a linear fashion. Hence the term *sequential.*

In most application programs, you only want to access a subset of the data at a given point in time, so rather than processing the entire file just to get a small piece of data, a random access file allows you to divide the file into chunks called *records.* (See "Organizing data in records," below for details.) Each record has a unique record number, which is determined by its relative position in the file. You can retrieve or update any record in the file by specifying the appropriate record number.

The key to making random access files work is that each record in the file is always the same size. This allows you to determine the location of the record by computing the starting byte of the record, just by knowing the size of the record and the relative record number in the file.

Even though a random access file may be organized differently than a sequential access file, you can also process a random access file sequentially by reading the records in order of their record numbers. This implies that you don't lose any functionality of a sequential access file if you choose to create your file as random access.

Organizing data in records

A record represents a chunk of data contained in a file and is organized into one or more *fields.* Each field has a specific name and *data type* associated with it. The name is used to uniquely identify the field in the record, and the data type describes what kind of information the field can hold.

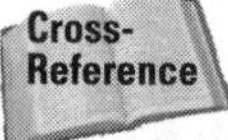

See "Columns and Data Types" in Chapter 2 for more information on this topic.

Because each record in the file always holds the same information, you can think of a file full of records as a table or grid, where each record corresponds to a row and each field corresponds to a column (see Figure 1-1). The table concept also conveys the concept of how the information is actually stored in the file, since the relative position of each field is fixed in relation to the other fields and the relative record number uniquely identifies the record's place in the table.

Name	Address	City	State	Zip Code
Christopher James	1234 Main Street	College Park	MD	20742
Samantha Ashley	2345 Central Avenue	College Park	MD	20742
Terry Katz	3456 Pennsylvania Ave	College Park	MD	20742
Robert Weiler	4567 Redwood Way	College Park	MD	20742
Wayne Freeze	5678 Baltimore Street	College Park	MD	20742
Bonnie Jean	6789 Oak Street	College Park	MD	20742
Jill Heyer	7890 Washington Drive	College Park	MD	20742
Raymond Bucky	8901 Souix Circle	College Park	MD	20742

Figure 1-1: A file with records looks like a grid or a table.

Concurrency

One of the most critical issues to consider when dealing with an application is ensuring that two or more concurrently-running programs don't interfere with each other while processing data. If the proper steps aren't taken, it would be easy for one program to destroy information that another program changed in the file. For instance, assume that you have a random access file that contains customers' checking account balances. Then assume that you have one program that debits the account for checks that the customer wrote, while another program credits customer deposits. While this scenario is unlikely, it is possible that the two programs may attempt to update the same customer record at the same time.

Now, consider the following sequence of events. The debit program reads the customer's record. Before the debit program has a chance to update the information, the credit program reads the customer's record and adds the deposit to the account's total balance. After the credit program updates the customer's information, the debit program completes its process by writing its updated account balance back to the file. In this scenario, the credit to the account was lost, since the update done by the debit program used an out-of-date account balance.

The proper way to prevent the concurrency problem is by controlling access to the data. Typically, this is done by *locking* the file to prevent other users from accessing any of the data in the file you want to use. The sequence of events in the above scenario would now look like this: The debit program would lock the file. Then it would read the customer record. The credit program would attempt to lock the file. Since the debit program already locked the file, the client program would be suspended. The debit program would complete its update and then release the lock on the file. The credit program would be resumed and the lock would be granted. It would then perform its update and release the lock, thus ensuring that the correct balance would be in the file.

Securing your data

In most computer systems, you can identify the users who are able to read or update a particular file, and deny access to all others using normal operating system security. However, it is often desirable to allow someone to see only part of a record — in a case, for instance, where you want to keep an employee's salary information in the same record with the employee's address and telephone number.

To prevent people from seeing salary information, you have to create another file that contains information about each person who can access your file and which fields they are permitted to access. Then your application programs must properly use this information to prevent unwanted access to data.

Of course this method is only as reliable as your application programming staff. One small mistake in a program could allow a user to read and/or change the value that they shouldn't have access to.

Performing backups and using transaction logs

No matter what you do to your data, you need to ensure that once a change has been made to it, it won't be lost. After all, it is possible that your hard disk could crash and destroy your files or your computer could suffer a power failure while the files were being updated.

There are a number of different ways to prevent your data from being lost. The most common practice is to back up your data on a regular basis. Of course you can't permit any users to update data while you're doing this, or your data files may be in an inconsistent state because someone changed a value in one file before the backup process copied the one file and after the backup process copied another file. Alternate ways to prevent you from losing your data include using redundant disk drives and/or database servers so that your data will still exist even if you lose a disk drive or server. However, I strongly recommend that you back up your data even if you use redundant equipment, just in case you lose both your primary copy and your redundant copy.

Most applications back up their data once a day, which limits the amount of data you might lose to a maximum of a single day. But losing even half a day's worth of information can be a big problem in most situations. For instance, in the case of a mail-order processing application, you always have the original order documents that you can reenter. However, in the case of a telephone order processing application, you may not even know which customers placed an order if you lose your files, and even if you did, do you really want to call all of your customers back to find out what they ordered?

There are a couple of solutions to this problem. First you can print every change you make to the files on a printer. This way, you will always have a paper record of the changes, and can reenter the information if you need to.

A better way would be to write all of your changes to a special file known as a *transaction log.* This file includes only the changes that were made to the file. Thus, if you have to restore the file from the previous day's backup, you could run a program that would read the values from the transaction log and reapply them to the main file.

Both of these approaches aren't 100% reliable, since the application programmer must explicitly send the information to the printer or write the changes to the transaction log. If the programmer forgets to include the appropriate calls in their program, the information is pretty much useless.

A database is the answer

While you can use files to hold your organization's data, you can see that there are a number of problems associated with this practice. A database system solves these problems and others that you may not have thought of.

Tables, rows, and columns

Recall that a database holds information in tables that correspond to random access files. Each record in the file corresponds to a row in the table. Each field in the file corresponds to a column in the table. Unlike a record, you can choose which columns you wish to retrieve from a table. By retrieving only the columns you need, you help to isolate your program from changes in the table. This means you can add and delete columns from a table, and as long as your program doesn't reference any of these columns, your program will continue to work without change.

The concept of a relative record number isn't available to locate a row in a table. It has been replaced with a more powerful concept known as the *primary key.* The primary key is a set of one or more fields whose values will uniquely identify a row in a table. Where you may have used an employee number or part number as the relative record number in a random access file, you can now use an arbitrary set of values to locate the row. This gives you a lot more flexibility when designing a table.

Locking

Just as you use locking to prevent two programs from accessing the same data in a file-oriented application, the database management system uses locking to prevent the same thing from happening. The database system automatically determines how to use locks to prevent two or more programs from accessing the same data at the same time. Unlike file-oriented applications, where the entire file is locked, the database system is smart enough to allow programs to update data in the same table at the same time as long as all of the programs are all accessing different rows.

You can get a big performance boost in your application because a database permits multiple programs to access data in the same table at the same time. With file-based applications, one program had to complete the read, process, and update sequence before the next program could start. This translates into longer and longer delays as more and more users try to access the files at the same time. Since the database system permits multiple, non-conflicting read, process, and update sequences to be active at the same time, the wait time is no longer a factor.

Security

Database systems are designed from the ground up to be secure. You can specify which users can access which data in which fashion. Since the security is moved outside the application, it is much easier to verify that only properly authorized users can access a piece of information.

Restoring lost data

Unlike a collection of random-access files, a database system has a comprehensive mechanism to ensure that once data has been written to the database, it isn't lost. A database system includes tools that will back up the database in a way that will prevent the problem where some of the changes are captured, while others aren't. This means that you can always restore your database to a consistent state.

Also, a database system includes an integrated transaction log that will automatically capture all of the changes to the database. When you have to restore a database, the restore process can automatically process the transaction log. All of the transactions written to the log will be recovered, which means that the data will be correct as of the moment before your disk crashed.

Database Architecture

Nearly all database systems available on the market today are implemented using a *client/server* architecture. This architecture defines two types of programs and how they interact with each other.

Servers and clients

A *client* is a program that generates requests that are sent to another program, called a *server,* for execution. When the server has finished the request, the results are returned to the client. In today's computing environment, many applications are implemented using client/server technology. For instance, your Web browser is a client program that talks to a Web server. A file server contains files that are made available to you over a network. Likewise, a print server allows a network manager to share a single printer with many different users.

Servers, clients, hardware, software, and confusion: The terms *client* and *server* are often used to describe both the software applications and the hardware they run on. This can lead to some confusion. It is quite possible that you may use a Web browser (client) application to access a Web server on the same computer. For example, I frequently test new Web pages on a test Web server running on the same computer as the browser before uploading them to a production Web server. In general, when I use the terms client and server I'm referring to the software applications and not the physical machines they run on.

Database servers and database clients

A *database server* is a program that receives *database requests* from a *database client* and processes the requests on the database client's behalf (see Figure 1-2). A database client is a program that generates database requests by interacting with a user, processing a data file or in response to a particular event in your computer. A database request is a specific operation that is to be performed by the database server, such as returning data from a table, updating one or more rows in a table, or performing some other database management task.

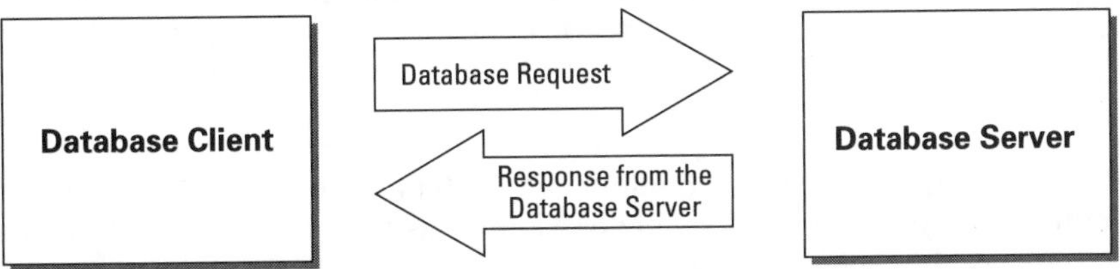

Figure 1-2: Database clients send database requests to a database server for processing.

Database servers

A database server typically runs on its own computer system and receives database requests across a network. If the request generates a response, then the response is returned to the database client computer over the network. This arrangement isolates the database server from each of the database clients, which improves the performance and reliability of the database system.

A special software package known as the *Database Management System* (DBMS) is run on the database server. It is this software that receives database requests, processes them, and returns the resulting information back to the database client.

The database server is typically run on an operating system designed to support servers, such as Windows 2000/NT Server or any of the various flavors of Unix. Desktop operating systems such as Windows 98/95 don't provide the reliability or stability necessary to run a database server.

In small environments, you can run several different servers on your server computer — such as a file server, Web server, mail server and transaction server — in addition to your database server. However, as your workload increases, it will become desirable to dedicate computers to each of these functions.

This type of arrangement would allow you to scale the size of each computer system to accommodate your workload. You can add more memory, faster CPUs and more disk space to keep pace with increases in your workload. Also, by dedicating a computer to running the database server, you run less of a risk of a system crash because of a software problem in another server such as the transaction server.

Database clients

The database client is simply an application running on the same network as the database server that requests information from the database. The application program generates database requests using an *Applications Programming Interface* (API), which is nothing more than a set of subroutine calls or set of objects that your program uses to send requests to the database and receive information from the database.

The API allows the program to communicate with more than one database system through the use of a special piece of code known as a *database driver*. A database driver represents a special program that is installed on the database client computer. It translates the standardized database requests made using the API into the special language used by the specific database server.

By using database drivers, the same application program can communicate with different database systems without changing the application itself. This level of independence is important since it allows an organization to replace one database system with another with only a minimal impact to the applications themselves.

Simple database systems

While most database systems fall into the client/server architecture I described above, a few simple database systems work differently. These are typically low-end database systems where performance and scalability issues are not a problem. These systems still communicate with your application via a standard API, but instead of passing requests onto a database server on a different computer, they pass the requests to code residing in the client computer.

This database code in the local client computer is designed to cooperate with other copies of the database code running in other computers to access a common file or set of files located somewhere on the network. The database files could be located on the same computer as one of the database clients, or located on a central file server. A low-end database system is also a good choice if you are designing a stand-alone application for a single user.

Administration of these database systems is fairly easy. Backing up the database is accomplished by backing up the file containing the database, and recovery processes are limited to restoring a backed-up version of the database.

Of course this approach can have a big impact on performance, because locking must now be done at the file level rather than based on the values selected from the database. While this will obviously hurt an application with many users, the overhead is low enough that for a handful of users, the performance may actually be better than the client/server architecture.

Types of Databases

There are four basic types of database systems: hierarchical, networked, indexed and relational. While each of the four types has many similar concepts, their differences result from how they store their data.

Hierarchical databases

The *hierarchical database* is the oldest form of database in existence. Data is arranged in a series of tree structures, which often reflect the natural relationship between data. IBM's IMS database, which is still available today, is the classic example of a hierarchical database.

A hierarchy models a data relationship known as *1 to many*. A 1 to many relationship means that one data value is related to one or more other data values. The classic example for this type of relationship is students and classes. When students attend school, they take many classes, a situation which can be described with a natural hierarchy (see Figure 1-3).

Networked databases

The *networked database* was developed as an alternative to the hierarchical database. While a lot of data can be organized using a hierarchical relationship, it is difficult to model other data relationships. Consider the case of students and their teachers. A student will take courses from many different teachers, whereas a teacher will teach more than one student (see Figure 1-4). This relationship is called *many to many*.

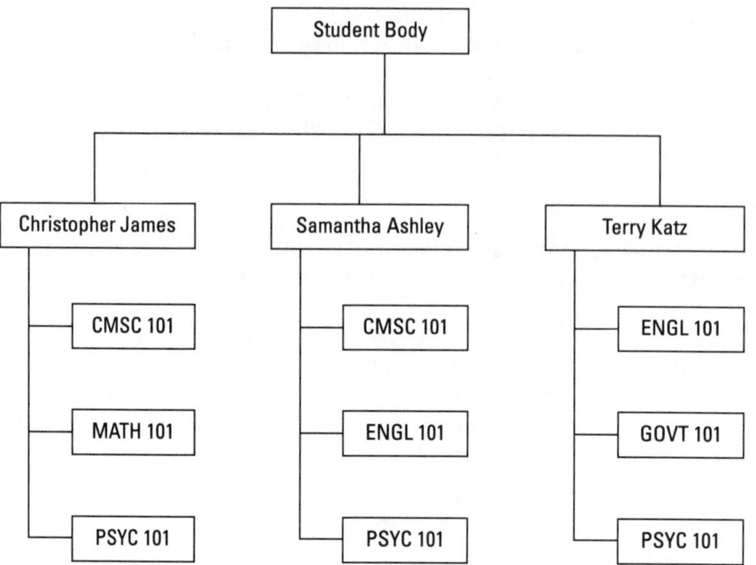

Figure 1-3: A hierarchical database reflects the natural relationship betw een data.

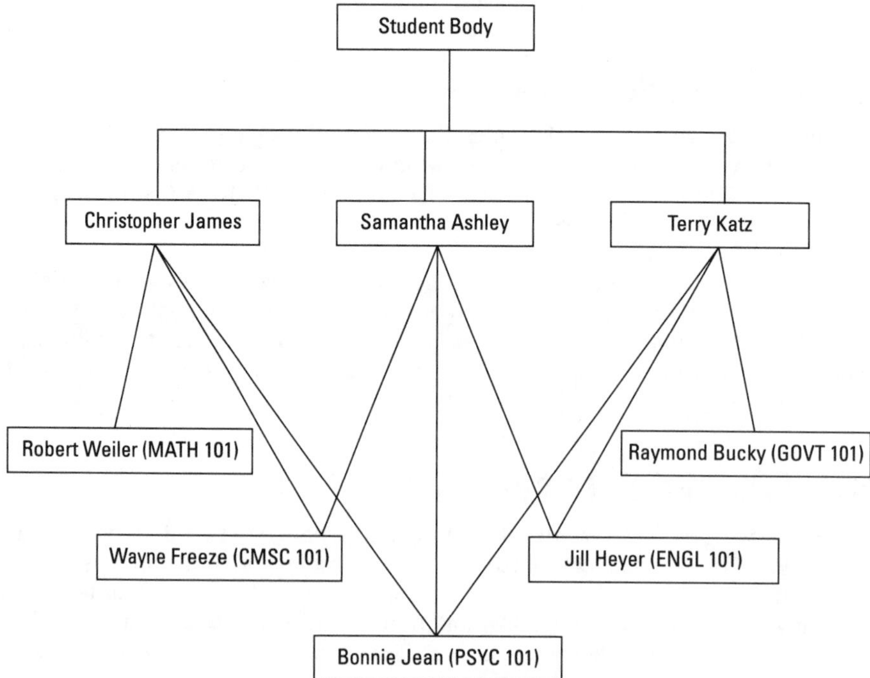

Figure 1-4: A networked database can handle situations that a hierarchical database cannot.

A networked database stores information in datasets, which are similar to files and tables. A record on one dataset that is related to a set of records in another dataset will have a set of physical pointers, also known as a link. Thus the record in the first dataset is linked to the records in the second dataset. The primary drawback to networked databases is that it can be quite complicated to maintain all of the links. A single broken link can lead to enormous problems in the database.

Indexed databases

While similar in concept to a networked database, an *indexed database* replaces links with an *inverted list.* An inverted list is another file that contains a list of unique values found in a particular field in a dataset, along with pointers to each record in which the value appears. This value is known as a *key value.* If you know the key value, you can quickly list all of the records in the dataset that contain that value. In practice, an indexed database is the most efficient database system in the marketplace today.

Relational databases

The concept of the *relational database management system* (RDBMS) goes back to the early 1970's, when IBM researchers were looking for a better way to manage data. One of the problems with hierarchical, networked, and indexed databases is that they all require pointers to connect data together. The researchers built a mathematical model, which discarded the pointers and used common values to link multiple records together. Thus, you weren't limited to hierarchical structures as in the hierarchical database model, and you didn't have to set links as in the networked database model. (The indexed model evolved after the original work was done on the relational database model.)

The primary drawback to the relational database model is that a relational database is very slow when compared to the other database models. Without pointers to help you quickly locate a particular record, you may have to read every record in a table to find one particular record. To help combat this problem, the concept of an *index* was introduced. Even with indexes, relational databases are generally less efficient than databases implemented using the other database models. However, the relational database gained popularity as computing began to shift from traditional mainframe computers to smaller mini-computers and personal computers. The initial applications of relational databases were far less demanding than the database systems running on mainframes, so the performance issues were not as much of a factor as they could have been. As time went on, the speed of mini-computers and personal computers increased to the point where they rivaled mainframe computers.

See Chapter 2 for a more in-depth discussion of relational databases.

Common Databases

In today's marketplace there are a number of relational database systems you can use. In this book, however, I'm going to focus on only three: Microsoft SQL Server 7.0, Microsoft Jet 3.5/4.0 and Oracle 8*i*. These three database systems make up the majority of the database systems in the world today, at least from the Visual Basic programmer's perspective. Although there are other database systems that run in the mainframe world, such as CA's IDMS and IBM's IMS, they aren't typically used by Visual Basic programmers.

SQL Server 7.0

One of Microsoft's major design goals with SQL Server 7.0 was to create a scalable product that ran the same on a Windows 98 system with limited memory and disk space, up to a large Windows 2000/NT Server system with multiple processors, gigabytes of main memory, and lots of disk space. To accomplish this, Microsoft created three versions of SQL Server. The Desktop Edition runs on Windows 98 and Windows 2000/NT Workstation. It's designed to handle smaller databases and is ideal for helping developers test their programs away from the production database server. The Standard Edition is the most common edition and provides the features that you really need for most applications. The Enterprise Edition expands the Standard Edition by adding features that help SQL Server handle applications with a lot of data and a large number of transactions.

Besides focusing on scalability, Microsoft also worked hard to reduce the total cost of ownership for a database system. Modern relational databases are often served by a group of specialists known as *database administrators*. These people are expensive to hire and difficult to keep, due to the increasing demand for their skills. SQL Server 7.0 addresses this problem by including a number of wizards that make it easy to perform routine tasks. Also the SQL Server Agent can be used to run various activities when your machine is left unattended.

A good primer: See *Microsoft SQL Server 7 for Dummies* by Anthony T. Mann for more detailed information about how to administer an SQL Server 7 database server.

Microsoft also addressed data warehousing applications by including two key features in SQL Server 7. The first is the *Data Transformation Services* (DTS). This feature makes it easy to move data from one place to another. This is particularly important, since the data in a data warehouse is usually taken from tactical applications like accounting and inventory systems, even if they exist on the corporate mainframe.

The second key feature is *OLAP Services* (OLAP stands for online analytical processing). These services bridge the gap between the data warehouse and the analysis tools running on the user's workstation. The data warehouse data is preprocessed in the OLAP server before the results are presented to the analysis tool. Microsoft has made the *application programming interface* (API) to OLAP Services available, so that other companies can design client tools to analyze OLAP data.

Microsoft Jet 3.5/4.0

Microsoft Access is a simple desktop database application development tool that is targeted at small- to medium-sized organizations. At the heart of Access is a true relational database engine known as Microsoft Jet. Like SQL Server, Jet is based on the SQL standard. Unlike SQL Server, the database code runs in the application itself rather than in a database server. Also, because Jet was developed independently of SQL Server, it isn't totally compatible with SQL Server.

Even though Jet is developed as part of Microsoft Access, Jet is included with Visual Basic. You can develop applications using Jet and freely distribute the Jet runtime code with your application. You can't do this with SQL Server applications.

Jet 3.5 is the version of Jet that shipped with Access 97 and Visual Basic 6, while Jet 4.0 is the version shipped with Access 2000. While Jet 4.0 offers some improvements over Jet 3.5, you should probably stick with Jet 3.5 unless you need to share your database with an Access 2000 application, since Access 2000 works only with Jet 4.0.

Oracle 8*i*

Oracle 8*i* is a high performance database system that runs on many different operating systems. While SQL Server is available only for Windows-based systems, Oracle 8*i* runs on everything from small Linux systems to large Sun Solaris-based systems and IBM mainframes running MVS/ESA or OS/390. Of course it also runs on Windows 2000/NT. Since the same code base is used for all of the different platforms, Oracle 8*i* applications need not worry about the computer that is hosting the database server.

Like SQL Server, Oracle 8*i* is available in several editions. The Standard Edition represents the most common form of Oracle 8*i*, and is suitable for most database applications. Oracle 8*i* Enterprise Edition is designed to support high-volume *online transaction processing* (OLTP) applications and query-intensive data warehouses. Oracle 8*i* Personal Edition is targeted at single user development and deployment applications.

Thoughts on Database Systems

Although the architecture of a database system may permit you to write an application program that will work with several different database systems, reality is a lot different than theory.

Most database systems offer assorted extensions that can improve the performance and abilities of most applications. However, if you take advantage of these extensions, your application becomes tied to a single database system. While this isn't necessarily bad, it is something to consider if you think you may change database systems in the future. The key to addressing this problem is to design your database and your application so that they only contain features that are common to all of the database systems you may use.

Isolating the database system from the application is even more important if you are developing applications for resale. Most likely your customers will already have an investment in a database system and would prefer that your application use that database system rather than having to invest in a totally new database system.

Isolating your application from your database system is more difficult than you might believe. This is especially true if you use only one type of database system. You'll often find yourself in situations that are easier to solve if you use a database system-specific feature than if you solve it in a more general-purpose way. This isn't necessarily bad, and often will allow you to build a better application in the long run.

If you plan to use only one database system, selecting the proper one is very important. Although many people pick a database by finding the one with the best set of features, you really should look for a database that will be around in five or ten years. Over time, a feature that is found in only one database management system will be included in the other systems in their next release. After a few releases, those features that you found very important when you picked your database vendor aren't all that important anymore.

Evaluate a database vendor in terms of their commitment to their database system. A vendor that is constantly improving their database is much better than a database vendor that doesn't. A lack of enhancements over a long period of time means that people will tend to select other databases to fit their needs. Eventually, if the enhancements stop, the vendor will stop supporting the database system and you may find yourself in a situation where all of your applications are so dependent on one database system that you can't move them to another database system.

Summary

In this chapter you learned that:

- Database systems have many advantages over using conventional files to hold your data, including better concurrency controls, better security, and better backup and recovery mechanisms.
- Database systems are usually implemented using client/server architectures.
- The different types of databases include the hierarchical, networked, indexed, and relational models.
- SQL Server 7.0, Oracle8*i* and Jet are three of the most common database systems that a Visual Basic programmer is likely to encounter.

✦ ✦ ✦

CHAPTER

The Relational Database Model

In This Chapter

Introducing the Structured Query Language

Business benefits of a relational database

Parts of a relational database

In this chapter, I'm going to introduce you to the development of SQL language and why it's important for relational databases. Then I'll give you a brief overview of the various structures in a relational database.

Introducing the Structured Query Language

Without the Structured Query Language (SQL), relational databases might not have become as popular as they are today. Their popularity is due mostly to how the relational database industry evolved and the standards that were an outgrowth of this evolution. Of course the business benefits of a relational database also had a great deal of impact on its acceptance.

Relational history

While the rise in popularity of relational databases appears to be tied to the personal computer revolution, the history of the relational database begins much earlier. And the origins of the relational database begin at the world's largest computer company rather than at M.I.T.S., the unknown company that designed the world's first personal computer.

The prequel to SEQUEL

In the early 1970's, one company dominated the computer business, much like Microsoft does today. That company was IBM. Today's IBM bears little resemblance to the IBM of that era. To many people at that time, computer meant IBM. IBM was a massive organization that planned things years in advance. This showed most dramatically in their research labs. They had researchers whose sole purpose was to think about alternate ways to perform computing tasks without regard to practicality. One of these researchers was Dr. E.F. Codd.

In June 1970, Dr. Codd published an article titled "A Relational Model of Data for Large Shared Data Banks" in the journal, *Communications of the Association for Computing Machinery*. This article presented a mathematical theory for storing and manipulating data using tabular data structures. This theory is the basis for the modern relational database.

SEQUEL and System/R

The idea of a relational database was appealing for many reasons and IBM authorized a research project in the mid-1970's to create a database system based on that theory. This project became known as System/R. Along with the work on the database itself, work was also underway to develop a query language for the database. The researchers developed several different languages, including one known as SEQUEL (Structured English QUEry Language).

In the late 1970's, IBM decided to release System/R to some of their key customers for evaluation. As part of this evaluation process, the query language was renamed SQL, although it continued to be pronounced SEQUEL. The System/R project came to a close in 1979, when IBM decided that the relational database theories developed by Codd ten years earlier were ready to be turned into a commercial product.

Ingres and Oracle

IBM was not the only company to work on relational databases during the 1970's. Some professors at the University of California's Berkeley computer labs also built a relational database known as Ingres. The query language for this database was known as QUEL, which is short for QUEry Language. Like SQL, this language was based on a highly structured form of the English language.

Ingres was also developed on a Unix platform, unlike System/R, which ran on an IBM mainframe operating system. At that time, Unix systems generally ran on small mini-computers such as Digital's VAX, which were much cheaper to acquire and operate than mainframes. This made the database popular with many universities that used the database to teach the fundamental concepts of relational database implementations.

Eventually, some of the professors left the Berkeley computer labs in 1980 and formed a company known as Relational Technology, Inc. to build a commercial version of Ingres. Ingres still exists as a commercial database, though it hasn't achieved the popularity of some other database implementations.

Another company called Relational Software, Inc. was formed in the late 1970's to create their own relational database system. Their database system, called Oracle, was first shipped in 1979, making it the first commercially available relational database system. Like IBM's System/R project, it was based on SQL, and like Ingres, it ran on a VAX mini-computer. Today, Oracle is the leading supplier of relational database systems in the world.

Back to IBM

In 1981, IBM shipped their first commercial relational database system, called SQL/Data System (SQL/DS). SQL/DS was available for the Virtual Machine (VM) operating system and was targeted primarily at computer centers that wanted to provide ad hoc query processing for relatively small databases.

IBM chose this approach for two main reasons. First, they didn't want to cannibalize sales of their highly successful hierarchical database system, Information Management System (IMS), which ran on the large Multiple Virtual Storage (MVS) based mainframes. Second, for any given workload, SQL/DS was much slower than IMS. By restricting relational database technology to a small niche, IBM was able to get practical experience with the technology without alienating its customers.

In 1983, IBM released the first relational database system to run on MVS, called Data Base/2, which is more commonly known as DB2. In the early days, DB2 gained a reputation for being a resource hog and for very slow performance. This was true when compared to the IMS database, which had many more years of tuning and optimization than DB2 had at that time. IBM's response was to suggest that DB2 should be used for ad hoc query processing, and to use IMS for high-volume transaction processing.

IBM also labeled DB2 as a strategic product. In IBM speak, this meant that a customer that was concerned about the future should be running DB2 today. While this helped DB2 sales, it didn't help DB2 performance. However, as time went on, two things helped to change DB2 performance dramatically. First, DB2 underwent several major version changes, with each change bringing a significant improvement in performance. At the same time, the price of hardware dropped immensely, which meant that customers could buy a lot more computing power for the same amount of money. And nothing solves a performance problem as well as more hardware.

A lot of memory is good and too much is just right: When dealing with a relational database, nothing improves performance as much as adding memory. Adding more RAM to a computer allows the database to reduce the amount of I/O needed to process a query. Adding RAM for a disk cache will also work wonders.

ANSI Standard SQL

In 1982, the American National Standards Institute (ANSI) began a process to determine a standard for a relational database query language. Over the next four years they reviewed several different languages, including SQL and QUEL; however, with IBM's weight behind DB2, SQL was eventually selected as the standard. Even though SQL was selected as the standard, there were some major differences between the actual syntax used by DB2 and the final syntax adopted by ANSI in 1986.

The final syntax adopted in 1986 had a lot of open holes, which prompted ANSI to revise the standard for a second time in 1989 and again in 1992. The standards have become known as SQL-86, SQL-89, and SQL-92. Because the standards allowed various levels of compliance, many database vendors could claim that their database supported the ANSI SQL standard.

Caution

A non-standard standard: The ANSI standard permits vendors to add their own proprietary extensions to their SQL implementations. In practice, this means that each vendor's implementation is significantly different from each other. While the really simple statements are compatible between vendors, many complex statements may not be compatible between database vendors. If you are trying to use the one-program fits all database systems approach to application design, you need to verify that the statements you use are appropriate for all database systems.

Ingres finally bowed to the pressure and in 1986, added support for SQL alongside QUEL. Since that time, nearly all database vendors have added support for SQL to their databases. Even some database vendors with non-relational database systems now support the Structured Query Language.

Other relational database vendors followed Oracle's lead and jumped on the SQL bandwagon, such as Sybase, Informix, Digital, and Microsoft. For the most part, these vendors ignored the high-end mainframes and concentrated their efforts on mini-computers and/or personal computer networked servers, which turned out to be the right decision since the demand for mainframe databases is declining as the demand for mainframes remains stagnant.

Note

Mainframes and Unix servers: Having worked with computers of many different sizes over the years, I've learned that there isn't as much difference between a mainframe and some of the largest Unix servers on the market as most people believe. Much of the technology used in the high-end Unix servers was first developed for the mainframe, while the innovative design approaches used to build affordable Unix servers were incorporated into mainframes. This blending of technology and design means that mainframes will continue to be around for a long time as an alternative to the high-end Unix servers.

Business benefits of a relational database

Obviously, SQL wouldn't have achieved its success unless it met people's expectations. SQL succeeded because of several key factors, such as the underlying relational database technology, the existence of an independent ANSI standard, and the fact that the language itself is very robust and that most of the database systems using SQL are based on modern client/server architectures.

Relational database technology

Designing a non-relational database can be a difficult task and using one can be even worse. In most non-relational database systems, creating a database is a difficult task due to the fact that the hierarchies must be completely described or all of the possible relationships must be thought out before the database is created. A relational database allows you to make changes easily and on the fly. You can add and remove database structures while the database is running.

The relational database model also permits people to use relationships that haven't been predefined. This lets an organization change their databases gradually over time, which reduces the impact and scope of any single change.

Pros and cons of the ANSI standard

Many people believe that the ANSI standard guarantees that programs written to use SQL can be moved from one database platform to another with minimal problems, in much the same way that people can move an ANSI C program from one machine to another. This gives many users the feeling that if they need to, they can switch database vendors. In reality, unless you make a special effort to design your application to the ANSI standard, most people will find moving from one database system to another more trouble than it's worth.

However, there are many advantages to having an independent standard than simply portability. One of the largest problems today is finding knowledgeable people to develop applications. Often people are hired with some of the skills, but need to be trained in others. While the details of the SQL syntax may vary from one database vendor to another, the basic statements are the same. This makes it possible to train someone in a new database system by focusing only on how their SQL is different from the standard rather than starting with a whole new language. This means that people can move from one database system to another with much less effort than would have been possible without an independent standard.

Powerful query language

Prior to SQL, most database systems used one method to access a database interactively and another method for programmatic access. This forced programmers to learn multiple languages to access their database. Also, the interactive query language wasn't powerful enough to answer certain types of questions. In addition, there was typically a third language that was used to define the structure of the database. This made it much harder than it really needed to be for many application programmers. SQL solves this problem by providing a single query language. This same language can be used interactively, programmatically and to define the database structures.

Client/server architecture

Another benefit of using database systems based on the SQL language is that most database systems have been developed using a client/server architecture. This makes it a natural fit for modern personal computer networks. This also makes it easy to scale the size of the computer running the database server, which in turn allows an organization to spend less money on computing resources.

Parts of a Relational Database

In order to understand how to access a relational database, you need to understand the basic parts of a relational database and how they fit together.

Separation of data: I often do my development directly on a Windows 2000/NT Server system, with a local database server. This way, I can test applications I'm working on against a test database without impacting my production database server.

Tables and rows of data

A database holds your data in a series of one or more *tables*. Each table is similar to a spreadsheet, with the data organized into a series of rows and columns. Each row corresponds to a record in a file and represents a unique instance of a piece of data. A column corresponds to a field in a file and represents a single attribute of a piece of data.

Consider a table that contains information about a customer. Each row in the table contains information about a single customer, while each column in the table contains a specific attribute about that customer, such as their name or street address.

Columns and data types

The data in a column is often called *atomic*, which implies that the data in the column can't be subdivided. For instance, consider a field called Name, which consists of three subparts: Name.First, Name.Middle, and Name.Last. The Name field is not atomic since it can be broken into smaller pieces. On the other hand, a field that contains an unstructured name value would be atomic since there is no structure to the field.

A *repeating group* is a field that contains more than one instance of a data value. Thus any field that is an array or a collection is a repeating group. Since a repeating group is also not atomic, it can't be represented by a single column.

Associated with each column is a *data type* that identifies the type of data you plan to store in the column. In general there are four main data types:

✦ **Numbers** — Integers, fixed decimal point and floating decimal point numbers fall into this category.

✦ **Character strings** — *Fixed-length* character strings always use the same amount of storage in your table, while *variable-length* character strings store only the characters in the string, plus some information that allows the database to track the length of the string.

✦ **Date/time values** — This data type contains a date value, a time value, or a combination date and time value. Each database server will determine the exact meaning of these values and how they are stored.

✦ **Binary values** — This is basically an unformatted, store-it-yourself field. You can store items such as images, sound clips, and even application programs using a binary data type.

Note

All binary data types are not the same: The database server you are using will determine the characteristics for a binary data type.

In addition to storing a data value in a column, a special flag known as **Null** is also available. This flag indicates whether the column contains a valid value. If the column has a valid value, this flag will be set to false and the column will be known as **Not Null**. However if you don't assign a value to this column, then the flag will be set to true and the column will be known as **Null**.

Note

Nulls aren't empty: Don't confuse an empty string with **Null**. An empty string represents a value, while **Null** means that no value is associated with the column.

Indexes and keys

In the theoretical relational database model there isn't any organization to how the rows are stored in the table. However, from a practical viewpoint, you need a mechanism that allows you to quickly select a row or set of rows. This mechanism is known as an *index*.

An index is a special database structure that maintains a set of column values, sorted in a way that minimizes the search time. Typically, an index is implemented as an inverted list, similar to that used in the indexed database model. This allows the database server to quickly search through the list of values in the index to select the desired rows from the table. Indexes are separate from the table and can be added and removed on the fly.

A column is said to depend on another field when there is only one possible value of the second field for a specific value of the first column. If this sounds confusing, consider the following: you have a table with a name column and a social security number column. Since the social security number is unique for each individual and each individual has only one name, the name field is dependent on the social security number. Note that the reverse isn't true, since it is possible to have more than one social security number for a given name. In other words, there may be more than one person with the name of John Smith in this country, and each will have their own unique social security number.

The list of columns included in the index is known as the *key*. Every table should have a key whose value is unique for each row in the table. This is known as the *primary key*. For example, a table that contains information about customers might have a column called CustomerId as the primary key. A key that contains more than one column is also known as a *composite key*.

Any other keys in the table are referred to as *secondary keys*. Unlike the primary key, secondary keys need not be unique. They merely help you locate a common subset of rows in a table.

When a group of columns in one table matches the primary key definition in another table, the group of columns is called a *foreign key*. Foreign keys are useful when you want to establish a relationship between two tables. For example, in the customer table, one of the columns might be zip code. You could add a ZIP code table to your database, which contains a list of ZIP codes each with their corresponding city name. Thus, for any given ZIP code, you could determine the name of the city where the customer lives. This way you could automatically fill in the city name when a customer enters their ZIP code.

You can choose to make a relationship—a required relationship—in which case the database server will prevent you from adding a row to the table unless the value in the foreign key columns is found as the primary key in the corresponding table. Thus if you choose to enforce the above relationship, you can only insert a row into the customer's table if the customer's ZIP code exists in the ZIP code table.

Another advantage of indexes is that you can use an index to ensure that a value in the table is unique. While the primary key of the table must be unique, in some cases you may want the secondary key to be unique as well.

Theory vs. Reality

One of the advantages of a relational database is the use of set theory to describe operations against its data. It allows a high degree of separation between how the data is viewed by the database user and how the data is actually stored internally. However, just because something makes sense in theory doesn't necessarily mean it's a good idea, because the theory doesn't take into consideration the physical limitations of your database server.

Without indexes, every query would have to read every row in a table. On small tables this wouldn't be a big handicap, since it doesn't take very long to read all of the rows. However, on large tables this can be a major problem.

Views

One of the most important concepts in a relational database is known as a *view*. A view is simply a "virtual table" created from one or more base tables in your database. Views come in two flavors: updateable and non-updateable. As their names imply, updateable views can be updated and are usually created from a single table. Non-updateable views are generally created from two or more tables or contain columns whose values are calculated in some fashion.

Normalization

Normalization is a way to classify your database structure. From a theoretical viewpoint, the more normalized you database is, the better. These are the four basic levels of normalization that are commonly found in normal database designs:

- **Unnormalized:** No rules are imposed on the database structure.
- **First normal form:** Each field must be atomic. Repeating groups and composite fields are not permitted.
- **Second normal form:** Every non-key field must depend on the entire primary key. A field must not depend on only part of a composite primary key. The database must also be in first normal form.
- **Third normal form:** A non-key field can't depend on another non-key field. The database must also be in the second normal form.

Relational database theory also describes a fourth normal form, a fifth normal form, and a Boyce/Codd normal form. These last forms often result in a database that has too many tables to offer good performance.

You can't build an unnormalized relational database since repeating groups and composite fields aren't permitted. (Of course there are ways around even these restrictions in most database servers.) The most important thing to understand is that as you move up the normalization ladder, the database's large tables become broken down into more and more small tables. This is done in the name of reducing data duplication.

For example, in a truly normalized database, you wouldn't store city and state information with someone's address, since you can get this information from the person's ZIP code. You would add another table to your database that uses the ZIP code as a primary key and have the corresponding city and state information for that ZIP code. However, to get someone's address, you now must access two different tables, which is far more expensive than accessing a single table with all of the customer's address information.

Thoughts on Relational Databases

Relational databases have a much longer history than most people would believe. However, I believe this history played a very important part in shaping the relational databases you use today.

Unlike other types of databases that were either developed by a committee or by a single vendor who were able to unilaterally impose their standards on their customers, relational databases were developed through intense competition. This competition has existed for nearly twenty years and shows no sign of letting up.

When selecting a database, rely less on the features of a particular relational database, and more on the database vendor's track record. Relational databases are usually updated every couple of years and sometimes more often than that. When one particularly innovative feature shows up in one database system, the other vendors will be quick to copy and improve on it and you'll most likely see it released in the next version of their database software.

Many customers will make a decision on which database to buy based on which database vendor has the best features at the time of their evaluation. I've seen organizations use this approach, only to have problems down the road when the vendor decided to freeze their product at a particular version and not enhance it any more. This left the organization heavily dependent on a dead-end product and forced them to undergo a major conversion effort to a similar product from another vendor. This cost a lot of time and effort that could have been used to develop new applications.

Carefully consider these issues when picking your database product. Remember that the investment you make in your database is not just for a year or two but for the next ten to twenty years. There are many vendors in today's market that have a long track record and have proven themselves over time. Choosing one of these vendors will save you time and money in the long run.

Summary

In this chapter you learned that:

✦ The evolution of the relational database resulted in many database vendors offering products that appear to be compatible because they are based on the SQL database language, but in reality they are highly incompatible.

✦ There are many business benefits to using relational database systems in your applications, including having a single language for data definition, data manipulation and query processing, and a client server architecture for efficient sharing of data.

✦ The major parts of a relational database include tables, columns, rows, indexes, and views.

✦ Normalizing a database is not necessarily a good thing.

✦ ✦ ✦

Designing a Relational Database

✦ ✦ ✦ ✦

In This Chapter

Stating the problem

Brainstorming

Modeling entities and relationships

Building the database

✦ ✦ ✦ ✦

In this chapter, I'm going to show you the way I design a database. While I'll use SQL Server tools in this chapter, the same concepts can be applied to any database system. The key to using this approach is to understand the techniques I'm going to show you and adapt them so that they work for you.

Overview of the Design Process

Designing a relational database can be as easy or as hard as you choose to make it. I generally use a seven-step approach as outlined below:

1. Stating the problem
2. Brainstorming for ideas
3. Modeling entities and relationships
4. Building the database
5. Creating the application

I'm going to discuss the first four steps in this chapter. The rest of this book will focus on step five.

See Chapter 2 for information about the relational database model.

Stating the Problem

While stating the problem may seem easy, it's a lot harder than it looks. The problem statement should present an understanding of what the organization is trying to accomplish, while at the same time trying to emphasize the most critical business needs. If you want to replace an existing application, you can use that application as a basis for the answer. But if you are building an application for the first time, it is very important to understand what problem you're trying to solve. After all, if you can't identify the problem, how are you going to know if you really solved it?

The problem should be stated as simply as possible. For example, if the people at Amazon.com were to state their problem, it might look like this: we want to establish Amazon.com as a brand name by selling books to consumers via the Internet at the lowest possible cost to the consumer and with the best possible service, while building market share that will ensure the long-term stability of the company. A specialty mail-order catalog company might want to solve this problem: we want to improve how we take customer orders over the telephone to reduce mistakes and improve service to our customers. A small electronics supplier might state their problem in this way: we need to improve our inventory control to increase the number of times the inventory is turned over each year and to prevent stockpiles of obsolete items. In this book, I'm going to use a common database for all of the examples I create. I'll also update an application I wrote a few years ago called Car Collector, which tracks a collection of toy cars. Since I originally wrote this program, the Internet has become very important to collectors. Web sites like eBay make it much easier for people to buy and sell collectibles. In fact, my wife likes to buy and sell collectible dolls and has been asking me to build her a version of Car Collector that is targeted at the doll market.

Taking this information into consideration, I can state my problem like this: I want to update Car Collector to include support for other types of toys and collectibles and add support for trading toys with other collectors over the Internet. With the new features I'm going to add, I'm going to change the name of the application to Toy Collector.

Note

It's almost realistic: Toy Collector as used in this book isn't meant to be a complete application, but rather a framework for showing you different techniques for building database applications in Visual Basic. Therefore, the database design may not be as complete as a commercial application, nor will all of the features found in the commercial application be present in Toy Collector. Some of the data structures I use, as well as the features included in the application, may seem like overkill, but they are necessary to illustrate various points along the way. So, focus on the techniques that I'm going to show you and try to understand why and how I do things, rather than focusing on why this feature was added or why that information is missing.

Brainstorming

Once you have a basic understanding of the problem your application needs to solve, you need to design the database to accommodate the information related to your application. The first step in this process it to take a look at your problem and try to determine all of the information and functions that might be needed to solve the problem. I call this step *brainstorming*.

Brainstorming is the act of discussing and recording ideas without regard to how feasible they are to implement. This helps you identify all of the information you need to keep and all of the tasks your application will need to perform.

I like to conduct brainstorming sessions that include everyone who will be involved with the project in a single room with a white board. It helps to have as wide a range of people present as possible. Everyone from end users, to programmers, to management should be involved in this process.

Every idea that is raised should be listed on the white board, even if it's similar to an idea that's already listed. After the meeting, the information should be organized, and similar ideas can be combined as a single item. The ideas should be classified as either a task that the application should perform or a piece of information that will need to be kept.

It's important to understand that some of the ideas that come out of the brainstorming session may not be practical. At this stage of the process, you shouldn't worry about practicality. It is far more important to be complete. Sometimes things that seem impractical at this stage may prove easy to implement later, while other ideas that seem easy to implement at first may not prove to be worth the time and effort.

Also, it's important not to make fun of any ideas, no matter how bad they seem. This is especially true for ideas coming from the less technical attendees. Quite often, their ideas and comments may lead to a better understanding of how the application should work.

Brainstorming Toy Collector

Since you can't actively participate in the brainstorming session, I sat down and held one myself, and came up with the following list of functions that need to be performed by Toy Collector application:

- ✦ Track items currently in the collection
- ✦ Create reports of items in the collection
- ✦ Locate a toy in the inventory

- Keep a mailing list of current and potential customers
- Create a Web page with a list of items currently for sale
- Create a Web page with a list of items wanted
- Create an HTML listing for eBay
- Evaluate the condition of a toy
- Track purchases and sales
- Process an order that sells one or more toys to a customer
- Process an order that purchases a toy from a customer

The functions will be used to maintain a database containing the following data elements:

- Toy name
- Manufacturer
- Description
- Year the toy was built
- Value
- Price paid
- Asking price
- Condition
- Condition questions
- Type of toy
- Order information
- Shipping cost
- Sales tax
- Date ordered
- Date received
- Date shipped
- Credit card number
- Expiration date
- Customer name
- Customer's first name
- Customer's last name
- Customer's middle initial
- Customer's address
- Customer's city
- Customer's state
- Image of the collectible

Reviewing the results

After conducting the brainstorming session, you need to review the information you collected and try to eliminate duplicate information and make sure that the information you have is complete. Quite often while you conduct this review, you'll realize that other related information might be useful and should be added to the list.

Examining the functions to be performed

Looking at the above results, you can see a few common threads. First, you need an inventory system that tracks all of the toys in the collection. This is a fairly common application, along with maintaining a mailing list.

The inventory part of an application usually requires a unique identifier for an item in inventory. This wasn't included as part of the original brainstorming session. In a traditional inventory system, the quantity of the item is also included. However, due to the fact that different toys may have different characteristics based on their condition, I choose to ignore the quantity issue and require that each item in the inventory must have its own unique record.

Processing orders isn't difficult. However, a few more items need to be added to what was already identified above. For instance, in order to compute sales tax, you need to know the sales tax rate. For the purposes of this book, I'm going to assume that the sales tax rate is uniform across a state, even though this isn't necessarily true. You also need to capture the customer's name on the credit card, since it may be different than the name they entered into your database. There should also be an option to ship to an alternate destination, rather than a regular mailing address.

The mailing list is pretty straightforward, except that you should give the customer the option to not receive mail. This is important, because even in today's marketplace, people will complain about unwanted mail. Also, you may want to include some additional comments about the customer that would let the user record problems that they may have had during previous transactions.

The customer's name is actually listed twice: once as simply name, and another time as first, middle, and last names. Which way is best really depends on you. Having a separate last name field makes it easy to search on someone's last name. However, using a single field lets you format a name more naturally, which is important when you have people that have suffixes such as Ph.D., Junior, Senior or III. It also allows someone to enter a title such as Mr., Ms., Dr., etc. with fewer problems. In the long run, it really doesn't matter which method you pick as long as you're consistent throughout your database.

Evaluating the condition of a toy can be a fairly complex process. One method is to assign the toy a point value, assuming that it's in mint condition. Then you would ask a series of questions about specific flaws that are possible in the toy. Depending on the response, points will be deducted from the maximum score. The resulting score can then be mapped onto condition value, which in turn allows you to determine the true value of the toy. Since the questions can vary by the type of toy, additional information is needed to determine the type of toy and the questions that will be used to determine the toy's overall condition.

Mapping the results to data types

The last step of the brainstorming session is to map the data elements onto a series of data types. After reviewing the brainstorming information, I like to assemble a list of the data elements that were derived from the session, along with Visual Basic data type and a short description of the elements, such as those shown in Table 3-1.

Table 3-1
Data Elements

Data Element	*Data Type*	*Description*
CustomerName	String	The name of the customer.
Street	String	The street on which the customer lives.
City	String	The city where the customer lives.
State	String	The state where the customer lives.
Zip	String	The proper ZIP code for the customer's address.
Phone	String	The customer's telephone number.
EMailAddress	String	The customer's e-mail address.
MailingList	Boolean	True if the customer wants to receive periodic notices.
OrderNumber	Long	A number that uniquely identifies the order.
OrderStatus	String	The current status of the order.
DateOrdered	Date	The date the order was placed.
DateShipped	Date	The date the order was mailed.
ShippingCost	Currency	The cost to ship the order.
SalesTax	Currency	The amount of sales tax collected.
CreditCardNumber	String	The credit card number used to purchase a toy.
ExpirationDate	String	The expiration date on the credit card.
InventoryId	Int	A unique identifier for an item in the collection.
ToyName	String	The name of the collectible toy.
Manufacturer	String	The toy's manufacturer.
ToyType	String	The type of toy.
ToyDescription	String	A description of the toy.

Data Element	Data Type	Description
MintValue	Currency	The value of the toy if it was in mint condition.
Condition	Long	A numeric description of the toy's condition.
Question	String	A question used to evaluate a toy's condition.
TrueValue	Currency	The true value of the toy based on its condition.
DatePurchased	Date	The date the toy was purchased.
Image	Picture	A picture of the toy.

US first: When building an e-commerce application, one of the first things you need to plan for is how to handle international issues. For the most part, the only way these issues would affect your database design is that additional data elements, such as Country and CurrencyType, would need to be included, plus you would need to allow additional space for other fields such as ZIP code. Just because I don't include these fields in Toy Collector isn't a good reason for you not to include them in your application.

Modeling Entities and Relationships

The next step in the process is translating the information from the brainstorming session into a database design.

Entity/relationship modeling

Entity/Relationship modeling (also known as E/R modeling) is a way of describing the *relationship* between *entities*. An entity is a thing that can be uniquely identified, such as a toy, a customer, or an order. Associated with the entity is a set of attributes, which helps to describe the entity. Each customer has a name and an address. Each toy has a name and a manufacturer. An order has an order number and a date ordered. Relationships are formed between two entities, such as customers and orders, where a customer places an order for a toy.

When drawing an E/R model, I use rectangles for entities, ellipses for attributes, and diamonds for relationships. In Figure 3-1, you can see a simple E/R model that has two entities (Customers and Orders), with each entity having two attributes (Customers-Address and Name, Orders-Order Number and Date Ordered) and a single relationship (Customer-Order).

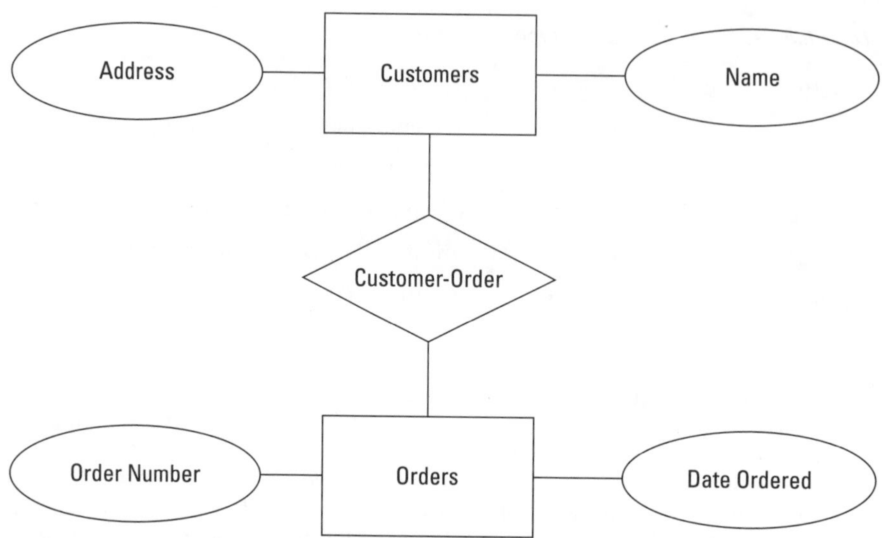

Figure 3-1: Designing a simple database using an E/R model.

Identifying entities and attributes

The first step in this process is to review the list of data elements found in Table 3-1 and look for common groupings. As you scan through the list of data elements, three main groupings jump out almost immediately: customer information, inventory information, and order information. Each of these groupings represents a major entity in the Toy Collector database.

At the same time, you need to look at the various entities and their attributes from an implementation point of view. You may find that a few other attributes are easy to include and will add value to the application from the user's point of view.

Dirt cheap disk drives: If you designed a database years ago, you will remember that disk space was very expensive, and you always tried to use the least amount of space possible. In today's marketplace, you can purchase a high-performance 9-gigabyte SCSI disk drive for less than $500. If you allow 2,000 bytes for each customer (which is very generous), you can store over 4 million customers on a single disk drive. Since most applications won't store this much data, don't let the cost of disk space drive your database decisions.

Customer information

Table 3-2 contains the list of data elements that are related to a customer, plus a few more that popped up while assembling the list. Finding some additional data elements at this stage is quite normal, since we now have a better understanding of the application's needs. In this case, I added fields to identify when the customer was originally added to the database (DateAdded) and the last time the information was updated (DateUpdated). I also added a field called Comments that allows the user to record any comments they may have about this particular customer.

Table 3-2
Customer Information

Column Name	*Data Type*	*VB Type*	*Description*
CustomerId	Int	Long	A unique identifier for the customer.
Name	Varchar(64)	String	The customer's name.
Street	Varchar(64)	String	The street address where the customer lives.
City	Varchar(64)	String	The name of the city where the customer lives.
State	Char(2)	String	The name of the state where the customer lives.
Zip	Int	Long	The ZIP code for the customer's address.
Phone	Varchar(32)	String	The customer's phone number.
EmailAddress	Varchar(128)	String	The customer's e-mail address.
DateAdded	Datetime	Date	The date the customer was added to the database.
DateUpdated	Datetime	Date	The date the customer's information was last updated.
MailingList	Bit	Boolean	When true means that the customer wishes to receive periodic mailings.
Comments	Varchar(256)	String	Comments about the customer.

Inventory information

The information about the inventory is a little more complicated than the customer information. While it is easy to identify the attributes that are directly related to an inventory item (see Table 3-3), there are a few cases where some of the information isn't directly related. For instance, the questions that you need to ask the user in order to determine the condition of a toy are related to the type of toy, not the actual toy itself. This implies that another entity called ToyTypes (see Table 3-4) will be needed to hold information about a type of toy. Also, because there are multiple questions for each toy type, you'll need yet another entity (ConditionQuestions) to hold the questions (see Table 3-5).

Table 3-3
Inventory Items

Column Name	Data Type	VB Type	Description
InventoryId	Int	Long	A unique identifier for the item in the collection.
ToyTypeId	Int	Long	A unique identifier for the type of toy in the collection.
Name	Varchar(64)	String	The name of the toy.
ManufacturerId	Int	Long	The name of the manufacturer who made the toy.
YearIssued	Datetime	Date	The date the toy was first manufactured.
Description	Varchar(256)	String	A description of the toy.
MintValue	Money	Currency	The value of the toy if it is in mint condition.
Condition	Int	Long	The condition of the toy using a numeric scale.
ConditionMask	Varchar(64)	String	Answers to the condition questions for this type of toy.
TrueValue	Money	Currency	The true value of the toy based on its current condition.
DatePurchased	Datetime	Date	The date the toy was added to the inventory.
PurchasePrice	Money	Currency	The amount of money paid for the toy.
AskingPrice	Money	Currency	The amount of money you are willing to sell the toy for. A value of zero means that you aren't willing to sell the toy at this time.
BuyingPrice	Money	Currency	The amount of money you are willing to pay for a similar toy.
Wanted	Bit	Boolean	If true means that you want to buy the toy.
ForSale	Bit	Boolean	If true means that you want to sell the toy.

Column Name	*Data Type*	*VB Type*	*Description*
Comments	Varchar(256)	Sting	Any comments that would be displayed along with the toy.
DateUpdated	Datetime	Date	The most recent time this information was updated.

Table 3-4
Toy Types

Column Name	*Data Type*	*VB Type*	*Description*
ToyTypeId	Int	Long	A unique identifier for the type of toy in the collection.
Description	Varchar(64)	String	A description of the type of toy.

Table 3-5
Condition Questions

Column Name	*Data Type*	*VB Type*	*Description*
TypeId	Int	Long	A unique identifier for the type of toy in the collection.
Seq	Int	Long	A sequence number that is used to distinguish between multiple questions for a specific type of toy.
Question	Varchar(64)	String	A question used to evaluate the condition of the toy.
Weight	Int	Long	The relative importance of the question when determining the toy's condition.
Responses	Int	Long	The highest possible value of the response.

Sometimes it is useful to codify a data value to ensure data consistency. A good example of a field that can easily get bad data is the Manufacturer field. Consider how many different ways someone can spell Mattel. One way to ensure that the mis-spelling doesn't happen is to encode each toy manufacturer as a numeric value and store the numeric value in the database. Then you need to add a translation table that can be used to translate the codified value into a text string. This is what the Manufacturers table accomplishes (see Table 3-6).

Table 3-6
Manufacturers

Column Name	*Data Type*	*VB Type*	*Description*
ManufacturerId	Int	Long	A unique identifier for the name of the manufacturer.
Name	Varchar(64)	String	The name of the manufacturer.

Another area of concern is that we need to store images for the toys. While I believe it is acceptable for you to store images in a database, I also believe that they should be stored in a separate table. Since I need to use a separate table for the image, I decided to add a sequence number column that will let me store multiple images for a single toy (see Table 3-7).

Table 3-7
Images

Column Name	*Data Type*	*VB Type*	*Description*
InventoryId	Int	Long	A unique identifier for the item in the collection.
Seq	Int	Long	A sequence number that is used to distinguish between multiple images for a single toy.
Image	Image	Picture	A large binary field that holds the actual image of the toy.

Order information

The final major entity that I identified in this application is the Orders entity. However, this entity needs to be subdivided so each order can have multiple items in the order. Thus, Table 3-8 lists the attributes of the Orders entity, while Table 3-9 lists the attributes associated with a single item that is in the order. I called this entity OrderDetails.

Storing Images in a Database

While many people recommend against storing an image in your database, I believe otherwise. By storing images in the database, it is much easier to secure and access them. Storing images outside the database means that you have to maintain a separate security system to protect the images. This can become very complicated if you permit the images to be accessed both by Web browser-based applications and traditional client/server applications.

While I believe in storing images in the database, I also believe that the images should be stored in their own table, away from any related data. Database performance is based mostly on how much information you can retrieve with a single disk I/O. The more rows you can retrieve, the better.

In a typical database table, you might be able to retrieve anywhere from 10 to 100 rows with a single disk I/O. However, if you include an image in the table, you may find that you only get one row for each disk I/O. By moving the image to a separate table, the performance of the main table isn't compromised.

Table 3-8
Orders

Column Name	*Data Type*	*VB Type*	*Description*
OrderId	Int	Long	A unique identifier for the order.
CustomerId	Int	Long	A unique identifier for a customer.
OrderType	Int	Long	1 = sale, 2 = purchase.
ShippingCost	Money	Currency	The total cost of shipping.
SalesTax	Money	Currency	The total cost of sales tax.
HowPaid	Int	Long	1 = credit card, 2 = check.
CreditCardNumber	Varchar(32)	String	The customer's credit card number.
ExpDate	Varchar(16)	String	The customer's credit card expiration date.
OrderStatus	Int	Long	1=order placed, 2=order shipped, 3=order received.
DateOrdered	Datetime	Date	The date and time the order was placed.
DateShipped	Datetime	Date	The date and time the order was shipped.
DateReceived	Datetime	Date	The date and time the order was received.

Table 3-9
OrderDetails

Column Name	*Data Type*	*VB Type*	*Description*
OrderId	Int	Long	A unique identifier for the order.
Seq	Int	Long	A sequence number that is used to distinguish between multiple items in a single order.
InventoryId	Int	Long	A unique identifier for the item in the collection.
PurchasePrice	Money	Currency	The amount paid for the toy.

The last entity I want to talk about is the States entity. This entity exists mostly to translate the two-character state abbreviation into a sales tax rate, which is used to compute the amount of sales tax that must be collected for an order. At the same time, I decided to add the StateName field to translate State into a more meaningful value.

Table 3-10
States

Column Name	*Data Type*	*VB Type*	*Description*
State	Char(2)	String	The two-character abbreviation for a state.
StateName	Varchar(64)	String	The proper state name.
SalesTaxRate	Decimal	Currency	The sales tax rate for the state.

Identifying Relationships

Once you have identified all of your entities and their attributes, identifying the relationships in your design is a piece of cake. You begin by looking at how the entities are related to each other.

There are three basic types of relationships: one-to-one, one-to-many, and many-to-many. These relationships refer to the number instances of data in one entity that are related to instances of data in another entity. In a *one-to-one relationship,* there is only one instance of data in one entity that is related to a single instance of data in another entity. For instance, assume that you have two entities—stores and managers. Each store has a single manager, while each manager has a single store. Thus each store has a unique manager and each manager has a unique store.

In a *one-to-many relationship,* one instance of data in the first entity is related to zero or more instances of data in the second entity. For example, assume that you have an entity for customers and an entity for orders. Each customer may place as many orders as they desire. They need not have placed any orders if they have signed up to be on a mailing list. For each order, there is exactly one customer who placed the order. Thus for each order there is only one customer and for each customer there may be zero or more orders.

In a *many-to-many relationship,* multiple instances of data in the first entity are related to multiple instances of data in the second entity. This can be illustrated by having an entity for parents and an entity for children. Each parent may have zero or more children, while each child may have multiple parents. (Remember, an orphan child has no parents, while a child with divorced parents, may have a mother, a father, a stepmother and a stepfather.)

Drawing the E/R model

Drawing the E/R model is a fairly simple task (see Figure 3-2) with the information found in Tables 3-2 to 3-10. While I didn't list the attributes for each entity because it would render the small drawing nearly unreadable, it is a fairly easy task. Of course, comparing the above tables to the diagram is probably even more meaningful.

Tip

When drawing an E/R model, I suggest using a tool like Visio rather than creating a drawing with a paper and pencil. Visio allows you to easily edit the drawing to accommodate the inevitable changes that will occur as various people review and comment on your document. Of course, there are some very expensive database design tools that offer similar capabilities, but I find Visio works nearly as well for most database designs.

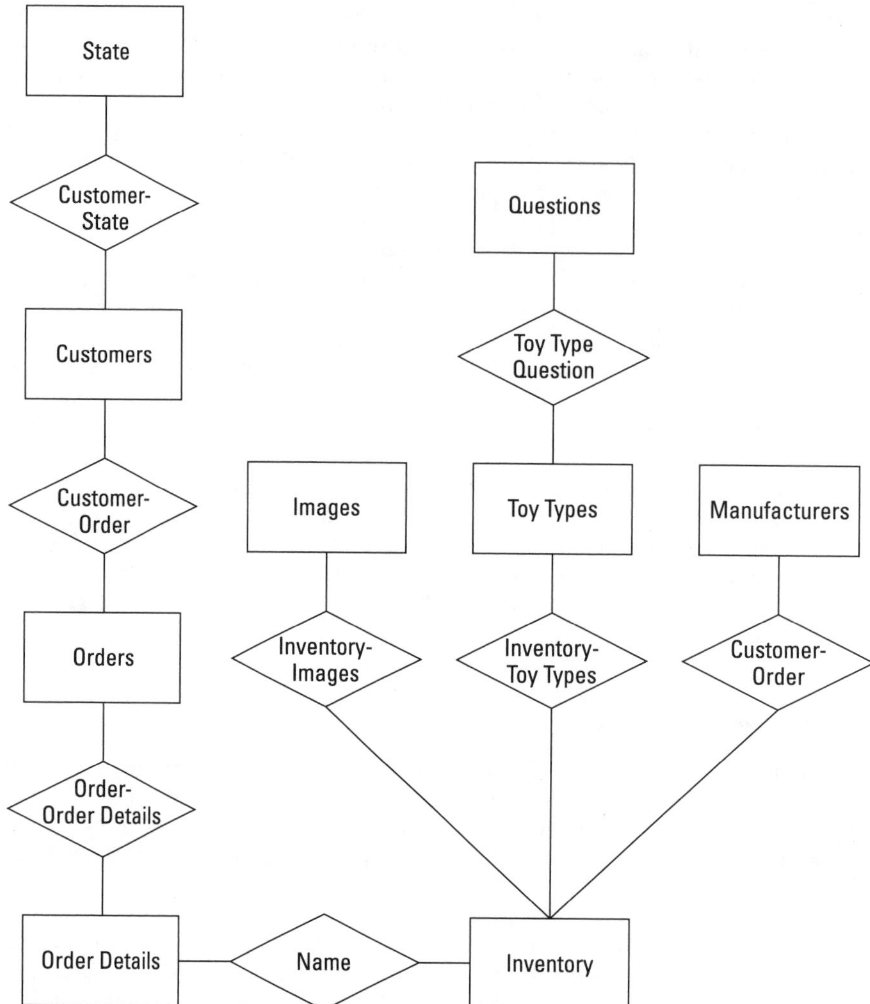

Figure 3-2: Viewing the final Entity/Relationship model for Toy Collector.

Building the Database

Translating an E/R model into a database is a pretty straightforward process. Each of the entities becomes a table and their attributes become columns in the table. You can see the final product in Figure 3-3 using the SQL Server database diagram facility.

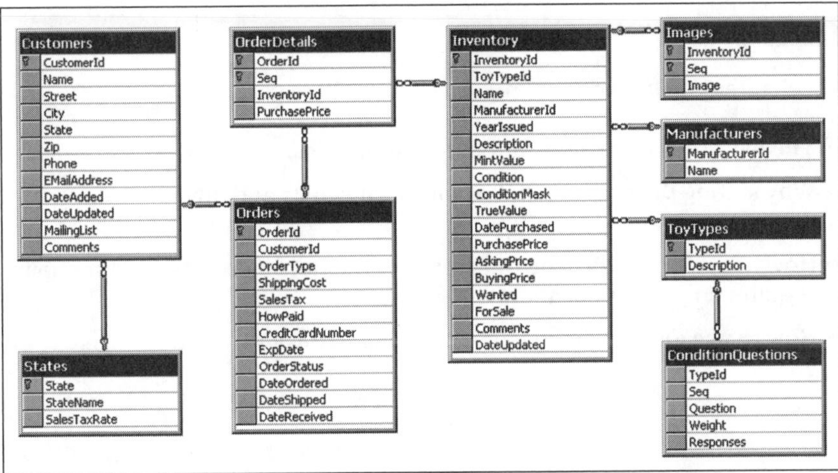

Figure 3-3: Looking at a database diagram of the Toy Collector database.

Thoughts on Database Design

Just because you have a valid database design doesn't mean that you will get the best performance from it. There are a number of factors that will affect performance, such as the number of tables in the database, the size of the columns, and the number of indexes you are using. However, the biggest single factor that affects your database's performance is the hardware you're using.

Believe it or not, having a faster CPU will not necessarily make your database server run faster. A database server is very I/O intensive. Anything that allows the database to retrieve data faster from disk will help the database server's overall performance.

Adding memory to your server allows the database server to cache more data in memory. After all, retrieving data from memory is much faster than retrieving it from disk. This is the biggest change you can make to improve database performance.

After adding memory to your system, using SCSI disk drives in place of IDE drives is the next place you should look for performance gains. Not only can you manage up to 15 disk drives on a single SCSI card, SCSI also allows you to perform concurrent operations on each drive. Thus you can have multiple disk drives performing seeks, while other drives are transferring data. SCSI-III can transfer data faster than SCSI-II or SCSI-I and should be used for best performance.

Using faster disk drives themselves will also improve performance. Disks that spin at 7,200 revolutions per minute (RPM) will transfer data faster than those that spin at 5,400 RPM, although two 5,400 RPM disk drives will probably perform better than one 7,200 RPM drive, assuming that you can split your workload evenly between the two drives. Of course, if you can spring for two of the new 10,000 RPM disk drives, you'll be better off in the long run.

Summary

In this chapter you learned:

- ✦ The five steps in an application design process.
- ✦ Why stating the program helps you clarify goals and objectives for the entire design process.
- ✦ How to use brainstorming to determine the data elements and functions required in your application.
- ✦ How to use Entity/Relationship modeling to design your database.

✦ ✦ ✦

SQL Statement Primer

✦ ✦ ✦ ✦

In This Chapter

The Select statement

The Insert statement

The Delete statement

The Update statement

The Create Table statement

The Create Index statement

The Create View statement

✦ ✦ ✦ ✦

In this chapter, I'm going to show you some of the key SQL statements that you will be using when you develop your applications. These statements will allow you to create tables, views, and indexes. The rest of the statements can be used to add, remove, change, and retrieve rows from your database.

Using SQL Statements

A detailed knowledge of SQL isn't necessary for most programmers. However, it will be impossible to write a database program without knowing a little bit about the language. The statements I'm going to cover in this chapter apply to all of the database systems that will be discussed in this book.

SQL for Dummies: If you really want to learn more about the SQL language, read the book SQL for Dummies, 3rd Edition, by Allen G. Taylor. This is a good introduction to the SQL language and covers all of the essential elements of the language. More advanced users should refer to the database vendor's documentation for their extensions to the SQL language.

SQL statements

The SQL language consists of a series of statements that perform specific tasks (see Table 4-1). There are statements to create databases and tables, statements to add and delete rows in a table, and statements to retrieve rows from a table or set of tables. There are other statements that deal with data security and data integrity. These statements are constructed according to a set of complex rules that vary slightly from one database system to another. However, for most users, these differences aren't all that important.

Table 4-1
Some Common SQL Statements

Statement Name	*Description*
`Create Index`	Builds an index on a set of columns on a table.
`Create Table`	Builds an empty table in a database.
`Create View`	Builds a view.
`Delete`	Removes rows from a table.
`Drop Index`	Deletes an index from a database.
`Drop Table`	Deletes a table from a database.
`Drop View`	Removes a view from a database.
`Insert`	Adds rows to a table.
`Select`	Retrieves rows from a table.
`Update`	Changes the data values of one or more columns in the table.

Data definition language statements

The **Create Table**, **Drop Table, Create View**, **Drop View, Create Index**, and **Drop Index** statements are known as *Data Definition Language* (DDL) statements, while the **Insert**, **Delete**, **Update**, and **Select** statements are known as *Data Manipulation Language* (DML) statements. In most database systems today, you rarely execute DDL statements when you want to create a database structure. Instead, you use a utility supplied with the database system that allows you to fill in all of the information into a table, or you use a wizard that will help you create your table or index.

This doesn't mean that the DDL statements aren't used. It merely means that you enter the information in a different fashion. The database utility usually includes a feature that will allow you to generate the SQL statements from the definitions you entered. Then you might use these SQL statements to create a copy of the database on another computer or include them in your application if you want your users to be able to create the database structures on the fly.

SQL data types

Each column in a table must have a data type associated with it. The data type you choose for a column must be compatible with a Visual Basic variable data type. Table 4-2 lists some of the most common data types used by SQL, along with their equivalent data types in Visual Basic.

Table 4-2
Some Common SQL Data Types

SQL Data Type	*Visual Basic Data Type*	*Description*
Char	String	A fixed-length string of characters.
Date	Date	A value containing a date and time value. (Available with Oracle only.)
Datetime	Date	A value containing a date and time value. (Available with SQL Server only.)
Decimal	Currency	An exact numeric value of the specified size.
Float	Double	A 64-bit floating-point number.
Int	Long	A 32-bit integer.
Money	Currency	An exact numeric value. (Available with SQL Server only).
Number	Currency	An exact numeric value. (Available with Oracle only.)
Real	Single	A 32-bit floating-point number.
Smallint	Integer	A 16-bit integer.
Varchar	String	Variable-length character string.

These data types can be loosely grouped into four main types: exact numeric values, floating point values, string values, and date values. Most database servers also offer many other data types to choose from.

For more detailed information about the data types available in a particular database, see Chapter 23, "Overview of SQL Server," Chapter 26, "Overview of Oracle 8*i*," or Chapter 29, "Overview of Microsoft Jet."

Exact numeric data types

Exact numeric data types represent numbers by using an exact value. These data types generally fall into two sub classes: *integer values* and *packed decimal values.* Integer values store their numbers as a binary value. This offers more efficient storage for large numbers than when you use a packed decimal value.

Money, money, money: If you need to perform calculations using currency values, you should always use an exact numeric data type.

Packed decimal values store numbers as a string of numeric digits. Four bits are used to represent a value from zero to nine. Most database servers will allow you to determine the number of digits you want when you specify the data type.

The advantage of exact numeric values is that when you perform arithmetic with them, you never lose accuracy. This isn't true with floating point values.

Floating point data types

Floating point data types represent numbers by breaking them into two pieces: a *mantissa* and an *exponent.* Floating point numbers are expressed in terms of a value time 10 to some power. For instance, the value 12,345 is written as 1.234×10^5 and often displayed on the computer as 1.2345E5, where E means 10 raised to this poser. In this example, the mantissa is 1.2345 and the exponent is 5.

Because of the way they are stored, floating point numbers are only accurate to so many decimal places. This allows you to represent very large numbers with much less storage than what would be required if you stored every single digit. Generally, *single values* have about five decimal places of accuracy, while *double values* are accurate to about ten decimal places.

Maybe, maybe not: You'll probably never need to use a floating point data type in your database, because most people don't appreciate adding 1,000,000.02 + 0.01 and getting 1,000,000 because the floating point value stored only 5 digits of information in the mantissa.

String data types

String data types hold character information. There are two different types of character strings: *fixed-length* and *variable-length.* The fixed-length strings always reserve the same amount of space in a table whether you store one character in the column or fifty. Variable-length strings, on the other hand, store only the characters you have in the string, plus some additional information that holds the length of the string.

In general, you should choose variable-length strings over fixed-length strings. This tends to save space in your database, especially if the amount of data you store in the column varies significantly from one row to the next. Using variable-length strings also allows you to create your strings with a larger maximum size. This is useful in situations where you may have an unusually large value that you don't want to truncate, such as a person's name.

Fixed-length strings are good when the size of each value remains relatively constant, as with a two-character abbreviation for a state or a product identifier code. This is especially true for small strings where the extra overhead to keep track of the true length of the string occupies more space then the string itself.

Date data types

Date data types are almost always unique to a particular database system. Even though there isn't much compatibility among the database vendors' implementations, the alternatives are worse. You could allocate an eight-character string and use the first four characters for the year, the next two for the month, and the last two for the year. You could also use an integer value to track the number of days since 1900 or since the day your organization was created.

Both of these methods have a drawback: the lack of integrated support for the values by the database server. If you store your date values as a character string instead of a date data type, when you use an interactive query tool, all you'll see is the raw, unformatted value. When using these values with Visual Basic, you'll have to manually convert your values to and from a **Date** variable in order to take advantage of the wide range of date and time functions already included in Visual Basic. In the long run, using the supplied date data types from the database server is a much better idea.

Testing SQL statements

One of the advantages of SQL is that the same language can be used interactively or embedded in your application. This means that you can code and test your SQL statements using an interactive query tool and then add them to your program. While the query tools differ depending on the database system you're using, they all do the same thing. You enter your statement and click on a button to execute it. The results will then be displayed on your computer.

For the examples in this chapter, I'm going to use the SQL Server database and the Query Analyzer tool to run the queries against the book's sample database. However, once you create and load the sample database in your database system of choice, you will be able to use the corresponding query tool to run the same examples.

The Select statement

Of the statements in the SQL language, the **Select** statement is the most commonly used. Its purpose is to identify the rows you want to retrieve from the database.

Here is the syntax for this statement:

```
Select [<selectoption>]<selectexpression>
[,<selectexpression>]...
From <tableref> [, <tableref>] ...
[Where <expression>]
[Order By <expression> [Asc|Desc]
   [,<expression> [Asc|Desc] ]...
```

where

```
<selectoption> ::= All | Distinct | Top <number>
<selectexpression> ::=  * | <selectitem> [ [As] <alias> ]
<selectitem> ::= <column> | <table>.<column> |
   <function> ( [Distinct]<expression> ) |  <expression>
<function> ::= Count | Max | Min | Sum
```

and

```
<alias> is an alternate name of a column or table.
<expression> is a valid expression.
<number> is a valid number.
```

The **Select** statement is the most complicated statement in SQL. The above syntax represents only a small part of the full **Select** statement syntax. However, you will rarely need anything beyond these clauses when building your application. A **Select** statement is composed of a series of clauses, such as **From**, **Where**, and so on. Only the **From** clause is required. I'm going to discuss how the basic Select statement works, and then discuss each of the clauses that work with it.

Simple Select statements

To use a **Select** statement, all you need to do is identify the table and the columns you want to retrieve from the database. Immediately following the **Select** keyword is the list of columns you want to retrieve, and the **From** clause specifies the name of the table you want to access.

Retrieving all columns

The following statement retrieves all of the columns from the Customers table in the sample database you'll find in the CD-ROM:

```
Select *
From Customers
```

The asterisk (*) implies that you want to retrieve every column from the table. Running this statement in Query Analyzer should generate results similar to those shown in Figure 4-1.

Retrieving a list of columns

If you only need a few specific columns, then you should replace the asterisk with the list of column names you want returned, as shown here:

```
Select CustomerId, Name, Zip
From Customers
```

Each column name should be separated from the previous column by a comma (see Figure 4-2).

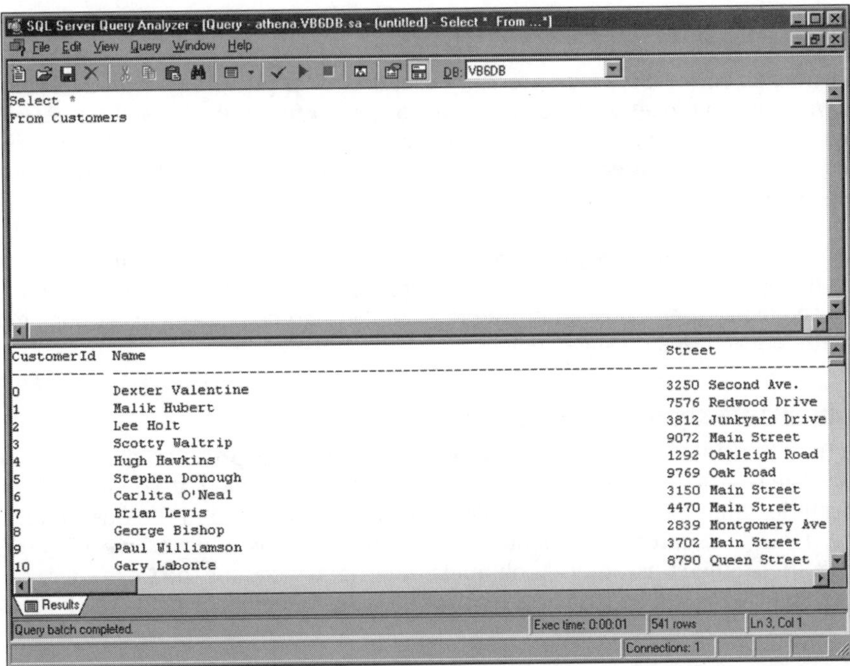

Figure 4-1: Running a simple query to retrieve all columns from the Customer table

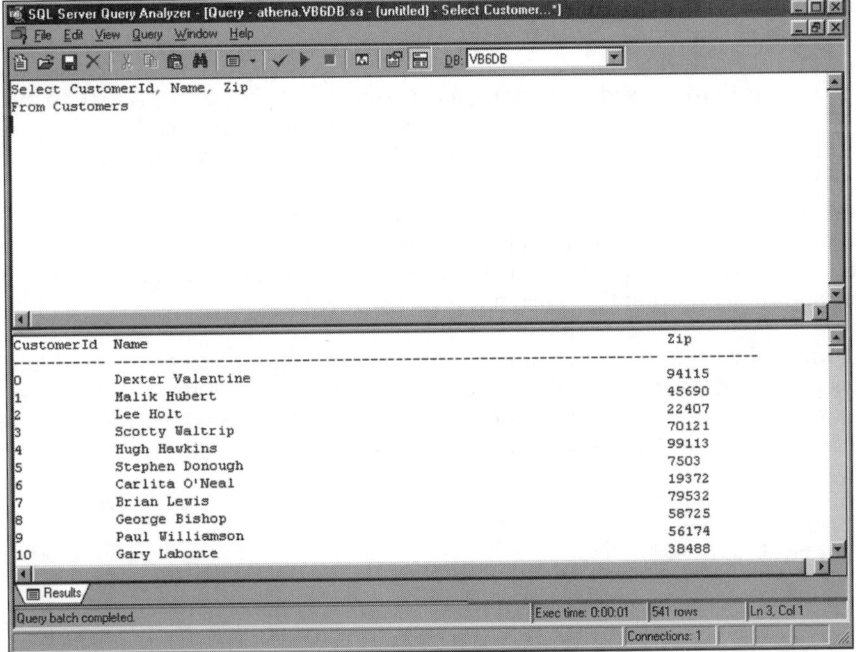

Figure 4-2: Running a simple query with a list of columns

Selecting a subset of a table

Returning an entire table is not terribly useful in an application program. Typically, you will want to retrieve only a single row or a handful of rows that are related to some other value. This is where the **Where** clause comes into play. The **Where** clause allows you to specify a search expression that identifies the set of rows you want to return.

Where oh where is my favorite clause: If the **Select** statement is the most commonly used statement in the SQL language, the **Where** clause is the most commonly used clause. It is used in a number of other statements, including the **Delete** and **Update** statements.

Using simple search expressions

The trick to using a **Where** clause is to create a search expression that will only return the row or rows you want. For instance, let's assume that you want all of the information about a customer 431. The information is stored in the Customers table. Thus, the search expression `CustomerId = 431` would retrieve all of this information. Since CustomerId column is the primary key for the Customers table, only a single row will be returned by the following **Select** statement (see Figure 4-3):

```
Select *
From Customers
Where CustomerId = 431
```

Searching for expressions with all the wrong operators: SQL supports all of the same operators that Visual Basic includes (=, <, >, <=, >=, <>, **Not**, **And**, and **Or**) to make it easy to build an expression. SQL also supports a few other operators, such as **In** (discussed in Nested Queries below) and **Like,** which is used to match a specified pattern, and which may include wild card characters. Of course, parentheses may also be used to ensure that the expression is evaluated properly.

Only those rows containing a CustomerId value of 431 will be returned. Since CustomerId is the primary key of this table, you know that each value of CustomerId is unique, so at most, one row will be returned. Note that if you specify a value for CustomerId that isn't in the table, no rows will be returned.

Of course, if you use an expression that is true for multiple rows, then multiple rows will be returned. The following **Select** statement may return multiple rows from the Customers table, since there may be multiple rows where the State column contains the value "MD" (see Figure 4-4):

```
Select *
From Customers
Where State = "MD"
```

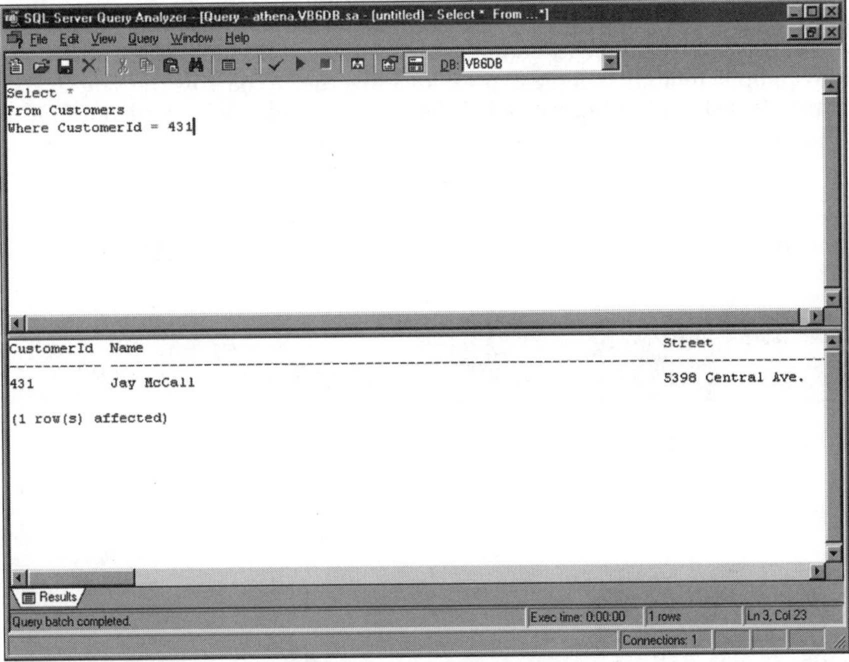

Figure 4-3: Selecting information about CustomerId 431

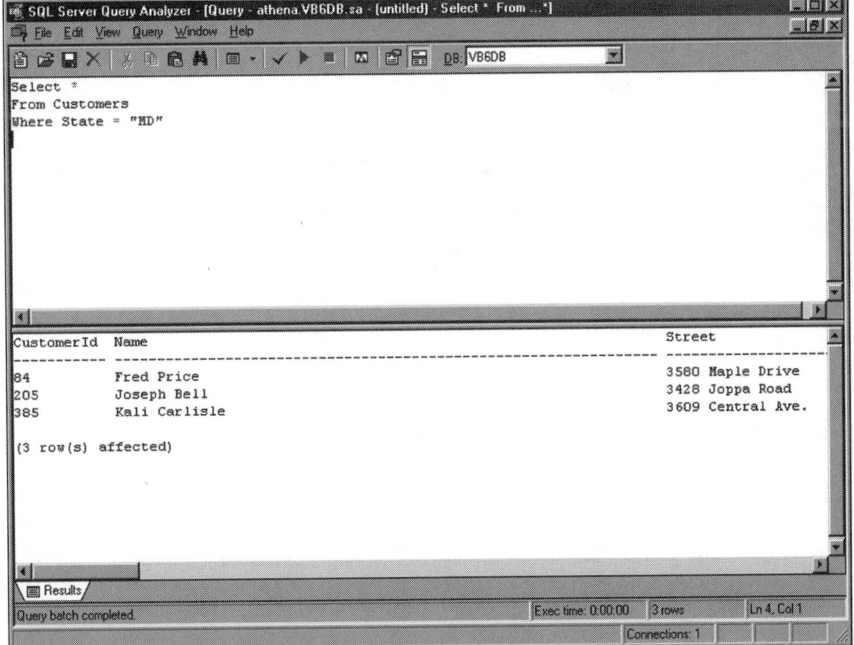

Figure 4-4: Selecting customers from Maryland

More complex search expressions

Search expressions can be as complicated as you want. You can use **And**, **Or,** and **Not** to compile multiple simple expressions together to narrow the search. The following **Select** statement returns all of the customers who were added to the database since 1999 and who also live in California (see Figure 4-5):

```
Select *
From Customers
Where State = "CA" And DateAdded >= "1-January-1999"
```

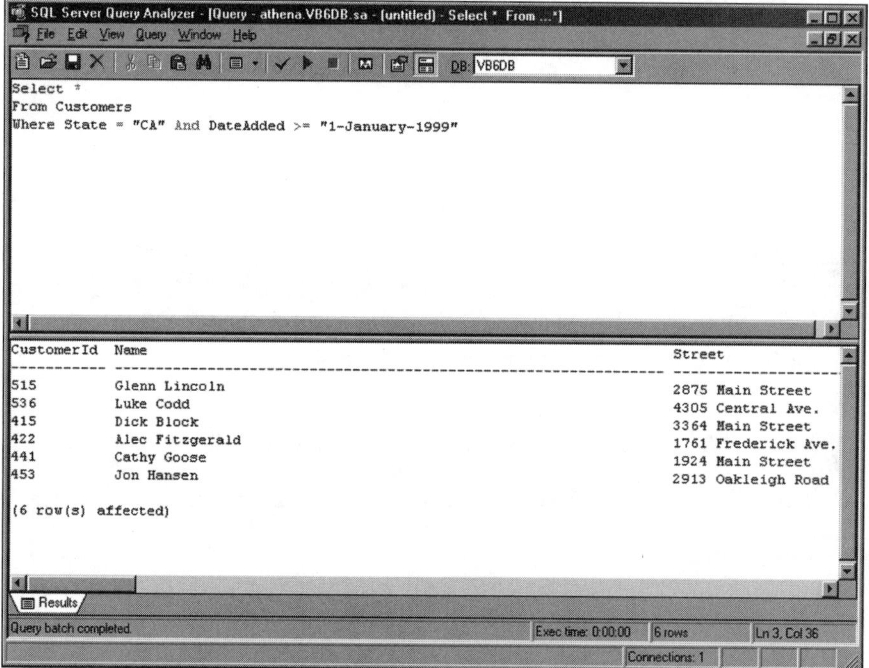

Figure 4-5: Retrieving all the customers living in California who were added since 1999

Waiting for it to end: Always try to include at least one column in your search expression that is part of an index. Otherwise, the database server will have to search through every row in the table to find the rows you want. While searching the whole table can be fairly quick for small tables, it can take a long time for large tables.

Sorting results

By default, the **Select** statement doesn't return rows in any particular order. In many cases this isn't a problem, but if you want to display these rows to the user, you might find it beneficial to sort them before they're displayed with the **Order By** clause.

Order By follows the **Where** clause and includes the list of columns that you want to use to sort the results. If you follow a column name with the key **Asc** or **Desc**, that particular column will be sorted in ascending or descending order, respectively. If you don't specify either keyword, the data will be sorted in ascending order. In the statement below, I'm going to retrieve all of the customers who live in North Carolina and sort them by their name (see Figure 4-6):

```
Select *
From Customers
Where State = "NC"
Order By Name
```

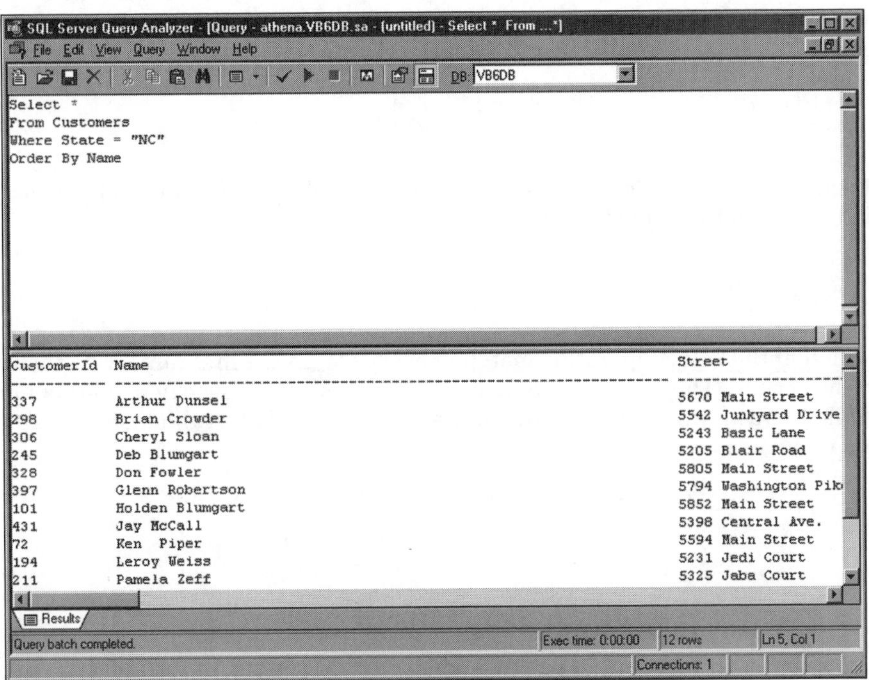

Figure 4-6: Sorting rows retrieved from a table

Note that since the data in the Name field is stored first name then last name, the results are sorted by the person's first name.

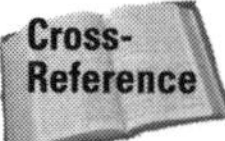

For more information about foreign keys and keys in general, refer to Chapter 2, "Indexes and Keys."

Using multiple tables

The **Select** statement allows you to combine information from multiple tables into a single "virtual table." This "virtual table" can't be updated, but it makes it easier when you need to collect information you want to display in your application.

Join operations: The technical term for combining the rows and columns in two or more tables is known as a *join operation.*

The wrong way to use two tables

The **Select** statement allows you to specify a list of tables in the **From** clause. However, the results are probably not what you would expect. Consider the following tables. Each table has three rows, with two columns in each row. Each letter represents a specific value in a particular column.

```
Table A: {{A, I}, {B, J}, {C, K}}
Table B: {{X, I}, {Y, J}, {Z, K}}
```

If you specify two tables in the **From** clause, the **Select** perform would look like this and you'll get the following result:

```
Select *
From A, B
```

Note that the **Select** operation matched every row in the first table with each row in the second. This created a table with nine rows, each row having four columns. While there may be cases where you want this result, I can't think of any off the top of my head.

```
{{A, I, X, I}, {A, I, Y, J}, {A, I, Z, K},
{B, J, X, I}, {B, J, Y, J}, {B, J, Z, K},
{C, K, X, I), {C, K, Y, J}, {C, K, Z, K}}
```

The right way to use two tables

Generally when you want to use two tables, it is because the two tables are related to each other. This means that the tables have one or more columns in common. These columns could be part of a foreign key relationship. Suppose that Table A and Table B have the Column2 in common, which is the second column in each table. Then the following Select statement would allow you to join the two tables together based on the rows that have a common value in their second column:

```
Select *
From A, B
Where A.Column2 = B.Column2
```

This **Select** statement would then generate the following result:

```
{{A, I, X, I}, {B, J, Y, J}, {C, K, Z, K}}
```

Note that even though Column2 values are identical, they are repeated twice because the rows were appended to each other. Also, if you look back at the previous set of results, you will find these three rows buried. The **Where** clause merely filtered out the rows where the values in Column2 didn't match.

Equijoins: A join that uses the **Where** clause to match column values in different tables is known as an *equijoin,* which is short for equality join.

Resolving column names

In the above example, I had two tables with the same column name. In order to know which column is associated with which table, it is necessary to qualify the column name by using the table name, as shown in the example below:

```
Select LastName, StateName
From Customers, States
Where Customers.State = States.State
```

To make life easier, you may want to use *table aliases,* which allow you to define an alternate name for your table. The table aliases are specified in the **From** clause by following the table name with the alternate name you want to use for the table. Personally, I prefer to use short one- or two-character abbreviations for table aliases, but you can choose whatever size name you want. Using table aliases, I can rewrite the previous query as follows:

```
Select LastName, StateName
From Customers C, States S
Where C.State = S.State
```

Note that using table aliases can shorten the expression in the **Where** clause. While this doesn't save much in this particular example, it can make a big difference in a very complex **Where** clause.

Nested queries

Of all the things you can do with the **Select** statement, *nested queries* are the most complex. In a nested query, you use a second (or third or fourth) **Select** statement nested inside your main statement. Typically, nested queries are used to return a set of values that can be used with the **In** operator.

Selecting rows using the In operator

Sometimes you want to compare a column to a list of values, as shown in the query below:

```
Select *
From Customers
Where State = "ND"
   Or State = "SD"
   Or State = "MN"
```

While this is fairly easy to write, imagine the problems you might have if you had a list of 15 or 20 different values to find. An alternative to writing a bunch of different clauses is the **In** operator. The **In** operator allows you to compare a column against a set of values, as shown in the query below. It will return a list of customer names that live in North Dakota, South Dakota, or Minnesota (see Figure 4-7).

```
Select *
From Customers
Where State In ("ND", "SD", "MN")
```

Sets of values

You can also create a set of values using a **Select** statement that can be used with the **In** operator. Consider the following query, which answers the question, "Which customers are in the same ZIP code as any of the customers that have been added since 1 January 1999?":

```
Select Name, Zip
From Customers
Where Zip In (Select Zip
              From Customers
              Where DateAdded >= "1-January-1999")
```

While this query is somewhat contrived, it gives you an alternate way to create a set of values. You may also think that this query is similar to the one listed below, but it isn't:

```
Select Name, Zip
From Customers
Where DateAdded >= "1-January-1999"
```

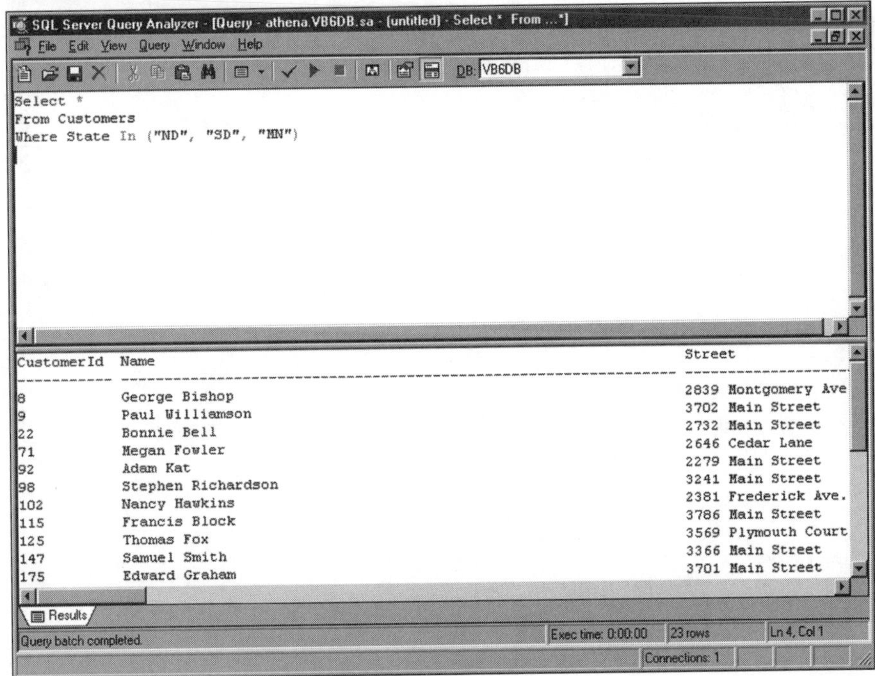

Figure 4-7: Finding customers in multiple states

The two queries could only be identical if each ZIP code had only one customer.

Complex to write, complex to debug: Nested queries often take a while to debug. The syntax errors will drive you nuts. I suggest that you avoid using them unless you can't do the query any other way. Unfortunately, there are some questions that you might want to ask that can only be answered using nested queries.

Using functions

You can also include various functions in your **Select** statement. For instance, the following **Select** statement counts the number of Customers who live in the state of Maryland (see Figure 4-8):

```
Select Count(CustomerId)
From Customers
Where State = "MD"
```

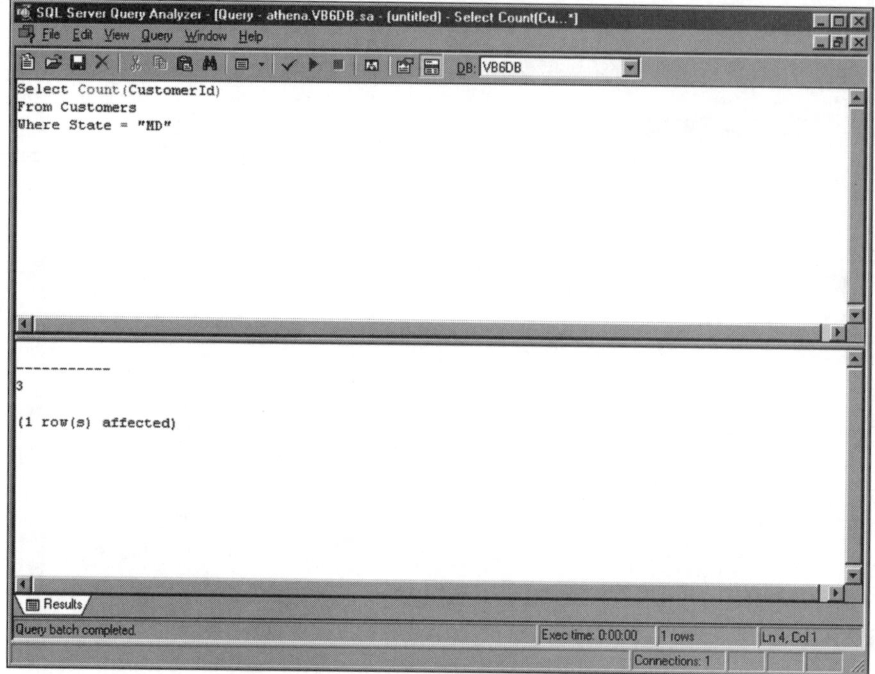

Figure 4-8: Counting the customers from Maryland

Other functions that you can use include **Min**, **Max,** and **Average**, which will compute the minimum, maximum, or average of a particular value across all of the rows selected from the database.

Not in my program, you don't: You probably aren't going to use functions in your application program. However, using functions in an interactive query program may help you decide if your program is working. You can use the **Count** function to determine the number of rows that you just added to your table, or you can use it to count the number of rows your program updated. Sometimes, just a quick check can help you identify if you actually processed all of the rows you thought you had.

Inserting Rows into a Table

The SQL **Insert** statement is used to add one or more rows to a table. Here is the syntax for this statement:

```
Insert [Into] <table> [(<column> [, <column>} ...])]   [ Values
(<value> [,<value>]...) |
As <selectstatement> ]
```

where

```
<table> is the name of where you want to insert new rows.
<column> is the name of a column in the table.
<value> is a value that you wish to insert into a column.
<selectstatement> is a valid Select statement.
```

The **Insert** statement adds a row into the specified table. You can specify a list of columns for which you will assign the values or use the list of columns specified when the table was created. You can either explicitly specify the list of values in the **Value** clause or use the **As** keyword to specify a **Select** statement that will retrieve values from another table.

Using the **Value** clause, you will specify the list of values to be inserted into the table. The position of each value corresponds to the order of the columns specified in the **Insert** statement, or if the list columns were not specified, the values will correspond to the order of the columns in the table definition.

Using the **As** clause with a **Select** statement allows you to populate a table with data from another table. Like the **Value** clause, the columns retrieved in the **Select** statement must match up with the columns specified after the table name.

Testing with copied data: When you are testing code that deletes or updates data in a table, it is often useful to create a temporary table with a copy of your test data and use that table for your testing. This allows you to easily refresh your data after your program deletes the wrong information. Using the **Insert** statement with the **As** clause makes this very easy to do.

A simple Insert statement

Here's a very simple **Insert** statement:

```
Insert Into Customers
   (CustomerId, Name, Street, City, State, Zip, Phone,
   EmailAddress, DateAdded, DateUpdated, MailingList,
   Comments)
Values (99999, "Christopher J. Freeze", "1234 Main Street",
   "Beltsville", "MD", 20705, "(800) 555-5555",
   "CFreeze@JustPC.net", "1-January-2000", "1-January-2000",
   1, "")
```

It adds a single row of information into the Customers table (see Figure 4-9). Note that I explicitly specify each of the columns in the table. Each of the values listed in the **Values** clause corresponds to the column listed in after the table name.

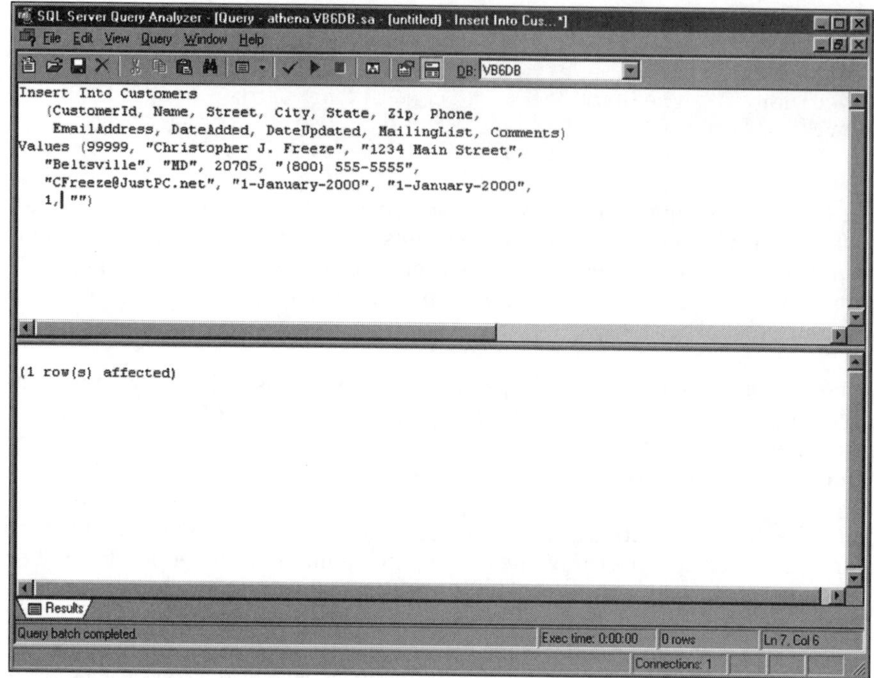

Figure 4-9: Adding a single row to the Customers table

The **Insert** statement listed below is identical to the previous one, but it assumes that the order of the columns as defined in the database is the same as the order of the data in the **Value** clause.

```
Insert Into Customers
Values (99999, "Christopher J. Freeze", "1234 Main Street",
   "Beltsville", "MD", 20705, "(800) 555-5555",
   "CFreeze@JustPC.net", "1-January-2000", "1-January-2000",
   1, "")
```

To run once is good, to run twice is bad: Running this statement more than once will cause an error. Since the CustomerId field is the primary key for the table and each row must have a unique value, attempting to add another row with the same value will cause an error.

Deleting Rows from a Table

The **Delete** statement is used to remove one or more rows from a table. Here is the syntax for this statement:

```
Delete From <table>
[Where <expression>]
```

where

```
<table> is the name of the database table from which you want
to delete the rows.
<expression> is an expression that is used to determine which
rows to delete.
```

The **Delete** statement is the opposite of the **Insert** statement. It is used to remove rows from a table. The **Delete** statement uses the **Where** clause from the **Select** statement to identify which rows should be deleted.

Deleting rows: When deleting a specific row from a table, use the primary key in the **Where** clause to identify the specific row you want to delete.

A Sample Delete Statement

The following **Delete** statement will delete the row I just added (see Figure 4-10):

```
Delete From Customers
Where CustomerId = 99999
```

You code the **Where** clause the same way you would the **Select** statement. In this case, I only want to delete the one row, so I need to code the **Where** clause to select the specific row I want to delete.

The **Delete** statement can also be very dangerous. The following statement will delete all of the rows in the Customers table:

```
Delete From Customers
```

Note that the only difference between this statement and the previous one is the missing **Where** clause.

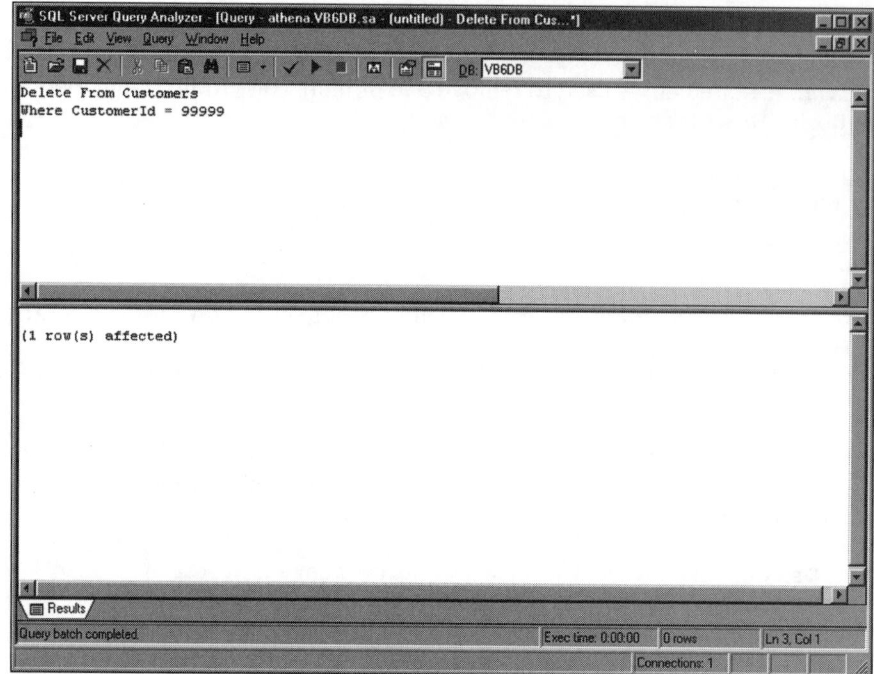

Figure 4-10: Deleting a single row from the Customers table

Don't delete everything: It is very easy to delete everything from a table. For that reason, you should exercise extreme caution whenever you use the **Delete** statement. Always use the **Where** clause when using the **Delete** statement. Failure to do so will delete all of the rows in your table. Unless you are deleting data as part of a transaction (see Chapter 16, "Transactions" for more information), you can't recover any deleted records.

Updating Rows in a Table

The **Update** statement allows you to change values in one or more columns in one or more rows. Here is the syntax for this statement:

```
Update <table>
Set <column> = <value> [, <column> = <value>] ...
Where <expression>
```

where

```
<table> is the name of the table you want to update.
<column> is a column name in the table you want to update.
```

```
<value> is an expression containing the new value for the
column.
<expression> is true for the rows you want to update in the
table.
```

The **Update** statement allows you to change any value in any row in a table. Like the **Delete** statement, you need to include a **Where** clause to isolate the effects of this statement only to the rows you want to update. Otherwise, you would apply the change to all of the rows in the table.

A Sample Update Statement

The following **Update** statement will search for all rows that have a **Null** value for DateUpdated in the Customers table and replace the value with a valid date (see Figure 4-11).

```
Update Customers
Set DateUpdated = "1-January-1997"
Where DateUpdated Is Null
```

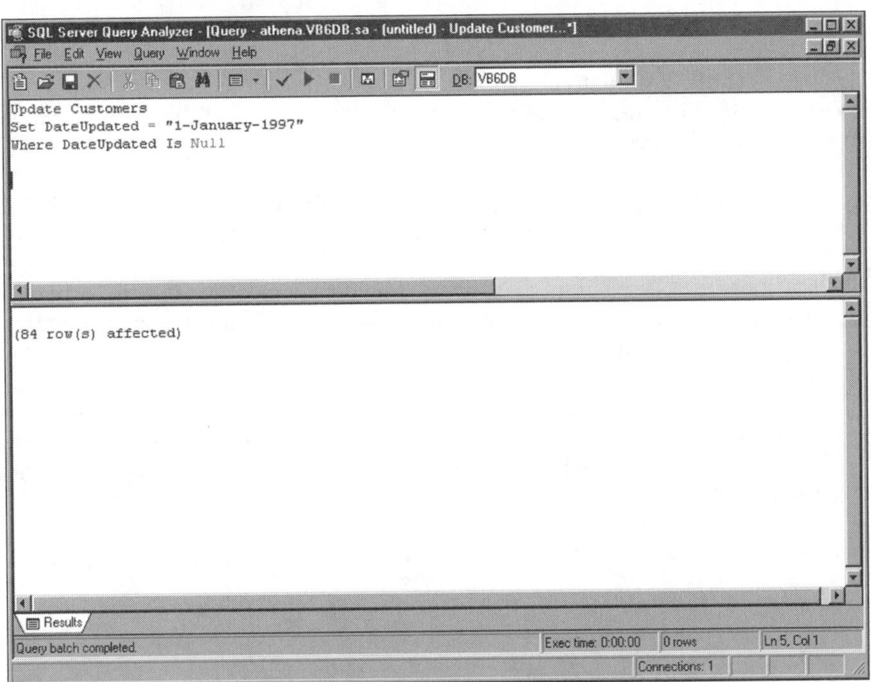

Figure 4-11: Changing **Nulls** to a valid date

The Create Table Statement

The **Create Table** statement is used to build a new table in your database.

There's more to this statement than meets the eye: Nearly all database vendors have added many vendor-specific extensions to the **Create Table** statement that I'll cover in more detail when I focus on the specific database systems in Chapters 23, 26, and 29.

Here is the syntax for this statement:

```
Create Table <tablename> (<columndef> [, <columndef>]...)
```

where

```
<columndef> ::= <columnname> <datatype> [Null | Not Null ]
```

and

```
<tablename> is the name of your table.
<columnname> is the name of a column in your table.
<datatype> is a valid data type.
```

The **Create Table** statement allows you to define the collection of columns that make up a table. The table must not already exist in your database, or you'll get an error message when you try to create it.

Each column must be assigned a valid data type. Table 4-2 earlier in this chapter lists some of the common data types available for a relational database.

For more detailed information about the data types available in a particular database, see Chapter 23, "Overview of SQL Server," Chapter 26, "Overview of Oracle 8*i*," or Chapter 29, "Overview of Microsoft Jet."

Gone with the table: To remove a table from your database, use the **Drop Table** <tablename> SQL statement. This statement will also delete any indexes associated with the table. Just be certain that you really want to delete the table, since it can't be undeleted.

The following SQL statement creates the Customers table for SQL Server:

```
Create Table Customers (CustomerId Int Not Null,
   Name Varchar(64), Street Varchar(64), City Varchar(64),
   State Char(2), Zip Int, Phone Varchar(32),
```

```
EMailAddress Varchar(128), DateAdded Datetime,
DateUpdated Datetime, MailingList Bit,
Comments Varchar(256))
```

Note that I declare the value CustomerId as **Not Null**, since this column is the primary key for this table.

The Create Index Statement

The **Create Index** statement is used to add an index to a table in your database.

Choose carefully, my child: Picking the right set of indexes can be difficult. You should use an index on the primary key of a table, especially if you plan to retrieve rows based on the primary key. However, adding any other indexes can severely impact your database's performance, since each time you add a row to the database, the database server has to update all of the indexes. The more indexes you have, the longer it will take to update your data.

Here is the syntax for this statement:

```
Create [Unique] Index <indexname> On <tablename> (<columnname>
[, <columnname>]...)
```

where

```
<indexname> is the name of your index.
<tablename> is the name of your table.
<columnname> is the name of a column in your table.
```

The **Create Index** statement adds an index to your table using the specified columns. Using an index can improve the performance of queries that use those columns at the cost of additional work the database server must do each time any of the values in the specified columns are changed.

Including the keyword **Unique** means that the set of values included in the index will be unique in the table. This is a useful feature if you need to ensure that you don't have two or more rows with the same value in the indexed columns.

Index be gone: To remove an index from your table, use the **Drop Index** <index-name> SQL statement.

A Sample Create Index Statement

The following SQL statement creates a **Unique** index on the CustomerId field of the Customers table:

```
Create Unique Index CustomerIndex
On Customers (CustomerId)
```

This ensures that each value of CustomerId in the table will be unique and also that queries using the CustomerId column in the **Where** clause will run faster.

The Create View Statement

The **Create View** statement creates a virtual table that can be used like any other table in your database. Here is the syntax for this statement:

```
Create View <viewname> [(<columnname> [, <columnname>]...)]
As <selectstatement>
```

where

```
<viewname> is the name of your view.
<columnname> is the name of a column in your view.
<selectstatment> is valid select statement that returns the
information in your view.
```

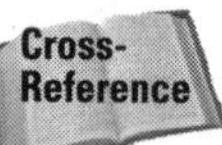

For more information about views, refer to "Views" in Chapter 2.

The virtual table that the **Create View** statement defines in your database is indistinguishable from a regular table for any operations involving a **Select** statement. The virtual table can often be updated, depending on how the view was created.

In order to update a view, the **Select** statement must only reference a single table known as the *base table,* and it must not return any calculated values using functions and/or mathematical formulas. Also, any columns not explicitly included in the view must be able to accept **Null** values. When you try to add a row to a view, any columns in the base table that are not part of the view will be set to **Null**.

Bye-bye view: To remove a view from your table, use the **Drop View** <viewname> SQL statement.

The following SQL statement creates a view that consists of the customer's name and the CustomerId column:

```
Create View CustomerNames As
   Select Name, CustomerId
   From Customers
```

Figure 4-12 shows the results of using a **Select** statement against the view. This view can be updated, since the columns that are not included will accept **Null** values. This technique is known as *vertical partitioning*, since only some of the columns are made available to the user.

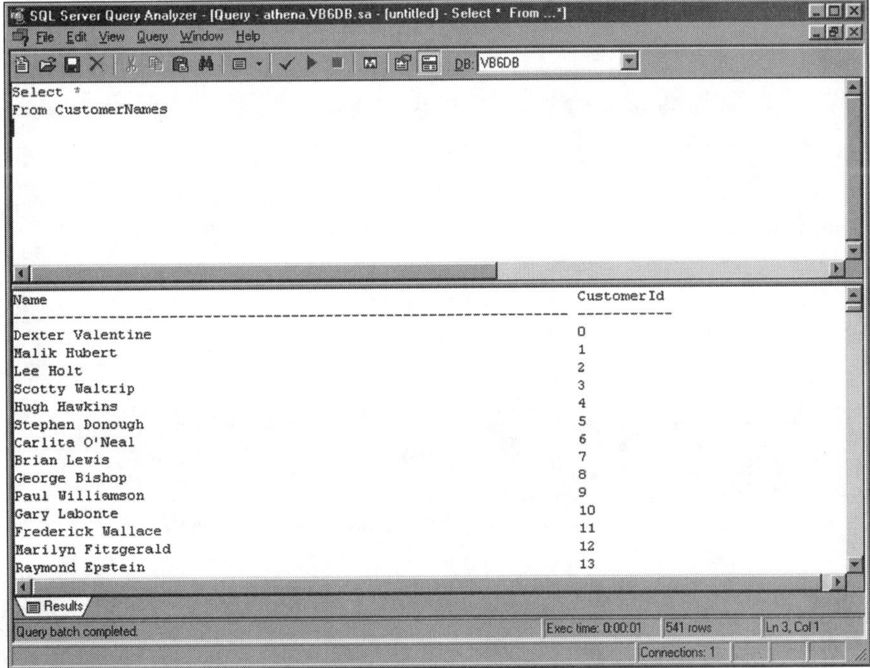

Figure 4-12: Preventing someone from seeing customer information beyond the customer's name and CustomerId

You can also use a **Where** clause to retrieve only some of the rows in a table. This technique is known as *horizontal partitioning*. Horizontal partitioning is useful if you need to create a view where only some of the rows in the table are retrieved. The following SQL statement creates a view containing only the customers found in Maryland (see Figure 4-13):

```
Create View MdCustomers As
    Select *
    From Customers
    Where State = "MD"
```

Note that this view is updateable, since all of the columns from the base table are present. Also, even though the view is restricted so that only customers from Maryland will be returned, you can insert rows using a different value for State. Thus, it is possible to add a row to the view that you will be unable to later retrieve.

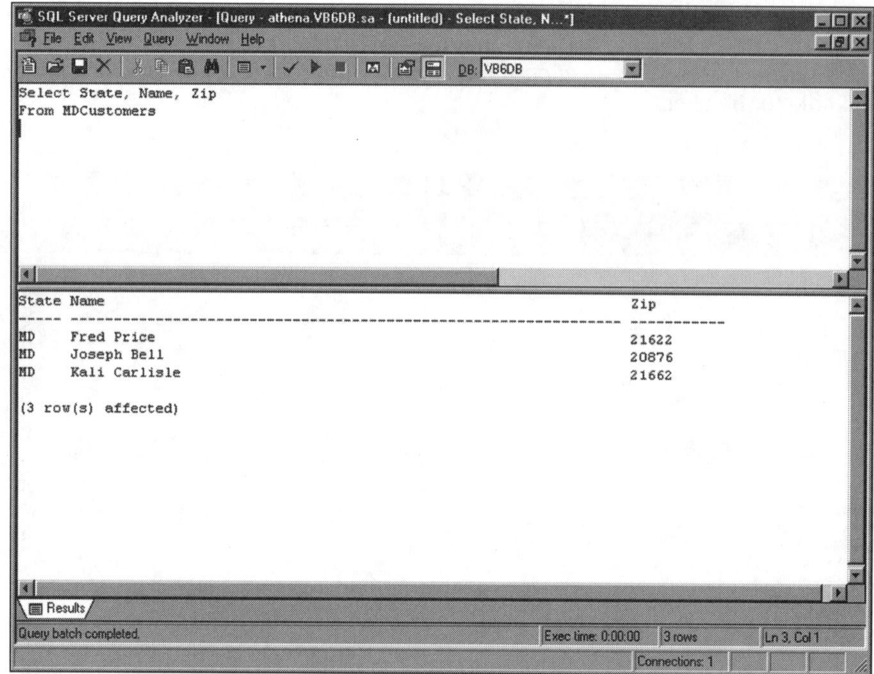

Figure 4-13: Restricting the view to only the customers from Maryland

Thoughts on Using SQL to Speed Your Development Process

The **Create Table**, **Create View**, and **Create Index** statements are known as *Data Definition Language* (DDL) statements, while the **Insert**, **Delete**, **Update**, and **Select** statements are known as *Data Manipulation Language* (DML) statements. In most database systems today, you rarely execute DDL statements when you want to create a database structure. Instead, you use a utility supplied with the database system that allows you to fill in all of the information into a table or use a wizard that will help you create your table or index.

This doesn't mean that the DDL statements aren't used. It merely means that you enter the information in a different fashion. The database utility usually includes a feature that will allow you to generate the SQL statements from the definitions you entered. Then you might use these SQL statements to create a copy of the database on another computer or include them in your application if you want your users to be able to create the database structures on the fly. Visual Basic includes several object models that isolate the programmer from the underlying SQL statements. So, while you may not need to know how to use the SQL statements to write a database application, you may find yourself backed into a corner, in terms of the technology.

Simply using an interactive query tool to retrieve information from your database will help you understand if your program is working properly or not. You can use the **Select** statement to return rows from a table and you can verify that they were updated properly. When used with the **Count** function, you can find out if your program processed the correct number of rows.

The **Insert** and **Create Table** statements can be used together to create test copies of a table, with which you can test updating and deleting rows repeatedly until you are satisfied that your program is running correctly.

Most database vendors supply a rich environment for executing SQL statements. Using this environment, it is possible to write multi-statement SQL programs called *stored procedures* that perform fairly complex operations. Since these stored procedures run totally on the database server, they may run significantly faster than executing them one statement at a time from your local computer. This is an important concept to keep in mind when developing a database application, and one that I'll explore in more depth when I talk about the stored procedures.

Also, keep in mind that many OLE DB providers translate the activities you perform into SQL statements that are sent to the database server for execution. This happens even if you don't explicitly include SQL statements in your program. So, in cases where every cycle counts, you might consider coding the SQL statements yourself rather than letting the provider do the work.

Another thing to keep in mind is that this chapter contains just enough information to get you started in learning how to use SQL. Since I feel that the best way to learn is by doing, I suggest you take the time to use Query Analyzer, SQL*Plus, or any other interactive SQL utility program to practice building and executing SQL statements. While I believe in the KISS rule (Keep it Simple Stupid!), there are times where it is appropriate to use very complex SQL statements. And the best way to write complex SQL statements that work is by practicing writing simple SQL statements.

Summary

In this chapter you learned:

- ✦ about the SQL statements and data types.
- ✦ how to use the **Select** statement to retrieve information from your database.
- ✦ how to use the **Insert**, **Delete,** and **Update** statements to manipulate the data in your database.
- ✦ how to use the **Create Table** statement to create a new table.

✦ how to use the **Create Index** to allow the database to find specific rows in your table more quickly.

✦ how to use the **Create View** statement to create a virtual table that can be used just like a real table, but whose contents are dynamically created from other tables in the database.

✦ ✦ ✦

Introducing Visual Basic

In This Chapter

Why use Visual Basic?

Visual Basic editions

Types of Visual Basic applications

In this chapter, I'm going to discuss why you should be using Visual Basic to develop your database applications. Then I'm going to quickly review the types of Visual Basic applications.

Why Use Visual Basic?

The easy answer to this question is that Visual Basic offers the best combination of features, efficiency, ease of use, and reliability of any programming language on the market today. However, the easy answer isn't always the obvious answer, so let's look at why you should be using Visual Basic for your database applications.

Basic history

Visual Basic is Microsoft's latest implementation of a language known as BASIC (Beginners All-purpose Symbolic Instruction Code) that was developed at Dartmouth College in 1964. It was designed to be an easy to use programming language for teaching students how to use a computer.

Jurassic BASIC

In the 1960's and 1970's, versions of BASIC were written for nearly every computer platform available, including everything from large-scale IBM mainframes and Cray supercomputers to the smallest mini-computers. It was extremely popular on the small mini-computers of that time, because both the computers and BASIC were interactive.

Most programming languages at that time were compiled in batch. In other words, you entered a bunch of statements into the computer and ran a compiler that checked the syntax and then ran the program if there were no syntax errors. Most often, you had to punch the statements onto punch cards using a special device known as a keypunch. Once you had created a deck of cards with your program on them, you had to submit the cards using a card reader to a faceless mainframe computer for executing. You then had to wait for the computer to run your batch job, at which time you got a printout that listed your errors. If you made a syntax error in the first line of the program, you got dozens of pages of errors, which had to be fixed before you could try again. If you were lucky, you could get two or three runs an hour, and if you were a lousy typist, you might spend several hours before you got far enough to actually run your program for the first time.

The key to BASIC's success was that BASIC would check each line of code when it was entered into the computer and report any errors immediately. This helped most programmers find their syntax errors and correct them before they tried to run the program. Then when the programmers were ready to run the program, they sat in front of a terminal and were able to immediately interact with the program. This helped immensely when testing a program, because you could test your program, find an error, and retest it in a matter of a minute or two, which allowed you to get meaningful results much quicker.

Of course this efficiency came with a cost. Most BASIC programs ran very slowly when compared to programs written in other programming languages. For the most part, this meant that the BASICs of that time were used mostly for teaching students how to program. After learning BASIC, most people would move onto real languages like COBOL or FORTRAN, which were more suited to building complex programs. This is where BASIC got a reputation for being a toy programming language that wasn't suitable for serious work.

BASIC jumps out of the Gates

In 1976, a small company known as MITS developed a computer from a handful of electronic parts, including a general-purpose calculator chip from a small, little-known company known as Intel. This computer was known as the Altair 8800. However, without a programming language, this computer was pretty useless. It did, however, provide an opportunity for a couple of Harvard students named Bill Gates and Paul Allen, who formed a company known as Microsoft. Their first product was a BASIC interpreter for the Altair that ran in 4,096 bytes of memory.

As other personal computers — such as the Apple II, the Commodore, the Atari, and a host of long-forgotten others — were designed, Microsoft was called upon to develop versions of BASIC for them as well. Before long, Microsoft was the standard of the industry, and every company that introduced a computer needed a Microsoft BASIC interpreter.

When IBM chose to enter the personal computer marketplace, they asked Microsoft to create a BASIC interpreter for their new machine. When discussions with another company for an operating system fell through, Microsoft was asked to create an operating system for the new computer also. This new operating system became known as PC-DOS, and later as MS-DOS.

By now Microsoft's BASIC had grown to the point where many people were using it to develop serious applications. The ability to read and write random files was a standard feature of the language, though the concept of database access was years away. BASIC had become a key product for the success of Microsoft and this generation of the personal computer industry.

Before BASIC was Visual

Over time, Microsoft realized that a compiler was necessary to improve performance of BASIC programs, so a new product known as QuickBasic was created. Another version called the Professional Development System was created for professional application developers and included a number of tools to make their life easier.

When Microsoft began building Windows, they decided to standardize on the C programming language. In order to build a serious program in the early versions of Windows, you really had to use C because that was the only practical way to access the operating system functions.

Microsoft didn't forget its roots, however, and created a special version of BASIC for Windows known as Visual Basic. It allowed programmers to include graphical interfaces for their BASIC applications. Version 1.0 of Visual Basic was the first and only version of Visual Basic to run on both DOS and Windows.

Data basics

Microsoft Access was developed to compete with similar products from Borland called Paradox, as well as products from Ashton-Tate called DBase. These products allowed people to build simple database applications quickly and easily. This was possible because of the functions provided by the databases that were at the heart of these tools.

Access came with a database known as Microsoft Jet. Unlike the databases used in the other tools, Jet was a true relational database. Since Jet was independent of Access, it was possible to use it in other programming languages. When Visual Basic 3 was released in 1993, it included an enhanced version of the Jet database, known as Jet 1.1. This tool became very popular with developers, and there are some people that are still using the original Visual Basic 3/Jet 1.1 combination to develop applications.

As time marched on, Microsoft released Visual Basic 4, which was the first version of Visual Basic to support 32-bit application development. It was also the last version of Visual Basic to support 16-bit application development. This dual nature was accomplished by two independent implementations of Visual Basic. However, the two versions were slightly incompatible with each other, because some of the controls weren't available in both versions. This usually caused a problem because Visual Basic 3 programmers couldn't move up to the 32-bit Visual Basic 4 compiler.

Another difference between the 16 and 32-bit version of Visual Basic was the Jet 2.5 and Jet 3.0 databases. Jet 2.5 was an improved version of the 16-bit Jet database included with Visual Basic 3, while the Jet 3.5 database was the same 32-bit database used by Access 95.

In Visual Basic 5, the 16-bit version was dropped, but numerous enhancements were made to the 32-bit version. The biggest enhancement was the ability to create your own ActiveX controls. Previously, if you wanted to create your own controls, you needed to write them in C++, which was time-consuming and complicated and often beyond the ability of the average Visual Basic programmer. However, with Visual Basic 5, anyone familiar with Visual Basic class objects could create their own controls.

The key to making ActiveX controls feasible was a native-mode compiler. Previous versions of Visual Basic compiled their programs into an intermediate code, which was executed at runtime by a special interpreter. The new native-mode compiler used components from the Visual C++ compiler to create the actual code. Now Visual Basic applications were almost as fast as Visual C++ applications.

BASIC today

Visual Basic 6 is the most recent version of Visual Basic. I like to think of Visual Basic 6 as Visual Basic 5 with every available factory option. While a few minor changes were made to the language itself, most of the changes added new features to the development environment. While Visual Basic 5 had only one type of application, Visual Basic 6 adds specialized applications that run on a Web server (IIS Application) and an application that runs on a Web browser (DHTML Application). Also, Visual Basic 6 includes a number of enhancements in the database area. These enhancements include the ability to drag and drop database definitions onto a form, a stored procedure debugger, and the ability to design databases directly in Visual Basic.

Database integration

The inclusion of the Jet database in Visual Basic doesn't necessarily mean that it's easy to use. However, the engineers at Microsoft worked hard to integrate database support into the Visual Basic language. This is accomplished through a few key features, such as a database object model, the ability to bind regular controls to the results of a database request, and specialized database controls.

Database object model

One of Visual Basic's strengths is the ability to create and use objects. Microsoft took advantage of this ability and created a set of objects that you can use to access the database. This isolates all of the low-level details from the average application and makes it easier to use the database.

Visual Basic currently supports three different object models:

- Data Access Objects (DAO)
- Remote Data Objects (RDO)
- ActiveX Data Objects (ADO)

DAO was originally released in Visual Basic 3 to support the Jet database and its design reflects that. While you could use DAO to access other databases, you had to define the other databases to Jet and access them through Jet. This extra overhead made a big impact on performance.

RDO was developed to eliminate the overhead and allow programmers to directly connect to SQL Server databases. The RDO object model was also much simpler than the DAO object model, making it easier to use. RDO was first introduced with Visual Basic 5.

Since neither DAO nor RDO offered a universal solution to database access, Microsoft developed the ADO object model with the intent to make it work everywhere. ADO was first shipped with Visual Basic 6, though you could download a copy from the Internet for use with Visual Basic 5. The ADO object model is similar to the RDO object model; however, some of the restrictions imposed by the RDO object model were removed, making it more flexible and easy to use.

Part III of this book is dedicated to the topic of ADO.

Bound controls

Most of the controls in Visual Basic can be tied to an open database, and automatically display the information in the current row of a table. The user can alter the contents of the bound control and the information will automatically be saved into the database. Using bound controls reduces the amount of code needed to display information from a database. And in general, the less code a programmer has to write, the more stable the program.

Database-oriented tools

Visual Basic 6 now includes a set of tools that helps the programmer perform database functions:

- **Data Environment Designer** helps you drag and drop database design information onto a form to quickly create database applications.
- **Data View Window** is available to view the contents of a database table or query at design time.
- **SQL Editor** is also available to help you create and debug stored procedures.
- **T-SQL Debugger** helps you debug stored procedures in SQL Server and Oracle8i systems.
- **Data Reporter** helps you build reports using information from the Data Environment Designer.

The Visual Database Tools integrated into Visual Basic, allowing you to create and modify database structures without leaving the Visual Basic development environment.

Database-oriented controls

Visual Basic also includes several controls that are designed primarily with database access in mind. The Data Control (which is available for both ADO and DAO) allows you to quickly build an application, which can scroll through the values in a database table or access the results of a database query.

Microsoft also took some common controls, such as the ComboBox and ListBox, and created database-specific versions of them with enhanced functions. These controls take their data directly from the database rather than requiring the programmer to load them explicitly. Microsoft also created a special control that allows a programmer to populate a spreadsheet grid with data from a database and allows the user to directly edit the values. These controls are available for both the ADO object libraries and the DAO object library.

A special control known as the DataRepeater control takes your custom ActiveX control, which displays information from a single row in a table, and repeats it as many times as necessary to display the results of a database query.

Visual Basic Editions

There are several different editions of Visual Basic that offer various features targeted at several audiences:

- Learning Edition
- Professional Edition

✦ Enterprise Edition

✦ Other flavors of Visual Basic

Fixes before the fact: Like most software today, Visual Basic isn't perfect. Since Visual Basic was first released, Microsoft has found and fixed several problems and put the fixes together in a service pack. The service pack can be downloaded from Microsoft's Web site at `www.Microsoft.com/Vbasic` by following the links to product updates and downloads. There, you will be able to download the service pack. While hardly any of these problems should affect you, it is a good idea to download and apply the service pack to prevent any known problems from happening.

Learning Edition

The Visual Basic Learning Edition is targeted at people who want to learn how to use Visual Basic. Only the most core features are found in this edition. While you can develop simple database applications using this edition, the lack of features will force you to upgrade to the Professional Edition rather quickly.

Professional Edition

The Professional Edition is the most common edition of Visual Basic. This edition includes such features at the Data Environment Designer, the Data View Window, which allows you to view the information found in a database table while designing your application, the special database controls described above. The Visual Database Tools and the SQL Editor described above are included only with the Enterprise Edition.

Tools, tools and more tools: In general, I prefer to use the tools found with the particular database system, rather than the Visual Database Tools. This is because the Database Tools are missing certain features that would eventually force you to learn the tools included with the database system anyway.

A full set of ActiveX tools are included in the Professional Edition that perform a wide range of functions useful for building your database, such as the TreeView and ListView controls, as well as tools that allow your programs to access resources over the Internet.

You can choose to build a number of different types of programs with the Professional Edition. You can create your own ActiveX controls, your own ActiveX objects, Web server applications and Web browser applications in addition to the normal executable programs. This edition also has a number of wizards that help you build applications more quickly, as well as a number of templates that you can easily modify to perform routine functions.

Enterprise Edition

The Enterprise Edition of Visual Basic includes all of the features found in the Professional Edition, but adds the Visual Database Tools and the SQL Editor to create stored procedures. A number of other facilities, such as the Visual Component Manager and Visual SourceSafe, are included to facilitate group-programming projects. An application Performance Explorer tool is also available to help you determine the efficiency of your application.

The other big difference between the Professional Edition and the Enterprise Edition of Visual Basic are the collection of tools that are included with the package. Personal versions of Internet Information Server, and Microsoft Transaction Server and SQL Server are included to help developers set up a test environment on their own computers.

Also, the Remote Data Objects are available only with the Enterprise Edition. This was true with Visual Basic 5 as well as Visual Basic 6, but is only important if you had older programs that used RDO. Otherwise, this really isn't that critical of a feature.

Other Variations

Microsoft is so strongly committed to Visual Basic that they find ways to incorporate it into many products, often without your knowledge. Besides the editions of Visual Basic that I've just introduced, you can find additional variations in many other places.

Visual Basic for Applications (VBA)

Most Office products include a product known as Visual Basic for Applications (VBA). This product is based on the same Visual Basic language that is used to develop application programs. The primary purpose of this variation is to help Office users build macros that make a particular application easier to use. The macros are really just calls to the object model exposed by the application itself. However, an application programmer can use this object model to create some rather complex programs that can be run from Word or Excel.

Visual Basic Script (VBScript)

Another variation of Visual Basic is known as Visual Basic Script or VBScript. VBScript is designed as a lightweight macro language. Many of the features found in regular Visual Basic and VBA are missing from this language. VBScript was originally implemented as part of Internet Explorer as an alternative to JavaScript; however, it can be incorporated into your own application programs as well.

VBScript and viruses: Recently, several different viruses that were written using VBScript have made the news. These viruses were included in e-mail messages as macros, which are automatically executed when someone opens the message. Just because VBScript is now associated with viruses doesn't mean that it's bad, but you should take appropriate precautions and treat all files that you receive from e-mail or otherwise as a potential virus source.

Windows Host Scripting (WHS)

The final variation of Visual Basic is really a variant of VBScript, known as Windows Host Scripting (WHS). WHS is used as a macro language for Windows itself. It allows you to build complex command line programs similar to those built by Unix programmers using csh or other Unix command interpreters. The best way to think of WHS is that it is really just a replacement for the old batch file procedures that people used to write for DOS.

Types of Visual Basic Programs

There are four main types of Visual Basic programs:

- ✦ Standard EXEs
- ✦ ActiveX Controls/DLLs/EXEs
- ✦ IIS Applications
- ✦ DHTML Applications

Many applications will use a combination of these program types in order to fully exploit the power of Visual Basic.

Standard EXEs

People have been building standard EXE applications for years. In this type of application, the programmer creates an EXE file that is run by the application's user, which in turn interacts with the user to perform a specific function.

When building database applications, I often refer to the standard EXE as the traditional client/server program, because it communicates with a database server using the client/server application model. This helps to distinguish this type of program from other Web-based application programs, such as IIS Applications and DHTML Applications and other multi-tier applications built using ActiveX components.

ActiveX DLLs/Controls/EXEs

ActiveX programs come in three flavors:

- ActiveX DLLs
- ActiveX Controls
- ActiveX EXEs

Each of these flavors represents a collection of Component Object Model (COM) objects that have been compiled and can be used by other programs.

ActiveX DLLs

ActiveX DLLs are simply a collection of COM objects that can be used by other programs. Since the objects are stored in a Dynamic Link Library (DLL), you need to create a program that can use them. They can't be used standalone. However, ActiveX DLLs are a great place to locate common elements that would be shared among multiple programs.

COM+ Applications are really just ActiveX DLL programs that have been designed to run under control of the Windows 2000 COM+ Transaction Server. The primary purpose of COM+ transactions is to create a middle tier of processing that is independent of both the client computer and the database server. While you can accomplish this by using an ActiveX EXE, the COM+ Transaction Server is far more scalable and reliable and can be extremely useful if you have a large application with a high volume of activity.

MTS + 1 = COM+: The COM+ Transaction Server is a major update to the old Microsoft Transaction Server version 2.0. While many of the features are similar, COM+ handles more of the details, making it easier to use than MTS.

ActiveX Controls

ActiveX Controls are nearly identical to ActiveX DLLs, except an ActiveX Control provides a visual presence on a Visual Basic form. You design an ActiveX Control by drawing a series of controls onto a form-like surface and adding the code necessary to manage the control.

ActiveX Controls are useful mostly when you want to put a combination of other controls and access them as a single unit. When combined with the DataRepeater control, you can display multiple rows of information on a form using the same format.

ActiveX EXEs

An ActiveX EXE combines the features of a Standard EXE with the objects found in an ActiveX DLL. Many programs you are familiar with are really implemented as an ActiveX EXE, such as Microsoft Word and Excel.

One advantage of an ActiveX EXE is that you can place the program on one computer and access the objects managed by the program from another program running on a different computer on the network. This program can offload work from both your database server and your client computer by adding a middle or third tier of processing.

IIS Applications

In today's world, many people are moving away from traditional client/server database applications to Web-based applications. These applications are really just programs that run on the Web server that return a string of HTML tags in response to a request from the Web browser.

An *IIS Application* is a special type of Visual Basic program that doesn't have any graphical components. Instead, it receives requests that originate from a Web browser via the same object model used by Active Server Programs (ASP) created by Visual Interdev. Then, the IIS Application constructs a Web page and returns it back to the Web browser for further processing by the user.

Since the IIS Application imposes very few requirements on the Web browser, it doesn't matter if the user has Internet Explorer, Netscape Navigator, or nearly any other type of Web browser running on any type of computer. This is the only type of Visual Basic program that will run on a Macintosh or a Sun workstation. However, as its name implies, IIS Applications will only work with an IIS Web server, so you must have a Windows 2000/NT server to run your IIS Application.

DHTML Applications

A *DHTML Application* is a Web page that contains an embedded ActiveX DLL, which can communicate with a database server or access other resources over the Internet. Its primary advantage is that it doesn't involve the Web server once the Web page and DLL have been downloaded. However, DHTML Applications only run on Internet Explorer 4.01 or higher.

Thoughts on Visual Basic

Microsoft claims that over three million people program in some form of Visual Basic. While this number undoubtedly includes people who write macros in Word and Excel, the true number of real Visual Basic programmers still exceeds one million individuals. I'm proud to be one of them.

I've been creating programs for over 25 years. I've used traditional programming languages like Fortran, COBOL, and Pascal for years. I've used specialized languages such as LISP, Prolog, GASP and SAS. I've used more assembly and systems programming languages than I can remember. I even used C before there was a C++. I've written compilers for my own programming languages, which were used by no one but myself. Yet I prefer Visual Basic to all of them.

There are many reasons why I prefer Visual Basic, but the most important one is that I'm more productive in Visual Basic than any other language, especially when writing Windows programs. I can start with nothing and end up with a comprehensive program faster in Visual Basic than any other language.

I wouldn't use Visual Basic to build a compiler, nor would I use Visual Basic to write an operating system, but I would use Visual Basic to write nearly any other type of program. And when it comes to database programs, Visual Basic is a clear winner to me. It is easy to create both traditional client/server and Web-based database programs, and by using ActiveX DLLs and COM+ transactions, you can gain a great deal of flexibility in how you actually create these programs.

Summary

In this chapter you learned that:

✦ Microsoft's first commercial product was an implementation of a programming language called BASIC.

✦ Visual Basic comes in multiple editions, of which only the Professional Edition and the Enterprise Edition have complete database support.

✦ You can create standard EXEs, ActiveX Controls, ActiveX DLLs and ActiveX EXEs using Visual Basic.

✦ You can develop Web server-based Visual Basic applications using IIS Applications.

✦ You can develop browser-based Visual Basic applications using DHTML Applications.

✦ You can develop Visual Basic to build n-tier applications using COM+ transactions.

✦ ✦ ✦

Accessing Databases from Visual Basic

In This Chapter

ODBC and OLE DB

DAO object model

RDO object model

ADO object model

Visual Basic database tools

In this chapter, I'm going to discuss how Visual Basic talks to a database server. ODBC and OLE DB are the low-level technologies that actually perform the work, while the DAO, RDO, and ADO object models encapsulate these technologies to make them easy for the Visual Basic programmer to use.

Microsoft Database Programming APIs

Just because your database server is based on SQL doesn't mean that you can easily access it from your favorite programming language. Many database vendors provide a special pre-compiler that translates embedded database statements into database subroutine calls that in turn communicate with the database server. The problem with this approach is that you need a different pre-compiler for each programming language the database vendor supports. Of course, since the pre-compilers are specific for each database server, you'll need a pre-compiler for each database server for which you develop programs. Rather than developing a large number of pre-compilers for each combination of database server and programming language, Microsoft developed a standard called *Open Database Connectivity* (ODBC), which later evolved into OLE DB.

ODBC

The ODBC standard defines an *Application Programming Interface* (API) for database programming. This allows you to write a program using standard subroutine calls for any database server that supports ODBC, making it possible for the same object code to access any ODBC-compatible database server.

ODBC architecture

ODBC is based on the idea that the calls to the API routines made by the application program are translated to lower calls that are passed onto a database driver (see Figure 6-1). The database driver in turn performs the necessary work to talk to the database server. Thus, the database vendor need only provide an ODBC-compatible driver for each client computer system and not for each compiler on each client operating system.

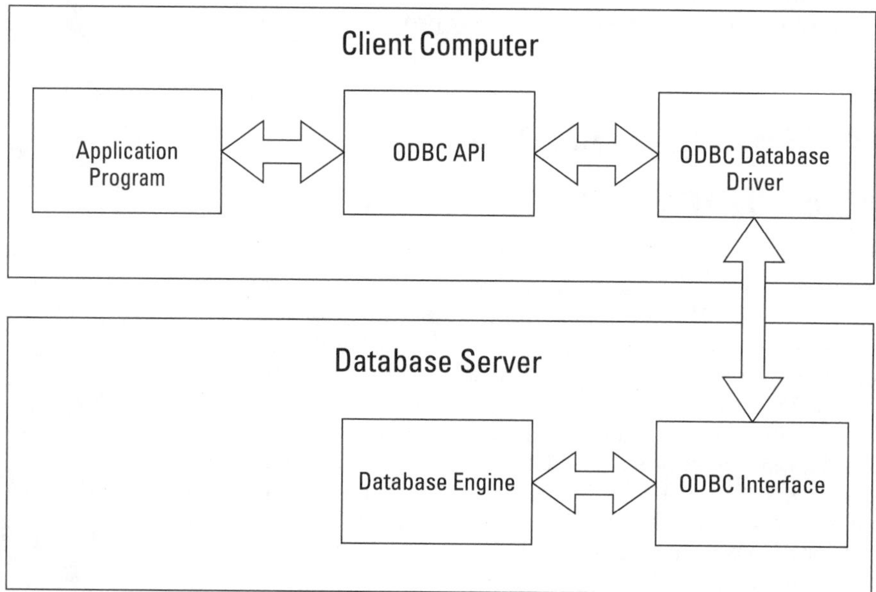

Figure 6-1: The client side of the ODBC architecture is based on the driver model.

On the database server side, all the database vendor needs to do is provide a single ODBC interface, which will be shared by all ODBC clients. This means that database vendors can preserve their native interface, plus any other specialized interfaces for other applications.

A utility program called the ODBC Administrator is included as part of the operating system to manage the set of ODBC drivers and database servers that are available to the ODBC API. This program allows you to add and remove ODBC drivers, specify how to connect to the database server, and include security information that will be used when the connection between the client computer and the database server is opened.

Drawbacks to ODBC

While the architecture of ODBC allows a great deal of flexibility on the part of the database vendor, there are several drawbacks to writing ODBC applications. First, the ODBC APIs are difficult to use, especially if you aren't programming in C. Second, the ODBC APIs are often slower than the native database interface. Third, the ODBC API often imposes restrictions on the SQL statements that can be used.

While the first drawback applies to all database servers, the second two drawbacks apply mainly to non-Microsoft database servers. Microsoft uses ODBC as the native interface to both the Jet database and SQL Server. They spent a lot of time tuning the interface for optimal results. While other database vendors support ODBC, their native interfaces may offer improved performance and functionality, especially for non-Microsoft compilers.

Database Access Objects (DAO)

Because the ODBC API is difficult to use, Microsoft chose to build an object-oriented interface to ODBC called *Data Access Objects* (DAO). DAO was originally developed for Access and Visual Basic programmers who needed to access the Jet database. Most of the functionality available in DAO mirrors features found in the Jet database.

While DAO can be used to access other databases, the process is often difficult to use and clumsy in its implementation. To access an SQL Server database, you need to create a Jet database and then go through the Jet database to access the remote database. While DAO allows you to access the ODBC database directly, each time you open the database, you must download a lot of information about the database structures that you might access. By using the Jet database, this information is saved locally and need not be downloaded each time you open the database.

Note

Visual Basic 6 and Access 2000: While Jet 3.51 is shipped with Visual Basic 6, Jet 4.0 is shipped with Access 2000. While it's possible to use Visual Basic 6 and DAO with Jet 4.0, many of the new features found in Jet 4.0 can only be used if you're using ADO.

Remote Database Objects (RDO)

The *Remote Database Objects* (RDO) object model was built to address the problems associated with accessing SQL Server from Visual Basic. First available with the Visual Basic 5 Enterprise Edition of Visual Basic, RDO offered a streamlined object model which in turn offered much better performance than DAO when used with a database such as SQL Server or Oracle. However, RDO doesn't work with the Jet database and other single-user database systems.

One feature lacking in RDO that is found in DAO is the ability to create a database by defining objects. Given that RDO is really targeted at large installations, this isn't nearly as limiting as it seems. These installations generally have a group of people known as *database administrators* (DBAs), whose sole responsibility is the creation and maintenance of database structures. DBAs often use specialized tools to help them design and document their databases.

OLE DB

After years of working with ODBC, Microsoft recognized that the database server to database client model used by ODBC could be generalized as a *data provider* to *data consumer* model (see Figure 6-2).

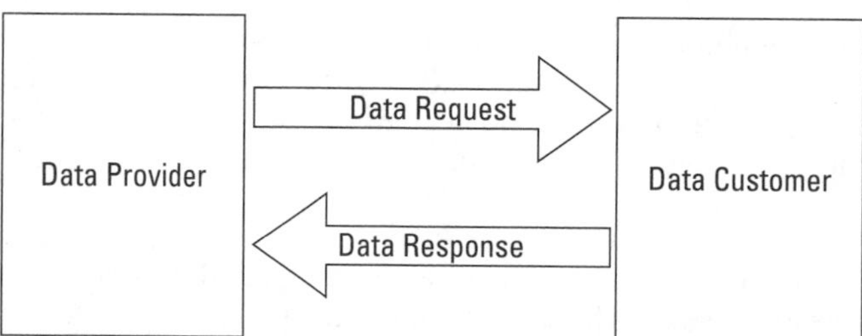

Figure 6-2: A data provider handles data requests from a data consumer.

Data providers

A *data provider* is a program that supplies data to another program. In the ODBC model, the data provider is the database server. However, in the OLE DB, nearly anything that can produce data could be considered a data provider. This allows programmers to treat such things as an Excel workbook, a flat file, or another custom-built program like a database server.

Data consumers

A *data consumer* is simply a client program that requests data from a data provider. Two types of information may be requested from the data producer: *data* and *metadata*. Data is the information used by an application, while metadata is information about the structures used to hold the data. Metadata includes such information as the name of each column returned, its size and data type, and other descriptive information.

ActiveX Data Objects (ADO)

The *ActiveX Data Objects* (ADO) object model was created to replace both DAO and RDO object models and was shipped for the first time in Visual Basic 6. It uses the newer OLE DB API rather than the older ODBC API. In addition, ADO has an even simpler object model than found in the DAO and RDO, which makes it easier to use.

ADO is modeled after RDO and includes many of the familiar objects found in DAO and RDO, such as the **RecordSet** object. However, where RDO maintains a relatively strict object hierarchy, ADO's object structure is much looser. This means that you generally need fewer objects in your program, and the resulting code is even simpler.

Like RDO, ADO doesn't include objects that you can use to define your database. However, with version 2.5 of ADO, Microsoft included a new set of objects known as ADOX, which can be used to define database structures and security. These objects would be useful if you want to write a general-purpose tool that allows you to create and manipulate database structures from multiple database vendors. They can help smooth over differences in how the various vendors implement their own SQL extensions.

ADO MD is another set of extensions to the base ADO objects. These objects allow you to work with a multidimensional database such as the OLAP Services bundled with SQL Server. You can use these objects to build your own programs for manipulating information from your own data warehouse.

OLE DB providers

Table 6-1 lists the OLE DB providers that are available with Visual Basic 6. Other OLE DB providers may be available from your specific database vendor.

Table 6-1
Common OLE DB Providers

Provider Name	*Description*
Microsoft Jet 3.51 OLE DB Provider	Supports Access 97/Jet 3.51 databases
Microsoft Jet 4.0 OLE DB Provider	Supports Access 2000/Jet 4.0 databases
Microsoft OLE DB Provider for SQL Server	Supports SQL Server 6.5 and 7.0
Microsoft OLE DB Provider for Oracle	Supports Oracle 7 and 8
Microsoft OLE DB Provider for Microsoft Active Directory Service	Supports Microsoft Active Directory Service found in Windows 2000 Server
Microsoft OLE DB Provider for Microsoft Index Service	Supports Microsoft Index Server 2.0 and newer
Microsoft OLE DB Provider for OLAP Services	Supports Microsoft OLAP Server
Microsoft OLE DB Provider for ODBC Drivers	Supports generic ODBC access

Even if your database server doesn't support OLE DB, that doesn't mean you can't access the database from ADO. There is a special provider known OLE DB Provider for ODBC. This allows you to connect your ADO-based application to any ODBC database. Of course, you should try to use a native OLE DB provider whenever possible.

Custom OLE DB providers

The architecture of OLE DB allows you to write your own OLE DB provider. This is an advanced technique that most people won't ever need to use. After all, how many people implement their own database management system? However, if you have a custom data storage application, you can create your own OLE DB provider for it. This will allow programmers to access it using tools with which they are already familiar.

Visual Basic Database Tools

To support database programming, Visual Basic includes a nice assortment of tools that will assist you in creating your application, including the following:

- ✦ Data Environment Designer
- ✦ Data View Window

- Database Designer
- SQL Editor
- T-SQL Debugger
- Query Designer
- Data Report Designer
- UserConnection Designer

With the exception of the UserConnection Designer, these tools will work only in an ADO programming environment. The UserConnection Designer works only with RDO objects.

Data Environment Designer

The Data Environment Designer (see Figure 6-3) is an interactive design-time tool that helps you create database objects for use at runtime. It is based on the ADO object model and will not work with RDO and DAO objects.

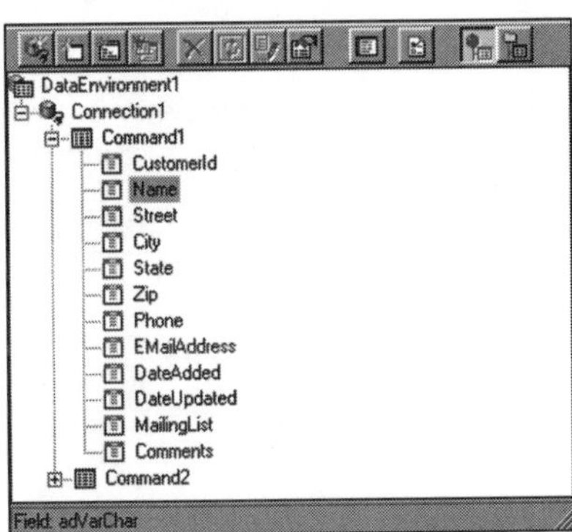

Figure 6-3: Using the Data Environment Designer

You can use the Data Environment Designer to perform the following tasks:

- Define **Connection** objects to your database using either OLE DB data sources or ODBC data sources.
- Define **Command** objects using tables, queries, and stored procedures from your database.
- Create hierarchies of **Command** objects that can be used with hierarchical tools like the **HFlexGrid** control and the **Data Reporter Designer**.

- Drag and drop fields and tables from a **Command** object in the designer onto a **Form** object or the **Data Reporter** designer that are automatically bound to the **Command** object.
- Specify default the type of control to be used as part of drag and drop operations.
- Bind data-aware controls to **Field** objects within a **Command** object.
- Attach code for **Connection** and **Recordset** objects in the Data Environment Designer.
- Trap all ADO events for the **Connection** and **Command** objects.

Data View Window

The Data View Window allows you to access your database system through Visual Basic instead of a particular database vendor's utility (see Figure 6-4). Through the Data View Window, you can access the Microsoft Visual Database Tools.

The Visual Database Tools are present only in the Enterprise Edition of Visual Basic. This not only includes the Data View Window, but the Database Designer, the Query Designer, the SQL Editor, and the T-SQL Debugger.

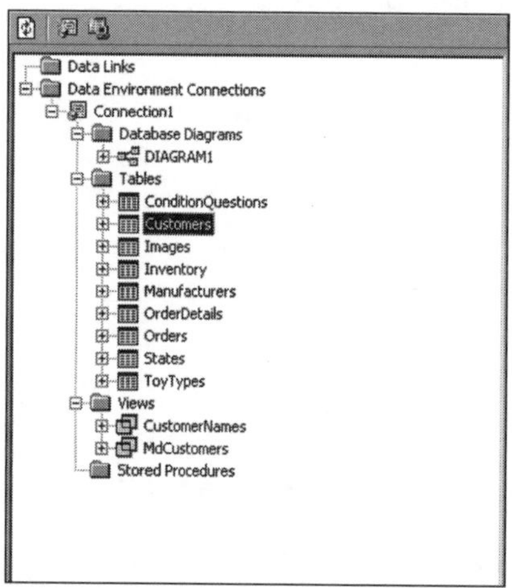

Figure 6-4: Using the Data View Window to browse and edit the database structures in your database

You can use the Data View Window to perform the following tasks:

- Create a **Connection** object that can be used to access your database while in design mode or at runtime.
- Design your database graphically using the Database Designer.

✦ View the contents of a table or view using a worksheet-like display.

✦ Create and edit stored procedures using the SQL Editor.

✦ Debug stored procedures using the T-SQL Debugger.

✦ Create views using the Query Designer.

✦ Generate reports using the Data Reporter Designer.

Database Designer

The Database Designer is a graphical tool that presents a database using a graphical diagram (see Figure 6-5). The Database Designer works with both Microsoft SQL Server and Oracle database systems.

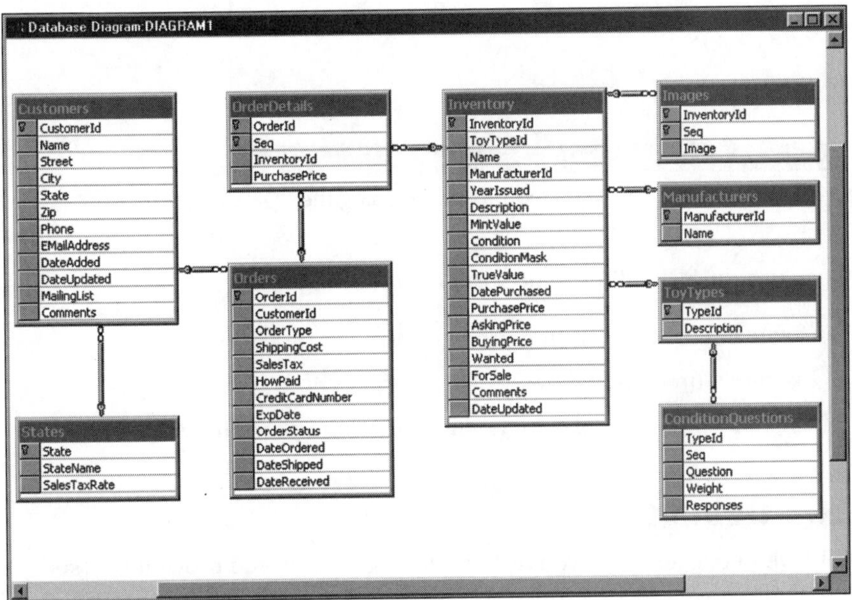

Figure 6-5: Designing a database graphically using the Database Designer

You can use the Database Designer to perform the following tasks:

✦ Create and modify tables.

✦ Add and delete indexes.

✦ Define relationships between tables.

✦ Save SQL scripts to create or update your database structures.

SQL Editor

The SQL Editor provides a simple editor to help you write stored procedures (see Figure 6-6).

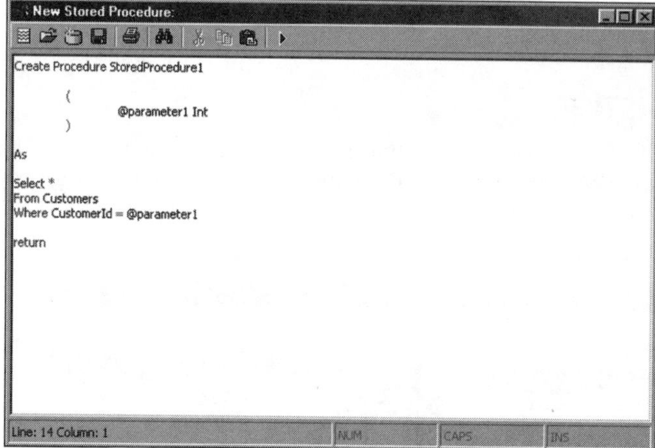

Figure 6-6: Editing a simple stored procedure using the SQL Editor

You can use the SQL Editor to perform the following tasks:

- ✦ Create and edit SQL stored procedures.
- ✦ Execute stored procedures.
- ✦ Use the T-SQL Debugger to debug your stored procedures.

T-SQL Debugger

The T-SQL Debugger helps you test and debug your stored procedures (see Figure 6-7).

You can use the T-SQL Debugger to perform the following tasks:

- ✦ Display the contents of local variables and parameters.
- ✦ Modify local variables and parameters while executing the stored procedure.
- ✦ Control execution by using breakpoints.
- ✦ Step through the stored procedure.
- ✦ View global variables.
- ✦ View the call stack.

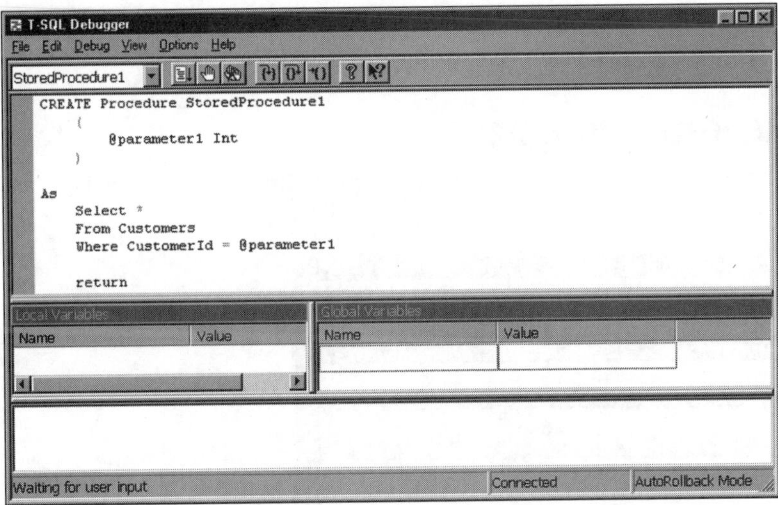

Figure 6-7: Testing a simple stored procedure using the T-SQL Debugger

Query Designer

The Query Designer is a tool that works with the Data View Window to drag and drop tables and columns to create a view or query (see Figure 6-8).

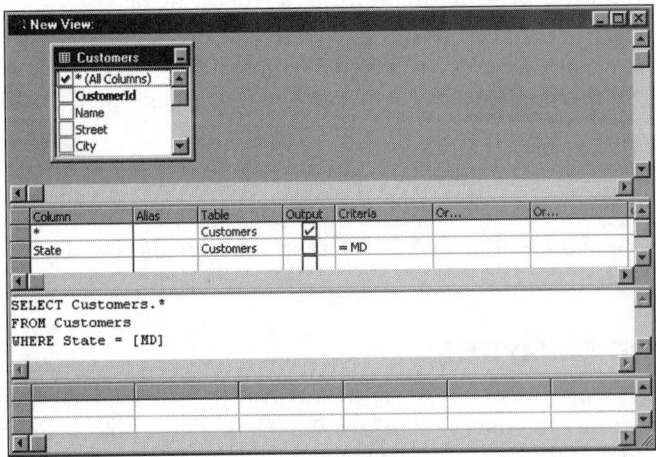

Figure 6-8: Creating a view using the Query Designer

You can use the Query Designer to perform the following tasks:

- ✦ Drag and drop tables from the Data View Window onto your query.
- ✦ Use a criteria grid to specify search criteria and sort order.

- Select the columns to be output as a result of the query.
- Browse and edit live views of your data in your view.

Data Reporter Designer

The Data Reporter Designer helps you build reports interactively (see Figure 6-9).

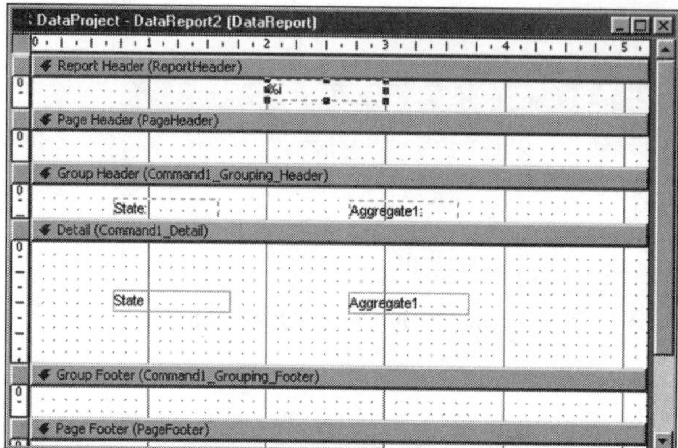

Figure 6-9: Building a report using the Data Reporter Designer

You can use the Data Reporter Designer to perform the following tasks:

- Create reports by dragging and dropping fields from the Data View Window.
- Add controls to your report, just like you add controls to a Form in a Visual Basic program.
- Implement a Print Preview function in your program to allow users to preview the report before sending it to the printer.
- Allow the user to resume working while the report is running (i.e., asynchronous execution of the report).

UserConnection Designer

The UserConnection Designer is a tool that assists the RDO programmer in building connection (**rdoConnection**) and query (**rdoQuery**) objects. These objects are made available at the project level and can be used anywhere in your program. A key part of these objects is that they have a simplified method for responding to database events. These objects also make it easier to call stored procedures at runtime.

RDO not ADO: The UserConnection Designer supports only the RDO object model. Do not try to use it with DAO or ADO object models. The Data Environment Designer is a much improved version of the UserConnection Designer and is available for use with ADO programs.

Thoughts on Visual Basic

Visual Basic programmers can choose from three different object models to access their databases: DAO, RDO, and ADO. Deciding which model is best for you may seem difficult, but it really shouldn't be. ADO is the model that Microsoft would prefer you to use. It is where they are placing the majority of their efforts and it is where you will see the most enhancements in the future.

Microsoft isn't going to abandon the DAO object model anytime soon. There are too many Visual Basic programs that still use it. Dropping support for DAO in a future release of Visual Basic would simply mean that many Visual Basic programmers wouldn't upgrade. (Consider the number of people still using Visual Basic 3 and 4 because Microsoft stopped supporting 16-bit versions with Visual Basic 5.) So if you're currently using DAO, you can continue to use it in the foreseeable future. However, if you're not currently using DAO, you probably shouldn't start.

Directly accessing SQL Server databases using DAO isn't really practical for large applications. As more and more people tried to do this, Microsoft developed RDO as a solution. Its low overhead offered much better performance in large-scale applications. However, RDO's time is also past, and if you're not using it now, don't start.

ADO is the wave of the future. You should be using it for new applications wherever practical. While you don't have to drop everything you're currently doing to convert your existing applications to ADO now, you should have a plan in place that ensures that they will all be converted over time. This is especially true in applications with high transaction rates or applications that are offering services over the Internet.

In the former case, many of the things that Microsoft will do to improve performance will be tied to ADO. This includes facilities such as the COM+ Transaction Server and future versions of SQL Server. In the latter case, Microsoft is already adding features, such as XML support to ADO, which will not be added to DAO and RDO. Also, all of the tools designed to make you more productive, such as the Data View Window and the Data Environment Designer, also require an ADO-based program.

Summary

In this chapter you learned that:

✦ ODBC was originally developed as an alternative to developing pre-compilers for each programming language to translate SQL statements into executable code.

✦ DAO was created to provide an object-oriented API to access Microsoft Jet as well as any ODBC database.

✦ RDO is a low-overhead, general-purpose ODBC interface.

✦ OLE DB is a general-purpose interface that allows data consumers to talk to data producers.

- ADO is the recommended way for Visual Basic programmers to access OLE DB.
- Visual Basic includes a number of specialized tools for the database programmer, which include the Data Environment Designer, Data View Window, Database Designer, SQL Editor, T-SQL Debugger, Query Designer, Data Reporter Designer, and the UserConnection Designer.

✦ ✦ ✦

PART

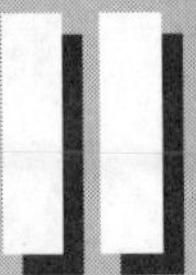

Beginning Database Programming

Many people believe that database programming is a black art that is programmed only by code wizards and magicians, but nothing can be further from the truth. In this Part, I'm going to show you how to build a database program without using a single line of code. This is possible through a concept known as bound controls, which I'll explore in detail as this Part progresses.

To simplify database programming in Visual Basic, Microsoft has included a tool known as the Data Environment Designer. This provides an interactive way to build tools that you can use in your application program. As a companion to the Data Environment Designer, Microsoft has also released a tool known as the Microsoft Data Reporter. This facility allows you to create reports interactively that can easily be incorporated into your application.

✦ ✦ ✦ ✦

In This Part

✦ ✦ ✦ ✦

CHAPTER 7

Codeless Database Programming

In This Chapter

How bound controls work

The ADO Data Control

Common bound controls

Connecting to a database

Building a program without code

Binding a text box to a data control

In this chapter, I'm going to show you how to create a working Visual Basic database program without writing a single line of code. I'll use the ADO Data Control and some common controls found in nearly every Visual Basic Program.

Data Binding

One of the most powerful concepts in Visual Basic is the concept of data binding. By using data binding, you can delegate many of the details of moving data between your database and your program.

What is data binding?

Data binding is a technique that allows a data source to be tied to a data consumer. Then when the data values associated with the data source change, the updated information is reflected in the data consumer. Likewise, data values that are updated in the data consumer are passed back to the data source for updating.

In the case of a Visual Basic program, both the data source and data consumer are typically ActiveX controls, although other types of COM objects may be used (see Part III, Hardcore ADO, for more information about this subject). The classic data source in a Visual Basic program is the data control, while the classic data consumer is a text box control.

One data control doesn't fit all: There are three different data controls, one for each object model (DAO, RDO, and ADO). The DAO control is simply known as the Data Control, while the RDO data control is also known as the RemoteData control. The ADO Data Control is also called the ADODC. You should pick the data control corresponding to the object model you wish to use and if you don't have a specific need to use the DAO or RDO object models, you should use the ADO Data Control to take advantage of the enhancements and features in the ADO object model.

How does data binding work?

Data binding is a two-step process. First, you create a data source and provide the information necessary for it to connect to the database server. Then you create one or more data consumers that are in turn connected to a specific database field returned by the data source. Since the data consumers are typically common controls such as the text box control, they are also known as bound controls.

The binding information is handled by setting various property values in the bound controls. Two properties in particular are very important when binding a control to a data source. The `DataSource` property identifies the name of the data source control, while the `DataField` property identifies which database field will supply the data for the bound control.

Then, when your application begins, the data control establishes a connection with the database server and each of the bound controls establishes a connection with the data control. Whenever the data control moves to a new record, the information in each of the bound controls can be updated automatically. Likewise, whenever the user changes a value in a bound control, the information is passed back to the data control, which in turn will automatically update the database when the user moves to a different record.

Connecting to the database

After binding the controls the user will interact with the data control, which needs to be connected to the database. Again, this is handled via a set of properties. The key property is the `ConnectionString` property, which holds the information needed to connect to the database server. This is a `String` value that contains four main pieces of information. The name of the database server and the name of the data provider are used to create a vehicle that can be used to link the program to the database server. Then the user name and password are used to authenticate the user and determine the user's privileges in the database.

Once you have a valid `ConnectionString`, you need to specify the source of the data. This is kept in the `RecordSource` property. This value can be the name of a database table, an SQL **Select** statement, or a stored procedure. Typically with a data control, you'll want to specify a table name, since it will make all of the records in the table available to the user. Also, by specifying a table name, you won't run into any complications with adding records to your database.

See Chapter 4 for details about **Select** statements.

Intrinsic bound controls

Visual Basic includes two main types of controls: *intrinsic* and *ActiveX*. Intrinsic controls are included with the Visual Basic runtime library and are always available to the Visual Basic programmer. While these controls are not true COM objects, they are much more efficient and the most frequently used. Many of these controls can be bound to a data control, including:

- **CheckBox**
- **ComboBox**
- **Image**
- **Label**
- **ListBox**
- **PictureBox**
- **TextBox**

Of these controls, probably the one you'll use most often is the `TextBox` control, since this control makes it easy to display a database value to a user and allows them to modify it. Other controls you might find yourself using are an `Image` or `Picture` control when you want to display a picture on your form and the `CheckBox` control when you want to display a `Boolean` value from your database. While you might think that the `ComboBox` control might also be heavily used, there is a more database-friendly ActiveX control called the `DataCombo` control that you will find yourself using in place of the `ComboBox` control in most applications.

ActiveX bound controls

Unlike the intrinsic bound control, the ActiveX bound controls are true COM objects and are external to the Visual Basic runtime libraries. Also, unlike the intrinsic bound controls, the ActiveX controls are more complex and have the ability to work with more than one database field at a time.

- **DataList**
- **DataCombo**
- **DataGrid**
- **DateTimePicker**
- **ImageCombo**
- **MaskEdit**
- **MonthView**
- **MSFlexGrid**
- **MSChart**
- **RichTextBox**

Of these controls, probably the most useful are the `DataCombo`, the `DateTimePicker`, the `MaskEdit`, and the `MonthView` control. All of these controls have one common feature: they make it harder for a user to enter an incorrect value into the program.

Keep the Garbage Out

You're probably familiar with the old expression "Garbage in, garbage out". One of the most important goals of a database programmer is to prevent bad data from getting into the database. When you get bad data in your database, you may find it hard to isolate and correct. I remember a situation where one slightly corrupted field in a database prevented a financial application from closing the books at the end of a fiscal year. It took nearly a week to track down and correct the bad piece of data. In the meantime, none of the other programs in the application would run correctly, and other processing involving the general ledger came to a complete halt. In a small business this may not be a big problem, but in a billion dollar a year organization, you can believe the top-level management wasn't very happy. So think about it this way, keeping bad data out of your database is a good way of keeping yourself happily employed.

Building the Codeless Program

Building a codeless program is an interesting exercise and one that is probably worth your time, especially if you are relatively new to Visual Basic. Bound controls will make your life much easier, especially in more complex applications. They definitely reduce the amount of code you have to write in your application and anything that reduces the amount of code you have to write appeals to the lazy programmer in everyone. For the rest of this chapter, I'm going to show you how to build a codeless program that allows you to access the Customers table in the database I designed in Chapter 3.

It's your turn: This program is available on the CD-ROM as `\VB6DB\Chapter07\NoCode\Project1.vbp`. To run this program, simply create a Data Link File as described in Configuring the ADO Data Control below for your `ADODC1` control that reflects your database server, database name, user name, and password information. Then run the program.

Preparing your project

When you start Visual Basic, you have a number of different project templates you can choose from. These templates allow you to build many different types of Visual Basic programs. For this program, I'm going to take the Standard EXE project and add everything I need to build the program (see Figure 7-1).

The next step is to add the ADO Data Control to the project. This is done using the Components dialog box. To open this dialog box, choose Project ➪ Components from the main menu. Then select the Controls tab if it isn't already selected and scroll down the list of controls until you find the Microsoft ADO Data Control (see Figure 7-2). Click on the checkbox and press OK to add the control to your Toolbox.

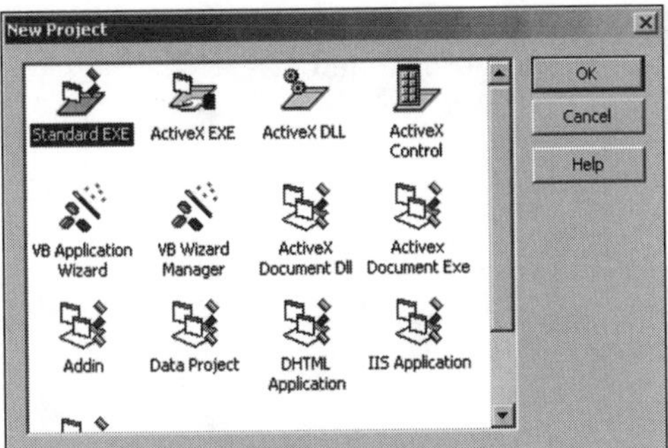

Figure 7-1: Selecting a Standard EXE project

The service pack game: Figure 7-2 reflects the names of the controls that were updated using Visual Studio Service Pack 3. This is identified by (`SP3`) in the name of the control.

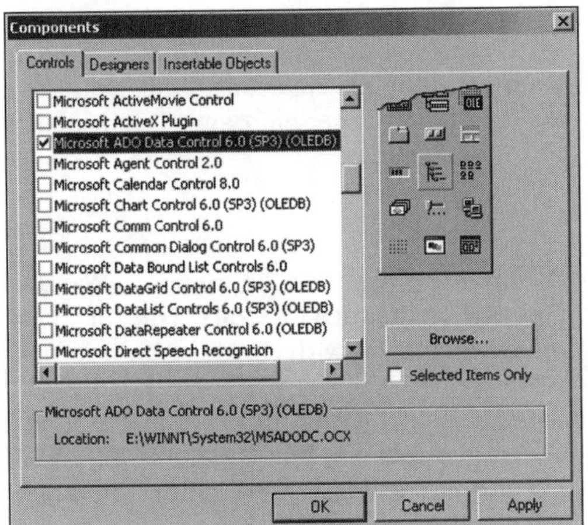

Figure 7-2: Adding the ADO Data Control to the project

Configuring the ADO Data Control

Once you add the ADO Data Control to your project, you need to place a copy of the data control on your form and set the properties so that it will access your database. You can either set the properties though the Visual Basic Properties Window, or you can right click on the control and select ADODC Properties from the popup menu. This will display a set of Property Pages for the control (see Figure 7-3).

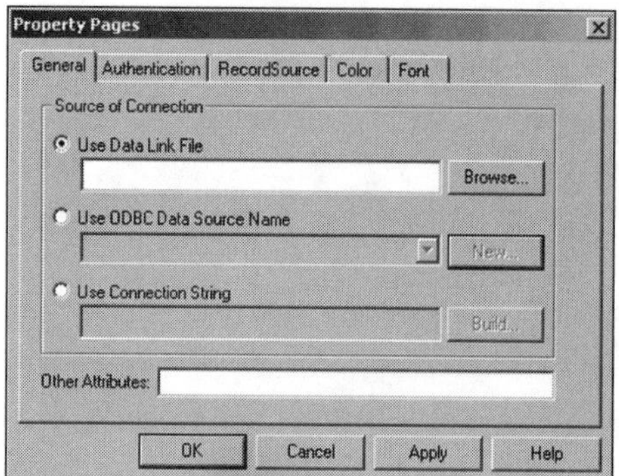

Figure 7-3: Setting the data control's properties

On the General tab, you'll see that there are three different ways to connect to a database server. You can use a Data Link File, an ODBC Data Source Name, or a Connection string. I'm going to show you how to build a Data Link File in this chapter and you can see how to create a Connection String in Chapter 9.

OLE DB, not ODBC: The ADO Data Control is based on the OLE DB architecture, which is more efficient and offers a more flexible architecture. While you can create an ODBC Data Source, you would be much better off using a Data Link File or creating a Connection string.

Selecting a Data Link File

After selecting Use Data Link File as the Source of Connection, press the Browse button to either select an existing Data Link File or create a new one. The Select Data Link File dialog box (see Figure 7-4) will be displayed with the default directory for data link files (`\Program Files\Common Files\System\OLE DB\Data Links\`). If you have an existing Data Link File, simply select it and press Open. If not, you can create one by right clicking in the file area of the dialog box and choosing New ➪ Microsoft Data Link. A new file called New Microsoft Data Link will be created.

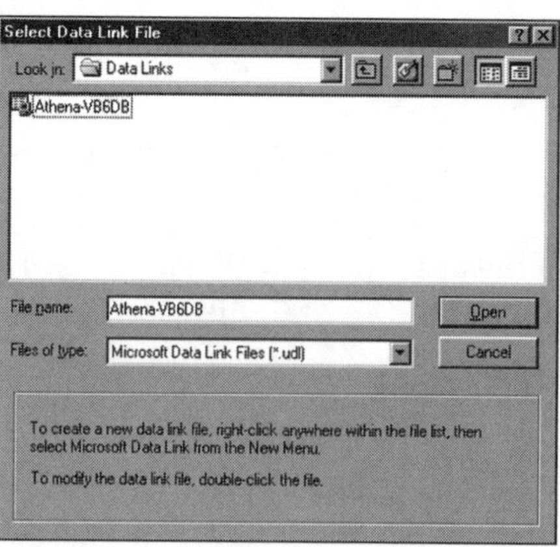

Figure 7-4: Choosing a Data Link File

Name of the game: I like to include the database server and the default database name in the name of my Data Link files. This makes it easy to identify the connection information.

Choosing an OLE DB provider

You can edit the properties in a Data Link File by right clicking on its icon and selecting Properties from the popup menu. This will display the Properties dialog box for the data link file. Select the Provider tab of the Properties dialog box to begin configuring your data link (see Figure 7-5).

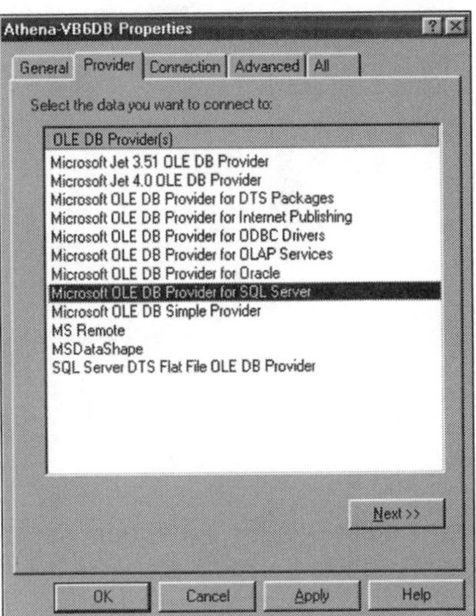

Figure 7-5: Viewing the properties of a Data Link File

Define me before you use me: If you just created this file, you must edit the properties before it can be used.

There are a number of choices for the data provider. For best performance, you should always choose the OLE DB provider for your database system. If you can't locate one for your specific database management system, then choose Microsoft OLE DB Provider for ODBC Drivers. Once you've chosen your provider, press the Next button.

It isn't there: Microsoft only supplies OLE DB providers for SQL Server and Oracle. If you are using a different database system, contact your database vendor to get their OLE DB provider.

Entering provider-specific information

Each OLE DB provider has a list of information it needs in order to connect to a database server. Figure 7-6 shows the information required for the Microsoft OLE DB Provider for SQL Server.

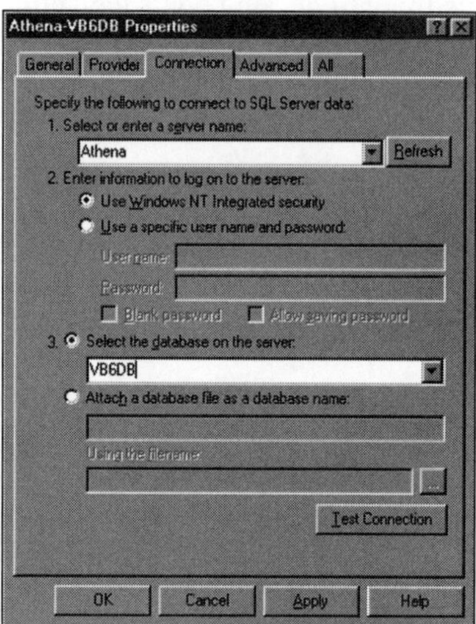

Figure 7-6: Selecting the database server and default database

There are three basic pieces of information needed in this form: the name of the database server, login information, and the name of the default database. In this example, I'm using `Athena` as my database server, Windows NT Authentication for my login information and `VB6DB` as the default database.

Testing the connection

Once you've finished entering the properties, press the Test Connection button to verify that you can connect to the database server. If the information you specify is correct, you should see a message box saying, "Test connection succeeded". If there is a problem, you will see an error message describing the problem. You should then correct the information you provided and try it again.

After you are able to test the connection successfully, you should press the OK button to close the Properties dialog box, and then press the Open button on the Select Data Link File dialog box to choose the data link file. This will return you to the data control's Properties window.

Choosing a RecordSource

The last step of configuring the data control is to choose a source of data. This information is stored in the `RecordSource` property. You can edit this property on the RecordSource tab of the Properties window. In this case, since you want to make the Customers available via this program, you should choose a `CommandType` of `adCmdTable` and then select the Customers table from the drop-down list found immediately below that field (see Figure 7-7). This will automatically be entered into the `RecordSource` property. Then I can press OK to close the Property Pages dialog box and save these values in the data control.

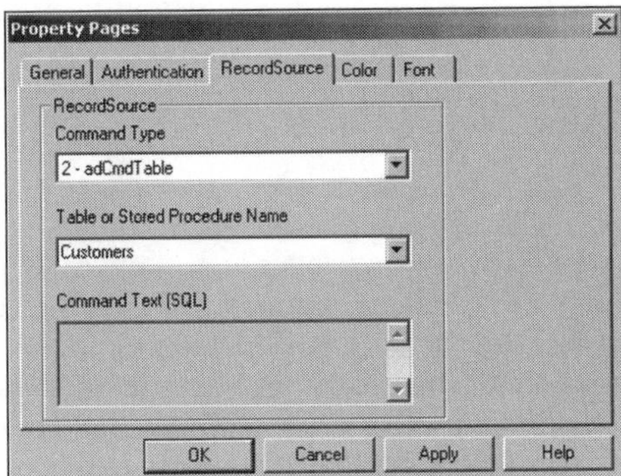

Figure 7-7: Selecting the Customers table as the RecordSource

Adding bound controls

After adding and configuring the ADO Data Control, it's time to add some bound controls. I'm going to start by adding a text box for the Name field and binding it to the data control (see Figure 7-8).

Drag a text box onto your form, and size it to hold a person's full name. Then view the Properties window and scroll it so that the `DataSource` and `DataField` properties are both visible. Select the `DataSource` property. A drop-down arrow will appear at the end of the property's value field. Press it and select the data control from the drop-down list. It should be the only item on the list.

Next, select the `DataField` property and press the drop-down arrow. A list of all of the fields in the table will be listed. Select the Name field to bind the text box to the Name column in the Customers table.

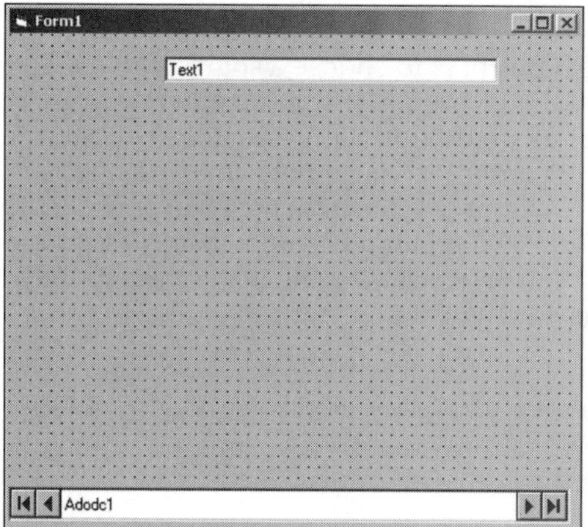

Figure 7-8: Adding the text box for the Name field to your form

The Database Connection: You may not have given this much thought at this point, but the Visual Basic development environment automatically uses the connection information you specified in the ADO Data Control to gather information about your database at development time. It then uses this information to help you avoid mistakes when you enter values into the various properties. Of course, you can enter all of the information for the bound controls manually and then configure the data control, but that isn't the lazy programmer's way of doing things.

Testing your program

Even though this program can only display the person's name from the Customers table, it is worth running it to verify that the program actually works. After choosing Run ➪ Start from the main menu, the program will load, establish a connection to the database, retrieve the first row from the Customers table, and display the value from the Name field in the text box (see Figure 7-9).

You can press the Next Row button on the data control to display the name from the second row in the table and you can return to the first row by pressing the Previous Row button. Pressing the Last Row button will take you to the last row of the table, while pressing the First Row button will return you to the first row in the table.

Finishing your program

Of course, a program that lists one field from a database table is a significant accomplishment in terms of all the little steps necessary to make it work, but it isn't a terribly useful program. So at this point, you need to add controls for the rest of the fields in the table. Also, you should take the time to place labels beside each field so that the user will understand the information displayed. When you've finished, your form might look like the one shown in Figure 7-10.

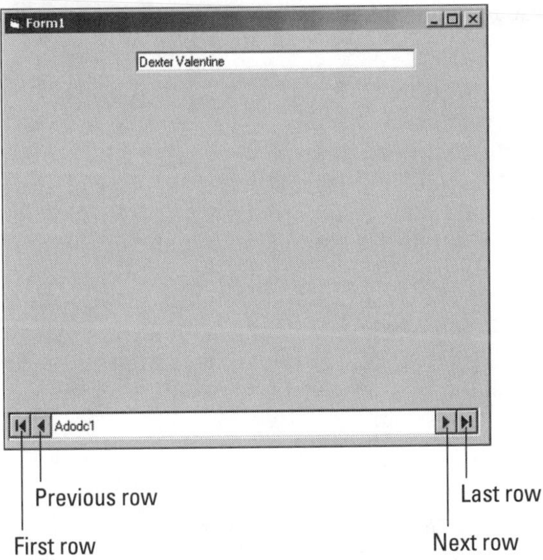

Figure 7-9: Running your codeless program for the first time

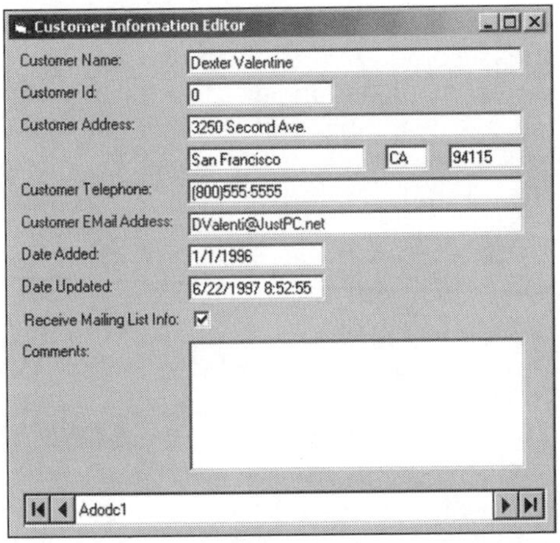

Customer Information Editor
Customer Name: Dexter Valentine
Customer Id: 0
Customer Address: 3250 Second Ave.
San Francisco CA 94115
Customer Telephone: (800)555-5555
Customer EMail Address: DValenti@JustPC.net
Date Added: 1/1/1996
Date Updated: 6/22/1997 8:52:55
Receive Mailing List Info: ☑
Comments:
Adodc1

Figure 7-10: Finishing your codeless program

Updating database information

To change a value in the database using this program, simply change the value in the field and move to another row. As you change the data displayed on the form, the bound controls pass the changes back to the data control, which will automatically update the row when it moves to another row. Of course, if there is an error with the update process, a message box will appear and you will remain on the current row until you correct the problem.

Using numeric fields

You may remember that the Zip field stores its information using a 32-bit integer rather than a character string. While you might think that some special code might be necessary to handle the data conversion from `Long` to `String` and back again, you would be wrong. The conversion is handled automatically by the text box control.

One limitation of using text boxes to display numeric information is that you can enter non-numeric information into the text box without immediately triggering an error. Of course, attempting to update the row will trigger a runtime error because you can't put a non-numeric value into a numeric field.

Using Boolean fields

`Boolean` fields are a natural fit for the `CheckBox` control. You set the `DataSource` and `DataField` properties just like the `TextBox` control. The control will display a `TRUE` value by placing a check mark in the check box and will clear the check box when the database value is `FALSE`.

Using Datetime fields

Like numeric values, date and time values also undergo a dynamic conversion process when information is displayed in the control. As long as the date and time information is properly formatted and legal, the control will automatically handle the conversion. If there is an error, the old Operation canceled message will be displayed, and the original values will be restored.

Adding new records

By default, the ADO Data Control doesn't allow you to add new records to the database. However, by changing one property value, you can easily include this capability in your codeless program. The `EOFAction` property determines what happens when the user attempts to move beyond the last row in the table.

By default, the data control will simply move the user back to the last row in the table if the user attempts to move beyond it. However, if you set `EOFAction` to `adDoAddNew` (2), the data control will automatically add a new blank row anytime the user attempts to move beyond the end of the file.

Once the user adds a record and enters the proper values into each of the fields, moving to another row will save the new row to the database. Of course, when you add a record using this technique, the final data must meet the database rules for acceptability. Any invalid values must be corrected before you can move to another row.

Thoughts on Codeless Programming

Okay, so a codeless program may not be perfect, but it will work and can often be useful in the early stages of building an application. If you're willing to add a little code to handle non-database functions, such as edit checking and menu management, Visual Basic offers a much better alternative to building a database application in Access.

Access is primarily an easy to use database forms generator with some scripting capabilities added. While it allows you to build simple database applications quickly, when building more complex applications you constantly run into situations that aren't easy to handle because of the many limitations in Access. However, Visual Basic is a true programming language and doesn't suffer from the same limitations.

The primary drawback to using a true programming language like Visual Basic is that it can be difficult to create programs that perform a complex task like accessing a database. However, by using bound controls and other tools in Visual Basic, you can easily create database programs that require very little code and that offer more power and flexibility than their Access counterparts.

I've added a record and I can't get out: One downside to using a codeless program to add records to your database is that there isn't a convenient method to abort the add process. In fact, the only way to abort the add process is to end the program, which is pretty drastic. Of course, this is a situation where a little code can go a long way towards making the program much easier to use.

Summary

In this chapter you learned the following:

- ✦ What data binding is and how it works.
- ✦ Which controls you can bind in your Visual Basic program.
- ✦ How you can use bound controls to build a meaningful program without any code.
- ✦ How to choose an OLE DB provider and build an ADO connection string to connect to your database.

✦ ✦ ✦

CHAPTER

More About Bound Controls

In the previous chapter, I showed you how to build a program without any code using only bound controls and the ADO Data Control. In this chapter, I will continue discussing bound controls by talking about some other properties and events that you can use to help ensure that only valid data is stored in your database. Then I'm going to discuss a few other useful controls that have special features to help ensure that your data is correct before it gets into the database.

Bound Controls Revisited

Bound controls are not as simple as I led you to believe in Chapter 7. There are several other properties, methods, and events that allow you to fine-tune how the user interacts with the control.

Key properties

All bound controls contain the properties listed in Table 8-1, which affect the way the control works with the user and with the database.

Key methods

While the SetFocus method isn't directly used in binding a control to a data source, it is sometimes used in performing data validation.

Table 8-1
Key Properties of Bound Controls

Property	*Description*
`CausesValidation`	A `Boolean` value, where `TRUE` means that the Validation event for the control previously focused will be fired before the focus is shifted to this control.
`DataChanged`	A `Boolean` value, where `TRUE` means that either the user has changed the value of the control or the program has changed the value of the control.
`DataField`	A `String` value containing the field name to which the control is bound.
`DataFormat`	An object reference to an `StdDataFormat` object which contains information about how to format the value displayed by the control.
`DataMember`	A `String` value that identifies which set of data should be used when a `DataSource` has more than one set of data.
`DataSource`	An object reference to an object that can act as a data source. Common data sources include the `ADO Data Control`, a `Recordset` object or a Class module where the `DataSourceBehavior` property is set to `vbDataSource` (1).

Object.SetFocus ()

The `SetFocus` method is used to transfer the focus to the control specified by *object*. If the control specified by *object* isn't visible or can't accept the focus, a runtime error will occur.

Key events

Most controls that can be bound have a set of events that will be fired as the user interacts with the control. These events can be used to verify that the information a user enters into the control is correct.

Event Change ()

The `Change` event is fired each time the value of a control changes. This can happen if the user updates the value in the control or explicitly sets the `Value`, `Caption`, or `Text` property in code.

Event GotFocus ()

The GotFocus event fired before a control receives the focus.

Event KeyDown (KeyCode As Integer, Shift As Integer)

The KeyDown event is fired whenever the user presses a key while the control has the focus, where KeyCode is an Integer value containing the key code of the key that was pressed. This value is not the ASCII character value associated with the key.

Shift is an Integer value that indicates the status of the Shift, Alt, and Ctrl keys.

Event KeyPress (KeyAscii As Integer)

The KeyPress event is fired whenever a key is pressed and released, where KeyAscii contains the ASCII code of the key that was pressed. Changing this value to zero in the event cancels the keystroke.

Event KeyUp (KeyCode As Integer, Shift As Integer)

The KeyUp event is fired whenever the user releases a key while the control has the focus, where KeyCode is an Integer value containing the key code of the key that was released. This value is not the ASCII character value associated with the key.

Shift is an Integer value that indicates the status of the Shift, Alt, and Ctrl keys.

Event LostFocus ()

The LostFocus event is fired just before the focus is transferred to another control.

Event Validate (Cancel As Boolean)

The Validate event is used to verify that the contents of a control are valid before the focus is shifted to another control. The Validate event will only be triggered if the destination control has the CausesValidation property set to TRUE. This is the case where Cancel is a Boolean value, and TRUE means that the focus should not be shifted to the next control. By default, Cancel is set to FALSE.

Data validation

There are basically four ways to verify that the user has entered the correct data into a control like a TextBox:

- Change event
- KeyPress, KeyUp, and KeyDown events
- GotFocus and LostFocus events
- Validate event

Each approach is discussed below, along with any of its advantages and disadvantages.

Using the Change event

The Change event is triggered each time the value of the control is changed. While at first this may be the ideal event with which to verify changes, it turns out it is the least practical approach.

Consider a TextBox control. Each time the user types a character into the text window, the change event is fired. Also, anytime you change the Text property in your program, you trigger the Change event. This can make things really complicated if you choose to change the value of the control while in the Change event.

Using the KeyPress, KeyUp, and KeyDown events

The KeyPress, KeyUp, and KeyDown events are fired whenever a user presses a key on the keyboard. Like the Change event, these events are somewhat limited in their usefulness for validating data. However, you can trap the keystrokes as they are entered and translate them into something or perform a special task.

For instance, you can include some code in the KeyPress event to translate any lowercase characters into their uppercase equivalents automatically. You can also define certain keystrokes, such as the Esc key, to perform special functions, like restoring the original value for the field from the database (see Listing 8-1).

Listing 8-1: The Text1_KeyPress event in Customer Information Editor

```
Private Sub Text1_KeyPress(KeyAscii As Integer)

If Chr(KeyAscii) >= "a" And Chr(KeyAscii) <= "z" Then
   KeyAscii = KeyAscii - 32

ElseIf (KeyAscii = 27) And Text1.DataChanged Then
   Text1.Text = Adodc1.Recordset.Fields("Name").OriginalValue
   KeyAscii = 0

End If

End Sub
```

Looking to the future: One of the properties of the ADO Data Control is a reference to the underlying Recordset object containing the data retrieved from the database. I'll cover the Recordset object in detail starting with Chapter 11.

Using the LostFocus event

You can also use the `LostFocus` event to perform edit checks. This event is triggered when the user or the program transfers the focus to another control. Since the `LostFocus` event of the current control is the last piece of processing that occurs before the next control gains the focus, it is an ideal place to verify that the data in the control is valid.

In Listing 8-2, I use the `LostFocus` event to determine if the user has left the field blank. If so, I turn the background red to indicate that this field has an error. After the user has entered some data and leaves the control again, I return the normal background color for the text box. Of course, since I only change the color in the `LostFocus` event, the error will still be flagged after the user returns the focus to the control. You can leave it this way, or you can add some code in the `GotFocus` event to reset the error flag.

Listing 8-2: The Text1_LostFocus event in Customer Information Editor

```
Private Sub Text1_LostFocus()

If Len(Text1.Text) = 0 Then
   Text1.BackColor = &HFFFF&

Else
   Text1.BackColor = &H80000005

End If

End Sub
```

Make an error stand out: No matter how you determine that the contents of a field are invalid, you should include some code to tell the user in no uncertain terms that the value is incorrect. You could include a line such as `Text1.BackColor = &HFF&` to turn the background of a text box red in the `LostFocus` event and use a line of code like `Text1.BackColor = &H80000005` to restore the proper background color. You could also use other colors to display different status conditions, such as yellow (&HFFFF&) to when a field should not be left blank.

Resetting focus in the `LostFocus` event: When your program handles the `LostFocus` event, the focus has already begun the process of shifting to the next control. If you try to use the `SetFocus` method inside the `LostFocus` event to bring the focus back to the current control, the next control will briefly receive the focus, and its `GotFocus` and `LostFocus` events will be fired.

Using the Validate event

Probably the best way to verify that the data entered by a user is acceptable is to put the test in the `Validate` event. When the user attempts to switch the focus to another control, the `Validate` event is fired. If the value in the control isn't acceptable, all you need to do is set the `Cancel` parameter to `TRUE` and the focus will remain with the current control without triggering the `GotFocus/LostFocus` events of the other control.

Unlike the other approaches to validating data which operate on a single control at a time, using the `Validate` method requires that you coordinate all of the controls on a single form. In general, all of the controls on the form that are capable of receiving the focus need the `CausesValidation` property set to `TRUE`. The only controls that shouldn't have `CausesValidation` set to `TRUE` are those that would allow the user to abort any changes.

For example, consider a form like the one in Figure 8-1. There are three text boxes and two command buttons that can receive the focus. Each of these controls has the `CausesValidate` property set to `TRUE`, except for the Cancel button. This means that the `Validate` event will be triggered when the user tries to shift the focus on any of the text boxes or the Update button.

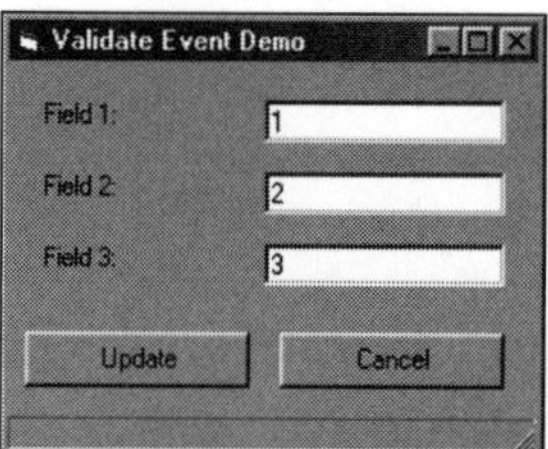

Figure 8-1: Validating data on a form

A typical `Validate` event is shown in Listing 8-3. In this routine, I merely verify that the text box is not empty. If it is, then I'll turn the background to red and display an error message in the status bar. Then I'll set the `Cancel` parameter to `TRUE` to prevent the user from moving the focus to another control.

Listing 8-3: The Text1_Validate Event in Validate Event Demo

```
Private Sub Text1_Validate(Cancel As Boolean)

If Len(Text1.Text) = 0 Then
   Text1.BackColor = &HFF&
   StatusBar1.SimpleText = "Field 1 is blank."
```

```
    Cancel = True
  End If
  End Sub
```

Since the Cancel button has the `CausesValidation` property set to `FALSE`, even if there is an error in one of the text boxes, the focus can be transferred to the Cancel button. Thus, you can use this button to undo any changes or reset the information displayed in the other controls to their default values.

Explain what caused the error: In addition to making your error stand out, you may want to explain the error in more detail. While you can always display the error message using a message box, consider adding a StatusBar control at the bottom of the form and displaying the error message inside one of the panels. This allows you to display the error message without unnecessarily disrupting the user's work.

Formatting data

Another ability of many bound controls is the ability to format automatically the data they display. You can specify the format information in the `DataFormat` property. You can specify the format information at design time (see Figure 8-2) or at runtime using the `StdDataFormat` object (see Table 8-2).

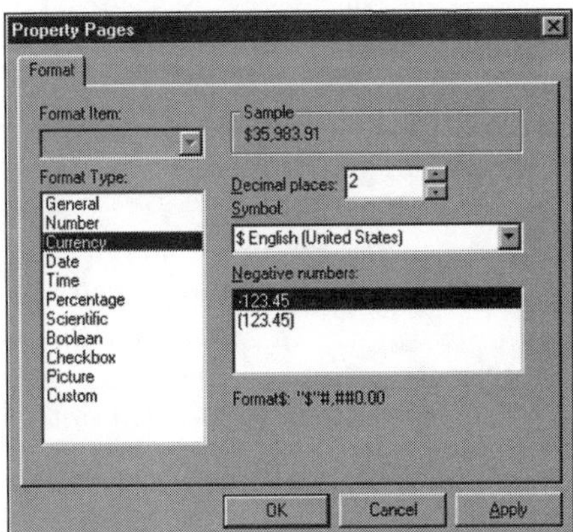

Figure 8-2: Specifying a format for your data

Typically, you're going to set the format for a field at design time. Simply choose the appropriate *Format Type* for the value you want to format and a set of options will appear under the *Format* heading corresponding to the *Format Type* you selected.

Table 8-2
Key Properties of the StdDataFormat Object

Property	*Description*
`FalseValue`	A `Variant` containing the value to be displayed when a `Boolean` field is `FALSE`.
`FirstDayOfWeek`	An enumerated value that contains the value of the first day of a week. This information is used to compute values such as the week of the year. Legal values are `fmtDayUseSystem` (0), `fmtSunday` (1), `fmtMonday` (2), `...` and `fmtSaturday` (7).
`FirstWeekOfYear`	An enumerated value that contains information about how to determine the first week of the year. Legal values are `fmtWeekUseSystem` (0), `fmtFirstJan1` (1), `fmtFirstFourDays` (2), and `fmtFirstFullWeek` (3).
`Format`	A `String` value containing a standard format string.
`NullValue`	A `Variant` containing the value to be displayed for a `Null` value.
`TrueValue`	A `Variant` containing the value to be displayed when a `Boolean` field is `TRUE`.
`Type`	An enumerated value that describes the type of information being displayed from the database. Legal values are: `fmtGeneral` (0), `fmtCustom` (1), `fmtPicture` (2), `fmtObject` (3), `fmtCheckbox` (4), `fmtBoolean` (5), and `fmtBytes` (6).

Numbers and names: Visual Basic often allows you to specify the value of a property by name rather than by number. This is known as an *enumerated value*. You should use enumerated values whenever possible to more clearly document the value you are using.

Using the Picture and Image Controls

Displaying graphic images in your database is very easy when you use a bound `Picture` or `Image` control. Unlike the other bound controls, these controls are strictly one way. They can display data from your database, but changing the image displayed in the control will not update the image in your database when the rest of the row is updated.

The key to using these controls is to bind them to a column in your database containing the raw image. The image can be in any format that is acceptable to the `LoadPicture` function, including `.BMP`, `.JPG`, and `.GIF`. The type of image will automatically be detected and picture will automatically be loaded into the control.

You can't assign an image stored in your database directly to the `Picture` property of the `Picture` or `Image` controls. You must either save the column's value to a file and then use the `LoadImage` function or bind the control directly to the database.

Aren't they the same? The `Image` and `Picture` controls can both be used to display images. All of the data binding properties are the same. However, the `Picture` control has the ability to act as a container for other controls, and it also includes a rich set of drawing methods that are not found on the `Image` control.

Using the Masked Edit Control

The `Masked Edit` control is an alternative to of the text box control. It includes the ability to compare incoming keystrokes against an input mask that determines whether the keystroke is valid or not. Using a simple mask can ensure that numeric fields will contain only numeric values, and with more complex masks, you can enter and display more complex values, such as telephone numbers and social security numbers (see Figure 8-3).

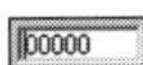

Figure 8-3: Entering a numeric value for the ZIP code.

Invalid social security numbers: The middle two digits of a social security number (AAA-BB-CCCC) are never 00. The programmers at the Social Security Administration use social security numbers with 00 in the middle to test their applications.

Key properties

The Masked Edit control contains all of the standard properties found in an average ActiveX control, such as Top, Left, Width, Height, Enabled, ToolTipText, etc. However there are a few key properties that affect the way the control works (see Table 8-3).

Table 8-3
Key Properties of the Masked Edit Control

Property	*Description*
AllowPrompt	A Boolean value, where TRUE means that PromptChar is a valid input character.
AutoTab	A Boolean value, where TRUE means that the control will automatically tab to the next field when this field is full.
ClipMode	An enumerated data type that determines if the literal characters displayed in the input mask will be included in a copy or cut operation. A value of mskIncludeLiterals (0) means that the characters will be included, while a value of mskExcludeLiterals (1) means that the characters will not be included.
ClipText	A String containing the contents of the control, without any literal characters.
Format	A String containing up to four format strings separated by semicolons that will be used to display the information in the control.
FormattedText	A String containing the text that will be displayed in the control when another control has the focus.
HideSelection	A Boolean value, where TRUE means that selected text will not be highlighted when the control loses focus.
Mask	A String value containing the input mask. Table 8-4 contains a list of legal mask characters. Any other character in the input mask is considered a literal character.
MaxLength	An Integer containing the maximum length of the input data.
PromptChar	A String containing a single character that is used to prompt the user for input.

Property	*Description*
`PromptInclude`	A `Boolean` value, where `TRUE` means that `PromptChar` is included in the `Text` property. For bound controls `TRUE` means that the value in the `Text` property will be saved in the database and `FALSE` means that the value in the `ClipText` property will be saved.
`Text`	A `String` value containing the value that is displayed in the control while the control has the focus.

Table 8-4
Mask Characters

Character	*Description*
#	A required numeric character.
.	A decimal point indicator as defined in Windows. It is treated as a literal.
,	A thousands separator as defined in Windows. It is treated as a literal.
/	A date separator as defined in Windows. It is treated as a literal.
:	A time separator as defined in Windows. It is treated as a literal.
\	Treat the next character as a literal.
&	A character placeholder.
>	Convert the following characters to uppercase.
<	Convert the following characters to lowercase.
A	A required alphanumeric character.
A	An optional alphanumeric character.
9	An optional numeric character.
C	Same as & (ensures compatibility with Microsoft Access).
?	A required alphanumeric character.
Other	Any other character is treated as a literal.

Creating an input mask

When programming the `Masked Edit` control, the first step is to build an input mask. The best way to start is to choose the mask characters that reflect how your users enter their data and insert them into the `Mask` property. You can add literal characters such as parentheses and dashes to make the input mask easier to use. Table 8-5 lists some sample values for the `Mask` property.

Table 8-5
Sample Masks

Input Mask	*Description*
(###) ###-####	A telephone number.
####-####-####-####	A credit card number.
###-##-####	A social security number.
>A<AAAAAAAA	A name field with the first character always in uppercase and the following characters always in lowercase.
>AAAAAAAAAA	A name field with all characters converted to uppercase.
?#:##	A time value.
##/##/##	A date value.

The mask didn't work: Just because you use an input mask to ensure the input is in the proper format doesn't mean that the value entered will always be correct. For instance, someone could enter (000) 000-0000 as a telephone number or they could enter 99/99/99 as a date. Both of these values are invalid, yet they meet the requirements specified by the input mask. In these cases, you can use the `Validate` event or another control, such as the `DateTimePicker`, to ensure that the user's data is correct.

As the user enters characters into the control at runtime, each character is validated against the input mask. Any literal characters are frozen on the screen and are automatically skipped over. If the user enters a character that isn't compatible with the input mask, it is ignored, unless you have coded the `ValidateError` event. Then the event will be fired and you can respond in whatever fashion you wish.

A real multimedia solution: I like to use the full multimedia capabilities of a PC/XT to let the user know that they typed an invalid character in the `Masked Edit` control. Therefore, in the `ValidateError` event, I'll include a Beep statement to generate an audible signal to the user.

Prompting the user

A prompt character can be defined using the `PromptChar` property. This character will be displayed in the each position of the field where the user is expected to enter a value. Generally, you will want to use the underscore (_) character as the prompt character, but you may want to supply a value like a zero or a space depending on the input mask. For instance, if you set `PromptChar` to 0 and Mask to ###-##-####, the user will see 000-00-0000 in the field. The user would then overtype the prompt characters with the appropriate values. Note that if you use a value for `PromptChar` that is also legal in the input mask, then you need to set the `AllowPrompt` property to `TRUE`.

Database considerations

When using the `Masked Edit` control as a bound control, you need to decide which value you want to store in the database. If you set the `PromptInclude` property to `TRUE`, the value in `Text` property, which will include any literal values from the input mask, will be saved in the database. Otherwise, the value from the `ClipText` property will be used.

Using the DateTimePicker Control

While you can use the `TextBox` or the `Masked Edit` controls to enter date and time values, using the `DateTimePicker` control is a much better way. The sole purpose of the `DateTimePicker` control is to help users enter legal date and time values. From a programming point of view, it works just like a `TextBox` control. You can use the standard data binding properties to connect it to your database.

Key properties

The `DateTimePicker` control contains all of the standard properties found in an average ActiveX control, such as `Top`, `Left`, `Width`, `Height`, `Enabled`, `ToolTipText`, etc. However, there are a few key properties that affect the way the control works (see Table 8-6).

Table 8-6
Key Properties of the DateTimePicker Control

Property	*Description*
`CalendarBackColor`	A `Long` value containing the background color of the calendar.
`CalendarForeColor`	A `Long` value containing the foreground color of the calendar.

Continued

Table 8-6 *(continued)*

Property	***Description***
CalendarTitleBackColor	A Long value containing the background color of the calendar's title bar.
CalendarTitleForeColor	A Long value containing the foreground color of the calendar's title bar.
CalendarTrailingForeColor	A Long value containing the foreground color for the dates before and after the current month.
CheckBox	A Boolean value. When TRUE, a check box will be displayed next to the value. If not checked, NULL will be returned as Value.
CustomFormat	A String value containing an alternate format to display date and/or time values chosen from the characters listed in Table 8-7. Also, you must set Format to dtpCustom (3).
Day	A Variant value containing the currently selected day of month.
DayOfWeek	A Variant value containing the currently selected day of week.
Format	An enumerated type specifying the standard or custom format that will be used to display the date and/or time value. Possible values are dtpLongDate (0) to display a date in a long format; dtpShortDate (1) to display a date in a short format; dtpTime (2) to display the time; and dtpCustom (3) to display the value using the format string in CustomFormat.
Hour	A Variant value containing the currently selected hour.
MaxDate	A Date value containing the maximum date value a user can enter.
MinDate	A Date value containing the minimum date value a user can enter.
Minute	A Variant value containing the currently selected minute.
Month	A Variant value containing the currently selected month.

Property	*Description*
`Second`	A `Variant` value containing the currently selected second.
`UpDown`	A `Boolean` value when `TRUE` displays an updown (spin) button to modify dates instead of a drop-down calendar.
`Value`	A `Variant` value containing the currently selected date.
`Year`	A `Variant` value containing the currently selected year.

Table 8-7
Mask Characters

Character	*Description*
D	Displays the day of month without a leading zero (1-31).
dd	Displays the day of month as two digits using a leading zero if necessary (01-31).
ddd	Displays the day of week as a three-character abbreviation (Sun, Mon, etc.).
dddd	Displays the day of week with its full name (Sunday, Monday, etc.).
H	Displays the hour without a leading zero (0-12).
hh	Displays the hour with two digits, using a leading zero if necessary (00-12).
H	Displays the hour in 24-hour format without a leading zero (0-23).
HH	Displays the hour in 24-hour format, using a leading zero if necessary (00-23).
M	Displays the month without a leading zero (1-12).
MM	Displays the month as two digits, using a leading zero if necessary (01-12).
MMM	Displays the month as a three-character abbreviation (Jan, Feb, etc.).
MMMM	Displays the month with its full name (January, February, etc.).
m	Displays the minutes without a leading zero (0-59).

Continued

Table 8-7 *(continued)*

Character	*Description*
mm	Displays the minutes as two digits, using a leading zero if necessary (00-59).
s	Displays the seconds without a leading zero (0-59).
ss	Displays the seconds as two digits, using a leading zero if necessary (00-59).
t	Displays AM or PM as a single character (A or P).
tt	Displays AM or PM as two characters (AM or PM).
x	Uses the Callback events (`CallbackKeyDown`, `Format`, and `FormatSize`) to get the information needed to format the custom date/time value.
y	Displays the day of year (1-365).
yy	Displays the year as a two-digit number (00-99).
yyyy	Displays the year as a four-digit number (0100-9999).

Choosing a user interface

The `DateTimePicker` control has two different ways to allow users to edit date and time values. If you want to edit only date values, you can display a drop-down calendar, which allows the user to select a particular date (see Figure 8-4). Set `UpDown` to `TRUE`.

Figure 8-4: Using a drop-down calendar to enter a date

If you want to edit only time values or date and time values, you can set `UpDown` to `FALSE` and the user can edit by clicking on a value and using the spinner arrows at the end of the field to adjust the value (see Figure 8-5). This option works with all formats, including any custom format you may choose to build.

Figure 8-5: Entering a date and time value

Using the DataCombo Control

The `DataCombo` control looks and works just like a regular `ComboBox` control, except that the data for the control comes directly from the database. This control is extremely useful when you want to translate a coded data value into its text equivalent. It uses two database tables: one table containing the data you want to edit, and a translation table that contains both the encoded and translated values. The beauty of this control is that no code is required to perform the translation process.

They come in pairs: The `DataList` control is very similar to the `DataCombo` control, in the same way a list box is the same as a combo box. Thus, they share many common properties and methods.

Key properties

The `DataCombo` control has a number of properties that affect the way the control works (see Table 8-8). It also supports all of the standard properties, methods, and events listed.

Table 8-8
Key Properties of the DataCombo Control

Property	Description
`BoundColumn`	A `String` value that contains the name of the column that will supply that value to the control.
`BoundText`	A `String` value that contains the current value of the `BoundColumn`.
`DataBindings`	An object reference to a `DataBindings` collection.
`ListField`	A `String` value that contains the name of the column used to fill the drop-down list.
`MatchedWithList`	A `Boolean` value that indicates the contents of the `BoundText` matches one of the entries in the list.

Continued

Table 8-8 (continued)

Property	*Description*
`MatchEntry`	An enumerated data type that controls how the user's keystrokes will be matched with the values in the control. A value of `dblBasicMatching` (0) means that when the user presses a key, the list of values is searched for by the first item whose first character matches the key that was pressed. If the same key is pressed again, the second item whose first character matches will be displayed. A value of `dblExtendedMatching` (1) means that the control will search for an item in the list whose value matches all of the characters entered. Typing additional characters refines the search.
`RowMember`	A `String` value that identifies which set of data should be used when a `RowSource` has more than one set of data.
`RowSource`	An object reference to an object that can act as a data source. Common data sources include the `ADO Data Control`, a `Recordset` object, or a Class module where the `DataSourceBehavior` property is set to `vbDataSource` (1).
`SelectedItem`	A `Variant` value containing a bookmark for the currently selected record.
`Style`	An `Integer` value that controls how the user interacts with the control. Values are `dbcDropdownCombo` (0), which allows the user to enter a value in the text box or select a value from the drop-down box; `dbcSimpleCombo` (1), which allows the user to enter a value into the text box or select a value from the list below the text box; and `dbcDropdownList` (3), which allows the user to only select a value from the drop-down list.

Sort, please: You should use a **Select** statement with the **Order By** clause when defining your data source so that the list of values can be displayed in sorted order.

Key methods

The `DataCombo` control supports the usual assortment of methods; however, the `ReFill` method is unique to this and the `DataList` control.

DataCombo.ReFill ()

The ReFill method gets a fresh copy of the data from the RowSource and recreates the list of items in the list.

It's not the same: Don't confuse the ReFill method with the Refresh method. The Refresh method merely repaints the data on the screen. It doesn't get a fresh copy of the data from the database.

Configuring the control

Using the DataCombo control is more complicated than most bound controls, because it needs to interact with two database tables. It also can be used in two different fashions. First, the user may choose a value from a list of values. Second, the user may choose from a list of values that are automatically encoded and decoded as needed.

Selecting from a list

To function as a normal bound control, you need to specify values for both the DataSource and DataField properties. The DataSource property must contain an object reference to an OLE DB data source such as an ADO Data Control or a Recordset object that references the table you want to update. The DataField property specifies the column name whose value is displayed in the text part of the combo box.

The list part of the combo box is populated using the RowSource and ListField properties. The RowSource property is an object reference to an ADO Data Control or a Recordset object corresponding to the list of entries to be displayed in the list part of the combo box. The ListField property contains the name of the column whose values will be displayed in the list part of the control. Before you can use the DataCombo control, you need to set one more property, BoundColumn. This property should be set to the same value as ListField.

Translating a value

When designing a database it is common to *codify* a value in order to reduce redundancy in your database. When you do this, you typically create a field called ManufacturerId in one table and use another table to translate ManufacturerId into the manufacturer's Name. Thus the ManufacturerId value is known as the *codified* value, while Name is known as the *translated* value.

In the example used in this book, each row in the Inventory table contains a reference to the ManufacturerId, while the Manufacturers table contains ManufacturerId and the Name associated with the ManufacturerId. Because ManufacturerId is a numeric value, it is difficult to remember which value is associated with each manufacturer's name. This situation is an ideal candidate for the `DataCombo` control.

The properties of the `DataCombo` control should be set as follows: `DataSource` = Adodc1 (the table with the raw data); `DataField` = ManufacturerId (the codified field in the raw data table); `RowSource` = Adodc2 (the translation table); `ListField` = Name (the translated field in the translation table); and `BoundColumn` = ManufacturerId (the codified field in the translation table).

When using the `DataCombo` control to automatically translate a value, you should set the `Style` property to `dbcDropdownList` (3) in order to prevent problems. The other values for `Style` allow the user to enter their own value into the control. This can cause a translation error, since the value in the codified column doesn't have translation value in the translation table. The easiest way to handle this situation is to place a button beside the `DataCombo` control to add the new value to the translation table and then refresh the data displayed in the control using the `Refill` method (see Figure 8-6).

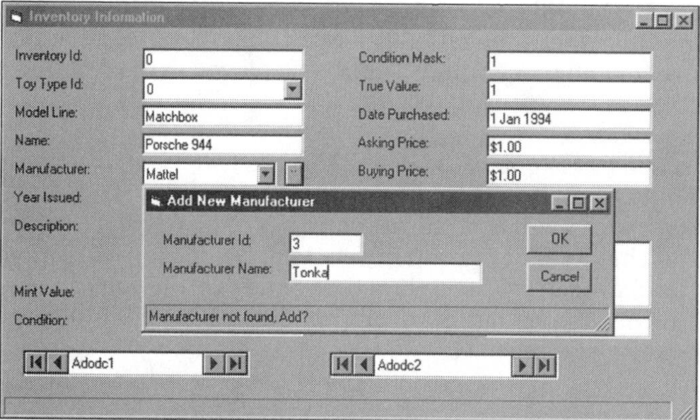

Figure 8-6: Adding a value to the translation table

In the `Command2_Click` event in the Add New Manufacturer form, which occurs when the OK button is pressed, you begin by adding the new manufacturer to the Manufacturers table (see Listing 8-4). Then you use the `Requery` method to get a fresh, reordered copy of the data from the database, and then use the data combo's `ReFill` method to get a fresh copy of the data for the drop-down line. Finally, you should save the newly added manufacturer into the data combo's `Text` property to save the user from having to select the newly added information.

Listing 8-4: The Command2_Click event in Inventory Information – Add New Manufacturer form

```
Private Sub Command2_Click()

Form1.Adodc2.Recordset.AddNew
Form1.Adodc2.Recordset.Fields("ManufacturerId").Value = _
   CLng(Text1.Text)
Form1.Adodc2.Recordset.Fields("Name").Value = Text2.Text
Form1.Adodc2.Recordset.Update
Form1.Adodc2.Recordset.Requery
Form1.DataCombo1.ReFill
Form1.DataCombo1.Text = Text2.Text
Unload Me

End Sub
```

Thoughts on Reducing Data Errors

If you were to write a database program in a different programming language, you would probably have to spend a lot of time moving data from database buffers to the various display fields. In some languages such as COBOL, you might spend as much as fifty percent of your programming effort writing this type of code.

By using bound controls in Visual Basic, you can do two things. First, you reduce the overall size of your program, since you don't have to move all that information to and from the database buffers. Second, you improve the reliability of your program, since the code that handles the data movement isn't yours. Of course, you might make a mistake when specifying which field is associated with a particular control, but this is much easier to find and fix than looking through a complex program and trying to find why a particular field wasn't updated.

Data validation is a big part of the process also. The best way to help prevent your database from becoming corrupt is to verify that all of the data that is entered into the database is acceptable. Using controls such as the `MaskedEdit` and the `DateTimePicker` control means that the data that is entered is at least of the right type and the proper format. This goes a long way towards preventing bad data from reaching your database.

Sometimes bad data will get into your database no matter how much you check and recheck your data before it is entered. For instance, someone could mistype an item number yet still end up with a bad record. Even though the item number was valid, it wasn't the product the customer wanted. To help prevent this type of problem, you should provide as

Continued

Continued

much visual feedback as possible. Perhaps you could display a picture of the item, which would allow the customer to see that they entered the wrong item. Izf a picture isn't practical, you should at least provide a description of the item from which the customer may be able to recognize their mistake.

While providing feedback isn't that important if the information is being entered by a person whose full-time job is to use this application, it is very important for a casual user. A casual user typically isn't very comfortable with the application and is prone to making more mistakes, yet with the proper feedback mechanisms, they will do a better job in the long run.

Summary

In this chapter you learned the following:

- ✦ You can validate data in a bound control by using the `Change`, `KeyPress`, `LostFocus`, and `Validate` events.
- ✦ You can use the `MaskEdit` control to prompt users for textual information.
- ✦ You can use the `DateTimePicker` control to help users select date and time values.
- ✦ You can use the `DataCombo` box in place of a normal `ComboBox` control to allow a user to select from a series of values extracted directly from your database.

✦ ✦ ✦

Programming with Data Environments

✦ ✦ ✦ ✦

In This Chapter

The Data Environment Designer

Connecting to databases

Creating and using commands

Using the Data View window

✦ ✦ ✦ ✦

In this chapter, I'm going to discuss how to use the Data Environment Designer to create a Data Environment, which simplifies many of the tasks of building a database application. It exploits the ADO object model and helps you create standardized ADO objects that simplify access to the database.

The Data Environment Designer

The Data Environment Designer is a tool in the Visual Basic IDE that helps a programmer create a database application more quickly than if they had to perform the same tasks manually. The Designer creates ADO objects corresponding to the tables in your database; it also provides other objects to help you manipulate your database. These objects are available as part of the Data Environment object at runtime.

ADO, not DAO and RDO: The Data Environment Designer only works with the ADO object model. The DAO and RDO object models are not supported. The UserConnection designer is a subset of the Data Environment Designer and supports the RDO object model.

See Chapter 6 for explanations of the ADO, DAO, and RDO models.

Enabling the Data Environment Designer

To add the Data Environment Designer to your project, choose Project ➪ Add Data Environment from the main menu. If you don't see it listed directly under the Project menu, try looking under the More ActiveX Designers menu (or Project ➪ More ActiveX Designers ➪ Data Environment from the main menu). This will display the main window for the Data Environment Designer.

If the Data Environment Designer doesn't appear in either location, you'll need to add it to Visual Basic. Choose Project ➪ Components from the main menu to display the Components dialog box, then select the Designer tab to see the window as shown in Figure 9-1. Place a check mark in the box next to Data Environment and press OK. This will add the Data Environment Designer to the Project menu. If you don't see Data Environment listed on the Designers tab, you need to install the Data Environment feature from your Visual Basic CD-ROM.

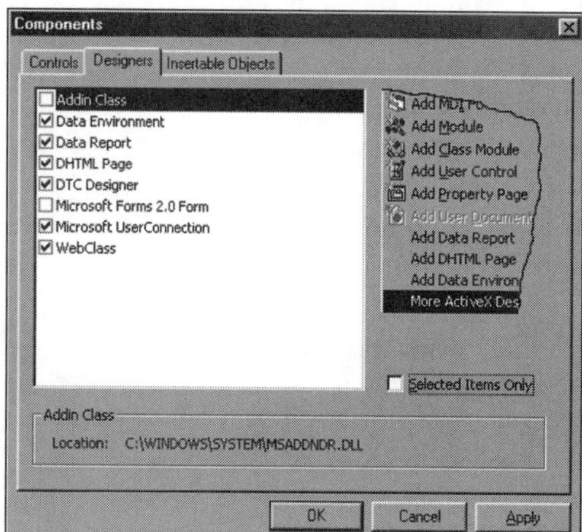

Figure 9-1: Adding the Data Environment Designer to the Visual Basic IDE

Exploring the Data Environment Designer

The main Data Environment Designer window (see Figure 9-2) includes a series of icons that are used to perform common operations, plus an icon tree view of the objects used in the Data Environment.

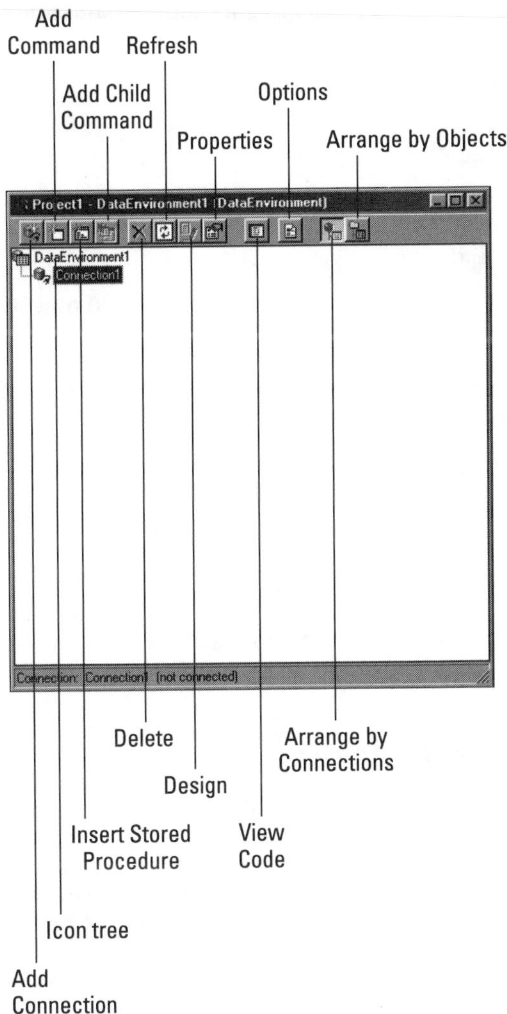

Figure 9-2: Exploring the Data Environment Designer window

- ✦ **Add Connection** – adds a new `Connection` object to the data environment, which will be used to access a database.
- ✦ **Add Command** – adds a new `Command` object to the data environment, which will be used to execute an SQL command.
- ✦ **Insert Stored Procedure** – adds a `Command` object with the information to call a stored procedure on the database server.

- **Add Child Command** – adds a Command object to another Command object to create a hierarchical structure of data.
- **Delete** – removes an object from the data environment.
- **Refresh** – refreshes the selected object. Connection objects are closed and reopened, while all of the metadata associated with a Command object will be rebuilt.
- **Design** – accesses the SQL query designer when you specify an SQL statement as the data source for a Command object.
- **Properties** – displays the properties associated with the selected object.
- **View Code** – displays the code associated with a particular object.
- **Options** – displays the Options dialog box that controls how the Data Environment Designer works.
- **Arrange by Connections** – arranges the objects in the icon tree by the Connection object they access.
- **Arrange by Objects** – arranges the objects in the icon tree by object type.
- **Icon Tree** – the list of objects associated with the data environment.

Many of these functions are also available via a pop-up menu that you can display by right clicking on an object in the icon tree.

Data Environment building blocks

The Data Environment Designer helps you create three main types of objects: Connections, Commands, and Recordsets. These objects are used at both design time and runtime to access your database. At design time, information about your database is extracted and made available to help you create your program. At runtime, these objects are used to perform typical database operations.

It's not what it seems: While these objects appear to be part of the Data Environment Designer, they are really normal ADO objects that the Data Environment Designer helps you create. For more information about all of the capabilities of these objects, please refer to Chapter 11.

Connection objects

A Connection object contains the properties and methods needed to access a database. Since the Connection object is used at both runtime and design time, a related object called the DECconnection is used by the Data Environment Designer to track information about each mode. This information contains the user name, password, how to prompt for password information, and whether to save password information at the end of the session for both runtime and design-time use.

Command objects

A Command object contains the information necessary to execute a command against your database. A command may be an SQL statement, a call to a stored procedure, or the name of a table. Some commands will require you to include a list of parameters when they are run. Some commands will return a set of rows, while others will return nothing but a status condition.

Recordset objects

Rows are returned from your database in a Recordset object. The Recordset object presents a single row of data, known as the *current record*. A *cursor* is used to point to the current record in the Recordset. You can manipulate the cursor by using various methods in the Recordset object.

If the rows in the Recordset object can be updated, there are other methods that allow you to add a new row, delete a row, and update a row. If you need to update multiple rows, you can easily create a Command object, which will call the appropriate SQL statement, or you can use the cursor to move through the rows in the Recordset object one at a time and use the appropriate methods to perform your updates.

Like the ADO Data Control, a Recordset object can be used as a data source with bound controls. This means that you can easily replace the ADO Data Control with the appropriate Recordset object by changing the DataSource property on each of the bound controls.

Hierarchical Recordsets

A hierarchical recordset is based on a normal Recordset, except that in place of one of the values in a row of data is another Recordset, known as a *child* recordset. The child recordset is created by a child Command, whose values are determined by a relationship with the parent recordset. It is also reasonable for a child recordset to have its own child recordsets, thus creating a multi-level hierarchy.

Hierarchical recordsets are useful when you want to retrieve data from multiple tables, but don't want to merge the data into a single table. The classic case of a hierarchical recordset is the customers, orders, and order items. A company has a collection of customers, each customer may have placed multiple orders, and each order a customer has placed may have multiple items.

Connecting to Your Database

The first step in working with the Data Environment Designer is to define a connection to the database. By default the Data Environment Designer creates a single Connection object called Connection1. This object is used at both design time and runtime to access information from the database.

Setting Connection properties

Selecting the Connection1 object and pressing the Properties button displays the Data Link Properties dialog box, as shown in Figure 9-3. While there are four tabs on the dialog box, only the Provider and Connection tab are typically used. The Advanced tab contains information regarding network settings, connection timeout, and access permissions whose default settings are almost always okay. The All tab lists all of the initialization parameters that will be used when establishing the database connection.

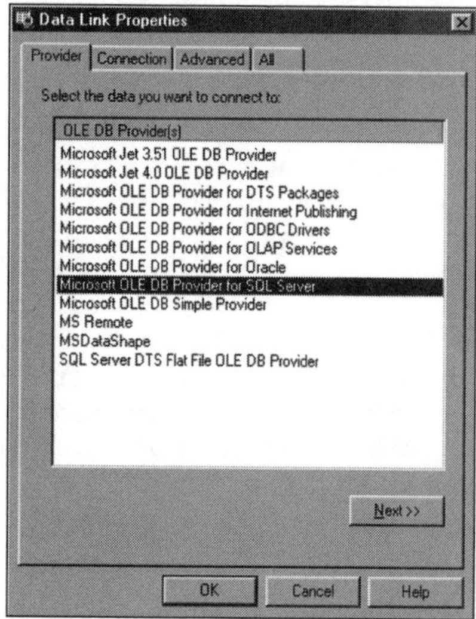

Figure 9-3: Setting Data Link properties for a Connection object

Selecting an OLE DB provider

The first step in defining your connection to the database is to choose an OLE DB provider on the Provider tab of the Data Link Properties dialog box. All of the providers available for your system will be listed. You should choose the native OLE DB provider for your database server, if one is available. Otherwise, you should choose the Microsoft OLE DB Provider for ODBC Drivers. Once you select the proper OLE DB provider, press Next to continue defining the connection properties.

Entering connection information

Since I chose the Microsoft OLE DB Provider for SQL Server in the previous step, pressing Next will request the information shown in Figure 9-4 using the Connection tab. In this case, my database server is on Athena. I'm going to use Windows NT integrated security and I want to use the VB6DB database as my default database.

Once I enter this information, I can press the Test Connection button to verify that everything is correct. If there is a problem, a message box will be displayed with a description of the error; otherwise, a message box saying Test connection succeeded will be displayed. After pressing OK on the test's message box, press OK to save the connection information.

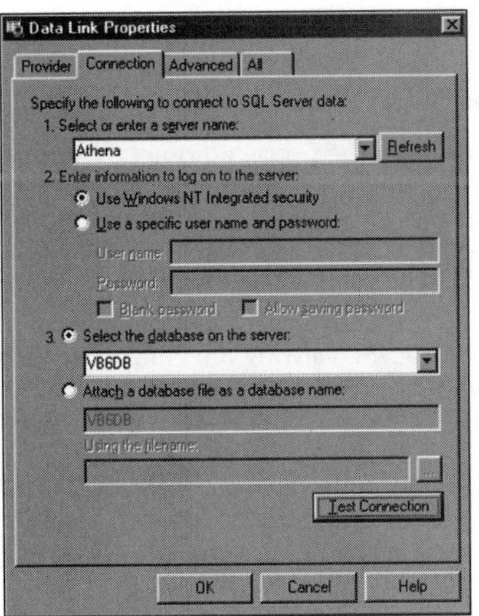

Figure 9-4: Entering connection information for the Microsoft OLE DB Provider for SQL Server

The information entered in the Data Link dialog boxes is used to build a *connection string*. This value is used anytime you want to connect an ADO object to a database. For more information about connection strings, see the `ConnectionString` property and the `Connection` object in Chapter 11. For details about how to connect to a specific database, see Connecting to SQL Server in Chapter 23, Connecting to Oracle8*i* in Chapter 26, or Connecting to Jet in Chapter 29.

Creating Commands with the Designer

After you have defined a `Connection` object, you can begin to define some `Command` objects. The Data Environment Designer treats `Command` objects in two different ways — as commands and as stored procedures. The difference is primarily how the information for the objects is obtained. If you choose to add a stored procedure, the designer will get a list of stored procedures from the database, you will need to enter a single, dynamically executed SQL statement as one of the properties of the `Command` object. Stored procedures are discussed later in this chapter under "Selecting a Database Object."

Adding a command

Adding a `Command` object by pressing the Add Command button on the Data Environment Designer toolbar simply adds a new command object beneath the currently selected `Connection`. All of the properties associated with the `Command` object are left at their default values and must be changed in order to use the command.

Setting general command properties

Pressing the Properties button or right clicking on the `Command` object will display the `Command1` Properties dialog box as shown in Figure 9-5. On the General tab, you can specify the name of the command, which connection will be used by the command, and the Source of Data for the command.

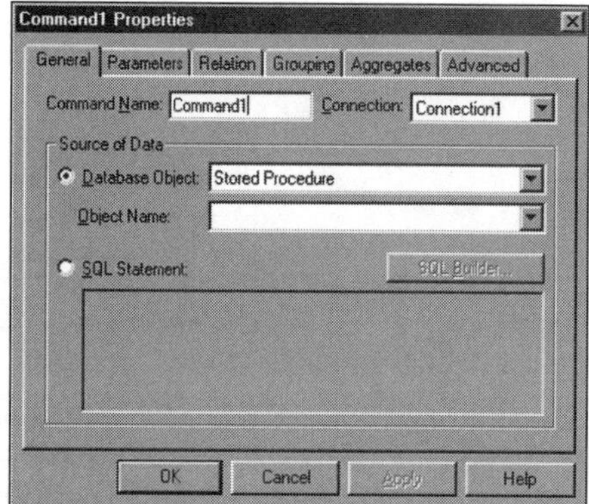

Figure 9-5: Viewing the general properties of the Command1 object

The Source of Data section is somewhat misleading since a `Command` object need not return data. It really depends on whether the database object you select or the SQL statement you enter returns any data.

Selecting a database object

You have a choice of four different database objects: a Stored Procedure, a Table, a View, or a Synonym. A *stored procedure* is nothing but a series of one or more SQL statements that are executed on the database server. Any data returned depends on whether the stored procedure includes a **Select** statement. Selecting Table or View will always return all of the data visible in the selected table or view. A *synonym* is an alternate name for a database object, such as a table or view.

Once you select which type of database object you want, you must specify the object name. The designer makes this easy because after you specify the type of database object you want, it will automatically connect to the database server using the specified `Connection` object and retrieve the list of available objects. These objects are then made available in the Object Name drop-down list directly below the Database Object drop down box. All you need to do is select the one you want.

Entering an SQL Statement

If you want the command to execute an SQL statement, simply enter the statement in the SQL Statement area in the dialog box. No other statement, except for the **Select** statement, will return data. To make it easier to create an SQL **Select** statement, you can press the SQL Builder button to display the Design window, which will help you build SQL queries.

One of the side effects of using an SQL statement or a stored procedure is that the designer doesn't know what fields will be returned. The only way for the `Command` object to know what fields are returned is to execute the command. Before executing the command, the designer will ask you for permission (see Figure 9-6), since the command could potentially update your database.

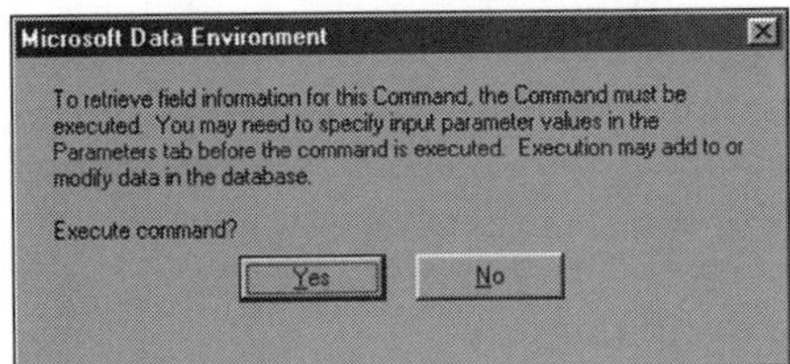

Figure 9-6: Asking for permission to execute an SQL statement

Test it first: You should take the time to verify that the SQL statement will work before you enter it into the SQL Statement area. The easiest way to do this is to use a tool like SQL Server's Query Analyzer.

Setting parameters

If you are using a stored procedure as your command, you will probably have one or more parameters associated with it. Consider the stored procedure in Listing 9-1. It will retrieve all of the information about the customer specified in `CustId`.

Listing 9-1: The GetCustomer stored procedure

```
Create Procedure GetCustomer (@CustId Int)
As
Select *
From Customers
Where CustomerId = @CustId
```

Figure 9-7 shows you the Parameters tab of the Properties dialog box. You can view the details about a particular parameter by clicking on it in the Parameters frame. The information related to it will be displayed in the Parameter Properties frame.

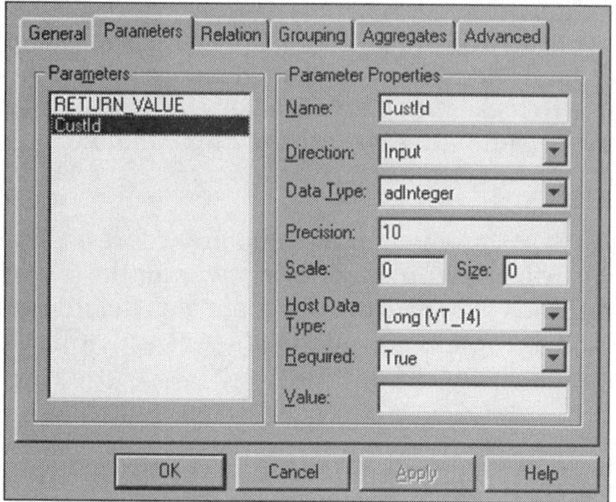

Figure 9-7: Looking at the parameters of a stored procedure

Each parameter has a number of different properties associated with it:

- ✦ **Name** – contains the formal name of the parameter.
- ✦ **Direction** – classifies the parameter as input, output, or input/output parameter.
- ✦ **Data_Type** – specifies the data type associated with the parameter.
- ✦ **Precision** – specifies the precision of a numeric data type.
- ✦ **Scale** – specifies the scale of a numeric data type. This field is disabled for non-numeric data types.
- ✦ **Size** – specifies the size associated with the data type. This field is disabled for non-numeric data types.
- ✦ **Host Data Type** – specifies the data type that will be used by the host. This value must be compatible with the value specified in the Data_Type field.
- ✦ **Required** – is `TRUE` when you must specify a value for the parameter before the command can be executed.
- ✦ **Value** – contains the default value for the parameter. It will be used at design time to test the `Command` object. At runtime, you will typically override this value with the real value you wish to use.

I can't change anything: If the type of command you are creating doesn't allow parameters, all of the fields on this tab will be blank, and even if the type of command does support parameters, some of the properties of the parameter may be disabled, meaning that you can't change them.

Setting advanced properties

The Advanced Properties tab (see Figure 9-8) contains a number of different properties that affect how the command will be executed and how the results will be returned. Depending on the type of command you choose, some or most of these properties may be disabled.

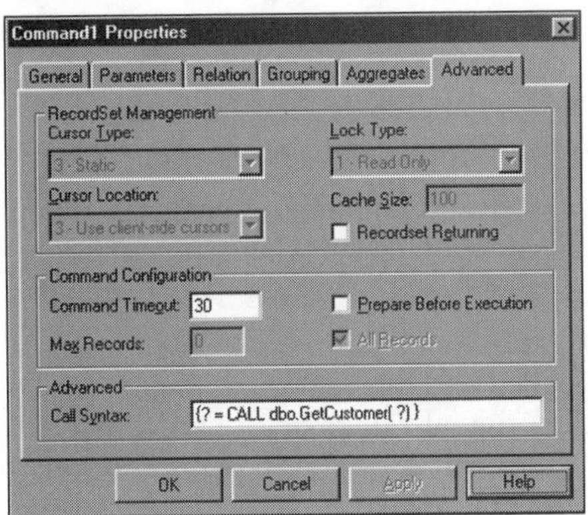

Figure 9-8: Reviewing advanced properties

Reviewing Recordset management properties

The four properties in the *RecordSet Management* section (`CursorType`, `CursorLocation`, `LockType` and `CacheSize`) control how the `Recordset` object will be created and how it can be accessed from your program.

See the `Recordset` object in Chapter 14 for a more complete discussion of cursors and locks.

The type of cursor used in a `Recordset` determines many of its characteristics. Client-side cursors are restricted to using only static cursors, while server-side cursors can use any of these four different types of cursors:

- ✦ **Forward Only** cursors point to a collection of rows that can only be accessed in a forward direction. Moving backwards isn't permitted. Otherwise, this cursor type is identical to Static.
- ✦ **Keyset** cursors point to a collection of rows that see all changes (including deletions) to the database, except for records that have been added after the `Recordset` was created.

✦ **Dynamic** cursors point to a collection of rows that see all changes (including additions and deletions) to the database after the `Recordset` was created.

✦ **Static** cursors point to a collection of rows that will not change until the `Recordset` is closed. Any rows that have been added, deleted, or updated by any other database user are not seen.

The `CursorLocation` property describes where the cursor is located. Choosing Use server-side cursors means that the cursor will be managed by the database management system, while choosing Use client-side cursors means that the cursor will be managed by a cursor library located on the same computer as the application. Client-side cursors are more flexible than server-side cursors, while server-side cursors are easier to use than client-side cursors.

The `LockType` property determines how you and other users can access the data in the database.

✦ **Read-only** locks mean that you can't alter any of the data in the `Recordset`.

✦ **Pessimistic** locks mean that the row is locked immediately when you begin to change the values in a row. The lock will be released when you complete your changes.

✦ **Optimistic** locks mean that the row is not locked until you have finished making your changes. Then the row is locked and the current values of the row in the database are checked against the original values before you changed them. If they are the same, your changes will be saved to the database, otherwise an error will be returned to your program.

✦ **Batch Optimistic** locks work just like optimistic locks, except that multiple rows of information are updated locally and are sent to the database server in a single batch. Any errors will be returned to your program. Your program must then identify the rows that weren't updated and take the appropriate action for each row.

Lock least: You should lock the least amount of data possible in order to make it easy to share data. If you don't need to update any of the data, you should use a read-only lock. In the beginning, you should use a pessimistic lock with a server-side cursor to prevent others from updating the data you are editing. Once you are comfortable with database programming, you should consider using client-side cursors with either optimistic or batch optimistic locking.

The `CacheSize` property determines how many rows are buffered in the client machine. Increasing this size allows the database server to operate more efficiently when returning data to the client system. It will also improve the performance of the client system, since most of the time, it will retrieve data from the local cache rather than request data from the server. However, the data in the cache will not be updated if changes are made to the same rows on the database server. The more rows you keep in the cache, the greater the chance that someone else may have updated the data. If you choose pessimistic locking, you should set the CacheSize property to one to prevent invalid records from sitting in your cache.

Reviewing other advanced properties

Like the properties in the *RecordSet Management* section, those in the *Command Configuration* section are taken from the Command object discussed in Chapter 11. However, the Command Timeout is important enough to discuss twice. This property contains the number of seconds the command is allowed to run before it is canceled. When dealing with large volumes of data or very complex stored procedures, the default value of 30 seconds may not be enough to allow the command to finish. If this happens, you will need to increase this value.

The *Call Syntax* section describes how a stored procedure will be called, including the list of parameters and the return value. While you can edit this value to change the number of parameters and presence of a return value, in general you should leave this field alone.

Saving the Command

To save your property settings and continue working with the properties, press the Apply button, or to save your changes and close the Command1 Properties dialog box, press the OK button. If the Apply button is grayed out, it indicates that the saved version of the environment is the same as the one you are viewing. Once your Command has been defined, you can see the list of fields that the command will return in the Data Environment by expanding the plus sign in front of the command's icon (see Figure 9-9).

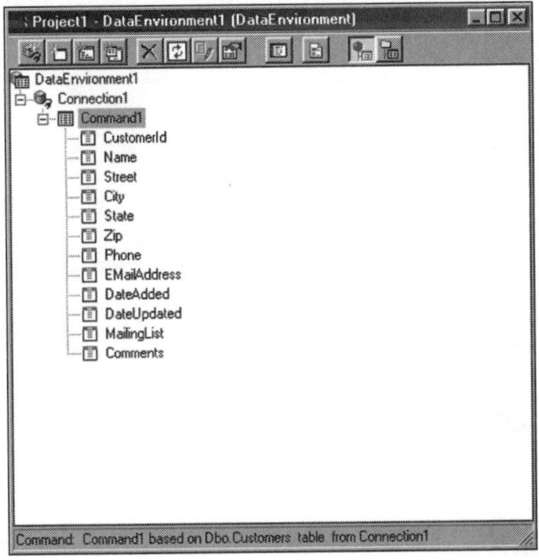

Figure 9-9: Viewing the fields returned by a command

Adding a Child Command

One of the nicer features of the Data Environment Designer is its ability to create hierarchical recordsets easily. Simply select the command you want to add the child to and press the Add Child Command button. This creates a new command that is nested at the same level as the fields on the parent command. Note that the command you choose as the parent command must return a `Recordset`, otherwise you will not be able to add the child command.

After selecting the child command, you can press the Properties button to define its properties. The first thing you must do in the Properties dialog box is to define the Source of Data. As with the parent command, you must choose a Source of Data that returns a `Recordset`. If you don't define a source of data, you'll receive a warning message if you try to access any of the other tabs in the Properties dialog box.

Once you've defined the Source of Data, you should define any properties on the Parameters and Advanced tabs that are needed to retrieve the data. Note that the `Recordset` object returned by the child command is always read-only. In fact, most of the properties on the Advanced tab will be disabled, and the properties will be set to be compatible with the properties selected for the parent command.

Defining a relationship

On the Relation tab (see Figure 9-10), you must define how the parent and child commands are related. At the top of the page, you'll see the Relate to a Parent Command Object check box and the Parent Command drop-down box. By default, the check box will be checked, meaning that this command is a child command, and its parent command will be the one that was selected when you pressed the Add Child Command button. Unchecking the check box will make this a regular command that is independent of any other commands in the Designer, while selecting a different parent command will make this command a child of the selected command.

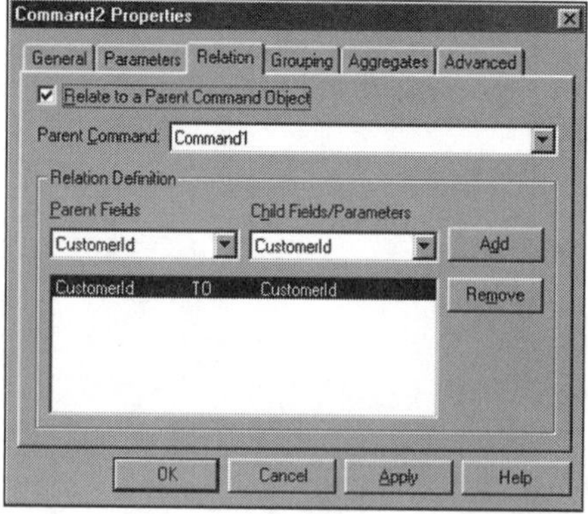

Figure 9-10: Defining a relationship between a child command and its parent

Once the parent has been selected, you need to choose the fields that establish the parent child relationship in the Relation Definition frame. Specifying pairs of fields, one in the parent and one in the child, defines the relationship between the two commands. For each row retrieved by the parent command, the child command will be executed and the values from the parent fields will be used to select only those rows with matching values in the child command. Since this is a somewhat complex concept, let's use an example from the sample database. Assume that the parent command retrieves all of the rows from the Customers table. Then the child command is set up to retrieve all of the rows from the Orders table. The relationship information specified on the Relation tab associates the CustomerId value in the Orders table with the CustomerId value in each row retrieved from the Customers table.

The information needed to build the sample database can be found in the \SampleDB directory on the CD-ROM.

The retrieved records would look like the information in Table 9-1. Notice that for each row retrieved from the Customers table (CustomerId and Name), one or more rows of information will be retrieved from the Orders table (OrderNumber and DateOrdered).

Table 9-1
A View of a Hierarchical Recordset

CustomerId	*Name*	*OrderNumber*	*DateOrdered*
0	Dexter Valentine	-	-
0	-	1000	1 Jan 2000
1	Malik Hubert	-	-
1	-	1001	1 Jan 2000
1	-	1004	1 Feb 2000
2	Lee Holt	-	-
2	-	1002	2 Jan 2000
2	-	1005	2 Feb 2000
3	Scotty Waltrip	-	-
3	-	1003	3 Jan 2000
3	-	1006	3 Feb 2000
3	-	1007	3 Mar 2000

Using groupings

An alternate way to create a hierarchical recordset is to define a grouping using the Grouping tab of the Properties dialog box (see Figure 9-11). A *grouping* allows you to take a single recordset and break it into two levels. A new level is created each time the values of the *Fields Used for Grouping* change.

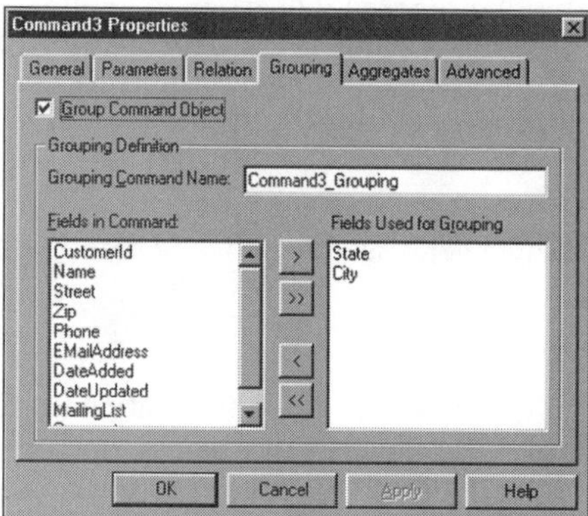

Figure 9-11: Selecting fields for grouping

To define your grouping, simply select the field or fields you want to move in the *Fields in Command* section of the form and press the > button to move them to the *Fields Used for Grouping*. You can move a field in the reverse direction by using the < button. The >> and << buttons move all of the fields in the direction of the arrows.

Aggregating data

In the Aggregates tab of the Command Properties dialog box (see Figure 9-12), you can create summary data for your recordset or hierarchical recordset. You can define aggregates that are based on grouping levels. You can also define grand totals for the entire recordset. The aggregated data will appear as part of a hierarchical recordset.

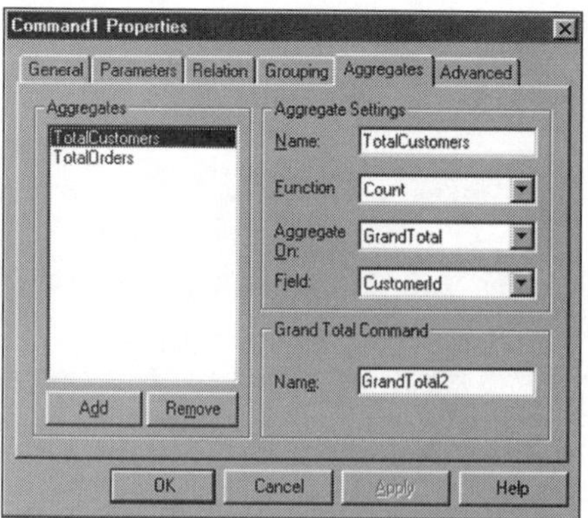

Figure 9-12: Selecting aggregations for a hierarchical recordset

To add a new aggregation, press the Add button to create a default aggregation. A new aggregation will appear in the Aggregation frame. Clicking on the aggregation will display all of its settings in the Aggregation Settings frame. Also, you can remove an aggregation by selecting it in the *Aggregates* frame and pressing the Remove button.

When working with a hierarchical recordset, you can define aggregations in two ways — as a grand total, which is computed over the entire recordset, or as a group summary over a child command. You can't define an aggregation on the lowest level of a hierarchical recordset. If you are working with a regular recordset, you can only define aggregations over the entire recordset for a grand total.

If you aggregate values over a child command, the aggregated values will be added to the current level of the hierarchical recordset. If you create a grand total, it adds a new level above the current level of the hierarchical recordset. When adding an aggregation, you need to give it a name and decide how to compute it. Remember that an aggregation will appear as a field in the recordset, so using a meaningful name is important.

To compute an aggregation, you need to define three pieces of information: the level of aggregation (the name of a child command or grand total), the name of the field that you want to aggregate, and the name of function that you want to use to perform the aggregation (see Table 9-2).

Table 9-2
Aggregation Operations

Operation	***Description***
Any	Performs the default operation for the field.
Average	Averages the values for a particular field.
Count	Counts the number of rows retrieved.
Maximum	Returns the highest value found in the field.
Minimum	Returns the lowest value in the field.
Standard Deviation	Computes the standard deviation of all of the values for the selected field.
Sum	Adds the values of the specified field together.

Inserting a stored procedure

Even though a stored procedure uses the same property window as regular `Command` objects, a special dialog box makes it easy to add multiple stored procedures to the Data Environment Designer. Clicking the Insert Stored Procedures button will display the dialog box shown in Figure 9-13. Simply select the stored procedures from the Available list and press the > button to add them to the Add list. You can use the >> button to add all of the stored procedures to the Add list. Pressing the < or << buttons will remove the selected or all of the stored procedures from the Add list respectively.

Once you've created the list of stored procedures you want to add, press the Insert button to add them to the Designer. When all of your selected stored procedures have been added, you can repeat the process to select additional stored procedures, or press the Close button to return to the Data Environment Designer.

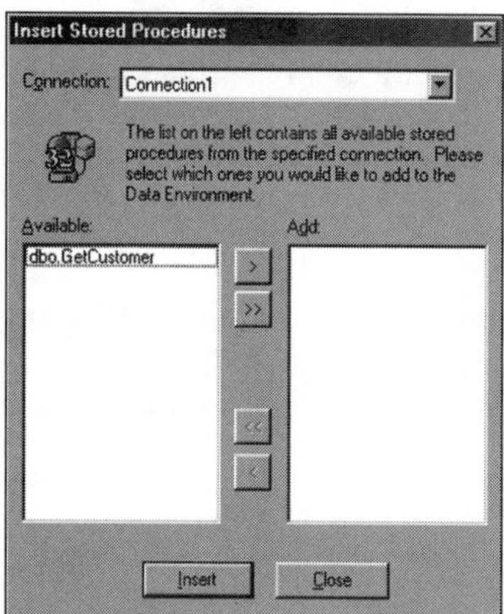

Figure 9-13: Inserting a stored procedure

Building Programs with the Designer

The true power of the Data Environment Designer is shown when you use it to design your forms. The Designer allows you to drag commands and fields from the Designer onto a Visual Basic form to create controls that are bound to the objects in the runtime component of the Data Environment Designer. Once the controls are positioned, you can write code to manipulate the information on the form.

Drawing controls

If you expand a `Command` object, you will see the list of fields in the object (see Figure 9-14). To add a field to your Visual Basic form, simply move the cursor to the field you want to add, press the left mouse button, and drag the field onto the form while still pressing the left mouse button. When the control is where you want it, release the left mouse button, and the control will be added to your form.

The new control is automatically bound to a `Recordset` object that is owned by the runtime component of the Data Environment Designer. The additional fields that are dragged onto the form from the same command will also be automatically bound to the same `Recordset` object. In addition to dragging fields, you can also drag a command onto your form. All of the fields that are contained in the command will be dropped on the form. Figure 9-15 shows the effect of dragging `Command1` from Figure 9-14 onto a blank form.

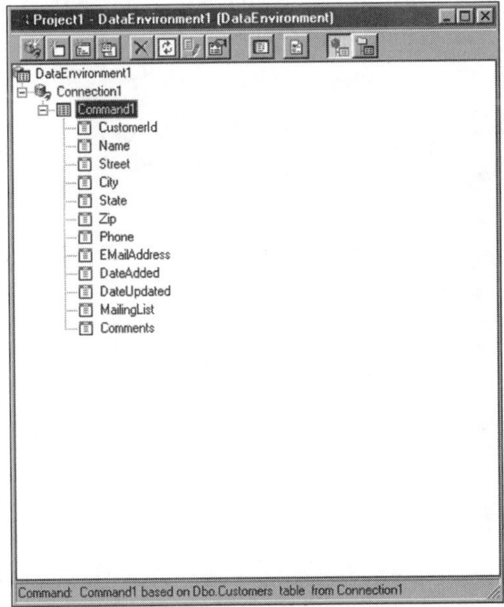

Figure 9-14: Viewing the fields in a command

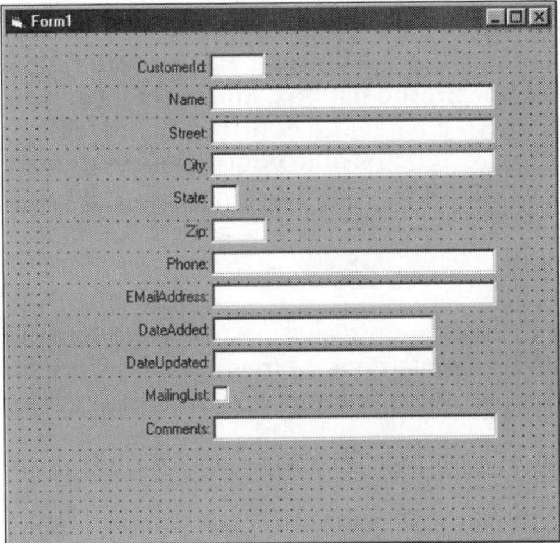

Figure 9-15: The result of dragging a command 8object onto a form

They're still in one piece: When you drop the fields onto your form object, all of the fields are selected. This makes it easy to move the fields around on the form until they fit.

Setting options

You can control how a field appears on a form by setting the Field Mapping on Data Environment Designer's Options dialog box (see Figure 9-16). Depending on the data type of the database field, the Designer will select a control type based on the information shown in the Default Control Association area of the dialog box.

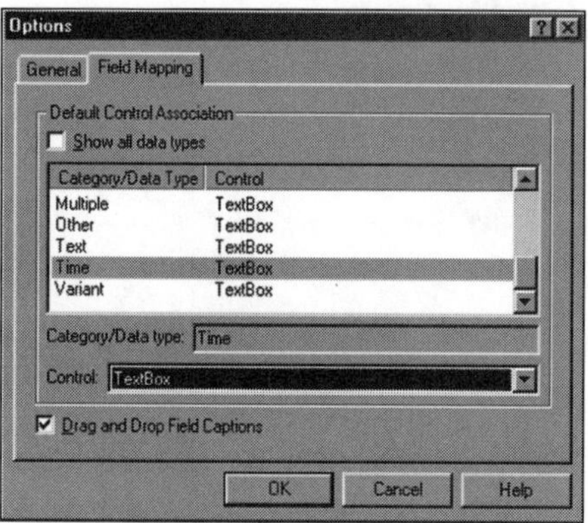

Figure 9-16: Changing the field mapping

If the Drag and Drop Field Captions check box is checked, a `Label` control will automatically be generated alongside the selected control. The `Caption` property of the `Label` control will be set to the name of field in the database.

You can change the control associated with a data type by selecting the data type under *Category/Data Type* in the list box area (see Figure 9-16). The data type will appear in the *Category/Data type* area beneath the list box, and the control will appear in the drop-down box below that. To change the control, simply press the drop-down arrow to display a list of choices. All possible controls on your system will be listed, whether or not they are available in your current project. If you choose a control that isn't available in your project, it will be added automatically. Press OK to save your changes.

There's more: On the General tab of the Options dialog box, there are some general options you can enable or disable. While none of these options have a big impact on how the Designer works, you might find that they make the Designer more comfortable to use.

Data Environment RunTime Object Model

The Data Environment Designer includes a runtime object called DataEnvironment for your program. The DataEnvironment object is basically just a container for all of the objects you created in the Designer.

DataEnvironment properties

The DataEnvironment object contains five main properties, which are listed in Table 9-3. The Commands and Connections are references to collection objects containing the commands and connections you defined using the Data Environment Designer.

Table 9-3
Properties of the DataEnvironment Object

Property	*Description*
Commands	An object reference to a collection object containing the set of Commands objects defined in the Data Environment.
Connections	An object reference to a collection object containing the set of Connection objects defined in the Data Environment.
Name	A String containing the name of the DataEnvironment object.
Object	An object reference to the DataEnvironment object.
Recordsets	An object reference to a collection object containing the set of Recordset objects defined in the Data Environment.

The Recordsets collection contains a series of Recordset objects. Each Command in the Commands collection will have a corresponding Recordset object in the Recordsets collection, which will hold the results of the Command. Adding the characters rs to the front of the Command object's name forms the name of the Recordset object.

Unlike traditional collection objects, you can't add or delete objects from these collections at runtime. The only way to add or delete objects from these collections is by using the Data Environment Designer at design time.

Using these collections can be a little difficult. The following line of code is used to retrieve the value of the CustomerId column:

```
DataEnvironment1.Recordsets("rsCommand1").Fields("CustomerId").
Value
```

You need to explicitly include the name of the Recordset when trying to access it through the collection object. Since this approach is pretty messy, Microsoft included a shortcut for each Recordset object in the DataEnvironment object. This allows you to rewrite the statement as:

```
DataEnvironment1.rsCommand1.Fields("CustomerId").Value
```

Then if you use the With statement, you can rewrite this statement as:

```
With DataEnvironment1.rsCommand1
    .Fields("CustomerId").Value

End With
```

With what: Using the With statement can be very useful if you need to perform multiple operations against the Recordset. Not only do you save yourself a lot of typing, your program will execute slightly faster. The better performance is a result of having to resolve the reference to the DataEnvironent1.rsCommand1 object once for the With block rather than once for each statement executed.

DataEnvironment methods

The default DataEnvironment object has no default methods. However, each time you add a command in the Data Environment Designer, a shortcut method will be added to the DataEnvironment object. This makes it easier to code your application.

Calling a command without parameters

There are two ways to call a Command object using the DataEnvironment object. You can access the command though the Commands property, like this:

```
DataEnvironment1.Commands("Command1").Open
```

Or you can use the shortcut method, like this:

```
DataEnvironment1.Commmand1
```

Calling a command with parameters

It isn't difficult to call a Command object with parameters. You can specify the parameters as part of the Command object's Parameters collection, as shown below:

```
DataEnvironment1.Commands("Command1").Parameters("Parm1").Value = 1
DataEnvironemnt1.Commands("Command1").Parameters("Parm2").Value = 2
```

```
DataEnvironment1.Commands("Command1").Parameters("Parm3").Value = 3
DataEnvironment1.Commands("Command1").Open
```

Or you can use the shortcut method, like this:

```
DataEnvironment1.Commmand1 1, 2, 3
```

See Chapter 11 for more information about the Parameters collection.

Data Environment events

The Data Environment Designer automatically creates a separate module to hold all of the code for the `DataEnvironment` object and all of the `Connection` and `Recordset` objects created beneath it.

Event Initialize ()

The `Initialize` event is called when the `DataEnvironment` object is accessed for the first time. Typically, this will be when your program is first started. This is a good place to include code that prompts the user for a user Id and password if you don't want to use the default login form.

Event Terminate ()

The `Terminate` event is called just before the `DataEnvironment` object is destroyed.

Viewing Databases with the Data View Window

The Data View Window is the central component of the Visual Database Tools (see Figure 9-17). It works with the Data Environment Designer to allow you to perform various tasks with your database, such as designing your database, editing data in the tables, creating **Views,** and managing stored procedures. These tools are based on the tools that ship with SQL Server 7, and work with both SQL Server and Oracle 8*i* database systems.

Why doesn't it work for me?: Some of the features of the Data View Window are only available with the Enterprise Edition of Visual Basic.

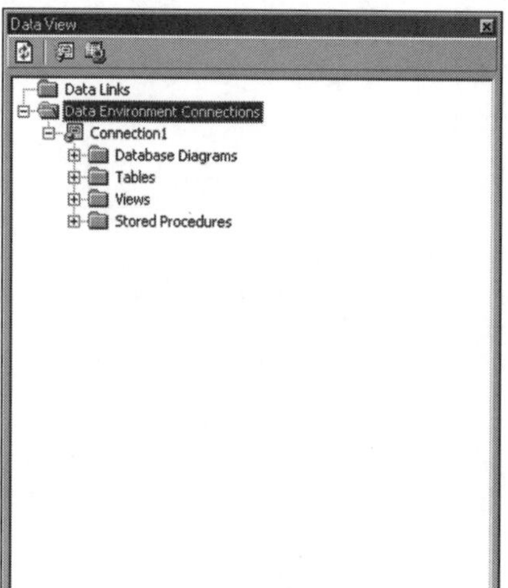

Figure 9-17: Viewing databases with the Data View Window

Configuring the Data View Window

To start the Data View Window, you can choose View ➪ Data View Window from the main menu or press the Data View Window icon on the toolbar. You can also display the Data View Window by pressing the Design button while in the Data Environment Designer.

All of the `Connection` objects you defined in the Data Environment Designer will be listed under the Data Environment Connections icon. Simply expand the icon to show icons for Database Diagrams, Tables, Views, and Stored Procedures. Expanding these icons will show you the list of database objects you can access through the Designer.

Data Environment Not: You don't need to use the Data Environment Designer with the Data View Window. You can create a Data Link by right clicking on the Data Links icon and selecting Add a Data Link from the pop-up menu. You'll see the familiar Data Link Properties dialog box that you've seen many times before. Simply select the OLE DB provider for your database and press the Next button. Then enter the rest of the information and you'll be all set to use the Data View Window.

Working with database diagrams

A *database diagram* is a visual representation of a database that you can modify (see Figure 9-18). You can add new tables, delete existing tables, or change any of the characteristics of a table.

The Database Diagram tool is identical to the Database Diagram tool in SQL Server 7's Enterprise Manager. See Chapter 24 for more information.

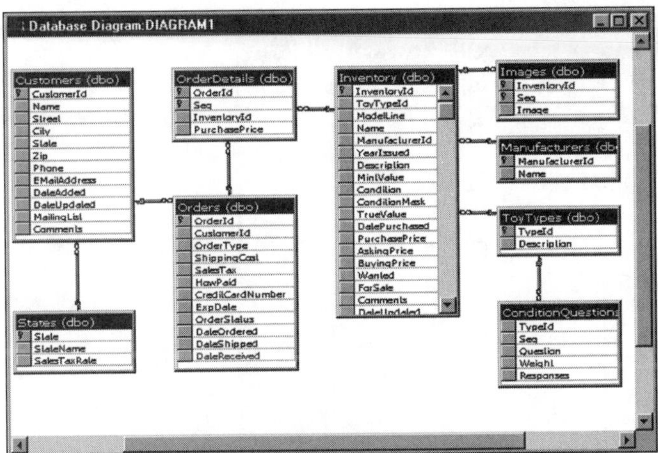

Figure 9-18: Working with a database diagram

Working with tables

There are two main functions you can perform with tables using the Data View Window. The first is to open a table in design mode (see Figure 9-19) by simply right clicking on the table name and selecting Design from the pop-up menu.

Each column in the table corresponds to a row of information displayed in the Design window, including the Column Name, its Data Type and size information, whether **Nulls** are allowed, etc. . . You can easily change most values directly by editing the value in the particular cell. For instance, you can changethe length of a **Varchar** field from 50 characters to 128 characters by changing the value 50 to 128. You can also add new columns to the table by simply adding them to the end of the list of columns.

But it's not empty: Even if your table has data in it, you can still make some changes to its structure in Design mode. Before the changes are applied to the database, the utility will verify that the data in the table is compatible with the changes. If it isn't, an error message will be displayed and you can opt to save your changes into a script file that can be applied later.

The other main function you can perform with a table is to view its data in a spreadsheet-like grid, similar to the `DBGrid` control (see Figure 9-20). You can open your table by right clicking on the table name and selecting Open from the pop-up menu.

You can change any value in the table by simply overtyping the data in the particular cell. The changes are committed to the database when you move your cursor to another row. If you move your cursor to the first blank row at the end of the grid, you can insert a new row into the table by right clicking on the table and choosing New from the pop-up menu.

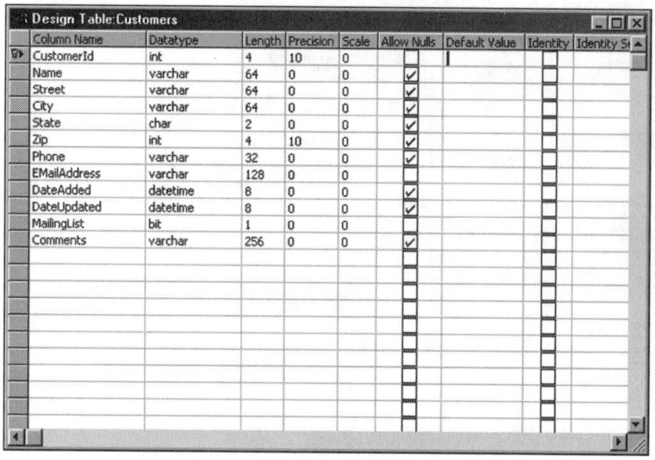

Design Table:Customers

Column Name	Datatype	Length	Precision	Scale	Allow Nulls	Default Value	Identity	Identity S
CustomerId	int	4	10	0	☐		☐	
Name	varchar	64	0	0	☑		☐	
Street	varchar	64	0	0	☑		☐	
City	varchar	64	0	0	☑		☐	
State	char	2	0	0	☑		☐	
Zip	int	4	10	0	☑		☐	
Phone	varchar	32	0	0	☑		☐	
EMailAddress	varchar	128	0	0	☐		☐	
DateAdded	datetime	8	0	0	☑		☐	
DateUpdated	datetime	8	0	0	☑		☐	
MailingList	bit	1	0	0	☐		☐	
Comments	varchar	256	0	0	☑		☐	

Figure 9-19: Working with a table in design mode

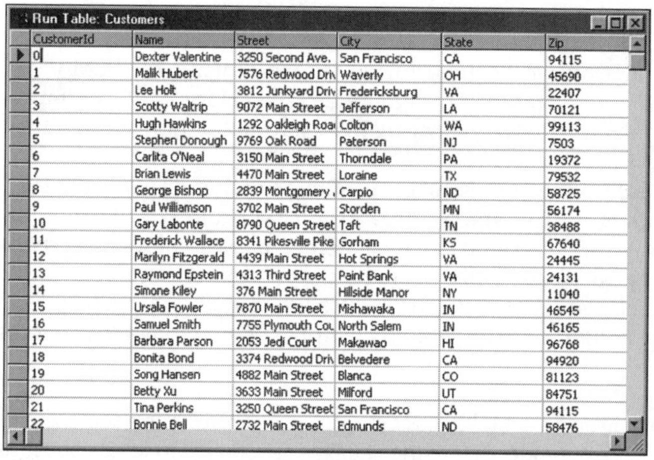

Run Table: Customers

CustomerId	Name	Street	City	State	Zip
0	Dexter Valentine	3250 Second Ave.	San Francisco	CA	94115
1	Malik Hubert	7576 Redwood Driv	Waverly	OH	45690
2	Lee Holt	3812 Junkyard Driv	Fredericksburg	VA	22407
3	Scotty Waltrip	9072 Main Street	Jefferson	LA	70121
4	Hugh Hawkins	1292 Oakleigh Roa	Colton	WA	99113
5	Stephen Donough	9769 Oak Road	Paterson	NJ	7503
6	Carlita O'Neal	3150 Main Street	Thorndale	PA	19372
7	Brian Lewis	4470 Main Street	Loraine	TX	79532
8	George Bishop	2839 Montgomery .	Carpio	ND	58725
9	Paul Williamson	3702 Main Street	Storden	MN	56174
10	Gary Labonte	8790 Queen Street	Taft	TN	38488
11	Frederick Wallace	8341 Pikesville Pike	Gorham	KS	67640
12	Marilyn Fitzgerald	4439 Main Street	Hot Springs	VA	24445
13	Raymond Epstein	4313 Third Street	Paint Bank	VA	24131
14	Simone Kiley	376 Main Street	Hillside Manor	NY	11040
15	Ursala Fowler	7870 Main Street	Mishawaka	IN	46545
16	Samuel Smith	7755 Plymouth Cou	North Salem	IN	46165
17	Barbara Parson	2053 Jedi Court	Makawao	HI	96768
18	Bonita Bond	3374 Redwood Driv	Belvedere	CA	94920
19	Song Hansen	4882 Main Street	Blanca	CO	81123
20	Betty Xu	3633 Main Street	Milford	UT	84751
21	Tina Perkins	3250 Queen Street	San Francisco	CA	94115
22	Bonnie Bell	2732 Main Street	Edmunds	ND	58476

Figure 9-20: Opening a table for viewing

You may select rows by clicking on the row header area, just before the first column. Pressing the delete key will display a dialog box asking if you really want to delete the selected rows from your database. Pressing Yes will remove the rows, while pressing No will return you back to the table.

Working with views

The same two main functions available with tables are also available for views. You can open a view just like you opened a table, and the results will be displayed the same way. You can also design a view using the Query Designer (see Figure 9-21).

You can enter your **Select** directly or use the interactive Designer to create the **Select** statement.

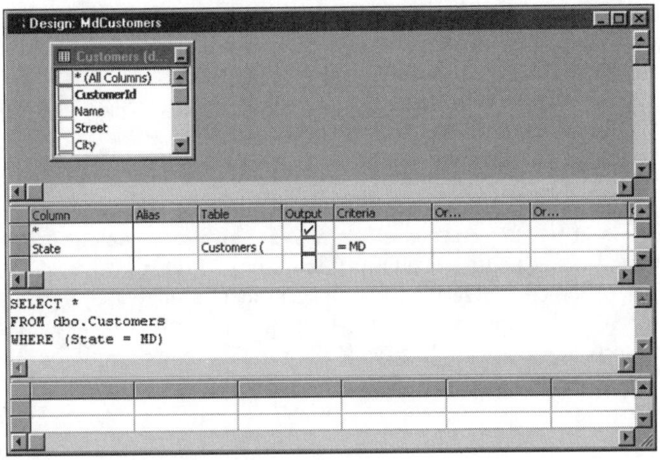

Figure 9-21: Designing a view

Working with stored procedures

You can design and debug stored procedures using the Data View Window. Right click on the stored procedure you want to edit and choose Design from the pop-up menu. This will display the Design window for the stored procedure (see Figure 9-22). You can type your changes into the window and save them as a disk file or back to the database. When you are finished, you can use the T-SQL Debugger to test it.

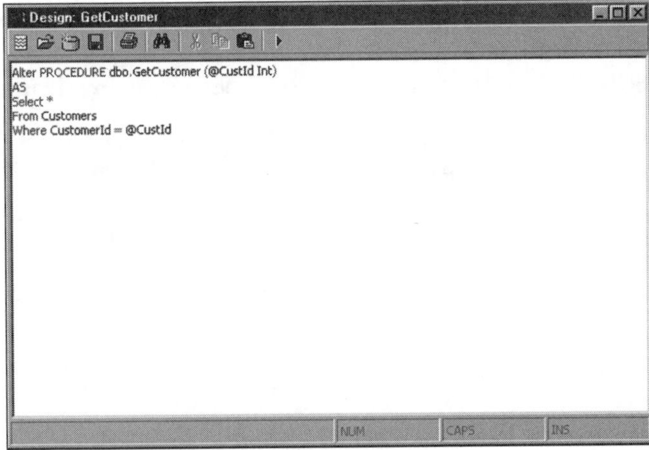

Figure 9-22: Changing a stored procedure

Thoughts on the Data Environment Designer

The Data Environment Designer is an alternate way to develop database applications. It is a step up in functionality from the ADO Data Control that was discussed in Chapter 7, but it is not as flexible as using the ADO objects, directly. The primary advantage to using the Data Environment Designer is that it allows you to drag and drop bound fields to your form objects. It is also useful when you want to create hierarchical recordsets for use with Microsoft Report, which I'll cover in Chapter 10.

The Data View Window allows Microsoft to reuse some of the code in SQL Server to provide some of the basic design facilities that exist in SQL Server's Enterprise Manager in Visual Basic. This means that you don't have to have the SQL Server software installed on your development computer. While this is an interesting tool in theory, I find myself using SQL Server's Enterprise Manager or Oracle's SQL*Plus for these functions anyway. I invariably need Enterprise Manager or SQL*Plus open to perform a function that isn't available in the Visual Database Tools or to look at a piece of data while I'm running my program, because the Data View Window is available only at design time.

Summary

In this chapter you learned the following:

- ✦ You can use the Data Environment Designer to simplify the process of creating various ADO objects that are used to access your database.
- ✦ You can create `Command` objects to execute SQL statements.
- ✦ You can explicitly specify an SQL statement for a `Command` object or create a reference to a table or stored procedure.
- ✦ You can use the Data View Window to view the contents and structure of a database.
- ✦ You can design SQL statements and create stored procedures directly from Visual Basic.

✦ ✦ ✦

CHAPTER 10

Building Reports with the Microsoft Data Report Designer

In This Chapter

The Data Report Designer

Adding the Data Report to your program

Previewing a report

Printing a report

Exporting reports

Presenting the data report object model

In this chapter, I'm going to talk about the Microsoft Data Report and show you how to incorporate it into your application.

Introducing the Microsoft Data Report

Contrary to popular belief, paper reports are far from dead. Your applications need the ability to produce reports from their database. Microsoft Data Report is the answer. Microsoft Data Report is a full-featured report generator whose features include:

- **Controls** – includes the familiar `Label`, `Shape`, `Image`, `TextBox`, and `Line` controls used in creating Visual Basic forms, plus the `Function` control that allows you to compute the sum, average, minimum or maximum value for a database field.
- **Drag and drop design** – works just like forms in Visual Basic. You select controls from a toolbox and drop them on your report. The controls support data binding and work with the Data Environment Designer to make it easy to define your data source.

✦ **Print preview** – allows your users to see what their reports will look like before they print them.

✦ **File export** – means that you can save the generated report as a text file or as an HTML file that can be displayed on your Web site.

✦ **Asynchronous operation** – permits your reports to run in the background while your users continue to use their application for other tasks.

Using the Data Report Designer

To create a data r eport, you use the Data Report Designer in Visual Basic. You start by creating a data source and an instance of the Data Report Designer. Typically, you will want to use the Data Environment Designer discussed in Chapter 9 to create the data source.

Getting your data

In order to create a report, you must first add a Data Environment Designer to your application. Then you need to create a `Command` object that will retrieve the data you want to include in your report. The `Command` object can contain child commands to create a hierarchical recordset.

Building a data report's structure

To add a data report to your application, choose Project ➪ Add Data Report. Then the Data Report Window will appear on your screen (see Figure 10-1). This window represents a virtual view of your report. It is broken into a series of sections that contains controls that will display the data from your data source. Note that I included each of the section types in Figure 10-1. The group header and footer sections must be manually added to the report.

✦ **Report header** – is printed only once at the very beginning of the report.

✦ **Page header** – is printed at the top of each page of the report. This section is generally used for things like page title.

✦ **Group header** – is printed at the beginning of a new group of data. A group section corresponds to a `Command` object in a hierarchical recordset, or may include the `RptFunction` control to summarize data from a column in another `Command` object.

✦ **Detail** – is printed for each row that is retrieved from the lowest level recordset in the hierarchical recordset.

✦ **Group footer** – is printed at the end of a group of data. It corresponds to the group header section.

✦ **Page footer** – is printed at the bottom of each page of the report.

✦ **Report footer** – is printed only once at the end of the report.

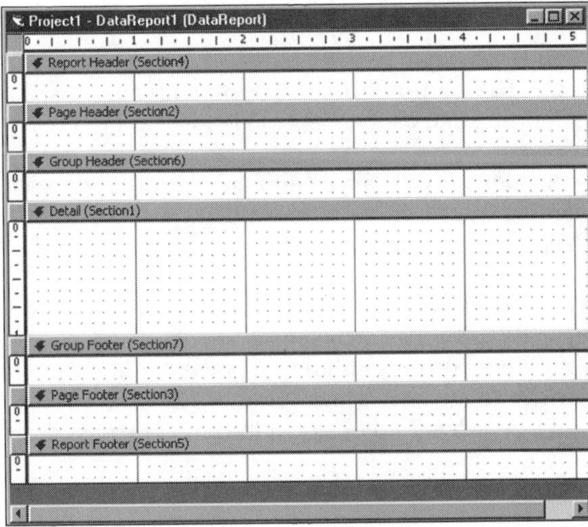

Figure 10-1: The Data Report Window

Growing groups: By default, no groups are included in your report. If you right click on the report and choose Insert Group Header/Footer, you can add a new group to the report.

Binding the data report to the data source

The very first thing you should do after creating a data report is to bind the data report to your data source. You do this by setting the values for the `DataSource` and `DataMember` properties in the normal Visual Basic Properties window. The `DataSource` property should be bound to the `DataEnvironment` object and the `DataMember` property should be bound to the `Command` object that retrieves the information you want to display in the report. All of the controls you use in your report will automatically use these values to retrieve the data for the report.

Grouping data: You should use a hierarchical `Command` object if you wish to define groups in your reports. Each level above the lowest level in the hierarchical command will correspond to a group section in the report.

Adjusting the structure to fit your data

Once you define the `DataSource` for your report, you can right click on the report and choose Retrieve Structure from the pop-up menu. This will add group sections to your report to accommodate the hierarchical recordset from your data source. Note that retrieving the structure will erase any controls you have on the report. You don't need to use the Retrieve Structure function when you're using a regular recordset, because the default report doesn't include any data.

You can also manually add or delete sections to your report by right clicking on the report and selecting or deselecting the section from the pop-up menu. This is useful when you don't want to use a section, such as the Report Header and Footer.

Tip

Where did that space come from?: If you only need a header or footer section but not both, you should set the height of the one you don't want to zero. This means that it won't take up space in your report.

You can use the Insert Group Header/Footer on the pop-up menu to add a group section to your report. If you already have a group on your report, a dialog box will be displayed, asking you where the new groups should be placed (see Figure 10-2). Simply press the up or down arrows to move the new group up or down in the group hierarchy. If the group can't be moved up or down in the hierarchy, the appropriate arrow will be disabled.

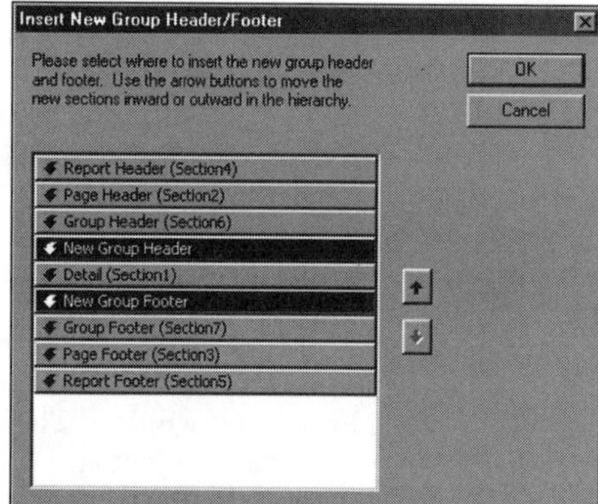

Figure 10-2: Placing a new group in your report

Placing controls on your report

There are two main ways to add controls to your report. The easiest method is to add them automatically by dragging `Command` objects and/or fields from the Data Environment Designer onto the report in the appropriate section and then move them to where you would like the information to appear. The other way is to add controls manually to your report from the Toolbox and then bind them to the data source.

Automatically adding controls

Once you have bound your report to a `Command` object in the Data Environment Designer, you can drag the object over to a section in your report and the designer will automatically add all of the fields in the section. If you had the Drag and Drop Field Captions check box marked in the Data Environment Designer Options window, labels for each field will also be created. The controls will be arranged in a single column, and the height of the section will automatically be adjusted to accommodate the controls if there isn't sufficient space (see Figure 10-3).

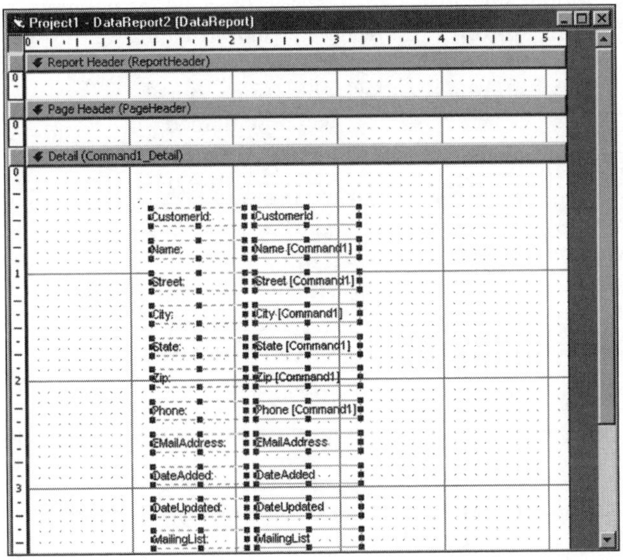

Figure 10-3: Dropping controls on a report

Once the controls are on the form, you will probably want to rearrange them to better use the space available. Since most reports tend to be columnar-based, you may want to try to arrange the controls to fit into a single line, or into a format that doesn't waste as much space. You can drag the columns around the screen. If you want to change their size, simply move the mouse pointer over the appropriate handle and press the left mouse button. Then you can just drag the mouse pointer around until the field is the size you want it to be.

Creating column headers: By default, dragging a field from the `Command` object will also drag along a `RptLabel` field with the name of the field. The `RptLabel` control is similar to a `Label` control in that it will always display a constant text value. In many cases, you will want to move the `RptLabel` control from the section in which you dropped the controls to a section higher in the report hierarchy. For instance, you might want to move the labels from the Detail section to the Page Header section or to a group section. See the next section, "Manually Adding Controls," for an explanation of the `RptLabel` control.

If you have a hierarchical recordset, you must move the `Command` objects one at a time into the appropriate sections. The designer won't let you move a `Command` object containing child commands to a Details section. It must be moved to either a group header or footer section.

You may also drag information from the Data Environment Designer one field at a time onto the report. I find this approach more useful than dragging all of the fields over at once, because it is easier to position each control where I want, and I don't have all of the other controls cluttering the work area.

Manually adding controls

In addition to dragging information from the Data Environment Designer, you can also manually add controls from the standard Visual Basic Toolbox. These controls are kept in a new section on the toolbox known as the DataReport section (see Figure 10-4). The controls available in the toolbox include:

- **RptLabel** – displays a label on your report with a fixed block of text.
- **RptTextBox** – displays a value from your database.
- **RptImage** – displays an image on your report. Note that this field can't be bound to a field in your database.
- **RptLine** – displays a line on your report. This is useful when you want to separate one area of your report from another.
- **RptShape** – displays a shape (rectangle, square, circle, or oval) on your report. This can be used to draw attention to a particular area on your report.
- **RptFunction** – computes the sum, average, minimum value, or maximum value of a column in your database. This control must be used only in a group footer or a report footer section.

These controls are discussed in their respective sections toward the end of this chapter.

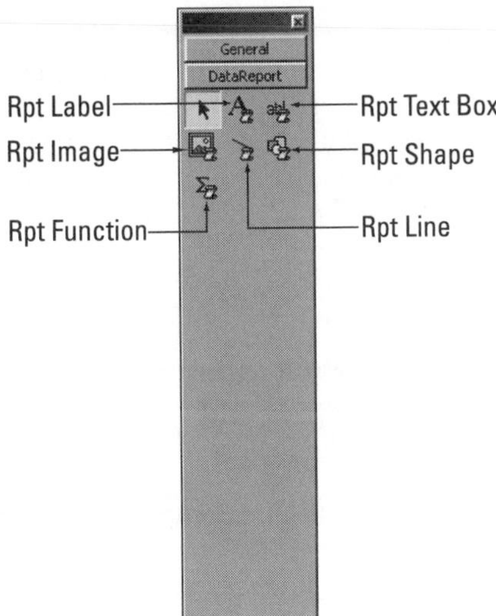

Figure 10-4: Viewing the DataReport toolbox

Setting control properties

Each of the Data Report controls has properties just like traditional controls. The properties for each control are displayed in the Properties window, just as they would be for any other control. You should review the properties of any control you add manually to make sure that their values are appropriate for how you plan to use them.

They're different too: While the names of the controls in the Data Report are similar to the names of the controls you use in a Visual Basic form, they are significantly different. The Data Report controls are often missing various properties or have slightly different definitions for others. For instance, while the `TextBox` control has a `Text` property, the `RptTextBox` control doesn't. Don't assume that the controls are the same. Refer to "The Data Report Object Model" later in this chapter for all of the details about each control.

Binding relationships: The `RptTextBox` and `RptFunction` controls are useless unless they are bound to a data source. Since the `DataReport` object itself is already bound to a data source, you need to bind the `RptTextBox` and `RptFunction` control's `DataField` property to the appropriate field from your data source. Also, you need to select the function that the `RptFunction` control will perform on the bound data.

Adding shortcut controls

In addition to the controls listed above, the Data Report Designer includes some useful shortcuts to predefined `RptLabel` controls. These shortcuts are not available in the toolbox, but can be accessed by moving your mouse pointer over the section of the report you wish to change and right clicking to display a popup menu. Then you can choose the shortcut you want. The following shortcuts may be available:

✦ **Current Page Number** – displays the current page number (%p).

✦ **Total Number of Pages** – displays the total number of pages in the report (%P).

✦ **Current Date (Short Format)** – displays the current date using the Windows short date format (%d).

✦ **Current Date (Long Format)** – displays the current date using the Windows long date format (%D).

✦ **Current Time (Short Format)** – displays the current time using the Windows short time format (%t).

✦ **Current Time (Long Format)** – displays the current time using the Windows long time format (%T).

✦ **Report Title** – displays the value in the `DataReport`'s `Title` property (%i).

Build your own: You can also add any of the format codes (%p, %P, and so on) listed above to your own `RptLabel` control.

Percent complete: In order to display a percent sign (%) in a `RptLabel` control, you need to enter it twice (%%).

Programming Your Report

Most of the work of building a report is done using the Data Report Designer. Very little code is required to use this facility.

Previewing a report

Displaying a report in a preview window requires nothing more than a call to the `Show` method, as shown below:

```
DataReport1.Show
```

This call is easily inserted as a menu item in your program or in the `Click` event of a command button. Running the `Show` method displays the first page of the report in the preview window, as shown in Figure 10-5. In addition to the scrollbars, users can press buttons to print the report, export the report to a disk file, control the zoom level, or select which page they want to view.

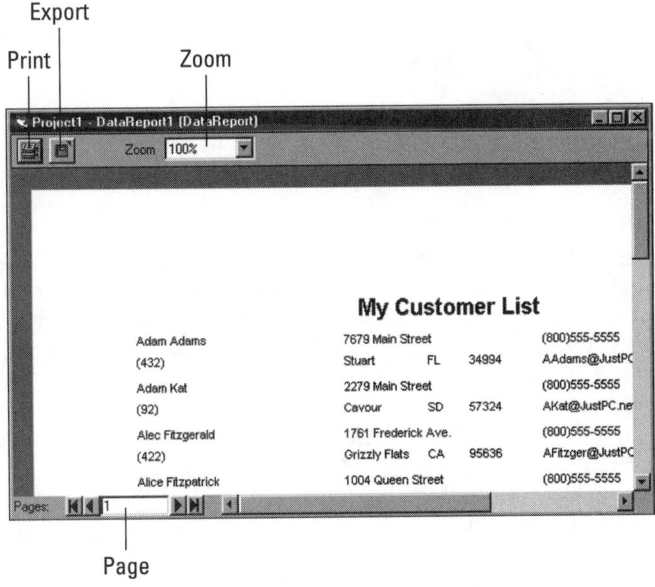

Figure 10-5: Showing the preview of your report

Window sizing: While this may seem obvious, the default size of the Data Report Preview window is the same size as the window used by the Data Report Designer. Also, remember to allow for the width of the margins for your printer when choosing the initial size of the Print Preview window.

Printing a Report

While the user can press the Print button on the Preview window to send the report to the printer, you can do the same thing in your own code by using the `PrintReport` method. The following code will show the Print dialog box displayed in Figure 10-6. If you don't display the Print dialog box (in other words, if the `ShowDialog` parameter is set to `False`), the report will be sent directly to the printer.

```
Cookie = DataReport1.PrintReport (True, rptRangeAllPages)
```

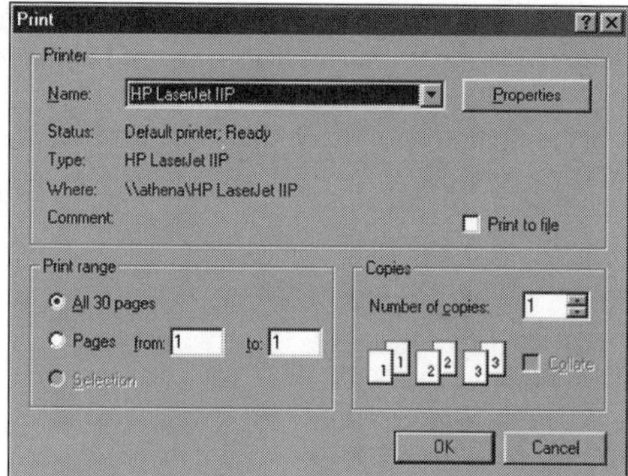

Figure 10-6: Showing the Print dialog box to the user

The value returned by the `PrintReport` method is known as a `Cookie`. It allows you to track this particular report task using the various events that occur while the report is being processed. This can be important, since it is possible to run several reports concurrently. Without the `Cookie` value, you wouldn't be able to identify which report triggered an event.

You can also specify which pages you want to print when you use the `PrintReport` method. If you display the Print dialog box by setting the `ShowDialog` parameter to `True`, the user can override any of the default parameters for the printer and any other values you specified as parameters.

Exporting reports

In addition to sending your reports to the printer, you can also export them to a disk file. You can create either a regular text file or an HTML file. Both types of files can be created with regular characters or with Unicode characters.

You can export a report by calling the `ExportReport` method, using code like this:

```
Cookie = DataReport1.ExportReport (rptKeyHTML, _
         "d:\vb6db\Chapter10\MSReport\report1.HTM", _
         True, False, rptRangeFromTo, 1, 3)
```

This will create a file called `report1.HTM` without showing the Export dialog box. If the file exists, it will be overwritten and only pages one through three will be exported. To understand the meaning of the various parameters in the ExportReport method, see the section on `DataReport` methods later in this chapter.

Tracking asynchronous activity

Recall that *asynchronous operation* permits your reports to run in the background while your users continue to use their application for other tasks. Also keep in mind that the Data Report facility operates independently of your application program. This means that your user can continue to work with your application while the report is being generated and printed. You can track the progress of the report in your application by using the AsyncProgress event, as shown in Listing 10-1. Note that one of the values passed to the event is the same Cookie value that was returned by the method that created the report or export task.

Listing 10-1: The DataReport_AsyncProgress event

```
Private Sub DataReport_AsyncProgress _
   (ByVal JobType As MSDataReportLib.AsyncTypeConstants, _
    ByVal Cookie As Long, ByVal PageCompleted As Long, _
    ByVal TotalPages As Long)

Form1.ProgressBar1.Min = 0
Form1.ProgressBar1.Value = PageCompleted
Form1.ProgressBar1.Max = TotalPages

End Sub
```

The Data Report object model

The Data Report Designer is based around an object called DataReport. This object contains a number of different properties, methods, and events that control how your report is generated.

Forming an object: The DataReport object is based on the Form object and it inherits all of the same properties, methods, and events.

DataReport properties

The DataReport object contains many different properties. I've listed the key ones for this object in Table 10-1.

Table 10-1
Properties of the DataReport Object

Property	*Description*
`AsyncCount`	A `Long` value containing the number of asynchronous operations still executing.
`BottomMargin`	A `Long` value containing the size of the bottom margin in twips.
`Caption`	A `String` value containing the value that will be displayed in the DataReport's title bar.
`DataMember`	A `Variant` value containing the data member of the `DataSource` that will be used to generate the report.
`DataSource`	A `Variant` containing the data source for the report.
`ExportFormats`	An object reference to an `ExportFormats` collection that contains the type of export formats available.
`Font`	An object reference to a `Font` object that will be used as the default font for the report.
`LeftMargin`	A `Long` value containing the size of the left margin in twips.
`ReportWidth`	A `Long` value containing the total width of the report in twips.
`RightMargin`	A `Long` value containing the size of the right margin in twips.
`Sections`	An object reference to a `Sections` collection containing information about the various sections of the report.
`Title`	A `String` value containing the title of the report.
`TopMargin`	A `Long` value containing the size of the top margin in twips.

Twips are for kids: Visual Basic uses the *twip* as the fundamental unit of measurement when placing controls on a form or report. A twip is 1/20 of a point or 1/1440 of an inch. A pixel is the smallest element that can be displayed on a screen or a printer. Pixels depend on the characteristics of the device they are being displayed on, while a twip is independent of any physical device.

DataReport methods

The DataReport object has a number of methods. Listed below are the ones that are the most important when using Data Report in your application.

Function ExportReport ([FormatIndexOrKey], [FileName], [Overwrite As Boolean = True], [ShowDialog As Boolean = False], [Range As PageRangeConstants], [PageFrom], [PageTo]) As Long

The ExportReport method writes the text part of a report to a disk file. The return value is known as a Cookie, which is used to identify the specific data report process. This value will be used in various events to allow you to identify which report triggered the event.

Not saved: Any images or shapes that you include in your printed report will not be saved in your exported report.

FormatIndexOrKey is a Variant containing either a reference for an ExportFormat object or a String that is one of the following: rptKeyHTML ("key_def_HTML"), export the report in standard HTML format; rptKeyText ("key_def_Text"), export the report as a regular text file; or rptKeyUnicodeHTML_UTF8 ("key_def_UnicodeHTML_UTF8). If this value is not specified, the Export dialog box will be displayed.

FileName is a String containing the name of the file to be displayed. If this value isn't specified, the Export dialog box will be shown.

Overwrite is a Boolean value when TRUE means that if the file specified by FileName exists, it will automatically be overwritten.

ShowDialog is a Boolean value when TRUE means that the Export dialog box will be displayed.

Range is an enumerated data type. A value of rptRangeAllPages (0) will print all of the pages in the report (default), while a value of rptRangeFromTo (1) will print only the pages specified in the PageFrom and PageTo parameters.PageFrom is a Long value containing the starting page number used when Range is set to rptRangeFromTo (1).

PageTo is a Long value containing the ending page number used when Range is set to rptRangeFromTo (1).

Function PrintReport ([ShowDialog As Boolean = False], [Range As PageRangeConstants], [PageFrom], [PageTo]) As Long

The `PrintReport` method is used to send a copy of the report to the default system printer. The return value is known as a `Cookie`, which is used to identify the specific data report process. This value will be used in various events to allow you to identify which report triggered the event.

`ShowDialog` is a `Boolean` value when `TRUE` means that the Print dialog box will be displayed.

`Range` is an enumerated data type. A value of `rptRangeAllPages` (0) will print all of the pages in the report (default), while a value of `rptRangeFromTo` (1) will print only the pages specified in the `PageFrom` and `PageTo` parameters.`PageFrom` is a `Long` value containing the starting page number used when `Range` is set to `rptRangeFromTo` (1).

`PageTo` is a `Long` value containing the ending page number used when `Range` is set to `rptRangeFromTo` (1).

Sub Refresh ()

The `Refresh` method is used to reprocess the report and repaint the display.

Sub Show ([Modal], [OwnerForm])

The `Show` method displays the Data Report form as the report's Print Preview window.

`Modal` is an `Integer` that determines how the Preview window is displayed. A value of `vbModal` (1) will freeze all activity in the application until the Preview window is closed, while `vbNormal` (0) allows the application to continue running while the Preview window is displayed. If not specified, `vbNormal` is assumed.

`OwnerForm` is a `String` containing the name of the owner form. The default value for this argument is `"Me"`.

Key DataReport events

The `DataReport` object contains a few events that allow you to monitor its progress as your report is being processed.

Event AsynchProgress (JobType as AsynchTypeConstants, Cookie As Long, PageCompleted As Long, TotalPages As Long)

The `AsynchProgress` event is called when the Data Report process has finished generating a page of the report.

Where am I?: You may want to use this event to update a progress bar that indicates how much of the report has been processed.

`JobType` is an enumerated data type whose value is `rptAsyncPreview` (0) when a preview operation is being processed, `rptAsyncPrint` (1) when a print report operation is being processed, or `rptAsyncReport` (2) when an export operation is being processed.

`Cookie` is a `Long` value that identifies the specific report job.

`PageCompleted` is a `Variant` containing the number of pages that have been completed.

`TotalPages` is a `Variant` containing the total number of pages to be processed.

Event Error (JobType as AsynchTypeConstants, Cookie As Long, ErrObj As RptError, ShowError As Boolean)

The `Error` event is called when the Data Report program encounters an error.

`JobType` is an enumerated data type whose value is `rptAsyncPreview` (0) when a preview operation is being processed, `rptAsyncPrint` (1) when a print report operation is being processed, or `rptAsyncReport` (2) when an export operation is being processed.

`Cookie` is a `Long` that identifies the specific report job.

`ErrObj` is an `RptError` object containing the details of the error that triggered this event.

`ShowError` is a `Boolean`, which when set to `TRUE` will display the error information to the user in a dialog box.

Event ProcessingTimeout (Seconds As Long, Cancel As Boolean, JobType as AsynchTypeConstants, Cookie As Long)

The `ProcessingTimeout` event is fired periodically while the report is being generated. You can examine the amount of time that the job has been running and choose whether or not to cancel the report process.

Seconds is a Long value containing the number of seconds since the report process was started.

Cancel is a Boolean, which when set to TRUE will cancel the report process.

JobType is an enumerated data type whose value is rptAsyncPreview (0) when a preview operation is being processed, rptAsyncPrint (1) when a print report operation is being processed, or rptAsyncReport (2) when an export operation is being processed.

Cookie is a Long value that identifies the specific report job.

Controls collection properties

The Controls collection is an object that contains object references to the controls stored in a particular Section object. Table 10-2 lists the properties of the Controls collection. Note that controls can't be added or deleted at runtime.

Table 10-2
Properties of the Controls Collection

Property	*Description*
Count	A Long value containing the number of controls in the collection.
Item	An object reference to one of the control objects (RptFunction, RptImage, RptLabel, RptLine, RptShape, and RptTextBox).

ExportFormat object properties

The ExportFormat object contains information about a single export format. Table 10-3 lists the various properties associated with the ExportFormat object.

ExportFormats collection properties

The ExportFormats object contains information about a single export format. Table 10-4 lists the various properties associated with the ExportFormat object.

Table 10-3
Properties of the ExportFormat Object

Property	*Description*
FileFilter	A String value containing the list of file extensions that will be used in the file filter. If more than one file extension is used, they must be separated by semicolons (;). For example: "*.HTM" is a valid value.
FileFormatString	A String value containing the text value displayed in the Export dialog box's Save As type box that corresponds to the list extensions listed in FileFilter. For example: "Web Report (*.HTM)" is a valid value for this property.
FormatType	An enumerated data type containing the type of export format. Legal values are: rptFmtHTML (0), export the report using the regular HTML format; rptFmtText (1), export the report as a text file; rptFmtUnicodeText (2), export the report as a Unicode text file; rptFmtUnicodeHTML_UTF8 (3), export the report using an HTML format with the UTF – 8 Unicode character set.
Key	A String that uniquely identifies the export format.
String	A String containing the template that will be used to export the report.

Table 10-4
Properties of the ExportFormat Object

Property	*Description*
Count	A Long value containing the number of objects in the collection.
Item (key)	An object reference to an ExportFormat object containing information about a particular export format, where key contains a reference to the ExportFormat object.

ExportFormats collection methods

The ExportFormats collection has no default methods. However, each time you add a command in the Data Environment Designer, a shortcut method will be added to the DataEnvironment object. This makes it easier to code your application.

Function Add (Key As String, FormatType As ExportFormatTypeConstants, FileFormatString As String, FileFilter As String, [Template]) As ExportFormat

The `Add` method creates a new `ExportFormat` object and inserts it into the `ExportFormats` collection.

`Key` is the key value that will be used to locate the new `ExportFormat` object.

`FormatType` is an enumerated data type describing the type of format stored in the object: `rptFmtHTML` (0), export the report using the regular HTML format; `rptFmtText` (1), export the report as a text file; `rptFmtUnicodeText` (2), export the report as a Unicode text file; `rptFmtUnicodeHTML_UTF8` (3), export the report using an HTML format with the UTF – 8 Unicode character set. If this value is not specified, the Export dialog box will be displayed.

`FileFormatStrong` is a `String` value containing the text value displayed in the Export dialog box's Save As type box that corresponds to the list extensions listed in `FileFilter`. For example: `"Web Report (*.HTM)"` would be a valid value for this argument.

`FileFilter` is a `String` value containing the list of file extensions that are associated with the export format. If more than one file extension is used, they must be separated by semicolons (;) and the first extension is the default extension. For example: `"*.HTM"` is a valid value.

`Template` is a `String` value containing the template that will be used when someone uses this export format. If not specified, an empty string will be assumed.

Sub Clear ()

The `Clear` method removes all of the members of the collection.

Sub Insert (Format As ExportFormat)

The `Insert` method adds an `ExportFormat` object to the collection. `Format` is an `ExportFormat` object containing information to be added to the collection.

Sub Remove (Key)

The `Remove` method deletes a member identified by `Key` from the collection. `Key` is the index or key value of the `ExportFormat` object to be removed from the collection.

RptError object properties

The RptError object contains error information about an error that occurred while processing a report. Table 10-5 lists the various properties associated with the RptError object.

Table 10-5
Properties of the RptError Object

Property	*Description*
Description	A String value containing a textual description of the error.
ErrorNumber	A Long value containing error number value.
HelpContext	A Long containing the help context for the error, which will contain more information about the error.
HelpFile	A String containing the name of the help file associated with HelpContext.
Source	An object reference to the object that caused the error.

RptFunction control properties

The RptFunction control is used to compute a value based on a series of values retrieved from the database. Table 10-6 lists the various properties associated with the RptFunction object.

Critical properties: DataField should be set to the appropriate field from your data source and FunctionType should be set to the calculation you would like to apply to the data prior to running a report.

Table 10-6
Properties of the RptFunction Control

Property	*Description*
Alignment	An enumerated value describing how the contents of the control will be displayed. Legal values are: rptJustifyLeft (0), rptJustifyRight (1), and rptJustifyCenter (2).
BackColor	A Long value containing the color value for the background of the control.

Continued

Table 10-6 *(continued)*

Property	***Description***
BackStyle	An enumerated data type containing the style of the background. Legal values are: rptTransparent (0) and rptOpaque (1).
BorderColor	A Long value containing the color value for the border surrounding the control.
BorderStyle	An enumerated data type describing the style of the border surrounding the control. Legal values are: rptBSTransparent (0), rptBSSolid (1), rptBSDashes (2), rptBSDots (3), rptBSDashDot (4), rptBSDashDotDot (5).
CanGrow	A Boolean value, when TRUE means that the height of the control will automatically be increased if the size of the text exceeds the default height of the control.
DataField	A String value containing the name of the database field which the function will be applied to.
DataFormat	An object reference to a StdDataFormat object containing the information on how to format the data displayed by the control.
DataMember	A String value containing the name of the data member of the data source that will be used as the source of data for the control.
Font	An object reference to a Font object that describes the font information used to display the value of the control.
ForeColor	A Long containing the color that the text will be displayed in.
FunctionType	An Integer value identifying the function used with the field specified by DataField to compute the value that will be displayed by this control. Legal values are: rptFuncSum (0), computes the sum of the values in DataField; rptFuncAve (1), computes the average of the values in DataField; rptFuncMin (2), finds the minimum value of the values in DataField; rptFuncMax (3), finds the maximum value of the values in DataField; rptFuncRCbt (4), counts the number of rows retrieved in this section; rptFuncVCnt (5), counts the number of rows retrieved in this section whose values are not **Null**; rptFuncSDEV (6), computes the standard deviation of the values in DataField; rptFuncSERR (7), computes the standard error of the values in DataField.
Height	A Long containing the height of the control in twips.
Left	A Long containing the distance between the left edge of the report and the left edge of the control.

Property	Description
Name	A String containing the name of the control.
RightToLeft	A Boolean, when TRUE means that the text will be displayed right to left in a bi-directional version of Windows.
Top	A Long containing the distance between the top edge of the section and the top edge of the control.
Visible	A Boolean, when TRUE means that the control will be displayed at runtime.
Width	A Long containing the width of the control in twips.

RptImage control properties

The RptImage control is used to display a static image on your report. Table 10-7 lists the various properties associated with the RptImage object.

Critical properties: You should set the Picture property to the image you want to see at design time. Then you should adjust the SizeMode and Picture Alignment if needed to make sure that the picture is displayed properly.

Table 10-7
Properties of the RptImage Control

Property	Description
BackColor	A Long value containing the color value for the background of the control.
BackStyle	An enumerated data type containing the style of the background. Legal values are: rptTransparent (0) and rptOpaque (1).
BorderColor	A Long value containing the color value for the border surrounding the control.
BorderStyle	An enumerated data type describing the style of the border surrounding the control. Legal values are: rptBSTransparent (0); rptBSSolid (1); rptBSDashes (2); rptBSDots (3); rptBSDashDot (4); rptBSDashDotDot (5).
Height	A Long containing the height of the control in twips.
Left	A Long containing the distance between the left edge of the report and the left edge of the control.

Continued

Table 10-7 *(continued)*

Property	***Description***
Name	A String containing the name of the control.
Picture	An object reference to an IPictureDisp object.
PictureAlignment	An enumerated data type describing how the picture will be positioned in the control. Legal values are: rptPATopLeft (0), position the image at the top left corner; rptPATop (1), position the image at the top center edge; rptPATopRight (2), position the image at the top right corner; rptPARight (3), position the image at the right center corner; rptPABottomRight (4), position the image at the bottom right corner; rptPABottom (5), position the image at the bottom center edge; rptPABottomLeft (6), position the image at the bottom left corner; rptPALeft (7), position the image at the left center edge; rptPACenter (8), center the image in the control.
SizeMode	An enumerated type describing how the image will be displayed in the control. Legal values are: rptSizeClip (0), the image will be clipped to fit inside the control; rptSizeStretch (1), the image will be stretched to fill the control; rptSizeZoom (2), the image will be stretched to fill the control, but the image's height to width proportion will remain unchanged.
Top	A Long containing the distance between the top edge of the section and the top edge of the control.
Visible	A Boolean, when TRUE means that the control will be displayed at runtime.
Width	A Long containing the width of the control in twips.

RptLabel control properties

The RptLabel control is used to display a constant text value on your report. Table 10-8 lists the various properties associated with the RptLabel object.

Critical properties: Enter the text you want to display in Caption. Next, set the Alignment property to position text properly within the label. If there is too much text for the label, then either resize the control on the Report Designer window or set the CanGrow property to TRUE to display all of the text.

Table 10-8
Properties of the RptLabel Control

Property	*Description*
Alignment	An enumerated value describing how the contents of the control will be displayed. Legal values are: rptJustifyLeft (0), rptJustifyRight (1), and rptJustifyCenter (2).
BackColor	A Long value containing the color value for the background of the control.
BackStyle	An enumerated data type containing the style of the background. Legal values are: rptTransparent (0) and rptOpaque (1).
BorderColor	A Long value containing the color value for the border surrounding the control.
BorderStyle	An enumerated data type describing the style of the border surrounding the control. Legal values are: rptBSTransparent (0), rptBSSolid (1), rptBSDashes (2), rptBSDots (3), rptBSDashDot (4), rptBSDashDotDot (5).
CanGrow	A Boolean value, when TRUE means that the height of the control will automatically be increased if the size of the text exceeds the default height of the control.
Caption	A String value containing the text that will be displayed by this control.
Font	An object reference to a Font object that describes the font information used to display the value of the control.
ForeColor	A Long containing the color that the text will be displayed in.
Height	A Long containing the height of the control in twips.
Left	A Long containing the distance between the left edge of the report and the left edge of the control.
Name	A String containing the name of the control.
RightToLeft	A Boolean, when TRUE means that the text will be displayed right to left in a bi-directional version of Windows.
Top	A Long containing the distance between the top edge of the section and the top edge of the control.
Visible	A Boolean, when TRUE means that the control will be displayed at runtime.
Width	A Long containing the width of the control in twips.

Tip

Fortune favors the bold: In most cases, you should display the text in a label in bold to help set apart column headers and other text from the data in the detail section.

RptLine control properties

The `RptLine` control is used to draw a line on your report. You define a rectangle using the `Height` and `Width` properties and the line will be drawn from one corner to the diagonal. Which corners are used depends on the `LineSlant` property. Table 10-9 lists the various properties associated with the `RptLine` control.

Tip

Critical properties: Adjust the `LineSlant` to change the direction of the line. Note that a control whose width is only one twip tall will be displayed as a horizontal line without a slant.

Table 10-9
Properties of the RptLine Control

Property	*Description*
`BorderColor`	A `Long` value containing the color value of the line.
`BorderStyle`	An enumerated data type describing how the line will be drawn. Legal values are: `rptBSTransparent` (0), `rptBSSolid` (1), `rptBSDashes` (2), `rptBSDots` (3), `rptBSDashDot` (4), `rptBSDashDotDot` (5).
`Height`	A `Long` containing the height of the control in twips.
`Left`	A `Long` containing the distance between the left edge of the report and the left edge of the control.
`LineSlant`	An enumerated type describing which corners will be used to draw the line. Legal values are: `rptSlantNWSE`, the line will be drawn from the top left to the bottom right; `rptSlantNESW`, the line will be drawn from the top right to the bottom left.
`Name`	A `String` containing the name of the control.
`Top`	A `Long` containing the distance between the top edge of the section and the top edge of the control.
`Visible`	A `Boolean`, when `TRUE` means that the control will be displayed at runtime.
`Width`	A `Long` containing the width of the control in twips.

RptShape control properties

The RptShape control is used to draw a shape on your report. You define a rectangle using the Height and Width properties and then choose the shape that will fill the rectangle using the Shape property. If you choose to draw a circle or a square, then the shape will start in the upper-left corner of the rectangle you drew and its size will be dictated by the width or height, whichever is smaller. Table 10-10 lists the various properties associated with the RptShape control.

Tip

Critical properties: Shape should be set to the shape you want to display.

Table 10-10
Properties of the RptShape Control

Property	***Description***
BackColor	A Long value containing the color value for the background of the control.
BackStyle	An enumerated data type containing the style of the background. Legal values are: rptTransparent (0) and rptOpaque (1).
BorderColor	A Long value containing the color value of the line.
BorderStyle	An enumerated data type describing how the shape will be drawn. Legal values are: rptBSTransparent (0), rptBSSolid (1), rptBSDashes (2), rptBSDots (3), rptBSDashDot (4), rptBSDashDotDot (5).
Height	A Long containing the height of the control in twips.
Left	A Long containing the distance between the left edge of the report and the left edge of the control.
Name	A String value containing the name of the control.
Shape	An enumerated data type that identifies the shape that will be drawn on the report. Legal values are: rptShpRectangle (0), rptShpSquare (1), rptShpOval (2), rptCircle (3), rptShpRoundedRectangle (4), rptShpRoundedSquare (5).
Top	A Long containing the distance between the top edge of the section and the top edge of the control.
Visible	A Boolean, when TRUE means that the control will be displayed at runtime.
Width	A Long containing the width of the control in twips.

RptTextBox control properties

The RptTextBox control is used to display a value from the database on your report. Table 10-11 lists the various properties associated with the RptTextBox object.

Critical properties: The DataField property should be set to the field from your data source that will be displayed in the text box.

Table 10-11
Properties of the RptLabel Control

Property	*Description*
Alignment	An enumerated value describing how the contents of the control will be displayed. Legal values are: rptJustifyLeft (0), rptJustifyRight (1), and rptJustifyCenter (2).
BackColor	A Long value containing the color value for the background of the control.
BackStyle	An enumerated data type containing the style of the background. Legal values are: rptTransparent (0) and rptOpaque (1).
BorderColor	A Long value containing the color value for the border surrounding the control.
BorderStyle	An enumerated data type describing the style of the border surrounding the control. Legal values are: rptBSTransparent (0), rptBSSolid (1), rptBSDashes (2), rptBSDots (3), rptBSDashDot (4), rptBSDashDotDot (5).
CanGrow	A Boolean value, when TRUE means that the height of the control will automatically be increased if the size of the text exceeds the default height of the control.
Font	An object reference to a Font object that describes the font information used to display the value of the control.
ForeColor	A Long containing the color that the text will be displayed in.
Height	A Long containing the height of the control in twips.
Left	A Long containing the distance between the left edge of the report and the left edge of the control.
Name	A String value containing the name of the control.
RightToLeft	A Boolean value, when TRUE, means that the text will be displayed right to left in a bi-directional version of Windows.

Property	Description
Top	A Long containing the distance between the top edge of the section and the top edge of the control.
Visible	A Boolean, when TRUE means that the control will be displayed at runtime.
Width	A Long containing the width of the control in twips.

Section object properties

The Section object contains information about how a section is displayed on the report. See Table 10-12 for the properties available in this object.

Table 10-12
Properties of the Section Object

Property	Description
Controls	An object reference to a Controls collection containing information about the set of controls displayed in the section.
ForcePageBreak	An enumerated type describing how page breaks will be taken for the section. Values are: rptPageBreakNone (0), no page breaks are taken; rptPageBreakBefore (1), the page break occurs before the section; rptPageBreakAfter (2), the page break occurs after the section; rptPageBreakBeforeAndAfter (3), the page break occurs before and after the section.
Height	A Long value containing the height of the section in twips.
KeepTogether	A Boolean value, which when set to TRUE forces the entire section to fit on the same page. If there isn't sufficient room, a new page will be started.
Name	A String value containing the name of the section.
Visible	A Boolean, which when set to TRUE means the report section is visible at runtime.

Sections collection properties

The Sections collection is an object that contains object references to the sections stored in your report. Table 10-13 lists the properties of the Sections collection. Note that sections can't be added or deleted at runtime.

Table 10-13
Properties of the Controls Collection

Property	*Description*
`Count`	A `Long` value containing the number of `Section` objects in the collection.
`Item`	An object reference to the `Section` object.

Thoughts on the Data Report Feature

A tool like Microsoft Data Report is important to many application developers. With the emphasis today on building graphical applications that can provide information on demand that eliminates the need for paper reports, programmers often forget that sometimes having a paper report is critical.

Some types of reports deserve to be archived on paper, even if they are never looked at. For example, consider an audit log. Having a paper audit trail may be the only way to prove that someone unauthorized changed information in your database. Also, for some high profile applications, having a paper report available may allow the user to continue operating in the event of a catastrophic system failure. Failure to plan for this type of situation is the sign of a poor job analyzing the user's true needs.

Of course, there are many cases where actual reports are critical. Printing receipts from a point of sale system, as well as printing packing lists for the warehouse and invoices for accounts receivable, are all cases where a well-designed paper report is important. While it is possible to do this by using the `Print` object in Visual Basic and manually building the code to do the job, using Data Report is a much more efficient use of a programmer's time.

While I'm not a big fan of the Data Environment Designer for designing forms, I've found that the Data Report Designer works best when you use the Data Environment Designer as a data source. This is especially true if you want to use hierarchical recordsets as input. This is because I find the drag and drop report design using the field objects from the Data Environment Designer much easier than manually binding the controls after I've created them.

Summary

In this chapter you learned the following:

- ✦ You can use the Data Report Designer to design a report graphically just like you design a form for a Visual Basic program.
- ✦ You can extract the information for the report using the Data Environment Designer.
- ✦ You can define various sections on the report to help you summarize your data.
- ✦ You can place fields on the report by dragging them from the Data Environment Designer.
- ✦ You can allow the user to preview the report before sending it to the printer.
- ✦ You can also export your report to a text file or an HTML file.

✦ ✦ ✦

PART III

Hardcore ADO

Developing efficient database programs requires a good understanding of how to access your data. ActiveX Data Objects (ADO) is the preferred way to access a database. Not only does it provide an object-oriented view of your database, it is independent of any single database vendor, which allows you to develop applications that can be used from a wide variety of database systems.

I'll begin this Part with an overview of the ADO Object Model. Then I'll focus on how to connect to a typical database system. Once connected, I'll show you how to execute SQL commands and stored procedures. Finally, I'll spend a lot of time showing you how to work with recordsets, which contain data retrieved from your database.

✦ ✦ ✦ ✦

In This Part

✦ ✦ ✦ ✦

The ADO Object Model

◆ ◆ ◆ ◆

In This Chapter

Introducing ADO 2.5

Using ADO objects

Working with the ADO Errors collection

◆ ◆ ◆ ◆

In this part of the book, I'm going to turn my attention from the tools that can make it easier to build your applications and focus on the underlying object model that they use. Over time, I found that using the ADO objects directly is often easier than using the tools. In this chapter, I'm going to present a brief overview of the ADO object model and explain how the various objects fit together. In the rest of Part III, I'll dig into each of the key objects and show you how easy they are to use.

Introducing ActiveX Data Objects 2.5

The ActiveX Data Objects (ADO) is Microsoft's way of implementing *Universal Data Access.* Universal Data Access allows you to use the same high-speed interface for both relational and non-relational data, while providing an easy-to-use, language-independent interface.

The ADO object model

ADO carries over some of the objects used in the older DAO and RDO object models discussed in Chapter 6. However, it uses a completely different approach that removes the strict hierarchy required when using the older object models (see Figure 11-1 and Table 11-1).

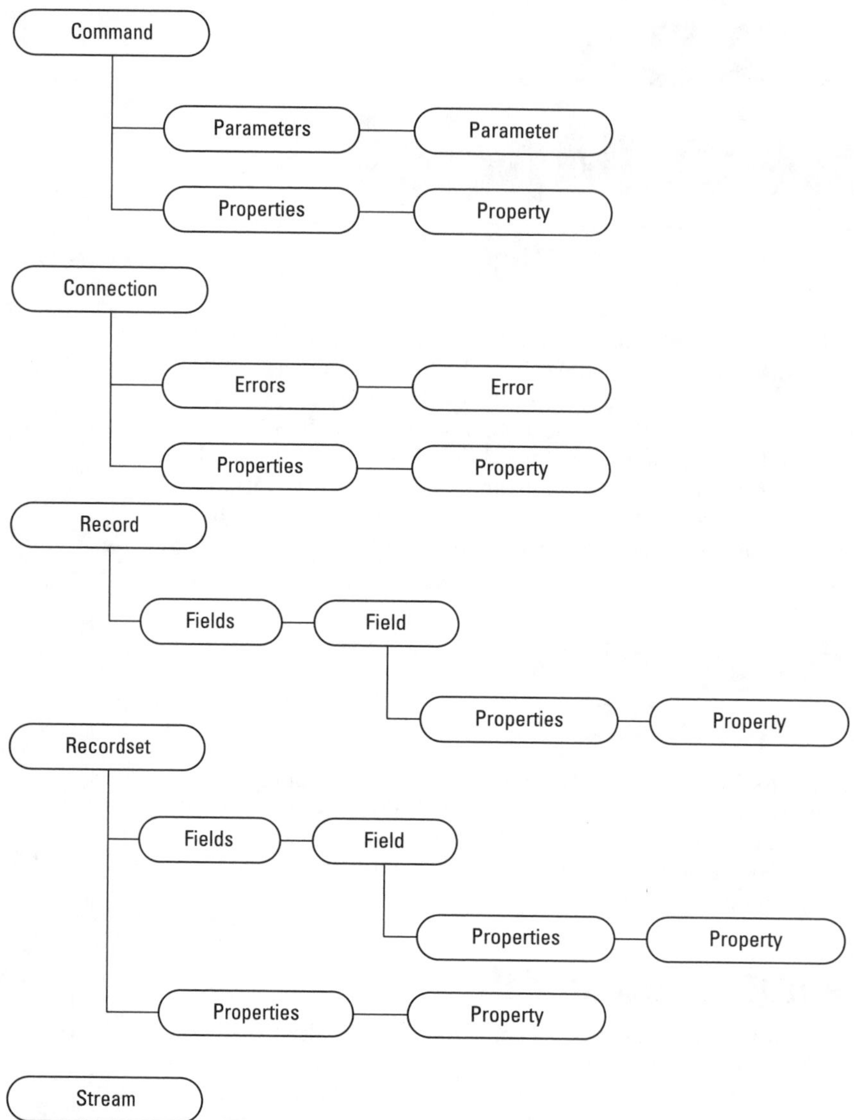

Figure 11-1: Presenting the ADO object model

There are three main objects in the ADO object model that are used for database access. The `Connection` object provides a path to the data source. The `Command` object contains the information necessary to execute an SQL Statement or a stored procedure. The `Recordset` object contains the results from a query. The `Command` and `Recordset` objects have the ability to create an implicit `Connection` object if desired, so you can access a set of records or perform a database function by creating only a single object.

Table 11-1
ADO Objects

Object	*Description*
`Command`	Executes an SQL Statement or stored procedure.
`Connection`	Used to manage the information necessary to connect to a database or other OLE DB data provider.
`Error`	Contains information about a specific error.
`Errors`	Contains a collection of `Error` objects.
`Field`	Contains information about a specific field in the database.
`Fields`	Contains a collection of `Field` objects.
`Parameter`	Holds information that is passed to or returned from a stored procedure or parameterized query.
`Parameters`	Contains a collection of `Parameter` objects.
`Property`	Contains a dynamic property that is defined by the OLE DB data provider.
`Properties`	Contains a collection of `Property` objects.
`Record`	Represents a row in `Recordset` object or a file or an e-mail message.
`Recordset`	Used to manage the set of rows generated by a query operation.
`Stream`	Represents a stream of binary data or text.

The `Record` and `Stream` objects are used primarily to support access to non-database resources. The `Record` object represents either a row in a `Recordset` or a file or an e-mail message. A `Stream` object provides the facilities to manipulate the data in a file or an e-mail message.

New in ADO 2.5

If you are familiar with the previous versions of ADO, here's a quick introduction to the new features.

The Record object

The `Record` object is used to represent information such as directories and files in a file system, and folders and messages in an e-mail system. A `Record` object can also be used to represent a row from a `Recordset` object.

The Stream object

The `Stream` object is used to read and write binary information to and from files and messages associated with the `Record` object.

URLs

URLs may now be used in place of connection strings (see the `Connection` object) and command text (see the `Command` object) as an alternative to using traditional connection strings and command text.

New properties and methods

Several new properties and methods have been added to the ADO library. The `Mode` property is available in the `Connection`, `Record`, and `Stream` objects and describes the permissions available for modifying data. The rest of the new properties and methods are used by the new `Stream` and `Recordset` objects to manage files and e-mail messages.

Introducing ActiveX Data Objects Extensions

While not exactly new in ADO 2.5, the ActiveX Data Objects Extensions (ADOX) gives you the capability to create and modify a database's structure (also known as a *schema*) and maintain security through an object-oriented approach. Since these objects are independent of any single data provider, it is possible to build a general-purpose program that would work with any data provider.

The ADOX object model (see Figure 11-2 and Table 11-2) was developed as an object-oriented way for someone to access a database schema. The schema provides access to all of the possible objects in a database: tables, indexes, stored procedures and views, as well as security information.

The `Catalog` is the root object. All other objects can be referenced from the `Catalog`. Beneath the `Catalog` object are the five main collections of database objects, the `Tables` collection, the `Groups` collection, the `Users` collection, the `Procedures` collection, and the `Views` collection.

The `Tables` collection documents the physical structure of the data. From the `Table` object, you can find out the details of the structure by examining the `Columns`, `Indexes`, and `Keys` collections. Note that the `Index` and `Key` objects also reference the `Columns` collection. However, before you can add a `Column` object to either the `Index` or `Key` object, it must already exist in the `Table` object.

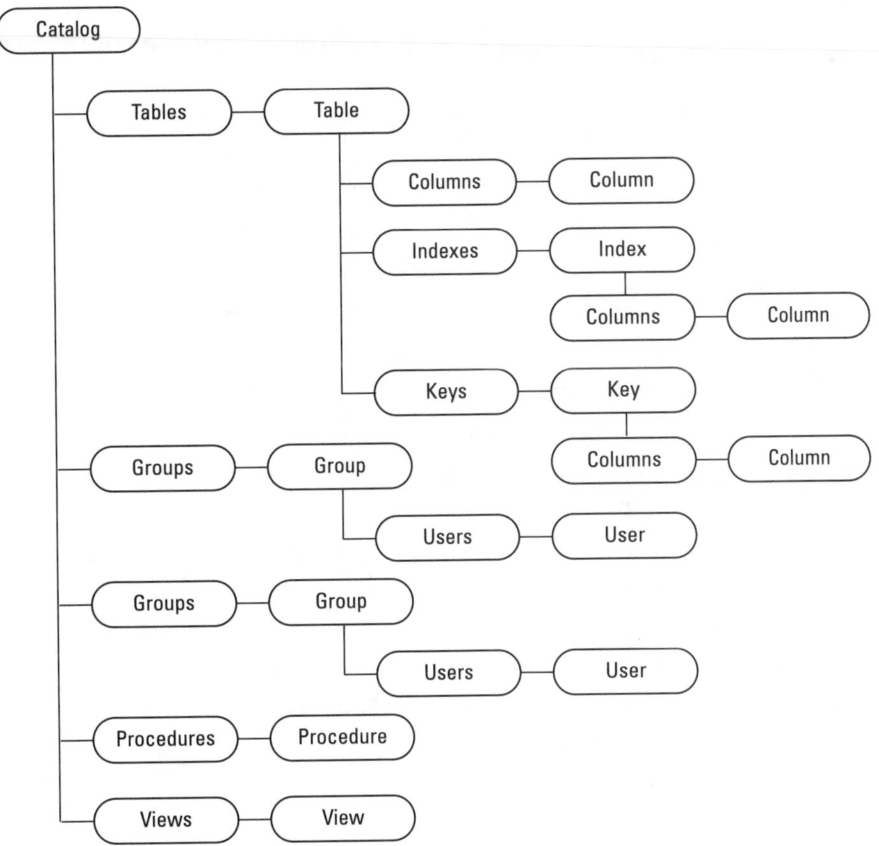

Figure 11-2: Presenting the ADOX object model

Table 11-2
ADOX Objects

Object	*Description*
`Catalog`	Contains the schema definition of the data source. This is the base object in ADOX.
`Column`	Contains information about a specific column from a table, index, or key.
`Columns`	Contains the `Column` definitions of a table, index, or key.

Continued

Table 11-2 *(continued)*

Object	***Description***
Group	Contains information about a security group.
Groups	Contains all of the security Group objects in the catalog.
Index	Contains information about an index for a database table.
Indexes	Contains the set of indexes associated with a table.
Key	Contains the definition of a key field from a table.
Keys	Contains the set of Key objects associated with a table.
Procedure	Contains information related to a stored procedure.
Procedures	Contains the set of stored procedures.
Table	Contains the definition of a table, including things like columns, indexes, and keys.
Tables	Contains the set of tables in the Catalog.
User	Contains security information about a user account and its database permissions.
Users	Contains the set of users associated with the Catalog.
View	Contains the schema definition of a database view.
Views	Contains the collection of View objects in the Catalog.

The Groups collection contains the set of security groups. Each Group object contains a reference to the collection of Users that are in that particular group. Before you can add a user to the Users collection, it must already exist in the Users group that is directly beneath the Catalog object.

The Users collection is similar to the Groups collection, except that the users associated with the database are stored in the Users collection, while the groups associated with a single User are stored in the Groups collection. As you might expect, in order to add a group to the Groups collection, you must first define it in the Groups object that is directly beneath the Catalog object.

The Procedures collection documents the set of stored procedures available in the database. A single Procedure object contains all of the information associated with a specific procedure. It also includes a reference to a Command object that can be used to execute the stored procedures.

The Views collection documents the set of views in the database. Each view is defined in the View object. Like the Procedure object, a reference to a Command object that will retrieve the values from the view is also included.

Basic ADO Programming

Writing a database program using the ADO object model is more work than using the ADO Data Control or the Data Environment Designer, but it is far more flexible in the long run.

Connecting to the data source

The first step in building an ADO based application is connecting to the database. The key to this step is creating a connection string that includes key information, such as the data provider, the location of the data, and your user name and password. In addition, you may need to provide additional information, such as the default database name that is required for a specific data provider.

The Connection object uses the connection string to create a way for your program to communicate to the database. Once opened, all database functions performed by your application must reference the Connection object, either explicitly or implicitly.

In addition to providing a gateway to a data source, the Connection object also serves as a common place to record error information by using the Errors collection. The Errors collection contains information about the most recent error encountered. If a new error occurs, the Errors collection will be cleared before any new information is added. It's important to note that a successful operation will not clear the Errors collection. Thus, the Errors collection may not apply to the most recently executed operation. The only way to be certain is to clear the Errors collection after handling the error or immediately before performing a critical operation.

The Connection object is discussed in detail in Chapter 12.

Executing a command

Once you have a connection to the data source, you may issue commands to perform database operations. The commands you issue are defined in a Command object, using the CommandText and CommandType properties. There are three basic types of commands: SQL Statements, table names, and stored procedures.

Once a Command is defined and you have an open Connection to a data source, you may execute the Command. The command may use a set of Parameters to control how it works. This information is kept in the Parameters collection. Parameters can contain values that are passed to the data source and values that are returned from the data source. In addition to returning values through a parameter, a Command may also return a Recordset object, containing a set of rows that were retrieved from the data source.

A Recordset will always be returned if you execute an SQL **Select** Statement or specify a table name for CommandText. All other SQL Statements will not return a Recordset. Stored procedure, on the other hand, may or may not return a Recordset depending on how the stored procedure was written.

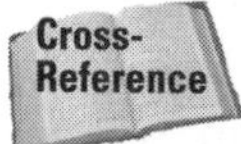

The Command object is discussed in detail in Chapter 13.

Playing with Recordsets

A Recordset object is the way you access the actual data stored in your database. The Recordset maintains a pointer to the current row that can be manipulated through the various methods available in the object. You can move to the next row or the previous row, using the MoveNext and MovePrevious methods. You can jump to the first row or to the last row with the MoveFirst and MoveList methods. You can save the current record pointer and later restore it using the Bookmark property.

Access to the information in a particular row is through the Fields collection. Each individual column in the Recordset is represented by a Field object. You can access the current value of the column though the Value property. If the Recordset was opened with update access, you can change the value of the column by assigning a value to the Value property. You can then save the changes to your database by using the Update method or discard the changes by using the CancelUpdate method.

Other functions are available to help you locate a particular row in the Recordset using the Find method , or you can filter the rows currently available in the Recordset to eliminate unwanted rows with the Filter property. You can also refresh the data in the Recordset by using the Requery or Resync method.

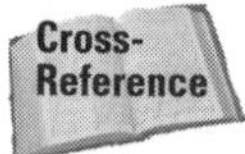

The Recordset object is discussed in detail in Chapters 14, 15, and 16.

Thoughts on ADO

Data bound controls are only really useful if you have a visible object. Some types of Visual Basic programs, such as an IIS Application or a COM+ transaction, don't have a visual component, so you can't use bound controls. In general, I find the ADO object model much easier to use than either the DAO or RDO object models. All you need to do is establish a connection to the database and open a recordset and you're ready to go.

When ADO was first released, it didn't contain an object-oriented way to create schemas and for some reason, the Microsoft Jet database (the core database used in Access and frequently used by Visual Basic programmers), didn't include the SQL Statements needed to define schemas. The only way to build a Jet database was to either use the DAO objects provided for schema definition or use a utility program such as the Visual Data Manager or Access to create an empty database. Because Microsoft wanted current DAO users to move up to ADO, they created the ADOX objects. Now there isn't any reason for someone to continue using DAO.

Summary

In this chapter you learned the following:

- ✦ You can use the ADO `Connection` object to access a database.
- ✦ You can use the ADO `Command` object to run SQL statements and stored procedures on a database server.
- ✦ You can use the ADO `Recordset` object to retrieve information from a database and update the information stored in the database.

✦ ✦ ✦

CHAPTER 12

Connecting to a database

✦ ✦ ✦ ✦

In This Chapter

Using the ADO Connection object

Working with the ADO Error object

Introducing the ADO Errors collection

Connecting to your database server

Analyzing errors

✦ ✦ ✦ ✦

In this chapter, I'm going to discuss the ADO `Connection` object in depth. Also, since the `Errors` collection and the `Error` object are tightly coupled with the `Connection` object, I'm going to cover them also. Access to a data provider is managed using the ADO `Connection` object. Thus, every program that uses a database server must include at least one `Connection` object. Unless you are using multiple data providers or accessing multiple database servers, one `Connection` object is sufficient.

The Connection Object

The `Connection` object is used to maintain a connection to a data source. It can be implicitly created through the `Command` and `Recordset` objects, or you can create an instance of the `Connection` object and share it among multiple `Command` and `Recordset` objects.

Connection object properties

Table 12-1 lists the properties associated with the `Connection` object.

Table 12-1
Properties of the Connection Object

Property	*Description*
`Attributes`	A `Long` value containing the transaction attributes for a connection (see Table 12-2). Note that not all data providers support this property.
`CommandTimeout`	A `Long` containing the maximum number of seconds for the command to execute before an error is returned. Default is 30 seconds.
`ConnectionString`	A `String` containing the information necessary to connect to a data source.
`ConnectionTimeout`	A `Long` containing the maximum number of seconds that the program should wait for a connection to be opened before returning an error. Default is 15 seconds.
`CursorLocation`	A `Long` containing the default location of the cursor service (see Table 12-3). This value will automatically be inherited by the `Recordset` object using this `Connection` object.
`DefaultDatabase`	A `String` containing the name of the default database.
`Errors`	An object reference to an `Errors` collection.
`IsolationLevel`	A `Long` containing the level of transaction isolation (see Table 12-4).
`Mode`	A `Long` containing the available permissions for modifying data (see Table 12-5).
`Properties`	An object reference to a `Properties` collection containing provider-specific information.
`Provider`	A `String` containing the name of the data provider. This value may also be set as part of the `ConnectionString`.
`State`	A `Long` describing the current state of the `Command` object. Multiple values can be combined to describe the current state (see Table 12-6).
`Version`	A `String` containing the current ADO version number.

See Chapter 22, "Integrating XML with Internet Explorer 5," for more information about SQL Server connection strings; Chapter 26, "Overview of Oracle 8i," for more information about Oracle 8i connection strings; and Chapter 30, "Creating Jet Database Objects," for more information about Jet connection strings.

Table 12-2
Values for Attributes

Constant	*Value*	*Description*
`adXactCommitRetaining`	131072	Calling `CommitTrans` automatically starts a new transaction.
`adXactAbortRetaining`	262144	Calling `RollbackTrans` automatically starts a new transaction.

Table 12-3
Values for CursorLocation

Constant	*Value*	*Description*
`adUseNone`	1	Does not use cursor services (obsolete).
`adUseServer`	2	Uses the server-side cursor library.
`adUseClient`	3	Uses the client-side cursor library.

Table 12-4
Values for IsolationLevel

Constant	*Value*	*Description*
`adXactUnspecified`	-1	The provider is using a different isolation level than specified.
`adXactChaos`	16	Pending changes from more highly isolated transactions can't be overwritten.
`adXactBrowse`	256	Can view uncommitted changes in other transactions.
`adXactReadUncommitted`	256	Same as `adXactBrowse`.
`adXactCursorStability`	4096	Can view only committed changes in other transactions.
`adXactReadCommitted`	4096	Same as `adXactCursorStability`.
`adXactRepeatableRead`	65536	Can't view changes in other transactions until you `Requery` the `Recordset` object.

Continued

Table 12-4 *(continued)*

Constant	*Value*	*Description*
`adXactIsolated`	1048576	Transactions are conducted in isolation from all other transactions.
`adXactSerializable`	1048576	Same as `adXactIsolated`.

Table 12-5
Values for Mode

Constant	*Value*	*Description*
`adModeUnknown`	0	Permissions are not set or can't be determined.
`adModeRead`	1	Requests read permission.
`adModeWrite`	2	Requests write permission.
`adModeReadWrite`	3	Requests read/write permission.
`adModeShareDenyRead`	4	Prevent other connections from opening with read permissions.
`adModeShareDenyWrite`	8	Prevent other connections from opening with write permissions.
`adModeShareExclusive`	12	Prevent other connections from opening.
`adModeShareDenyNone`	16	Permit other connections with any permissions.
`adModeRecursive`	32	Used with `adModeShareDenyRead`, `adModeShareDenyWrite`, and `adModeShareDenyNone` to propagate sharing restrictions to all sub-records of the current `Record`.

Connection object methods

The `Connection` object has many methods that allow you to manage your connection to a data source.

Table 12-6
Values for State

Constant	*Value*	*Description*
adStateClosed	0	The Command object is closed.
adStateOpen	1	The Command object is open.
adStateConnecting	2	The Command object is connecting to the database.
adStateExecuting	4	The Command object is executing.
adStateFetching	8	Rows are being retrieved.

Function BeginTrans () As Long

The BeginTrans method marks the beginning of a transaction. The return value corresponds to the nesting level of the transaction. The first call to BeginTrans will return a one. A second call to BeginTrans, without a call to CommitTrans or RollbackTrans, will return two.

Sub Cancel ()

The Cancel method is used to terminate an asynchronous task started by the Execute or Open methods.

Sub Close ()

The Close method closes the connection to the data provider. It will also close any open Recordset objects and set the ActiveConnection property of any Command objects to Nothing.

Sub CommitTrans ()

The CommitTrans method ends a transaction and saves the changes to the database. Depending on the Attributes property, a new transaction may automatically be started.

Function Execute (CommandText As String, [RecordsAffected], [Options As Long = -1]) As Recordset

The Execute method is used to execute the specified command. A Recordset object will be returned as the result of the function, which will contain any rows returned by the command.

`CommandText` is a `String` containing an SQL Statement, stored procedure, table name, or other data provider-specific command to be executed.

`RecordsAffected` optionally returns a `Long` value with the number of records affected by the command.

`Options` optionally passes a combination of the values specified in Table 11-5 found in the section on the `Command` object.

Sub Open ([ConnectionString As String], [UserID As String], [Password As String], [Options As Long = -1])

The `Open` method initializes the `Connection` object by establishing a connection to a data provider.

`ConnectionString` is a `String` value containing the same connection information found in the `ConnectionString` property. The value in this parameter will override the value in the property.

`UserID` contains a `String` value with the UserID needed to access the database. This value will override any UserID information included in the `ConnectionString` parameter or property.

`Password` contains a `String` value with the password associated with the specified UserID. This value will override any password information included in the `ConnectionString` parameter or property.

`Options` optionally passes one of the values specified in Table 12-7. If you specify `adAsyncConnect`, the `ConnectComplete` event will be fired when the connection process has finished.

Table 12-7
Values for Options

Constant	*Value*	*Description*
`adConnectUnspecified`	-1	Opens the connection synchronously. Default.
`adAsyncConnect`	16	Opens the connection asynchronously.

Function OpenSchema (Schema As SchemaEnum, [Restrictions], [SchemaID]) As Recordset

The `OpenSchema` method returns database information from the data provider. A `Recordset` object will be returned as the result of the function, which will contain any rows returned by the command.

`Schema` is an enumerated value specifying the type of information to be returned.

`Restrictions` contains an array of query constraints.

`SchemaID` optionally contains a GUID for a provider-schema query not defined in the OLE DB specification. This parameter is only used when the `Schema` parameter is set to `adSchemaProviderSpecific`.

So you want to write a database utility: The `OpenSchema` method can be used to perform nearly forty different queries against a database catalog. Each query returns a different `Recordset` containing the relevant information. Since this information is extremely complex and not generally used by database programmers, you should reference the OLE DB documentation for detailed information about this method.

Sub RollbackTrans ()

The `RollbackTrans` method ends a transaction and discards any changes to the database. Depending on the `Attributes` property, a new transaction may automatically be started.

Connection object events

The `Connection` object contains events that allow you to intercept status information and determine error conditions while you have a connection to your data source.

Event BeginTransComplete (TransactionLevel As Long, pError As Error, adStatus As EventStatusEnum, pConnection As Connection)

The `BeginTransComplete` is called after the `BeginTrans` method has finished running in asynchronous mode.

`TransactionLevel` is a `Long` value containing the new transaction level.

`pError` is an object reference to an `Error` object if the value of `adStatus` is set to `adStatusErrorsOccured`.

`adStatus` is a `Long` value that contains one of the status values listed in Table 12-8.

`pConnection` is an object reference to the `Connection` object associated with the `BeginTrans` method.

Table 12-8
Values for adStatus

Constant	Value	Description
adStatusOK	1	The operation completed successfully.
adStatusErrorsOccured	2	The operation failed. Error information is in pError.
adStatusCantDeny	3	The operation can't request the cancellation of the current operation.
adStatusCancel	4	The operation requested that the operation be canceled.
adStatusUnwantedEvent	5	Setting the value of the adStatus parameter to this value while in the event will prevent subsequent events from being fired.

Event CommitTransComplete (pError As Error, adStatus As EventStatusEnum, pConnection As Connection)

The CommitTransComplete is called when the CommitTrans method has finished running in asynchronous mode.

pError is an object reference to an Error object if the value of adStatus is set to adStatusErrorsOccured.

adStatus is a Long value that contains one of the status values listed in Table 12-8 in the BeginTransComplete event.

pConnection is an object reference to the Connection object associated with the CommitTrans method.

Event ConnectComplete (pError As Error, adStatus As EventStatusEnum, pConnection As Connection)

The ConnectComplete is called when the Connect method has finished running in asynchronous mode.

pError is an object reference to an Error object if the value of adStatus is set to adStatusErrorsOccured.

adStatus is a Long value that contains one of the status values listed in Table 12-8 in the BeginTransComplete event.

pConnection is an object reference to the Connection object associated with the Connect method.

Event Disconnect (adStatus As EventStatusEnum, pConnection As Connection)

The Disconnect event is called when the connection has been dropped from the data source.

adStatus is a Long value that always contains adStatusOK.

pConnection is an object reference to the Connection object associated with the CommitTrans method.

Event ExecuteComplete (RecordsAffected As Long, pError As Error, adStatus As EventStatusEnum, pCommand As Command, pRecordset As Recordset, pConnection as Connection)

The ExecuteComplete event is called when the Execute method has finished running in asynchronous mode.

RecordsAffected is a Long value containing the number of records affected by the command executed by the Execute method.

pError is an object reference to an Error object if the value of adStatus is set to adStatusErrorsOccured.

adStatus is a Long value containing one of the status values listed in Table 12-8 in the BeginTransComplete event.

pCommand is an object reference to a Command object, if a Command object was executed.

pRecordset is an object reference to a Recordset object containing the results of the command's execution.

pConnection is an object reference to the Connection object associated with the ExecuteComplete method.

Event InfoMessage (pError As Error, adStatus As EventStatusEnum, pConnection as Connection)

The `InfoMessage` event is called when a warning message is received by the current connection.

`pError` is an object reference to an `Error` object if the value of `adStatus` is set to `adStatusErrorsOccured`.

`adStatus` is a `Long` value containing one of the status values listed in Table 12-8 in the `BeginTransComplete` event.

`pConnection` is an object reference to the `Connection` object associated with the message.

Event RollbackTransComplete (pError As Error, adStatus As EventStatusEnum, pConnection as Connection)

The `RollbackTransComplete` event is called when the `RollbackTrans` method has finished running in asynchronous mode.

`pError` is an object reference to an `Error` object if the value of `adStatus` is set to `adStatusErrorsOccured`.

`adStatus` is a `Long` value containing one of the status values listed in Table 12-8 in the `BeginTransComplete` event.

`pConnection` is an object reference to the `Connection` object associated with `RollbackTrans` method.

Event WillConnect (ConnectionString As String, UserID As String, Password As String, Options As Long, adStatus As EventStatusEnum, pConnection as Connection)

The `WillConnect` event is called before the process to establish that a connection is started. You can override any of the values in the `ConnectionString`, `UserID`, `Password`, and `Options` properties. By default, the value of `adStatus` is set to `adStatusOK`. If you set `adStatus` to `adStatusCancel`, you will terminate the connection request. This will trigger the `ConnectComplete` event with an `adStatus` of `adStatusErrorsOccurred`.

`ConnectionString` is a `String` containing the same connection information found in the `ConnectionString` property.

`UserID` contains a `String` value with the UserID needed to access the database.

Password contains a String value with the password associated with the specified UserID.

Options optionally passes one of the values specified in Table 12-7 in the Open method above.

adStatus is a Long value containing one of the status values listed in Table 12-8 in the BeginTransComplete event.

pConnection is an object reference to the Connection object associated with the connection that triggered this event.

Event WillExecute (Source As String, CursorType As CursorTypeEnum, LockType As LockTypeEnum, Options As Long, adStatus As EventStatus Enum, pCommand As Command, pRecordset As Recordset, pConnection as Connection)

The WillExecute event is called before a command is executed. You can override any of the values in the Source, CursorType, LockType and Options properties. By default, the value of adStatus is set to adStatusOK. If you set adStatus to adStatusCancel, you will terminate the connection request. This will trigger the ConnectComplete event with an adStatus of adStatusErrorsOccurred.

Source is a String containing the SQL Statement, stored procedure name, or other command to be executed.

CursorType contains a CursorTypeEnum value describing the type of cursor to be used in the Recordset (see Table 12-9).

LockType contains a LockTypeEnum value (see Table 12-10).

Options optionally passes one of the values specified in Table 12-7 in the Open method above.

adStatus is a Long value containing one of the status values listed in Table 12-7 in the BeginTransComplete event.

pCommand is an object reference to a Command object, if a Command object is about to be executed.

pRecordset is an object reference to a Recordset object, if a Recordset object was the source of the function to be executed.

pConnection is an object reference to the Connection object associated with the connection that triggered this event.

Table 12-9
Values for CursorType

Constant	Value	Description
adOpenUnspecified	-1	The type of cursor isn't specified.
adOpenForwardOnly	0	A forward-only cursor is used, which permits you only to scroll forward through the records in the Recordset.
adOpenKeyset	1	A keyset cursor is used, which is similar to a dynamic cursor, but doesn't permit you to see records added by other users.
adOpenDynamic	2	A dynamic cursor is used, which allows you to see records added by other users, plus any changes and deletions made by other users.
adOpenStatic	3	A static cursor is used, which prevents you from seeing any and all changes from other users.

Table 12-10
Values for LockType

Constant	Value	Description
adLockUnspecified	-1	The type of locking isn't specified.
adLockReadOnly	1	Doesn't permit you to change any values.
adLockPessimistic	2	Records are locked at the data source record by record once the data in the record has been changed.
adLockOptimistic	3	Records are locked only when you call the UpdateMethod.
adLockBatchOptimistic	4	Records are not locked, and conflicts will be returned for resolution after the UpdateBatch method has completed.

The Error Object

The `Error` object contains information about a specific error condition.

Error object properties

Table 12-11 lists the properties associated with the `Error` object.

Table 12-11
Properties of the Error Object

Property	*Description*
`Description`	A `String` value containing a short text description of the error.
`HelpContext`	A `Long` value containing the help context ID reference within the help file specified by `HelpFile`. If no additional help can be found, this value will contain a zero.
`HelpFile`	A `String` containing the name of the help file where a more detailed description of the error may be found. If no additional help is available, this value will contain an empty string.
`NativeError`	A `Long` containing a provider-specific error code.
`Number`	A `Long` containing the OLE DB error code number. This value is unique to this specific error condition.
`Source`	A `String` containing the name of the object or application that caused the error. ADO errors will generally have `Source` values of the format ADODB.*objectname*, ADOX.*objectname,* or ADOMD.*objectname*, where *objectname* is the name of the object that caused the error.
`SQLState`	A `String` containing the standard five-character ANSI SQL error code.

The Errors Collection

The `Errors` collection contains the set of errors generated in response to a specific failure. If an operation fails, the `Errors` collection is cleared and all of the individual errors are recorded in the collection.

If you are using the Resync, UpdateBatch, or CancelBatch methods on a Recordset object, you may generate a set of warnings that will not raise the On Error condition in Visual Basic. Thus, it is important to check for warnings when using these methods and take the appropriate action.

I'm certain it didn't error again: Successfully performing a function will not clear the Errors collection. Thus, the information from a previous error will remain in the collection until it is either explicitly cleared or another error occurs. For this reason, it is very important that you clear the Errors collection after you handle the error condition and before you resume normal processing. Otherwise, you may falsely detect an error condition.

Errors collection properties

Table 12-12 lists the properties associated with the Errors collection.

Table 12-12
Properties of the Errors Collection

Property	*Description*
Count	A Long value containing the number of errors in the collection.
Item(index)	An object reference to an Error object containing information about a particular error. To locate an error, specify a value in the range of 0 to Count –1.

Errors collection methods

The Errors collection contains methods to manage the collection of error information.

Sub Clear ()

The Clear method initializes the Errors collection to the empty state.

Sub Refresh ()

The Refresh method gets a fresh copy of the error information from the data provider.

Connecting To Database Server

In the previous chapters, I provided all of the information necessary to connect to either the ADO Data Control or the Data Environment Designer and they took care of connecting to the database server. However, if you plan to use the ADO objects directly, you need to deal with a few issues yourself.

Connection strings

A *connection string* contains the information necessary to connect your application to a data source. This value is stored in the `ConnectionString` property of the `Connection` object. It consists of a series of keyword clauses separated by semicolons (;). You create a keyword clause by specifying a keyword, an equal sign (=), and then the value of the keyword. If the same keyword is specified more than once, only the last occurrence will be used, except in the case of the `provider` keyword, in which the first occurrence will be used.

Spaces are permitted: A keyword always ends with an equal sign, so special characters, such as a space or a period, are legal.

Consider the following connection string:

```
provider=sqloledb;data source=Athena;initial catalog=VB6DB
```

It uses the `sqloledb` provider and then specifies `Athena` as the data source and `VB6DB` as the initial catalog. Note the spaces inside both the data source and the initial catalog keywords are legal.

Connection strings the easy way: Building a connection string to a new database system can be a real headache, making sure that you have all the needed keywords to make the connection. Try building a dummy application using the ADO Data Control. Then configure the `ConnectionString` property using the Properties dialog box. This creates the connection string and puts it in the `ConnectionString` property. Then all you need to do is copy the connection string to your application.

Provider keyword

The `Provider` keyword specifies the name of the OLE DB provider that will be used to connect to the data source. If this keyword is not included in the connection string, the `OLD DB Provider for ODBC` will be used. Table 12-13 lists some common databases and their OLE DB providers.

Table 12-13
Common OLE DB Providers

Database	*Provider*
OLE DB Provider for ODBC	`MSDASQL.1`
Jet 3.51 (Access 97)	`Microsoft.Jet.OLEDB.3.51`
Jet 4.0 (Access 2000)	`Microsoft.Jet.OLEDB.4.0`
Oracle	`MSDAORA.1`
SQL Server 7	`SQLOLEDB`

Common keywords

Nearly all data providers support the keywords listed in Table 12-14. In many cases, these keywords will be all you need to connect to the data source.

Table 12-14
Common Keywords for SQLOLEDB

Keyword	*Alias*	*Description*
`Data Source`	`Server`	Specifies the location of the database server or the name of the file containing the data, depending on the specific provider.
`Initial Catalog`	`Database`	Specifies the name of the default database on the database server.
`Password`	`PWD`	Specifies the password associated with the User Id keyword.
`User Id`	`UID`	Specifies the user name that will be used to connect to the database server.

Keywords for SQLOLEDB

Accessing an SQL Server database is very straightforward. All you need to do is include the `Data Source` keyword and either specify the user name and password or set the `Trusted_Connection` keyword to `yes`. However, there are a number of other keywords that can provide additional functions. Table 12-15 lists the set of keywords that are specific to SQL Server.

Table 12-15
Common Keywords for SQLOLEDB

Keyword	*Description*
`Application Name`	Contains the name of the application program.
`Connect Timeout`	Specifies the number of seconds in which the database server must respond before the connection will timeout.
`Integrated Security`	When set to `SSPI`, Windows NT Authentication will be used.
`Trusted_Connection`	Contains `yes` if you are using Windows NT Authentication.
`Workstation ID`	Contains name of the client machine.

Keywords for Microsoft.Jet.OLEDB.4.0

When accessing a Jet database, you need to remember that there isn't really a database server involved, like there is with most other database systems. The database is a specially formatted disk file, which you reference in the `Data Source` keyword. The other keywords have the normal meaning, and the list of specific keywords for the Microsoft Jet provider is listed in Table 12-16.

Table 12-16
Common Keywords for SQLOLEDB

Keyword	*Description*
`Jet OLEDB:System Database`	Contains the fully qualified file name for the workgroup information file.
`Jet OLEDB:Registry Path`	Specifies the registry key that contains values for the database engine.
`Jet OLEDB:Database Password`	Contains the database password.

Opening a connection

Opening a database connection is merely a matter of declaring an object, creating a new instance of it, and then opening the connection. The key is using the proper connection string when you open the connection.

Declaring a Connection object

The following line of code declares the variable db as a `Connection` object.

```
Dim db As ADODB.Connection
```

You can use any of the methods or properties associated with the `Connection` object, but not any of the events. This is perfectly fine for most programs. The events only provide status information that can be safely ignored by most programs.

Globally speaking: When creating applications with multiple forms, I often add a module to the program to hold objects that I want to access, including things like the `Connection` object, which can easily share among multiple forms.

Sometimes, however, you might want to track this status information. This is a great place to include extra security checks, since you have the opportunity to review various functions before they are actually performed, and cancel them. To include events with the `Connection` object, you need to use the `WithEvents` keyword in the `Dim` statement as in the statement below:

```
Dim WithEvents db As ADODB.Connection
```

Qualifying for clarity: I usually use the `ADODB` prefix for all ADO objects. This eliminates confusion with other objects (such as the DAO) that have the same name.

The `WithEvents` keyword imposes some restrictions on how you can declare your object. You can only use it in `Form` modules and `Class` modules. You can't use it in a regular `.BAS` module. You also can't use the `New` keyword. You must instantiate the object using a `Set` statement with the `New` keyword.

Faster objects: While you can use the `New` keyword in a `Dim` statement to create an object the first time it's used, it adds code to every statement to see if the object exists and create it if necessary.

Coding the Connection object

One of the things I like best about using the ADO objects directly, rather than using the Data Environment Designer or the ADO Data Command, is that the database isn't opened for me when the program is started. This allows me the opportunity to ask the user for their user name and password before I open the database.

The Connect Demo program shown in Figure 12-1 is a very simple program that demonstrates how to connect to an SQL Server database. It consists of two command buttons that are used to connect and disconnect from the database, plus two text boxes that allow the user to enter their user name and password.

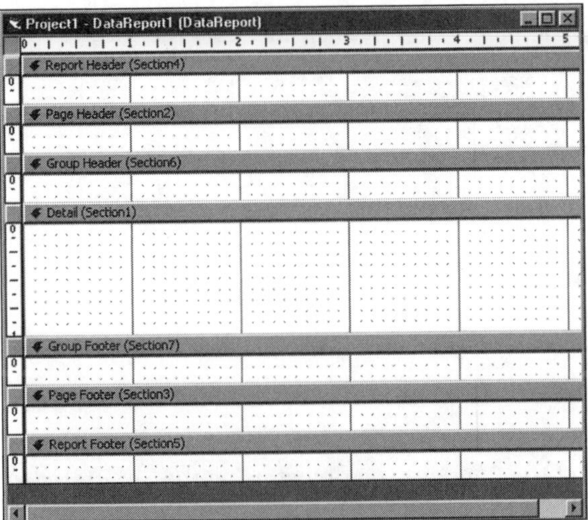

Figure 12-1: The Connect Demo program

Clicking the button labeled Connect will fire the `Command1_Click` event, as shown in Listing 12-1. I begin the routine by using the `On Error Resume Next` statement, which prevents a run-time error from killing the program. However, I need to be careful to explicitly check for error conditions, or an undetected error could cause havoc with my program.

Listing 12-1: The Command1_Click event in Connect Demo

```
Private Sub Command1_Click()

Dim p As ADODB.Property

On Error Resume Next
Set db = New ADODB.Connection
db.ConnectionString = "provider=sqloledb;" & _
   "data source=Athena;initial catalog=VB6DB"

db.Properties("User Id").Value = Text1.Text
db.Properties("Password").Value = Text2.Text

db.Open
```

Continued

Listing 12-1 (continued)

```
If db.State = adStateOpen Then
   Command1.Enabled = False
   Command2.Enabled = True

Else
   WriteError

End If

End Sub
```

Next, I create a new instance of the Connection object using the Set statement. Then I set the various properties in the Connection before I open the connection. While I can set the ConnectionString property directly, I need to set the values for User Id and Password through the Properties collection. For these values, I simply use the name of the property as the index in the Properties collection and assign the values I want to the Value property. Of course, these properties are specific to the provider that is used, so you need to see which of these custom properties you really need.

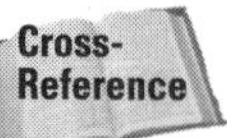

Check "The Parameter Object" and "The Parameters Collection" in Chapter 13 for more details about these objects.

Opening the connection

Once the properties are set, I invoke the Open method to connect to the database server. Another way to handle the connection would be to specify all of the information as part of the call to the Open method, as shown below:

```
db.Open "provider=sqloledb;data source=Athena; " & _
   "initial catalog=VB6DB", Text1.Text, Text2.Text
```

This has the advantage of fewer lines of text, which means fewer places where something can go wrong.

After I've used the Open method, I need to know if it was successful. Had I not used the On Error statement, I could safely assume that the Open method was successful, because the program would had gotten a run-time error and died. Here I can do one of two things. First, I can check the Errors object to see if there was an error and check the error code for the appropriate action. Second, I can check the State property to make sure that the object's state is open. If the connection is open, I'll disable the button that connects to the database and enable the button that closes the connection. If it isn't, I'll display an error message to the user with the WriteError routine.

Closing a connection

Closing a Connection object is merely a matter of using the Close method and releasing the resources associated with the object, which you can see in Listing 12-2. If I was able to close the connection, I will disable the Disconnect button and reenable the Connect button so the user can try connecting to the database again. If the Close method generated an error, I'll display the error using the WriteError routine.

Listing 12-2: The Command2_Click event in Connect Demo

```
Private Sub Command2_Click()

db.Close
If db.State = adStateClosed Then
   Set db = Nothing
   Command2.Enabled = False
   Command1.Enabled = True

Else
   WriteError

End If

End Sub
```

Analyzing Errors

The Connection object's Errors collection contains the information about the most recent error that occurred. When performing database functions, it is quite possible that a single request may generate multiple errors. Usually, the first error is the most significant error, and the rest of the errors are secondary effects of the main error.

Retrieving error informationThe WriteError subroutine in Listing 12-3 is designed to update a StatusBar control with the results of the most recent error. I check the Count property to see how many errors are in the collection, and if there's only one, I display it in the status bar. If I have multiple errors, I'll display the first error in the status bar just like I displayed the single error, and then use a For Each loop to display each of the individual error messages.

Listing 12-3: The WriteError subroutine in Connect Demo

```
Private Sub WriteError()

Dim e As ADODB.Error

If db.Errors.Count = 1 Then
   StatusBar1.SimpleText = "Error: " & db.Errors(0).Description

Elseif db.Errors.Count > 1 Then
   StatusBar1.SimpleText = "Multiple errors:" & _
      db.Errors(0).Description

   For Each e In db.Errors
      MsgBox e.Description

   Next e

End If

db.Errors.Clear

End Sub
```

It is important to clear the Errors collection before you issue the next database request. The Errors collection is only cleared automatically the next time an error is encountered. If you don't clear the collection before you issue a database request, and then check it afterwards, you can't be certain that the errors in the Errors collection were caused by the most recent database request.

There are two places where you should clear the Errors collection. The first is immediately after handling an error condition, as I did in the WriteError routine. This ensures that Error object is clear after processing an error condition. However, since it is possible that you may not check every place there can be an error, you should also clear the Errors collection before any call that might result in an error.

Watching connection activity

The events associated with the Connect object provide a way to catch an activity before and after it executes. This will allow you to grab information and display it to the user, or to review the request and deny it.

Displaying status information

The db_ConnectComplete event shown in Listing 12-4 will be fired after the user connects to the database. I begin by checking the adStatus parameter to see if the connection completed without an error. If it did, I let the user know that they're connected to the database. Otherwise, I get the error message from the pError object and display it in the status bar.

Listing 12-4: The db_ConnectComplete event in Connect Demo

```
Private Sub db_ConnectComplete(ByVal pError As ADODB.Error, _
   adStatus As ADODB.EventStatusEnum, _
   ByVal pConnection As ADODB.Connection)

If adStatus = adStatusOK Then
   StatusBar1.SimpleText = "Connected."

Else
   StatusBar1.SimpleText = "Error: " & pError.Description

End If

End Sub
```

Canceling a request

The Complete events in the Connection object merely indicate the current status of a request. The Will events, on the other hand, are the perfect place to review a request and cancel it if desired. Listing 12-5 takes advantage of the db_WillConnect event to see if the user really wants to connect to the database server.

Listing 12-5: The db_WillConnect event in Connect Demo

```
Private Sub db_WillConnect(ConnectionString As String, _
   UserID As String, Password As String, Options As Long, _
   adStatus As ADODB.EventStatusEnum, _
   ByVal pConnection As ADODB.Connection)

If MsgBox("Do you really want to connect?", vbYesNo, _
      "Connect to remote database") = vbYes Then
   StatusBar1.SimpleText = "Will connect."

Else
   adStatus = adStatusCancel

End If

End Sub
```

I begin this routine by displaying a message box that asks the user if they really want to connect to the database server. If the user responds no, I'll cancel the request by setting the `adStatus` parameter to `adStatusCancel`. This will trigger an error condition, which is intercepted by both the `WriteError` routine and the `ConnectComplete` event. If the user responds yes, the status bar is updated, and the `Open` method will be allowed to continue.

So it's contrived: The example here is somewhat contrived; however, in a real application, you may want to restrict connections based on the time of date, day of week, or particular value of the user name.

Thoughts on the Connection Object

The `Connection` object manages the path to your database server. In most cases, you'll open the connection when your program begins and close it when it ends. You won't bother with any of the events and you may not even specify any of the connection properties other than the connection string. After all, the main reason you want to use the `Connection` object is to connect to the database. The real work of your application will be done with the other objects in the ADO library.

Summary

In this chapter you learned the following:

✦ You can use the `Connection` object to establish a link between the database client program and the database server.

✦ You can use connection strings to specify the parameters that are passed to the OLE DB provider to establish the connection to the database server.

✦ You can use the `Error` object to determine why the most recent database request failed.

✦ You can use the events in the `Connection` object to gather information about the various database requests sent to the database server and cancel them if desired.

✦ ✦ ✦

CHAPTER 13

Using Commands and Stored Procedures

✦ ✦ ✦ ✦

In This Chapter

Presenting the ADO Command Object

Introducing the ADO Parameter Object

Working with the ADO Parameters Collection

Creating and executing commands

Using stored procedures

✦ ✦ ✦ ✦

In this chapter, I will cover how to create and use ADO Command objects. The Command object allows you to specify a command that will retrieve data from your database. Typically this object is used with stored procedures and SQL queries that include a series of parameters.

Introducing the ADO Command Object

After you have an open connection, the first thing you're going to want to do is to execute some commands. Commands are defined in the Command object and can be SQL statements or calls to stored procedures. Some commands, particularly those that use stored procedures, may have parameters that supply additional information to the command or return information after the command was executed. Parameter information is stored in the Parameters collection, with each parameter having its own Parameter object. Also, depending on the particular command, it may or may not return a Recordset object containing rows of information from your database.

Discussing Command objects without talking about Recordset objects can be difficult, since the primary reason for using Command objects is to create Recordsets. See Chapter 14 for more information about Recordset objects.

The Command Object

The Command object contains information about an SQL statement or stored procedure you wish to execute against a database. You may optionally include a list of parameters that will be passed to the stored procedure. If the command returns a set of rows, the Command object will return a Recordset object containing the results.

Command object properties

Table 13-1 lists the properties associated with the Command object.

Table 13-1
Properties of the Command Object

Property	*Description*
ActiveConnection	A Variant array containing an object reference to the Connection object used to access the database. May also contain a valid connection string that will dynamically create a connection to your database when you use the Execute method.
CommandText	A String value containing an SQL statement, a stored procedure name, or other provider command to be executed.
CommandTimeout	A Long value containing the maximum number of seconds for the command to execute before an error is returned. Default is 30 seconds.
CommandType	An enumerated type (see Table 13-2) describing the type of command to be executed.
Name	A String containing the name of the object.
Parameters	An object reference to a Parameters collection containing the parameters that will be passed to a stored procedure or a parameterized query.
Prepared	A Boolean, when TRUE, means that the command should be prepared before execution.
Properties	An object reference to a Properties collection containing additional information about the Command object.
State	A Long describing the current state of the Command object. Multiple values from Table 13-3 can be combined to describe the current state.

Table 13-2
Values for CommandType

Constant	*Value*	*Description*
adCmdUnspecified	-1	CommandType should be automatically determined.
adCmdText	1	CommandText contains either an SQL statement or stored procedure call.
adCmdTable	2	CommandText contains the name of a table in the database.
adCmdStoredProcedure	4	CommandText contains the name of a stored procedure.
adCmdUnknown	8	The type of command isn't known.
adExecuteNoRecords	128	Indicates that the command will not return any rows or will automatically discard any rows that are generated. Must be used with adCmdText or adCmdStoredProcedure.
adCmdFile	256	CommandText is the name of a persistently stored Recordset.
adCmdTableDirect	512	CommandText contains the name of a database table.

Table 13-3
Values for State

Constant	*Value*	*Description*
adStateClosed	0	The Command object is closed.
adStateOpen	1	The Command object is open.
adStateConnecting	2	The Command object is connecting to the database.
adStateExecuting	4	The Command object is executing.
adStateFetching	8	Rows are being retrieved.

Command object methods

The `Command` object contains only three methods: `Cancel`, `CreateParameter`, and `Execute`.

Sub Cancel()

The `Cancel` method is used to terminate an asynchronous task started by the `Execute` method.

Function CreateParameter ([Name As String], [Type As DataTypeEnum = adEmpty], [Direction As ParameterDirectionEnum = adParamInput], [Size As Long], [Value]) As Parameter

The `CreateParameter` method creates a new `Parameter` object, which may be added to the `Parameters` collection using the `Parameters.Append` method.

`Name` specifies the name of the parameter.

`Type` specifies the data type of the parameter.

`Direction` specifies whether the parameter is input only, output only, or both input and output.

`Size` specifies the length of the parameter. This parameter is only important when you have a variable length data type, such as a string or an array.

`Value` specifies the value of the parameter.

Function Execute ([RecordsAffected], [Parameters], [Options As Long =-1]) As Recordset

The `Execute` method runs the SQL statement or stored procedure specified in the `Command` object. A `Recordset` object will be returned as the result of the function, which will contain any rows returned by the command.

`RecordsAffected` optionally returns a `Long` value with the number of records affected by the command.

`Parameters` optionally passes a `Variant` array containing a list of parameters to be used by the command. Note that output parameters will not return correct values through this parameter. Instead, you should use the `Parameters` collection to get the correct values for output parameters.

`Options` optionally passes a combination of the values specified in Table 13-4. Note that some of these values are the same as those available for the `CommandType` property.

Table 13-4
Values for Options

Constant	*Value*	*Description*
`adOptionUnspecified`	-1	No options are specified.
`adCmdText`	1	`CommandText` contains either an SQL statement or stored procedure call.
`adCmdTable`	2	`CommandText` contains the name of a table in the database.
`adCmdStoredProcedure`	4	`CommandText` contains the name of a stored procedure.
`adCmdUnknown`	8	The type of command isn't known.
`adAsyncExecute`	16	The command should be executed asynchronously.
`adAsyncFetch`	32	After the number of rows specified in the `CacheSize` property of the `Recordset` object are returned, the remaining rows will be returned asynchronously.
`adAsyncFetchNonBlocking`	64	The main thread isn't blocked while retrieving rows. If the current row hasn't been retrieved, the current row will be moved to the end of the file.
`adExecuteNoRecords`	128	Indicates that the command will not return any rows or will automatically discard any rows that are generated. Must be used with either the `adCmdText` or `adCmdStoredProcedure` values.
`adCmdFile`	256	`CommandText` is the name of a persistently stored `Recordset`.
`adCmdTableDirect`	512	`CommandText` contains the name of a database table.

The Parameter Object

The Parameter object contains information about a parameter used in a stored procedure or parameterized query defined in a Command object.

Parameter object properties

Table 13-5 lists the properties associated with the Parameter object.

Table 13-5
Properties of the Parameter Object

Property	*Description*
Attributes	An enumerated type describing the characteristics of the parameter (see Table 13-6).
Direction	An enumerated type that describes whether the parameter is an input-only, input/outpu, or output-only parameter (see Table 13-7).
Name	A String value containing the name of the parameter.
NumericScale	A Byte value containing the number of digits to the right of the decimal point for a numeric field.
Precision	A Byte value containing the total number of digits in a numeric field.
Properties	An object reference to a Properties collection containing provider-specific information about a parameter.
Type	An enumerated type (see Table 13-8) containing the OLE DB data type of the field.
Value	A Variant array containing the current value of the parameter.

Table 13-6
Values for Attributes

Constant	*Value*	*Description*
adFldUnspecified	-1	The provider doesn't supply field attributes.
adFldMayDefer	2	The field value is not retrieved with the whole record, but only when you explicitly access the field.

Constant	Value	Description
adFldUpdateable	4	The field's value may be changed.
adFldUnknownUpdateable	8	The provider can't determine if you can change the field's value.
adFldFixed	16	The field contains fixed-length data.
adFldIsNullable	32	The field will accept **Null** values.
adFldMayBeNull	64	The field may contain a **Null** value.
adFldLong	128	The field contains a long binary value and you should use the `AppendChunk` and `GetChunk` methods to access its data.
adFldRowID	256	The field contains an identity value that can't be changed.
adFldRowVersion	512	The field contains a time stamp value that is used to track updates.
adFldCacheDeferred	4096	This field is cached by the provider and subsequent reads and writes are done from cache.
adFldIsChapter	8192	The field contains a chapter value, which specifies a specific child `Recordset` related to this parent field.
adFldNegativeScale	16384	The field contains a numeric column that supports negative scale values.
adFldKeyColumn	32768	The field is (or is at least part of) the primary key for the table.
adFldIsRowURL	65536	The field contains the URL that names the resource from the data store represented by the record.
adFldIsDefaultStream	131072	The field contains the default stream for the resource represented by the record.
adFldIsCollection	262144	The field contains a collection of another resource, such as a folder, rather than a simple resource, such as a file.

Table 13-7
Values for Direction

Constant	*Value*	*Description*
`adParamUnknown`	0	The direction of the parameter is unknown.
`adParamInput`	1	The parameter is an input-only parameter.
`adParamOutput`	2	The parameter is an output-only parameter.
`adParamInputOutput`	3	The parameter is both an input and an output parameter.
`adParamReturnValue`	4	The parameter contains a return value.

Table 13-8
Values for Type

Constant	*Value*	*Description*
`adEmpty`	0	This field has no value (`DBTYPE_EMPTY`).
`adSmallInt`	2	This field has an `Integer` value (`DBTYPE_I2`).
`adInteger`	3	This field has a `Long` value (`DBTYPE_I4`).
`adSingle`	4	This field has a `Single` value (`DBTYPE_R4`).
`adDouble`	5	This field has a `Double` value (`DBTYPE_R8`).
`adCurrency`	6	This field has a `Currency` value (`DBTYPE_CY`).
`adDate`	7	This field has a `Date` value (`DBTYPE_DATE`).
`adBSTR`	8	This field has a null-terminated Unicode string (`DBTYPE_BSTR`).
`adIDispatch`	9	This field has a pointer to an `IDispatch` interface in a COM object (`DBTYPE_IDISPATCH`).
`adError`	10	This field has a 32-bit error code (`DBTYPE_ERROR`).
`adBoolean`	11	This field has a `Boolean` value (`DBTYPE_BOOL`).

Constant	*Value*	*Description*
adVariant	12	This field has a Variant value (DBTYPE_VARIANT). Note that this type is not supported by ADO and causes unpredictable results.
adIUknown	13	This field has a pointer to an IUnknown interface in a COM object (DBTYPE_IUNKNOWN).
adDecimal	14	This field has an exact numeric value with a fixed precision and scale (DBTYPE_DECIMAL).
adTinyInt	16	This field has a one byte signed integer (DBTYPE_I1).
adUnsignedTinyInt	17	This field has a one byte unsigned integer (DBTYPE_UI1).
adUnsignedInt	18	This field has a two byte unsigned integer (DBTYPE_UI2).
adUnsignedInt	19	This field has a four byte unsigned integer (DBTYPE_UI4).
adBigInt	20	This field has an 8-byte signed integer (DBTYPE_I8).
adUnsignedBigInt	21	This field has an 8-byte unsigned integer (DBTYPE_UI8).
adFileTime	64	This field has a 64-bit date-time value represented as the number of 100-nanosecond intervals since 1 January 1601 (DBTYPE_FILETIME).
adGUID	72	This field has a globally unique identifier value (DBTYPE_GUID).
adBinary	128	This field has a Binary value (DBTYPE_BYTES).
adChar	129	This field has a String value (DBTYPE_STR).
adWChar	130	This field contains a null-terminated Unicode character string (DBTYPE_WSTR).
adNumeric	131	This field contains an exact numeric value with a fixed precision and scale (DBTYPE_NUMERIC).

Continued

Table 13-8 *(continued)*

Constant	*Value*	*Description*
adUserDefined	132	This field contains a user-defined value (DBTYPE_UDT).
adDBDate	133	This field has a date value using the YYYYMMDD format (DBTYPE_DBDATE).
adDBTime	134	This field has a time value using the HHMMSS format (DBTYPE_DBTIME).
adDBTimeStamp	135	This field has a date-time stamp in the YYYYMMDDHHMMSS format (DBTYPE_DBTIMESTAMP).
adChapter	136	This field has a 4-byte chapter value that identifies the rows in a child rowset (DBTYPE_HCHAPTER).
adPropVariant	138	This field has an Automation PROPVARIANT (DBTYPE_PROP_VARIANT).
adVarNumeric	139	This field contains a numeric value. (Available for Parameter objects only.)
adVarChar	200	This field has a String. (Available for Parameter objects only.)
adLongVarChar	201	This field has a long character value. (Available for Parameter objects only.)
adVarWChar	202	This field has a null-terminated Unicode character string value. (Available for Parameter objects only.)
adLongVarWChar	203	This field has a long null-terminated character string value. (Available for Parameter objects only.)
adVarBinary	204	This field has a binary value. (Available for Parameter objects only.)
adLongVarBinary	205	This field has a long binary value. (Available for Parameter objects only.)

Parameter object methods

There is only one method available for the `Parameter` object: the `AppendChunk` method.

Sub AppendChunk (Data As Variant)

The `AppendChunk` method is used to add data to a large text or binary field. The first time the `AppendChunk` method is used, the value in `Data` will overwrite any existing data in the field. For subsequent calls, simply append data to the end of the existing data. `Data` is a `Variant` array containing the data to be appended to the end of the field.

The Parameters Collection

The `Parameters` collection contains the set of parameters associated with a `Command` object.

Parameters collection properties

Table 13-9 lists the properties associated with the `Parameters` collection.

Table 13-9
Properties of the Parameters Collection

Property	*Description*
`Count`	A `Long` value containing the number of `Parameter` objects in the collection.
`Item`(index)	An object reference to a `Parameter` object containing information about a particular field in the `Recordset`. To locate a field, specify a value in the range of 0 to `Count` –1 or the name of the `Parameter`.

Parameters collection methods

The method available for the `Parameters` collection allows you to manage the set of `Parameter` objects.

Sub Append (Object As Object)

The `Append` method adds a `Parameter` object to the collection. The `Type` property of the `Parameter` object must be defined before you can add it to the collection. `Object` is a `Parameter` object containing the new parameter.

Tip

Use the `CreateParameter` method of the `Command` object to create a new `Parameter` object, then use the `Append` method to add it to the collection.

Sub Delete (Index As Variant)

The `Delete` method removes an object specified by `Index` from the collection. `Index` is either a `String` value containing the name of the parameter or a `Long` value containing the ordinal position of the `Parameter` object to be deleted.

Sub Refresh()

The `Refresh` method can be used to retrieve information about the parameters in a stored procedure from the data provider. To use `Refresh` in this fashion, you need a valid `Command` object with an active connection to the data source. Then all you need to do is specify values for `CommandText` and `CommandType` and use the `Parameters.Refresh` method. This will retrieve all of the information for the stored procedure from the data provider. Note that this works only if your data provider supports stored procedures or an SQL query with embedded parameters (also known as a *parameterized query*).

Running SQL Statements

A `Command` object contains all of the information necessary to send a command to the database server for execution. Sometimes the command will need parameters, while at other times it will not. Depending on the command you want to execute, it may return nothing or a `Recordset` object containing the set of rows selected from the database. No matter what the command is, the approach you use to define it and run it is basically the same.

Running a simple command

Every `Command` you execute needs at least two pieces of information before you can use it. You must set the `CommandText` to the command you want to execute and you must set the `ActiveConnection` property to an open `Connection` object.

While not as important, you should set the `CommandType` property to the value appropriate for the command you want to execute. If this value is not specified, or set to `adCmdUnknown`, the database server must determine if the command is an

SQL statement, a stored procedure, or a table name before it can execute it. While this extra overhead isn't large by itself, it can be significant when you multiply it by the number of requests the server must execute.

The Command Demo program (see Figure 13-1) is based on the Connection Demo program from Chapter 12. All of the code and form elements are carried over intact, although I added a few new command buttons and `Click` events to demonstrate how to use the `Command` object.

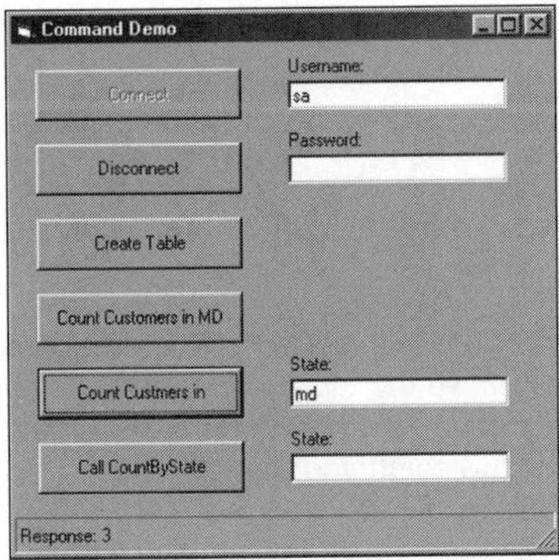

Figure 13-1: Running the Command Demo program

The Command Demo program can be found on the CD-ROM in the \VB6DB\Chapter13\CommandDemo directory.

.

Listing 13-1 shows how you can use a `Command` object to create a database table. In this example, I create a table called `MyTable`. However, this technique can be used to execute any SQL statement except for the **Select** statement. (The **Select** statement will return a `Recordset` object, which requires some additional code.)

Listing 13-1: The Command5_Click event in Command Demo

```
Private Sub Command5_Click()

Dim c As ADODB.Command

On Error Resume Next
```

Continued

Listing 13-1 *(continued)*

```
Set c = New ADODB.Command
Set c.ActiveConnection = db
c.CommandText = "Create Table MyTable (MyColumn Char (10))"
c.CommandType = adCmdText

db.Errors.Clear
c.Execute
If db.Errors.Count > 0 Then
   WriteError

End If

End Sub
```

Once is okay, twice isn't: Since this routine creates a table in your database, running it a second time will fail unless you remove the table manually. You should use a query tool to delete the table before you try it a second time or try it again to see the error that will result from executing this command twice.

The routine begins by creating a new instance of the `Command` object and setting the `ActiveConnection` property to the same `Connection` object I created in Chapter 12. Then I assign the SQL statement I want to execute to the `CommandText` property. Since I'm executing an SQL statement, I'll set the `CommandType` to `adCmdText` to prevent the server from trying to determine if it is the name of a table or stored procedure.

Once the command is defined, executing is easy. I `Clear` the `Errors` collection to make sure that any errors in the collection are caused by the `Execute` method. Then I use the `Execute` method to run the command on the database server. If there are any errors in the `Errors` collection, I'll call the `WriteError` routine to display the information.

Returning a Recordset

Working with `Recordsets` is basically the same as working with simple commands except that the `Execute` method returns a reference to `Recordset` object. In Listing 13-2, I create a `Connection` object the same way as in Listing 13-1, but instead of the **Create Table** SQL statement, I use a **Select** statement.

Listing 13-2: The Command4_Click event in Command Demo

```
Private Sub Command4_Click()

Dim c As ADODB.Command
Dim rs As ADODB.Recordset

On Error Resume Next

Set c = New ADODB.Command
Set c.ActiveConnection = db
c.CommandText = "Select Count(*) From Customers "& _"
Where State = 'MD'"
c.CommandType = adCmdText

db.Errors.Clear
Set rs = c.Execute
If db.Errors.Count > 0 Then
   WriteError

Else
   StatusBar1.SimpleText = "Response: " & _
      FormatNumber(rs.Fields(0).Value, 0)

End If

End Sub
```

Since the call to `c.Execute` will return an object reference, I need to use a `Set` statement to assign the object reference to the `Recordset` object. Note that I didn't need to create an instance of the `Recordset` object. The `Execute` method took care of this for me.

Next, I check for errors in the `Errors` collection and call the `WriteError` routine if I find any. Otherwise, I output the value of the first field in the first row of the `Recordset` in the status bar. You can verify that the value is correct by executing the same query using your database query tool.

Tip

Quick and dirty: Building and debugging a database application can be difficult. If you're truly paranoid, like me, you don't trust your application until you can verify that it worked properly using an independent tool. This is where a tool like SQL Server's Query Analyzer comes in handy. You can use it to execute any type of query you like. Thus, you can test your **Select** statement to ensure that the right number of rows was returned or to verify that an update to the database was made properly. You can also use it to test various SQL statements, and when you're satisfied that they're correct, you can copy them to the `CommandText` property of a `Command` object.

Running with parameters

While knowing the number of customers in Maryland is nice, a better approach than creating a `Command` object for each state would be to create one that accepts parameters. This is also an easy process, as you can see in Listing 13-3. This routine is based on the one shown in Listing 13-2. The only differences are the ones needed for parameters.

Listing 13-3: The Command3_Click event in Command Demo

```
Private Sub Command3_Click()

Dim c As ADODB.Command
Dim p As ADODB.Parameter
Dim rs As ADODB.Recordset

On Error Resume Next

Set c = New ADODB.Command
Set c.ActiveConnection = db
c.CommandText = "Select Count(*) From Customers "& _"
Where State = MD"
c.CommandType = adCmdText

Set p = c.CreateParameter("State", adChar, adParamInput, 2)
c.Parameters.Append p

c.Parameters("State").Value = Text3.Text

db.Errors.Clear
Set rs = c.Execute
If db.Errors.Count > 0 Then
   WriteError

Else
   StatusBar1.SimpleText = "Response: " & _
      FormatNumber(rs.Fields(0).Value, 0)

End If

End Sub
```

The first difference you might have noticed is that I assigned the **Select** statement to the `CommandText` property. In place of the MD, there is now a question mark (?). Question marks are used to identify the place where a parameter will be substituted into the statement. In this case, the parameter is the two-character state abbreviation.

Next, I use the `CreateParameter` method to create a new `Parameter` object called `State`. I'll save the object reference in a temporary variable called `p`. It has a type of **Char(2)** and is an input-only parameter. The last argument of the method is omitted. Had I wanted to assign a default value for the parameter, I would have specified it as the last parameter. After creating the parameter, I use the `Append` method of the `Parameters` collection to add the object to the collection.

Order in the parameters: The order in which you add the parameters to the collection is the same order that will be used to match the parameters to the question marks in the `CommandText`. The first parameter is mapped to the first question mark, while the second parameter is mapped to the second question mark, and so on.

Once the parameter has been defined, you can use the `Parameters` collection to identify the parameter by name and assign it a value. Then you can use the `Execute` method to generate the `Recordset` object and display the results.

An alternate way to execute a command with parameters is to supply the parameter values as part of the `Execute` method, as shown in the following line of code:

```
Set rs = c.Execute(, Array(Text3.Text))
```

The second argument of the `Execute` method allows you to specify a `Variant` array containing a list of parameters that will be used by the command. The easiest way to construct a `Variant` array is to use the `Array` function, which takes a list of values and returns a `Variant` array containing the values. If you have already specified a parameter directly in the `Parameters` collection, the value specified in the `Execute` method will override that value.

Stored Procedures

Stored procedures are useful tools that allow you to execute a set of SQL statements on the database server by issuing a single command with a series of parameters. Information can be returned via the `Parameters` collection or in a `Recordset` object. Stored procedures are highly dependent on the database system on which they run. However, the benefits of using stored procedures often far outweigh having SQL statements that are independent of a particular database system.

Advantages of stored procedures

Many people use stored procedures in their database applications for three main reasons: faster performance, application logic, and security.

Faster performance

Using stored procedures is typically faster than issuing the equivalent SQL statements from your application, for several reasons. The first reason is that stored procedures are stored on the database server in a prepared format. This avoids the overhead of preparing a statement on the fly. Also, if you repeatedly execute the same statement, most database servers will prepare the statement each time you execute it, imposing a lot of extra overhead on the database server.

Note

Prepared for speed: Before any SQL statement can be executed, it must be prepared. Preparing a statement involves parsing the words in the statement, compiling them into a package, and then optimizing the package based on the data in the database.

In addition, stored procedures often contain multiple SQL statements, which means that you don't have to wait for a response across the network before you send the next command. The individual statements are executed in sequence until the stored procedure is complete. This means that the intermediate recordsets you would have transmitted to the client computer, and the commands you would have issued in response, aren't necessary. Which in turn reduces the amount of time needed to perform the function.

Application logic

Stored procedures are written using a language that allows you to have local variables, perform computations, call other stored procedures, and process recordsets — as well as execute SQL statements. In short, you can think of a stored procedure much like you would think of a Visual Basic program, but one whose execution is tightly coupled with the database server.

Since many developers find this concept appealing, they code their business logic as stored procedures and make them available for application programmers to use. This ensures that each program can take advantage of the business logic, and as long as the calling sequence isn't changed, you won't have to recompile your Visual Basic program each time a stored procedure is changed.

Security

Using a stored procedures can be more secure than granting someone direct access to a database. Since stored procedures are database objects, they are usually secured using the same tools that you would use for a table or a view for user access, yet you can allow the stored procedure to run using someone else's database privileges. This allows you to put code in a stored procedure to perform a specific function that the user might not otherwise be able to perform. The user will not be able to see or change this code.

Stored procedures and the Data View Window

In Chapter 9, I talked about how to use the Data View Window (see Figure 13-2) to access your database while using the Data Environment Designer. It's possible to use the Data View Window without the Data Environment Designer. Unlike the Data Environment Designer, the Data View Window isn't integrated into your program. It is a design-time only tool that allows you to access your database design, tables, views, and stored procedures tasks using a database vendor independent tool.

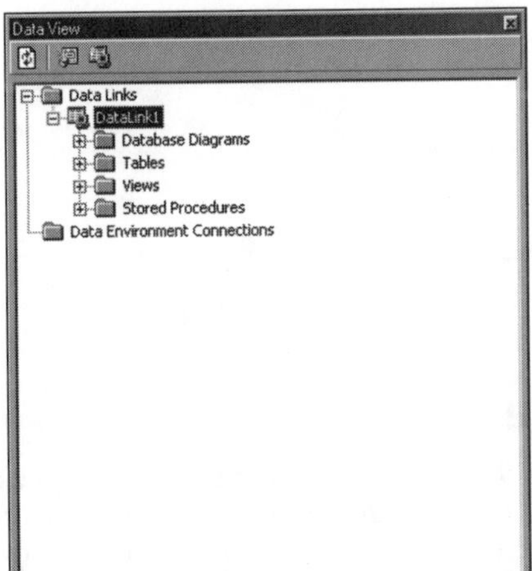

Figure 13-2: Adding the Data View Window to your application

Exclusively Enterprise Edition: The Data View Window features I'm going to cover apply to the Enterprise Edition of Visual Basic. If you have the Professional Edition, you will need to create and debug your stored procedures using tools provided by your database vendor. This isn't entirely bad, as I feel these tools are often better than the ones supplied with Visual Basic.

Creating a Data Link

Before you can use the Data View Window, you need to create a link to the database. After opening the Data View Window, right click on the Data Link icon and select Add a Data Link from the pop-up menu. This will display the same Data Link Properties dialog box that you've seen many times by now (see Figure 13-3). Simply select the proper OLE DB provider for your database, enter the connection information, and press OK to return to the Data View Window.

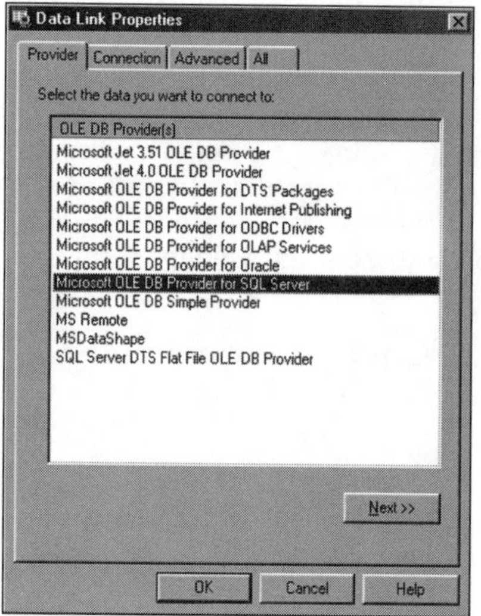

Figure 13-3: Viewing the Data Link Properties window yet again

Creating a stored procedure

If you expand your newly created Data Link icon, you'll see each of the four types of objects available for you to manipulate: Database Diagrams, Tables, Views and Stored Procedures. Double clicking on the Stored Procedures icon will display the list of stored procedures in the database, and right clicking on the same icon and selecting New Stored Procedure from the po-up menu will allow you to create a new stored procedure (see Figure 13-4).

The New Stored Procedure window is a simple editor with a series of buttons across the top of the screen. The same window will be used to edit an existing stored procedure. The only difference is that the name of the existing stored procedure will be displayed in the title bar. The icons that appear in the toolbar are explained below:

- ✦ **New Stored Procedure** – prompts you to save your changes and then displays a skeleton stored procedure for you to edit.
- ✦ **Open Text File** – asks if you want to overwrite the existing text and then displays a File Open dialog box to load a text file into the edit window.
- ✦ **Save to Database** – saves your stored procedure to the database.

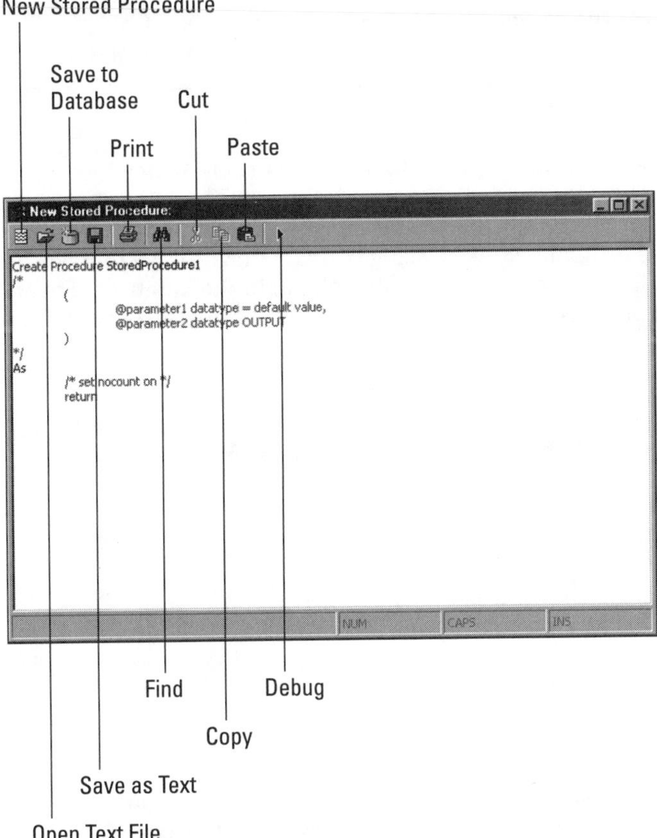

Figure 13-4: Creating a stored procedure

- **Save as Text** – saves your stored procedure to a text file.
- **Print** – sends your stored procedure to the default Windows printer.
- **Find** – displays a Find dialog box.
- **Cut/Copy/Paste** – performs the standard editing function using the clipboard.
- **Debug** – starts the stored procedure debugger.

Coding the stored procedure

Writing a stored procedure is highly dependent on the database server you use. The example I'm going to use here is for the SQL Server 7. However, no matter whose database system you're using, all stored procedures have some things in common. First, they are all created using the **Create Procedure** SQL statement, and can be deleted with the **Drop Procedure** statement. The identifier that follows the **Create Procedure** statement is the name of the stored procedure. Second, all stored procedures accept arguments that allow you to pass parameters to them and return values from them. After the arguments are defined, you enter the statements that comprise the stored procedure.

The Stored Procedure window allows you to build the **Create Procedure** statement that will create your stored procedure. Listing 13-4 shows a stored procedure that performs the same function as the **Select** statement I've been using throughout this chapter in the sample program. It takes a single parameter, `@State` that has a type of **Char(2)**, which is the same type as the State column in the database. The `@State` parameter is used in place of the question mark in the parameterized **Select** statement in the previous example.

Listing 13-4: The CountByState stored procedure

```
Create Procedure CountByState (@State Char(2)) As

Select Count(*)
From Customers
Where State = @State
Return
```

Saving the stored procedure

Pressing the Save to Database button will execute the **Create Procedure** statement on the database server and will create a stored procedure using the name `CountByState`. If you want to edit the stored procedure, simply expand the Stored Procedures icon on the Data View window and double click on `CountByName`. This will display the same SQL statement, with one minor difference. The words **Create Procedure** will be replaced with **Alter Procedure**.

Debugging stored procedures

The T-SQL Debugger allows you to debug stored procedures directly from Visual Basic. This tool only works with SQL Server 6.5 and later databases. The debugger can be called directly from Visual Basic. Before you can use the debugger, you must install the appropriate code on your database server.

Installing the SQL Server debugging support

The setup program is contained in the `\SQDBG_SS` directory on disk 2 of the Visual Basic installation CD-ROMs. You can even run the setup program while your SQL Server database is running.

When you start the setup program, you'll see a dialog box similar to the one shown in Figure 13-5 reminding you that this utility is not part of SQL Server, but part of Visual Basic. If you agree with the license information, press the Continue button.

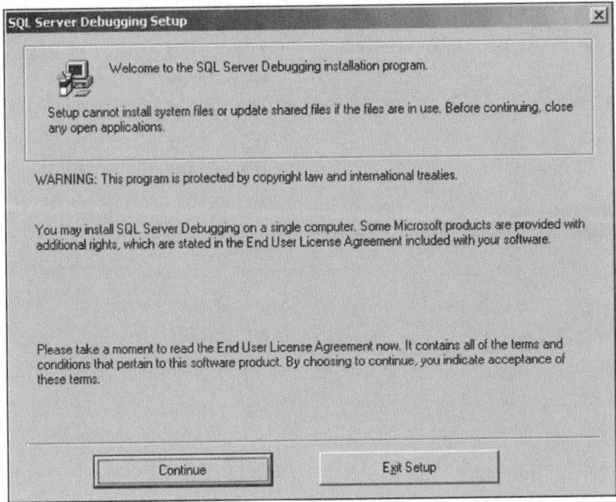

Figure 13-5: Reviewing license information for the SQL Server Debugging facility

The next few dialog boxes will ask you to verify your name and organization information and to enter the CD Key from the back of your Visual Basic CD-ROM case. Enter the information as requested and press OK or Continue at each step of the wizard until you reach the Installation dialog box shown in Figure 13-6. You can change the directory where the software will be installed by pressing the Change Folder button. When you're ready to begin, press the square Server button. The setup program will then install the debugging support feature.

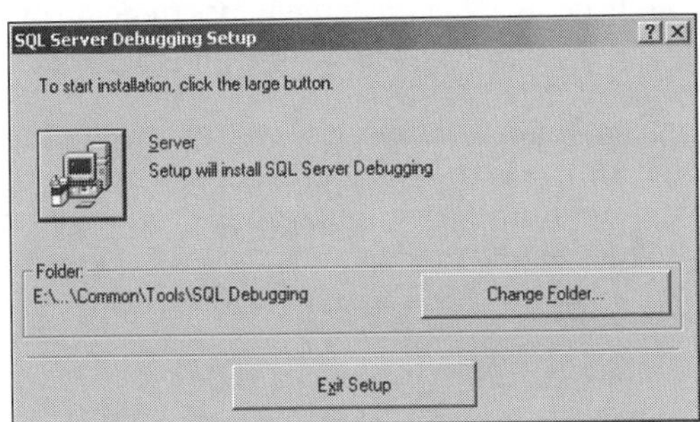

Figure 13-6: Starting the installation program

I got this weird error: If you get a strange error while trying to start the T-SQL Debugger and it instructs you to look in the client log on the database server, most likely the SQL Server Debugging support has not been installed.

Setting T-SQL Debugging Options

Before you use the T-SQL Debugger, you should review the options. To display the options, choose Tools ➪ T-SQL Debugging Options from the Visual Basic main menu. This will bring up the T-SQL Debugging Options dialog box, as shown in Figure 13-7.

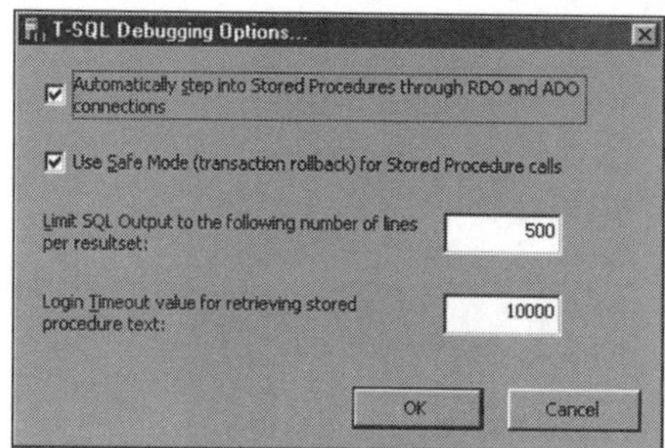

Figure 13-7: Setting debugging options

There are four options you can set. Checking the *Automatically step into Stored Procedures through RDO and ADO connections* will automatically start the debugger anytime you execute a stored procedure while running your Visual Basic program. If this box is not checked, the debugger will not be used at runtime. Checking *Use Safe Mode (transaction rollback) for Stored Procedure calls* means that any changes made by the stored procedure while in debug mode are discarded.

Sometimes it works and sometimes it doesn't: I've noticed that changing these properties don't always take effect the next time you run your program in the IDE. I suggest running your program and ending it before you attempt to do anything. Then run the program again, and the debugger should behave properly.

The *Limit SQL Output to the following number of lines per resultset* determines the upper limit in the number of rows that will be retrieved while debugging the procedure. This value helps to ensure that your stored procedure doesn't run out of control. The *Login Timeout value for retrieving stored procedure text* sets the maximum amount of time the debugger will wait to connect to the database server.

Starting the T-SQL Debugger

You can run the T-SQL Debugger directly from Visual Basic by choosing Add-Ins ÿ T-SQL Debugger from the main menu. This will display the Visual Basic T-SQL Batch Debugger dialog box (see Figure 13-8). You need to provide the information in this window to connect to the database to select and run your stored procedure.

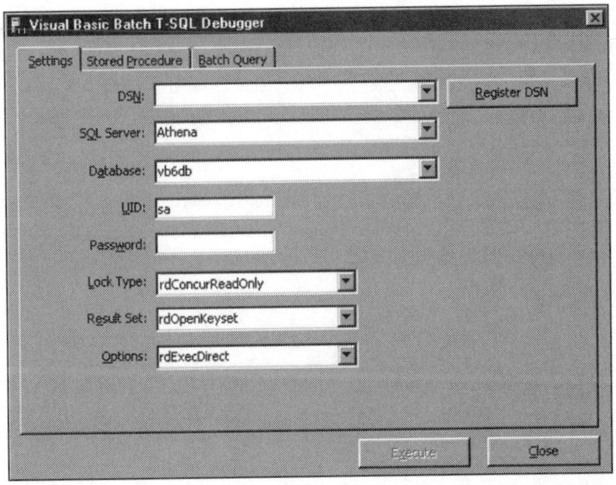

Figure 13-8: Setting options in the T-SQL Debugger window

To connect to an SQL Server database using OLE DB, simply enter the name of your database server in the SQL Server drop-down box, specify the name of the database you want to use in the Database drop down box, and supply your user name and password in the *UID* and *Password* fields. You can also define an ODBC connection by pressing the Define DSN button.

Once these values are set, the Stored Procedure and Batch Query tabs will be enabled. To debug a stored procedure, select the Stored Procedure tab (see Figure 13-9) and choose the stored procedure you want to debug in the Procedure Name drop-down box. Then select each of the parameters listed in the *Parameters* area and assign them the values you want to use during the execution.

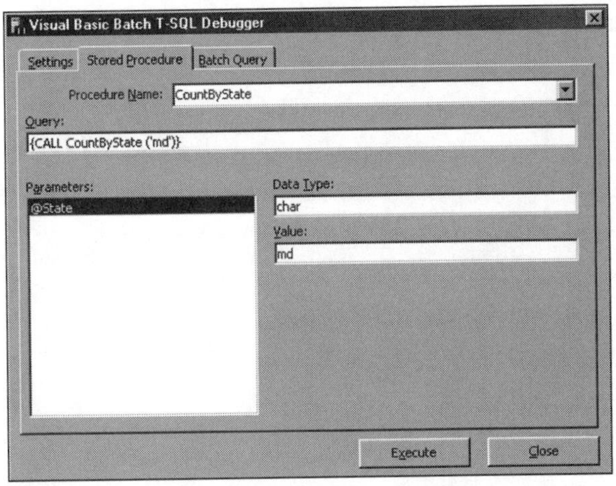

Figure 13-9: Selecting the stored procedure and entering its parameters

Run simple queries: You can use the Batch Query tab in the Visual Basic T-SQL Debugger to run any block of SQL statements you may choose using the T-SQL Debugger.

Running the Debugger

After you have finished entering values for all of the parameters, press the Execute button on the Stored Procedure tab of the Visual Basic Batch T-SQL Debugger to start a debugging session. The T-SQL Debugger window will be displayed (see Figure 13-10).

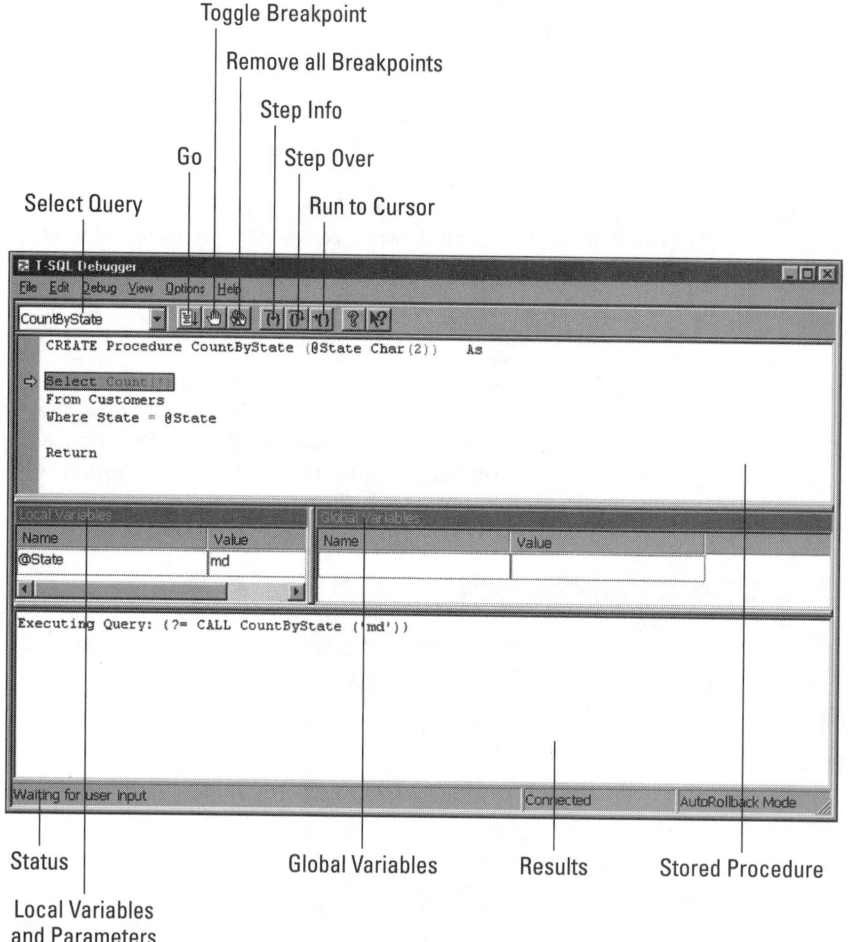

Figure 13-10: Running the T-SQL Debugger

✦ **Select Query** – allows you to choose from multiple queries you may be debugging at the same time.

✦ **Go** – runs the query to completion from the current statement or to the next breakpoint.

✦ **Toggle Breakpoint** – enables or disables a breakpoint at the specified line of code.

✦ **Removes All Breakpoints** – removes all of the breakpoints in the stored procedure.

✦ **Step Into** – runs the stored procedure until the specified subexpression is reached

✦ **Step Over** – runs the selected subexpression.

✦ **Run To Cursor** – runs the stored procedure up to where the cursor is pointing.

✦ **Stored Procedure** – contains the text of the stored procedure. This area is used to display the currently active statement and any breakpoints that have been set.

✦ **Local Variables and Parameters** – this section contains variables local to the stored procedure and their current values. You can edit a value by double clicking on the value to select it and entering a new value.

✦ **Global Variables** – this section contains the global variables for the stored procedure and their current values. These values may also be changed while the stored procedure is waiting for user input.

✦ **Results** – displays any rows returned by a **Select** statement and also describes the current state of execution.

✦ **Status** - describes the current state of the debugger. If the message *Waiting for user input* is displayed, the debugger is in break mode and waiting for you to resume execution.

Calling a stored procedure

As you might expect, defining a stored procedure in a `Command` object isn't much different than defining an SQL statement (see Listing 13-5). In place of the SQL statement, you will need to specify the name of the stored procedure in the `CommandText` property. You should specify `adCmdStoredProc` as the value of `CommandType`.

One advantage of using stored procedures is the ability to automatically retrieve the parameter definitions rather than manually defining each `Parameter` object and adding it to the `Parameters` collection. Simply use the `Refresh` method of the `Parameters` collection to retrieve the definitions from the database. Then you may assign values to each parameter by name as you did when you explicitly defined the parameters.

Listing 13-5: The CountByState stored procedure

```
Private Sub Command6_Click()

Dim c As ADODB.Command
Dim p As ADODB.Parameter
Dim rs As ADODB.Recordset

On Error Resume Next

Set c = New ADODB.Command
Set c.ActiveConnection = db
c.CommandText = "CountByState"
c.CommandType = adCmdStoredProc

c.Parameters.Refresh
c.Parameters("@State").Value = Text4.Text

db.Errors.Clear
Set rs = c.Execute
If db.Errors.Count > 0 Then
   WriteError

Else
   StatusBar1.SimpleText = "Response: " & _
      FormatNumber(rs.Fields(0).Value, 0)

End If

End Sub
```

Thoughts on Stored Procedures

Using stored procedures is very important when building applications for Oracle. They can make a significant difference in how your application performs. However, stored procedures are not as important for SQL Server 7 databases. SQL Server 7 prepares an SQL statement the first time it encounters it during your program's execution and retains it so that the next time you use it, it won't have to prepare it again. This doesn't mean that you shouldn't use stored procedures in SQL Server 7, because they don't make as big of a difference as they do with an Oracle database.

`Command` objects are necessary when you want to execute a stored procedure or any SQL statement other than a **Select** statement. Also, `Command` objects are important when you want to use parameter-based queries. The rest of the time, you can perform the same function directly using the `Recordset` object, a topic that will be covered in the next chapter.

Summary

In this chapter you learned the following:

- ✦ You can define a `Command` object to hold a frequently executed SQL statement or stored procedure.
- ✦ You can define `Parameter` objects which contain information that is passed to a stored procedure or parameterized query for execution.
- ✦ You can easily create and edit stored procedures directly in Visual Basic.
- ✦ You can install the stored procedure debugger routines into your database server so that you can debug stored procedures directly from Visual Basic.

✦ ✦ ✦

Working with Recordsets – Part I

In This Chapter

The Recordset object

Exploring various types of locks

Choosing a cursor type

Opening a recordset

Of all of the objects in ADO, the `Recordset` object is the one you'll use the most. It contains the actual data from your database. You can use this object to retrieve, insert, update, and delete information from the database. It can be used as a data source for other controls, just like the ADO Data Control. In fact the ADO Data Control exposes a reference to the `Recordset` object, you can access the information contained in the underlying recordset directly.

This chapter and the next two are dedicated to the topic of recordsets. In this chapter, I'm going to discuss the various properties, methods, and events in a `Recordset` object. Then I'll discuss how to open and use a `Recordset` object. In the next chapter, I'll continue discussing the `Recordset` object and cover how to move around inside recordsets and how to access the individual fields. Finally, in Chapter 16 I'll cover the issues related to updating the data contained in a recordset.

The Recordset Object

The `Recordset` object contains the set of rows retrieved from a database query. Various properties and methods instruct the OLE DB provider on how the rows should be returned from the database and how the provider should handle updates and locking to ensure proper access to the data. Other properties and methods in the `Recordset` object allow you to access the set of rows retrieved.

Birds of a Feather aren't at the first record of the Recordset: There is a common misconception that when BOF is TRUE, you are at the first record of the Recordset. This isn't true. When BOF is TRUE, the current record pointer is before the first record in the Recordset, and there isn't a current record. The same is true for EOF, except in that case, the current record pointer is beyond the last record in the Recordset.

Recordset object properties

Table 14-1 lists the properties associated with the Recordset object. Tables 14-2 through 14-8 contain additional information about individual properties in the Recordset object.

Table 14-1
Properties of the Recordset Object

Property	*Description*
AbsolutePage	A Long value containing the absolute page number of the current record in the Recordset ranging from 1 to PageCount. This value may also be adPosBOF (-2) if the current record is at the beginning of the file or adPosEOF (-3) if the current record is at the end of the file. A value of adPosUnknown (-1) may be used if the Recordset is empty or the provider doesn't support this property.
AbsolutePosition	A Long value containing the absolute position of the current record in the Recordset ranging from 1 to RecordCount. This value may also be adPosBOF (-2) if the current record is at the beginning of the file or adPosEOF (-3) if the current record is at the end of the file. A value of adPosUnknown (-1) may be used if the Recordset is empty or the provider doesn't support this property.
ActiveCommand	An object reference to the Command object that created the Recordset. If the Recordset wasn't created using a Command object, this property will have a **Null** object reference.
ActiveConnection	A Variant array containing either a String value with a valid connection string or an object reference to a Connection object.
BOF	A Boolean value that is TRUE when the current record position is before the first record in the Recordset.

Property	Description
Bookmark	A Variant that sets or returns a value that uniquely identifies the current record in the current Recordset object. You can save this property and move to a different record. Then you can restore the value to return back to the original record.
CacheSize	A Long value containing the number of records kept in the provider's cache. The default value for this property is 1.
CursorLocation	An enumerated value that indicates where the cursor is maintained (see Table 14-2).
CursorType	An enumerated value that specifies the type of cursor that will be used on the Recordset. (see Table 14-3).
DataMember	A String containing the name of the data member that will be retrieved using the DataSource property. Works with the DataSource property to bind a Recordset to a control.
DataSource	An object reference that indicates the data source when using bound controls.
EditMode	An enumerated value containing the edit mode of the current record (see Table 14-4).
EOF	A Boolean value that is TRUE when the current record position is after the last record in the Recordset.
Fields	An object reference to a Fields collection containing the fields associated with the current record.
Filter	A Variant value containing one of the following: a String value containing an expression similar to that in a **Where** clause that will select only those records meeting the specified criteria; an Array of bookmarks; or a Long value selected from Table 14-5.
Index	A String containing the name of an index that is used in conjunction with the Seek method.
LockType	An enumerated value containing the locking mode used by the Recordset when retrieving records (see Table 14-6).
MarshalOptions	An enumerated value that indicates how records are to be marshaled back to the server. Applies only to Recordsets with client-side cursors (discussed later in this chapter). The default value is adMarshalAll (0), which returns all rows back to the server for processing, while adMarshalModifiedOnly (1) returns only the modified rows.

Continued

Table 14-1 *(continued)*

Property	*Description*
`MaxRecords`	A `Long` value that specifies the maximum number of rows to be returned. A value of zero implies there is no maximum limit.
`PageCount`	A `Long` value containing the number of pages of data in the `Recordset`. The number of records in a page is specified by the `PageSize` property, while the current page number is specified in the `AbsolutePage` property.
`PageSize`	A `Long` value containing the number of records in a single page.
`Properties`	An object reference to a `Properties` collection containing provider specific information.
`RecordCount`	A `Long` value containing the number of records retrieved. If the provider is not able to determine the number of records retrieved or a forward-only cursor is selected, this property will have a value of –1.
`Sort`	Specifies a list one or more of field names on which the `Recordset` will be sorted. Multiple fields need to be separated by commas, and each field name may be followed by ASC or DESC to sort the fields in either ascending or descending order. The syntax is basically the same as the **Order By** clause in the **Select** statement. This property is only valid when you use a client-side cursor (discussed later in this chapter).
`Source`	A `Variant` which can either be a `String` containing the name of a table, a SQL Statement, or the name of a stored procedure or an object reference to a `Command` object.
`State`	A `Long` value describing the current state of the `Recordset` object. Multiple values can be combined to describe the current state (see Table 14-7 for a list of values).
`Status`	A `Long` value describing the current status of a record in a batch update (see Table 14-8).
`StayInSync`	A `Boolean` value that when `TRUE` means that the reference to child records in a hierarchical `Recordset` will automatically be changed when the parent row's position changes. The default value for this property is `TRUE`.

Table 14-2
Values for CursorLocation

Constant	*Value*	*Description*
`adUseNone`	1	Doesn't use cursor services. This value should not be selected and exists solely for compatibility.
`adUseServer`	2	The cursor services are provided by the data provider.
`adUseClient`	3	The cursor services are provided by a local cursor library, which may provide more features than the data provider's cursor library provides.

Table 14-3
Values for CursorType

Constant	*Value*	*Description*
`adOpenUnspecified`	-1	The type of cursor isn't specified.
`adOpenForwardOnly`	0	A forward-only cursor is used, which permits you only to scroll forward through the records in the `Recordset`.
`adOpenKeyset`	1	A keyset cursor is used, which is similar to a dynamic cursor, but doesn't permit you to see records added by other users.
`adOpenDynamic`	2	A dynamic cursor is used, which allows you to see records added by other users, plus any changes and deletions made by other users.
`adOpenStatic`	3	A static cursor is used, which prevents you from seeing any and all changes from other users.

Table 14-4
Values for EditMode

Constant	*Value*	*Description*
adEditNone	0	Editing is not active; the data in the current record hasn't been changed.
adEditInProgress	1	The data in the current record has been changed, but not yet saved.
adEditAdd	2	The AddNew method has been used to create a new record, but the record hasn't been saved yet.
adEditDelete	4	The current record has been deleted.

Table 14-5
Values for Filter

Constant	*Value*	*Description*
adFilterNone	0	Removes all filtering criteria.
adFilterPendingRecords	1	Selects only those records that have been changed, but not sent to the server for updating. Applies to batch update mode only.
adFilterAffectedRecords	2	Selects only those records that have been affected by the last CancelBatch, Delete, Resync, or UpdateBatch.
adFilterFetchedRecords	3	Selects only those records in the current cache.
adFilterConflictingRecords	5	Selects only those records that have failed the last batch update.

Table 14-6
Values for LockMode

Constant	*Value*	*Description*
adLockUnspecified	-1	The type of locking isn't specified.
adLockReadOnly	1	Doesn't permit you to change any values.

Constant	Value	Description
adLockPessimistic	2	Records are locked at the data source record by record once the data in the record has been changed.
adLockOptimistic	3	Records are locked only when you call the UpdateMethod.
adLockBatchOptimistic	4	Records are not locked, and conflicts will be returned for resolution after the UpdateBatch method has completed.

Table 14-7
Values for State

Constant	Value	Description
adStateClosed	0	The Command object is closed.
adStateOpen	1	The Command object is open.
adStateConnecting	2	The Command object is connecting to the database.
adStateExecuting	4	The Command object is executing.
adStateFetching	8	Rows are being retrieved.

Table 14-8
Values for Status

Constant	Value	Description
adRecOK	0	The record was successfully updated.
adRecNew	1	The record is new.
adRecModified	2	The record has been modified.
adRecDeleted	4	The record has been deleted.
adRecUnmodified	8	The record has not been modified.
adRecInvalid	16	The record wasn't saved because its bookmark was invalid.

Continued

Table 14-8 (continued)

Constant	*Value*	*Description*
adRecMultipleChanges	64	The record wasn't saved because it would have affected multiple records.
adRecPendingChanges	128	The record wasn't saved because it refers to a pending insert.
adRecCanceled	256	The record wasn't saved because the operation was canceled.
adRecCantRelease	1024	The new record wasn't saved because the existing record was locked.
adRecConcurrencyViolation	2048	The record wasn't saved because optimistic concurrency was in use.
adRecIntegrityViolation	4096	The record wasn't saved because the data violated an integrity constraint.
adRecMaxChangesExceeded	8192	The record wasn't saved because there were too many pending changes.
adRecObjectOpen	16384	The record wasn't saved because of a conflict with an open storage object.
adRecOutOfMemory	32768	The record wasn't saved because the computer ran out of memory.
adRecPermissionDenied	65536	The record wasn't saved because the user doesn't have sufficient permissions.
adRecSchemaViolation	131072	The record wasn't saved because it violates the underlying database structure.
adRecDBDeleted	262144	The record has already been deleted from the data source.

Recordset object methods

The Recordset object contains many different methods to manipulate the data in the Recordset.

Sub AddNew ([FieldList], [Values])

The AddNew method is used to add a new empty record to the Recordset. This will set the EditMode property to adEditAdd. After assigning values to each of the fields, you can use the Update method to save the changes. If you specify the FieldList and Values parameters, the values are immediately saved to the database and no call to Update is needed.

In batch update mode, you proceed as above. The changes will be saved locally in the Recordset, but not sent to the server. After adding the last record of the batch, you must call the UpdateBatch method to save the changes to the database. Then you should set the Filter property to adFilterConflicting and take the appropriate action for the records that weren't posted to the database properly.

FieldList is optional and is either a String value containing a single field name or a String Array containing a list of field names.

Values is an optional Variant containing a single value corresponding to a single field name or Array of values corresponding to the Array of field names.

Sub Cancel()

The Cancel method is used to terminate an asynchronous task started by the Open method.

Sub CancelBatch ([AffectRecords As AffectEnum = adAffectAll])

The CancelBatch method is used to cancel a pending batch update. If the current record hasn't been saved, CancelBatch will automatically call CancelUpdate to discard any changes. As with all batch operations, you should verify the Status property for all of the affected records to ensure that they were properly canceled.

AffectRecords is an enumerated type that describes which records will be affected by the cancel operation (see Table 14-9).

Table 14-9
Values for AffectRecords

Constant	*Value*	*Description*
adAffectCurrent	1	Affects only the current record in the Recordset.
adAffectGroup	2	Affects only those records selected by the current value of the Filter property.
adAffectAll	3	Affects all records in the Recordset.
adAffectAllChapters	4	Affects all records in all chapters of the Recordset.

Sub CancelUpdate ()

The CancelUpdate method is used to abandon all of the changes made to a record and to restore its values to the original values before the Update method is called. If you use CancelUpdate to undo a row added with the AddNew method, the newly added row will be discarded, and the current record will become the row that was the current row before the AddNew method was used.

Function Clone ([LockType As LockTypeEnum = adLockTypeUnspecified]) As Recordset

The Clone method is used to create a duplicate of a Recordset object. LockType allows you to specify that the new Recordset object is read-only. The only permissible values are adLockUnspecified and adLockReadOnly.

Sub Close

The Close method closes an open Recordset and frees all of its associated resources. If you are editing a record in the Recordset, an error will occur, and the Close method will be terminated. You need to call either Update or CancelUpdate first. If you are working in batch mode, all changes since the last UpdateBatch will be lost.

Sub CompareBookmarks(Bookmark1, Bookmark2) As CompareEnum

The CompareBookmarks method compares two bookmarks and returns information about their relative positions. Both bookmarks must come from the same Recordset object or from clones of the same Recordset object. Table 14-10 contains a list of possible return values.

Bookmark1 and Bookmark2 are valid bookmarks.

Table 14-10
Values for CompareEnum

Constant	*Value*	*Description*
adCompareLessThan	0	The first bookmark is before the second bookmark.
adCompareEqual	1	The two bookmarks are equal.
adCompareGreaterThan	2	The first bookmark is after the second bookmark.
adCompareNotEqual	3	The two bookmarks are different and not ordered.
adCompareNotComparable	4	The bookmarks can't be compared.

Sub Delete ([AffectRecords As AffectEnum = adAffectCurrent])

The `Delete` method is used to delete one or more records from a `Recordset` object.

`AffectRecords` is an enumerated type that describes which records will be deleted by this operation (see Table 14-9). The default value is `adAffectCurrent`, which means only the current row will be deleted.

Sub Find (Criteria As String, [SkipRows As Long], [SearchDirection As SearchDirectionEnum = adSearchForward], [Start])

The `Find` method is used to locate the specified criteria in a `Recordset`. Note that you must have a valid current record before calling the `Find` method, so you may want to call `MoveFirst` before using this method.

`Criteria` is a `String` value that specifies a field name, a comparison operator, and a value. Only one field name may be specified.

`SkipRows` is a `Long` value that specifies the number of rows to skip relative to the current row before starting the search. The default value is zero, which means the search will begin with the current row.

`SearchDirection` is an enumerated type that indicates the direction of the search. You can specify `adSearchForward` (1) to search to the end of the `Recordset`, or you can specify `adSearchBackward` (-1) to search to the beginning of the `Recordset`.

`Start` is a `Variant` containing a bookmark for the first record to be searched.

Function GetRows ([Rows As Long = -1], [Start], [Fields]) As Variant

The `GetRows` method retrieves multiple records from a `Recordset` object into a two-dimensional array.

`Rows` is the number of rows to be retrieved. The default value is `adGetRowsRest` (-1), which will retrieve the rest of the rows in the table.

`Start` is an optional `Variant` containing a bookmark for the first row to be retrieved. If you do not specify values for both `Rows` and `Start`, all of the rows in the table will be retrieved.

`Fields` is an optional `Variant` containing a `String` with a single field name, a `String` array with multiple field names, the index of the field, or an array of field index values.

Function GetString ([StringFormat As StringFormatEnum = adClipString], [NumRows As Long = -1], [ColumnDelimiter As String], [RowDelimiter As String], [NullExpr As String]) As String

The `GetString` method returns a `String` containing the values from the `Recordset`.

`StringFormat` is a `Long` value containing the value `adClipString` (2). This is the only legal value for this method.

`NumRows` is a `Long` value containing the number of rows to be saved in the string. A value of –1 means that all of the rows will be retrieved.

`ColumnDelimiter` is a `String` containing the delimiter to be used between each column. If not specified, a tab character will be used.

`RowDelimiter` is a `String` containing the delimiter to be used between each row. If not specified, a carriage return character will be used.

`NullExpr` is a `String` containing the value to be displayed in place of a null value. If it is not specified, nothing will be output.

To CSV or not to CSV: I often find it useful to create Comma Separated Value files from a database. These files can be easily imported into a program like Excel for analysis and testing. The `GetString` method makes it easy to write a program to save your data into a CSV file. Simply specify a comma for `ColumnDelimiter` and `vbCrLf` for the `RowDelimiter`.

Sub Move (NumRecords As Long, [Start])

The `Move` method is used to move the current record pointer to a different location in the `Recordset`. If the `Recordset` is already at `BOF`, an attempt to move backwards will generate a runtime error. Similarly, if the `Recordset` is already at `EOF`, an attempt to move forward will also generate a runtime error.

`NumRecords` is a `Long` value containing the number of records to be moved. If a value of zero is specified, the current record pointer remains unchanged, and the current record is refreshed. A value greater than zero means that the current record position will be moved to the end of the `Recordset`, while a value less than zero will move the current record pointer towards the beginning of the `Recordset`.

`Start` is a `Variant` containing a bookmark that will be used as the starting position for the move.

Forward-NOT-only: Even if you specify a forward-only cursor, you can still move backward using the `Move` method, as long as you do not move beyond the records in the current cache.

Sub MoveFirst ()

The MoveFirst method moves the current record pointer to the first record in the Recordset.

MoveFirst first: I usually find it a good idea to call MoveFirst after opening a Recordset to ensure that I have a valid record ready for processing.

Sub MoveLast()

The MoveLast method moves the current record pointer to the last record in the Recordset. Note that you can't use the MoveLast method with a forward-only cursor.

Sub MoveNext ()

The MoveNext method moves the current record pointer to the next record in the Recordset. If the current record pointer is at the last record in the Recordset, the current record pointer will be moved to EOF. If the current record pointer is already at EOF, a call to MoveNext will cause a runtime error.

Sub MovePrevious ()

The MovePrevious method moves the current record pointer to the previous record in the Recordset. If the current record pointer is on the first record in the Recordset, the current record pointer will be moved to BOF. If the current record pointer is already at BOF, a call to MovePrevious will trigger a runtime error.

Function NextRecordset ([RecordsAffected]) As Recordset

The NextRecordset method clears the current Recordset object and returns the next Recordset that resulted from a query or stored procedure that returned multiple Recordsets. RowsAffected is a Long value containing the number of records affected.

Sub Open ([Source As Variant], [ActiveConnection As Variant], [CursorType As CursorTypeEnum = adOpenUnspecified], [LockType As LockTypeEnum], [Options As Long = -1])

The Open method opens a new Recordset object.

Source is a Variant containing an object reference to a valid Command object; an object reference of a valid Stream object containing a persistently stored Recordset; or a String containing a SQL statement, a table name, the name of a stored procedure, a URL, or the name of a file.

`ActiveConnection` is a `Variant` that contains an object reference to an open `Connection` object or a `String` value that contains the same connection information found in the `ConnectionString` property.

`CursorType` is an enumerated value (see Table 14-11) that specifies the type of cursor that will be used on the `Recordset`.

`LockType` is an enumerated value (see Table 14-12) containing the locking mode used by the `Recordset` when retrieving records.

`Options` optionally passes one of the values specified in Table 14-3.

Table 14-11
Values for CursorType

Constant	*Value*	*Description*
`adOpenUnspecified`	-1	The type of cursor isn't specified.
`adOpenForwardOnly`	0	A forward-only cursor is used, which permits you only to scroll forward through the records in the `Recordset`.
`adOpenKeyset`	1	A keyset cursor is used, which is similar to a dynamic cursor, but doesn't permit you to see records added by other users.
`adOpenDynamic`	2	A dynamic cursor is used, which allows you to see records added by other users, plus any changes and deletions made by other users.
`adOpenStatic`	3	A static cursor is used, which prevents you from seeing any and all changes from other users.

Table 14-12
Values for LockType

Constant	*Value*	*Description*
`adLockUnspecified`	-1	The type of locking isn't specified.
`adLockReadOnly`	1	Doesn't permit you to change any values.
`adLockPessimistic`	2	Records are locked at the data source record by record once the data in the record has been changed.

Constant	Value	Description
adLockOptimistic	3	Records are locked only when you call the UpdateMethod.
adLockBatchOptimistic	4	Records are not locked, and conflicts will be returned for resolution after the UpdateBatch method has completed.

Sub Requery ([Options As Long = -1])

The Requery method gets a fresh copy of the data in a Recordset by re-executing the query that originally generated the Recordset.

Options is a Long value that describes how to execute the query. You may set its value to any combination of the following values described in Table 14-13: adAsyncExecute, adAsyncFetch, adAsynchFetchNonBlocking, and adExecuteNoRecords. If omitted, none of these values will be selected.

Table 14-13
Values for Options

Constant	Value	Description
adOptionUnspecified	-1	No options are specified.
adCmdText	1	CommandText contains either a SQL statement or a stored procedure call.
adCmdTable	2	CommandText contains the name of a table in the database.
adCmdStoredProcedure	4	CommandText contains the name of a stored procedure.
adCmdUnknown	8	The type of command isn't known.
adAsyncExecute	16	The command should be executed asynchronously.
adAsyncFetch	32	After the number of rows specified in the CacheSize property of the Recordset object are returned, the remaining rows will be returned asynchronously.

Continued

Table 14-13 (continued)

Constant	Value	Description
adAsyncFetchNonBlocking	64	The main thread isn't blocked while retrieving rows. If the current row hasn't been retrieved, the current row will be moved to the end of the file.
adExecuteNoRecords	128	Indicates that the command will not return any rows or will automatically discard any rows that are generated. Must be used with either the adCmdText or adCmdStoredProcedure values.
adCmdFile	256	CommandText is the name of a persistently stored Recordset.
adCmdTableDirect	512	CommandText contains the name of a database table.

Sub Resync ([AffectRecords As AffectEnum], [ResyncValues As ResyncEnum)

The Resync method gets any updates to the data that may have happened while using a static or forward-only cursor. Unlike the Requery method, the Resync method does not re-execute the query associated with the Recordset, so any rows added since the original query was executed will not be visible.

AffectRecords is an enumerated type that describes which records will be affected by the cancel operation (see Table 14-9).

ResyncValues is an enumerated type that determines how changed records in the Recordset will be handled. A value of adResyncUnderlyingValues (1) means that all pending updates are saved, while a value of adResyncAllValues (2) means that all pending updates are canceled (default).

Sub Save ([Destination], [PersistFormat As PersistFormatEnum])

The Save method is used to save a local copy of an open Recordset (including any child recordsets associated with it) to a disk file or a Stream object. If you have an active filter on the Recordset, only the filtered records will be saved. After the first time you call the Save method, you should omit the Destination parameter, because the destination remains open. If you specify the same value for Destination a second time, a runtime error will occur. If you specify a different value, both destinations will remain open. Closing the Recordset will also close the Destination.

Destination is a Variant value containing either an object reference to a Stream or a String containing the fully qualified filename where the data will be stored.

PersistFormat is an enumerated data type whose value is either adPersistADTG (0), which will save the Recordset in the Advanced Data TableGram (ADTG) format (default), or adPersistXML (1), which will save the Recordset using XML format.

Sub Seek (KeyValues, [SeekOption As SeekEnum])

The Seek method is used to move the cursor to a new location in the Recordset. It works with the Index property to search the specified index for a particular value.

KeyValues is an array of Variant values, corresponding to the columns in the index.

SeekOption is an enumerated data type that specifies how to perform the comparison (see Table 14-14).

Table 14-14
Values for SeekOption

Constant	*Value*	*Description*
adSeekFirstEQ	1	Seeks the first row with a key value equal to KeyValues.
adSeekLastEQ	2	Seeks the last row with a key value equal to KeyValues.
adSeekAfterEQ	4	Seeks the first row with a key value greater than or equal to KeyValues.
adSeekAfter	8	Seeks the first row with a key value greater than KeyValues.
adSeekBeforeEQ	16	Seeks the first row with a key value just less than or equal to KeyValues.
adSeekBefore	32	Seeks the first row with a key value just less than KeyValues.

Clients not wanted: The Seek method will not work with client-side cursors (discussed later in this chapter), so select adUseServer for the CursorType property.

Function Supports (CursorOptions As CursorOptionEnum) As Boolean

The `Supports` method returns `TRUE` if the data provider supports the combination of values specified in `CursorOptions`. `CursorOptions` is a `Long` value whose value is created by adding one or more values of the values listed in Table 14-15 together.

Table 14-15
Values for CursorOptions

Constant	*Value*	*Description*
`adHoldRecords`	256	The provider will retrieve more records or changes to another position without committing all pending changes.
`adMovePrevious`	512	The provider supports the `MoveFirst`, `MovePrevious`, `Move`, and `GetRows` methods to move the cursor backwards without requiring bookmarks.
`adBookmark`	8192	The provider supports the `Bookmark` property.
`adApproxPosition`	16384	The provider supports the `AbsolutePosition` and `AbsolutePage` properties.
`adUpdateBatch`	65536	The provider supports the `UpdateBatch` and `Cancel` batch methods.
`adResync`	131072	The provider supports the `Resync` method.
`adNotify`	262144	The provider supports notifications, which implies that `Recordset` events are supported.
`adFind`	524288	The provider supports the `Find` method.
`adSeek`	4194304	The provider supports the `Seek` method.
`adIndex`	8388608	The provider supports the `Index` property.
`adAddNew`	16778240	The provider supports the `AddNew` method.
`adDelete`	16779264	The provider supports the `Delete` position.
`adUpdate`	16779984	The provider supports the `Update` method.

Sub Update ([Fields], [Values])

The `Update` method saves any changes you make the current row of a `Recordset`. You can either update the row directly by accessing each field by using the `Recordset`'s `Fields` collection, or you can specify a list of fields and their values by using the `Fields` and `Values` properties.

If you move to another row in the Recordset, ADO will automatically call the Update method to save your changes. You must explicitly call the CancelUpdate method to discard any changes you may have made before moving to another row.

Fields is a Variant value containing a single field name or a Variant array containing a list of field names.

Values is a Variant value containing a single value or a Variant array containing a list of values, whose position in the array correspond to the field names in the Fields parameter.

All or none: You must specify both the Fields and Values parameters or neither. Specifying only one will cause an error. Also if you pass an array for Fields, the Values property must also be an array of an identical size.

Sub UpdateBatch ([AffectRecords As AffectEnum])

The UpdateBatch method saves all pending batch changes to the database. AffectRecords is an enumerated data type indicating which rows in the Recordset will be affected (see Table 14-9).

It sort of worked: You must check the Errors collection after performing a UpdateBatch to determine which rows weren't properly updated. You can set the Filter property to adFilterAffectedRecords and move though the remaining records to identify those with problems by checking the Status property.

Recordset object events

The Recordset object contains many different events to handle various conditions encountered in the Recordset.

Event EndOfRecordset (fMoreData As Boolean, adStatus As EventStatusEnum, pRecordset As Recordset)

The EndOfRecordset event is triggered when the program attempts to move beyond the end of the Recordset. This is most likely triggered by a call to MoveNext. You can use this event to acquire more rows from the database and append them to the end of Recordset to allow the MoveNext to succeed. If you do this, you must set the fMoreData parameter to TRUE to indicate that the cursor is no longer at the end of the Recordset.

fMoreData is a Boolean value where TRUE means that more rows have been added to the Recordset.

adStatus is an enumerated value that indicates the action that should be taken when the event returns (see Table 14-16). When the event is triggered, this value will be set to either adStatusOk or adStatusCantDeny. If it is set to adStatusCantDeny, you can't set the parameter to adStatusCancel.

Table 14-16
Values for EventStatusEnum

Constant	Value	Description
AdStatusOK	1	The operation that triggered the event was successful.
adStatusErrorsOccured	2	The operation that triggered the event failed.
adStatusCantDeny	3	The operation can't be canceled.
adStatusCancel	4	Requests that the operation that triggered the event be canceled.
adStatusUnwantedEvent	5	Prevents subsequent notifications before the event method has finished executing.

pRecordset is an object reference to the Recordset that triggered the event.

Event FetchComplete (pError As Error, adStatus As EventStatusEnum, pRecordset As Recordset)

The FetchComplete event is triggered after all of the rows have been retrieved during an asynchronous operation.

pError is an object reference to an Error object containing any error information. This property is only valid if adStatus is set to adStatusErrorsOccured.

adStatus is an enumerated value that indicates the action that should be taken when the event returns (see Table 14-16). You may also set this value to adStatusUnwantedEvent before the event completes to prevent it from being called again.

pRecordset is an object reference to the Recordset that triggered the event.

Event FetchProgress (Progress As Long, MaxProgress As Long, adStatus As EventStatusEnum, pRecordset As Recordset)

The FetchProgress event is fired periodically during an asynchronous operation to report how many rows have been retrieved.

Progress is a Long value indicating the number of records that have been retrieved so far.

MaxProgress is a Long value indicating the number of records that are expected to be retrieved.

adStatus is an enumerated value that indicates the action that should be taken when the event returns (see Table 14-16).

pRecordset is an object reference to the Recordset that triggered the event.

Event FieldChangeComplete (cFields As Long, Fields, pError asError, adStatus As EventStatusEnum, pRecordset As Recordset)

The FieldChangeComplete event is called after the values of one or more Field objects have been changed. This can happen if the program assigns a value to the Value property of the Field object or by using the Update method and specifying a list of fields and values.

cFields is a Long value indicating the number of fields in Fields.

Fields is an array of object pointers that point to Field objects that were changed.

pError is an Error object containing any error that may have occurred. This value is valid only if adStatus is set to adStatusErrorsOccured.

adStatus is an enumerated value that indicates the action that should be taken when the event returns (see Table 14-16).

pRecordset is an object reference to the Recordset that triggered the event.

Event MoveComplete (adReason As EventReasonEnum, pError As Error, adStatus As EventStatusEnum, pRecordset as Recordset)

The MoveComplete event is called after the current record has changed to a new position in the Recordset.

Counting rows: If you want to display the relative position of the cursor in the Recordset, the MoveComplete event is an ideal place for this. You can easily use the AbsolutePosition property to display the current record number and the RecordCount properties to display the total number of records retrieved.

adReason is an enumerated data type indicating the operation that originally caused the move (see Table 14-17).

Table 14-17
Values for EventReasonEnum

Constant	*Value*	*Description*
adRsnAddNew	1	The operation executed an AddNew method.
adRsnDelete	2	The operation used the Delete method.
adRsnUpdate	3	The operation performed an Update method.
adRsnUndoUpdate	4	The operation reversed an Update method.
adRsnUndoAddNew	5	The operation reversed an AddNew method.
adRsnUndoDelete	6	The operation reversed a Delete method.
adRsnRequery	7	The operation performed a Requery.
adRsnResync	8	The operation performed a Resync.
adRsnClose	9	The operation closed the Recordset.
adRsnMove	10	The operation moved the current record pointer to a different record.
adRsnFirstChange	11	The operation made the first change to a row.
adRsnMoveFirst	12	The operation moved the current record pointer to the first record in the Recordset.
adRsnMoveNext	13	The operation moved the current record pointer to the next record in the Recordset.
adRsnMovePrevious	14	The operation moved the current record pointer to the previous record in the Recordset.
adRsnMoveLast	15	The operation moved the current record pointer to the last record in the Recordset.

pError is an Error object containing any error that may have occurred. This value is only valid if adStatus is set to adStatusErrorsOccured.

adStatus is an enumerated value that indicates the action that should be taken when the event returns (see Table 14-16).

pRecordset is an object reference to the Recordset that triggered the event.

Event RecordChangeComplete (adReason As EventReasonEnum, cRecords As Long, pError As Error, adStatus As EventStatusEnum, pRecordset as Recordset)

The `RecordChangeComplete` event is called after one or more records in the `Recordset` have been changed.

`adReason` is an enumerated data type indicating the operation that originally caused the change (see Table 14-17). Possible values are the following: `adRsnAddNew`, `adRsnDelete`, `adRsnUpdate`, `adRsnUndoUpdate`, `adRsnUndoAddNew`, `adRsnUndoDelete`, and `adRsnFirstChange`.

`cRecords` is a `Long` value containing the number of records that were changed.

`pError` is an `Error` object containing any error that may have occurred. This value is only valid if `adStatus` is set to `adStatusErrorsOccured`.

`adStatus` is an enumerated value that indicates the action that should be taken when the event returns (see Table 14-16).

`pRecordset` is an object reference to the `Recordset` that triggered the event.

Event RecordsetChangeComplete (adReason As EventReasonEnum, pError As Error, adStatus As EventStatusEnum, pRecordset as Recordset)

The `RecordsetChangeComplete` event is called after a change to the `Recordset`.

`adReason` is an enumerated data type indicating the operation that originally caused the move (see Table 14-17). Possible values are the following: `adRsnClose`, `adRsnReQuery`, and `adRsnReSync`.

`pError` is an `Error` object containing any error that may have occurred. This value is only valid if `adStatus` is set to `adStatusErrorsOccured`.

`adStatus` is an enumerated value that indicates the action that should be taken when the event returns (see Table 14-16).

`pRecordset` is an object reference to the `Recordset` that triggered the event.

Event WillChangeField (cFields As Long, Fields, adStatus As EventStatusEnum, pRecordset As Recordset)

The `WillChangeField` event is called before an operation that will change the values in one or more `Field` objects is started. After the changes have been made, the `FieldChangeComplete` event is fired. You can choose to cancel the operation by setting the `adStatus` property to `adStatusCancel`.

`cFields` is a `Long` value indicating the number of fields in `Fields`.

`Fields` is an array of object pointers that point to `Field` objects that are to be changed.

`adStatus` is an enumerated value that indicates the action that should be taken when the event returns (see Table 14-16).

`pRecordset` is an object reference to the `Recordset` that triggered the event.

Event WillChangeRecord (adReason As EventReasonEnum, cRecords As Long, pError As Error, adStatus As EventStatusEnum, pRecordset as Recordset)

The `WillChangeRecord` event is called before one or more records in the `Recordset` will be changed.

`adReason` is an enumerated data type indicating the operation that caused the change (see Table 14-17). Possible values are the following: `adRsnAddNew`, `adRsnDelete`, `adRsnUpdate`, `adRsnUndoUpdate`, `adRsnUndoAddNew`, `adRsnUndoDelete`, and `adRsnFirstChange`.

`cRecords` is a `Long` value containing the number of records will be changed.

`adStatus` is an enumerated value that indicates the action that should be taken when the event returns (see Table 14-16).

`pRecordset` is an object reference to the `Recordset` that triggered the event.

Event WillChangeRecordset (adReason As EventReasonEnum, pError As Error, adStatus As EventStatusEnum, pRecordset as Recordset)

The `WillChangeRecordset` event is called before the `Recordset` is changed.

`adReason` is an enumerated data type indicating the operation that caused the change (see Table 14-17). Possible values are the following: `adRsnClose`, `adRsnReQuery`, and `adRsnReSync`.

pError is an Error object containing any error that may have occurred. This value is only valid if adStatus is set to adStatusErrorsOccured.

adStatus is an enumerated value that indicates the action that should be taken when the event returns (see Table 14-16).

pRecordset is an object reference to the Recordset that triggered the event.

Event WillMove (adReason As EventReasonEnum, adStatus As EventStatusEnum, pRecordset as Recordset)

The WillMove event is called before the current record pointer is changed to a new position in the Recordset.

adReason is an enumerated data type indicating the operation that originally caused the move (see Table 14-16).

adStatus is an enumerated value that indicates the action that should be taken when the event returns (see Table 14-16).

pRecordset is an object reference to the Recordset that triggered the event.

Before Opening a Recordset

Before you open a recordset there are a number of issues you need to consider. For instance, you need to decide whether or not you plan to update the database. Then you need to decide what type of cursor you want to use. Finally, you need to decide where the cursor should be located. These issues have a big impact on how your application performs, not only for a single user, but for all of the users that access your database server.

Locking considerations

One of the problems of running an application where multiple users are accessing the same collection of information is controlling access to the information so that two people aren't trying to update the same information at the same time.

To understand why locking is important consider the following example. Assume that your bank runs two programs to update their accounts at the same time (see Figure 14-1). One program applies deposits, while the other applies withdrawals. As luck would have it, both programs attempt to update your account at the same time. Without locking, the withdrawal program may read the current balance in your account and begin to process the withdrawal. Then the deposit program reads the current balance and updates the database with the new balance. Finally, the withdrawal program posts the balance it computes. This is a serious problem (although I wish it worked the other way).

Without Locking

Withdrawal Program	Read Account Balance			Apply Withdrawal of $700
Deposit Program		Read Account Balance	Apply Deposit of $5000	
	Time			
Account Balance	$1,426.55	$1,426.55	$6,426.55	$726.55

Figure 14-1: Processing concurrent database updates without locks

To avoid this problem, you need to prevent all other users from accessing this particular account until after the update has been completed. Figure 14-2 shows how the same sequence of actions would work with locks. The withdrawal program is able to read the account balance immediately, and it places a lock on the account so no other programs can access the information. When the deposit program attempts to read the balance, it is forced to wait for the lock to be released. This allows the withdrawal program to finish its processing uninterrupted and release the lock it placed on the account. Once the lock is released, the account balance will be returned to the deposit program, which can then complete its updates accurately.

With Locking

Withdrawal Program	Read Account Balance With Lock		Apply Withdrawal of $700	Release Lock		
Deposit Program		Read Account Balance	Wait for Lock to be Released		Apply Deposit of $5000	Release Lock
	Time					
Account Balance	$1,426.55	$1,426.55	$726.55	$726.55	$5,726.55	$5,726.55

Figure 14-2: Processing concurrent database updates with locks

As you can see, locking is necessary to ensure that changes to the database are applied in the correct order. In most cases, the order of the changes against the database isn't important as long as the changes are made sequentially rather than concurrently. After all, it doesn't matter whether the deposit is made first or the withdrawal is made first as long as they aren't made at the same time.

The ADO `LockType` allows you to choose from one of four different types of locks: read-only, pessimistic, optimistic, and batch optimistic. You need to choose the one that best suits your needs.

Read-only locks

While locks are necessary when performing updates, it is useful to tell the database server that you are never going to update the data in the database. In a sense, a *read-only lock* is not a lock at all, but specifying a read-only lock ensures that you can't update the database.

Pessimistic locks

A *pessimistic lock* is the most conservative lock available in ADO. When you begin to edit a record by assigning a new value into one of the existing fields in the row, a lock is placed on the row so that no other users can access it. The row remains locked until you update it using the `Update` method.

One problem with using pessimistic locking is that in addition to the row you are modifying, all of the rows stored in the same physical block of storage (typically called a *database page*) are also locked, which makes them unavailable for other users also.

In days of old: The current version of most popular database systems supports row-level locking, which means that a lock affects only the row that it was intended for and not the other rows in the same physical block of storage.

However, a bigger problem with pessimistic locking is that the lock is held during the entire time you are editing the row. Depending on how your application works, the lock could be held anywhere from a few moments to many minutes. In some applications this may not be critical, but in others it could cause serious problems because other applications may be forced to wait until you complete the edit. Also the database server may take the lock away from you if you held it too long, which will cause an error when you eventually get around to finishing the update.

In general, the more rows you have in a table, the fewer problems you will have with conflicting pessimistic locks. Likewise, performing fewer updates and having fewer users also reduces the likelihood of a lock conflict.

Optimistic locks

Optimistic locks still ensure that your update is performed correctly. Unlike pessimistic locks, however, optimistic locks aren't placed until you call the `Update` method, so a lock is not placed on the row when you begin editing the row. When the update is performed, the row is locked, and the current value of each field in the database server is compared to the original value of each field taken when the application program retrieved the row. If there aren't any differences, the update will proceed normally. Otherwise an error will be returned to your program. It will be up to your program to decide whether to reapply the changes or restart the update from the beginning.

Batch optimistic locks

Batch optimistic locks are similar to optimistic locks, except you can update multiple rows before returning them to the database server for updating using the `UpdateBatch` method. After performing a batch update, you need to review each of the rows you updated to ensure that the changes were applied to the database.

This type of lock is useful when you want to add lots of rows to a table. It is impossible for anyone to update any of the values in these rows, since the data hasn't been sent to the database yet.

Choosing a cursor type

While locks affect how you update data, cursor types affect how your application will see changes in the database that are made by other users. Choosing the appropriate cursor type is important and depends mostly on how you plan to use the data. ADO supports four types of cursors: forward-only cursors, static cursors, keyset cursors, and dynamic cursors.

Forward-only cursors

A *forward-only cursor* is the most restrictive of all of the cursors available. It is available only in combination with a read-only lock. It presents a static view of the data in the `Recordset` that can't be addressed randomly. Any changes, additions, or deletions to the underlying data will not be visible to your program.

You must scroll through the `Recordset` one row at a time from the beginning to the end. If you need to move backwards or start over again, you will have to close the `Recordset` and reopen it.

Typically this type of cursor is most useful for reports or for translation tables that are never updated. Forward-only cursors have less overhead and offer better performance than the other types of cursors.

Static cursors

Like the forward-only cursor, a *static cursor* also provides a static view of your data. Records that have been added, deleted, or updated will not be visible to your program. However, you may move the current record pointer to any location in the `Recordset` without restriction.

Client-side only: A static cursor is your only choice for client-side cursors, though it may be used with a server-side cursor as well.

Keyset cursors

A *keyset cursor* allows you to see any updates or deletions, but not additions made to the underlying data that have been made after you opened the `Recordset`. Bookmarks are supported, and you may move anywhere in the `Recordset` you choose.

Keyset cursors work by keeping a list of bookmarks in a temporary table on the server. As you move from one row to another, the provider will retrieve the most current values associated with the particular row. In general, I avoid keyset cursors because they are slower than static cursors and don't provide all of the updates to the database as does a dynamic cursor.

Dynamic cursors

Dynamic cursors allow you to view any changes made to the database, including additions, deletions, and updates. All forms of movement through the `Recordset` that don't rely on `Bookmarks` are always supported. Note that most data providers include bookmark support even though it isn't required.

Dynamic cursors are useful if you want to see all of the changes in the underlying data you retrieved from the database. They are only appropriate if you are using a server-side cursor and there is more overhead when using a dynamic cursor because the provider has to check continually for changes in the database. However, if you are only retrieving a few rows from the database, then dynamic cursors may be appropriate.

Picking a cursor location

The last major choice you have to make when opening a recordset is choosing between a server-side cursor and a client-side cursor. This choice is made using the `CursorLocation` property.

Server-side cursors

A *server-side cursor* is the traditional cursor used in a database system. It directly accesses data on the server. A request to move the current record pointer to a different record results in a request to the database server (unless, of course, you set `CacheSize` to a value greater than one, and the record is in the local cache). Server-side cursors can be used with keyset and dynamic cursors to allow your program to see changes in the live database.

Client-side cursors

A *client-side cursor* is a special type of cursor that allows you a richer environment with which to build your application than a server-side cursor does. Data is buffered locally, and you can operate in disconnected mode from the database server. After retrieving your data from the database, you can break the connection and work with the information in the recordset locally. Later you can reconnect and apply whatever changes you made locally to the database server.

I can't see it: The `UnderlyingValue` property is not available on `Field` objects using a client-side cursor, since all of the records are buffered locally.

Opening a Recordset

There are three main ways to create a `Recordset`. As you saw in Chapter 13, you can create a `Command` object and use the `Execute` method to return a reference to a `Recordset` object. A second way to create a `Recordset` is by storing a SQL statement, stored procedure name, or table name in the recordset's `Source` property and then using the `Open` method to populate the recordset. The last way is to set the `Source` property to an active `Command` object and then use the `Open` method. Because I already covered the first way in Chapter 13, I'll cover the last two ways here.

Using Source strings

For many applications all you need to use is a `Connection` object and a `Recordset` object. Listing 14-1 is similar to the program in Chapters 13 and uses the same `Connection` object from Chapter 12. Instead of creating a `Command` object with the **Select** statement, I assign the **Select** statement to the `Source` property of the `Recordset`.

I then specify values for `CursorLocation`, `CursorType`, and `LockType`. While these values aren't critical to the way this routine runs, it is a good idea to specify them always and ask only for the resources you really need. Then after clearing the

Errors collection, I issue the Open method. If there's a problem, I write the error message using the WriteError routine from Chapter 12. Otherwise, I display the first value from the first column of the recordset in the status bar just like I did in the previous version of the program.

Listing 14-1: The Command7_Click event in Recordset Demo

```
Private Sub Command7_Click()

Dim rs As ADODB.Recordset

On Error Resume Next

Set rs = New ADODB.Recordset
Set rs.ActiveConnection = db
rs.Source = "Select Count(*) From Customers Where State = 'MD'"
rs.CursorLocation = adUseServer
rs.CursorType = adOpenForwardOnly
rs.LockType = adLockReadOnly

db.Errors.Clear
rs.Open
If db.Errors.Count > 0 Then
   WriteError

Else
   StatusBar1.SimpleText = "Response: " & _
      FormatNumber(rs.Fields(0).Value, 0)

End If

End Sub
```

Using Command objects

Another way to populate a Recordset object is to create a Command object with the command to extract the information from the database and assign it to the recordset's Source property. Listing 14-2 is essentially a combination of the code from Listing 14-1 and Listing 13-5. It takes the steps I used to build a Command object that references the stored procedure CountByState and marries it to the code to create and open the Recordset. The only difference in the steps is that I used a Set statement to assign the Command object to the recordset's Source property instead of assigning a **Select** statement to the Source property.

Listing 14-2: The Command8_Click event in Recordset Demo

```
Private Sub Command8_Click()

Dim c As ADODB.Command
Dim p As ADODB.Parameter
Dim rs As ADODB.Recordset

On Error Resume Next

Set c = New ADODB.Command
Set c.ActiveConnection = db
c.CommandText = "CountByState"
c.CommandType = adCmdStoredProc

c.Parameters.Refresh
c.Parameters("@State").Value = Text5.Text

Set rs = New ADODB.Recordset
Set rs.Source = c
rs.CursorLocation = adUseServer
rs.CursorType = adOpenForwardOnly
rs.LockType = adLockReadOnly

db.Errors.Clear
rs.Open
If db.Errors.Count > 0 Then
   WriteError

Else
   StatusBar1.SimpleText = "Response: " & _
      FormatNumber(rs.Fields(0).Value, 0)

End If

End Sub
```

Thoughts on Opening a Recordset Object

Of the three approaches I talked about in the last two chapters to create a recordset, the two I described in this chapter are the ones I use, typically. I like the simplicity of just using the `Recordset` object and the `Connection` object to access the database. I also like the ability to open the recordset with the options Especially, I really want the options for the type of cursor and locking strategy. Of course, I can't use this technique to execute any commands that have parameters, which is why I use the other approach. As with the other approach, I have the freedom to set all of the key values in the `Recordset` object before I open it.

Summary

In this chapter you learned the following:

✦ You can use a server-side cursor when you want to manipulate the recordset on the database server.

✦ You can use a client-side cursor when you want to manipulate the recordset on the database client.

✦ You can use read-only locks to prevent others from changing the data while your recordset is open.

✦ You can use pessimistic locks to prevent others from changing the values in the current record in your recordset. This technique however incurs a significant amount of overhead in the database server.

✦ You can use optimistic locking when you don't expect others to change the data in the current row while you are editing it. Of course you have to handle the error condition that may arise if someone does change the data while you are accessing it.

✦ You can use batch optimistic locking when making changes in a group of records. This approach has the least overhead of all of the locking methods, but requires you to verify each row you changed to insure that the data wasn't changed by another database client before you made your changes.

✦ ✦ ✦

Working with Recordsets – Part II

✦ ✦ ✦ ✦

In This Chapter

Accessing fields in a recordset

Moving around in a recordset

Sorting and filtering rows

Collecting recordset information

Getting information from fields

Working with large values

✦ ✦ ✦ ✦

In this chapter, I'll continue my discussion of the ADO `Recordset` object by covering how to access the information contained in the various fields. Then I'll explain how to move around and locate records in the `Recordset`.

More About Recordsets

As you know, a `Recordset` object contains a collection of rows returned from the database. Rather than make all of the rows available to you at one time, it maintains a pointer to the current row that you can move through the recordset using various methods and properties. The information contained in the row's columns is made available through the `Fields` collection. Depending on your cursor type, you can change the values locally and then commit the values to the database using the appropriate methods.

The Field Object

The `Field` object contains information about a specific column in a `Recordset`. It is part of the `Fields` collection, which contains the set of columns retrieved from the database.

Field object properties

Table 15-1 lists the properties associated with the Field object. Tables 15-2 and 15-3 contain additional information about specific properties listed in Table 15-1.

Values, values and more values: Each field has three properties that describe its value. Value contains the current value of the field. OriginalValue contains the value as it was originally retrieved from the database. UnderlyingValue contains the current value for the field, which may reflect changes made by other transactions.

Table 15-1
Properties of the Field Object

Property	*Description*
ActualSize	A Long value containing the actual length of a field's value.
Attributes	An enumerated type describing the characteristics of the column (see Table 15-2).
DataFormat	An object reference to a StdDataFormat object containing information about how to format the data value.
DefinedSize	A Long containing the maximum length of a field's value.
Name	A String value containing the name of the field.
NumericScale	A Byte value containing the number of digits to the right of the decimal point for a numeric field.
OriginalValue	A Variant containing the original value of the field before any modifications were made.
Precision	A Byte value containing the total number of digits in a numeric field.
Properties	An object reference to a Properties collection containing provider-specific information about a field.
Type	An enumerated type containing the OLE DB data type of the field (see Table 15-3).
UnderlyingValue	A Variant containing the current value of the field in the database as it exists on the database server.
Value	A Variant containing the current value of the field.

Table 15-2
Values for Attributes

Constant	*Value*	*Description*
adFldUnspecified	-1	The provider doesn't supply field attributes.
adFldMayDefer	2	The field value is not retrieved with the whole record, but only when you explicitly access the field.
adFldUpdateable	4	The field's value may be changed.
adFldUnknownUpdateable	8	The provider can't determine if you can change the field's value.
adFldFixed	16	The field contains fixed-length data.
adFldIsNullable	32	The field will accept **Null** values.
adFldMayBeNull	64	The field may contain a **Null** value.
adFldLong	128	The field contains a long binary value and you should use the AppendChunk and GetChunk methods to access its data.
adFldRowID	256	The field contains an identity value which can't be changed.
adFldRowVersion	512	The field contains a time stamp value that is used to track updates.
adFldCacheDeferred	4096	This field is cached by the provider and subsequent reads and writes are done from cache.
adFldIsChapter	8192	The field contains a chapter value, which specifies a specific child Recordset related to this parent field.
adFldNegativeScale	16384	The field contains a numeric column that supports negative scale values.
adFldKeyColumn	32768	The field is (or at least part of) the primary key for the table.
adFldIsRowURL	65536	The field contains the URL that names the resource from the data store represented by the record.

Continued

Table 15-2 (continued)

Constant	Value	Description
`adFldIsDefaultStream`	131072	The field contains the default stream for the resource represented by the record.
`adFldIsCollection`	262144	The field contains a collection of another resource such as a folder rather than a simple resource such as a file.

Table 15-3
Values for Type

Constant	Value	Description
`adEmpty`	0	This field has no value (OLE DB data type value: `DBTYPE_EMPTY`).
`adSmallInt`	2	This field has an `Integer` value (OLE DB data type value: `DBTYPE_I2`).
`adInteger`	3	This field has a `Long` value (OLE DB data type value: `DBTYPE_I4`).
`adSingle`	4	This field has a `Single` value (OLE DB data type value: `DBTYPE_R4`).
`adDouble`	5	This field has a `Double` value (OLE DB data type value: `DBTYPE_R8`).
`adCurrency`	6	This field has a `Currency` value (OLE DB data type value: `DBTYPE_CY`).
`adDate`	7	This field has a `Date` value (OLE DB data type value: `DBTYPE_DATE`).
`adBSTR`	8	This field has a null-terminated Unicode string (OLE DB data type value: `DBTYPE_BSTR`).
`adIDispatch`	9	This field has a pointer to an `IDispatch` interface in a COM object (OLE DB data type value: `DBTYPE_IDISPATCH`).
`adError`	10	This field has a 32-bit error code (OLE DB data type value: `DBTYPE_ERROR`).
`adBoolean`	11	This field has a `Boolean` value (OLE DB data type value: `DBTYPE_BOOL`).

Constant	Value	Description
adVariant	12	This field has a Variant value (OLE DB data type value: DBTYPE_VARIANT). Note that while this type is supported by OLE DB, but it is not supported by ADO. Using it may cause unpredictable results.
adIUnknown	13	This field has a pointer to an IUnknown interface in a COM object (OLE DB data type value: DBTYPE_IUNKNOWN).
adDecimal	14	This field has an exact numeric value with a fixed precision and scale (OLE DB data type value: DBTYPE_DECIMAL).
adTinyInt	16	This field has a one byte signed integer (OLE DB data type value: DBTYPE_I1).
adUnsignedTinyInt	17	This field has a one byte unsigned integer (OLE DB data type value: DBTYPE_UI1).
adUnsignedInt	18	This field has a two byte unsigned integer (OLE DB data type value: DBTYPE_UI2).
adUnsignedInt	19	This field has a four byte unsigned integer (OLE DB data type value: DBTYPE_UI4).
adBigInt	20	This field has an 8-byte signed integer (OLE DB data type value: DBTYPE_I8).
adUnsignedBigInt	21	This field has an 8-byte unsigned integer (OLE DB data type value: DBTYPE_UI8).
adFileTime	64	This field has a 64-bit date-time value represented as the number of 100-nanosecond intervals since 1 January 1601 (OLE DB data type value: DBTYPE_FILETIME).
adGUID	72	This field has a globally unique identifier value (OLE DB data type value: DBTYPE_GUID).
adBinary	128	This field has a Binary value (OLE DB data type value: DBTYPE_BYTES).
adChar	129	This field has a String value (OLE DB data type value: DBTYPE_STR).
adWChar	130	This field contains a null-terminated Unicode character string (OLE DB data type value: DBTYPE_WSTR).
adNumeric	131	This field contains an exact numeric value with a fixed precision and scale (OLE DB data type value: DBTYPE_NUMERIC).

Continued

Table 15-3 (continued)		
Constant	***Value***	***Description***
adUserDefined	132	This field contains a user-defined value (DBTYPE_UDT).
adDBDate	133	This field has a date value using the YYYYMMDD format (OLE DB data type value: DBTYPE_DBDATE).
adDBTime	134	This field has a time value using the HHMMSS format (OLE DB data type value: DBTYPE_DBTIME).
adDBTimeStamp	135	This field has a date-time stamp in the YYYYMMDDHH MMSS format (OLE DB data type value: DBTYPE_ DBTIMESTAMP).
adChapter	136	This field has a 4-byte chapter value that identifies the rows in a child rowset (OLE DB data type value: DBTYPE_HCHAPTER).
adPropVariant	138	This field has an Automation PROPVARIANT (OLE DB data type value: DBTYPE_PROP_VARIANT).
adVarNumeric	139	This field contains a numeric value. (Available for Parameter objects only.)
adVarChar	200	This field contains a String. (Available for Parameter objects only.)
adLongVarChar	201	This field has a long character value. (Available for Parameter objects only.)
adVarWChar	202	This field has a null-terminated Unicode character string value. (Available for Parameter objects only.)
adLongVarWChar	203	This field has a long null-terminated character string value. (Available for Parameter objects only.)
adVarBinary	204	This field has a binary value. (Available for Parameter objects only.)
adLongVarBinary	205	This field has a long binary value. (Available for Parameter objects only.)

Field object methods

The Field object contains two methods that help you deal with large fields.

Sub AppendChunk (Data as Variant)

The `AppendChunk` method is used to add data to a large text or binary field. The first time the `AppendChunk` method is used, the value in `Data` will overwrite any existing data in the field. For subsequent calls, simply append data to the end of the existing data.

`Data` is a `Variant` containing the data to be appended to the end of the field.

Function GetChunk (Length as Long) as Variant

The `GetChunk` method is used to retrieve data from a large text or binary field. The first time `GetChunk` is called, the data will be retrieved from the start of the field. Only the number of bytes (or Unicode characters) specified will be retrieved. Subsequent calls will retrieve data from where the previous call left off. If you specify a length greater than the remaining data, only the remaining data will be returned without padding.

A long, long chunk ago: You can only use the `GetChunk` and the `AppendChunk` methods when the `adFldLong` bit is set in the `Attributes` property.

`Length` is a `Long` containing the number of bytes or characters of data to be retrieved.

The Fields Collection

The `Fields` collection contains the set of columns being returned in a `Recordset` object.

Fields collection properties

Table 15-4 lists the properties associated with the `Fields` collection.

Table 15-4
Properties of the Fields Collection

Property	*Description*
`Count`	A `Long` value containing the number of `Field` objects in the collection.
`Item`(index)	An object reference to a `Field` object containing information about a particular field in the `Recordset`. To locate a field, specify a value in the range of 0 to `Count` –1 or the name of the `Field`.

Special fields: The two special fields that are defined for a Record object are the default Stream object (index = adDefaultStream) and the absolute URL for the Record (index = adRecordURL).

Fields collection methods

The Fields collection contains methods that are used to maintain the set of Field objects.

Sub Append (Name As String, Type As DataTypeEnum, [DefinedSize As Long], [Attrib As FieldAttributeEnum = adFldUnspecified], [FieldValue As Variant])

The Append method creates a new Field object and adds it to the Fields collection.

Name is a String value containing the name of the field.

Type is the data type that will be associated with the new field.

DefinedSize is a Long containing the size of the new field.

Attrib is a bit pattern containing values that determine the characteristics of the field (see Table 15-2 for the possible values for this property).

FieldValue is a Variant that contains the value for the new field. If this value isn't specified, then the field will be **Null**.

Sub Delete (Index As Variant)

The Delete method removes a Field from the collection. Index is either a String containing the name of the field or a Long value containing the ordinal position of the Field object to be deleted.

Sub Refresh()

The Refresh method has no real effect on the Fields collection. To see a change in the underlying database structures, you need to issue a Requery method of the Recordset object.

Sub Update()

The Update method is used to save the changes you make to the Fields collection.

Moving Around a Recordset

You can use the `Recordset` object to gain access to the set of rows selected from the database. You can only access one row at a time with the *current record pointer,* which allows you to use various methods and properties to change the record that the current record pointer is pointing to.

The Recordset Movement Demo program

To demonstrate the different ways to move around in a `Recordset`, I wrote the Recordset Movement Demo program (see Figure 15-1). This program might not win the award for the World's Most Cluttered window, but it would certainly place in the top five. However, it does accomplish its goal of presenting the maximum amount of information about what happens when you move around in a `Recordset`.

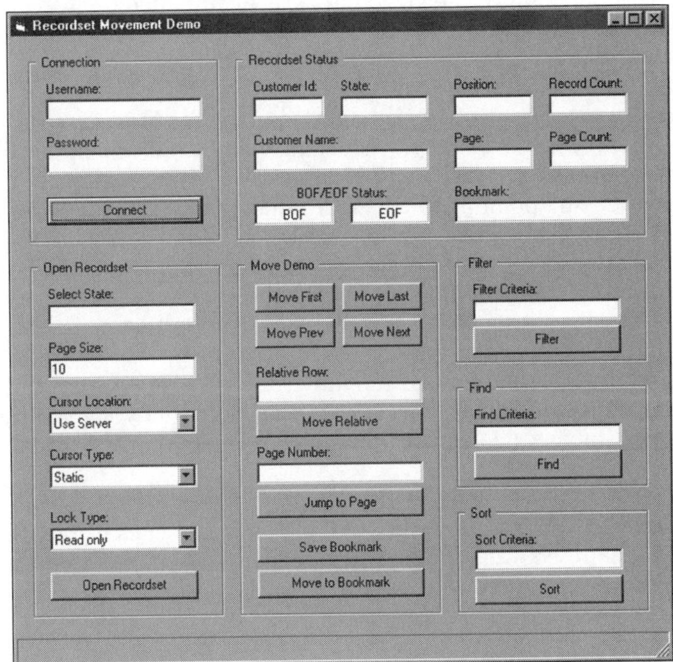

Figure 15-1: Running the Recordset Movement Demo program

This program can be found on the CD-ROM in the `\VB6DB\Chapter15\RecordsetMovementDemo` directory.

Running the program

In order to try moving around in a recordset with this program, you must first connect to your database. Enter your user name and password information in the appropriate blanks in the Connection frame and press the Connect button. Respond Yes to the message box that asks "Do you really want to connect?". If you were able to successfully connect to the database server, the message "Connected" will be displayed in the status bar at the bottom of the form.

Once you're connected to the database server, you can open the `Recordset` in the Open Recordset frame. You may enter a two-character state name in the field called Select State to restrict the `Recordset` so that it only contains customers from the specified state. Otherwise, the recordset will contain all of the customers from the database.

You can also specify the number of records you want per page in the Page Size field. The default value is ten. Then you can choose values for Cursor Location, Cursor Type, and Lock Type properties. Pressing Open Recordset will open the recordset. You can change any of these values and press the Open Recordset button to close the current recordset and open it again with the new parameters.

The current status of the `Recordset` object is recorded in the Recordset Status frame. The values from three fields are displayed, along with the current status of the `BOF` and `EOF` properties. Normally the BOF or EOF boxes will be black, indicating that the current record pointer isn't pointing to either extreme. When you read either BOF or EOF, the appropriate box will be displayed in yellow. If you are already on BOF or EOF and attempt to move beyond the end of the recordset a second time, the box will be displayed in red. Also displayed are the values from the `AbsolutePosition`, `RecordCount`, `AbsolutePage`, `PageCount`, and `Bookmark` properties.

Once you have opened the `Recordset`, you can move around using the controls in the Move Demo, Filter, Find, and Sort frames of the form. Note that you can't update any of the fields in the database. I'll discuss updating information in a recordset in Chapter 16.

Check before you click: I don't check most of the input parameters before using them, so don't be surprised if the program gets a fatal error or does something unpredictable if you enter the wrong value.

Module level declarations

The Recordset Movement Demo program includes a few variables declared at the module level, making them global to the entire module (see Listing 15-1). These include the `Customers Recordset` object, the `db Connection` object and the `SaveBookmark` variable. Note that I declared both the `Recordset` and `Connection` objects `WithEvents`, which allow me to monitor the status of both objects with the appropriate events to track their status.

Listing 15-1: Module level declarations for Recordset Movement Demo

```
Option Explicit

Dim WithEvents Customers As ADODB.Recordset
Dim WithEvents db As ADODB.Connection
Dim SaveBookmark As Variant
```

Moving sequentially

The current record is a pointer to one of the rows in the `Recordset`. Assume that you retrieve a `Recordset` from your database with seven rows. Before the first row in the recordset is a special marker known as the BOF, while the EOF marker is beyond the end of the last row. The current record pointer can point to any of these locations (see Figure 15-2).

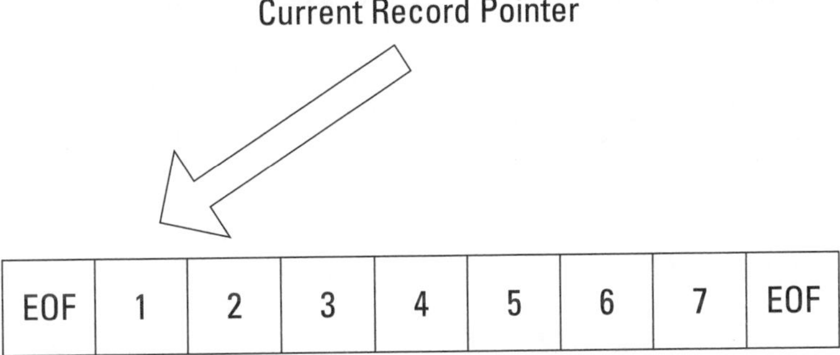

Figure 15-2: A logical view of the current record pointer

Absolutely addressed: The record numbers shown in Figure 15-2 correspond to the values of the `AbsolutePosition` property, except for BOF and EOF, which don't have a corresponding value for `AbsolutePosition`.

When you first open a `Recordset`, the current record pointer is pointing to the first record (assuming of course that there is at least one record in the recordset). From this location, you can move to the next record (record number 2) in sequence using the `MoveNext` method. Using the `MoveLast` method will take you to record number 7, which is the last record in the recordset. You can return to the first record by using the `MoveFirst` method, and you can move to the previous record using the `MovePrevious` method.

Moving beyond the ends

One problem with the `MoveNext` method is that if you are at the last record in the recordset, there is nothing to prevent you from trying to move beyond the end. When this happens, the current record pointer is moved to EOF. While the current record pointer points to EOF, any attempt to access column information results in an error. The same problem occurs with the `MovePrevious` method and the beginning of the `Recordset`.

The solution to this problem is to not leave the current record pointer pointing to EOF or BOF. This condition can be detected by using the EOF and BOF properties. The `EOF` property is `TRUE` only when the current record pointer is pointing beyond the last record, while the `BOF` property is only `TRUE` if the current record pointer is pointing before the first record. Note that if both properties are `TRUE`, the `Recordset` doesn't contain any records.

Using the MoveNext method

Using these methods is very straightforward. All you really need to do is to call the desired method; however, this isn't really practical since it doesn't do any error checking. A more practical example is shown in Listing 15-2. This routine verifies that the `Recordset` isn't already at the end of file marker before it calls the `MoveNext` method. This ensures that you can't move beyond EOF.

Listing 15-2: The MoveNextDemo routine

```
Sub MoveNextDemo()

If Not Customers.EOF Then
   Customers.MoveNext

End If

End Sub
```

An alternate MoveNext

Another way to handle the `MoveNext` method is shown in Listing 15-3. This routine uses the `On Error Resume Next` statement and the `Err` object to detect when the `MoveNext` fails. If it does fail, then my old friend `WriteError` is used to display the database message.

Listing 15-3: The Command5_Click event in Recordset Movement Demo

```
Private Sub Command5_Click()

On Error Resume Next

StatusBar1.SimpleText = ""
Err.Clear

Customers.MoveNext
If Err.Number <> 0 Then
   WriteError

End If

End Sub
```

However, to make the Command5_Click event work properly, I also have to code the `WillMove` event to detect and cancel any attempt to move beyond the BOF or EOF (see Listing 15-4). This routine detects when you are at EOF or BOF and are about to perform a method that would trigger an error, and sets the `adStatus` parameter to `adStatusCancel` to return an error condition.

Listing 15-4: The Customers_WillMove event in Recordset Movement Demo

```
Private Sub Customers_WillMove( _
   ByVal adReason As ADODB.EventReasonEnum, _
   adStatus As ADODB.EventStatusEnum, _
   ByVal pRecordset As ADODB.Recordset)

If Customers.BOF And adReason = adRsnMovePrevious Then
   adStatus = adStatusCancel

End If

If Customers.EOF And adReason = adRsnMoveNext Then
   adStatus = adStatusCancel

End If

End Sub
```

Moving randomly

There are several ways to move around the Recordset randomly. The one you should use depends on what you are trying to accomplish. The Bookmark property allows you to save the location of a row and be able to return to that row at some future point in time. The Move method allows you to move forward or backward the specified number of rows. The AbsolutePage property allows you to jump to the specified page number in the Recordset. If your recordset supports it, you can also use the AbsolutePosition property to position the cursor at a specific location in the recordset.

Using bookmarks

The Bookmark property contains the current location of a record in a Recordset. It is a Variant value that is highly dependent on the data provider. It is possible to have multiple bookmarks that point to the same record, but each bookmark is a different value. The only way to compare bookmarks is to use the CompareBookmarks method. Also, a Bookmark is specific to the Recordset that it came from. You can't use it with any other recordsets, even if they were created with the same command.

Cloned again: A Bookmark can be used with any copy of a Recordset that was created using the Clone method.

To save a bookmark, simply declare a Variant variable and save the value of the Bookmark property to it, as shown below.

```
SaveBookmark = Customers.Bookmark
```

This saves the location of the current record. Then after moving to a different record, you can move the current record pointer back to the bookmarked location by assigning the value you saved back to the Bookmark property. When you add some error-handling logic, you end up with code like you see in Listing 15-5.

Listing 15-5: The Command8_Click of Recordset Movement Demo

```
Private Sub Command8_Click()

On Error Resume Next

StatusBar1.SimpleText = ""
Err.Clear

Customers.Bookmark = SaveBookmark
```

```
If Err.Number <> 0 Then
   WriteError

End If

End Sub
```

Moving forward and backward

The Move method takes two parameters: the number of rows to move and an optional Bookmark that will be used as the starting location. The number of rows may be either positive or negative. A positive value will move the specified number of rows toward the last row of the Recordset, while a negative value will move toward the first row. If you specify a value of zero, the current record will be refreshed.

Specifying the bookmark computes the offset relative to that record rather than the current record. Of course, the Recordset must support bookmarks in order to use this parameter.

Listing 15-6 shows how easy it is to call the Move method. While you might think that the error checking in this routine isn't necessary, think again. If you specify too large of a value (for example, one that would take you beyond the end of the recordset), a run-time error will be triggered.

Listing 15-6: The Command7_Click event of Recordset Movement Demo

```
Private Sub Command7_Click()

On Error Resume Next

StatusBar1.SimpleText = ""
Err.Clear

Customers.Move CLng(Text14.Text)
If Err.Number <> 0 Then
   WriteError

End If

End Sub
```

Reading pages

One of the more interesting features of ADO is its ability to manage data in terms of pages. A *page* is a group of records from the database. The `PageSize` property determines the number of records in a page, while the `PageCount` property tells you the number of pages in your `Recordset`. The `AbsolutePage` property contains the relative number of the current in the recordset.

You can reposition the current record pointer by setting the `AbsolutePage` property to a particular page, as shown below:

```
Customers.AbsolutePage = CLng(Text18.Text)
```

This will move the current record pointer to the first record on that page. You can even change the `PageSize` property while the `Recordset` object is open, which makes it easy to change the number of records displayed per page on the fly.

Internet ready: The page properties are often useful in an Internet or transaction-oriented environment where a user scrolls though a recordset one page at a time. You can use the `AbsolutePage` property to determine which page needs to be displayed, and then use the `MoveNext` method to retrieve the remaining rows on the page.

Absolute positioning

If your recordset supports the `AbsolutePosition` and `RecordCount` properties, you can determine the current record number and the total records in your `Recordset`. The `AbsolutePosition` property will also allow you to move the cursor to the specified location.

Absolute ain't accurate: You should not use the `AbsolutePosition` property in place of bookmarks. Depending on the options you select when you open your recordset, the actual record pointed to by the `AbsolutePosition` may change as other records are added and deleted from the recordset. Don't assume that if you haven't added or deleted a record, this value won't change. Remember—depending on the type of cursor you select, changes made by other database users may affect the value of `AbsolutePosition` associated with a particular row.

Searching, Sorting, and Filtering

Another common need is the ability to find and organize the information within a recordset. The `Recordset` object includes a method to find a particular row by searching for a value, and a method to sort the records contained in the recordset by a specified list of fields.

Finding a row

One common problem with retrieving a large number of records is trying to find a particular value in the Recordset. The easiest way to address this problem is to use the Find method.

The Find method allows you to specify a search string consisting of a column name, a relational operator, and a value. If the value is a string, it must be enclosed in either single quotes (') or pound signs (#). Double quotes (") may not be used. Pound signs must enclose date values.

If you use the **Like** operator, you may also use an asterisk (*) as a wild card character in any string value. However, the asterisk must be the last character in the value or the only character in the value. Otherwise a run-time error will occur.

The Find method has several arguments in addition to the search condition. Specify the number of rows to skip before beginning your search; otherwise, the search will begin with the current row. So, you should specify a value of one if you want to find the next occurrence of a value.

You can also specify whether you want to search backwards (toward the beginning) or forwards (toward the end) of the recordset, and you may specify a bookmark from where the search will begin.

Like most of the Recordset methods I've talked about so far, you simply call the method with the list of arguments you wish to use, and include the appropriate error checking to prevent a run-time error from occurring if you can't find the record or your search condition contains an error (see Listing 15-7).

Listing 15-7: The Command10_Click event of Recordset Movement Demo

```
Private Sub Command10_Click()

On Error Resume Next

StatusBar1.SimpleText = ""
Err.Clear

Customers.Find Text17.Text, 1
If Err.Number <> 0 Then
   WriteError

End If

End Sub
```

For client-side cursors only: The Seek method provides an alternative to the Find method, but is only available when you are using client-side cursors (discussed in Chapter 14). You begin by specifying the name of an index in the Index property and then supplying a list of values to search for that corresponds to the columns in the index (i.e., if your index has only one column, only one value may be supplied). Note that not all providers support this feature, including the one for SQL Server, so you may want to use the Supports method to determine if the Seek method is supported.

Sorting rows

The Sort property contains the list of columns that are used to sort your recordset. Thus, one way you can sort the recordset in the sample program is by setting the Sort property to the following value:

```
State, Name Desc
```

This sort key will sort the rows by State in ascending order and then by the Name column in descending order.

The Sort property is available only for client-side recordsets, which means you may want to do a little extra error checking, especially if you use multiple cursor types. The error message that would normally be issued ("Object or provider is not capable of performing requested operation") doesn't fully describe what caused the error.

Listing 15-8 contains some sample code that will sort the information in a recordset. The routine begins by getting the sort key from the form and assigning it to the Sort property. Then I check for errors and display the appropriate error message. An error code of 3251 implies that the user attempted to sort the recordset without using a client-side cursor.

Listing 15-8: The Command13_Click event in Recordset Movement Demo

```
Private Sub Command13_Click()

On Error Resume Next

Err.Clear
Customers.Sort = Text19.Text
If Err.Number = 3251 And _
   Customers.CursorLocation = adUseServer Then
      StatusBar1.SimpleText = _
```

```
            "Can't sort while using server cursors."

   ElseIf Err.Number <> 0 Then
      WriteError

   End If

   End Sub
```

Filtering rows

One of my favorite tools available in a Recordset object — one that will help you locate a particular record — is the Filter property. Only those rows that meet the filter criteria you specify will be visible in the recordset.

You can filter your recordset using a string which is similar to the condition you would specify in the **Where** clause of a **Select** statement. A *condition* is composed of one or more simple expressions composed of column names, relational operators, and values that can be grouped together, as in this example:

```
State = 'MD' And CustomerId > 100
```

To remove a filter, simply set the Bookmark property to zero or the constant adFilterNone. The original contents of the recordset will now be accessible.

If you create an array of bookmark values and assign it to the Filter property, only the rows in the array will be visible in the recordset. You can also assign the Filter property a value from the FilterGroupEnum data type. Aside from adFilterNone, these values are used primarily for reviewing the results of batch updates, which I'll talk about in the next chapter.

Why did it change?: Using the Filter property will change the values in the AbsolutePosition, AbsolutePage, RecordCount, and PageCount properties for a specific row. If you need to remember where a particular row is located, you should use the Bookmark property, which will remain unchanged no matter what the value of the Filter property.

Listing 15-9 describes a routine that applies the value specified in the Text16 text box as a filter to the Customers recordset. If the length of the text is zero, then I explicitly remove the filter by assigning the Filter property the value adFilterNone.

Listing 15-9: The Command9_Click event in Recordset Movement Demo

```
Private Sub Command9_Click()

On Error Resume Next

StatusBar1.SimpleText = ""
Err.Clear

If Len(Text16.Text) = 0 Then
   Customers.Filter = adFilterNone

Else
   Customers.Filter = Text16.Text

End If

If Err.Number <> 0 Then
   WriteError

End If

End Sub
```

Collecting recordset information

There are two events associated with changing the position of the current record pointer in the Recordset object. I talked about the WillMove event earlier in this chapter (see Listing 15-4), and now I want to talk about the MoveComplete event. This is an excellent place to display the current status of a recordset.

You don't need to do this: In this sample program, I wanted to demonstrate clearly how the various status fields change while you perform various tasks using a Recordset. The easiest way for me to do this was to trap the state of the object using the MoveComplete event. However, this isn't something you need to do in your own programs. You can easily test the various properties directly after you perform a task. Thus, you don't need to use the MoveComplete event.

Listing 15-10: The Customers_MoveComplete event in Recordset Movement Demo

```
Private Sub Customers_MoveComplete( _
   ByVal adReason As ADODB.EventReasonEnum, _
   ByVal pError As ADODB.Error, _
   adStatus As ADODB.EventStatusEnum, _
```

```
    ByVal pRecordset As ADODB.Recordset)

On Error Resume Next

If Customers.BOF And adStatus = adStatusErrorsOccurred Then
   Text5.BackColor = RGB(255, 0, 0)

ElseIf Customers.BOF Then
   Text5.BackColor = RGB(255, 255, 0)

Else
   Text5.BackColor = RGB(0, 0, 0)

End If

If Customers.EOF And adStatus = adStatusErrorsOccurred Then
   Text6.BackColor = RGB(255, 0, 0)

ElseIf Customers.EOF Then
   Text6.BackColor = RGB(255, 255, 0)

Else
   Text6.BackColor = RGB(0, 0, 0)

End If

Text9.Text = FormatNumber(Customers.AbsolutePosition, 0)
Text10.Text = FormatNumber(Customers.RecordCount, 0)
Text11.Text = FormatNumber(Customers.AbsolutePage, 0)
Text12.Text = FormatNumber(Customers.PageCount, 0)

Err.Clear
Text13.Text = Customers.Bookmark
If Err.Number <> 0 Then
   Text13.Text = "The bookmark isn't available."

End If

End Sub
```

This routine starts out by displaying information about the BOF and EOF flags. The code for both is the same. There are three possible conditions. First, if the current record pointer is not pointing to either BOF or EOF, I have a normal record and don't want to do anything. Second, if the current record pointer is pointing to either BOF or EOF, then I want to turn the background of the associated text box to yellow (`RGB(255,255,0)`). The third condition arises if the most recent move operation had an error. I assume that the current record pointer was at BOF or EOF before the mast operation. Then I want to display the background in red (`RGB(255,0,0)`).

This means that the user attempted to move past the BOF or EOF marker. The easiest way to implement this in code is to start with the last condition (because it's the most restrictive) and work my way backwards.

After I set the BOF and EOF flags, I display the properties for AbsolutePosition, RecordCount, AbsolutePage, and PageCount. Then I attempt to grab the current bookmark. If the Bookmark isn't available, I'll trigger a run-time error and display a message that indicates this.

Getting Information From Fields

Moving around a recordset is important, but retrieving information from a field is equally important. Each of the sample programs in Part III of this book has used the Fields collection and some Field objects to display data. In some cases, this was done explicitly through statements like this:

```
Text1.Text = FormatNumber(rs.Fields(0).Value, 0)
```

while other programs used the Recordset object as the data source and bound various controls on the form to the individual Field objects.

Binding a field to a control

The same properties that you use to bind a control to the ADO Data Control are also used to bind to a Recordset. However, unlike the ADO Data Control, you can't bind the controls at design time, since the Recordset object doesn't exist. So you need to set these properties at runtime. In fact, you can only set these properties while the Recordset object is open. This means that if you close a recordset and reopen it, you need to rebind all of your controls.

Shown below is a code fragment that contains the key properties you need to set in order to bind a field to a control. The DataField property contains the name of the column you want to bind the control to, while the DataSource property contains an object reference to the Recordset object. Note that you must use the Set statement to make this assignment.

```
Text3.DataField = "Name"
Set Text3.DataSource = Customers
```

Accessing field values

Assuming that you don't want to bind your data using a control, you can access each field directly using the Fields collection and the Field object.

Referencing a field's value

Visual Basic provides many different ways for you to retrieve a value from a Field object. You can use the traditional object-oriented way by specifying the Recordset object and working your way down to the lowest level object. The following expressions take advantage of the default properties of the Recordset object and the Fields and Items collections to return the value of the "Name" field. Note that you can replace the value "Name" with the numeric position of the field in the Fields collection.

```
Customers.Fields.Items("Name").Value
Recordset.Fields.Items("Name")
Recordset.Fields("Name").Value
Recordset.Fields("Name")
Recordset("Name")
```

Tip

Fewer is faster: The fewer periods (.) included in an object reference, the faster it will run. Each period means that a call must be made to the object to determine if the following property is valid and to get a reference to the code that will process it. The information needed to call the object's default property is automatically retrieved when the object is created.

An alternate way to retrieve a value is by using an exclamation mark (!), as shown below.

```
Recordset!Name
```

Note that in this format, the field name must be specified without single quotes (') and spaces. You also can't use a numeric reference to the field. However, if you enclose the field name using square brackets ([]), you can use any of these values as shown below.

```
Recordset![First Name]
```

Other field values

There are two other value properties associated with a Field object: the OriginalValue and the UnderlyingValue. The OriginalValue field contains the value of the Field object as it was when it was retrieved from the database. This value is useful when you want to restore the original value after you change it. The UnderlyingValue contains the value for this field in this row, as it currently exists in the database when you access this property.

Working with large values

When you declare a column as **NText**, **Text,** or **Image**, you can't use the Value property to access the data. Instead, you must use the GetChunk method to retrieve information from the field, and the AppendChunk method to save values to the field. These methods work basically the same for all three types of data, so I'm just going to talk about **Image** fields in this section. Most people are going to use them for graphic images, binary documents (such as RTF files, Excel Worksheets, and so on) or other forms of binary data.

Bound controls

Chances are, the reason you're using large columns is that you want to hold an image or a large text document. If that's true, then you should take advantage of controls like the Image, Picture, and the Rich Text Box that are capable of being bound to a field in a recordset and can handle large volumes of data.

Imperfect images: Changing the image in either the Picture control or the Image control will not update the field in the recordset. You must explicitly load the image into the field. Even if you were able to save the image in the control, you would be better off storing the image in either .GIF or .JPG format in the database, rather than storing the uncompressed bit map image used by the Picture and Image controls.

Loading images

One of the most common questions I've heard people ask is how to load an image into an **Image** database field from a Visual Basic program. The answer is shown in Listing 15-11. The real trick is to use a Byte array and Redim the size so that the array has the same number of bytes as the image file. Then it's merely a matter of opening the file for binary access and using the Get statement to read the image into the array in a single chunk. Once you've loaded the image into memory, you can use the AppendChunk method to copy it into the Field object, and then Update to save it to the database.

You can find the Recordset Update Demo program on the CD-ROM in the \VB6DB\Chapter16\RecordsetUpdateDemo directory.

Listing 15-11: The Command14_Click event in Recordset Update Demo

```
Private Sub Command14_Click()

Dim f As String
Dim img() As Byte

f = InputBox("Enter image file name:")
```

```
f = App.Path & "\" & f

If Len(Dir(f)) > 0 Then
   Open f For Binary Access Read As #1
   ReDim img(FileLen(f) - 1)
   Get #1, , img()
   Close #1

   Images("Image").AppendChunk img
   Image1.Picture = LoadPicture(f)

Else
   Image1.Picture = LoadPicture()

End If

End Sub
```

Zero counts, too: When moving data from a file to a `Byte` array, remember that the array will start with zero, so the size of the array must be one byte less than size of the file to allow for the zeroth byte in the array.

While it is possible to use a loop like the one shown below to load an image, I feel that it isn't worth the effort for files smaller than a megabyte or so. However, you can use the following code to replace the statements in Listing 15-11 from the `Open` statement to the `Close` statement to perform a loop. Note that this routine begins by copying the odd size block first and then copying chunks in a fixed block size. Otherwise, you'd have to keep track of the number of bytes transferred to determine when you are about to read the last block so you may `ReDim` the `Byte` array in order to transfer only the appropriate amount of data.

```
Open f For Binary Access Read As #1
ReDim img(FileLen(f) Mod 1024 - 1)
Get #1, , img()

Do While Not EOF(1)
   Images.Fields("Image").AppendChunk img
   ReDim img(1023)
   Get #1, , img

Loop
Close #1
```

Saving images

The code to save the value in a long field isn't very different than it is to load the data into the field. If possible, it's best to try to deal with the data in a single chunk, as shown in Listing 15-12.

Listing 15-12: The Command15_Click event in Recordset Update Demo

```
Private Sub Command15_Click()

Dim f As String
Dim img() As Byte

f = InputBox("Enter image file name:")
f = App.Path & "\" & f

ReDim img(Images.Fields("Image").ActualSize - 1)
Open f For Binary Access Write As #1
img = Images.Fields("Image").GetChunk(UBound(img) + 1)
Put #1, , img
Close #1

End Sub
```

Thoughts on Designing Database Applications

There are two basic ways to design a database application. One way is to permit the user to scroll through from one record to another through the entire recordset. The second way is to ask the user for a key value, which will return only the records related to the key. Both approaches have strengths and weaknesses, and you can build effective programs using either technique.

The first method works well if you want to use the ADO Data Control. The ADO Data Control opens a connection to the database and its `Recordset` object as soon as the form containing it is shown. However, this isn't practical for large, multi-user applications. It can be difficult for a user to find a particular row in the data, while at the same time consuming a lot of database resources. However, this approach is ideal for small databases, where the number of records is small enough that the scrolling ability is appreciated and you have a sufficiently small number of users that won't overwhelm the database server.

A better approach for large databases is one that allows the user to retrieve data based on a key value, such as CustomerId or IntentoryId. If the user doesn't know the exact value, they can perform a limited search on a field like Name to get the appropriate key value. This approach has the advantage of using fewer resources on the database server, since you are accessing far fewer records at any point in time. It also allows you to think of your application in terms of transactions. This allows you to take advantage of stored procedures and COM+ transactions, which would allow you to isolate the application logic, and in turn makes your application far more scalable. This approach is the only way you can build applications that run in a user's browser.

Summary

In this chapter you learned the following:

- ✦ You can use the `Fields` collection to access the collection of columns retrieved from the database.
- ✦ You can use the `Field` object to access the information associated with a single column.
- ✦ You can use many different methods to select a record from the recordset, including `MoveFirst`, `MoveNext`, `MovePrev`, `MoveLast`, `Move`, `Bookmark`, `AbsoluteRecord` and `AbsolutePage`.
- ✦ You can use the `Sort` property to sort the information in a recordset and the `Find` method to locate a particular row in a recordset.
- ✦ You can use the `GetChunk` and `AppendChunk` methods to retrieve and store information in large values in your recordset, such as images.

✦ ✦ ✦

CHAPTER 16

Working with Recordsets – Part III

✦ ✦ ✦ ✦

In This Chapter

Updating fields in a recordset

Adding and deleting records in a recordset

Batching changes

Using transactions

Working with disconnected recordsets

Working with other recordset functions

✦ ✦ ✦ ✦

In this chapter, I'll wrap up my coverage of the ADO `Recordset` object by discussing how to update the information in a particular record, and then I'll explain other more advanced ideas such as batch updates and transactions. I'll conclude the chapter by covering how to clone recordsets, resync, and requery recordsets, and how to return multiple recordsets. I'll also show you some alternate ways to get data, and finally, how to set the cache size for recordsets.

Up until this point, I've focused on how to move the current record pointer around in a `Recordset` object and how to access individual fields in it. Now it's time to discuss how to change the information in a recordset. You can insert, delete, and update the individual records in a recordset by using the `AddNew`, `Delete` and `Update` methods.

Updating Recordsets

Updating records in a `Recordset` can involve no more than selecting the appropriate `LockType` when you open the recordset. After the user has updated the field using bound controls or with code in your program that explicitly changes a field's `Value` property, using any of the move methods will automatically save the changes. However, having a deeper understanding of how the update process works will help you fine-tune your application to run faster and better.

Recordset Update DemoThe Recordset Update Demo program (see Figure 16-1) is designed to let you try different approaches to updating a recordset while watching the various indicators.

While this program is similar to the Recordset Movement Demo program (and uses much of the same code), it is more complicated to use. In the Recordset Movement Demo program, most of the activities require only one button click in order to perform a function. The Recordset Update Demo program usually requires a number of separate steps in order to accomplish a task successfully. This process merely reflects the number of individual steps it takes to update a database record.

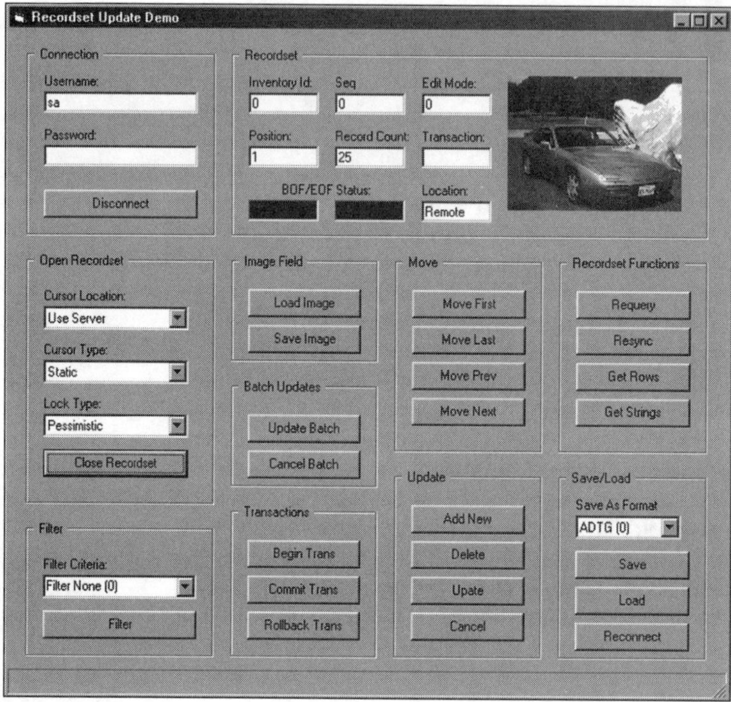

Figure 16-1: Running the Recordset Update Demo program

You can find the Recordset Update Demo program on the CD-ROM in the `\VB6DB\Chapter16\RecordsetUpdateDemo` directory.

Like the Recordset Movement Demo program, the Recordset Update Demo program relies on bound controls to display information from the database. I used a different table in this program to show you how to use an image to display a picture from an Image field in the table. Unfortunately, you can only display an image from the database with the `Image` control. You must manually load the image file from disk to update the value in the database. See Chapter 15 for more details about how to use the `AppendChunk` method to load a file to the **Image** field.

In a typical update scenario, you press the Add New button to create a new record in the database and then fill in values for the two bound fields (InventoryId and Seq). Next, you press the Load Image button to fill in a value for the image field. Finally, you press the Update button to save the image to the database. Of course, this simple example assumes that you have opened the recordset with a cursor that can be updated.

Tip

I did it first: I often find myself writing small programs that allow me to explore the various features of an object. The program usually starts out simple and often ends up fairly complex. The Recordset Update Demo and the Recordset Movement Demo programs provide examples of applications that I wrote to test various features in ADO. Rather than write your own small programs to try combinations of things in ADO, I suggest you use these programs instead. They'll save you a lot of time and energy.

Updating an existing record

The update process begins as soon as you move the current record pointer to a new row. If you selected pessimistic locking when you opened the recordset, the database server will immediately place a lock on the row, preventing any other user from accessing the row until you have finished working with it.

Note

The read-only and the batch: This section addresses only what happens when you use pessimistic or optimistic locking with a server-side cursor. Obviously, you can't update a recordset that was opened in read-only mode, and I'll cover batch optimistic locks and client-side cursors later in this chapter under "Performing batch updates" and "Working with Disconnected Recordsets," respectively.

When the row is retrieved from the database server, its values will be made available to you in the `Fields` collection of the `Recordset` object. As you saw in Chapter 15, each `Field` object in the collection keeps the original value of the field as it was retrieved separate from the current value as seen by your program. The current value is stored in the `Value` property, while the original value is stored in the `OriginalValue` property. A third value, which is available on demand, allows you to retrieve the value of the field as it currently exists in the database server at that instant. The `UnderlyingValue` property is useful only with optimistic locking, since it is impossible for the value of the field to change while the row is locked using pessimistic locking.

Note

Binding effects: Bound controls work exactly the same with `Recordset` objects as they do with the `ADO Data Control`. When the user changes a value in a bound control, the `Value` property of the `Field` object will be changed automatically. This action triggers all of the associated processes for the `Recordset`.

Initially, the EditMode property will be set to adEditNone (0), which means that no changes have occurred to the record. The moment one of the values changes, the EditMode property will be set to adEditInProgress (1), which means that one or more values of the current record have been changed.

Once you've finished changing the values in the current row, you can decide whether to save your changes or to discard them. In database terms, you either perform a *commit* to save your changes or a *roll back* to undo all of your changes. If you choose to roll back your changes, you must call the Cancel method (see Listing 16-1). This method takes care of undoing your changes in the database. While it is unlikely, it is possible that you may get a run-time error when using the Cancel method.

Listing 16-1: The Command12_Click event in Recordset Update Demo

```
Private Sub Command12_Click()

On Error Resume Next

Images.Cancel
If Err.Number <> 0 Then
   WriteError

End If

Text10.Text = FormatNumber(Images.EditMode, 0)

End Sub
```

Updating the data is a lot more complex than canceling the update, even though the code is similar (see Listing 16-2). What happens under the covers depends on the locking mode you chose. If you chose pessimistic locking, the values will be returned to the database server and applied to the database. The EditMode property will be reset to adEditNone. The lock on the record at the database server will remain in place until you move to a new row.

If you chose optimistic locking, a series of activities will take place. First, a lock is placed on the row at the database server. Then, for each field in the recordset's Fields collection, the OriginalValue property will be compared to the UnderlyingValue property. If there are any differences, the Update method will be terminated, an error will be returned in the Errors collection and the lock will be released. If the original values are the same as the underlying values, the changed values in the Value property will be saved to the database server. Then the lock on the current row will be released, and EditMode will be reset to adEditNone.

Listing 16-2: The Command10_Click event in Recordset Update Demo

```
Private Sub Command10_Click()

On Error Resume Next

Images.Update
If Err.Number <> 0 Then
   WriteError

End If

Text10.Text = FormatNumber(Images.EditMode, 0)

End Sub
```

No matter which locking strategy you chose, it is still possible for the update to fail. You may have changed the primary key so that it duplicates another value in the table. It is possible that you may have used a set of values that violates a foreign key constraint, or you may have triggered another constraint. In these situations, the update will not be made to the database, and the `Update` method will fail. Your current data will remain in the `Fields` collection, and you may attempt to correct the problem and try the `Update` method again.

Adding a new record

Adding a new record is similar to updating an existing record, except that no locks are required. The `AddNew` method creates a new database record by creating an empty row, which then becomes the current record (see Listing 16-3). All of the `Field` objects will automatically be set to **Null** or the default value as specified in the table definition. The `EditMode` property will be set to `adEditAdd`, indicating you're editing a newly accessed record. Your program is then free to change the values as desired.

Listing 16-3: The Command7_Click event in Recordset Update Demo

```
Private Sub Command7_Click()

On Error Resume Next
```

Continued

Listing 16-3: *(continued)*

```
Images.AddNew
If Err.Number <> 0 Then
   WriteError

End If

Text10.Text = FormatNumber(Images.EditMode, 0)

End Sub
```

When your program is ready to save the new record to the database, you need to call the `Update` method. The new record will be sent to the database server for processing. If you have an identity field, its value will be computed before it is saved to the database. If there are any errors with the values in the record, such as a duplicate primary key, invalid foreign key reference, not **Null** constraints, or any other constraint violations, an error will be returned, and the record won't be added. However, the values will remain in the `Fields` collection, and you can correct them to try again. Alternately, you can call the `Cancel` method to undo the `AddNew` method.

The newly added record may or may not be visible in the `Recordset` depending on your provider and the cursor type. You may have to use the `ReQuery` method to make it visible.

Yet another way to add: If you specify a list of field names and their values as part of the call to `AddNew`, the new record will be created, the listed values will be applied to their associated fields, and the record will be saved to the database. There's no need to call the `Update` method. Note that this method may still fail for the reasons I discussed earlier, at the end of "Updating an existing record."

Deleting an existing record

Deleting the current record is as easy as calling the `Delete` method (see Listing 16-4). Of course, you must lock the record before deleting it, so it is possible for the `Delete` method to fail if you are using optimistic locking. It is also possible for the `Delete` method to fail if deleting the record would trigger a constraint.

Once the record is deleted, it remains the current record, although if you try to access any of the `Field` objects, a run-time error will occur. As soon as you move the current record pointer to another record, the deleted record will no longer be visible. Once a record has been deleted, you can't undelete it using the `Cancel` method.

Listing 16-4: The Command8_Click event of Recordset Update Demo

```
Private Sub Command8_Click()

On Error Resume Next

Images.Delete
If Err.Number <> 0 Then
   WriteError

End If

Text10.Text = FormatNumber(Images.EditMode, 0)

End Sub
```

The `Delete` method has an interesting capability that allows you to delete multiple rows with a single call. You can delete all of the rows in the `Recordset`, or you can delete only those records selected by the `Filter` property. You can also delete the rows in the current chapter of a hierarchical recordset.

Performing batch updates

The idea behind optimistic locking is that with enough data, the odds that two or more people would try to access the same record are so low as to be nonexistent. Suppose you have an application that falls into this group that performs operations on groups of records rather than just individual records. Perhaps, you have a table that you use to hold the line items entry from an order. So if someone is likely to access one of these rows, that person is likely to access all of them. The same argument could hold true for the course records in a student information system, the transaction records against a single financial account, or the payroll records of a single employee. Each of these groups could be considered a batch, which is updated as a single unit.

ADO supports the concept of batch updating with a *batch optimistic* locking strategy. It uses the same locking strategy that is used for an optimistic lock, but it allows you to create a group of changes that are sent to the database server for processing at a single time. By transmitting the group of changes as a single group, you can get better response time because you don't have to wait on each individual row to be updated. Also, this means less work for the server as it can update the group of rows more intelligently.

In terms of using batch optimistic locks in your application, you need to open the Recordset object with LockType equal to adLockBatchOptimistic. Next you should set CursorLocation to adUseClient and CursorType to adStatic. While other combinations of these properties may work, these will give you the best results. All of the data will be buffered locally in the client computer, which will give you the best performance because you only communicate with the database server at the beginning and the end of the process.

After you open your Recordset, you can use it as you normally would. You can add new records, delete existing ones, or change any values you choose. However, as you make these changes, they are held and not transmitted to the database server for processing. Instead, they are held locally until you explicitly commit them or discard them.

You can discard your changes with the CancelBatch method (see Listing 16-5), or you can save the changes with the UpdateBatch method (see Listing 16-6). However, since the changes are applied with an optimistic lock, you need to check for errors to see if all of your changes were successfully applied. Even if you use the CancelBatch method, it is possible for you to get a warning or an error if someone else deleted some or all of the records you would have updated before you canceled the update.

Listing 16-5: The Command13_Click event in Recordset Update Demo

```
Private Sub Command13_Click()

On Error Resume Next

Images.CancelBatch
If Err.Number <> 0 Then
   WriteError

End If

Text10.Text = FormatNumber(Images.EditMode, 0)

End Sub
```

You can check the status of your data after you use the CancelBatch or the UpdateBatch by setting the Filter property to adFilterConflictingRecords. The filter limits the recordset so that only the records that couldn't be updated during the call to UpdateBatch are visible. You should then scan through the entire recordset and check the Status property to learn why the records weren't properly updated.

Listing 16-6: The Command11_Click event in Recordset Update Demo

```
Private Sub Command11_Click()

On Error Resume Next

Images.UpdateBatch
Images.Filter = adFilterConflictingRecords
Images.MoveFirst
Do While Not Images.EOF
   If Images.Status <> 0 Then
      MsgBox "Error " & FormatNumber(Images.Status,0) & _
         " in: " & _
         FormatNumber(Images.Fields("InventoryId").Value, 0)

   End If

   Images.MoveNext

Loop

Text10.Text = FormatNumber(Images.EditMode, 0)

End Sub
```

Making Transactions

An important feature in ADO is the ability to use *transactions* while processing your data. They allow you to identify a series of individual database operations all of which must be successful or all of their effects must be completely removed from the database.

Why do I need transactions?

Think back to Chapter 14 where I was discussing why locking is necessary in a database system. I discussed an example where you needed to serialize the debits and the credits to a bank account to prevent an invalid value from being created. Yet you could create an invalid amount in another way, even with proper locking.

Consider what happens when you transfer money from one account to another. You withdraw money from one account and credit it to another. With locking, you can make sure that each operation ensures that the appropriate values are created in both tables. However, what happens if one operation happens and the other doesn't. If you do the withdrawal first, the money will disappear if it isn't properly credited, while if the credit is made first, the money appears to come out of nowhere.

This is a situation where you have two database operations that must be successful or both operations must fail together. If only one fails, you have a serious problem. The problems that cause the failure of one operation and not the other can range from a simple application error, through a networking problem, and to a major database server problem. While you might think that this example is a little contrived, there are many situations where you have a series of database operations where you want all of them to succeed or none of them.

The solution to this program is to group the set of operations into a package known as a transaction. A transaction is an *atomic* unit because it can't be subdivided. The entire transaction must be applied to the database, or the entire transaction is aborted.

Yet a transaction need not be limited to a single recordset. Most applications update multiple recordsets as a routine part of their processing. Consider the order portion of the sample database. The Orders table contains information that is specific to the order such as the CustomerId and the date the order was placed. Each item in the order has a separate record in the OrderDetails table. To place an order, you have to add one record to the Orders table and one or more records to the OrderDetails table. This is another situation where you want both tables properly updated or neither.

ADO and transactions

Transactions are implemented using the `Connection` object and not the `Recordset` object. You can involve any number of `Recordset` objects and operations as long as they are all using the same `Connection` object. Of course, the single connection limitation implies that a transaction can't span more than one database server, though you may be able to access multiple databases on a single database server.

A transaction involves three basic methods. The `BeginTrans` method (see Listing 16-7) marks the beginning of a transaction. The `CommitTrans` method (see Listing 16-8) marks the successful conclusion of a transaction, while the `RollbackTrans` method (see Listing 16-9) discards all of the changes made and leaves the database untouched.

Note

Transactions aren't batch locks: Don't confuse batch optimistic locks with transactions. They serve two different purposes. Batch optimistic locks are a performance enhancement that can be used successfully on large databases where you don't expect multiple users to try to access the same group of rows. Transactions are used to ensure that the database remains consistent. They can be used in any situation where you have a group of database operations that must be performed together or not at all.

Listing 16-7: The Command21_Click event in Recordset Update Demo

```
Private Sub Command21_Click()

On Error Resume Next

db.BeginTrans
If Err.Number <> 0 Then
   WriteError

Else
   Text11.Text = "Active"

End If

End Sub
```

Listing 16-8: The Command20_Click event in Recordset Update Demo

```
Private Sub Command20_Click()

On Error Resume Next

db.CommitTrans
If Err.Number <> 0 Then
   WriteError

Else
   Text11.Text = "Committed"

End If

End Sub
```

Listing 16-9: The Command19_Click event in R ecordset Update Demo

```
Private Sub Command19_Click()

On Error Resume Next
db.RollbackTrans
If Err.Number <> 0 Then
```

Continued

Listing 16-9 *(continued)*

```
    WriteError
Else
    Text11.Text = "Rollback"

End If

End Sub
```

If you set the `Connection` object's `Attribute` property to either `adXactAbortRetaining` or `adXactCommitRetaining` or both, a new transaction will be started automatically when you call either the `RollbackTrans` or the `CommitTrans` method. While this can be useful in some types of programs, I like the idea of explicitly marking the beginning and end of a transaction. Not only does this make the code that forms the transaction clearer to the next programmer who may have to modify your program, but it also allows you the freedom to perform database activities outside the scope of a transaction.

Working with Disconnected Recordsets

Client-side cursors let you do more of your database work on your local machine rather than continually communicating with the database server for each and every request. However, it is possible to do all of your work locally if you're willing to do a little extra work and then upload your work to the database server when you're finished.

What is a disconnected recordset? The basic idea behind a *disconnected recordset* is that you make a local copy of the data in the recordset and then break the connection to the database server. You can then perform your updates against the local copy, and when you're finished, you can reconnect to the database server and upload the changes.

The key to making this work is the ability to use a client-side cursor and batch optimistic locking. Using these tools, you would go ahead and process your data normally and all of the changes would be buffered locally until you execute the `UpdateBatch` method to transmit them to the database server. So while you might have a connection to the database server, it's not absolutely necessary since there are no communications traveling between the database client and the database server.

Disconnected from the net: Disconnected recordsets are ideal for situations where you need to make changes to your database from a laptop that is not permanently attached to your network. You can collect these changes into a single batch while the computer is away from the network and upload them when the computer is reattached to the network.

Making a recordset local

A Recordset object can be saved as a local disk file by using the Save method. You can save the recordset using either the ADTG (Advanced Data Table Datagram) or XML (Extensible Markup Language). ADTG is a Microsoft proprietary format that is somewhat more efficient than the XML format and can handle all types of Recordsets. XML is an open standard supported by multiple vendors, but there are some situations (primarily dealing with hierarchical recordsets) where you may lose some functionality. When saving a Recordset for local processing, either format is fine, though XML would be preferred if you want to share the file with someone else.

Saving the recordset

In the example in Listing 16-10, I constructed a filename using the directory path to the application and the first three characters of the file type described in the combo box. Then I used the value from the ItemData list for the current combo box to determine the format used to save the Recordset.

Listing 16-10: The Command18_Click event of Recordset Update Demo

```
Private Sub Command18_Click()

On Error Resume Next

Images.Save App.Path & "\localrs." & _
   Left(Combo5.Text, 3), _
   Combo5.ItemData(Combo5.ListIndex)

If Err.Number <> 0 Then
   WriteError

End If

End Sub
```

Expensive words: The process of saving a copy of a Recordset locally so it can be reopened while not connected to the database server is known as *persisting the recordset.*

I'll talk about XML in more detail starting with Chapter 21.

Once the Recordset has been saved, you can disconnect it from the database server by setting the ActiveConnection property to Nothing. Then you can close the Recordset object and the Connection object. As long as the recordset is connected to the database, you will continue to operate as before.

Opening the saved recordset

Once you have saved the Recordset as just described, you can reopen it using the file you just saved without specifying a connection to the database server (see Listing 16-11). You'll need a valid instance of a Recordset object in order to open the file. When you code the Open method, you need to specify the name of the file as the Source parameter and adCmdFile for the Options parameter. The file will then be copied by the client cursor library into memory and can be accessed as a normal Recordset object, and you can also use bound controls.

Listing 16-11: The Command22_Click event of the Recordset Update Demo

```
Private Sub Command22_Click()

On Error Resume Next

If Images Is Nothing Then
   Set Images = New Recordset

Else
   Images.Close

End If

Err.Clear
Images.Open App.Path & "\localrs." & Left(Combo5.Text, 3), , _
   adOpenStatic, adLockBatchOptimistic, adCmdFile

If Err.Number <> 0 Then
   WriteError

Else
   Text8.Text = "Local"

   Text4.DataField = "InventoryId"
   Set Text4.DataSource = Images
   Text7.DataField = "Seq"
   Set Text7.DataSource = Images
   Image1.DataField = "Image"
   Set Image1.DataSource = Images

End If

End Sub
```

Reconnecting to the database server

Once you've finished updating your recordset locally, you need to reconnect to the database server. This can be a few minutes or a few days after you originally saved the data. If you haven't opened the recordset with batch optimistic locks, you need to close the recordset and reopen it.

With the open copy of the local recordset, you then have to set the `ActiveConnection` property to a valid connection object (see Listing 16-12). This will restore your connection to the database server. Then you can use the `UpdateBatch` method to send the changed records to the database server. It is very important that you check the results of the `UpdateBatch` method; since it is possible someone else may have updated the records while you were editing the recordset locally.

Listing 16-12: The Command25_Click event in Recordset Update Demo

```
Private Sub Command25_Click()

On Error Resume Next

Set Images.ActiveConnection = db
If Err.Number <> 0 Then
   WriteError

End If

Images.UpdateBatch
Images.Filter = adFilterConflictingRecords
Images.MoveFirst
Do While Not Images.EOF
   If Images.Status <> 0 Then
      MsgBox "Error " & FormatNumber(Images.Status,0) & _
         " in: " & _
         FormatNumber(Images.Fields("InventoryId").Value, 0)

   End If

   Images.MoveNext

Loop

End Sub
```

Working with Other Recordset Functions

There are few other functions available for recordsets, which I want to briefly touch on in this chapter. For the most part, these functions aren't used very often, but they can add value to your application in the right situation.

Cloning a recordset

Sometimes it is useful to create an identical copy of a `Recordset` object. This may arise if you need multiple current record pointers in the same recordset or if you want to use two different filters at the same time.

In order to clone a recordset, your provider must support bookmarks. The side effect of this is that a bookmark from one recordset will work in all of its clones as long as no filters have been applied or you haven't executed the `Resync` or `Requery` methods. This has yet another side effect; changes made to one recordset will be seen immediately by the other recordsets.

Resyncing and requerying a recordset

When you access a `Recordset` with a static or forward-only cursor, you can't see the changes that someone else may have made in the database. The `Resync` method allows you to get a fresh copy of the values from the database without executing the query again. This means that the `Resync` method is more efficient.

Of course, `Resync` has its limitations. It won't detect when a new record has been added. If any of the records in the `Recordset` are deleted, an error will be generated in the `Error` collection, and you will need to use the `Filter` property to examine these records to determine how you want to handle them.

The `Requery` method on the other hand forces the database server to re-execute the query that was originally used to retrieve the records from the database. This means that records that have been added, deleted, and updated will be properly reflected in your `Recordset`. Calling `Requery` is the equivalent of calling the `Close` and `Open` methods. Obviously, using `Requery` is more expensive (in terms of resources and time) than using `Resync`, but there are times when it is necessary.

Returning multiple recordsets

A stored procedure has the ability to return multiple recordsets with a single call; however, only one recordset is accessible at a time through the `Recordset` object. You can also specify multiple **Select** statements in a `Command` object to return multiple recordsets.

When you execute the Command object, the first recordset is generated, and the server waits to generate the next recordset until you call the NextRecordset method. If you close the Recordset object before retrieving all of the recordsets, the remaining statements are not executed.

Alternate ways to get data

While you can retrieve information from a recordset using the Fields collection, there are a couple of other methods of which you should be aware. They are the GetRows method and the GetString method. Both return one or more rows of information from the Recordset object in a single call.

The GetRows method returns a Variant containing a two-dimensional array where each row of the array corresponds to a row of information from the recordset and each column of the array corresponds to a column in the recordset. The dimensions of the array are automatically resized to handle the amount of data that you request.

You can also specify the field you want to extract by including the name of the field as a parameter to the method. You can specify an array containing list of fields that you want to retrieve.

The GetString method performs the same basic function as the GetRows method, but it returns the data as a single String rather then the cells of an array. You can specify the delimiter that will be used between columns and the delimiter between rows. For example, you can create a CSV (comma separated value) file by specifying a comma (,) as the column delimiter and a carriage return/line feed pair (vbCrLf) for the row delimiter.

Both methods start with the current record and return the specified number of records. The GetRows method allows you to specify the starting position if your Recordset supports bookmarks.

Comma Separated Value files, the easy way: The GetString method makes it really easy to create the data for a CSV file.

Note that with either method, you may get an error number 3021 when reading the last block of data. This error number means that you reached the end of the file; however, this is expected, if you read multiple records at a time. In this case, it means that you requested more records than were available, hence the end of file error.

Setting the cache size

One of the problems when building a client/server database is that all of the communications between the client program and the database server are routed through a network. By default, only one record is transmitted between your application and the database server each time you move the current record pointer. However, this value is tunable by using the `CacheSize` property.

The `CacheSize` determines the number of records that are buffered locally by the OLE DB provider. A value of one means that only one record is quickly available to your program. Increasing this size to more than one means that the provider will keep multiple records locally. This means that the provider will not request additional data from the server until you reference a record outside of the cache. As long as your program requests from within the cache, the provider doesn't need to communicate with the database server. When your program does reference a record outside of the cache, the provider will flush the local cache and fill it again with new records from the database server.

Depending on your program, changing the `CacheSize` property can make a big difference, either good or bad. If you are reading through the `Recordset` sequentially, then you'll get the biggest performance boost, especially if you open the recordset in read-only mode with a forward-only cursor. In many cases, the cost of retrieving records is proportional to the number of calls the provider has to make to the database server. Thus, if you retrieve more records from the database server with each call, the fewer calls you will need to make to satisfy the query.

However, if your program is reading records randomly throughout the recordset, having a large cache is a detriment. The database server must retrieve more records from the database and transmit them over the network, which is work that is essentially wasted.

There is another issue using a large cache, which can cause other problems if you are not careful. Since the provider and server are not in contact until you need to retrieve additional records, it is possible that someone else will have changed or deleted a record after the records were retrieved. Your program will need to be able to handle this situation. For read-only access with a forward-only cursor, this shouldn't be a big problem. But if your program is attempting to update records using a `CacheSize` greater than one, you may have problems. I suggest that you either use batch optimistic locking and handle the errors after the fact or drop the `CacheSize` back to one.

Thoughts on Updating Recordsets

Updating `Recordsets` is one of the most important functions that a database program PERFORMS. ADO provides a wide range of tools to make this process as painless as possible. Once you get comfortable using the ADO object library to access your data, using other tools will feel downright awkward.

Most of the time when I need to build a simple program to update a database, I just open a `Recordset` object and then bind a bunch of controls to it to display the information. While there is a little more code involved with this process than using something like the ADO Data Control, I don't mind the extra work because I prefer to open the `Recordset` after I open the form that uses it.

But while it is easy to update a database using a `Recordset`, you'll probably be better off using stored procedures and a `Command` object. Depending on the database server and the OLE DB provider, many `Recordset` operations have to be translated to explicit SQL Statements that are executed directly against the database. While this extra work isn't much, if you have a high-volume application, anything you can do to reduce work will make your application run better. After all, while machine resources are relatively cheap, someone has to pay for them, and if you don't really need the resources, you shouldn't use them.

Summary

In this chapter you learned the following:

- ✦ You can change the values in a row by using the `Fields` collection and then save the new values using the `Update` method.
- ✦ You can use the `AddNew` method to insert a new row and the `Delete` method to remove a row from a recordset.
- ✦ You can group changes into batches for better performance.
- ✦ You can define transactions in your application, in which all of the changes must succeed or all of the changes will be discarded.
- ✦ You can use disconnected recordsets to access information from the database without having an active connection to the database.
- ✦ You can perform a number of other useful functions with a `Recordset` object such as returning multiple recordsets and multiple rows.

✦ ✦ ✦

COM+ Transactions and Message Queues

P A R T

IV

✦ ✦ ✦ ✦

In This Part

✦ ✦ ✦ ✦

For the advanced Visual Basic program, this Part explores three very interesting subjects: first, how to build your own bound controls, including controls that can act as a data source and a data consumer; second, how to build a transaction for the COM+ Transaction Server (COM+ Transactions are important in many large applications where you need scalability and high performance); and finally, an introduction to Microsoft Message Queues, which provide you with a way to process transactions asynchronously.

CHAPTER 17

Building Your Own Bound Controls

◆ ◆ ◆ ◆

In This Chapter

Building class objects

Building user controls

Implementing data binding

◆ ◆ ◆ ◆

In this chapter, I'll show you how to build your own COM components that can be bound to a data source. I'll also cover how to create your own data source, which can be used in place of the ADO Data Control.

Introducing Data Sources and Consumers

In the ADO world, everything can be classified into one of two groups: data sources and data consumers. A *data source* produces data that can be read by a data consumer. A *data consumer* may update data provided by a data source. The technique used to connect the data source to the data consumer is known as *data binding*. This is the same technique that you use to bind a text box control (data consumer) to the ADO Data Control (data source).

Data sources and data consumers are just COM objects that support a few special properties and events. COM objects can take the form of ActiveX controls, ActiveX DLLs, and ActiveX EXEs. The form you choose depends on how you want your objects to work. The same principles of binding apply equally to all three types of COM components.

Data sources

A data source is responsible for generating an ADO `Recordset` object, which is accessed by a data consumer. A common example of a data source in Visual Basic is the ADO Data Control. While you might think that the ADO Data Control is very complicated, it really isn't. I'll show you how to build one later in this chapter, in the section called "Building a Data Source".

A data source has two key elements: the `DataSourceBehavior` property and the `GetDataMember` event. When the `DataSourceBehavior` property has a value of `vbDataSource` (1), the object becomes a data source. The `GetDataMember` event will be triggered whenever the data source needs an object pointer to the `Recordset` object. Whenever the current record in the `Recordset` object changes, the data consumer will be notified and it can update its information.

The data source has the option of making more than one recordset available to a data consumer. The `DataMember` property is used to identify the specific recordset that the data consumer wants to access. This value is passed to the object using the `GetDataMember` event. If your data source only returns a single `Recordset` object, then this property can be ignored.

Data consumers

A data consumer receives data generated by a data source. It doesn't deal with the `Recordset` object directly, but rather it identifies one or more fields of data that it wants to access and the properties that will receive it. Then, as the current record pointer in the `Recordset` moves, the data source will assign the updated data to the specified properties in the data consumer.

Data consumers come in two flavors: simple and complex. A *simple data consumer* binds only a single property to a data source, while a *complex data consumer* can bind multiple properties to a data source. The type of data consumer is identified by the `DataBindingBehavior` property. A value of `vbSimpleBound` (1) means that the object has one property bound to the data source, while a value of `vbComplexBound` (2) means that the object has multiple properties bound to the data source.

After selecting the type of data consumer, you need to adjust the attributes for each of the properties you want to bind to the data source. This involves using the Procedure Attributes dialog box to mark the property as data bound. If you're not familiar with this tool, see "Setting Property Attributes," later in this chapter.

While a simple data consumer can specify the necessary binding information directly in the object's properties, a complex data consumer can't. It uses the `DataBindings` collection and the `DataBinding` object to hold the definitions. The `DataBinding` object contains all of the properties that would have been used in the object itself had the object been a simple data consumer. Thus, you need one `DataBinding` object for each property you wish to bind. The `DataBindings` collection holds the set of `DataBinding` objects for the data consumer.

A Brief Introduction to COM Components

Many database applications, which are written as a series of large programs, could benefit from rewriting them to use COM (component object model) components. COM components are ideal for isolating commonly used functions from the programs that use them. You can use them to hold your application logic, such as how to validate a particular data element, or you can use them to hold your database logic, such as how to retrieve a set of information from the database.

By isolating commonly used routines away from your main programs, you make it easier to update your application. Since COM components live in files external to your program's EXE file, you can replace one component without necessarily affecting the others. This will let you replace one small file, rather than replacing all of the program files that make up your application.

What is a COM component?

A COM component is an object module that contains executable code that can be dynamically loaded into memory at runtime. Communication with a COM component follows a fairly strict set of rules, the details of which a Visual Basic programmer really doesn't have to worry about. The Visual Basic programmer only has to worry about properties, methods, and events that form the interface to the COM component.

Recall that COM components come in three flavors: ActiveX DLLs, ActiveX EXEs, and ActiveX Controls. Every Visual Basic programmer is familiar with ActiveX controls, which are placed on their forms to perform various functions. ActiveX DLLs (Dynamic Linking Libraries) and ActiveX EXEs (Executables) are really just a series of one or more Visual Basic `Class` modules that are compiled into a single file.

The key difference between an ActiveX control and ActiveX DLLs and EXEs is that a control has a visible presence that can be included on a Visual Basic form. ActiveX DLLs and EXEs are built using the Visual Basic `Class` modules, while an ActiveX control is built using a `UserControl` module.

Using class modules

Class modules are used to build both ActiveX DLLs and ActiveX EXEs. Which of these you choose depends on how you plan to use them. The code in an ActiveX DLL runs inside your program's address space and responds quicker to processing requests than an ActiveX EXE. An ActiveX EXE runs independently of your program and need not reside on the same computer. This allows you to spread your processing over multiple computers.

A `Class` module is just a template for an object. It describes the public properties, methods, and events that other programs will use, and it contains the code and local data storage definitions that are used to respond to various processing requests.

Properties appear to the user as a variable that is part of the object. They are implemented as either a public module level variable that is visible to the users of the object or as a special routine that is called when you want to return or set a property value. Property values are returned using the `Property Get` statement, which is equivalent to the `Function` statement. The `Property Set` statement is used to assign object values to a property, while the `Property Let` is used to assign values to all other types of variables. While it is legal to use a set of parameters with the `Property` statements, you should make the PropertyGet and Let statements have the same parameter list.

Methods are normal functions and subroutines that are used to perform actions using information in the object. These routines must be declared as Public in order to be accessed by the object's user. Otherwise, they may only be called by other routines in the object itself.

Events are subroutines external to the object that can be called from within the object. The subroutine header must be included in the `Class` module in order to define the parameters that may be passed to the subroutine, while the actual subroutine will be coded by the object's user and will reside in the user's program.

Eventless: Even though you have the ability to use events in your class module, you shouldn't use them, because they limit the usefulness of your objects.

Persistable objects

It is often desirable to create objects that have a memory of their property values. This means that while you run a program, you can create an object and save its values so that the next time you run the program, those values will be restored.

Queuing for bytes: When using message queuing, it is important for you to make any objects you send persistent. If you don't, you will lose your data when the receiving program re-creates your object (see Chapter 19 for more information about message queuing).

Persistence is managed though the `PropertyBag` object. When you create an instance of the object for the first time, you must provide initial values for each of the properties. As part of the process of destroying the object, you can save the property values into the `PropertyBag` object. Then when the object is re-created, you can restore the property values saved in the `PropertyBag`, which means that the object has all of the same values that it had before it was destroyed.

Consider for a moment how Visual Basic implements ActiveX controls. While in design mode, VB actually creates an instance of the control and lets you manipulate its properties through the Properties window. Then, when you go to run the program, the design time instance of the control is destroyed, but before it is destroyed, it saves a copy of its properties in the `PropertyBag`.

When you run the program, a run-time instance of the control is created, which reads its property settings from the PropertyBag. All of your design time settings are present in the new instance of the control, so the control can draw itself on the form in the proper location, as dictated by the Left, Top, Width, and Height properties. This also means that the rest of the property values are available so the control should behave as per your design.

Class module properties

Table 17-1 lists the internal properties for a class object. These properties determine how the object will behave. Note that these properties will not be visible to the user, but merely determine some of the capabilities of your object.

Table 17-1
Properties for a Class Module

Property	*Description*
DataBindingBehavior	An enumerated data type which can be vbSimpleBound (1), meaning that only a single property can be bound; vbComplexBound (2), meaning that multiple properties can be bound; or vbNone (0), meaning that the object isn't a data consumer.
DataSourceBehavior	An enumerated data type which can be vbDataSource (1), meaning the object will act as a data source; or vbNone (0), meaning the object isn't a data source.
Instancing	An enumerated data type which describes how an object will be reused. A value of Private (0) means that even though your object may have Public members, no programs outside your current project can access it. PublicNotCreatable (1) means that other programs can use this object but can't create it. MultiUse (5) means that other programs can create and use this object. GlobalMultiUse (6) is identical to MultiUse, but the properties and methods of this class can be used without explicitly creating an instance of the object first.
Persistable	An enumerated data type that allows you to keep property values between instances. If you set this property to Persistable, additional events will be available in your class module to initialize, save, and restore property values. NotPersistable implies that the object's properties will be reinitialized each time an instance of the object is created.

Class module property routines

When you set the DataBindingBehavior property to vbComplexBound (2), the four property routines described below will automatically be added to your class object to handle the binding issues.

Public Property Get DataSource() As DataSource

The DataSource Propety Get routine is used to return the current data source.

Public Property Set DataSource(ByVal objDataSource As DataSource)

The DataSource Property Set routine is used to assign a new value to data source, where objDataSource is an object reference to a data source.

Public Property Get DataMember() As DataMember

The DataMember Property Get routine is used to return the current data member.

Public Property Let DataMember(ByVal DataMember As DataMember)

The DataMember Property Let routine is used to assign a new data member to the object, where DataMember is an object reference to a data member.

Class module events

By default, a Class module has two events: Initialize and Terminate, which are called when the object is created and destroyed. However, if you make the object a data source, the GetDataMember event is also included.

Event GetDataMember(DataMember As String, Data As Object)

The GetDataMember event is triggered when a user requests a recordset by specifying a value for DataMember. Note that this event is present only when the DataSourceBehavior property is set to vbDataSource.

DataMember is a String value that contains the name of the data member that the event should return.

Data is an object reference that you must return containing a Recordset object associated with the DataMember value specified.

Event Initialize()

The Initialize event is triggered when a new instance of the object is created. You should initialize your local variables and allocate any module level objects that your object will be using.

Event InitProperties()

The `InitProperties` event is triggered when a new instance of the object is created. You should use this routine to initialize properties, rather than the `Initialize` event, to avoid conflicts that may occur when using the `Initialize` event and the `ReadProperties` event.

Event ReadProperties(PropBag As PropertyBag)

The `ReadProperties` event is triggered when an old instance of an object needs to restore its properties, where `PropBag` is an object reference to a `PropertyBag` object, which is used to store the property values.

Event Terminate()

The `Terminate` event is triggered when the object is about to be destroyed. You should set all of the object variables that still exist to `Nothing`, so that you can reclaim the memory and other resources they are using. If you don't do this, the objects will remain in memory until the user program for an ActiveX DLL or the ActiveX EXE ends.

Event WriteProperties(PropBag As PropertyBag)

The `WriteProperties` event is triggered before a persistent object is destroyed. In this event, you must use the `PropertyBag` object to save the values of your properties so that later they may be restored using the `ReadProperties` event. `PropBag` is an object reference to a `PropertyBag` object, which is used to store the property values.

The PropertyBag object

The `PropertyBag` object contains the information that needs to be saved between instances of an object. It works with the `InitProperties`, `ReadProperties`, and `WriteProperties` events in the `Class` module and `UserControl` module. The sole property for the `PropertyBag` object is `Contents`, which is a `Byte()` containing the data that is stored in the `PropertyBag`.

Function ReadProperty(Name As String, [DefaultValue]) As Variant

The `ReadProperty` method is used to retrieve a property value from the property bag.

`Name` is a `String` containing the name of the property value stored in the property bag. `DefaultValue` is a `Variant` containing the default value of the property.

Sub WriteProperty(Name As String, Value, [DefaultValue])

The `WriteProperty` method is used to store a property value in the property bag.

`Name` is a `String` containing the name of the property value stored in the property bag.

`Value` is a `Variant` containing the value of the property.

`DefaultValue` is a `Variant` containing the default value of the property.

Default consistently: You must specify the same value for `DefaultValue` in the `ReadProperty` and the `WriteProperty` methods, since the property value is stored only when it is different from the specified default value. By doing this, Microsoft reduces the amount of data you need to store in the property bag. However, if you're not careful, you can get different property values each time you save and restore an object.

Building a Data Source

The classic data source that everyone builds when creating the first data source is a clone of the ADO Data Control. It's an ideal control to build, since it offers a visual component that the user can interact with, and not much code is necessary beyond what is required to manage the `DataBindings` collection. My implementation of this control is called the `DataSpinner` control (see Figure 17-1).

The `DataSpinner` control consists of two command buttons and a text box. The command buttons are used to scroll forward and backward through the data in the control, while the text box simply represents a way to display information in the control.

UserControls vs. Classes: All of the steps described here apply equally when creating a UserControl data source or a Class module data source.

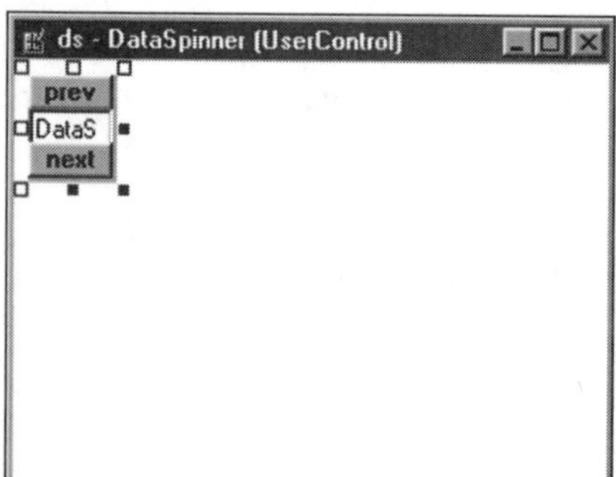

Figure 17-1: Designing the DataSpinner control

Module-level declarations

Before I dig into the code for the DataSpinner control, I want to go over the module-level declarations (see Listing 17-1). Of the six variables declared, four are used to hold property values. The ConnectionString is stored in cn; Recordsource is kept in ds; UserName is stored in us; and Password is stored in pw. The other two variables hold a connection to the database server and the current recordset that supplies the bound data.

Listing 17-1: Module-level declarations in DataSpinner

```
Private cn As String
Private db As ADODB.Connection
Private ds As String
Private pw As String
Private rs As ADODB.Recordset
Private us As String

Event Click()
Event Scroll()
```

Two events are also defined. The Click event is triggered whenever someone clicks in the text box, while the Scroll event is triggered whenever someone presses either the prev or next button.

Binding data

Since the DataSpinner control is a data source, you must set the DataSource Behavior to vbDataSource (1) in the UserControl properties. This will expose the names of the columns retrieved from the database and allow them to be bound to the control. This information is gathered from the GetDataMember event (see Listing 17-2).

Listing 17-2: The UserControl_GetDataMember Event in DataSpinner

```
Private Sub UserControl_GetDataMember _
   (DataMember As String, Data As Object)

If db Is Nothing Then

   If Len(cn) > 0 And Len(us) > 0 Then
      Set db = New ADODB.Connection
```

Continued

Listing 17-2 (continued)

```
        db.Open cn, us, pw

        Set rs = New ADODB.Recordset
        rs.Open ds, db, adOpenStatic, adLockPessimistic
        If Not (rs.EOF And rs.BOF) Then
           rs.MoveFirst
        End If

     End If

  End If

  Set Data = rs

  End Sub
```

The `GetDataMember` event is called whenever Visual Basic needs a reference to the underlying `Recordset` object. This allows the caller to find out the names of the columns returned at design time or to retrieve the current row of information to be displayed in the bound controls.

This event will also be called each time the `DataMember` property in the control is changed. Typically, you would return a different `Recordset` based on the value of `DataMember` argument: however, in this case, I'm always going to return the same `Recordset` no matter what value is supplied in the `DataMember` argument.

I start this event by checking to see if the module-level variable `db` is `Nothing`. If it is, it means that I haven't opened a connection to the database yet. Then I can verify that someone entered a connection string (`cn`) and a user name (`us`) before opening a database connection.

Once the connection is open, I can open the `Recordset` object. In this case, I choose to always specify a static cursor and pessimistic locking. However, I could have easily created properties for these values also. Then I do a `MoveFirst` to ensure that the current record pointer is pointing to the first record in the `Recordset`.

At the end of the routine, I'll return an object pointer to the `Recordset` object using the `Data` parameter. If I couldn't open the `Recordset`, then the `rs` will have a value of `Nothing` and the program trying to bind to the control will get an error. Otherwise, the information contained in `rs` will be used in the binding process.

Moving through the recordset

Once the control has been initialized, you write your program just like you would normally write a Visual Basic program. For instance, in Listing 17-3, the code you see would be very typical of routine to move current record pointer to the next record in a recordset.

Listing 17-3: The Command2_Click event in DataSpinner

```
Private Sub Command2_Click()

If Not rs Is Nothing Then
   rs.MoveNext
   If rs.EOF Then
      rs.MoveFirst

   End If
   RaiseEvent Scroll

End If

End Sub
```

The only part of the code that is different is the `RaiseEvent` statement. In this case, the `RaiseEvent` statement is used to trigger the `Scroll` event that was declared in the module-level declarations. This event allows someone using this control to detect when the current record pointer has changed.

Exporting recordset information

A programmer using this control might find it useful to look at the underlying `Recordset` object from time to time. The easiest way to handle this is to create a `Property Get` routine, like the one shown in Listing 17-4. This routine merely returns an object reference to `rs`. Because I don't want anyone changing the object, I didn't include a `Property Set` routine. This makes the `Recordset` property read-only, and the programmer using the control can't substitute their recordset for the one in the control.

Listing 17-4: The Recordset Property Get routine in DataSpinner

```
Public Property Get Recordset() As ADODB.Recordset

Set Recordset = rs

End Property
```

Using the DataSpinner control

Adding the `DataSpinner` control to your application is merely a matter of dragging the control onto your form and setting a few properties. In this case, I set the `Connection` property to `provider=sqloledb;data source=athena;initial catalog=VB6DB` and the `RecordSource` property to `Select * From Customers`. This will return all of the records in the Customer table.

The `Scroll` event is a good place to display the `AbsolutePosition` property of the underlying `Recordset` (see Listing 17-5). Note that I use the `Recordset` property described previously in this chapter under "Exporting Recordset Information" to access this information.

Listing 17-5: The DataSpinner1_Scroll event in Customer Viewer

```
Private Sub DataSpinner1_Scroll()

DataSpinner1.Text = _
   FormatNumber(DataSpinner1.Recordset.AbsolutePosition, 0)

End Sub
```

Building a Data Consumer

To go along with the data source I just built, I created a simple data consumer called `AddressDisplay` (see Figure 17-2). The control is composed of six text boxes and six label controls. Each text box has its own unique property. Assigning a value to any of these properties simply displays the value in the appropriate text box.

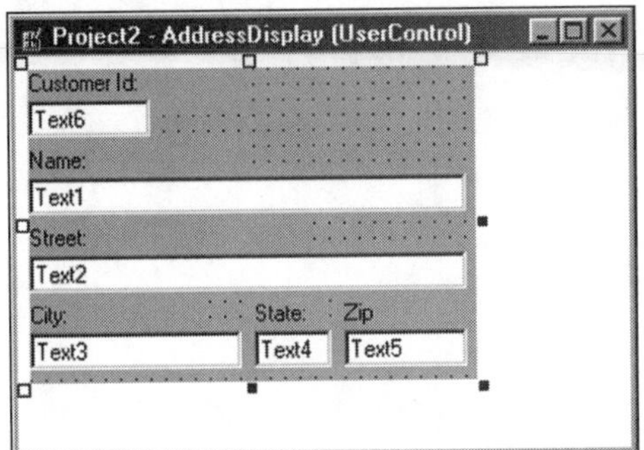

Figure 17-2: Designing the AddressDisplay control

Exposing properties

Each text box on the control has a `Property Get` routine and `Property Let` routine that manage the information associated with each control. Listing 17-6 shows a typical `Property Get` routine that retrieves the value from the text box that is used to display the `Name` field from the database.

Listing 17-6: The CName Property Get routine in AddressDisplay

```
Public Property Get CName() As String

CName = Text1.Text

End Property
```

What's in a name: You may be wondering why I named this property `CName`, rather than calling it `Name` after the database field. The reason is simple. Each ActiveX control already comes with a property called `Name`, and you can't override this property.

Changing a property is somewhat more complicated than you might expect. In the `CName Property Let` routine (see Listing 17-7), you notice that I call the `CanPropertyChange` method to determine if I can change the value. This prevents errors from occurring if someone chooses to bind the control to a read-only `Recordset`.

Listing 17-7: The CName Property Let routine in AddressDisplay

```
Public Property Let CName(s As String)

If CanPropertyChange("CName") Then
   Text1.Text = s
   PropertyChanged "CName"

End If

End Property
```

I also use the `PropertyChanged` method to notify the control that this property has changed. This is important, since it ensures that the control knows when a property has changed. If the control isn't aware that the property has changed, it may not properly save the property values in the `Recordset`.

You should closely examine your code and the objects on your `UserControl` to make sure that the value of the property can't be changed without calling the `PropertyChanged` method. In the case of this control, it is possible for a user to change the contents of the text box on the control. So I need to include a `Change` event for each text box to indicate that the value of the property has been changed (see Listing 17-8).

Listing 17-8: The Text1_Change event in AddressDisplay

```
Private Sub Text1_Change()

PropertyChanged "CName"

End Sub
```

Setting property attributes

In order to allow a property to be bound to a data source, you have to identify the property as data bound. To set the attribute on the property, you need to use the Procedure Attributes tool (see Figure 17-3). To start the tool, choose Tools ➪ Procedure Attributes from the Visual Basic main menu.

To mark a property as data bound, select the name of the property in the Name drop-down box and press the Advanced button. This will display a window similar to the one shown in Figure 17-4. At the bottom of the window is the Data Binding section.

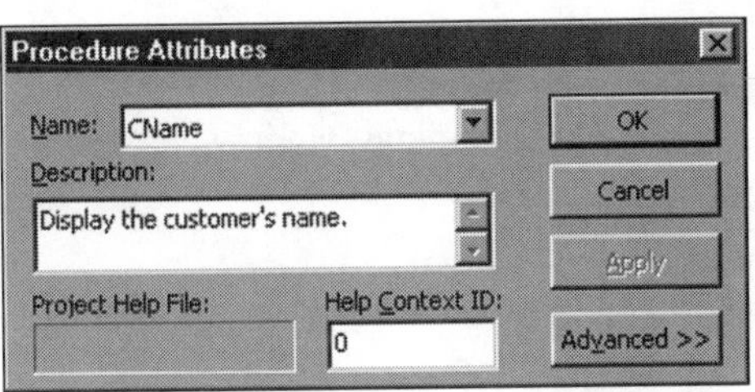

Figure 17-3: Setting property attributes

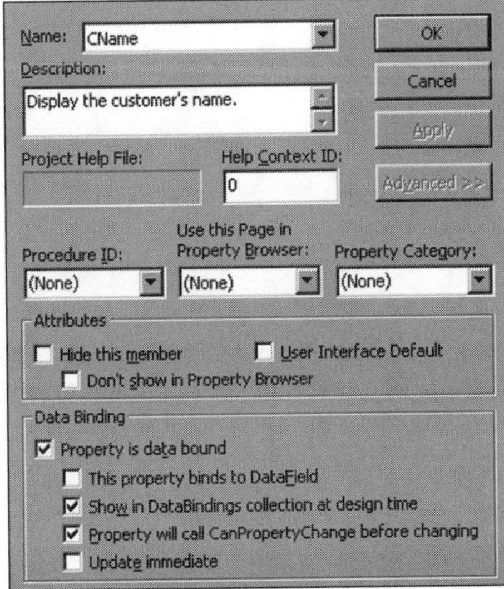

Figure 17-4: Viewing advanced procedure attributes

In the Data Binding section, place a check mark in the Property is data bound check box. This will enable the check boxes below it. Then you should check Show in DataBindings collection at design time and Property will call CanPropertyChange before changing check boxes. This will allow you to bind the property to a data source at design-time and let Visual Basic know that you are using the `CanPropertyChange` method in the property routines.

You don't have to close the window after selecting the information for a single property. Just select a different property in the Name drop-down box and set the desired values. Once you enter all of this information, you can verify it by adding your control to a simple program and displaying the Data Bindings window (see Figure 17-5).

If you check the This property binds to DataField check box in the window shown in Figure 17-4, you can bind the property to the control's `DataField` property. This means that the programmer using your control doesn't have to use the Data Bindings window to bind a field in a data source to this property.

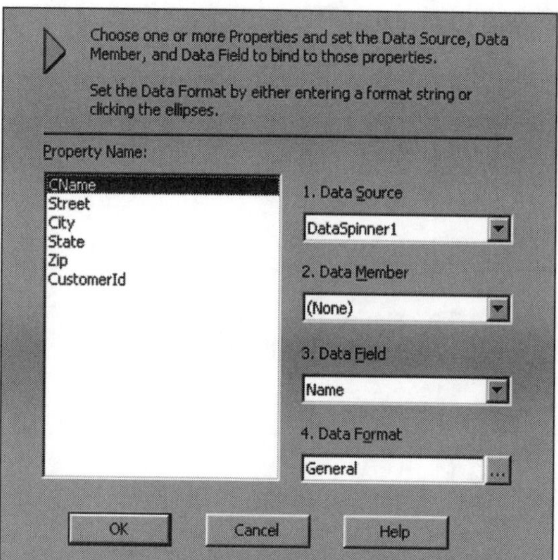

Figure 17-5: Binding properties in the Data Bindings window

Data binding and other stuff too: The Procedure Attributes tool performs many useful functions, in addition to allowing you to mark a property as data bound. You can add a description to each property that will show up when you view the component in the Object Browser window. You can mark a property as hidden, assign the property to a specific property page (if you implement custom property windows) and you can assign the property to a specific category so that it can be separated out in the Properties window.

Persisting properties

One of the important housekeeping duties you need to worry about in an ActiveX control is making sure that the values someone assigns to the control at design-time are properly saved between development sessions, and also available at run-time. This is managed by using the `PropertyBag` object (introduced earlier in this chapter under "Persistable Objects") and the `InitProperties`, `ReadProperties`, and `WriteProperties` events.

Initializing properties for the first time

The `InitProperties` event is triggered the first time a control (or any other persistent ActiveX component) is instantiated. You should include code in this event to make sure that all of the property values are properly initialized. In this example, I choose to assign descriptive values for each of the fields in the control (see Listing 17-9).

While I could have assigned these values directly using the Properties window for each of the controls used in this control, I wanted to show you the types of things you might do in this event.

Listing 17-9: The UserControl_InitProperties event in AddressDisplay

```
Private Sub UserControl_InitProperties()

Text1.Text = "CName"
Text2.Text = "Street"
Text3.Text = "City"
Text4.Text = "State"
Text5.Text = "Zip"
Text6.Text = "CustomerId"

End Sub
```

Saving property values

When the control is destroyed, the `WriteProperties` event is triggered so you can save your current property values (see Listing 17-9). A `PropertyBag` object is passed to this event to hold all of the property values. To save the current value of each property, you must call the `WriteProperties` event and specify the property name, the property value, and the default value.

Listing 17-9: The UserControl_WriteProperties event in AddressDisplay

```
Private Sub UserControl_WriteProperties(PropBag As PropertyBag)

PropBag.WriteProperty "CName", Text1.Text, "CName"
PropBag.WriteProperty "Street", Text2.Text, "Street"
PropBag.WriteProperty "City", Text3.Text, "City"
PropBag.WriteProperty "State", Text4.Text, "State"
PropBag.WriteProperty "Zip", Text5.Text, "Zip"
PropBag.WriteProperty "CustomerId", Text6.Text, "CustomerId"

End Sub
```

If the current value of the property is different than the default value, it will be saved in the property bag. Otherwise, the value will be discarded. While this saves space in the `PropertyBag` object, it may cause problems if you don't use the same default value consistently.

Reading properties after the first time

The `InitProperties` event is only called once, when the control is instantiated for the first time. Each time after that, the `ReadProperties` event will be called. In this event, you just need to load the properties you saved in the WriteProperties event (see Listing 17-10). As you might expect, you need to use the ReadProperty method to retrieve each property value from the PropertyBag object.

Listing 17-10: The UserControl_ReadProperties event in AddressDisplay

```
Private Sub UserControl_ReadProperties(PropBag As PropertyBag)

Text1.Text = PropBag.ReadProperty("CName", "CName")
Text2.Text = PropBag.ReadProperty("Street", "Street")
Text3.Text = PropBag.ReadProperty("City", "City")
Text4.Text = PropBag.ReadProperty("State", "State")
Text5.Text = PropBag.ReadProperty("Zip", "Zip")
Text6.Text = PropBag.ReadProperty("CustomerId", "CustomerId")

End Sub
```

Initialize ain't gone: The Initialize event is still present in a persistent component and you should use it to initialize various aspects to the control that need to be initialized each time the control is instantiated. You should save the ReadProperties and InitProperties events for situations where you want to keep a memory of various property values.

Pulling It All Together

With both the Data Spinner and the Address Display controls available, it is a simple matter to create a test program (see Figure 17-6). In this case, I simply created a new program and added both controls to the form. I then entered the appropriate values for the Connection, RecordSource, Username, and Password properties in the DataSpinner control, and bound the various properties of the AddressDisplay control to the DataSpinner control. I also added the code for the Scroll event to display the current record number.

Figure 17-6: Running the Customer Viewer program

Thoughts on Using ActiveX DLLs

Building your own COM components isn't difficult once you have a working template to follow. In this chapter I focused on how to create a data source and a data consumer using ActiveX controls. However, the steps I went through to expose the properties of a data consumer and returning `Recordset` information from a data source can be used to build other types of COM components.

In many ways, you'll find that ActiveX DLLs may be even more useful in database programming than ActiveX controls. After all, ActiveX controls are much more useful in a regular Visual Basic program than in an IIS Application. ActiveX DLLs can be used to represent information abstracted from a database rather than just presenting the collection of `Fields` from a `Recordset` object. They also are a convenient place to include application logic that can be used to validate information in the object or perform useful calculations with the data in the object. ActiveX DLLs are also easy to migrate to COM+ transactions, a topic that I'll explore in Chapter 18.

Summary

In this chapter you learned the following:

- ✦ You can easily create your own data sources similar to the ADO Data Control selecting the appropriate property values.
- ✦ You can build data consumers by configuring the properties of the object using the Procedure Attributes window.
- ✦ You can build COM components using the Visual Basic Class module.
- ✦ You can make an ActiveX control persistable by using the `PropertyBag` object to save and restore the values for each property.

✦ ✦ ✦

Using COM+ Transactions

In This Chapter

Reviewing the COM+ transaction architecture

Meeting the ACID test

Constructing COM+ transactions

Building a test program

In this chapter, I'll show you how to create a COM+ transaction. These transactions can be used to implement an *n*-tier application system, which can offer significant performance improvements when compared with more traditional client/server applications.

A Brief Overview of COM+

Writing a COM+ program isn't difficult. If you understand how to create and use a Class module, then writing a COM+ transaction isn't much more difficult than that. However, to write an effective COM+ application means that you need to know what COM+ is and how it works.

Multi-tier applications

In a traditional client/server application, the client computer communicates directly with the database server (see Figure 18-1). This is also known as a 2-tier application program.

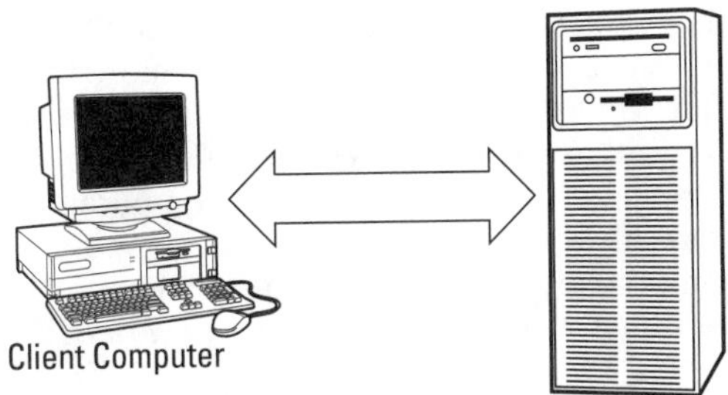

Figure 18-1: A 2-tier application

By using COM+ transactions, you can implement a 3-tier solution. In practice, you have a computer for the client, a second one for the COM+ transaction server, and a third one for the database server (see Figure 18-2). Note that the transaction server generally sits between the application client and the database server.

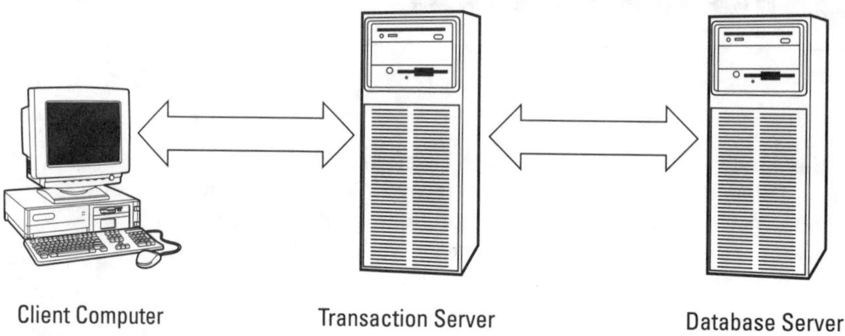

Figure 18-2: A 3-tier application

The transaction server is a place where you can move your application logic away from the client program yet keep it independent of the database server. This allows more flexibility when designing your application, because you can provide an object-oriented view of your data, while making available facilities that allow you to share resources for better performance and permit transaction support for better reliability.

A more interesting solution is shown in Figure 18-3. While I've labeled it a 4-tier processing solution, most people consider it just another variation of a 3-tier solution, because they feel that the client computer running a Web browser is not a true tier. However, given how easy it is to add VBScript or JavaScript to the Web page to perform basic functions like data validation, why not consider it a true tier?

In general, you can refer to multi-tier solutions as *n*-tier, where *n* refers to the number of levels of computers used in the application design. Note that I don't simply count the number of computers, because it is quite possible to have more than one Web server, more than one transaction server or more than one database server that provides the same basic services, but are implemented on multiple computers to better handle the workload. With *n*-tier solutions, each level of computers provides a new type of service. In practice, however, each new level of computers introduces additional overhead and beyond the four computers shown in Figure 18-3, it is doubtful that you would gain any additional benefit from adding a new tier.

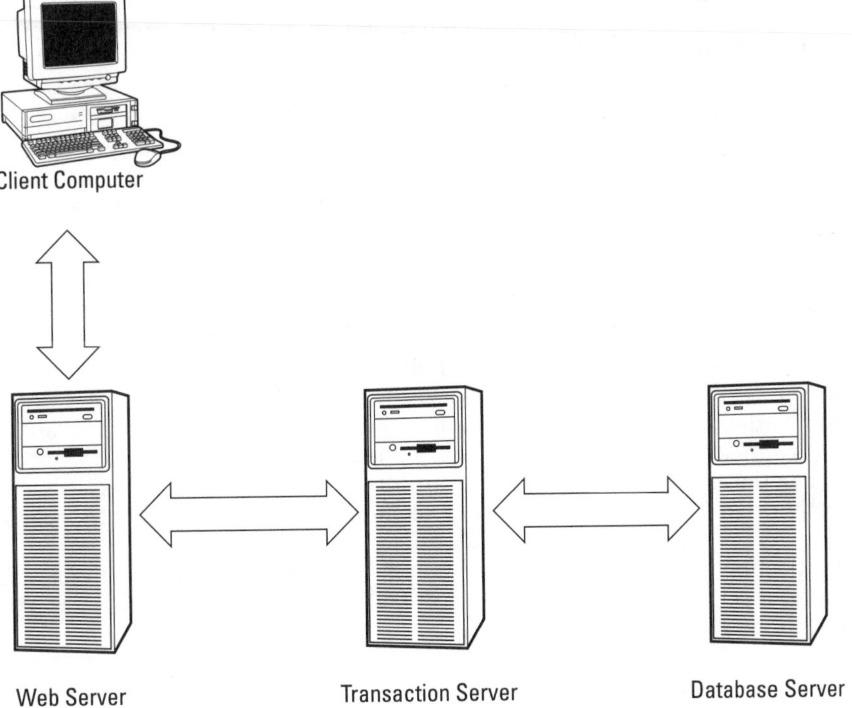

Figure 18-3: A 4-tier application

Transaction Servers

The transaction server receives requests from the program running on the client and starts a transaction to process it. If information is needed from the database server, the transaction will communicate with the database server. When the transaction has finished processing, it will return back to the calling program.

Adding the third tier, you offload some of the work from the database server, which allows the database server to perform additional work on the same hardware configuration. It also simplifies updating the application, since it is possible to make changes to a transaction on the transaction server without changing the client program that calls the transaction.

In a 4-tier solution, using a transaction server makes even more sense. It allows you to offload work from both the Web server and the database server onto a separate computer system, which serves to improve response time on both machines. This allows you to increase the available memory for Web page caching and database record caching.

Typically, the database server, transaction server, and Web server (if present) are all connected via a very high-speed connection. At least a 100 MHz Ethernet, if not a gigahertz Ethernet or other specialized networking technology, is used to connect these computers together. Often this network is isolated from the other networks to improve security and performance. This means that there are very few delays caused by the network. Yet by spreading the work around, you can ensure that no one system is overloaded. You can even add additional Web servers and transaction servers transparently if you really need them without requiring changes to your application.

COM+ applications

A COM+ transaction is basically a COM object that has been coded and compiled to run under the COM+ transaction server. In Visual Basic, you create a COM+ transaction by building an ActiveX DLL application. You need to include a few special objects and add a little code to perform some handshaking with the transaction server and use a special tool to define your transaction to the transaction server. But other than that, you're free to take advantage of the Visual Basic language.

A COM+ application is just a collection of one or more COM+ transactions that are grouped together into a single ActiveX DLL file. There are four basic types of COM+ applications:

- ✦ **Server applications:** A server application is the more common form of a COM+ application. It runs under control of the transaction server. The application can interact with the transaction server through the objects associated with the transaction's context.
- ✦ **Library applications:** A library application is a specialized form of a COM+ application that runs locally on the client computer. It runs in the same address space as the client program that created it. This means less overhead to the client program, because several COM+ applications can use the same components. However, because this object isn't running under the control of the transaction server, it can't take advantage of some of the features of the transaction server.
- ✦ **Application proxies:** An application proxy contains the registration information necessary for an application to remotely access a server application. If you run it on the client computer, all of the information necessary to access a specific remote server application will be installed on the client computer.
- ✦ **COM+ preinstalled applications:** COM+ comes with a set of applications that help you configure and administer your COM+ system. These applications include COM+ System Administration, COM+ Utilities, and IIS System Applications.

Of these types of COM+ applications, I'm going to focus on server applications, since they are the most useful of all.

The COM+ transaction server

The COM+ Transaction Server provides a framework to execute transactions on an *n*-tier application system. Included with the Server are facilities that allow you to share resources, such as ASO `Connection` objects, and provide additional security on your transaction.

You can only run the COM+ Transaction Server under Windows 2000 Server. You can't run it under Windows 9x, Windows NT, or even Windows 2000 Professional. It relies on facilities, such as the Active Directory, to manage much of the information it needs to run your transactions. Because the COM+ Transaction Server represents only one tier in an application, you can use any database server you choose, even if it runs under a different operating system such as Unix. The only restriction is that the database server must be supported by ADO.

Serving transactions under Windows NT: If you want to run transactions under Windows NT Server, you need to use a tool called Microsoft Transaction Server, usually called MTS. Many of the basic facilities in MTS were upgraded to create COM+, but COM+ is not upwards compatible with MTS. COM+ requires less code to interact with the transaction server and is easier to administer than MTS.

The object context

Every COM+ transaction that is run under control of the COM+ Transaction Server is associated with a set of objects known as a *context*. A context represents the smallest possible unit of work for a component. Each instance of a COM object is assigned to a context. Multiple objects can use the same context depending on how they were defined and created.

The object context contains information about how the object was created and the status of the work that is currently active. You can access these facilities through the `ObjectContext` object. All of the other objects in the context can be referenced from this object either directly or indirectly.

The Component Services utility

The Component Services utility is used to manage and configure COM+ transactions (see Figure 18-4). You can start it in Windows 2000 by choosing Programs ➪ Administrative Tools ➪ Component Services from the Start button. This tool will be used frequently while testing your application to change the characteristics of the transaction, as well as to install updated copies of the COM component that makes up your COM+ application.

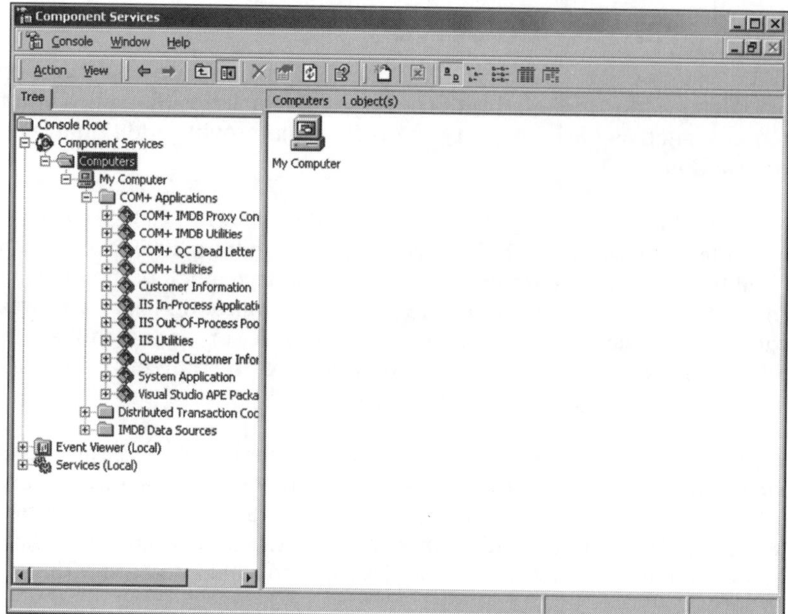

Figure 18-4: Running the Component Services utility

Introducing COM+ Transactions

COM+ transactions are a feature of Windows 2000 that you can use when building scalable, *n*-tier applications. COM+ is built on top of COM and integrates features such as the Microsoft Transaction Server and Microsoft Message Queues into a single technology.

COM+ is built using C++ and some of its features can only be accessed from C++. However, this doesn't mean that you can't use COM+ from Visual Basic 6. In fact, many of the features are actually very easy to use, once you understand how to work with them. Because this book is aimed at Visual Basic programmers, I'll focus on the features you can exploit today and leave the rest for the C++ programmers.

A view of things to come: As I write this, there are many rumors surrounding the features that will be present in Visual Basic 7. While it isn't clear exactly what features will be present, you can bet that support for COM+ will be at the top of the list.

In Chapter 16, I talked about how to use the `BeginTransaction`, `CommitTransaction`, and `RollbackTransaction` methods to define a transaction over a database connection. These transactions represented a fundamental unit of work for the application.

They could contain the database calls necessary to make a withdrawal from your savings account, register you for a college course, or even order a book over the Internet.

Simply looking at a transaction from a database perspective may be a bit too limiting for many applications. In addition to manipulating data in the database, transactions often perform validation along with the database activities. For example, before making a withdrawal from your checking account, you must first verify that the account number is valid, and second, that there are sufficient funds in the checking account before subtracting the money from that account.

There are a several ways to implement a transaction. The most common way is to write complex stored procedures that run on the database server. This approach imposes extra work on the database server, which may detract from the database server's overall performance. In Windows 2000, you have the option of building COM+ transactions that run under control of a transaction server, which you can easily run on a separate machine.

The ACID test

Each COM+ transaction must meet the ACID test. The letters in ACID stand for Atomicity, Consistency, Isolation, and Durability, and serve to identify the different criteria that a transaction must meet.

Atomicity

Atomicity means that either all or none of a transaction is completed. In other words, the work a transaction performs can't be subdivided. If the transaction completes successfully, all of the changes it makes will remain. If the transaction fails, then all of the changes it made must be undone.

Consider an airline reservations system. When you make a reservation, you specify the date, flight number, number of seats you want, plus a number of parameters such as first class or economy. You want the reservation to succeed only if all of these parameters are met. Otherwise you want the reservation to fail, so you can try again. Either all of the seats you requested are available or none of them.

Consistency

Another aspect of a transaction is that it must always leave the system in a consistent state. Consider what happens if you move money from your savings account to your checking account. You have to read the current balance from the savings account, subtract the amount of money you want to move, and update the account with the new balance. Then you have to read the current balance from the checking account, add the money to it, and update the account with the new balance.

Consider what happens if the process fails after the first update is finished, but before the second update is made. The database will automatically ensure that the first update is saved, but it will not save an incomplete update. This means that the money would be removed from your saving account but not added to your checking account. For all practical purposes, the money would be lost and the database left in an inconsistent state.

By placing the two updates into a transaction, you can ensure that the database is left in a consistent state. Either both updates are completed or both updates are not completed. In this example, whether the transaction succeeds or fails, the money won't be lost.

Isolation

While not as obvious as the previous characteristics of a transaction, isolation is also very important. Each transaction lives in its own world, where it can't see any of the processing performed by another active transaction. The concept of isolation is important because it allows the system to recover from failures. While the system is actively processing transactions, you may have dozens or even hundreds of active transactions at any point in time. However, with transaction isolation, these transactions can be viewed as a single stream of transactions, where one transaction is completed before the next one begins. This process allows recovery programs to work, and makes it possible to implement distributed database systems.

Durability

The last characteristic of a transaction is its ability to survive system failures. Once a transaction has been completed, it is critical that the changes it made aren't lost. For this reason, it's important that the system keep logs and backups of all the transactions that were processed. These files make it possible for work to be recovered in case of a catastrophic system failure.

Class module properties for transactions

In order to identify a Visual Basic class module as a COM+ transaction, you need to adjust some of its properties. These properties control how Visual Basic will compile your program.

In order to run a transaction under control of COM+ you need to specify the value of the `MTSTransactionMode` property in the class module. While this value can be overridden by the Component Services utility, you should choose the proper value before you try to install it under COM+. Table 18-1 lists the Visual Basic constant that you can set using the Properties window for the class module.

Table 18-1
MTSTransactionMode Values

Visual Basic Constant	*COM+ Transaction Support*	*Numeric Value*
`NotAnMTSObject`	Disabled	0
`NoTransactions`	Not Supported	1
`RequiresTransaction`	Required	2
`UsesTransaction`	Supported	3
`RequiresNewTransaction`	Requires New	4

- **NotAnMTSObject** implies that the object isn't supported under COM+ Transaction Server. You should use this value when you do not expect to run your component under control of the Transaction Server.
- **NoTransactions** means that the object doesn't support transactions. When a new instance of the object is created, its object context is created without a transaction.
- **RequiresTransaction** means that the component's objects must execute without the scope of a transaction. When a new instance of the object is created, the object context is inherited from the object context of the client. If the client doesn't have a transaction, a new transaction is created for the object. If the client is a COM+ transaction, then a new transaction will not be started because one is already active.
- **UsesTransaction** means that the component's objects can execute within the scope of a transaction. When a new instance of the object is created, its object context is inherited from the object context of the client. If the client doesn't have a transaction, the new object will run without a transaction.
- **RequiresNewTransaction** means that the component's objects must execute within their own transactions. When a new instance of the object is created, a new transaction will automatically be created for the object, even if the calling object is already executing within a transaction.

The ObjectContext object

The `ObjectContext` object is the most important object when implementing a COM+ transaction. Through this object, you will control how the transaction behaves. You can use this object to communicate with the transaction server and find out information about the environment in which it is running.

You can get access to this object by selecting the COM+ Services Type Library from the References window by choosing Project ÿ References from the Visual Basic main menu (see Figure 18-5) and then declaring and calling the `GetObjectContext` function, as shown below:

```
Dim MyContext As ObjectContext
Set MyContext = GetObjectContext()
```

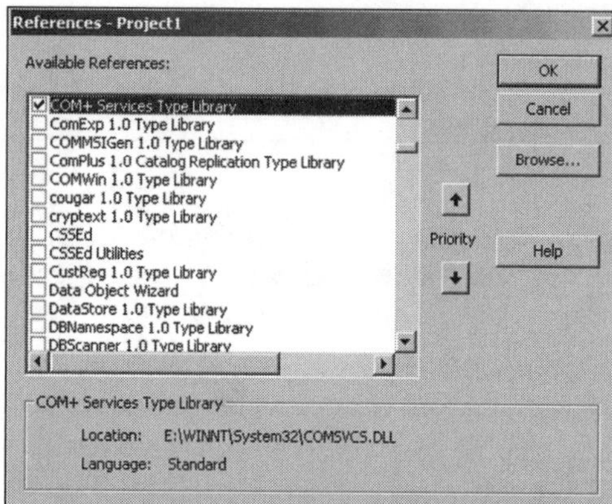

Figure 18-5: Selecting the COM+ Services Type Library

ObjectContext object properties

Table 18-2 lists the properties of the `ObjectContext` object.

Table 18-2
Properties of the ObjectContext Object

Property	*Description*
`ContextInfo`	An object reference to the `ContextInfo` object.
`Count`	A `Long` value containing the number of property objects.
`Item`	An object reference to a specific property object.
`Security`	An object reference to the `SecurityProperty` object.

ObjectContext object methods

Of the methods available for the `ObjectContext` object, the most important are `SetAbort` and `SetComplete`. These instruct the transaction server whether to allow the transaction's activities to be saved or undone.

Function CreateInstance (bstrProgID As String) As Variant

The `CreateInstance` method returns an object reference to a new instance of the specified object using the current object's context. This function should be used in place of the `CreateObject` function, because it implements the current context for its execution. If the object isn't registered with COM+, the object is merely created and no context will be assigned. If the object is registered with COM+, it will be created according to the COM+ Transaction Support value and the `MTSTransactionMode` property. `bstrProgID` is a `String` value containing the name of the object to be created.

Sub DisableCommit()

The `DisableCommit` method tells the transaction server that the object's work has left the system in an inconsistent state.

Sub EnableCommit()

The `EnableCommit` method tells the transaction server that the object's work may not be complete, but that the system is now in a consistent state.

Function IsCallerInRole(bstrRole As String) As Boolean

The `IsCallerInRole` method returns `True` when the object's direct caller is in the specified role, either individually or as part of a group. `bstrRole` is a `String` value containing the security role.

Function IsInTransaction() As Boolean

The `IsInTransaction` method is `True` when the object is executing inside a transaction.

Function IsSecurityEnabled () As Boolean

The `IsSecurityEnabled` method is `True` when security is enabled.

Sub SetAbort()

The `SetAbort` method instructs the transaction server to undo any of the transaction's actions. This may be because an unrecoverable error has occurred or the system is in an inconsistent state.

Sub SetComplete()

The `SetComplete` method instructs the transaction server to commit all updates to the system because the transaction has completed its work successfully.

Constructing a COM+ Transaction

Constructing a COM+ transaction is fairly easy. You start by creating an ActiveX DLL project to hold the transaction. If you want to pass any objects between the transaction and the program, you will need a second ActiveX DLL to hold the type information. Finally, to test your transaction, you'll need a simple application that calls the transaction.

For this example, I'm going to use the Customers table and create COM+ transactions to retrieve a single customer and to update a single customer. The information will be passed back and forth between the client and the transaction server using the Customer object. To demonstrate the transactions, I'm also going to build a simple IIS Application and run it through the IIS Web server.

Holding type information

One problem you will encounter when you begin using COM+ transactions is that you can't rely on global variables to pass information back and forth to the routines you may call. Everything must be passed as a parameter. Depending on the data you want to share with a routine, this can be a problem.

Using Visual Basic's class modules, you can create an object that contains a lot of information in a single entity. When using some of the more advanced features in Windows, such as COM+ transactions and message queuing, this is my favorite way to pass information around.

The downside to using class modules to pass information around in a COM+ transaction is that you really have to deal with two different programs. The COM+ transaction operates independently of the application program using the transaction. Therefore, both programs need a copy of the definitions. The only reasonable way to handle this situation is to introduce a third code module that holds the type definitions for your transactions. This third module exists on both the client machine and the transaction server machine.

Creating storage for property values

Like any object, the Customer object consists of a series of `Public Property Get` and `Property Let` routines, which are used to access a bunch of `Private` variables defined at the module level. Listing 18-1 contains the list of `Private` variables. Note that each of the variable names begins with an `X`. This is because I wanted the object's user to see the field names I used in the database rather than use a cryptic abbreviation. Since I'm the only person who expects to see inside the Customer object, I don't consider this a real hardship.

Listing 18-1: The module level declarations in Customer

```
Option Explicit

Private XCustomerID As Long
Private XName As String
Private XStreet As String
Private XCity As String
Private XState As String
Private XZip As Long
Private XPhone As String
Private XEMailAddress As String
Private XDateAdded As Date
Private XDateUpdated As Date
Private XMailingList As Boolean
Private XComments As String
Private XIsDirty As Boolean
```

You should note that in addition to the various fields from the database, I also added one more value, called `XIsDirty`. The `XIsDirty` property is used to indicate when the data in the object has been changed. It's a quick and easy way to determine if the information was changed and the database should be updated.

Managing property values

The `Property Get` routine just returns the value of the corresponding `X` variable (see Listing 18-2), while the `Property Let` routine is a little more complicated (see Listing 18-3).

The `Property Let` routine determines if the value of the property is different than the value already in private storage. If the value is different, then I save the new value, set the `XIsDirty` property, and mark the property as changed. Otherwise, I ignore the assignment. While checking the assignment is a little extra work, it allows someone to reassign the current value to the property without resetting the `XIsDirty` flag.

Listing 18-2: The CustomerId Property Get routine in Customer

```
Public Property Get CustomerId() As Long

CustomerId = XCustomerID

End Property
```

Listing 18-3: The CustomerId Property Let routine in Customer

```
Public Property Let CustomerId(c As Long)

If c <> XCustomerID Then
   XCustomerID = c
   XIsDirty = True
   PropertyChanged "CustomerId"

End If

End Property
```

Property May I: The `CanPropertyChange` method isn't required when dealing with properties in the `Customer` object, since the `Customer` object can't act as a data consumer.

Initializing property values

I chose to make the Customers object a persistable object. This will have a big benefit later when I talk about message queuing in Chapter 19. However, for normal COM+ transactions, you don't really need persistent objects. Once the object is instantiated, it will remain instantiated until you destroy it.

Listing 18-4 contains the statements necessary to initialize the variables in local storage. Note that I just use reasonable default values for all of these properties except for `XDateAdded` and `XDateUpdated`. For these values, I use the function `Now` to save the current date and time into these variables. This makes it easier for someone to create a new Customer object and not worry about assigning values to these two fields. It also won't cause a problem when the COM+ transaction returns information from the database, since these initial values will be overlaid with the live values from the database.

Listing 18-4: The Class_InitProperties event in Customer

```
Private Sub Class_InitProperties()

XCustomerID = -1
XName = ""
XStreet = ""
XCity = ""
XState = ""
```

```
XZip = 0
XPhone = ""
XEMailAddress = ""
XDateAdded = Now
XDateUpdated = Now
XMailingList = False
XComments = ""
XIsDirty = False

End Sub
```

As you would expect, the `ReadProperties` and `WriteProperties` events are pretty simple, just a series of statement that use the `ReadProperty` and `WriteProperty` methods to restore and save these values. Listing 18-5 shows the `ReadProperties` event.

Listing 18-5: The Class_ReadProperties event in Customer

```
Private Sub Class_ReadProperties(PropBag As PropertyBag)

XCustomerID = PropBag.ReadProperty("CustomerId", 0)
XName = PropBag.ReadProperty("Name", "")
XStreet = PropBag.ReadProperty("Street", "")
XCity = PropBag.ReadProperty("City", "")
XState = PropBag.ReadProperty("State", "")
XZip = PropBag.ReadProperty("Zip", 0)
XPhone = PropBag.ReadProperty("Phone", "")
XEMailAddress = PropBag.ReadProperty("EMailAddress", "")
XDateAdded = PropBag.ReadProperty("DateAdded", 0)
XDateUpdated = PropBag.ReadProperty("DateUpdated", 0)
XMailingList = PropBag.ReadProperty("MailingList", False)
XComments = PropBag.ReadProperty("Comments", "")
XIsDirty = False

End Sub
```

Note that even though I assign the current date and time in the `InitProperties` event to the `DateAdded` and `DateUpdated` properties, I use a default value of zero. This just means that these properties will always be stored in the property bag, which is likely to happen anyway, given the nature of the data stored in the properties.

Installing the DLL

Once you build your program, you need to compile it to an ActiveX DLL (Dynamic Linking Library) and then register it in the Windows Registry. When you register your DLL, selected information about the DLL will be loaded into the Registry, including the location of the DLL file, the name of the objects available, and the Globally Unique Identifiers (GUID) that are used to locate them.

When your program references an object, it presents the object's GUID to Windows, which in turn uses it as a key to locate information about the object in the Registry. This means that the actual location of the file can be independent of the application.

To register your file, you need to use the RegSvr32 utility program. To run it, choose Start ➪ Run from the Windows taskbar. Then enter the `RegSvr32` followed by the fully qualified path name to the DLL file, as shown below:

```
RegSvr32 d:\VB6DB\Chapter18\CustomerObjects\cust.dll
```

and press Enter. The registration program will run for a split second and display a message box saying that RegisterDLL Server succeeded.

If you need to make a change to the DLL after you have registered it, you must run the following command:

```
RegSvr32 /u d:\VB6DB\Chapter18\CustomerObjects\cust.dll
```

It will acknowledge the request by saying DLLUnregister Server succeeded.

DOS ain't dead: After using DOS and many other character operating systems over the years, I actually like typing my commands and seeing the results. I often use DOS to display directory information and to copy files, and as a result, I usually have a DOS window open. So rather than choosing Start ➪ Run, I usually just toggle to my DOS window to run the RegSvr32 command. Besides, if the DLL is in the current directory, I need only type the file name rather than the fully qualified path name.

Accessing the database with transactions

Now that I have an object I can pass back and forth to COM+ transactions, I want to build some transactions. For all practical purposes, building a COM+ transaction is just like building any other COM component that accesses a database — with two exceptions. First, you need to use the `ObjectContext` object to inform the transaction server of the transaction's status. Second, you need to grab and release database resources, such as the Connection object, quickly.

Getting customer information

The GetCustomer method (see Listing 18-6) retrieves the customer information for the customer specified in the CustomerId parameter and returns it to the calling program using the Customer object. While a method that strictly reads information from the database doesn't benefit from the COM+ transaction server's ability to manage complex transactions, it does allow this routine to operate more efficiently than it would if you embedded the code directly in your application program.

Listing 18-6: The GetCustomer method of CustomerInfo

```
Public Function GetCustomer(CustomerId As Long) As Customer

Dim c As Customer
Dim cmd As ADODB.Command
Dim db As ADODB.Connection
Dim o As ObjectContext
Dim parm As ADODB.Parameter
Dim rs As ADODB.Recordset

Set o = GetObjectContext()

Err.Clear
Set db = New ADODB.Connection

db.Provider = "sqloledb"
db.ConnectionString = "Athena"
db.CursorLocation = adUseNone
db.Open , "sa", ""
db.DefaultDatabase = "VB6DB"

Set cmd = New ADODB.Command
Set cmd.ActiveConnection = db
cmd.CommandText = "Select * from Customers " & _
   "Where CustomerId = ?"
Set parm = cmd.CreateParameter("CustomerId", adInteger, _
      adParamInput, 4)
cmd.Parameters.Append parm

Err.Clear
cmd.Parameters("CustomerId").Value = CustomerId
Set rs = cmd.Execute
If Err.Number <> 0 Then
   App.LogEvent "CustomerInfo(GetCustomer): " & _
      "Can't retrieve the " & _
      "record for CustomerId " & _
      FormatNumber(CustomerId, 0) & ". Error: " & _
      Err.Description & "-" & _
      Hex(Err.Number)
```

Continued

Listing 18-6 (continued)

```
      Set c = Nothing

   Else
      Set c = New Customer
      c.CustomerId = rs.Fields("CustomerId")
      c.Name = rs.Fields("Name")
      c.Street = rs.Fields("Street")
      c.City = rs.Fields("City")
      c.State = rs.Fields("State")
      c.Zip = rs.Fields("Zip")
      c.Phone = rs.Fields("Phone")
      c.EMailAddress = rs.Fields("EMailAddress")
      c.DateAdded = rs.Fields("DateAdded")
      c.DateUpdated = rs.Fields("DateUpdated")
      c.MailingList = rs.Fields("MailingList")
      c.Comments = rs.Fields("Comments")

   End If

   Set GetCustomer = c
   rs.Close
   db.Close
   Set rs = Nothing
   Set db = Nothing
   Set c = Nothing
   Set o = Nothing

   End Function
```

The `GetCustomer` method begins by declaring a number of objects that I'll use in this program. Next, I'll get an object reference to the `ObjectContext` for this transaction. While I don't really need it, it isn't a bad idea to get in the habit of starting every method by getting the context.

Next, I establish a connection to the database. Rather than creating a connection once and using it for all transactions that this object might execute, it is more efficient to get a connection, use it, and then release it as quickly as possible. The COM+ transaction server intercepts your call and satisfies your request with an existing connection from a pool of connections it maintains. When you release the connection, the COM+ transaction server adds it back to the pool and makes it available for someone else to use. By sharing connections in this fashion, both your application and the database server have a lot less work to do.

After the connection is opened, I create a Command object with a parameterized **Select** statement and its associated Parameter object. I chose to use the Command object rather than a Recordset because the Command object will be more efficient in the long run. SQL Server 7 will parse the query the first time it sees it, and the next time I use the query, it will be able to use the already parsed version. This makes it nearly as fast as a stored procedure, without the headaches of creating a stored procedure.

When I execute the Command, it will return a Recordset object containing the value I requested, in which case I'll save the values into a Customer object and return it as the value of the function. If executing the Command generated an error, I'll write the error to the application's log file and return Nothing as the value of the function.

At the end of the function, I close the Recordset and Connection objects and destroy all of the objects I used in the routine. Note that I destroy the ObjectContext object, since it is no longer necessary. A call to SetComplete or SetAbort isn't necessary since I didn't modify any data.

Saving customer information

The PutCustomer method shown in Listing 18-7 follows the same basic logic flow as the GetCustomer method you saw in 18-6. I begin by acquiring a connection to the database. Then I create a Command object that executes an SQL **Update** statement. Next I assign the appropriate values from the Customer object to the parameters in the command and then execute the **Update** statement. Finally, I return any error information as the value of the function, signal the ObjectContext that the transaction is complete and destroy the objects I used.

Listing 18-7: The PutCustomer method of CustomerInfo

```
Public Function PutCustomer(c As Customer) As Long

On Error Resume Next

Dim cmd As ADODB.Command
Dim db As ADODB.Connection
Dim o As ObjectContext
Dim parm As ADODB.Parameter

Set o = GetObjectContext()

PutCustomer = 0
Err.Clear
```

Continued

Listing 18-7 *(continued)*

```
Set db = New ADODB.Connection
db.Provider = "sqloledb"
db.ConnectionString = "Athena"
db.CursorLocation = adUseNone
db.Open , "sa", ""
db.DefaultDatabase = "VB6DB"

Set cmd = New ADODB.Command
Set cmd.ActiveConnection = db
cmd.CommandText = "Update Customers Set Name=?, Street=?, " _
      "City=?, State=?, " & _
      "Zip=?, Phone=?, EMailAddress=?, DateAdded=?, " & _
      "DateUpdated=?, MailingList=?, Comments=? " & _
      "Where CustomerId=?"

Set parm = cmd.CreateParameter("Name", adVarChar, _
      adParamInput, 64)
cmd.Parameters.Append parm

Set parm = cmd.CreateParameter("Street", adVarChar, _
      adParamInput, 64)
cmd.Parameters.Append parm

Set parm = cmd.CreateParameter("City", adVarChar, _
      adParamInput, 64)
cmd.Parameters.Append parm

Set parm = cmd.CreateParameter("State", adChar, _
      adParamInput, 2)
cmd.Parameters.Append parm

Set parm = cmd.CreateParameter("Zip", adInteger, _
      adParamInput, 4)
cmd.Parameters.Append parm

Set parm = cmd.CreateParameter("Phone", adVarChar, _
      adParamInput, 32)
cmd.Parameters.Append parm

Set parm = cmd.CreateParameter("EMailAddress", adVarChar, _
      adParamInput, 128)
cmd.Parameters.Append parm

Set parm = cmd.CreateParameter("DateAdded", adDBDate, _
      adParamInput)
cmd.Parameters.Append parm
```

```
Set parm = cmd.CreateParameter("DateUpdated", adDBDate, _
     adParamInput)
cmd.Parameters.Append parm

Set parm = cmd.CreateParameter("MailingList", adBoolean, _
     adParamInput)
cmd.Parameters.Append parm

Set parm = cmd.CreateParameter("Comments", adVarChar, _
     adParamInput, 256)
cmd.Parameters.Append parm

Set parm = cmd.CreateParameter("CustomerId", adInteger, _
     adParamInput, 4)
cmd.Parameters.Append parm

cmd.Parameters("CustomerId").Value = c.CustomerId
cmd.Parameters("Name").Value = c.Name
cmd.Parameters("Street").Value = c.Street
cmd.Parameters("City").Value = c.City
cmd.Parameters("State").Value = c.State
cmd.Parameters("Zip").Value = c.Zip
cmd.Parameters("Phone").Value = c.Phone
cmd.Parameters("EMailAddress").Value = c.EMailAddress
cmd.Parameters("DateAdded").Value = c.DateAdded
cmd.Parameters("DateUpdated").Value = c.DateUpdated
cmd.Parameters("MailingList").Value = c.MailingList
cmd.Parameters("Comments").Value = c.Comments
cmd.Execute

If Err.Number <> 0 Then
   App.LogEvent _
      "Customer(PutCustomer): Can't update the record " & _
      "for CustomerId " & _
      FormatNumber(c.CustomerId, 0) & ". Error: " & _
      Err.Description & "-" & _
      Hex(Err.Number)
   PutCustomer = Err.Number
End If

db.Close
o.SetComplete
Set cmd = Nothing
Set db = Nothing
Set o = Nothing

End Function
```

You may be wondering why I chose to use the **Update** statement, rather than update the database using a `Recordset` object. The answer is really simple: the **Update** statement is more efficient in this situation. In order to use a `Recordset`, you would have to retrieve the records a second time. Then you would have to change the values in the current record and use the `Update` method to send the changes back to the database. In this case, simply send the update directly to the server.

Installing the transaction into COM+

The COM+ transaction server is managed by using the Component Services utility. You can access this utility by choosing Start ➪ Programs ➪ Administrative Tools ➪ Component Services (see Figure 18-4).

To add your application to the COM+ transaction server, you need to perform these steps:

1. Choose Start ➪ Programs ➪ Administrative Tools ➪ Component Services from the Windows taskbar.
2. Under Console Root, open COM+ Applications by selecting Component Services, then Computers and the name of the computer on which you want to create service.
3. Right click on Component Services and choose New ➪ Application from the pop-up menu. This starts the COM Application Install Wizard.
4. Press Next from the welcome screen and then click on the Create an empty application button.
5. On the Create Empty Application window, enter the name for your new application and choose Server Application (see Figure 18-6).
6. Click Next to display the Set Application Identity window shown in Figure 18-7. Choose the user account under which the application will run. You can choose to use the security of the user name who is logged onto the server's console (the interactive user) when the application is run. You may also enter the name and password of a specific user. Click Next to go to the last step of the wizard.
7. Click Finish to install the empty application.

Note

Security can be difficult: For testing purposes, I suggest that you use the user name of the interactive user logged onto the server's console. Then you should sign on as Administrator (or another user name with the same privileges as Administrator). This will remove most of the security restrictions on your transactions. Once the transactions have been debugged, you can go back and create a specific user name with only the privileges needed to run the transaction.

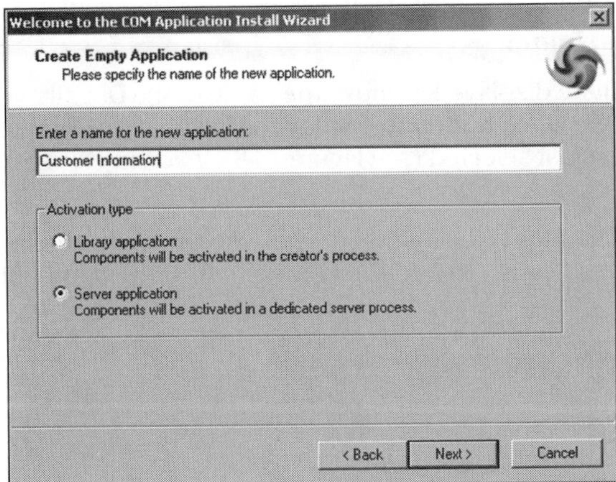

Figure 18-6: Entering the name of the application

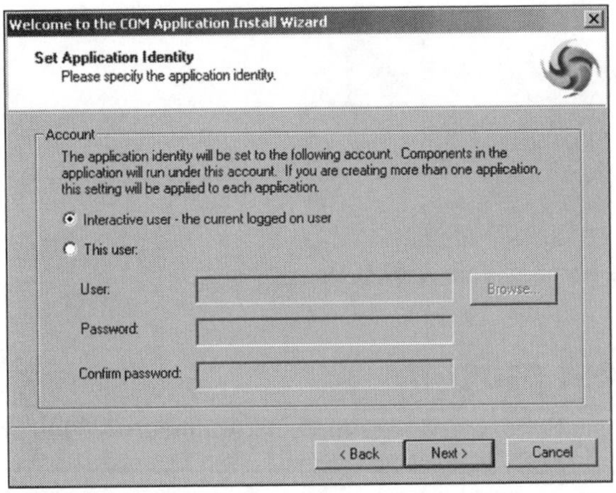

Figure 18-7: Associating the application with a user name

Once you have an empty application, you need to import your ActiveX DLL using these steps in the Component Services utility (choose Start ➪ Programs ➪ Administrative Tools ➪ Component Services in Windows 2000).

1. Expand the application you just created to display the Components and Roles folders beneath it.
2. Right click on the Components folder and select New ➪ Component from the pop-up menu. This will start the COM Component Install Wizard.

3. Click Next to move to the Import or Install a Component step and click on Install New Component(s) button.

4. A File Open dialog box will be displayed. Choose the name of the DLL file you just created and click on the Open button to display the Install New Components dialog box with the file you just selected (see Figure 18-8). If you need to install more than one file, press the Add button.

5. After you have selected the files to be installed, click Next to go to the last step of the wizard and press Finish to add the component to the application.

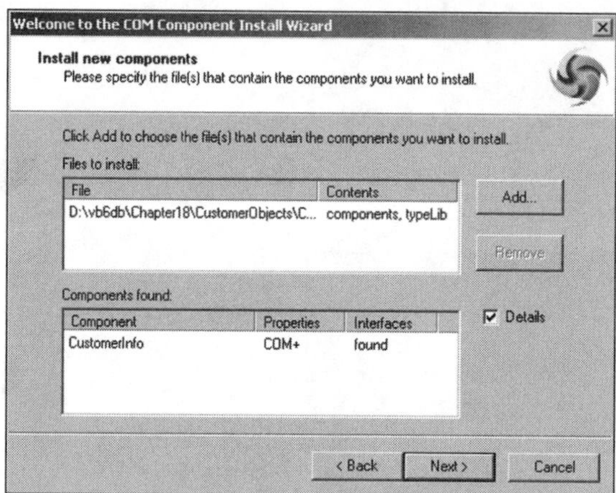

Figure 18-8: Selecting the name of your ActiveX DLL

Building a simple test program

In order to test the COM+ transactions, I created simple IIS Application. This program responds to the URL `http://Athena/VB6DB18/VB6DB18.ASP` with a Web page, as shown in Figure 18-9.

IIS Applications are neat: My favorite feature in Visual Basic 6 is the ability to create a compiled, Web server-based application using IIS Applications. IIS Applications are generally more efficient than ASP applications and they are more secure because the source code is separate from the executable program.

When someone enters the URL to run the IIS Application, IIS will trigger the `WebClass_Start` event shown in Listing 18-8. Depending on the request, one of three things will happen. If no form information is included, a blank Web form will be displayed, with default values for the `Customer` object. If a `GetCustomer` request is made, then the `CustomerId` value from the form will be passed to the `GetCustomer` transaction to retrieve the specified customer. If a `PutCustomer` request is made, then the information on the form will be passed to the `PutCustomer` method to update the database. A form with the information about the current customer is returned in both the `PutCustomer` and `GetCustomer` requests.

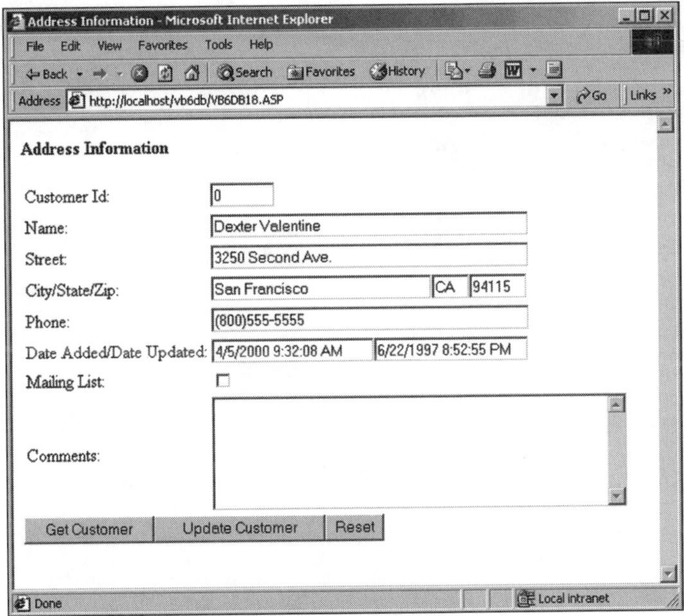

Figure 18-9: Viewing address information returned by the COM+ transaction

Listing 18-8: The WebClass_Start event in Address Information

```
Private Sub WebClass_Start()

Dim c As Cust.Customer
Dim ci As Object

If Len(Request.Form("GetCustomer")) > 0 Then
   Set ci = CreateObject("CustInfo.CustomerInfo")
   Set c = ci.GetCustomer(CLng(Request.Form("CustomerId")))
   Set ci = Nothing

ElseIf Len(Request.Form("PutCustomer")) > 0 Then
   Set ci = CreateObject("CustInfo.CustomerInfo")
   Set c = New Cust.Customer
   c.CustomerId = Request.Form("CustomerId")
   c.Name = Request.Form("Name")
   c.Street = Request.Form("Street")
   c.City = Request.Form("City")
   c.State = Request.Form("State")
   c.Zip = Request.Form("Zip")
```

Continued

Listing 18-8 *(continued)*

```
      c.Phone = Request.Form("Phone")
      c.EMailAddress = Request.Form("DateAdded")
      c.DateUpdated = Request.Form("DateUpdated")
      If Request.Form("MailingList") = "ON" Then
         c.MailingList = True
      Else
         c.MailingList = False
      End If
      c.Comments = Request.Form("Comments")
      ci.PutCustomer c
      Set ci = Nothing

   Else
      Set c = New Cust.Customer
      c.CustomerId = 9999

   End If

   With Response
      .Write "<html>"
      .Write "<head>"
      .Write "<title>Address Information</title>"
      .Write "</head>"
      .Write "<body>"
      .Write "<strong>Address Information</strong>"
      .Write "<form align=""left"" name=""AddressInfo"" "
      .Write "action=""VB6DB18.ASP"" method=""post"">"
      .Write "<table border = ""0"">"
      .Write "<tr>"
      .Write "<td>Customer Id:</td>"
      .Write "<td>"
      .Write "<input type=""text"" name=""CustomerId"""
      .Write " size=""6"" value="
      .Write FormatNumber(c.CustomerId, 0, , , vbFalse) & ">"
      .Write "</td>"
      .Write "</tr>"
      .Write "<tr>"
      .Write "<td>Name:</td>"
      .Write "<td>"
      .Write "<input type=""text"" name=""Name"""
      .Write " size=""45"" value=""" & c.Name & """>"
      .Write "</td>"
      .Write "</tr>"
      .Write "<tr>"
      .Write "<td>Street:</td>"
      .Write "<td>"
      .Write "<input type=""text"" name=""Street"""
      .Write " size=""45"" value=""" & c.Street & """>"
      .Write "</td>"
```

```
.Write "</tr>"
.Write "<tr>"
.Write "<td>City/State/Zip:</td>"
.Write "<td>"
.Write "<input type=""text"" name=""City"""
.Write " size=""30"" value=""" & c.City & """>"
.Write "<input type=""text"" name=""State"""
.Write " size=""2"" value=""" & c.State & """>"
.Write "<input type=""text"" name=""Zip"""
.Write " size=""5"" value="
.Write FormatNumber(c.Zip, 0, , , vbFalse) & ">"
.Write "</td>"
.Write "</tr>"
.Write "<tr>"
.Write "<td>Phone:</td>"
.Write "<td>"
.Write "<input type=""text"" name=""Phone"""
.Write " size=""45"" value=""" & c.Phone & """>"
.Write "</td>"
.Write "</tr>"
.Write "<tr>"
.Write "<td>Date Added/Date Updated:</td>"
.Write "<td>"
.Write "<input type=""text"" name=""DateAdded"""
.Write " size=""21"" value=""" & c.DateAdded & """>"
.Write "<input type=""text"" name=""DateUpdated"""
.Write " size=""20"" value=""" & c.DateUpdated & """>"
.Write "</td>"
.Write "</tr>"
.Write "<tr>"
.Write "<td>"
.Write "Mailing List:"
.Write "</td>"
.Write "<td>"
If c.MailingList Then
   .Write "<input type=""checkbox"" "
   .Write "name=""MailingList"" value=""ON"" checked>"
Else
   .Write "<input type=""checkbox"" "
   .Write "name=""MailingList"" value=""ON"">"
End If
.Write "</td>"
.Write "</tr>"
.Write "<tr>"
.Write "<td>Comments:</td>"
.Write "<td>"
.Write "<textarea rows=""6"" name=""Comments"""
.Write " cols=""45"">"
.Write c.Comments
.Write "</textarea>"
.Write "</td>"
.Write "</tr>"
```

Continued

Listing 18-8 *(continued)*

```
        .Write "</table>"
        .Write "<input type=""submit"" value=""Get Customer"" "
        .Write "name=""GetCustomer"">"
        .Write "<input type=""submit"" value=""Update Customer""  "
        .Write "name=""PutCustomer"">"
        .Write "<input type=""reset"" value=""Reset""
        .Write " name=""Reset"">"
        .Write "</form>"
        .Write "</body>"
        .Write "</html>"
    End With

    Set c = Nothing

    End Sub
```

This program is a little tricky in the way it works. It relies on the fact that the `Request.Form` method doesn't return an error when I try to access a particular field that isn't present, plus the fact that the value of a button is present in the form data only when it is pressed. So I can check `Request.Form("GetCustomer")` to see if someone pressed the Get Customer button and know that the value will only be there when someone pressed that button.

This means that I can use a compound `If` statement to determine which of the buttons on the form were pressed, if any. If the user pressed the Get Customer button, I can create an instance of the `CustomerInfo` object and call the `GetCustomer` method to return the specified customer value. Likewise, I can create a `CustomerInfo` object to call the `PutCustomer` method if I find the Put Customer button in the `Form.Request` method.

If neither button on the form was pressed, I can simply create an empty `Customer` object. This means that no matter how I start the form, I'll have a valid `Customer` object to use when I generate the form.

The second half of the routine is devoted to creating the HTML tags necessary to display the form. I embedded the references to the `Customer` object where necessary to display information on the form.

Developing IIS Application forms the lazy way: I used Microsoft FrontPage 2000 to create the basic form and then I copied the HTML tags in WordPad and added the appropriate calls to `Write`. Finally, I copied the statements into Visual Basic and added the code to reference the various objects I created.

Thoughts on COM+

The COM+ Transaction Server isn't appropriate for all applications. While COM+ transactions help large applications, they may actually hurt small ones. First, it adds another level of complexity that isn't necessary in a small application. Second, it may actually perform slower, depending on the hardware configuration.

However, there is no substitute for COM+ if you are building a high-volume application. This is especially true if you support multiple user interfaces to the data, such as a traditional Visual Basic form-based client/server program and a Web based application using an IIS Application.

There is a flaw in the update logic of the sample application. You may run into a conflict when multiple users try to update the data. Consider the case where Christopher gets a copy of the data, then Samantha gets a copy of the data and updates it, and then Christopher performs his update. Samantha's update would be lost and Christopher would not have seen her changes. For many applications this approach is fine, but it may cause a problem with others.

This problem is similar to the problem with optimistic locks, and you can use a similar approach to correct it. You could modify the `Customer` object to store both the original values for each field and the current values for each field. Then, when you update the database, you can compare the original values to the values in the database and abort the transaction if there is a difference.

Summary

In this chapter you learned the following:

✦ You can build applications by using multiple tiers of processing. This is known as *n*-tier processing.

✦ You can use transaction servers to improve the performance of your application.

✦ You can use the Component Services utility to add transactions to a COM+ Transaction Server.

✦ You can use the ACID test to determine if you have a valid transaction.

✦ You can use the `ObjectContext` object to communicate from your transaction to the transaction server.

✦ You can control security on a transaction so that it can perform tasks with the authority of someone other than the user name that called the transaction.

✦ ✦ ✦

CHAPTER 19

Using Message Queues

✦ ✦ ✦ ✦

In This Chapter

Introducing the Queuing Object Model

Accessing message queues

Building client and server programs

Viewing message queue information

✦ ✦ ✦ ✦

In this chapter, I want to talk about Microsoft Message Queues, including what they are, how they work, and when they might be useful for your applications.

How Message Queuing Works

Message queuing is a tool that helps two programs communicate with each other in an asynchronous fashion. This means that a client program can send a request to a server and then continue processing without waiting for the server process to complete. When the server process has finished processing the request, it will return the message to the client program, which will be notified with the response it available to be processed.

Well, kinda, sorta: While not strictly a part of the COM+ programming environment, Microsoft Message Queuing works closely with COM and COM+ components to implement high-performance applications.

Synchronous processing

Normally, when you are using a COM component and you issue a method, or request the information in a property, your program must wait until the method or property returns control to your program. This is called *synchronous processing*.

In synchronous processing, the client program begins by sending a request to the server to perform a specific task. The server program receives the request, performs the task, and returns the result back to the client. During the time the server is processing the client's request, the client program is in a wait state, where it can't perform any processing. It will only resume processing after the server has returned its response (see Figure 19-1).

Synchronous processing made simple: When thinking about synchronous processing, visualize how a Web browser works. The URL is used to generate a request to the Web server and then the browser waits for the Web page to be returned.

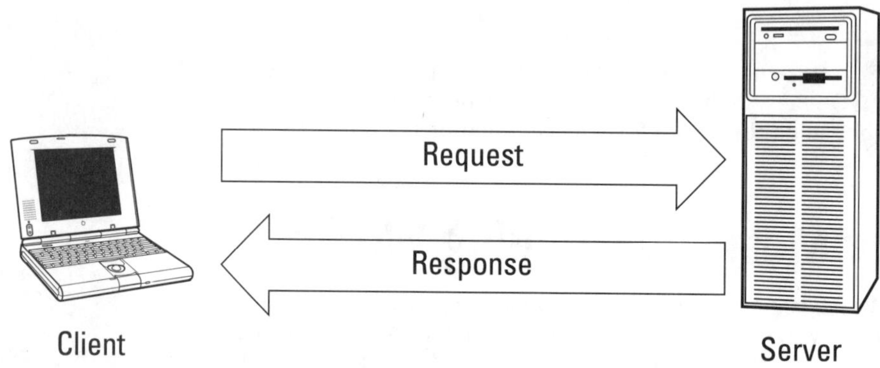

Figure 19-1: Processing a synchronous request

Asynchronous processing

In some cases, it's useful for your program to issue a request for information and then perform other tasks while your program waits for the response. This is called *asynchronous processing*.

In asynchronous processing, the client program begins by sending a request to the server to perform a specific task and then resumes its normal processing. The server receives the request, processes it, and returns the result. When the result is received, the client program is notified that the result is available and ready for the client program to use (see Figure 19-2).

Asynchronous processing made simple: One way to understand how asynchronous processing works is to compare it to electronic mail. You can send a message to someone requesting a piece of information and then continue reading and sending other e-mail until you receive a response to your original message.

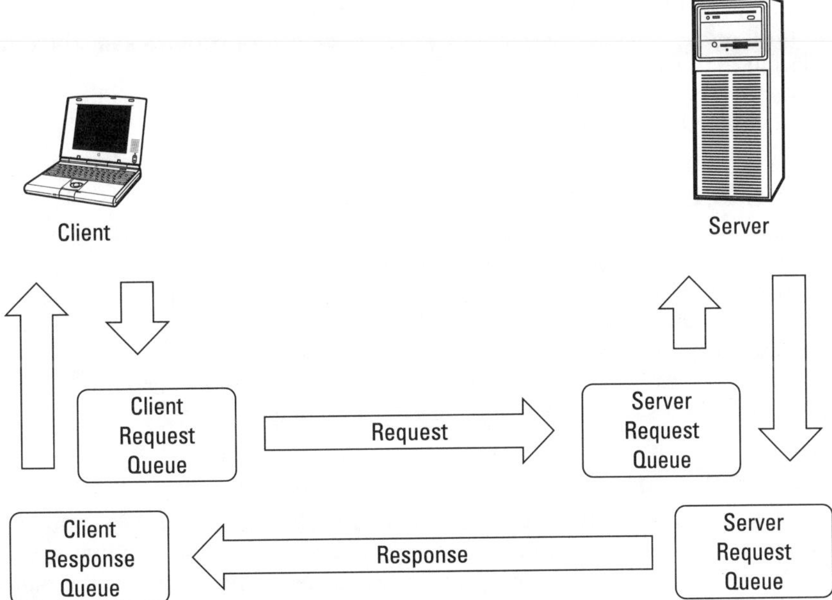

Figure 19-2: Processing an asynchronous request

Since the client is no longer tightly coupled to the server, the server has the freedom to process requests in the most efficient manner. Since it is quite possible that multiple clients will be sending requests, all of the messages are stored in a queue as they are received. As the server finishes processing one request, it will pull the next request from the queue. This ensures that all of the messages are processed in the order in which they were received.

Benefits of message queuing

Using message queues will increase the complexity of your application. In addition, not all applications will benefit from using message queuing. However, the benefits of message queuing may outweigh the extra complexity.

Component availability

Just because you have a full-time connection to the server doesn't mean that the server will always be available. The server's operating system or the application running on the server may have crashed. Networking problems are probably more common, especially if the server is located in another building or across the country from your client machines.

If you are unable to reach the server for any reason, all of the requests are buffered locally until the server can be reached. When the server becomes available, the information that was buffered locally will be transmitted to the server for processing. Also, any results that the server may have processed will be received into local storage for the client to process.

Component performance

By queuing requests for processing, the user need not wait for the server to finish processing one request before starting on the next request. Thus, you can create your application to prioritize how the processing is done. This is important when your server becomes overloaded. Those tasks that need an immediate response, such as checking inventory levels, can be handled as a normal COM+ object. Those tasks that are not as time-sensitive, such as printing an invoice, can be deferred until the server is less busy by using message queuing.

Component lifetimes

Delays caused by transmitting information over the network and interacting with the user extend the amount of time that an object actually exists inside the transaction server. By using message queuing, the exchange of information is handled outside the transaction server. This means that the object exists for far less time than it would without using message queuing. This translates into better performance in the transaction server, because fewer system resources are needed to process the actual transaction.

Disconnected applications

If you create queues that go in both to the server and to the client, you may not need a full-time connection to the server. Requests can be queued up until a connection to the server is established. Then the requests are transmitted to the server for processing using the server queue. Any responses that the server has for the client can be queued in the client queue. When the connection is established, both queues will be transmitted to the other machine. If the connection remains up for enough time, the server may actually be able to respond to the requests sent by the client and return them via the reverse queue.

Message reliability

Message queuing relies on a database to store the requests. This ensures that the requests are protected from system failures. If and when the database needs to be recovered, the requests in the queues would also be recovered. Since the time to transmit and add the request to a queue is much less than the time a normal object would exist, it is less likely that a failure would occur in the middle of a specific request.

Server scheduling

Another advantage of message queuing is the ability to shift the work sitting in a queue to a time when the server is less busy. Thus, message queues have the ability to duplicate the batch-processing features of the mainframe world by making it easy to shift work to a less busy time.

Load leveling

One problem with most server-driven application systems is that their workload can vary greatly over time, which may have an adverse impact on performance. In a synchronous environment, a server can easily get overwhelmed for a few moments at a time. If this happens occasionally, the server can catch up and nobody will notice. On the other hand, if this happens frequently, the operating system and the server application will be forced to spend extra resources managing the extra work, which means that there are less resources to process the extra work.

This extra overhead can be eliminated by using message queuing (asynchronous processing). You would tune the server and the application to get the highest performance. Then you would stage the requests in a message queue until the server can process them. Most of the time, the requests would be pulled from the message queue as fast as they arrive. However, when the requests arrive faster than the server can process them, they will remain in the message queue until the server can process them.

In real terms, the slight penalty imposed by using message queuing will not make a big difference in the time it takes to process a request until the server becomes overloaded. Then, depending on how overloaded the server is, using message queuing will increase the time to process each request. However, because the application is continuing to process requests at optimal speed, the time the request spends in the message queue, plus the time it takes the application to process the request, will most likely be less than the time it takes to process the request while the server is overloaded.

Note

Too much is just right: A long time ago, I ran into a situation where one of the computers I was responsible for was running at maximum capacity. The CPU utilization would stay at 100% for several minutes at a stretch. Response time was horrible. Upgrading to a CPU that was twice as fast solved the problem. However, the CPU utilization was about 40%, rather than the expected 50%. After a lot of digging and analysis, I determined that the old CPU was wasting nearly 20% of its capacity trying to manage the extra requests. With the faster CPU, the overload condition never arose and the CPU cycles were never wasted. While it is not always possible to double your CPU capacity, you may be able to use a tool like message queuing to ensure that the your CPU isn't wasting extra cycles trying to manage too much work.

Microsoft Message Queuing

In order to use message queues in a Windows environment, you need a piece of software called Microsoft Message Queuing (often abbreviated MSMQ). It runs on Windows 9x, Windows NT, and Windows 2000, though you may need the appropriate patches to run it. It is considered a base component of these operating systems; thus, there isn't a separate charge for the software.

Requests and responses

A request is sent to the server using an object containing all of the information needed to process the request. The object must be persistable and be less than four megabytes in length.

There are four basic responses to a request.

- **No response is necessary** – this means that the message sent by the client either doesn't need a response or the response will be returned using a different technique. For instance, the message sent by the client may request a report that will be returned by e-mail.
- **Trigger an event in the client application** – this means that the server application will fire an event in the client program when the server application has finished processing the message.
- **Use a synchronous method to check on the status** – this means that the server application may expose a property that a client application can access to determine if their message has been processed.
- **Use message queuing to receive a response** – this is probably the most common way to determine the outcome of processing a request. Consider the case of a salesperson that enters orders into a laptop computer while at a customer's site. At the end of the day, the salesperson could connect the laptop to the company's application server. Then MSMQ would transfer the local messages to the message queues on the server, while downloading any responses from the server into local storage for the salesperson to browse at his or her leisure.

Types of queues

Queues are really just storage that is allocated to contain messages along with the information needed to manage the information in the queue. Different types of requests receive different types of responses. Also, in order to operate a message queue, the software on the client and server ends of the message queue need to exchange information. This information is typically sent using message queues.

There are six basic types of queues. The type of queue dictates how the queue will be used, but underneath, the same basic technology is used to support all of these types:

✦ **Message** – this is the most common type of queue and is used primarily by applications. Clients can send messages to the queue, while server applications can retrieve messages from the queue.

✦ **Administration** – this type of queue is used by an application to retrieve status information about messages in a message queue. For example, an acknowledgement message indicates that a message was received or retrieved from the application at the queue's destination.

✦ **Response** – this type of queue is used by client applications to receive responses from the server application.

✦ **Report** – this type of queue tracks the progress of the messages as they move through the system.

✦ **Journal** – this type of queue holds messages that have been retrieved at their destination.

✦ **Dead-letter** – application messages that can't be delivered are stored in this type of queue.

Public and private queues

Queues can also be labeled as public or private. *Public queues* are registered in the Active Directory and can be located by anyone with access to the Active Directory. You can search for various properties of a queue in the Active Directory so that you can locate the correct one. Thus public queues can only be implemented on a Windows 2000 Server based system.

Combining the name of the computer with the name of the queue creates the name of a public queue. So, the queue `MyQueue` on the `Athena` would be known as `Athena\MyQueue`.

Actively seeking directory information: The Active Directory facility in Windows 2000 Server is a tool that stores information about the resources on the local computer, or resources that can be found elsewhere on the network. Windows 2000 makes extensive use of this facility to store information about the operating system, such as user names, like public queues, other specialized services, and so on. *Private queues* are registered on an individual computer and can be found by anyone who knows the names of the computer and the queue. You must also include the keyword `\Private$` in the name of the queue, so a private queue on Athena called `MyQueue` would be written as `Athena\Private$\MyQueue`.

By default, all queues are public. To make a queue private, you must include `\Private` in the name of the queue when it is created. You must have access to an Active Directory server to do this, however. Note that private queues can be created on Windows 98- and Windows NT-based machines.

Message queuing and COM+ transactions

COM+ transactions using message queues work automatically with the COM+ transaction server and the `ObjectContext` object. Getting the `ObjectContext` object and performing the `SetComplete`, or `SetAbort`, method automatically rolls back any operations you made to the queues. In other words, no messages are removed from the queues or physically sent until the transaction is either committed or rolled back.

There is one big issue about using message queues and transactions. While inside a transaction, you can only send messages to transactional queues — queues that were created with the `IsTransactional` parameter of the `MSMQQueueInfo.Create` method set to `True`. Also, any messages that are sent automatically have their `MSMQMessage.Priority` value set to zero. This ensures that the messages are processed in the order in which they were received.

The message queues also include their own version of transaction support in case you don't want to use the COM+ transaction server or want to work outside its control. You need to use the `MSMQCoordinatedTransactionDispenser` to begin a transaction while under control of the COM+ transaction server. Use the `MSMQTransactionDispenser` object if you're not under control of the COM+ transaction server. Then use the `MSMQTransaction` object to either commit the transaction or abort the transaction.

Message Queuing Object Model

Like most Windows tools, the MSMQ is accessed via a series of COM components. Figure 19-3 shows a brief overview of the objects and how they are related to each other.

- **MSMQQuery** – is used to search the Active Directory for public queues. It returns an `MSMQQueueInfos` collection containing the set of message queues that met the search criteria.
- **MSMQQueueInfos** – contains a set of `MSMQQueueInfo` objects. This component contains the results of an `MSMQQuery` operation.
- **MSMQQueueInfo** – is used to create and open queues as well as containing other information about a specific queue.

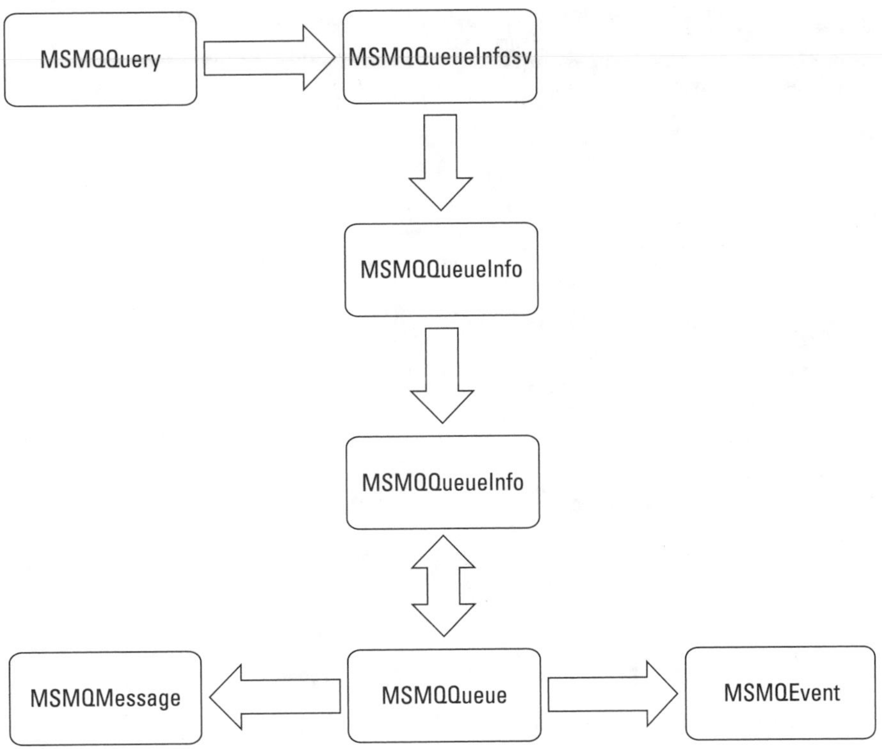

Figure 19-3: The Message Queuing Object Model

✦ **MSMQQueue** – is the base object in the object model. You use this object to access the individual messages in the queue.

✦ **MSMQMessage** – holds a message that is put in a queue or received from a queue.

✦ **MSMQEvent** – is used to define queuing events in your application. These events are fired as information arrives at your application.

Making it simpler: To simplify this discussion of message queues, I'm going to focus on private queues, which means that I'm going to ignore the `MSMQQuery` and `MSMQQueueInfos` objects. The only function lost by omitting the discussion of these objects is the ability to dynamically locate the proper queue by name only. To access a private queue, you must know the its name as well as the computer where it exists.

To add message queuing to your application, you need to select the Microsoft Message Queue 2.0 Object Library in the References dialog box (see Figure 19-4). To display this dialog box, choose Project ➪ References from the main menu.

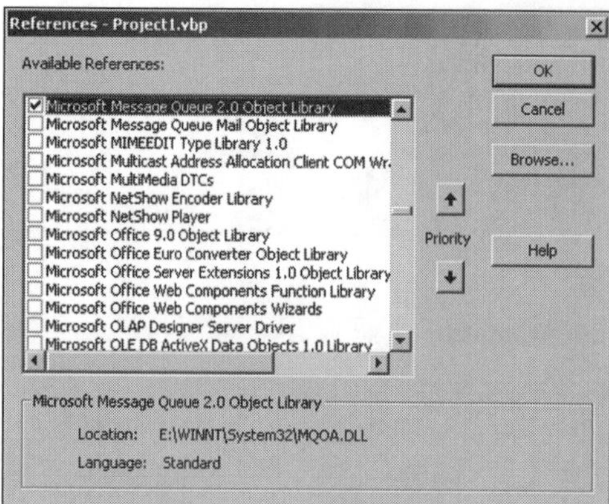

Figure 19-4: Selecting the Microsoft Message Queue Object Library

The MSMQQueueInfo Object

The `MSMQQueueInfo` object is used to create or open a message queue. It can also set and return information about a particular queue.

MSMQQueueInfo object properties

Table 19-1 lists the properties of the `MQMQQueueInfo` object.

Table 19-1
Properties of the MSMQQueueInfo Object

Property	*Description*
`Authenticate`	A `Long` value that specifies whether the queue accepts only authenticated messages.
`BasePriority`	A `Long` that specifies a base priority for all messages sent to a public queue.
`CreateTime`	A `Date` value containing the date and time the public queue was created.
`IsTransactional`	A `Boolean` value when `True` means only messages from transactions will be accepted into the queue.
`IsWorldReadable`	A `Boolean` when `True` indicates that everyone can read the messages in the queue.

Property	Description
Journal	A Long when set to MQ_JOURNAL (0) means that the messages aren't saved; MS_JOURNAL (1) means that when a message is removed from the queue, it is stored in the journal queue.
JournalQuota	A Long containing the size in kilobytes of the journal queue.
Label	A String value containing up to 124 characters that describe the queue.
ModifyTime	A Date value containing the date and time when the properties of the queue were last modified.
PathName	A String containing the path name of the queue. This value is in the form of \system\queue or \system\PRIVATE$\queue.
PathNameDNS	A String containing the path name of the queue, where the system name is fully qualified.
PrivLevel	A Long when set to MQ_PRIV_LEVEL_NONE (0) means that the queue accepts only unencrypted messages; MQ_PRIV_LEVEL_OPTIONAL (1) means that the queue doesn't enforce privacy (default); or MQ_PRIV_LEVEL _BODY (2) accepts only encrypted messages.
QueueGuid	A String containing the GUID of the queue.
Quote	A Long containing the maximum size of the queue in kilobytes.
ServiceTypeGuid	A String containing the type of service provided by the queue.

MSMQQueueInfo object methods

The MSMQQueueInfo object contains methods for managing queues.

Sub Create ([IsTransactional], [IsWorldReadable])

The Create method creates a new queue based on the properties defined in this object.

IsTransactional is a Boolean when True means only messages from transactions will be accepted into the queue.

IsWorldReadable is a Boolean when True indicates that everyone can read the messages in the queue.

Sub Delete()

The Delete method deletes the queue associated with this object.

Function Open(Access As Long, ShareMode As Long) As MSMQQueue

The Open method returns an object reference to MSMQQueue specified by the PathName property.

Access is a Long value specifying the level type of access to the queue. Multiple values may be combined by adding them together. Values are MQ_RECEIVE_ACCESS (1) means that messages can be received or peeked at in the queue; MQ_SEND_ACCESS (2) means that messages can be sent to the queue; and MQ_PEEK_ACCESS (32) means that you can peek at messages in the queue, but not remove them.

ShareMode is a Long specifying how the queue is shared. A value of MQ_DENY_NONE (0) means that the queue is shared with everyone (you must use this value if you specify MQ_SEND_ACCESS or MQ_PEEK_ACCESS); or MQ_DENY_RECEIVE_SHARE (1) prevents anyone except those in this process from accessing the queue (this value should be used when you specify MQ_RECEIVE_ACCESS).

Sub Refresh()

The Refresh method gets a fresh copy of the properties associated with this queue.

Sub Update()

The Update method updates the Active Directory for a public queue or the local computer with the current property values for this queue.

The MSMQQueue Object

The MSMQQueue object is a fundamental object when dealing with message queuing. This object has the necessary properties and methods to access the information in the queue. The MSMQQueueInfo object is used to open the queue and return an object reference to this object.

MSMQQueue object properties

Table 19-2 lists the properties of the MQMQQueue object.

Table 19-2
Properties of the MSMQQueue Object

Property	*Description*
Access	A Long value indicating whether you can send messages, peek at messages, or receive messages from the queue.
Handle	A Long containing a handle of the open queue.
IsOpen	A Boolean value when True means that the queue is open.
QueueInfo	An object reference to a MSMQQueueInfo object containing additional information about the queue.
ShareMode	A Long that indicates whether the queue is available to everyone or whether only this process.

MSMQQueue object methods

The MSMQQueue object contains methods for examining the contents of the queue.

Sub Close()

The Close method closes the queue.

Sub EnableNotification(Event As MSMQEvent, [Cursor], [ReceiveTimeout])

The EnableNotification method instructs the message queuing software to trigger events using the MSMQEvent object. Note that this object needed to be declared using the WithEvents keyword in order to receive the events. You can specify that the event will be fired when there is a message in the queue, when a message is at the queue's current location, or when a message is at the queue's next location. Note that it may be possible that multiple messages may be in front of the message that triggered the event.

Event is an object reference to an MSMQEvent object that has been declared WithEvents, which will be fired as needed.

`Cursor` is an enumerated type that specifies the action of the cursor. A value of `MQMSG_FIRST` (0) means that the event will be fired when a message is in the queue. A value of `MQMSG_CURRENT` (1) means that the event will be fired when a message is at the current location of the cursor. A value of `MQMSG_NEXT` (2) means that the event will be fired when a message is at the new cursor location.

`ReceiveTimeout` is a `Long` containing the number of milliseconds that MSMQ will wait for a message to arrive.

Function Peek([WantDestinationQueue], [WantBody], [ReceiveTimeout]) As MSMQMessage

The `Peek` method returns the first message in the queue without receiving the message from the queue. If the queue is empty, it will wait for a message to arrive.

`WantDestinationQueue` is a `Boolean` when `True` means that the `MSMQMessage.DestinationQueueInfo` property will be updated to contain the information about the destination queue. If not specified, a value of `False` will be assumed.

`WantBody` is a `Boolean` when `True` means that the body of the message should be returned (default). Set this value to `False` to reduce the amount of time to return the message.

`ReceiveTimeout` is a `Long` containing the number of milliseconds that MSMQ will wait for a message to arrive.

Function PeekCurrent([WantDestinationQueue], [WantBody], [ReceiveTimeout], [WantConnectorType]) As MSMQMessage

The `PeekCurrent` method returns the current message in the queue without receiving it.

`WantDestinationQueue` is a `Boolean` when `True` means that the `MSMQMessage.DestinationQueueInfo` property will be updated to contain the information about the destination queue. If not specified, a value of `False` will be assumed.

`WantBody` is a `Boolean` when `True` means that the body of the message should be returned (default). Set this value to `False` to reduce the amount of time to return the message.

`ReceiveTimeout` is a `Long` containing the number of milliseconds that MSMQ will wait for a message to arrive.

`WantConnecterType` is a `Boolean` when `True` means that connector information will also be retrieved. If not specified, a value of `False` will be assumed.

Function PeekNext([WantDestinationQueue], [WantBody], [ReceiveTimeout], [WantConnectorType]) As MSMQMessage

The `PeekNext` method returns the next method in the queue without receiving the message.

`WantDestinationQueue` is a `Boolean` value when `True` means that the `MSMQMessage.DestinationQueueInfo` property will be updated to contain the information about the destination queue. If not specified, a value of `False` will be assumed.

`WantBody` is a `Boolean` when `True` means that the body of the message should be returned (default). Set this value to `False` to reduce the amount of time to return the message.

`ReceiveTimeout` is a `Long` value containing the number of milliseconds that MSMQ will wait for a message to arrive.

`WantConnecterType` is a `Boolean` when `True` means that connector information will also be retrieved. If not specified, a value of `False` will be assumed.

Function Receive([Transaction], [WantDestinationQueue], [WantBody], [ReceiveTimeout], [WantConnectorType]) As MSMQMessage

The `Receive` method returns the first message in the queue and removes it from the queue.

`Transaction` is an `MSMQTransaction` object or one of these values: `MQ_NO_TRANSACTION` (0), which means that call is not part of a transaction; `MQ_MTS_TRANSACTION` (1), which means that the call is made as part of the current MTS or COM+ transaction; `MQ_XA_TRANSACTION` (2), which means that the call is part of an externally coordinated, XA-compliant transaction; or `MQ_SINGLE_MESSAGE` (3), which means that the call retrieves a single message.

`WantDestinationQueue` is a `Boolean` when `True` means that the `MSMQMessage.DestinationQueueInfo` property will be updated to contain the information about the destination queue. If not specified, a value of `False` will be assumed.

`WantBody` is a `Boolean` when `True` means that the body of the message should be returned (default). Set this value to `False` to reduce the amount of time to return the message.

`ReceiveTimeout` is a `Long` containing the number of milliseconds that MSMQ will wait for a message to arrive.

WantConnecterType is a Boolean when True means that connector information will also be retrieved. If not specified, a value of False will be assumed.

Function ReceiveCurrent([Transaction], [WantDestinationQueue], [WantBody], [ReceiveTimeout], [WantConnectorType]) As MSMQMessage

The ReceiveCurrent method returns the current message in the queue and removes it from the queue.

Transaction is an MSMQTransaction object or one of these values: MQ_NO_TRANSACTION (0), which means that call is not part of a transaction; MQ_MTS_TRANSACTION (1), which means that the call is made as part of the current MTS or COM+ transaction; MQ_XA_TRANSACTION (2), which means that the call is part of an externally coordinated, XA-compliant transaction; or MQ_SINGLE_MESSAGE (3), which means that the call retrieves a single message.

WantDestinationQueue is a Boolean when True means that the MSMQMessage.DestinationQueueInfo property will be updated to contain the information about the destination queue. If not specified, a value of False will be assumed.

WantBody is a Boolean when True means that the body of the message should be returned (default). Set this value to False to reduce the amount of time to return the message.

ReceiveTimeout is a Long containing the number of milliseconds that MSMQ will wait for a message to arrive.

WantConnecterType is a Boolean when True means that connector information will also be retrieved. If not specified, a value of False will be assumed.

Sub Reset()

The Reset method moves to the current message cursor to the start of the queue.

The MSMQMessage Object

The MSMQMessage object contains the message that is sent and received using message queuing.

MSMQMessage object properties

Table 19-3 lists the properties of the `MSMQMessage` object.

Set not for the body of a message: Don't use the `Set` statement to assign an object to the `Body` property of an `MSMQMessage` object. The `Set` statement creates a reference to an object. You should use an assignment statement to copy the entire contents of the object into the `Body` property.

Table 19-3
Properties of the MSMQMessage Object

Property	*Description*
`Ack`	A `Long` value that specifies the type of acknowledgement that is returned.
`AdminQueueInfo`	An object reference to the `MSMQQueueInfo` object that is used for acknowledgement messages.
`AppSpecific`	A `Long` value containing application-specific information.
`ArrivalTime`	A `Date` value containing the date and time the message arrived at the queue.
`AuthenticationProviderName`	A `String` value containing the name of the cryptographic provider used to generate the digital signature for the message.
`AuthenticationProviderType`	A `Long` value containing the type of the cryptographic provider.
`AuthLevel`	A `Long` value that specifies whether or not the message should be authenticated when received.
`Body`	A `Variant` value containing the message to be sent. Typically, this will be either a `String` or apersistent COM component.
`BodyLength`	A `Long` value containing the number of bytes in the message.
`Class`	A`Long` value containing the type of message being sent.

Continued

Table 19-3 *(continued)*

Property	***Description***
`ConnectorTypeGUID`	A `String` value containing the GUID associated with the component that was used to externally set some of the message properties that are typically set by MSMQ.
`CorrelationId`	A `Variant` value containing a 20-byte application-defined value that can be used to link messages together.
`Delivery`	Specifies how the message is delivered. Possible values are `MQMSG_DELIVERY_EXPRESS` (0), which is default and specifies a normal delivery process where it may be possible to lose the message in case of system failure; or `MQMSG_DELIVERY_RECOVERABLE` (1), which means that a more reliable system is used.
`DestinationQueueInfo`	An object reference to an `MSMQQueueInfo` object that will be used as the destination queue.
`DestinationSymmetricKey`	A `Variant` value containing the symmetric key used to encrypt messages.
`EncryptAlgorithm`	A `Long` value, which specifies the encryption algorithm used to encrypt the body of the message.
`Extension`	A `Variant` value containing additional application-specific information associated with the message.
`HashAlgorithm`	A `Long` value containing the hash algorithm used to authenticate a message.
`Id`	A `Variant` value containing the identifier for this message. This value is automatically generated by MSMQ.
`IsAuthenticated`	An `Integer` value that specifies whether the local queue manager authenticated the message.
`IsFirstInTransaction`	An `Integer` value that specifies whether the message is the first message sent in a transaction.
`IsLastInTransaction`	An `Integer` value that specifies whether the message is the last message sent in a transaction.

Property	Description
Journal	A Long value that specifies whether a copy of the message was stored in the journal queue.
Label	A String value containing an application-specific value describing the message.
MaxTimeToReachQueue	A Long value containing the maximum number of seconds that can elapse before the message must reach the queue before it will be canceled and an error message returned to the sender.
MaxTimeToReceive	A Long value containing the maximum number of seconds that can elapse before the message must be received before it will be canceled and an error message returned to the sender.
MsgClass	A Long value containing the message type.
Priority	A Long value containing the relative priority of the message.
PrivLevel	A Long value containing how the message is encrypted.
ResponseQueueInfo	An object reference to an MSMQQueueInfo object that specifies the response queue used to send response information.
SenderCertificate	A Byte() array containing the security certificate information.
SenderId	A Byte() array containing the name of the user who sent the message.
SenderIdType	A Long value that specifies whether the SenderId value was included in the message.
SenderVersion	A Long value containing information about the version of MSMQ that was used to send the message.
SendTime	A Date value containing the date and time the message was sent.
Signature	A Byte() containing the digital signature used to authenticate the message.
SourceMachineGuid	A String array value containing the GUID of the computer, which sent the message.

Continued

Table 19-3 *(continued)*

Property	Description
Trace	A Long value that specifies where a message will be returned to the sender in the report queue for each hop taken by the message in the delivery process.
TransactionId	A Byte() array that identifies the transaction that sent the message.
TransactionStatusQueueInfo	An object reference to a transaction status queue used for transactional messages.

MSMQMessage object methods

The MSMQMessage object contains methods for sending a message to a queue.

Sub AttachCurrentSecurityContext()

The AttachCurrentSecurityContext method retrieves the security information needed to attach a certificate to the message when requesting authentication.

Sub Send(DestinationQueue As MSMQQueue, [Transaction])

The Send method transmits the message to the specified queue.

DestinationQueue is an object reference to an open MSMQQueue object.

Transaction is a Variant which can be a reference to a MSMQTransaction object or one of these constants: MQ_NO_TRANSACTION (0), which means that this call isn't part of a transaction; MQ_MTS_TRANSACTION (1), which means that this call is part of the current MTS or COM+ transaction; MQ_XA_TRANSACTION, which means that this call is part of an externally coordinated, XA-compliant transaction; or MQ_SINGLE_TRANSACTION (3), which means the message comprises a single transaction.

MSMQEvent object events

The MSMQEvent object is used to define the events in your program that will be fired when a message arrives in the queue. These events are defined by the EnableNotification method of the MSMQQueue object.

Event Arrived (Queue As Object, Cursor As Long)

The `Arrived` event is triggered when an `MSMQMessage` object arrives in the associated queue.

`Queue` is an object reference to the queue containing the newly arrived message.

`Cursor` is a `Long` value for `Cursor` as specified in the `EnableNotification` method.

It's not automatic: You must call the `EnableNotification` method after processing the newly arrived message in order to be notified when the next message arrives.

Event ArrivedError (Queue As Object, ErrorCode As Long, Cursor As Long)

The `ArrivedError` event is triggered when an error occurs.

`Queue` is an object reference to the queue containing the newly arrived message.

`ErrorCode` is a `Long` value containing the cause of the error.

`Cursor` is a `Long` value for `Cursor` as specified in the `EnableNotification` method.

Timeout for an error: The most common error returned in the ArrivedError event is a timeout, where no messages were received in the specified amount of time. As with the `Arrived` event, you must use the `EnableNotification` method again to receive the next event.

Accessing Message Queues

While the object model for message queuing looks complicated, it isn't that difficult to master, especially if you use private queues. To demonstrate message queuing, I built a pair of programs. One originates requests, while the other responds to them. The client program (see Figure 19-5) retrieves information about a customer, while the server program (see Figure 19-6) processes the requests. I decided to use the COM+ transaction to get the information because it demonstrates how the various pieces can fit together into a robust application design.

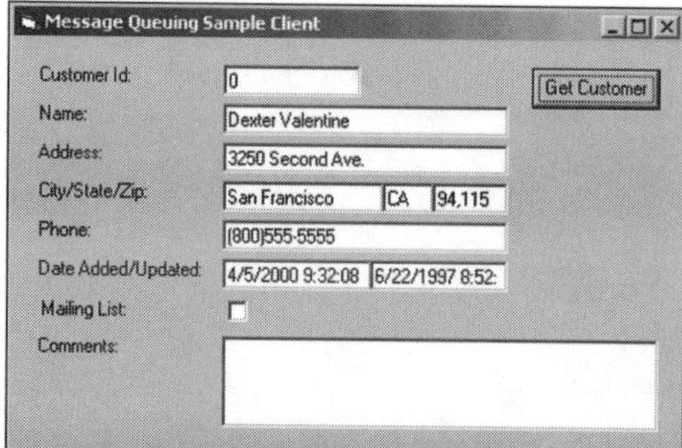

Figure 19-5: Running the message queuing client

Figure 19-6: Running the message queuing server

Building the client program

The client program is a relatively simple Visual Basic program that communicates with the server using two message queues. The first queue is the request queue, which is used to pass information to the server, while the second queue is the response queue, which is used to receive information from the server.

Starting the client

When the client program loads, I initialize both the request queue (`ReqQueue`) and the response queue (`RespQueue`) (see Listing 19-1). The process to open both queues is the same. I create a new `QueueInfo` object, specify the `PathName` of the queue, and then use the `Open` method to get access to the queue.

Listing 19-1: The Form_Load event in MSMQ Client

```
Private Sub Form_Load()

Set ReqInfo = New MSMQQueueInfo
ReqInfo.PathName = ".\Private$\VB6DB19Req"
Set ReqQueue = ReqInfo.Open(MQ_SEND_ACCESS, MQ_DENY_NONE)

Set RespInfo = New MSMQQueueInfo
RespInfo.PathName = ".\Private$\VB6DB19Resp"
Set RespQueue = RespInfo.Open(MQ_RECEIVE_ACCESS, _
   MQ_DENY_RECEIVE_SHARE)

Set RespEvent = New MSMQEvent
RespQueue.EnableNotification RespEvent, , 1000

End Sub
```

When I open the request queue, I specify `MQ_DENY_NONE` to allow other programs to share the request. However, when I open the response queue, I don't permit anyone else to receive data from it by specifying `MQ_DENY_RECEIVE_SHARE`. In general, each user should have their own unique response queue. This permits the server to send information to multiple users, even though the users may not be around to receive the information.

Once the response queue is opened, I create an `MSMQEvent` object, whose `Arrived` event will be fired when a message arrives in the response queue. I use the `EnableNotification` method to associate the Event object with the response queue. I also specify a timeout value of 1000 milliseconds (or 1 second). If no messages arrive in this amount of time, the `ArrivedError` event will be fired.

Requesting a customer's information

After the user enters a CustomerId value and presses the Get Customer button, the `Command1_Click` event will be triggered (see Listing 19-2). This routine verifies that a numeric value was entered into the `Text1` text box, and then constructs and sends a message to the server.

I begin by creating a new `Customer` object and assigning the value of the text box to the `CustomerId` property. Then I create a new `MSMQMessage` object. I set the `ResponseQueueInfo` property to point to the `QueueInfo` object associated with the response queue.

Listing 19-2: The Command1_Click event in MSMQ Client

```
Private Sub Command1_Click()

Dim msg As New MSMQMessage

If IsNumeric(Text1.Text) Then
   Set c = New Customer
   c.CustomerId = CLng(Text1.Text)
   Set msg = New MSMQMessage
   Set msg.ResponseQueueInfo = RespQueue.QueueInfo
   msg.Body = c
   msg.Send ReqQueue

End If

End Sub
```

The next statement is very critical. You must assign the object to the message's `Body` property. This saves a copy of the object in the `Body` property rather than merely saving a pointer to the object. Once you've populated the message, you can use the `Send` method to place the message in a queue.

Set not: By now, if you see an assignment with an object on the right side of the equal sign (=), you expect to see a `Set` statement before the variable on the left side. If you try to use the `Set` statement with the `Body` property of a message, your information will be lost as soon as the message is sent. Message queuing saves the persistent information from an object and then destroys it. The persistent information is then sent to the destination, where it is recreated when the program receives the object.

Getting the results

Because message queuing is asynchronous in nature, you don't know if the message will be returned in milliseconds, seconds, hours, or days. Thus, it is useful for an event to be fired when the message arrives. The `Arrived` event is triggered when a message is ready to be received (see Listing 19-3). If no messages arrive before the timeout limit is reached, the `ArrivedError` event will be fired (see Listing 19-4).

The `Arrived` event begins by receiving the first message from the queue. The queue that the message arrives in is specified by the `Queue` parameter and the `Receive` method is used to retrieve the message. I specify a value of 1000 milliseconds to retrieve the message before returning an error.

Listing 19-3: The RespEvent_Arrived event in MSMQ Client

```
Private Sub RespEvent_Arrived(ByVal Queue As Object, _
      ByVal Cursor As Long)

Dim r As Customer
Dim msg As MSMQMessage

Set msg = Queue.Receive(, , , 1000)
If Not (msg Is Nothing) Then
   Set r = msg.Body
   Text2.Text = r.Name
   Text3.Text = r.Street
   Text4.Text = r.City
   Text5.Text = r.State
   Text6.Text = FormatNumber(r.Zip, 0)
   Text7.Text = r.Phone
   Text8.Text = FormatDateTime(r.DateAdded, vbGeneralDate)
   Text9.Text = FormatDateTime(r.DateUpdated, vbGeneralDate)
   Check1.Value = CLng(r.MailingList) * -1
   Text10.Text = r.Comments

End If

RespQueue.EnableNotification RespEvent, , 1000

End Sub
```

Once I have the message, it is a very simple matter to get a reference to the `Customer` object from the `Body` property and assign its values to each of the fields on the form.

What happened to all my requests?: When receiving messages in the `Arrived` event, it is possible to process the messages too quickly. In this example, I assumed that the user would submit one request at a time, but there is nothing to prevent the user from requesting information on multiple customers before the response to the first message is received. If this happens, it is quite possible that the server will retrieve the next response before the user has finished viewing the first response. In this case, it may be useful to save the messages into a `Collection` object as they are received. Another approach would be to examine the information in each response using the `Peek` methods, and only receive the message from the message queue when you're ready to delete it.

Before I leave this event, I need to reset the trigger so that the next message is received. This is done using the same `EnableNotification` method that I originally used to enable this event.

Tip

But it worked once: If you can receive the first message, but your program doesn't process any other messages after that, verify that you re-enabled the response event after processing a message.

The `ArrivedError` event is fired when a message doesn't arrive in the message queue before its timeout value. If you are expecting a steady stream of messages, you may want to re-enable the event in the `ArrivedError` event (see Listing 19-4).

Listing 19-4: The RespEvent_ArrivedError event in MSMQ Client

```
Private Sub RespEvent_ArrivedError(ByVal Queue As Object, _
     ByVal ErrorCode As Long, ByVal Cursor As Long)

RespQueue.EnableNotification RespEvent, , 1000

End Sub
```

Building the server program

The server program is designed to receive requests from a client in the request queue, call the `GetCustomer` transaction I wrote in Chapter 18, and return the data to the client in the response queue. It also includes tools to create and delete the queues that the client program will use.

Creating queues

When the user presses the Build Queues button, the `Command1_Click` event will be triggered (see Listing 19-5). For each queue, this routine creates a new `QueueInfo` object, specifies the `PathName` of the queue, and then calls the `Create` method to define the queue.

Tip

Deleting is simple: To delete a queue, use the same logic as shown in Listing 19-5, but substitute `Delete` for `Create`.

Listing 19-5: The Command1_Click event in MSMQ Server

```
Private Sub Command1_Click()

Dim RespInfo As MSMQQueueInfo

Set RespInfo = New MSMQQueueInfo
RespInfo.PathName = ".\Private$\VB6DB19Resp"
RespInfo.Create

Set ReqInfo = New MSMQQueueInfo
ReqInfo.PathName = ".\Private$\VB6DB19Req"
ReqInfo.Create

Set respinfo = Nothing
Set ReqInfo = Nothing

End Sub
```

Starting the server

The server will not process any messages until the user presses the Run Server button. This triggers the `Command2_Click` event, as shown in Listing 19-6. This routine begins by writing that the server is active to the text box on the form, and then it opens the request queue and enables notification using the `ReqEvent` object. At this point, the server will respond to messages as they are sent, using the `ReqEvent_Arrival` events.

Listing 19-6: The Command2_Click event in MSMQ Server

```
Private Sub Command2_Click()

Text1.Text = FormatDateTime(Now, vbGeneralDate) & _
   " Server active." & vbCrLf
Set ReqInfo = New MSMQQueueInfo
ReqInfo.PathName = ".\Private$\VB6DB19Req"
Set ReqQueue = ReqInfo.Open(MQ_RECEIVE_ACCESS,
MQ_DENY_RECEIVE_SHARE)

Set ReqEvent = New MSMQEvent
ReqQueue.EnableNotification ReqEvent, , 60000

End Sub
```

Processing messages

The heart of the server is the ReqEvent_Arrived event (see Listing 19-7). This event is responsible for receiving the request, calling the COM+ transaction, and returning the data to the user via the response queue. This routine begins by appending an entry to the text box with the date and time that the message was received. This information is useful in monitoring the server's activities while testing the program, though it should be eliminated in a production application.

Listing 19-7: The ReqEvent_Arrival event in MSMQ Server

```
Private Sub ReqEvent_Arrived(ByVal Queue As Object, _
      ByVal Cursor As Long)

Dim c As Customer
Dim ci As CustInfo.CustomerInfo
Dim msg As MSMQMessage
Dim xc As Customer
Dim xmsg As MSMQMessage
Dim xqueue As MSMQQueue

Text1.Text = Text1.Text & FormatDateTime(Now, vbGeneralDate) _
   & " Message received." & vbCrLf

Set msg = Queue.Receive(, , , 1000)
If Not (msg Is Nothing) Then
   Set c = msg.Body

   Set ci = CreateObject("CustInfo.CustomerInfo")
   Set xc = ci.GetCustomer(c.CustomerId)
   Set ci = Nothing

   Set xmsg = New MSMQMessage
   xmsg.Body = xc

   Set xqueue = msg.ResponseQueueInfo.Open(MQ_SEND_ACCESS, _
      MQ_DENY_NONE)
   xmsg.Send xqueue
   Set xqueue = Nothing
   Set xc = Nothing

End If

ReqQueue.EnableNotification ReqEvent, , 60000

End Sub
```

Next, I receive the message using the `Queue` parameter. Once I have the message, I can extract the `CustomerId` value from the message's body and call the `CustInfo.CustomerInfo` transaction to get the requested information. Then I create a new `MSMQMessage` object and save the `Customer` object into the `Body` property. Note that I didn't use a `Set` statement, since I want a copy of the document rather than a reference for the object.

To send the message, I open the response queue contained in the original message and use the `Send` method to put the message into the response queue. Then I reset the message notification so that the next time a message arrives, I will be ready to process it. The program also includes a `ReqEvent_ArrivedError` similar to the one used in the MSMQ Client program to allow the server to continue to receive messages after a timeout condition.

Viewing Message Queue Information

You may find it useful to have an independent tool to see messages as they arrive in a message queue for processing. If you are running Windows 2000 Server, you can use the Computer Management utility (Start ➪ Programs ➪ Administrative Tools ➪ Computer Management) to examine the contents of a message queue.

After starting this program, you'll see the typical Microsoft Management Console with a tree of icons on the left side with details about the currently selected icon on the right (see Figure 19-7). By expanding the Services and Applications icon, you can expose the Message Queuing icon. Then by drilling down, under Private Queues, you can see the queues that are used by the MSMQ Client and MSMQ Server programs.

Within each queue, you can select Queue messages to see the messages that are in the queue waiting to be processed. The easiest way to try this, using the sample programs from this chapter, is to run the client program without running the server. Any messages sent from the client program will accumulate in the queue, and if you then run the server program, you can see the messages quickly disappear—returned to the client program via the response queue.

Where did my message go?: If your program isn't working properly, this utility will help you discover whether or not the program is sending the messages properly.

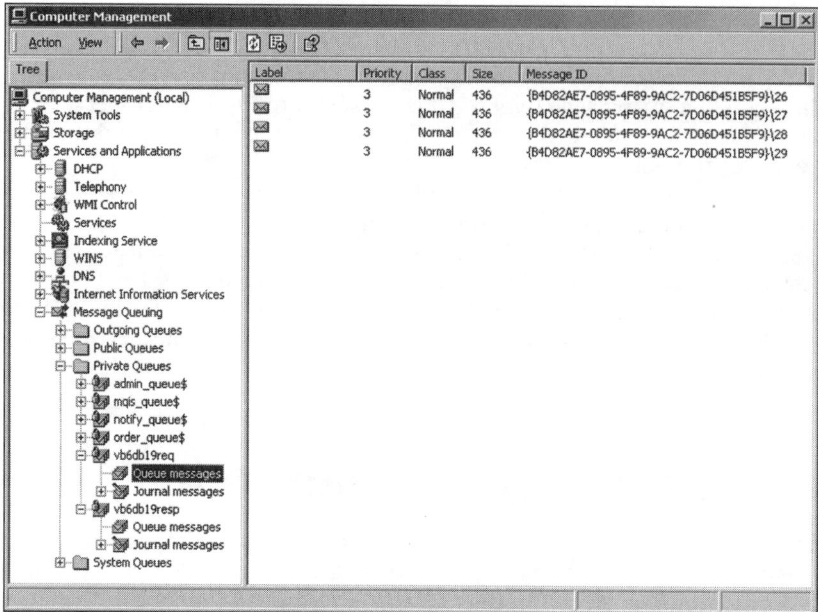

Figure 19-7: Running the Computer Management utility

Thoughts on Message Queuing

This chapter is just a brief introduction to what you can do with message queuing. I find message queuing a fascinating tool that makes it easy to implement asynchronous processing.

Consider this example. You have a group of salespeople out in the field with laptop computers. Since it's not practical for them to stay in constant contact with the home office, you build a stand-alone application that keeps track of the items in the sales catalog and allows them to enter orders that can be printed out and submitted later.

If you were to include message queuing in the application, you could modify the application so that it automatically queues orders to be sent to the home office the next time the salesperson connects to the organization's network. The application could also receive updates to the local sales database, as well as updates to customer orders that have already been placed.

Another situation where you might find message queuing useful is when you have long-running tasks like report generators, or complex database queries where an immediate response isn't necessary. By using message queuing, you can collect these requests and then process them as time and resources permit. In the mainframe world, this is referred to as batch processing. However, I suggest that you refer to this process by another name so that your users don't think you're a relic from the olden days — like me.

Summary

In this chapter you learned the following:

- ✦ You can use the Microsoft Message Queuing to send information asynchronously from one computer to another.
- ✦ You can use message queues to smooth the workload in a heavily loaded server.
- ✦ You can use public queues only on Windows 2000 servers, while private queues can be used on Windows 98 and NT as well as Windows 2000.
- ✦ You can open a queue with the `MSMQQueueInfo` object.
- ✦ You can send messages using the `MSMQQueue` object.
- ✦ You can receive messages via the `MSMQEvent` object.
- ✦ You can view the messages in a message queue by using the Computer Management utility to verify if your application is properly sending messages.

✦ ✦ ✦

PART

V

The Impact of XML

XML is one of the hottest technologies in the marketplace today. In this Part, I will introduce you to XML and explain how you should use it in your applications. Then, I'll cover the Document Object Model, which are a series of objects you can use from your Visual Basic program to parse existing XML documents and create new ones. Finally, I'll show you how to fit it all together by building a Visual Basic IIS Application that works with Internet Explorer 5 to send and receive database requests formatted in XML.

✦ ✦ ✦ ✦

In This Part

✦ ✦ ✦ ✦

CHAPTER 20

Introducing XML

◆ ◆ ◆ ◆

In This Chapter

Writing XML documents

Working with XML and ADO

Understanding the benefits of using XML

◆ ◆ ◆ ◆

Unless you've been living on the moon for the last several years, you've undoubtedly heard of XML. It's been hailed as the future of the Web, the foundation for e-commerce and the universal information exchange medium. In reality, XML is merely a language used to describe information. In this chapter, I'll talk about how to create an XML document, how XML works with ADO, and why you might want to use XML in your applications.

Documenting Information

XML stands for Extensible Markup Language. It is part of the family of languages developed from the *Standardized General Purpose Markup Language* (SGML) that includes the various dialects of *HyperText Markup Language* (HTML). These languages are used to describe the structure of a document, but not the actual information contained in the document.

Tagging information

All SGML languages, including XML and HTML, are based on the concept of tags. A *tag* is formed by inserting a keyword inside a less than and greater than symbol pair (<>), such as `<HEADER1>`. Most tags work in pairs such as `<HEADER1>` and `</HEADER1>`, where the slash in front of the keyword is used to mark the end of that tag pair. In XML, this combination is known as an *element*. An element is used to mark the beginning and end of a piece of information. Sometimes the information is a single value, while at other times, it may be a collection of elements.

Elements may be nested and the information inside inherits the characteristics of all of the outer elements. In HTML, for instance, the tag `<I>` identifies a block of text that should be displayed in italics, while the tag <B> identifies a block of text that should be displayed in bold. Thus, the following HTML statement will display the text in both bold and italics:

```
You may display text in <B>bold</B>, <I>italics</I>, and both
<B><I>bold and italics</I></B> by using different combinations
of tags.
```

Adding attributes

SGML also allows you to refine the meaning of a tag by including one or more attributes inside the tag. For instance, the <IMG> tag is used in HTML to mark the place where an image will be placed. Yet knowing that an image is to be placed in a document isn't sufficient unless you know which image is to be used. This information is specified with the SRC attribute. Thus, the following tag would display the image CJ&Sam.JPG in a Web page:

```
<IMG SRC="CJ&Sam.JPG">
```

Many tags support multiple attributes. The following tag not only specifies the name of the image to be displayed, but its height and width:

```
<IMG SRC="CJ&Sam.JPG" HEIGHT="640" WIDTH="480">
```

Grouping and formatting tags

Tags are grouped together in a document. With very few exceptions, how the tags are placed in the document doesn't matter, as long as the order of the tags remains constant. Thus, this set of tags

```
You may display text in <B>bold</B>, <I>italics</I>, and both
<B><I>bold and italics</I></B> by using different combinations
of tags.
```

and this set of tags

```
You may display text in
<B>bold</B>,
<I>italics</I>,
and both
<B><I>bold and italics</I></B>
by using different combinations of tags.
```

and even this set of tags

```
You may display text in
     <B>bold</B>,
     <I>italics</I>,
and both
     <B><I>bold and italics</I></B>
by using different combinations of tags.
```

have exactly the same meaning and will result in exactly the same display. This allows you to format your documents and make them easy to read without impacting the meaning of the information contained in the document.

Using XML tags

Unlike the HTML generic tags, which describe how information is to be formatted in a document, XML uses meaningful tags that describe the information they contain. A tag can refer to a single field or to a collection of fields, which correspond to a field name in a table, a database table, or a hierarchical view that is constructed from multiple database tables.

Helpful hierarchies: Theoretically, it is possible to describe any combination of data in a hierarchy. In fact, some of the earliest databases, such as IBM's Information Management System (IMS), were based on a hierarchical data model. When extracting data from a database to send to another application, it is often useful to arrange it as a hierarchy. This eliminates redundant information and makes it easier for the receiving application to reformat the data to fit its own database structures.

A Simple XML document

Figure 20-1 shows a diagram of my family. It describes the family name (Freeze), the father (me), the mother (Jill), our children (Christopher and Samantha), and our pets (Kokomo, Pixel, Terry, Cali, Dusty and Raymond).

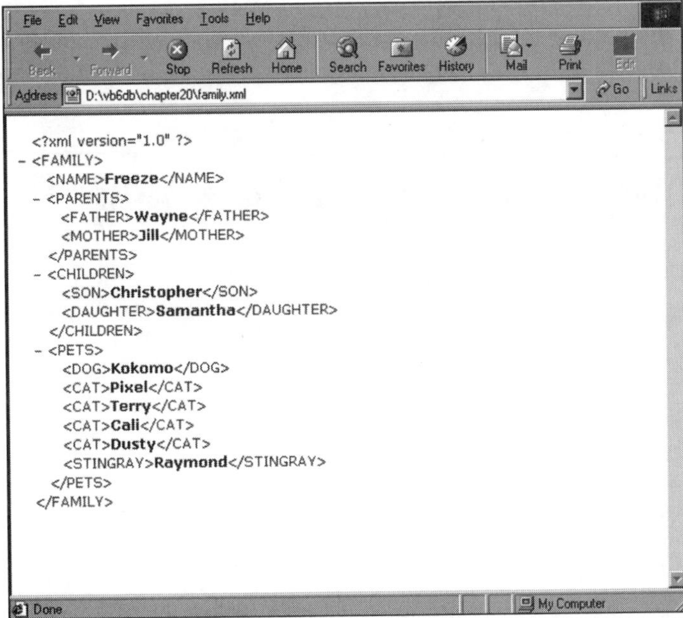

Figure 20-1: My family

Listing 20-1 contains the SQL statements that would create a database to hold this information. The database consists of four tables: one with the family name, one with information about the parents, another with the family's children, and a fourth with information about the family's pets.

Listing 20-1: A family database

```
Create Table Family (
   Name Char(32))

Create Table Parents (
   Name Char(32),
   Parent Char(32),
   Type Char(32))

Create Table Children (
   Name Char(32),
   Child Char(32),
   Type Char(32))

Create Table Pets (
   Name Char(32),
   Pet Char(32),
   Type Char(32))
```

You can also easily translate this information into an XML document (see Listing 20-2). Notice that the database tables had to flatten the information to fit into three distinct tables, while the XML document maintained the original hierarchical structure.

Listing 20-2: An XML document for the Freeze family

```
<?xml version="1.0"?>
<FAMILY>
   <NAME>Freeze</NAME>
   <PARENTS>
  <FATHER>Wayne</FATHER>
         <MOTHER>Jill</MOTHER>
   </PARENTS>
   <CHILDREN>
      <SON>Christopher</SON>
      <DAUGHTER>Samantha</DAUGHTER>
   </CHILDREN>
   <PETS>
      <DOG>Kokomo</DOG>
      <CAT>Pixel</CAT>
```

```
        <CAT>Terry</CAT>
        <CAT>Cali</CAT>
        <CAT>Dusty</CAT>
        <STINGRAY>Raymond</STINGRAY>
    </PETS>
</FAMILY>
```

You can find the FAMILY.XML document as \VB6DB\Chapter20\XML\FAMILY.XML on the CD-ROM.

The XML tags are used either to identify a single item, such as the name of the father or mother, or to identify a collection of tags that are logically grouped together, such as the children or pets.

Some of the latest generation of Web browsers, such as Internet Explorer 5.0, can display XML files directly (see Figure 20-2). If you look at Figure 20-2 carefully, you'll see a minus sign (-) in front of the <FAMILY>, <PARENTS>, <CHILDREN>, and <PETS> tags, in addition to the raw HTML. By clicking on the minus sign next to a tag, you can hide all of the tags below it in the hierarchy. The minus sign will change to a plus sign (+), which you can click on to show the tags again.

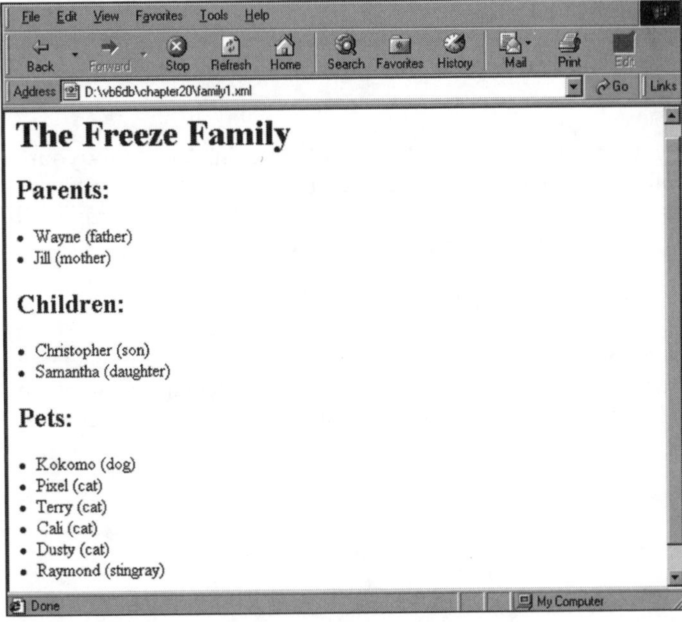

Figure 20-2: Viewing XML data in Internet Explorer 5.0

XML attributes

Another way to include information in an XML document is to use attributes. Like element names, you determine which attributes you want to include in the document. I've taken the XML document from Listing 20-2 and rewritten it to move the information about the type of family member to an attribute within an element, as shown in Listing 20-3.

Listing 20-3: An XML document for the Freeze family

```
<?xml version="1.0"?>
<FAMILY Name="Freeze">
<PARENT Type="Father">Wayne</PARENT>
   <PARENT Type="Mother">Jill</PARENT>
   <CHILD Type="Son">Christopher</CHILD>
   <CHILD Type="Daughter">Samantha</CHILD>
   <PET Type="Dog">Kokomo</PET>
   <PET Type="Cat">Pixel</PET>
   <PET Type="Cat">Terry</PET>
   <PET Type="Cat">Cali</PET>
   <PET Type="Cat">Dusty</PET>
   <PET Type="Stingray">Raymond</PET>
</FAMILY>
```

Using attributes lets you include more information in a single element. The downside is that it makes the document more complicated to read; it may also hide some hierarchy information.

For the most part, you should use attributes to hold information about your data. For example, the following element uses the attribute `Currency` to describe the type of currency used in the value for `LISTPRICE`. This is a good example of using attributes to clarify the information for a particular data value.

```
<LISTPRICE Currency="USD">29.99</LISTPRICE>
```

Extendable elements: If you're not sure whether to code a value as an element or an attribute, you should probably code the value as an element. This approach is more flexible, which is important if you plan to include new elements and attributes in the future.

Writing XML Documents

The rules for XML are fairly straightforward, and if you want, you can create your XML documents in any old text editor, including Notepad. However, for the most part, you should use an alternate way to load a file. Probably the best way is to write a program that generates the document for you. By doing this you can ensure that the document is generated properly. See Chapter 21 for one method you might use in Visual Basic.

Extensive XML: I highly recommend the *XML Bible* by Elliotte Rusty Harold, published by IDG Books. This well-written book goes into all of the details you should know before you build an XML-based application.

Creating an XML document

At the top of an XML document is a header tag, which describes information about the document (see Listing 20-4). Typically, all you will code is the version level, though the XML standard defines several other attributes that you may want to include.

Listing 20-4: A minimal XML document

```
<?xml version="1.0"?>
<root_element_tag>
</root_element_tag>
```

Following the header tag is the root level element. Every XML document is a hierarchy, with one and only one root element. In Listing 20-4, the root level element is `<root_element_tag>` and `</root_element_tag>`, while in Listing 20-2 the root level element is `<FAMILY>` and `</FAMILY>`.

Identifying XML elements

Unlike HTML, you must create the XML elements you use in your document. For instance, I created the following element to identify my son:

```
<SON>Christopher</SON>
```

The tag <SON> marks the beginning of a block of data, while the tag </SON> marks the end of the tag. You can nest pairs of tags within each other, like this:

```
<CHILDREN>
   <SON>Christopher</SON>
   <DAUGHTER>Samantha</DAUGHTER>
</CHILDREN>
```

The <CHILDREN> tag marks the collection of elements that comprises the children in my family. Elements can and should be nested to describe groups of data. A group of data might be something as simple as identifying a record, a collection of records, or a table.

The following element

```
<CHILDREN></CHILDREN>
```

can be written as

```
<CHILDREN/>
```

In this case, it means that there is no information associated with that particular element.

In order to be considered a well-formed XML document, the start and stop tags must not overlap. They need to be closed in the reverse order in which they were opened. The following statement is legal in HTML, but will cause an error in XML:

```
<B><I>Hi Jill</B></I>
```

Thus, you need to rewrite the statement as follows:

```
<B><I>Hi Jill</I></B>
```

Creating XSL Style Sheets

The Extensible Style Sheet Language (XSL) is used to format an XML document. An XSL Style Sheet is similar in concept to a Cascading Style Sheet for an HTML document. Both tools allow you to create a template that can be used to provide a common formatting to a document.

And that ain't all: This is an overly abbreviated section that describes what you can do with just a few XSL statements. XSL is a very rich language, which can be used to format some very complex documents.

The basic approach used in the XSL is that the first element in the document applies to the root element of the XML document. The rest of the elements on the XML document are formatted recursively from the root element. All XSL elements have a prefix of `xsl:`.XSL is derived from SMGL and XML, so it is a tag-oriented language that has to follow the same basic rules used for any XML document. Unlike some other languages, XSL is case sensitive, so all tags must be entered using lowercase characters. Figure 20-3 shows the same FAMILY.XML document from Listing 20-2, but it uses the style codes from the XSL document shown in Listing 20-5.

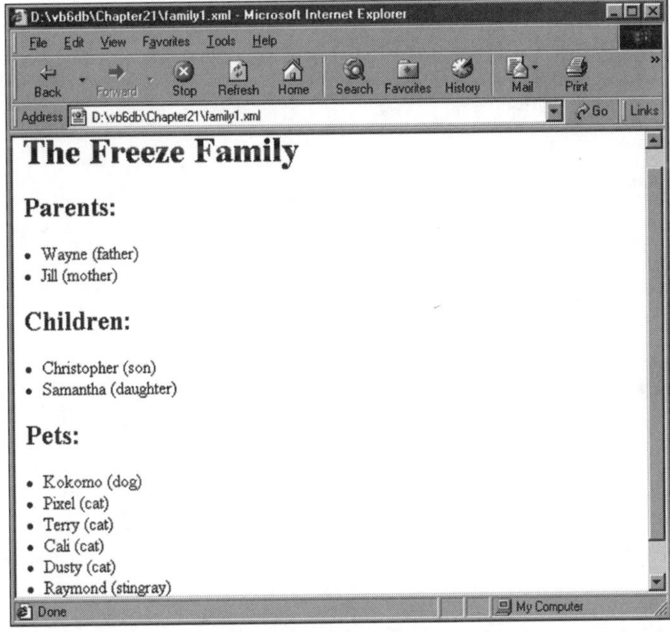

Figure 20-3: Formatting an XML document with an XSL style sheet

Listing 20-5: An XSL style sheet for the FAMILY.XML document

```
<?xml version="1.0"?>
<xsl:stylesheet xmlns:xsl="http://www.w3.org/TR/WD-xsl">
<xsl:template match="/">
     <html>
     <head>
     </head>
     <body>
     <xsl:apply-templates/>
     </body>
     </html>
```

Continued

Listing 20-5 *(continued)*

```
</xsl:template>

<xsl:template match="FAMILY">
     <h1>
     The
     <xsl:value-of select="NAME"/>
     Family
     </h1>
     <xsl:apply-templates/>
</xsl:template>

<xsl:template match="PARENTS">
     <p>
     <h2>Parents:</h2>
     <xsl:apply-templates/>
     </p>
</xsl:template>

<xsl:template match="FATHER">
     <li>
     <xsl:value-of select="."/>
     (father)
     </li>
</xsl:template>

<xsl:template match="MOTHER">
     <li>
     <xsl:value-of select="."/>
     (mother)
     </li>
</xsl:template>

<xsl:template match="CHILDREN">
     <p>
     <h2>Children:</h2>
     <xsl:apply-templates/>
     </p>
</xsl:template>

<xsl:template match="SON">
     <li>
     <xsl:value-of select="."/>
     (son)
     </li>
</xsl:template>

<xsl:template match="DAUGHTER">
     <li>
```

```
        <xsl:value-of select="."/>
        (daughter)
        </li>
</xsl:template>

<xsl:template match="PETS">
        <p>
        <h2>Pets:</h2>
        <xsl:apply-templates/>
        </p>
</xsl:template>

<xsl:template match="DOG">
        <li>
        <xsl:value-of select="."/>
        (dog)
        </li>
</xsl:template>

<xsl:template match="CAT">
        <li>
        <xsl:value-of select="."/>
        (cat)
        </li>
</xsl:template>

<xsl:template match="STINGRAY">
        <li>
        <xsl:value-of select="."/>
        (stingray)
        </li>
</xsl:template>

</xsl:stylesheet>
```

The XSL style sheet is found on the CD-ROM in the `\VB6DB\CHAPTER20\FAMILY.XSL` **file. I've also included a modified version of the FAMILY.XML file, called FAMILY1.XML, that will use this style sheet to format the information.**

The xsl:stylesheet element

The `xsl:stylesheet` element is the root element of an XSL style sheet. The primary attribute to this element is the `xlsnm:xsl`, which is used to specify the name space for the document. The name space identifies all of the elements and their attributes. This is a URL reference to a Web site like the one below. However, most XML vendors only verify the name; they don't actually look up the document on the Web.

```
http://www.w3.org/TR/WD-xsl
```

Name spaces are used in XML to help clarify a reference. For instance, if you have a tag called name, it may have many different meanings depending on the context in which it is used. By adding the name space and a colon in front of the element, you can clarify which name space the element was used from. In fact, the `xsl:` in front of the `xsl:stylesheet` element identifies the element as belonging to the xsl name space.

The xsl:template element

The `xsl:template` element is the fundamental element to control how a particular part of your XML document is formatted. Consider the following fragment from the FAMILY.XSL document:

```
<xsl:template match="STINGRAY">
    <li>
    <xsl:value-of select="."/>
    (stingray)
    </li>
</xsl:template>
```

This code will process the following `STINGRAY` element from the XML document:

```
<STINGRAY>Raymond</STINGRAY>
```

The `match` attribute identifies the XML element that will be processed by this XSL element. Note that there are many other ways to associate the XSL template with an XML element. The `match` attribute is just one of the easier ones to use.

Once the particular template element has been defined, the information inside the element will be displayed and any XSL elements will be executed. In this case, the following information will be output:

```
<li>Raymond (stingray)</li>
```

Where the text `<li>` comes directly from this element, the word `Raymond` will be generated by the `<xsl:value-of>` element, followed by the text `(stingray)` and `</li>`. There is no reason that I couldn't have included other HTML elements, such as an `IMG` element, to display a picture of a stingray or a hyperlink to another document. Also, you should note that the information is processed in order of how it is listed. Thus, you can perform tasks before and after any other XSL tags you wish to use.

Office-oriented: The `xsl:template` element is similar to the concept of Style, used in Microsoft Office. In a typical Word document for example, you may use specific styles for headers, body text, tables, etc. . If you want to change the font used in a header, all you have to do is update the style with the new font. Then all of the headers in the document will automatically be updated. Without styles, you would have to manually update each individual header.

The xsl:value-of element

The xsl:value-of element returns the value of an element. If you use the select attribute and specify a period as the value, then the value of the current element will be returned. Thus, for this XSL template

```
<xsl:template match="DAUGHTER">
    <li>
    <xsl:value-of select="."/>
    (daughter)
    </li>
</xsl:template>
```

and this XML element

```
<DAUGHTER>Samantha</DAUGHTER>
```

the <xsl:value- of select="."/> will return the value Samantha.

The xsl:apply-templates element

The xsl:apply-templates element processes templates for all of the elements within the current element. In the following XSL template

```
<xsl:template match="PARENTS">
    <p>
    <h2>Parents:</h2>
    <xsl:apply-templates/>
    </p>
</xsl:template>
```

an HTML header would be created containing the word Parents, and then the FATHER and MOTHER elements beneath the PARENTS tag would be processed from the XML document fragment shown below:

```
<PARENTS>
 <FATHER>Wayne</FATHER>
    <MOTHER>Jill</MOTHER>
</PARENTS>
```

Any information output by processing the templates associated with these elements would follow the information output before the <xsl-apply-templates> element was reached in the XSL template. After all of the templates have been processed, the </p> tag would be output.c

Other XML tools

There are a few other tools that you should be aware of when creating an XML document. These tools help ensure that your XML documents are created properly, as well as help other users understand your document.

XML parsers

One tool that you'll find valuable is an XML parser. Given the nature of the XML language, it can be a real pain for you to write code to convert the XML elements into something a bit more meaningful, much less verify that the XML document you received is well formed.

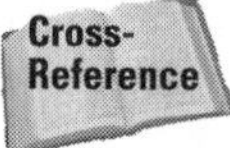

Microsoft has released an XML parser called MSXML that you can call from your program. I'll talk about this parser in more detail in Chapter 21.

Document Type Definitions

Another feature of XML is the ability to create a set of rules that governs how an XML document is created. These rules are known as *Document Type Definitions,* or DTD. This information can be useful when creating XML documents, since it ensures that you can't create an invalid document. You don't have to include a DTD with your XML document, and in practice, many tools, such as Internet Explorer 5.0, don't bother to use it even if you do include it.

XLinks and XPointers

The *Extensible Linking Language* (XLL) helps you locate XML resources outside the local document. XLL has two main parts: XLinks and XPointers. XLL is similar in concept to an HTML link. An XPointer is a way to identify a location in an XML document, while an XLink uses a URL, and perhaps an Xpointer, to locate a section of a document.

Working with XML and ADO

ADO has the ability to save information from a `Recordset` object into an XML file. This makes it easy to create ADO documents that can be sent to other applications. But while the file is formatted according to XML rules, there are a few unique characteristics that you should understand.

Creating an XML File with ADO

Consider the following **Select** statement:

```
Select CustomerId, Name
From Customers
Where State = 'MD'
```

You can easily use it to populate a `Recordset` with data from the sample database and save the results to an XML file with the statements in Listing 20-6.

Listing 20-6: The Command1_Click event in SaveXML

```
Private Sub Command1_Click()

Dim db As ADODB.Connection
Dim rs As ADODB.Recordset

Set db = New ADODB.Connection
db.Open "provider=sqloledb;data source=Athena;" & _
      "initial catalog=VB6DB", "sa", ""

Set rs = New ADODB.Recordset
rs.Open "Select CustomerId, Name From Customers " & _
      "Where State='MD'", db, adOpenForwardOnly, adLockReadOnly

rs.Save App.Path & "\results.xml", adPersistXML

rs.Close

db.Close

End Sub
```

The SaveXML program and a copy of the `Results.XML` file can be found on the CD-ROM in the `\VB6DB\Chapter20\SaveXML` directory.

Looking at the XML file

The XML file will contain all of the information necessary to reconstruct the `Recordset`, including a description of each `Recordset` and each row of information retrieved from the database (see Listing 20-7).

Listing 20-7: A sample XML file created by ADO

```
<xml xmlns:s='uuid:BDC6E3F0-6DA3-11d1-A2A3-00AA00C14882'
   xmlns:dt='uuid:C2F41010-65B3-11d1-A29F-00AA00C14882'
   xmlns:rs='urn:schemas-microsoft-com:rowset'
   xmlns:z='#RowsetSchema'>

<s:Schema id='RowsetSchema'>

   <s:ElementType name='row' content='eltOnly'
         rs:CommandTimeout='30'>

      <s:AttributeType name='CustomerId' rs:number='1'
         s:writeunknown='true'>

         <s:datatype dt:type='int' dt:maxLength='4'
               rs:precision='10'
            rs:fixedlength='true' rs:maybenull='false'/>

      </s:AttributeType>

      <s:AttributeType name='Name' rs:number='2'
         rs:nullable='true' rs:writeunknown='true'>

         <s:datatype dt:type='string' rs:dbtype='str'
            dt:maxLength='64'/>

      </s:AttributeType>

      <s:extends type='rs:rowbase'/>

   </s:ElementType>

</s:Schema>

<rs:data>

   <z:row CustomerId='84' Name='Fred Price'/>
   <z:row CustomerId='205' Name='Joseph Bell'/>
   <z:row CustomerId='385' Name='Kali Carlisle'/>

</rs:data>

</xml>
```

It looks different on disk: While the XML file generated by ADO is human readable, it isn't very printer friendly. Therefore, I've restructured how the elements are displayed in Listing 20-5, without changing any of the content.

The root element of the XML document is the `xml` element. It is used to define the name spaces that are used within the document. Four name spaces are typically defined:

- `s` defines the schema
- `dt` defines data types
- `rs` defines `Recordset` information
- `z` contains row information

The XML file is broken into two main elements: the schema element and the recordset element. The schema element is denoted by the tag `<s:schema>`, while the recordset element is denoted by the `<rs:data>` tag.

In the `s:schema` element, global recordset information is defined in the `s:ElementType` element. Within this element, information about each of the columns is defined. The `s:AtrributeType` element is used to define the column name that will be used in the recordset's `z:row` element, along with its data type.

Then each row of data in the recordset is listed in the `rs:data` element. This is the most understandable element in the file. Each row in the recordset is identified with the `z:row` element name. Within the row, each column is listed as an attribute, with its corresponding data value.

Understanding the Benefits of Using XML

So, now you know that XML is a way that you can intelligently describe data. But why would you want to use it in your applications? In short, not all applications will benefit from XML, but many will.

Data interchange

XML is based on the concept that a document is the best way to exchange information between organizations. All kinds of documents are used in a business: purchase orders, invoices, contracts, product specifications, and so on. A document created by one organization must then be read and understood by another. Documents contain two parts: the framework for presenting the information and the information itself.

Consider a product catalog. It consists of a number of individual specification sheets. For a group of similar products, each of the categories in the specification sheet is the same, inviting the reader to make apples-to-apples comparisons between products.

There are many different ways to exchange data between applications, each with its limitations and problems. In order to understand why you would use XML, you should understand the more traditional methods of data interchange.

Binary files

Binary files typically contain a raw dump of the data from your application. No information about the data structure of the file is contained in the file, and usually a custom program needs to be written to read the information from the file and reformat it into something that the receiving application can use.

Once the file is created, it is transported to another computer via a network, floppy disk, or some other method, then loaded into the second computer. Any errors or problems encountered on the remote computer are usually returned back to the first computer, using the same technique that was used to send the data in the first place. However, this technique means that there is a delay between the time the data is created in the sending application and the time before the receiving application has posted the changes. In many cases this doesn't matter, but in some cases it can be a big problem.

There are other drawbacks to using binary files. Different computers use different ways of storing numeric data. Intel computers, for instance, store a 16-bit integer low byte then high byte, while other types of computers may store the same value high byte then low byte. This means that you may have to transform the actual values in order to accurately process the file.

Text files

Text files are also known as *flat files.* These files usually contain a formatted dump of data from the sending application. When dealing with mainframe-based applications, these files typically use a fixed data format, where each field occupies the same column positions in each line of the file.

PC-based applications typically use delimited files, such as *Comma Separated Value* (CSV) files or tab delimited files, where each field in a line is separated from the next field by a special character, such as a comma or tab. Each record in the file is separated from the next by a carriage return, line feed, or carriage return line feed pair.

Like binary files, text files usually don't contain information about the data itself. Sometimes the first line of the file will contain the names of the fields, but other information, such as data type and size information, is almost never included. Also, like binary files, text files need to be transported to the remote computer either through a network or through removable media, such as a floppy disk or magnetic tape.

COM components

Using COM to exchange data is merely a matter of building a COM component in the receiving application that can be called by the sending application as the data is created. This makes is easier to send the data, since the receiving application is able to process the data as it is received. There is no problem parsing the various fields that are being transported, since each field is stored in its own property with its own specific data type.

One problem encountered when using COM for data interchange revolves around the real-time nature of COM. As the data is generated in the sending application, the receiving application must be available to process it. If necessary, you can use a message queue between the COM components that allows the two applications to process data at their own speed. This prevents the sending application from transmitting data faster than the receiving application can process it.

You don't have to worry about byte order or any other compatibility issues like that because the COM specification ensures that those problems can't arise. Of course, using COM components means that you have to run in a Windows environment. While there are techniques that allow you to run COM on non-Windows systems, they generally aren't as stable as using COM natively.

Separating content from formatting

It is possible to build generic Web pages that load and display the information found in an XML document, however it is often desirable to create a program that reads the HTML document and extracts meaningful information from the document. By using an XML document, you can easily extract the information you need.

Better searches

It is possible to perform better searches of an XML file when compared to an unstructured file. You can use the tags to ignore data you don't want to search. For instance, if you have an XML file containing a list of books, you can search only the author tags if you're looking for a book written by a particular author. While this may not make a big difference when searching for someone named Elizabeth Thornberry, it may help to eliminate false hits when searching for titles written by Red Book.

Local access

For all practical purposes, you could use an XML document as a primitive database. All of the information needed to describe the data is kept within the document, so it would be easy to retrieve data from a remote database server and save it locally in an XML file which could be used as input to various tools, such as a report writer or statistical analysis program. Because you have a local copy of the data, you don't impact the database server's performance when you process the data as you try various report formats or create complex statistical analysis programs.

Easily compressed

Because XML tags and data are stored using normal common ASCII characters, the data is easily compressed. Thus tools, such as a dial-up modem that automatically includes data compression helps to compensate for the fact that XML documents are much larger than a straight binary file. Note that even with compression, the XML document will most likely still be larger than the equivalent binary file, but using data compression goes a long way toward eliminating the extra overhead.

Vendor independence

XML is independent of any particular vendor and has the benefit of being incorporated into many different products. Thus, it is easily incorporated into applications. Unlike comma separated value files that have to be parsed, there are many different XML parsers available to help you read an XML document. So as long as you can agree on the elements in the XML document, it doesn't matter whether a COBOL program running on an IBM mainframe or a Visual Basic program running on Windows 2000 processes the XML document.

Industry acceptance

Many industry-specific groups are being formed to determine the elements and organization for document exchange. This is very important, since it will allow you to exchange information with other applications and not worry if, for example, someone chooses to call someone's name `FIRST_NAME`, `FIRSTNAME` or `FNAME`.

There are a number of industry groups currently working on standardizing XML tags so that organizations can exchange documents with the knowledge that they will understand the structures used in the documents.

Thoughts on Using XML

Not every application will benefit from XML. Specifically, adding XML support to closed applications (for example, those applications that don't share data with other applications) is probably a waste of time and money. There are better ways to share data within an application, such as a database or a COM object. However, if you have an open application that needs to exchange data with other applications, XML may be the solution for you.

It's my opinion that XML is one of the most over-hyped technologies in the market today. Every vendor is scrambling to demonstrate their commitment to XML and claim that their products are XML-enabled. In reality, XML is only a tool for facilitating data exchange. The real power of XML comes from the fact that many industries are defining XML-based standards for information interchange. Having a standard that describes how to submit a purchase order for automotive parts or return information about your checkbook is what is really important.

Summary

In this chapter you learned:

- how XML documents are formatted.
- about XML tags and attributes.
- how to translate a database design into an XML document.
- how to create an XML document with an editor.
- how to view an XML document with Internet Explorer 5.
- about XSL style sheets.
- how ADO saves recordsets in XML format.
- about the benefits of using XML

✦ ✦ ✦

CHAPTER 21

The Document Object Model

In This Chapter

Introducing the Document Object Model

Understanding the document hierarchy

Using the DOM Objects

Microsoft has developed a tool for creating and parsing XML documents called MSXML. MSXML implements the XML Document Object Model (DOM) as defined by the Worldwide Web Consortium (usually called W3C). W3C is an international standards body that is responsible for the standards (such as HTML, XML, XSP, and so on) that are used to access the Web.

The DOM stores an XML document as a series of objects that can be easily accessed by an application program. MSXML implements DOM as a series of COM objects for use on Windows-based computers. This means that these objects are independent of any programming language and database server and can be used with Visual Basic, Visual C++, ASP script files, SQL Server, and Oracle 8i without problems.

In this chapter, I'll discuss how to use the Document Object Model to create and parse XML documents.

Note

Basically beta: The version of the Document Object Model discussed in this book is based on the March 2000 beta release of MSXML. At the time I wrote this chapter, the W3C hadn't finalized the specifications for DOM, and as a consequence, Microsoft's implementation of it in MSXML is still subject to change.

The Document Object Model

Microsoft's implementation of the Document Object Model conforms fairly closely to the W3C's recommendation, but recommendations can be fairly complex to understand. The DOM is based on a hierarchical organization of object nodes whose types vary, as different types of information are stored in the document hierarchy. In addition, a number of other objects are stored there that contain specific pieces of information or utility functions.

Document hierarchy

The basic DOM hierarchy is shown in Figure 21-1. The root node of the hierarchy is the `DOMDocument` object, which encompasses the entire XML document. As you descend through the tree structure, other nodes represent a particular piece of information or group of information in the XML document.

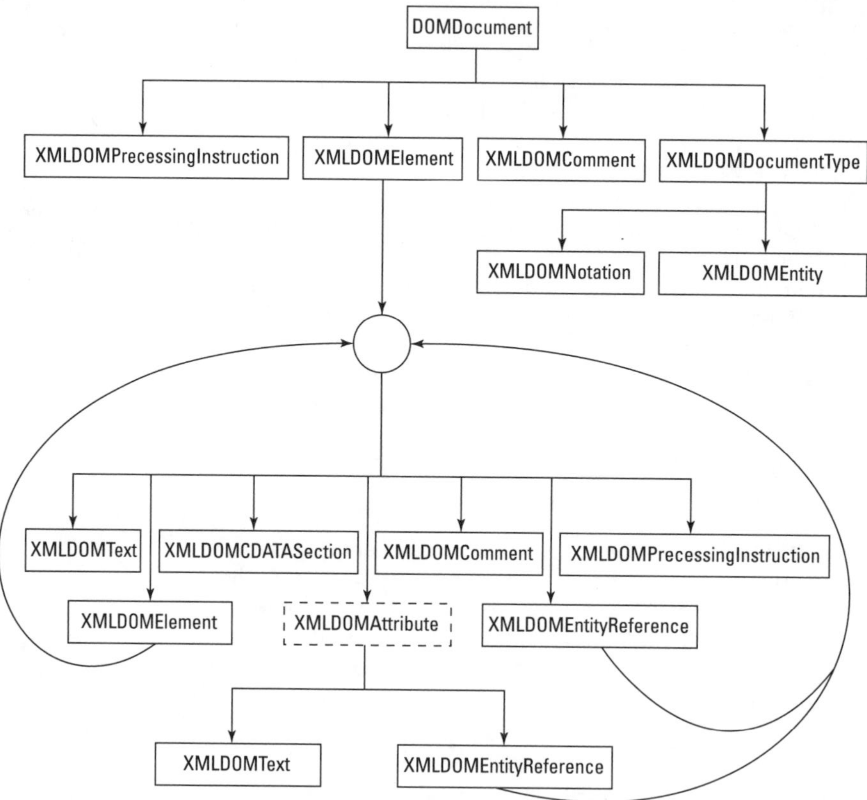

Figure 21-1: Viewing the Document Object Model object hierarchy

The basic object is the `XMLDOMNode` object, from which all of the other nodes are derived. In total, there are a dozen different types of nodes. Aside from the `DOMDocument` object, all of the other objects begin with `XMLDOM`.

- `DOMDocument` – This is the highest-level object in the hierarchy. It encompasses the entire XML document. It also includes additional methods and properties that can be used to obtain an XML document or to create other nodes.
- `XMLDOMAttribute` – This object is used to hold information about a single attribute in an element. It is not considered a true node value since it is referenced through the `attributes` property, rather than the `childNodes` property.
- `XMLDOMCDATASection` – This object is similar to the `IXMLDOMText` object, except it contains data that was stored in a CDATA section in the XML document. The CDATA section begins with the `<[[` string and ends with the `]]>` string. Any characters in between the two CDATA delimiters are treated as normal text. This lets you include any text into a text field, including elements that would normally be processed by the XML parser.
- `XMLDOMComment` – This object holds an XML comment element, which is the string of characters between the `<!--` and `-->`.
- `XMLDOMDocumentType` – This object contains information about the Document Type Declarations included in an XML document.
- `XMLDOMElement` – This object contains information about a single element in an XML document. If the element in the document contains other, nested elements, then the `childNodes` property will contain references to these objects. The `attributes` property can be used to find the `IXMLDOMAttribute` objects, which contain information about the attributes found in this element.
- `XMLDOMEntity` – This object contains information about a parsed or unparsed entity in the XML document.
- `XMLDOMEntityReference` – This object contains information about an entity reference in the XML document.
- `XMLDOMNode` – This object is the fundamental object of the Document Object Model. All of the other objects that can act as a node in the hierarchy are derived from this object.
- `XMLDOMNotation` – This object contains notation information from a Document Type Declaration or a schema.
- `XMLDOMProcessingInstruction` – This object contains processing information for the XML document. For example, this object will store the information found in the `<?xml version="1.0"?>` tag that is found at the start of most XML documents.
- `XMLDOMText` – This object contains the text value found in between the `<element>` and `</element>` tags in a document.

To IXMLDOM or not to IXMLDOM: Microsoft frequently prefixes the node names with an I in their implementation of the object model. The I prefix is a C++ convention that indicates that the object is a COM Interface, which just another object to a Visual Basic programmer.

Other objects

Here are a few other objects that you may find interesting. These objects cannot be used in place of a node object, but offer specialized support services.

- XMLDOMDocumentFragment – This object is used to store part of an XML document. You might find it useful if you want to restructure an XML object hierarchy.
- XMLDOMImplementation – This object allows you to detect various features included in a particular implementation of the Document Object Model.
- XMLDOMNodeList – This object is a container for a collection of nodes. This object is typically returned by several methods that you can use to search for specific elements in the document hierarchy.
- XMLDOMParseError – This object contains information about any errors that occurred while parsing your XML document.
- XMLHttpRequest – This object allows you to send and receive information using an HTTP connection.

The XMLDOMNode Object

The XMLDOMNode object is the fundamental object in the Document Object Model. It forms the basis of all the other node objects that hold your XML document. Each of those objects will inherit the XMLDOMNode's properties and methods, to which it may add unique properties, methods, and events.

XMLDOMNode object properties

Table 21-1 lists the properties associated with the XMLDOMNode object.

Table 21-1
Properties of the XMLDOMNode object

Property	***Description***
`attributes`	An object reference to a node containing the attributes. Returns `NULL` if this node doesn't have any attributes.
`baseName`	A `String` value containing right side of a fully qualified name of the document.
`childNodes`	An object reference to one of several different collections depending on the value of `nodeType` (see Table 21-2).
`dataType`	A `Variant` value that is either a `String` containing the name of the data type associated with the node or `VT_NULL` if no data type is defined.
`definition`	An object reference to a node in the document type definition or schema, if included.
`firstChild`	An object reference to the first child node of this node. Returns `NULL` if this node doesn't have any children.
`lastChild`	An object reference to the last child node of this node. Returns `NULL` if this node doesn't have any children.
`namespaceURI`	A `String` containing the Universal Resource Identifier (URI) of the namespace.
`nextSibling`	An object reference to the next sibling of this node. If there are no more siblings, then this value is `NULL`.
`nodeName`	A `String` value containing the name of the node.
`nodeType`	An enumerated data type containing the type of the node (see Table 21-2).
`nodeTypedValue`	A `String` value containing the node's value in its defined data type.
`nodeTypeString`	A `String` value containing a value corresponding to the value of `nodeType`. See Table 21-2 for the string values that correspond to the `nodeType` value.
`nodeValue`	A `String` value containing the text associated with the node.
`ownerDocument`	An object reference to the root `DOMDocument` object or the `DOMDocument`, which created this object.

Continued

Table 21-1 (continued)

Property	Description
parentNode	An object reference to the parent object of this node.
parsed	A Boolean when True means that this node and all of its descendents have been parsed.
prefix	A String containing the namespace prefix.
previousSibling	An object reference to the previous sibling of this node. If this is the first node, then this value will be NULL.
specified	A Boolean value when True means that the value was specified, rather than being derived from a default value in the DTD or schema.
text	A String containing the text value of the current node and all of its subtrees.
xml	A String containing the XML statements that make up the current document.

XMLDOMNode object methods

The XMLDOMNode object has a number of methods that are used to manage the child nodes associated with it.

Function appendChild (newChild As IXMLDOMNode) as IXMLDOMNode

The appendChild method is used to add a node object as a child of the current node. It returns an object to the newly added child node. This method is the equivalent of calling insertBefore (newChild, NULL). newChild is an object reference to a node, which will be added as a child to the current node.

Function cloneNode (deep As Boolean) as IXMLDOMNode

The cloneNode method is used to create a copy of the current node. deep is a Boolean, when True means that all of the child nodes of the current node are to be cloned also.

Table 21-2
Values for nodeType

Constant	*Integer*	*String*	*Description*
`NODE_ELEMENT`	1	`element`	Represents an element. Can be a child of the `Document`, `DocumentFragment`, `EntityReference` and `Element` nodes. Can have one or more `Element`, `Text`, `Comment`, `ProcessingInstruction`, `CDATASection`, and `EntityReference` nodes as children.
`NODE_ATTRIBUTE`	2	`attribute`	Represents an attribute. Referenced though an `Entity` node. Can have the `Text` and the `EntityReference` nodes as children. Technically, an `Attribute` is not considered a child of the `Element` node, since it is referenced through the `attributes` property.
`NODE_TEXT`	3	`Text`	Represents the text content of a tag. Can be a child of the `Attribute`, `DocumentFragment`, `Element`, and `EntityReference` nodes. Cannot have any child nodes.
`NODE_CDATA_SECTION`	4	`cdatasection`	Represents a CDATA section, which is used to escape blocks of text that might be recognized as markup. Can be a child of the `DocumentFragment`, `EntityReference`, and `Element` nodes. Cannot have any child nodes.
`NODE_ENTITY_REFERENCE`	5	`Entityreference`	Represents an entity. Can be a child of the `Attribute`, `DocumentFragment`, `Element`, and `EntityReference` nodes. Can have the `Element`, `ProcessingInstruction`, `Comment`, `Text`, `CDATASection`, and `EntityReference` nodes as children.
`NODE_ENTITY`	6	`Entity`	Represents an expanded entity. Can be a child of the `DocumentType` node. Can have other nodes as child nodes.

Continued

Table 21-2 (continued)

Constant	Integer	String	Description
`NODE_PROCESSING_INSTRUCTION`	7	`processinginstruction`	Can be a child of the `Document`, `Document Fragment`, `Element`, and `EntityReference` nodes. Cannot have any child nodes.
`NODE_COMMENT`	8	`comment`	Represents a comment. Can be a child of the `Document`, `DocumentFragment`, `Element`, and `EntityReference` nodes. Cannot have any child nodes.
`NODE_DOCUMENT`	9	`document`	Represents an XML document. Cannot be a child of any other nodes. Can have exactly one child node, which can be an `Element`, a `ProcessingInstruction`, a `Comment`, or a `DocumentType` node.
`NODE_DOCUMENT_TYPE`	10	`Documenttype`	Represents a document type declaration. Can be a child of the `Document` node. Can have `Notation` and `Entity` nodes as child nodes.
`NODE_DOCUMENT_FRAGMENT`	11	`documentfragment`	Represents a node or subtree with a document without being contained within the document. Cannot be a child of any other nodes. Can have `Element`, `ProcessingInstruction`, `Comment`, `Text`, `CDATASection`, and `EntityReference` nodes as child nodes.
`NODE_NOTATION`	12	`notation`	Represents a notation in the document. Can be a child of the `DocumentType` node. Cannot have any child nodes.

Function hasChildNodes () as Boolean

The hasChildNodes method returns True if the current node has children.

Function insertBefore (newChild As ICMLDOMNode, refChild) as IXMLDOMNode

The insertBefore method is used to add a child node to the current node. The node will be inserted before the node specified in refChild. An object reference to newChild will be returned as the value of the method.

newChild is an object reference to the node to be added. refChild is an object reference to a node that is a child of the current node. If this parameter is NULL, then the node will be added to the end of the collection.

Function removeChild (childNode as ICMLDOMNode) as IXMLDOMNode

The removeChild method is used to remove the specified node from the current node's child nodes. The node is not destroyed, so you should set the node to Nothing to free the node's resources if you really want to delete it. An object reference to the removed node will be returned by the method. childNode is an object reference to the node to be removed.

Function replaceChild (newChild As ICMLDOMNode, oldChild As ICMLDOMNode) as IXMLDOMNode

The removeChild method is used to replace an existing node with a new node. The method will return an object reference to the old node.

newChild is an object reference to a new node. oldChild is an object reference to one of the current node's child nodes that will be replaced with newChild.

Function selectNodes (queryString As String) as IXMLDOMNodeList

The selectNodes method searches the current object and its children for elements that match the specified XSL pattern string, and returns them as an IXMLDOMNodeList. queryString is a String value containing an XSL Pattern query.

Function selectSingleNode (queryString As String) as IXMLDOMNode

The selectSingleNode method searches the current object and its children for the first element that matches the specified XSL pattern string, and returns it as an IXMLDOMNode. queryString is a String value containing an XSL Pattern query.

Function transformNode (stylesheet As IXMLDOMNode) as String

The `transformNode` method returns a `String` value containing a formatted XML document using the specified XSL style sheet. `stylesheet` is an object reference to an `IXMLDOMNode` object containing the root of the XSL style sheet.

Sub transformNodeToObject (stylesheet As IXMLDOMNode, outputObject)

The `transformNodeToObject` method creates a `DOMDocument` structure containing the formatted XML document using the specified XSL style sheet. `stylesheet` is an object reference to an `IXMLDOMNode` object containing the root of the XSL style sheet. `outputObject` is an object reference to a `DOMDocument` object which will contain the root object of the formatted document.

The DOMDocument Object

The `DOMDocument` object is the fundamental object in the Document Object Model. It represents a single XML document.

DOMDocument object properties

The `DOMDocument` object has all of the properties of the `XMLDOMNode` object (see Table 21-1), plus the additional ones listed in Table 21-3.

Table 21-3
Unique Properties of the `DOMDocument` Object

Property	*Description*
`async`	A `Boolean` value when `True` means that the `Load` method will return control to the caller before the load is complete. You must use the `readyState` property or the `onReadyStateChange` event to determine when the load process is finished.
`doctype`	An object reference to an `XMLDOMDocumentType` object (specified with the <!DOCTYPE> tag) containing the document type definition.
`documentElement`	An object reference to the root element of the document.
`implementation`	An object reference to the `XMLDOMImplementation` object, which contains information about the features that are supported in this implementation of DOM.

Property	Description
namespaces	An object reference to an XMLDOMSchemaCache object that contains the collection of namespaces used in this XML document.
ondataavailable	A Boolean value, when True means that the ondataavailable event is enabled.
onreadystatechange	A Boolean value, when True means that the onreadystatechange event is enabled.
ontransformnode	A Boolean value, when True means that the ontransformnode event is enabled.
parseError	An object reference to the XMLDOMParseError object, which contains information about the last parsing error.
preserveWhiteSpace	A Boolean, when True means that the parsing process will retain the blanks that are included in the XML source document.
readyState	A Long value describing the state of the document, when loading the document asynchronously (see the async property). A value of LOADING (1) means that the XML source document is being loaded; a value of LOADED (2) means that the document is loaded, but none of the objects are available for access; a value of INTERACTIVE (3) means that some objects are available for use; a value of COMPLETED (4) means that the document has been loaded and all objects are available for access. Note that a value of COMPLETED doesn't imply that the document loaded successfully.
resolveExternals	A Boolean value, when True means that external definitions such as namespaces, DTD external subsets, and external entity references should be resolved at parse time.
schemas	An object reference to an XMLSchemaCache object containing a list of schemas that should be used when loading an XML document.
url	A String value containing the URL that was used to load the XML document.
validateOnParse	A Boolean, when True means that the document's structure should be validated during parsing.

Enabled, but impossible: Simply setting the ondataavailable, onreadystatechange, and ontransformnode properties to True is not sufficient to enable the corresponding events. You must declare the Document object using the WithEvents keyword at the module level in your program in order to include code for the events.

DOMDocument object methods

The `DOMDocument` object has a number of unique methods that are used to create and access the information in an XML document.

Sub Abort ()

The `Abort` method will cancel an asynchronous download. This will return an error in the `XMLDOMParseError` object indicating that the download was aborted.

Function createAttribute (name As String) as IXMLDOMAttribute

The `createAttribute` method creates an empty attribute object with the specified name. Note that the newly created node must be added to another node using the `appendChild` method. `name` is a `String` value containing the name of the attribute.

Function createCDATASection (data As String) as IXMLDOMCDATASection

The `createCDATASection` method creates an empty `IXMLDOMCDATASection` object with the specified data. Note that the newly created node must be added to another node using the `appendChild` method. `data` is a `String` value that will be stored in the new object's `nodeValue` property.

Function createNode (type, name As String, namespaceURI As String) as IXMLDOMNode

The `createNode` method creates an empty node in the document. Note that the newly created node must be added to another node using the `appendChild` method. `type` is either a `String` value containing the type of the node or an `Integer` containing the numeric value corresponding to the type of the node (see Table 21-2) `name` is a `String` value containing the name of the node that will be stored in the `nodeName` property. `namespaceURI` is a `String` containing the URI of the namespace.

Function createProcessingInstruction (target As String, data As String) as IXMLDOMProcessingInstruction

The `createProcessingInstruction` method creates an empty `IXMLDOMProcessingInstruction` object with the specified data. Note that the newly created node must be added to another node using the `appendChild` method. `target` is a `String` value containing the name of the processing instruction. `data` is a `String` value that will be stored in the new object's `nodeValue` property.

Output version: Use this method to generate the <?xml version="1.0"?> element at the start of your XML document. Use `xml` as `target`, and `version="1.0"` as `data`.

Function createTextNode (data As String) as IXMLDOMTextNode

The `createTextNode` method creates an empty TextNode object with the specified data. Note that the newly created node must be added to another node using the `appendChild` method. `data` is a `String` value that will be stored in the new object's `nodeValue` property.

Function getElementsByTagName (tagName As String) as IXMLDOMNodeList

The `getElementsByTagName` method searches the current object and its children for the specified elements and returns them as an `IXMLDOMNodeList`. `tagName` is a `String` value containing the element name to be found. If you specify an asterisk (*), all elements will be returned.

Function getProperty(name As String)

The `getProperty` method returns a property value set by the `setProperty` method. `name` is a `String` value containing the name of the property. `SelectionLanguage` is a `String` value, which can be either Xpath or XSLPattern. It determines the type of query that the user specifies in the `selectNodes` or `selectSingleNode` methods.

Function load (url As String) as Boolean

The `load` method loads the specified XML document into the `DOMDocument`, parses it, and then creates the appropriate child objects to represent the XML document. If the load was successful, this method will return `True`. `url` is a `String` value containing a URL that specifies the location of the XML document to be loaded.

Function loadXML(xmlString As String) as Boolean

The `loadXML` method loads parses and then creates the appropriate child objects to represent the XML document specified in `xmlString`. If the load was successful, this method will return `True`. `xmlString` is a `String` value containing the XML statements to be loaded.

Function nodeFromId (idString As String) as IXMLDOMNode

The `nodeFromId` method returns the node, which has an ID attribute with the supplied value. The ID attribute is supposed to appear only once in an element, and the value of each ID attribute is supposed to be unique within an XML document. `idString` is a `String` value containing the ID value to be searched for.

Sub save (destination)

The `save` method is used to write the XML to the specified location. `Destination` is a `Variant` which can be a `String` value containing a file name or an ASP Response object, which can be used to send the document over the Internet in a VB IIS Application.

Sub setProperty(name As String, value)

The `setProperty` method allows you to set the value of the `SelectionLanguage` property described earlier in this chapter under "Function getProperty(name As String)." `name` is a `String` value containing the name of the property, whose value is to be changed with the `SelectionLanguage` property.. `value` is the value to be assigned to the property.

Sub validate()

The `validate` method verifies the currently loaded document against the currently loaded DTD or schema. Without a DTD or schema, the validate method will cause a run-time error.

DOMDocument object events

The `DOMDocument` object is unique in this object model in that it is the only object to have events. These events assist you in processing XML documents asynchronously.

Event ondataavailable ()

The `ondataavailable` event is called as soon as the first object containing data is available during an asynchronous load process. The `ondataavailable` event will be called as additional chunks of data become available. Note that the `ondataavailable` property must be set to `True`, and the `DOMDocument` object must be declared `WithEvents`, in order for the event to be fired.

Event onreadystatechange ()

The `onreadystatechange` event is called each time the `readyState` property changes value. Note that the `onreadystatechange` property must be set to `True`, and the `DOMDocument` object must be declared `WithEvents`, in order for the event to be fired.

Event Function ontransformnode (nodeCode, nodeData) As Boolean

The `ontransformnode` event is called before each node in the style sheet is applied to each node in the XML document. If you return `True`, the transformation process will continue, while returning False will abort the transformation process. nodeCode is an object reference to the current node in the style sheet. nodeData is an object reference to the current node in the XML document.

Visual Basic, not: This event is not supported in Visual Basic due to the way it was implemented.

The XMLDOMAttribute object

The XMLDOMAtribute object holds information about a specific attribute in an element. Unlike the other node objects, the XMLDOMAttribute nodes are referenced through the attributes property.

XMLDOMAttribute object properties

Table 21-4 lists the unique properties associated with the XMLDOMAttribute object. All of the properties associated with the XMLDOMNode object (see Table 21-1) are also available in this object.

Table 21-4
Unique Properties of the XMLDOMNode object

Property	*Description*
Name	A String value containing the name of the attribute.
Value	A String containing the attribute's value.

XMLDOMAttribute object methods

The XMLDOMAttribute object has no unique methods. It inherits all of the methods found in the XMLDOMNode object.

The XMLDOMCDATASection Object

The XMLDOMComment object holds information about a CDATA section in your XML document.

XMLDOMCDATASection object properties

Table 21-5 lists the unique properties associated with the `XMLDOMCDATASection` object. All of the properties listed in the `XMLDOMNode` object (see Table 21-1) are also available for this object.

Table 21-5
Unique Properties of the XMLDOMCDATASection Object

Property	*Description*
`Data`	A `String` value containing the characters from the CDATA section of the XML document.
`Length`	A `Long` value containing the number of characters in `data`.

XMLDOMCDATASection object methods

The `XMLDOMCDATASection` object has two unique methods that are used to access the information from a CDATA section in your XML document. All of the methods found in the `XMLDOMNode` object are available for this object as well.

Function splitText (offset As Long) as IXMLDOMText

The `splitText` method splits the node into two nodes at the specified offset from the beginning of the text and automatically inserts the new node into the document hierarchy immediately following the current node. `offset` is a `Long` value containing the location where the split will take place. Specifying an offset value of zero will move all of the text in the current node to the new node.

Function substringData (offset As Long, count As Long) as String

The `substringData` method extracts a block of text from the node. `offset` is a `Long` value containing the location where the extraction will begin. The first character in the string has an offset of zero. `count` is a `Long` containing the number of characters to be extracted.

The XMLDOMComment Object

The `XMLDOMComment` object holds information about a comment in your XML document.

XMLDOMComment object properties

Table 21-6 lists the properties associated with the XMLDOMComment object. It also inherits the properties from the XMLDOMNode object (see Table 21-1).

Table 21-6
Unique Properties of the XMLDOMComment Object

Property	*Description*
Data	A String value containing the characters in the Comment section of the XML document.
Length	A Long value containing the number of characters in data.

XMLDOMComment object methods

The XMLDOMComment object has a method that you can use to extract information from a Comment section in your XML document. The methods available in the XMLDOMNode object are also available in this object.

Function substringData (offset As Long, count As Long) as String

The substringData method extracts a block of text from the node. offset is a Long value containing the location where the extraction will begin. The first character in the string has an offset of zero. count is a Long containing the number of characters to be extracted.

The XMLDOMDocumentType Object

The XMLDOMDocumentType object holds information about a document type declaration.

XMLDOMDocumentType object properties

Table 21-7 lists the unique properties associated with the XMLDOMDocumentType object.

Table 21-7
Unique Properties of the XMLDOMNode Object

Property	*Description*
`Entities`	An object reference to an `XMLDOMNameNodeMap` containing the collection of entities used in the document type declaration.
`Name`	A `String` value containing the name of the document type.
`Notations`	An object reference to an `XMLDOMNameNodeMap` containing the collection of `XMLDOMNotation` objects.

XMLDOMDocumentType object methods

The `XMLDOMDocumentType` object has no unique methods. It inherits all of the methods found in the `XMLDOMNode` object.

The XMLDOMElement Object

The `XMLDOMElement` object holds information about an entity from your XML document.

XMLDOMElement object properties

The unique property of the `XMLDOMElement` object is `tagName`, which is a `String` value containing the name of the tag that is used to identify the element. The `XMLDOMElement` object also inherits the properties from the `XMLDOMNode` object (see Table 21-1).

XMLDOMElement object methods

The `XMLDOMElement` object provides several methods that make it easy to access the information from the attributes associated with this object. Note that the methods available in the `XMLDOMNode` object (see Table 21-1) are also available in this object.

Function getAttribute (name as String) as Variant

The `getAttribute` method returns a `String` containing the value of the attribute. An empty string means that the attribute doesn't have a specified or default value. `name` is a `String` containing the name of the attribute.

Function getAttributeNode (name as String) as IXMLDOMAttribute

The `getAttributeNode` method returns a reference to an `XMLDOMAttribute` object containing the specified attribute. `name` is a `String` value containing the name of the attribute.

Sub normalize()

The `normalize` method combines all of the text nodes below this object into normal form, where each text node is separated by an element, a comment, a processing instruction, a CDATA section, or an entity reference. You can do the same thing by saving the document to a disk file, deleting all of the objects below the `DOMDocument` object, and loading the document back from the disk file.

Sub setAttribute (name as String, value)

The `setAttribute` method assigns a new value to an attribute. If the attribute doesn't exist, it will automatically be created for you. `name` is a `String` value containing the name of the attribute. `value` is a `Variant` value containing the value to be assigned to the attribute.

Function setAttributeNode (DOMAttribute as IXMLDOMAttribute) as IXMLDOMAttribute

The `setAttributeNode` method is used to create or replace an attribute node in the document hierarchy. It will return `Null` if the attribute didn't exist, or it will return an object pointer to the old attribute's node. `DOMAttribute` is an object reference to an `XMLDOMAttribute` object that contains the new attribute.

The XMLDOMEntity Object

The `XMLDOMEntity` object holds information about an entity from your XML document.

XMLDOMEntity object properties

Table 21-8 lists the unique properties of the `XMLDOMEntity` object. This object also inherits all of the properties from the `XMLDOMNode` object (see Table 21-1).

Table 21-8
Unique Properties of the XMLDOMEntity Object

Property	*Description*
notationName	A String value containing the name of the notation, if the entity is unparsed or an empty string once the entity has been parsed.
publicId	A String containing the public identifier associated with the entity.
systemId	A String containing the system identifier associated with the entity. If the system identifier isn't specified, this property will contain the empty string.

XMLDOMEntity object methods

The XMLDOMEntity object has no unique methods. It inherits all of the methods found in the XMLDOMNode object.

The XMLDOMEntityReference Object

The XMLDOMEntityReference object holds information about an entity from your XML document. This object is created based on the information from the XMLDOMEntity object. Due to the nature of the XML parser included in the object library, external entities may not be parsed and expanded in their own objects until they are needed, which means that two different objects are needed to hold the information.

No difference: The XMLDOMEntityReference object doesn't have any unique properties, methods, or events, when compared to the XMLDOMNode object. All of the standard properties and methods of the XMLDOMNode object are available in this object.

The XMLDOMNotation Object

The XMLDOMNotation object holds information about a notation that was declared in the data type declaration or schema section of your XML document.

XMLDOMNotation object properties

Table 21-9 lists the unique properties of the XMLDOMNotation object. This object also inherits all of the properties from the XMLDOMNode object.

Table 21-9
Unique Properties of the XMLDOMNotation Object

Property	Description
publicId	A String value containing the public identifier associated with the notation.
systemId	A String containing the system identifier associated with the notation. If the system identifier isn't specified, this property will contain the empty string.

XMLDOMNotation object methods

The XMLDOMNotation object has no unique methods. It inherits all of the methods found in the XMLDOMNode object (see Table 21-1).

The XMLDOMProcessingInstruction Object

The XMLDOMProcessingInstruction object contains processing directives, such as the <?xml version=1.0?>.

XMLDOMProcessingInstruction object properties

Table 21-10 lists the unique properties of the XMLDOMProcessingInstruction object. This object also inherits all of the properties from the XMLDOMNode object (see Table 21-1).

XMLDOMProcessingInstruction object methods

The XMLDOMProcessingInstruction object has no unique methods. It inherits all of the methods found in the XMLDOMNode object.

Table 21-10
Unique Properties of the XMLDOMProcessingInstruction Object

Property	*Description*
data	A String value containing the data associated with the processing instruction. In other words, this would be the version="1.0" part of the processing instruction. This value is identical to that in the nodeValue property.
target	A String containing the application that contains the processing instruction. For example, this would be xml from the <?xml version="1.0"?> processing instruction.

The XMLDOMText Object

The XMLDOMText object holds information about the text value associated with an XMLDOMElement or XMLDOMAttribute node.

XMLDOMText object properties

Table 21-11 lists the unique properties associated with the XMLDOMText object. All of the properties listed in the XMLDOMNode object are also available for this object.

Table 21-11
Unique Properties of the XMLDOMText Object

Property	*Description*
data	A String value containing the text characters that make up the value of an element or an attribute.
length	A Long value containing the number of characters in data.

XMLDOMText object methods

The XMLDOMText object includes a rich set of methods to manipulate the data stored in the node. It also includes all of the methods found in the XMLDOMNode object.

Sub appendData (data as String)

The `appendData` method adds the specified string value to the end of the existing data already in the node. `data` is a `String` value containing the new information to be added to the node's value.

Sub deleteData (offset as Long, count as Long)

The `deleteData` method removes the specified number characters from the node starting with the specified location. `offset` is a `Long` value containing the location where the characters will be deleted. The first character in the string has an offset of zero. `count` is a `Long` containing the number of characters to be deleted.

Sub insertData (offset as Long, data as String)

The `insertData` method inserts the specified data into the data already starting with the specified location. `offset` is a `Long` containing the location where the characters will be inserted. The first character in the string has an offset of zero. `data` is a `String` containing the characters to be added.

Sub replaceData (offset as Long, count as Long, data as String)

The `replaceData` method deletes the specified number of characters starting at the specified location, then inserts the specified data starting at the same location. `offset` is a `Long` containing the location where the characters will be replaced. The first character in the string has an offset of zero. `count` is a `Long` containing the number of characters to be deleted. `data` is a `String` containing the characters to be added.

Function splitText (offset as Long) as IXMLDOMText

The `splitText` method splits the node into two nodes at the specified offset from the beginning of the text, and automatically inserts the new node into the document hierarchy immediately following the current node. `offset` is a `Long` containing the location where the split will take place. Specifying an offset value of zero will move all of the text in the current node to the new node.

Function substringData (offset as Long, count as Long) as String

The `substringData` method extracts a block of text from the node. `offset` is a `Long` value containing the location where the extraction will begin. The first character in the string has an offset of zero. `count` is a `Long` containing the number of characters to be extracted.

The XMLDOMParseError Object

The XMLDOMParseError object contains information about the first error encountered while parsing your XML document.

XMLDOMParseError object properties

Table 21-12 lists the properties of the XMLDOMParseError object.

Table 21-12
Properties of the XMLDOMParseError object

Property	*Description*
ErrorCode	A Long value containing the error code.
Filepos	A Long containing the absolute position in the file where the error occurred.
Line	A Long containing the line number where the error occurred.
Linepos	A Long containing the position in the line where the error occurred.
Reason	A String value containing a text description of the error.
SrcText	A String containing the line with the error.
url	A String containing the URL of the document with the error.

XMLDOMParseError bject methods

The XMLDOMParseError object doesn't have any methods.

The XMLHttpRequest Object

The XMLHttpRequest object allows you to transfer XML documents using HTTP. This is primarily a client-side tool that can be used in a JavaScript or VBScript Web page to transmit a request to a server and process its response. The properties and objects that return information about the result are only valid if the send method has completed successfully.

XMLHttpRequest object properties

Table 21-13 lists the properties of the XMLHttpRequest object.

Table 21-13
Properties of the XMLHttpRequest Object

Property	*Description*
onreadystatechange	An object reference to an event handler in a scripting language.
readyState	A Long value describing the state of the transport, when loading the document asynchronously (see the async property). A value of UNINITIALIZED (0) means that the object has been created but nothing has been transferred. A value of LOADING (1) means that the source document is being loaded; a value of LOADED (2) means that the document is loaded, but none of the objects in the document hierarchy are available for access; a value of INTERACTIVE (3) means that some objects are available for use; a value of COMPLETED (4) means that the document has been loaded and all objects are available for access. Note that a value of COMPLETED doesn't imply that the document loaded successfully.
responseBody	A Variant value containing the response to the HTTP request.
responseStream	An object reference to a Stream object containing the raw data from the response to the HTTP request.
responseText	A String value containing the response to the HTTP request.
responseXML	An object reference to a DOMDocument object containing the parsed XML document that was received in response to the HTTP request.
status	A Long containing the HTTP status code returned by the HTTP server.
statusText	A String containing the HTTP line status.

XMLHttpRequest object methods

The XMLHttpRequest object includes methods for creating and sending an HTTP request to a Web server.

Sub abort()

The abort method terminates an active HTTP request.

Function getAllResponseHeaders () as String

The getAllResponseHeaders method returns the header information from the HTTP result as a single string. Each header is separated by a carriage return/line feed pair (vbCrLf).

Function getResponseHeader (bstrHeader as String) as String

The getResponseHeader method returns the specified header from the HTTP response where bstrHeader is a String value containing the particular header you wish to retrieve.

Sub open(bstrMethod as String, bstrUrl As String, [varAsync], [bstrUser], [bstrPassword])

The open method initializes an HTTP request. After the request is initialized, the send method must be used to transfer the document and wait for the response. bstrMethod is a String value that identifies the HTTP transfer method. This is usually one of the following: GET, POST, PUT, or PROPFIND. bstrUrl is a String containing the URL that will be used to process the request. varAsync is a Boolean value when True means that the call is asynchronous. If this value isn't specified, it will default to True. bstrUser is a String containing the userid to log onto the Web server. If this parameter is missing and the Web server requires a userId and password to log on, the user will be prompted for this information. bstrPassword is a String containing the password associated with bstrUserid.

Sub send ([varBody])

The send method transmits the request to the remote host and optionally waits for the host's response if the user specified False for varAsync on the open method. varBody is a Variant value containing the document to be sent. If this parameter isn't specified, then the current document is transmitted.

Sub setRequestHeader(bstrHeader as String, bstrValue as String)

The setRequestHeader method sets the value of the various header fields before the document request is sent. bstrHeader is a String value containing the header to be set. Note that the trailing colon (:) on the header should not be specified. bstrValue is a String containing the value to be assigned to the header.

Thoughts on the XML Object Model

As I said in the previous chapter, XML is far more complex than I have room to cover. This is really obvious when you look at the object model. However, much of the complexity isn't necessary for most programmers. As with most things in life, the eighty-twenty rule applies: eighty percent of the time, only twenty percent of the capabilities are needed or used.

In this case, the object model is designed to cover all sorts of situations that might not normally be encountered in most applications. In the next chapter, I'm going to use this object model in a simple example that shows you how you can generate an XML request and satisfy it with a Web server.

Summary

In this chapter you learned:

- about the XML Document Object Model
- how an XML document is mapped into the Document Object Model.

✦ ✦ ✦

CHAPTER 22

Integrating XML with Internet Information Server Applications

✦ ✦ ✦ ✦

In This Chapter

Requesting information using the Document Object Model

Building a simple Web page

Updating customer information

✦ ✦ ✦ ✦

In this chapter, I'll show you how to use the Document Object Model by building a Web page using VBScript. That Web page will communicate with a Web server application built with Internet Information Server (IIS) Applications.

Requesting Information

How often have you wanted to import a particular piece of information via the Web into your program for analysis? Perhaps you're interested in getting a stock quote on a periodic rate or following mortgage rates? Maybe you want to download information about how well the Orioles are playing.

By defining an XML document for requesting information and another document to contain the response, you can build a new breed of server that responds to XML requests for information. The fact that you can leverage existing HTTP technologies, such as Web servers and Web development tools, makes it easier to build these applications.

Getting Customer Information With XML

In this chapter, I'm going to focus on how to build an XML client program that requests information from an XML Server program. I've decided to build a Web page using a little VBScript as the client and an IIS Application as the server (see Figure 22-1). This application supports two basic types of requests: retrieving information about a customer and updating information about a customer.

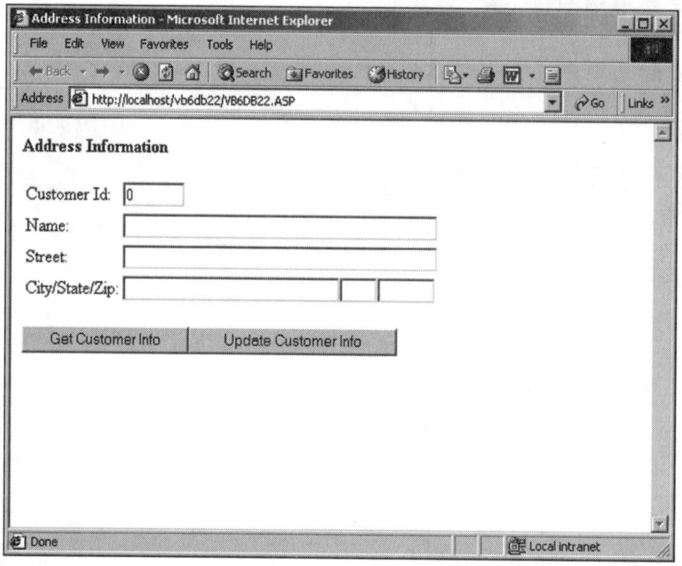

Figure 22-1: Running the XML Server application

Building the Simple Web Page

The sample Web page shown in Figure 22-1 is a fairly simple Web page that uses a table to line up the captions and the fields I use to display the data, as you can see in Listing 22-1. It is broken into three main sections: the `<head>`, the `<body>`, and the `<script>`. While I've left the tags for `<script>` in Listing 22-1, I omitted the code, since I'll discuss it later in this section.

Listing 22-1: HTML for the XML client Web page

```
<html>
   <head>
      <title>Address Information</title>
   </head>
```

```
  <body>
    <strong>Address Information</strong>
    <form align="left" name="AddressInfo">
      <table border = "0">
        <tr>
          <td>Customer Id:</td>
          <td><input type="text" name="CustomerId" size="6"
            value="0"></td>
        </tr>
        <tr>
          <td>Name:</td>
          <td><input type="text" name="Name" size="45"
              value=""></td>
        </tr>
        <tr>
          <td>Street:</td>
          <td><input type="text" name="Street" size="45"
              value=""></td>
        </tr>
        <tr>
          <td>City/State/Zip:</td>
          <td>
            <input type="text" name="City" size="30" value="">
            <input type="text" name="State" size="2" value="">
            <input type="text" name="Zip" size="5" value="">
          </td>
        </tr>
      </table>
    </form>
    <button onClick="GetCustomerInfo()">Get Customer Info</button>
    <button onClick="UpdateCustomerInfo()">Update Customer
          Info</button>
  </body>
  <script language="VBScript">

  </script>
</html>
```

Note that the form declaration differs from most Web pages that use forms. In this case, I don't need attributes that describe how to send the form data to the server. Specifically, I didn't code the `action` and `method` attributes. This is because I simply don't need them. The routines that will handle the conversion to XML will also handle the interactions with the Web server.

At the bottom of the form, I declared buttons that will call the `GetCustomerInfo` and `UpdateCustomerInfo` VBScript routines. This is where the actual work of converting the information from the form into an XML document and sending it to the server for processing takes place.

Requesting Customer Information

Retrieving customer information involves determining how the request and response XML documents should look and then building the code to process the documents.

Defining the XML documents

The `GetCustomerInfo` script routine takes the `CustomerId` field from the form on the Web page and assembles the XML document shown in Listing 22-2. This document defines the `GETCUSTOMERINFO` element to identify the request. Within the `GETCUSTOMERINFO` element are one or more `CUSTOMER` elements with the `CustomerId` attribute coded. This attribute specifies the customer you want to retrieve.

Listing 22-2: A sample request for customer information

```
<?xml version="1.0"?>
<GETCUSTOMERINFO>
   <CUSTOMER CustomerId="0"/>
</GETCUSTOMERINFO>
```

Listng 22-3 shows how the server should respond to the request. I use the same basic document that was used to request the customer's information, but I expand the `CUSTOMER` element to include elements for the Name, Street, City, State, and Zip fields from the Customers table. I also include another attribute called `Get`, which indicates the status of the request. A value of OK means that the information was retrieved properly. Otherwise, `Get` will contain an error message.

Listing 22-3: A sample response to the request for customer information

```
<GETCUSTOMERINFO>
   <CUSTOMER CustomerId="0" Get="OK">
```

```
      <NAME>
         Dexter Valentine
      </NAME>
      <STREET>
         3250 Second Ave.
      </STREET>
      <CITY>
         San Francisco
      </CITY>
      <STATE>
         CA
      </STATE>
      <ZIP>
         94115
      </ZIP>
   </CUSTOMER>
</GETCUSTOMERINFO>
```

Requesting a customer

Pressing the Get Customer Info button on the Web page will trigger the `GetCustomerInfo` VBScript routine in the `<script>` section of the HTML document (see Listing 22-4). This routine performs three separate tasks. First, it must create an XML document similar to the one shown in Listing 22-2. Next, it must take the document and transmit it to the Web server. Finally, it must take the response document (see Listing 22-3) from the Web server and fill in the various fields on the form.

Listing 22-4: The GetCustomerInfo routine in XML Client

```
Sub GetCustomerInfo()

Set XMLReq = CreateObject("MSXML2.DOMDocument")
Set p = XMLReq.createProcessingInstruction("xml", _
      "version=""1.0""")
XMLReq.appendChild p

Set node = XMLReq.createElement("GETCUSTOMERINFO")
Set subnode = XMLReq.createElement("CUSTOMER")
subnode.setAttribute "CustomerId", _
      Document.AddressInfo.CustomerId.Value

node.appendChild subnode
```

Continued

Listing 22-4 *(continued)*

```
XMLReq.appendChild node

MsgBox XMLReq.xml

set http=CreateObject("MSXML2.XMLHTTP")
http.open "Post", _
   "http://athena/VB6DB22/VB6DB22.ASP?wci=GetCustomer",
   false
http.setRequestHeader "Content-Type", "text/xml"
http.send XMLReq

Set XMLResp = CreateObject("MSXML2.DOMDocument")
XMLResp.LoadXML http.responsetext

MsgBox XMLResp.xml

Set nl = XMLResp.getElementsByTagName("CUSTOMER")
i = 0
Do While (i < nl.length) And _
   (nl(i).getAttribute("CustomerId") <_> _
      Document.AddressInfo.CustomerId.Value)
  i = i + 1
Loop

If i < nl.length Then
   If nl(i).getAttribute("Get") = "OK" Then
      Set nx = nl(i).getElementsByTagName("NAME")
      Document.AddressInfo.Name.Value = nx(0).text

      Set nx = nl(i).getElementsByTagName("STREET")
      Document.AddressInfo.Street.Value = nx(0).text

      Set nx = nl(i).getElementsByTagName("CITY")
      Document.AddressInfo.City.Value = nx(0).text

      Set nx = nl(i).getElementsByTagName("STATE")
      Document.AddressInfo.State.Value = nx(0).text

      Set nx = nl(i).getElementsByTagName("ZIP")
      Document.AddressInfo.Zip.Value = nx(0).text

   Else
      MsgBox "The customer wasn't found: " & _
         nl(i).getAttribute("Get")

Else
   MsgBox "The customer wasn't found."
```

```
End If

End Sub
```

The format's changed to protect the guilty: I admit it. I've reformatted all of the HTML and script code from the actual documents to make them more readable. However, changing the formatting does not change how the Web page works.

Building the request document

The `GetCustomerInfo` routine begins by creating a `DOMDocument` object called `XMLReq` to hold the XML document I want to send to the server. Note that I can't use the normal `Dim` and `Set` statements to create the object, because VBScript can't reference the object libraries directly from code. The only way to create an object in VBScript is to use the `CreateObject` function.

After creating the base document, I add the `<?xml version="1.0"?>` element by using the `createProcessingInstruction` and `appendChild` methods. While this isn't absolutely necessary, since the MSXML parser is smart enough to figure out how your document is structured without it, it is good form to include this element in case you choose to use a different XML server in the future.

Once the XML document is initialized, I create the `GETCUSTOMERINFO` element that really defines this document by using the `createElement` method. This returns an object reference to an `XMLDOMElement` object, which I save in the variable called `node`. Then I create another `XMLDOMElement` object for `CUSTOMER` in the variable `subnode`. I use the `setAttribute` method to create the `CustomerId` attribute with the value from the `CustomerId` field in the form. Then I connect the `subnode` object to the `node` object by using the `node.appendChild` method. Next, I use the `XMLReq.appendChild` method to link the `node` object to the root document.

I should point out that the order in which I append the processing and element instructions to the root object is important. All of the objects stored below a particular hierarchy are stored in the order where they were inserted. Thus, if you want element A to be displayed before element B when the XML document is generated, you must append element A before you append element B. Since I want the `GETCUSTOMERINFO` element to follow the processing instruction element, I have to append the processing instruction first.

After creating the document, I use the `MsgBox` statement (see Figure 22-2) and the `XMLReq.xml` method to display the document to the user. While this wouldn't be included in a production version of this application, it allows the programmer to see the XML request before it is sent.

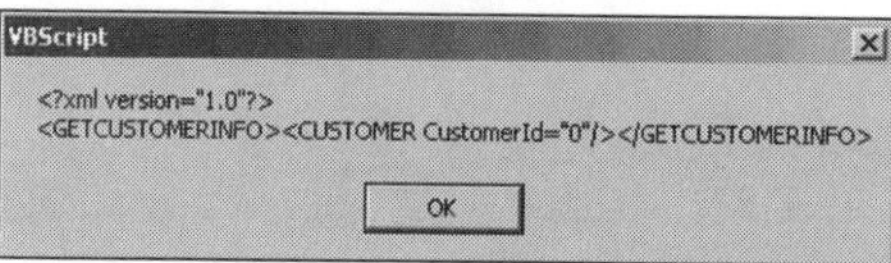

Figure 22-2: Viewing the XML GETCUSTOMERINFO request document

Sending the request document

In the next section of the routine, I create an `XMLHttp` object called `http` to perform the actual data transfer. After creating `http`, I use the `open` method to establish an HTTP connection to the Web server. I specify that I want to perform an HTTP Post operation to send the document, and I include the URL of the program that will process the request. Finally, I choose not to do an asynchronous transfer. This means that the `send` method won't return until a response has been received from the Web server. This approach simplifies the programming involved, since I don't have to enable the `onreadystatechange` event to determine when the response document has been received.

Before I send the document, I use the `setRequestHeader` method to set the Content-Type HTTP header explicitly to `text/xml`. While this isn't important in this application, since both sides are expecting XML documents to be transferred, it may be important in other situations where different processing paths may be taken depending on the document type.

When the code reaches the `send` method, a warning message may be displayed to the user letting them know that the Web page is accessing external information (see Figure 22-3). You can configure the Web browser to allow programs to disable this error message by changing the security level to low for the particular zone that you are accessing.

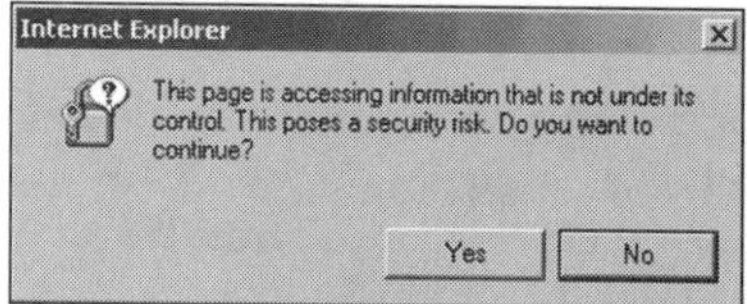

Figure 22-3: Getting permission to end the XML document

Do I really want to do this?: Changing the security level in your browser to allow you to use the `send` method in your Web page allows any Web page in the same content zone to use this function. Before you change this option, be sure you really want to take this security risk.

After using the `send` method to transmit the document, I create a new `DOMDocument` object that will hold the response from the Web server. Then I use the `LoadXML` method to create the document from the `http.responsetext` property and then use the `MsgBox` statement to display the response document to the user (see Figure 22-4).

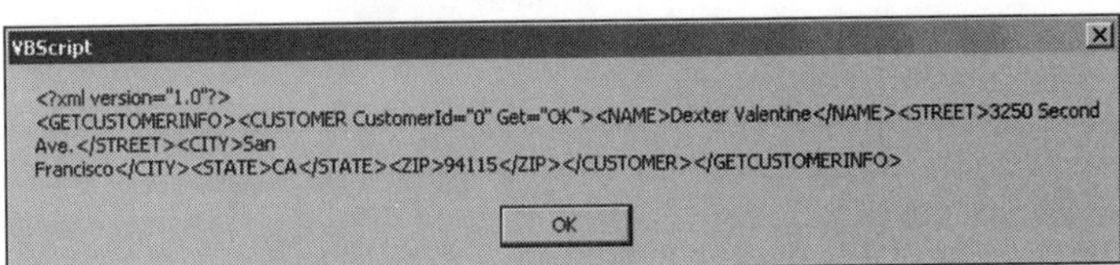

Figure 22-4: Viewing the GETCUSTOMERINFO response document

Displaying the response document

Displaying the information is merely a matter of working your way through the response from the Web server and extracting the information you want to display. This is easier said than done, however. You need to traverse the document hierarchy to find the `CUSTOMER` element that matches the CustomerId value from the form. Then you need to determine if the request was successful. Once this is done, you can take the information associated with the request and update the form.

In this case, I begin by creating a `nodeList` object that contains all of the `CUSTOMER` elements using the `getElementsByTagName` method. Since it is possible that the `nodeList` object may have more than one `CUSTOMER` element, I'll set the variable `i` to zero and use a `Do While` loop to check each of the elements to find the first one that matches the CustomerId value from the form.

When the loop finishes, the variable `i` will either point to the proper element or it will contain a value that is one larger than the number of elements in the `nodeList` object. (Remember that the `nodeList` object is a zero-based collection, so if it contains only one element, the element will have an index value of zero while the collection has a `length` of one.)

Next, I check the value of `i` to see if it is less than the length of the collection and issue the appropriate message if it isn't. Then I can see if the value of the `Get` attribute is `OK`. If it isn't, I need to issue the appropriate error message.

If everything worked correctly, I can retrieve the information for each of the fields on the form by creating a new `nodeList` object by searching for a particular element within the current node (`nl(i)`). Since the format of the document allows only one element with a particular name within the `CUSTOMER` element, I can safely access the first value in the returned `nodeList` since I know it must be the only element in the list. Then I can use the `text` property to extract the value of the `XMLDOMText` node below it and save it in the appropriate field on the form. This results in the updated Web page shown in Figure 22-5.

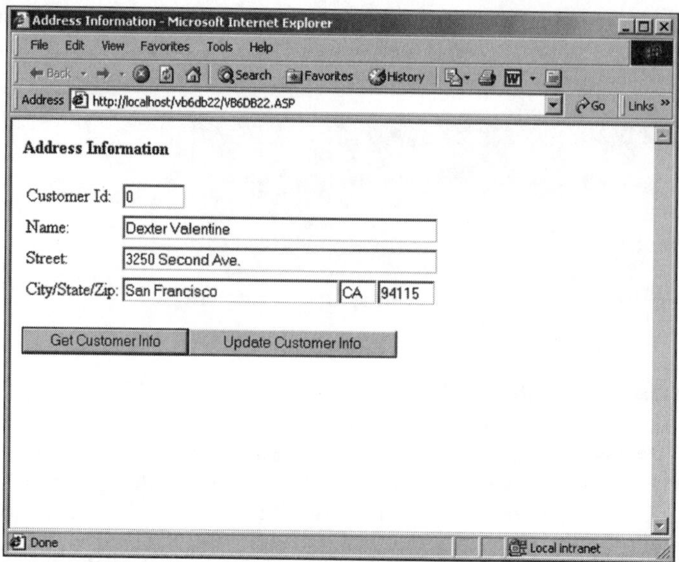

Figure 22-5: Viewing the customer's information

Getting a customer from the database

Now that you understand the client side, it's time to dig into the server side. Since this is an IIS Application, it responds to requests sent to an Internet Information Server (IIS) Web server. In this case, it must respond to an XML document that is transmitted using the `Post` method. It must parse the incoming XML document to determine the information that is requested and then construct a new XML document with the appropriate response.

The `GetCustomer_Respond` event in the XML Server program is triggered any time someone requests a document using the following URL:

```
http://Athena/VB6DB22/VB6DB22.ASP?wci=GetCustomer
```

This URL points to a computer called `Athena` and looks in the `VB6DB22` directory for the file called `VB6DB22.ASP`. It passes the `wci=GetCustomer` parameter to the file, which will trigger the `GetCustomer_Respond` event in the IIS Application (see Listing 22-5).

Listing 22-5: The GetCustomer_Respond event in XML Server

```
Private Sub GetCustomer_Respond()

Dim attr As IXMLDOMAttribute
```

```
Dim el As IXMLDOMElement
Dim nl As IXMLDOMNodeList
Dim node As IXMLDOMElement
Dim p As IXMLDOMProcessingInstruction
Dim subnode As IXMLDOMElement
Dim subsubnode As IXMLDOMElement
Dim XMLReq As DOMDocument
Dim XMLResp As DOMDocument
Dim z() As Byte

Dim db As ADODB.Connection
Dim rs As ADODB.Recordset

z = Request.BinaryRead(10000)
Set XMLReq = New DOMDocument
XMLReq.loadXML StrConv(z, vbUnicode)
Set nl = XMLReq.getElementsByTagName("CUSTOMER")

Set XMLResp = New DOMDocument
Set p = XMLResp.createProcessingInstruction("xml", _
   "version=""1.0""")
XMLResp.appendChild p

Set node = XMLResp.createElement("GETCUSTOMERINFO")
XMLResp.appendChild node

Set db = New ADODB.Connection
db.Open _
   "provider=sqloledb;data source=Athena "& _" ;
   initial catalog=VB6DB", _"sa", ""

Set rs = New ADODB.Recordset
Set rs.ActiveConnection = db

For Each el In nl
   rs.Source = "Select * From Customers Where CustomerId = " & _
         el.getAttribute("CustomerId")
   rs.Open

   If Not ((rs.BOF) And (rs.EOF)) Then
      Set subnode = XMLResp.createElement("CUSTOMER")
      Set attr = XMLResp.createAttribute("CustomerId")
      attr.Text = rs("CustomerId").Value
      subnode.Attributes.setNamedItem attr
      Set attr = XMLResp.createAttribute("Get")
      attr.Text = "OK"
      subnode.Attributes.setNamedItem attr
```

Continued

Listing 22-5 *(continued)*

```
         node.appendChild subnode

         Set subsubnode = XMLResp.createElement("NAME")
         subsubnode.Text = rs("Name").Value
         subnode.appendChild subsubnode

         Set subsubnode = XMLResp.createElement("STREET")
         subsubnode.Text = rs("Street").Value
         subnode.appendChild subsubnode

         Set subsubnode = XMLResp.createElement("CITY")
         subsubnode.Text = rs("City").Value
         subnode.appendChild subsubnode

         Set subsubnode = XMLResp.createElement("STATE")
         subsubnode.Text = rs("State").Value
         subnode.appendChild subsubnode

         Set subsubnode = XMLResp.createElement("ZIP")
         subsubnode.Text = rs("Zip").Value
         subnode.appendChild subsubnode

      Else
         Set subnode = XMLResp.createElement("CUSTOMER")
         Set attr = XMLResp.createAttribute("CustomerId")
         attr.Text = el.getAttribute("CustomerId")
         subnode.Attributes.setNamedItem attr

         Set attr = XMLResp.createAttribute("Get")
         attr.Text = "Not found"
         subnode.Attributes.setNamedItem attr

         node.appendChild subnode

      End If

      rs.Close

   Next el

   XMLResp.Save Response

   db.Close

   Set XMLResp = Nothing
   Set XMLReq = Nothing
   Set rs = Nothing
```

```
Set db = Nothing

End Sub
```

Preparing to respond to the request

After declaring a whole lot of local variables, I begin processing by using the `Request.BinaryRead` to get the input document into a byte array. Next, I create a new instance of the `DOMDocument` object that will hold the request, and use the `loadXML` method to build the document object hierarchy. Note that I used the `StrConv` function to convert the ASCII encoded string into Unicode before loading it with the `loadXML` method. Finally, I use the `getElementsByTagName` method to create a list of all of the `CUSTOMER` elements.

Then I create a new instance of the response document (`XMLResp`) and initialize it with the standard XML version information. Next, I will append a `GETCUSTOMERINFO` object that will contain the individual `CUSTOMER` elements that form the response.

In order to access the database, I create a new instance of the `ADODB.Connection` object and use the `Open` method to log onto the database server. Then I create a new instance of the `ADODB.Recordset` object and set the `ActiveConnection` property to the `Connection` object I just opened.

Building the response

After all of the prep work, I use a `For Each` loop to access each `CUSTOMER` element in the `nodeList` collection. Using the information from the `CustomerId` attribute, I build a **Select** statement to retrieve information about the specified CustomerId value and then open the `Recordset` object.

If the `Recordset` object contains at least one record (`Not (rs.BOF And rs.EOF)` is `True`), I'll create a new `CUSTOMER` element node using the `createElement` method, and set the `CustomerId` to the current value of CustomerId and the `Get` attribute to `OK`.

For each of the fields that I want to return, I create a new element node and assign it the value from the corresponding database field. Then I add it to the `CUSTOMER` element I created earlier. After I add all of the elements, I close the `Recordset` object.

If the **Select** didn't return any rows, I'll create a `CUSTOMER` element with the `CustomerId` and `Get` attributes as before, but rather than assigning the `Get` attribute a value of `OK`, I'll return `"Not found"`. Afterwards, I'll close the `Recordset` object for the particular `CUSTOMER` element and repeat the `For Each` loop until I'm out of `CUSTOMER` elements to process.

Finally, I'll use the XMLResp.Save method against the Response object. This will automatically take the XML document stored in the document object model and output the XML tags to the HTTP return stream. Once the document is returned, I can close the database connection and destroy the various objects I created while processing this request.

Updating Customer Information

You've seen one way to handle a transaction using XML documents to carry the request and the response. This is the basic way most XML data exchanges will occur. It doesn't matter if the document exchange returns information or performs a function. As long as the proper information is contained in the document, it really doesn't matter.

However, the GetCustomerInfo and GetCustomer_Respond routines are based on documents that are element-oriented. Each individual field is stored in a separate element. In the update process, I choose to store each field as an element of the CUSTOMER element.

Defining the update XML documents

When requesting an update, you need to include all of the fields that need to be updated in the requesting document. By using attributes instead of elements, you can get a slightly smaller document which probably won't make much of a difference in the long run, but it does result in a flatter hierarchy which can be easier to process with your application program.

Listing 22-6 contains a sample XML document that would be transmitted from the XML client to the XML server to update a particular value. Each of the fields to be updated are stored in a separate attribute, and the CustomerId attribute is used to identify the customer's information in the database.

Listing 22-6: An XML document containing update information

```
<?xml version="1.0"?>
<UPDATECUSTOMERINFO>
   <CUSTOMER CustomerId="0" Name="Dexter Valentine"
      Street="3250 Second Ave." City="San Francisco"
      State="CA" Zip="94115"/>
</UPDATECUSTOMERINFO>
```

The document to return the status of the update is based on the same document that was used to request the update (see Listing 22-7). The main differences are that the individual attributes containing the data to be updated are not returned, while a new attribute called `Update` is added that will report the status of the update.

Listing 22-7: An XML document containing the results of the update

```
<?xml version="1.0"?>
<UPDATECUSTOMERINFO>
   <CUSTOMER CustomerId="0" Update="OK"/>
</UPDATECUSTOMERINFO>
```

Requesting an update

Clicking on the Update Customer Info button will trigger the `UpdateCustomerInfo` routine shown in Listing 22-8. This routine begins by creating an object called `XMLReq`, which will hold the XML request document and insert the XML version processing instruction.

Listing 22-8: The UpdateCustomerInfo routine in XML Client

```
Sub UpdateCustomerInfo()

Set XMLReq = CreateObject("MSXML2.DOMDocument")
Set p = XMLReq.createProcessingInstruction("xml", _
"version=""1.0""")
XMLReq.appendChild p

Set node = XMLReq.createElement("UPDATECUSTOMERINFO")
Set subnode = XMLReq.createElement("CUSTOMER")

subnode.setAttribute "CustomerId", _
      Document.AddressInfo.CustomerId.Value
subnode.setAttribute "Name", Document.AddressInfo.Name.Value
subnode.setAttribute "Street",
Document.AddressInfo.Street.Value
subnode.setAttribute "City", Document.AddressInfo.City.Value
subnode.setAttribute "State", Document.AddressInfo.State.Value
```

Continued

Listing 22-8 *(continued)*

```
subnode.setAttribute "Zip", Document.AddressInfo.Zip.Value
node.appendChild subnode

XMLReq.appendChild node

MsgBox XMLReq.xml

set http=CreateObject("MSXML2.XMLHTTP")
http.Open "Post", _
   "http://athena/VB6DB22/VB6DB22.ASP?wci=UpdateCustomer", _
   false
http.setRequestHeader "Content-Type", "text/xml"
http.send XMLReq
Set XMLResp = CreateObject("MSXML2.DOMDocument")
XMLResp.LoadXML http.responsetext

MsgBox XMLResp.xml

End Sub
```

Next, I create the `UPDATECUSTOMERINFO` and `CUSTOMER` elements, which will hold the request. Then I can use the `setAttribute` method to add the various attribute values to the `CUSTOMER` element. Note that the `setAttribute` method will automatically create the `XMLDOMAttribute` object for the attribute if it doesn't exist and automatically append it to the element. If the attribute object already exists, then this method will merely update the value.

Before I send the document to the server, I display it using a MsgBox statement (see Figure 22-6). Then I use the same technique I used earlier to send the request to the XML server and wait for its response. When I receive the response, I display the response to the user to let them know if the update was successful or not (see Figure 22-7).

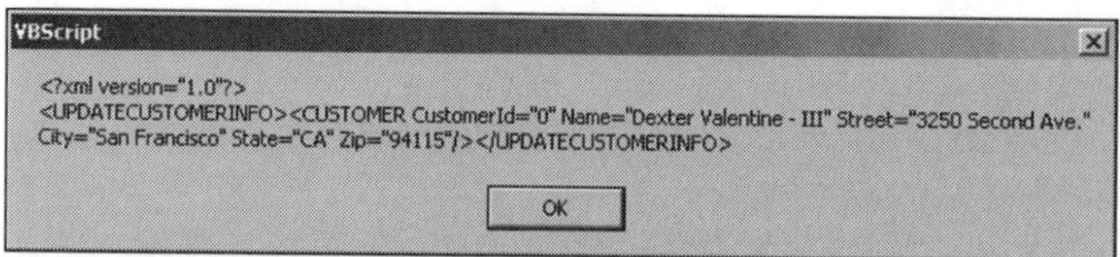

Figure 22-6: Displaying the update request

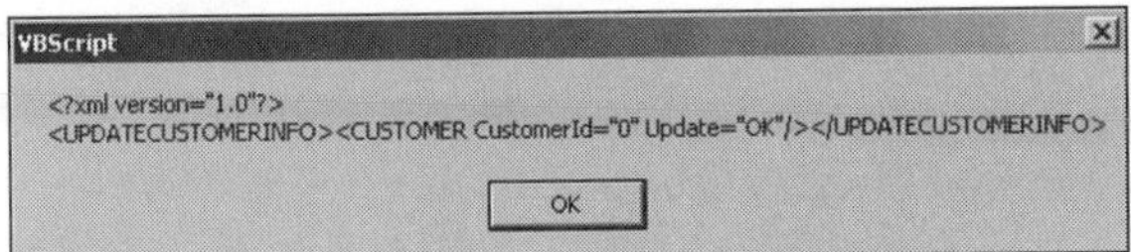

Figure 22-7: Displaying a successful update

Processing an update

On the server side, the `UpdateCustomer_Respond` event will be triggered when an XML document arrives (see Listing 22-9). It uses the same process that the `GetCustomer_Respond` method used to receive the XML document, initialize the return XML document, and open a database connection. I also select all of the elements named `CUSTOMER` and save them in a `nodeList` object. However, from this point on, the two routines differ significantly.

Listing 22-9: The UpdateCustomer_Respond in XML Server

```
Private Sub UpdateCustomer_Respond()

On Error Resume Next

Dim attr As IXMLDOMAttribute
Dim el As IXMLDOMElement
Dim nl As IXMLDOMNodeList
Dim node As IXMLDOMElement
Dim p As IXMLDOMProcessingInstruction
Dim parm As ADODB.Parameter
Dim subnode As IXMLDOMElement
Dim subsubnode As IXMLDOMElement
Dim XMLReq As DOMDocument
Dim XMLResp As DOMDocument
Dim z() As Byte

Dim db As ADODB.Connection
Dim cmd As ADODB.Command

z = Request.BinaryRead(10000)
Set XMLReq = New DOMDocument
XMLReq.loadXML StrConv(z, vbUnicode)

Set nl = XMLReq.getElementsByTagName("CUSTOMER")

Set XMLResp = New DOMDocument
```

Continued

Listing 22-9 *(continued)*

```
Set p = XMLResp.createProcessingInstruction("xml", _
      "version=""1.0""")
XMLResp.appendChild p

Set node = XMLResp.createElement("UPDATECUSTOMERINFO")
XMLResp.appendChild node

Set db = New ADODB.Connection
db.Open _
   "provider=sqloledb;data source=Athena;initial catalog=VB6DB", _
    "sa", ""

Set cmd = New ADODB.Command
Set cmd.ActiveConnection = db
cmd.CommandText = "Update Customers Set Name=?, Street=?, " & _
      "City=?, State=?, Zip=? Where CustomerId=?"

Set parm = cmd.CreateParameter("Name", adVarChar, adParamInput, 64)
cmd.Parameters.Append parm

Set parm = cmd.CreateParameter("Street", adVarChar, _
      adParamInput, 64)
cmd.Parameters.Append parm

Set parm = cmd.CreateParameter("City", adVarChar, adParamInput, 64)
cmd.Parameters.Append parm

Set parm = cmd.CreateParameter("State", adChar, adParamInput, 2)
cmd.Parameters.Append parm

Set parm = cmd.CreateParameter("Zip", adInteger, adParamInput, 4)
cmd.Parameters.Append parm

Set parm = cmd.CreateParameter("CustomerId", adInteger, _
   adParamInput, 4)
cmd.Parameters.Append parm

For Each el In nl
   cmd.Parameters("CustomerId").Value = _
      el.getAttribute("CustomerId")
   cmd.Parameters("Name").Value = el.getAttribute("Name")
   cmd.Parameters("Street").Value = el.getAttribute("Street")
   cmd.Parameters("City").Value = el.getAttribute("City")
   cmd.Parameters("State").Value = el.getAttribute("State")
   cmd.Parameters("Zip").Value = el.getAttribute("Zip")
   db.Errors.Clear
   cmd.Execute
```

```
      Set subnode = XMLResp.createElement("CUSTOMER")
      subnode.setAttribute "CustomerId", _
         cmd.Parameters("CustomerId").Value
      If db.Errors.Count = 0 Then
         subnode.setAttribute "Update", "OK"

      Else
         subnode.setAttribute "Update", db.Errors.Item(0).Description

      End If
      node.appendChild subnode

   Next el

   XMLResp.Save Response

   Set XMLResp = Nothing
   Set XMLReq = Nothing

   db.Close
   Set cmd = Nothing
   Set db = Nothing

   End Sub
```

I chose to create a parameterized `Command` object, which uses the **Update** statement to change the contents of the database. So, after creating a new instance of the `Command` object, I create an **Update** statement listing each of the fields I want to update and assigning them a value of question mark (?). The question mark is really a placeholder that will be replaced with the parameters associated with the `Command` object.

Then I create the `Parameter` objects for the `Command` object using the `CreateParameter` method. I specify the name, data type, direction, and length for each parameter as I create it, then I `Append` it to the `Command`'s `Parameters` collection. Note that I create the `Parameter` objects in the same order that the question marks appear. This is very important, since the only way to associate a parameter with the statement is the order of the parameters.

Once I've done all of this setup work, I'm ready to use a `For Each` loop to process the list of `CUSTOMER` elements. I use the `getAttribute` method to return the value of each of the attributes from the XML request document and save it as the value in the corresponding `Parameter` object.

After defining the parameters, I clear the `Connection` object's `Errors` collection and `Execute` the command. Then I create the `CUSTOMER` element in the return document and set the `CustomerId` property. If there were no database errors (`db.Errors.Count = 0`), I'll set the `Get` attribute to `OK`; otherwise, I'll set the `Get` attribute to the `Description` property from the first element in the `Errors` collection.

Now I `Append` the `CUSTOMER` element to the `XMLResp` document and retrieve the next node in the `nodeList` object. This process will continue until all of the elements in the `nodeList` object have been processed. I end the routine by saving the `XMLResp` object to the `Response` stream, closing the database connection and destroying the objects I used in this routine.

Thoughts about Programming XML Documents

Without XML at your disposal, getting information across the Web programmatically can be difficult. You have to build complicated programs that will download a Web page containing the information you want, and then try to parse it looking for the proper value. In addition, you have to update your program each time someone updates the format of the Web page. However, XML offers an easier solution.

Using XML it is reasonable to build a pair of applications that communicate with each other via the Internet using XML documents. The client program may be a traditional Visual Basic program, or perhaps a JavaScript-based Web page, that generates an XML document containing a request for information. This request is then passed to a Web server, which receives the XML document, decodes it, and returns the data to the client program. Finally, the client program extracts the information it wants from the return XML document.

The nice thing about this approach is that you can use any tools you want on the client and the server side. The only issue is that both programs must agree on the elements in the XML documents that are exchanged. But as long as XML is used in the middle, the details of the programs on each side aren't important.

The programs can be coded in Visual Basic, VBScript, Java, C++, or even COBOL for that matter. They can run on Windows 2000 Server, Solaris, Linux, or OS/390. The point is, as long as the XML is properly constructed, you have a vendor-independent solution.

You should consider the application I built here merely as a toy to explore what you can do with a little XML, HTML, and a Visual Basic program. I'm not saying that you should run out and convert all of your applications to XML anytime you need to pass information. However, XML is the wave of the future, and anything you can do now to learn more about how to use it will make your life easier in the future.

One of the problems with message queues is that you need a way to pass information between the client application and the transaction server. While you can pass persisted objects back and forth, they can be a pain to develop and debug. Since XML is human readable, it is easier to debug (trust me – debugging a COM+ based message queue application can be a real nightmare) without losing any of the flexibility of objects it would replace.

You could easily combine tools such as an IIS Application, COM+ transactions, message queues, and XML to build a complex, high-performance application that accepts vendor-neutral requests coded in XML. This allows you to develop clients for different platforms, including such operating systems as Linux, Solaris, Macintosh, and even the occasional OS/390 IBM mainframe.

Summary

In this chapter you learned:

- how to design XML documents to request and receive information from a Web server.
- how to build an IIS Application that sends an XML request to a Web server.
- how to build an IIS Application to parse an XML document.
- how to update a database using an XML document.

✦ ✦ ✦

PART

VI

SQL Server

SQL Server is Microsoft's premier database system. It is scalable from very small applications to extremely large applications. In this Part, I'm going to cover the fundamentals of using SQL Server with Visual Basic, including its architecture, how to connect to the database using ADO, and how its data types map into Visual Basic. Then, I'll cover how to use Enterprise Manager to create databases, tables, indexes, and security. Finally, I'll discuss how to build and debug stored procedures using Enterprise Manager and Query Analyzer.

✦ ✦ ✦ ✦

In This Part

✦ ✦ ✦ ✦

CHAPTER 23

Overview of SQL Server

✦ ✦ ✦ ✦

In This Chapter

Summarizing SQL Server

Introducing SQL Server utilities

Understanding the database architecture

Connecting to SQL with ADO

Examining the security model

✦ ✦ ✦ ✦

In this chapter, I'll introduce you to Microsoft SQL Server 7, including the key features of the product. Then I'll cover its architecture and security model. Finally I'll cover specific issues related to using ADO to access SQL Server, such as building a connection string and mapping data types.

Overview of SQL Server 7

Microsoft SQL Server 7 is Microsoft's premier database management system. It is easy to install and administer, and it comes with tools and wizards that make it easy to develop applications. As you might expect, SQL Server runs only on Microsoft Windows operating systems. Unlike previous versions of SQL Server, however, SQL Server 7 runs on both Windows 2000/NT and Windows 98/95 platforms.

SQL Server 7 has these key features:

- ✦ High performance relational database
- ✦ Scalable from small databases to very large databases
- ✦ Easy to install and use
- ✦ Reasonably priced
- ✦ Tightly integrated with Windows
- ✦ Built-in support for data warehousing

SQL Server editions

SQL Server comes in three different editions: Desktop, Standard, and Enterprise. All three editions are built on the same code base, so applications that are developed to run on the Desktop Edition are guaranteed to be 100% compatible with the Standard and Enterprise Editions. Likewise, you may take an application running on the Enterprise Edition and run it on the Desktop Edition so long as you don't use any of the advanced features present in the Enterprise Edition.

The Desktop Edition

The Desktop Edition is new in SQL Server 7 and is targeted at small databases that reside on a workstation. This edition might be useful for programmers who want to debug and test their applications locally before running them on a larger, shared database. You might also use it when you keep a local database to cache information or for use with a stand-alone application. You could also use database replication to keep this database synchronized with a larger database.

You can install the Desktop Edition only on Windows 98/95 systems, Windows NT Workstation and Windows 2000 Professional Systems. You are limited to a maximum of two CPUs in the same system and a maximum database size of 4GB. Also, some features that are found in the Standard Edition and Enterprise Edition, such as the OLAP Services and full-text indexing, aren't included in the Desktop Edition.

While the Desktop Edition uses the same code base as the Standard and Enterprise Editions, a lot of effort has gone into optimizing the database server for a workstation environment. The amount of main memory needed to run the database server has been minimized, and other changes have been made to get the optimal performance out of this configuration.

Don't blame me: While the Desktop Edition of SQL Server will run on a Windows 98/95 platform, you should not expect the same level of stability that you would find on a Windows 2000/NT platform.

The Standard Edition

The Standard Edition is the traditional version of SQL Server that has been in use for years. This edition can be installed only on Windows 2000/NT Server. It can be used on systems with up to four CPUs, and there is no limit to the size of your database.

A lot of effort has gone into making SQL Server 7 easy to use. Many configuration options that existed in prior releases have been replaced with internal code that makes changes dynamically based on the workload. For parameters that still exist, intelligent wizards are available to help you choose the appropriate values.

In addition to all of the features present in the Desktop Edition, the Standard Edition includes support for parallel queries, read-ahead scans, and hash and merge joins, which makes your database programs much more efficient. Other features, such as full-text indexes, which make it easy to locate information in your database, and OLAP Services, which makes it easy to build data warehouses, are also included in the Standard Edition.

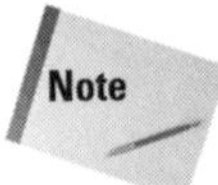

Data warehouses without programming: Believe it or not, you can combine SQL Server Standard Edition with tools like Microsoft Excel 2000 and Microsoft MapPoint 2000 to create data warehouses without writing a single line of code. Don't believe me? Check out a copy of my book *Unlocking OLAP with SQL Server and Excel 2000* published by IDG Books Worldwide, Inc. I hope you like it.

The Enterprise Edition

The Enterprise Edition is not for everyone. It is targeted at very large and/or high-activity database servers. It requires Windows 2000/NT Server, Enterprise Edition, which supports more than 2GB of main memory and more than four CPUs in a single server. It includes advanced features, such as fail over clustering facilities and the ability to partition an OLAP cube across multiple servers, which are designed to handle large workloads in a multiserver environment.

SQL Server utilities

SQL Server includes several utilities to help you configure, manage, and use your database server. Of these tools, you're probably going to use the Enterprise Manager and the Query Analyzer most of all, with the Data Transformation Services (DTS) close behind. These are the tools with which you can create your database and its structures and extract information on the fly.

Enterprise Manager

Enterprise Manager is a multipurpose utility that you use to manage your database. With this utility, you can start and stop the database server and set configuration properties for the database server. This utility allows you to define logon ids and manage security. You can even use it to create databases and their objects, including tables, indexes, stored procedures, and so on, using an interactive graphical design tool.

The Enterprise Manager uses the Microsoft Management Console (MMC) as its basic interface (see Figure 23-1). The display consists of an icon tree on the left side of the window and a display area that contains more detailed information about the selected icon in the icon tree.

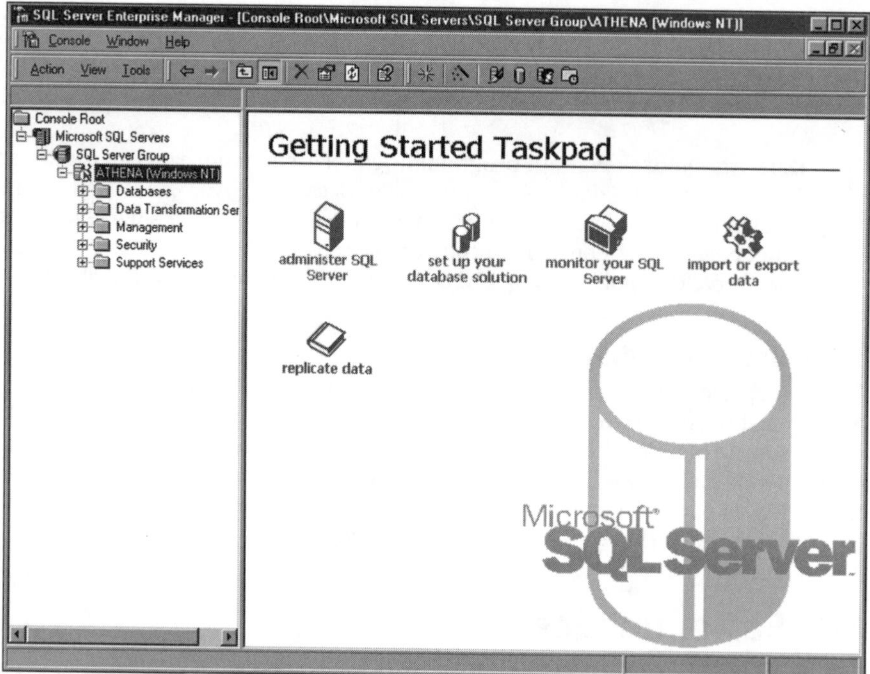

Figure 23-1: Running the Enterprise Manager

The Enterprise Manager contains a large number of wizards to help you perform common tasks such as creating databases, tables, and logon ids. Also, it contains wizards that help you define a maintenance schedule for tasks such as backing up your database, reorganizing indexes, and checking database integrity. Once the list of tasks has been selected, you then define a schedule for them, and SQL Server will take care of scheduling and running them. It will also keep records of the activities so that you can review them for potential problems.

Query Analyzer

The Query Analyzer is a utility that allows you to execute SQL statements interactively, which is useful for testing SQL statements before you include them in your application (see Figure 23-2). You can also use this utility to extract information from the database, and you can use that information to validate the changes your application makes to your database.

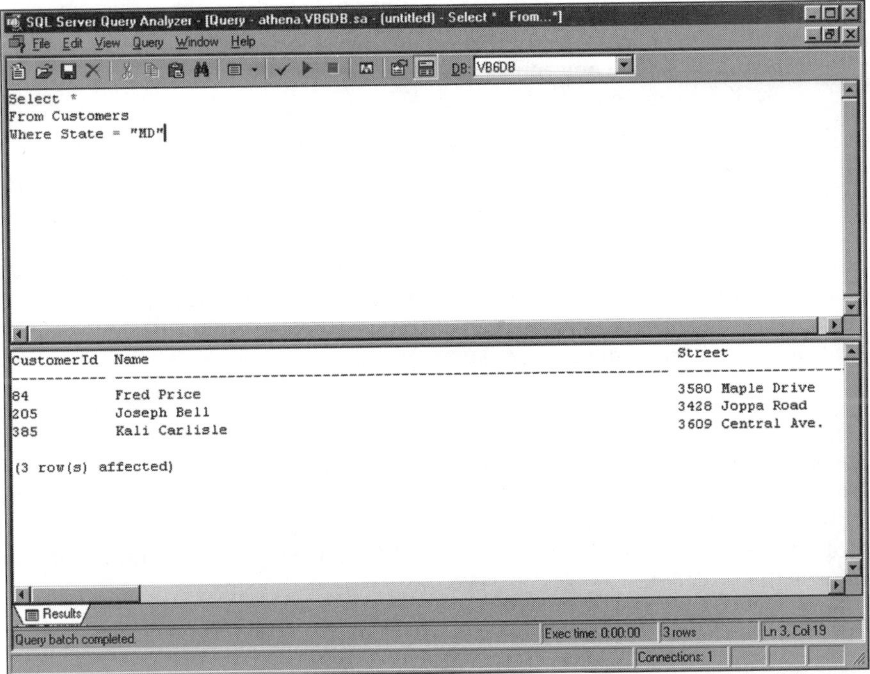

Figure 23-2: Running the Query Analyzer

Testing, testing, testing: Since you can call stored procedures from within Query Analyzer, you may want to use it to test your stored procedures before trying to call them from your Visual Basic application.

Data Transformation Services

I found that the Data Transformation Services is one of the most useful tools in SQL Server 7, since it makes it easy to move data from one place to another. It is extremely fast and flexible and can communicate with SQL Server databases, Oracle databases, Excel files, text files, and just about any other type of file that you can access using OLE DB or ODBC.

One of the nicest features included with DTS is the ability to transform your data while copying it. You can specify how each source column is mapped to the destination column. DTS will handle the most common data type transformations. DTS even has the ability to use a VBScript macro to transform one column to another, which may prove useful if a simple data type conversion isn't sufficient.

But wait, there's more: If your source and destination databases are both in SQL Server 7, you can copy all of the components of a database, including security information, stored procedures, and so on. This makes it easy to make a complete copy of a database for testing purposes.

OLAP Services

OLAP (Online Analytical Processing) Services fulfills a critical need when implementing a data warehouse. It allows you to reorganize the data from a regular relational database into a multidimensional data store that can be easily used by data analysis tools such as Excel 2000. By including the ability to aggregate selected parts of the data, OLAP Services can offer much better performance than if a conventional database storage system were used.

English Query

English Query is a series of COM components that allows you to translate an English language question into an SQL Statement. This ability makes it easy to build tools that let inexperienced users retrieve information from their databases. It also includes a tool that can automatically create a simple Web page that accepts questions and returns their results.

The English Query utility is used to collect information about the database you want to access. This utility is driven by a series of wizards that asks you detailed questions about the words that can be used to describe your data. This information is collected and saved in a domain that is used by the COM components to translate the user's question into a SQL **Select** statement.

Database Architecture

SQL Server uses a true client/server architecture, where the database server runs in its own address space. While it can run on Windows 98/95 platform, you will get the best results running on multiprocessor computers with Windows 2000/NT Server. It is designed to be remotely administered and to exploit facilities that already exist in Windows such as e-mail, Internet access, etc.

SQL Server is arranged as a single Windows service that operates a collection of databases. Four of the databases are known as system databases, because they provide services critical to the database server itself. The other databases are known as user databases, because they contain user data.

System databases

The system databases are *master*, *tempdb*, *msdb* and *model*. The master database contains information about the databases that the database server manages. This information includes the database name and physical files that are used. It also includes security information that allows users to access the database server itself.

Tempdb holds temporary tables and temporary stored procedures. It also supplies temporary storage for tasks such as holding the intermediate results of a query. Since none of the information stored in tempdb needs to exist beyond the current database server session, each time SQL Server is started, tempdb is erased.

The msdb database is used to maintain information about scheduled activities in the database, such as database backups, DTS jobs, and so on.

The model database is used as a template whenever SQL Server creates a new database. As part of the process to create a database, the contents of the model database are copied to the new database. Then the rest of the space in the database is filled with empty database pages.

Database objects

Within a database there are several different types of database objects that can be manipulated. The most fundamental object within a database is a table. Tables come in two flavors, *system tables* and *user tables*. A system table contains information about the database. For instance a system table called `sysobjects` contains information about the various objects in the database. The database server itself updates system tables, though if you wish, you can read the information from the system tables to determine information about the database itself. User tables on the other hand are created by a database user and contain the user's information.

Database destroyer: Updating a system table directly is one of the fastest ways to destroy a database's integrity. Any mistake you may make may result in corrupting your database beyond repair. If you happen to be updating a system table in the master database, you've corrupted the entire database server.

Another type of database object is the *index*. The index holds information that allows the database server to quickly locate a row or set of rows in a table. Besides tables and indexes, objects such as stored procedures, users, roles, and so on are also stored in the database. However, unlike tables and indexes, which are stored directly in the database files, these objects are stored in system tables.

Database storage

Each database is composed of two types of files: *data files* (`.MDF`) and *log files* (`.LDF`). Data files hold information kept in the database, while log files keep a history of the changes made to the database. A minimal database consists of one data file and one log file. Additional files can be used as needed. Data files consist of a series of 8KB pages. There are six types of pages (see Table 23-1). Each page has a 96-byte header, which contains system information like the type of page, the amount of free space on the page, and information about whose data is on the page. Pages can't be shared and are assigned to a single table or index or are used to hold allocation information.

Table 23-1
Page Types

Page Type	*Description*
Data	Contains one or more of rows of information, except for large columns.
Index	Contains index entries.
Text/Image	Contains values stored in **Text, nText,** and **Image** columns.
Global Allocation Map	Contains information about allocated extents.
Index Allocation Map	Contains information about the extents used by a table or index.
Page Free Space	Contains information about the free space available on pages.

A *data page* is used to store information about one or more rows. A row can't exceed the maximum size of a page. Since the page header size is 96 bytes and the additional information used to manage row information takes 32 bytes, the largest row you can store is 8,060 bytes. Note that if a row contains large columns (Text, nText, or Image), these columns do not count towards the 8,060-byte limit. Large columns are stored in their own pages and will occupy as many pages as needed to store the entire column's information.

An *extent* is eight pages. This is the primary unit of allocation for a table or index. If the size of a table or index is less than eight pages, it is assigned to a mixed extent that shares the extent with other tables and indexes. Once a table or index grows larger than eight pages, it is moved to a uniform extent, which is not shared with other database objects.

For better performance: If possible, you should keep your database files on an NTFS (NT file system) formatted disk drive with 64KB disk extents.

Log files consist of a series of log records. Each log record contains information necessary to undo a change made to a row. This consists of before and after values for every changed column, plus additional information that allows the records to be grouped together in transactions and to identify when and how the changes were made. When combined with a database backup, you can use the information in a log file to recover all of the changes to a database up to a specific point in time or when the database server stopped working.

Database capacities

In an ideal world, a database would be able to store as much information as you would like. However, in the real world, there are always limits. Table 23-2 displays a list of limitations in SQL Server 7.

Table 23-2
Database Capacities

Item	*Capacity*
Bytes per index	900
Bytes per key	900
Bytes per row	8,060
Clustered indexes per table	1
Columns per index	16
Columns per key	16
Columns per base table	1,024
Columns per **Select** statement	4,096
Columns per **Insert** statement	1,024
Database size	1,048,516TB
Databases per server	32,767
Files per database	32,767
File size, data file	32TB
File size, log file	4TB
Foreign key table references per table	253
Identifier length in characters	128
Nested stored procedure calls	32
Nested subqueries	32
Nonclustered indexes per table	249
Parameters per stored procedure	1024
Rows per table	limited by available storage
Tables per **Select** statement	256

SQL Server data types

SQL Server supports a wide variety of data types as shown in Table 23-3.

Table 23-3
SQL Server Data Types

SQL Server Data Type	*Visual Basic Data Type*	*Comments*
`Binary`	`Byte Array`	Contains a fixed length binary string up to 8,000 bytes long.
`Bit`	`Boolean`	**Null** values can't be used with a `Bit` field.
`Char`	`String`	Since `Char` fields always have a fixed length, the length of the `String` value will be the same as the length of the field.
`Datetime`	`Date`	A date and time value that is more accurate than the `Date` data type. The value will be rounded as needed.
`Decimal`	`Currency`	A packed decimal number with up to 38 digits of accuracy. Same as `Numeric`.
`Float`	`Double`	A 64-bit floating point number.
`Image`	`Byte Array`	A variable-length binary field containing up to $2^{31}-1$ bytes.
`Int`	`Long`	A 32-bit integer.
`Money`	`Currency`	An 8-byte scaled integer with four digits of accuracy. Values can range from –922,337,203,685,477.5808 to +922,337,203,685,477.5807.
`NChar`	`String`	Contains a fixed length Unicode string up with up to 4,000 characters.
`Ntext`	`String`	Contains large blocks of Unicode text, with up to $2^{30}-1$ characters.
`NvarChar`	`String`	Contains a variable-length Unicode string with up to 4,000 characters.

SQL Server Data Type	Visual Basic Data Type	Comments
Numeric	Currency	A packed decimal number with up to 38 digits of accuracy. Same as Decimal.
Real	Single	A 32-bit floating point value.
SmallDatetime	Date	A date and time value ranging from 1 Jan 1900 to 6 Jun 2079 and accurate to the minute.
Smallint	Integer	A 16-bit integer.
SmallMoney	Currency	A 4-byte scaled integer with four decimal digits of accuracy. Values can range from −214,748.3648 to +214,748.3647.
Sysname	String	Sysname is really a synonym for Nchar(128) and is used to hold the name of a database object.
Text	String	Contains large blocks of text data, up to $2^{31}-1$ characters.
Timestamp	Byte Array	Contains a unique identifier that can be used to order a sequence of events. However, it doesn't contain a value that corresponds to a date or time.
Tinyint	Byte	An 8-bit integer.
VarBinary	Byte Array	If you declare a Byte Array without bounds and assign the value to it, you may then use the Len or UBound functions to determine the size of the field.
VarChar	String	The length of the String will be the length of the field. It has a maximum length of 8,000 characters.
UniqueIdentifier	String	Contains the hex equivalent of a GUID.

Connecting to SQL Server with ADO

Creating a connection string for SQL Server is a fairly straightforward process. You must specify the name of the provider, which is `SQLOLEDB` when connecting to an SQL Server database; the name of the data source, which is the name of the database server; and the initial catalog, which is the name of the name of the database you want to access. The first keyword in the list must be the `Provider=` keyword. The rest of the connection string is passed to the provider for interpretation. A sample connection string is shown below.

```
Provider=SQLOLEDB;Data source=Athena;Initial catalog=VB6DB
```

Besides specifying the database server and initial catalog, you can also include security information. If you're using SQL Server Authentication, you can include the `User Id=` keyword and the `Password=` keyword of the login you want to use to access the database. Otherwise, Windows NT Authentication will be used. You can also force the `SQLOLEDB` provided to use Windows NT Authentication by including `Trusted_Connection=yes` as part of the connection string.

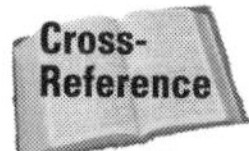

Authentication is discussed in the next section, "SQL Server Security."

Hacking security systems: You should never hardcode a user id and password in a connection string. A hacker might view your program with a binary editor, which can display the contents of the program file in both ASCII and hex. A simple search on `SQLOLEDB` or `User Id` will let the hacker find these values. In the same vein, storing the user id and password in the Registry is also vulnerable to a smart hacker. Better alternatives would be to use Windows NT Authentication, which doesn't use user id and password to access the database, or to prompt the user for the user id and password and then insert them into the connection string.

SQL Server Security

Everyone that accesses a SQL Server database must present login information that is verified before the user is granted access to the database server. This process is known as *authentication*.

Authentication in SQL Server

SQL Server has two different modes of authenticating a user: SQL Server Authentication and Windows NT Authentication. You can use Windows NT Authentication by itself or in combination with SQL Server Authentication, which is also known as Mixed Mode Authentication. This authentication value is set for the entire database server level and affects all databases. While changing from Windows NT Authentication to Mixed Mode Authentication isn't difficult, converting Mixed Mode Authentication to Windows NT Authentication can be very difficult due to the number of logins that may need to be converted to Windows NT accounts.

Windows 2000 or NT only: In order to use Windows NT Authentication, SQL Server must be running on a Windows 2000/NT platform. You must use SQL Server Authentication if you are running your database server on Windows 98/95.

SQL Server Authentication

When a user connects to an SQL Server database using SQL Server Authentication, that user needs to provide a login id and a password. This information is presented when the user attempts to connect to the database. It is validated against the information in the master database. If the login information is correct, the user is granted access to the database server. If the login information is incorrect, the connection to the database is terminated.

No Windows, no options: If you want to connect from a non-Windows computer to an SQL Server database, you must use SQL Server Authentication.

A SQL Server login can range in size from 1 to 128 characters and may contain any combination of letters, numbers, and special characters other than a backslash (\). From a practical viewpoint, using some special characters such as spaces in the login may force you to use double quotes (") or square brackets ([ ]) around the login id when you try to reference the login id in a SQL Statement. Logins are also case-insensitive, unless you selected a case-sensitive sort order when you installed SQL Server.

Windows NT Authentication

Windows NT Authentication is based on Window 2000/NT login techniques. The same user name that you use to sign onto Windows becomes your login id. A password isn't needed, since the user name was validated when you signed onto Windows. However, just because your user name has been validated, doesn't mean that you automatically have access to SQL Server. SQL Server maintains information in the master database that identifies the users who are permitted to access the database server.

The primary advantage to using Windows NT Authentication is that you can use NT security groups. You can create a security group and add it to SQL Server in place of the user name. Then anyone who is a member of the security group automatically has access to the SQL Server database server.

Simplify your services: You should always use Windows NT Authentication for services such as an IIS Application or a COM+ transaction. This eliminates the need to store a database password in the application, which allows you to change passwords for these user names on a periodic schedule without recompiling the programs.

Mixed Mode Authentication

Mixed Mode Authentication is a combination of both SQL Server Authentication and Windows NT Authentication. If a login id is specified when you connect to the database server, SQL Server Authentication is used. If no login id is specified, Windows NT Authentication is used. In both cases, the login information must be correct, or the connection to the database server will be dropped.

You may not have a choice: While Windows NT authentication is more secure, you must use Mixed Mode Authentication if you plan to let users from non-Windows based computers access your database.

SQL Server authorization

Just because the user has been granted access to the database, doesn't mean that the user can access any information inside the database or perform any database tasks. The user must be *authorized* to access resources and perform tasks. Each login must be mapped onto a specific user id in each database. Without this mapping, the login will be denied access to the database.

Within each database, each user is granted access to the various objects inside, such as tables, indexes, and stored procedures. The type of access granted to an object is known as a *permission*. The permissions available depend on the type of database object. For instance, on a table you can permit someone to select rows, insert rows, update rows, delete rows, or access the table as part of a referential integrity constraint.

In addition to granting access to database objects, you can also grant access to the SQL Statements that allow you to create, alter, and destroy various database objects, such as tables, views, and stored procedures. The same facility also controls the ability to back up and restore databases and database log files.

SQL Server roles

In order to simplify security administration, SQL Server allows you to define *roles* in a database. Roles are similar to security groups in Windows 2000/NT. They represent a collection of users who are granted similar permissions. A role can be used in place of a user id when granting permissions.

Roles come in three flavors, *fixed server, fixed database,* and *user defined.* The fixed server roles determine the functions a login can perform at the database server level (see Table 23-4). The fixed database roles define groups of standard capabilities available to a user within a single database (see Table 23-5).

Table 23-4
Fixed Server Roles

Role	*Description*
Sysadmin	has permission to perform any activity in SQL Server.
Serveradmin	has permission to set server-wide configuration options and to shut down the database server.
Setupadmin	has permission to manage linked servers and startup procedures.
Securityadmin	has permission to create and destroy logins, to set **Create Database** permissions, and to read error logs.
Processadmin	has permission to manage processes running in the database server.
Dbcreator	has permission to create and alter databases.
Diskadmin	has permission to manage the disk files used by SQL Server.

Table 23-5
Fixed Database Roles

Role	*Description*
db_owner	has permission to perform any activity and access any data in the database.
db_accessadmin	has permission to create and destroy user ids.
db_securityadmin	has permission to manage all database permissions, object ownerships, roles, and role memberships.
db_ddladmin	has permission to create and destroy database objects, but doesn't have permission to manage permissions.
db_backupoperator	has permission to backup the database.
db_datareader	has permission to read data from any user table in the database.
db_datawriter	has permission to modify data in any user table in the database.
db_denydatareader	has permission to deny read access to any database object.
db_denydatawriter	has permission to deny modify access to any database object.

You can create user defined roles as needed to simplify security management. You can assign security permissions to a role, and every user associated with that role automatically inherits those permissions. As with fixed database roles, user defined roles are restricted to a single database.

Also, a user may be associated with multiple roles in the same database. This means that when you design your database, you can define roles for each basic function that a user can perform in the database. You can define roles that permit users to read information from different groups of tables, plus other roles that allow users to perform different types of updates. For instance, you may define a `Clerk` role that permits someone to enter order information, but prevents him or her from updating price information, while defining a `Manager` role that permits someone to change price information.

Thoughts on SQL Server

SQL Server is a modern relational database management system that is more than competitive with any other database management system in the market today. It is well integrated into the Windows environment, which makes it ideal for those organizations where one or two people are responsible for the full range of IT services from IT Manager and Database Administrator to Systems Analyst, Programmer, and Computer Operator. The wide range of automated wizards allows you to install, build, and operate database applications much easier than with most other database management systems, yet SQL Server's performance is among the highest available, meaning that it will scale well into even the largest environments.

Summary

In this chapter you learned:

- ✦ about SQL Server and its various editions.
- ✦ that Enterprise Manager is used to create and maintain SQL Server databases.
- ✦ that Query Analyzer is used to perform ad-hoc queries against an SQL Server database.
- ✦ that Data Transformation Services is a high performance data import and export utility.
- ✦ about the architecture of SQL Server.
- ✦ about the datatypes available in SQL Server.
- ✦ how to connect to SQL Server with ADO.
- ✦ how security is implemented in SQL Server.

✦ ✦ ✦

CHAPTER 24

Creating Database Objects with SQL Server

✦ ✦ ✦ ✦

In This Chapter

Introducing Enterprise Manager

Creating databases and tables

Constructing indexes and database diagrams

Controlling security

Managing logins and users

✦ ✦ ✦ ✦

In this chapter I'm going to show you how to use SQL Server 7's Enterprise Manager utility to create various objects in your database. These objects include databases, tables, indexes, database diagrams, and stored procedures. You can also use Enterprise Manager to manage security by creating logins, map them to users and assign security to the various database objects.

Introducing Enterprise Manager

Enterprise Manager is the primary utility that you use to manage an SQL Server database system. It has the ability to create databases and database objects, control the database's security, and perform routine operational activities like database backups and reorganizations. It can control the properties of the database server itself, as well as start and stop the server from a remote location. In short, it is a very powerful utility that is used by several different types of users to administer an SQL Server database.

Security dictates function: Anyone with a valid login can use Enterprise Manager. However, the functions available at the database server level are based on the login's capabilities and functions on the corresponding user's system.

Enterprise Manager fundamentals

Enterprise Manager is a Microsoft Management Console (MMC) application, meaning that it shares its look and feel with many other system management tools provided by Microsoft (see Figure 24-1). To start Enterprise Manager, choose Start ➪ Programs ➪ Microsoft SQL Server 7.0 ➪ Enterprise Manager. Like many tools available from Microsoft, most of its operations can be performed by using a wizard or by manually configuring property windows.

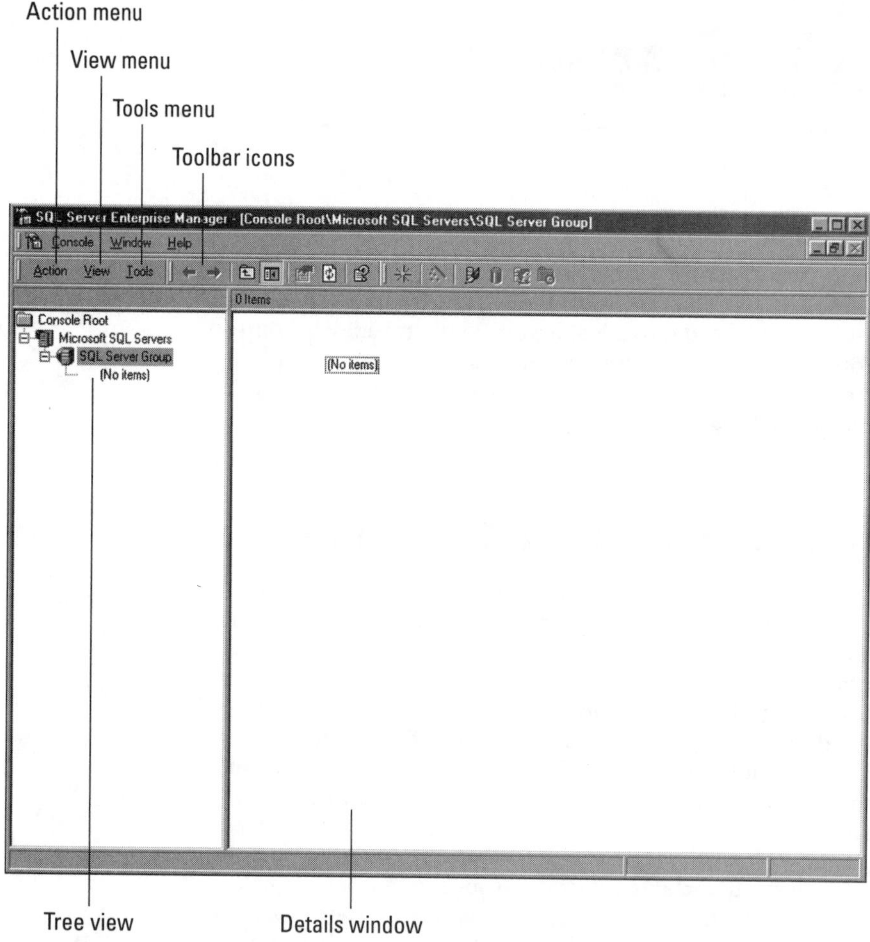

Figure 24-1: Viewing the Enterprise Manager window

✦ **Tree view** contains a hierarchical list of the database servers, databases, and classes of database objects that can be viewed or changed.

✦ **Details window** provides additional information for the selected icon in the tree view.

✦ **Action menu** contains a list of menu items that can be performed based on the context.

✦ **View menu** controls how the information will be displayed using MMC. Typically, all of the items will be selected including Console Tree, Description Bar, Status Bar, and the toolbars. You can also choose to display how the information is displayed in the details window using the Large, Small, Details, and List formats.

✦ **Tools menu** provides a list of shortcut menu items to help you perform most common tasks quickly.

✦ **Toolbar icons** provides a list of shortcut icons for the most popular pop-up menu items.

Registering a database server

Enterprise Manager is capable of managing several SQL Server database servers across multiple remote computers. These computers are listed under the SQL Server Group icon in the tree view. However, before you can access a remote server, you must register the server with Enterprise Manager.

Duh: In order to run Enterprise Manager on your computer, you first have to install it. If you are using the same computer on which you are running the database server, Enterprise Manager is already installed. If you are using a different computer, you can either choose to install the desktop version of SQL Server or just the SQL Server utilities from the server version.

Registering a server is very easy. Just follow these steps:

1. Right click on the SQL Server Group icon in the tree view and right click to display the pop-up menu. Choose New SQL Server Registration. You can also choose Action ⇨ New SQL Server Registration. After choosing either option, the Register SQL Server Wizard will be displayed.

2. After pressing Next, the wizard will display a list of available database servers (see Figure 24-2). Select one and press the Add button. If the server you want to use isn't listed, type the name in the text box at the top of the list and press Add. Then press Next to continue.

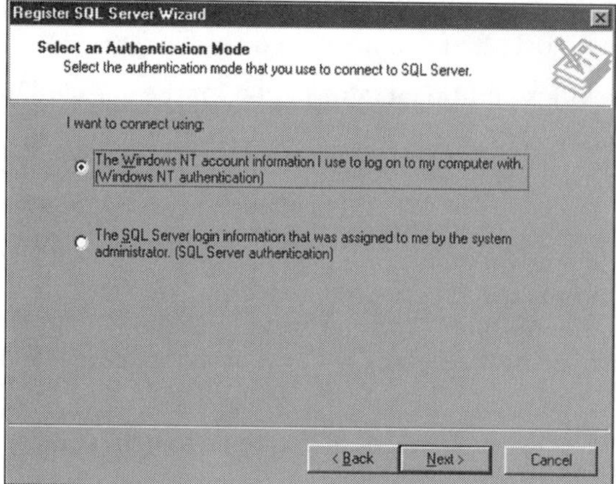

Figure 24-2: Choosing the database server to add

3. In the next step, you have a choice of which authentication system to use (see Figure 24-3). Since you are already using a Windows computer (it doesn't matter whether it's Windows 98 or Windows 2000/NT), you should probably use Windows NT account information. However, you must use a login that is already defined on the server. If you choose SQL Server authentication, the wizard will then prompt you for how you want to log in to the server. You can supply your login information, which Enterprise Manager will use each time it starts, or you can choose to be prompted for the information.

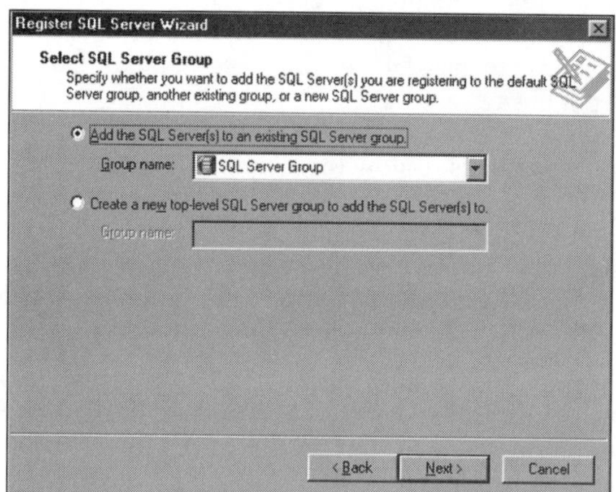

Figure 24-3: Selecting an authentication method

4. After you finish specifying how Enterprise Manager should log in to the database server, you can choose where the icon for the server will be stored (see Figure 24-4). By default, it will be stored under the SQL Server Group, but you can choose another group or create a new group.

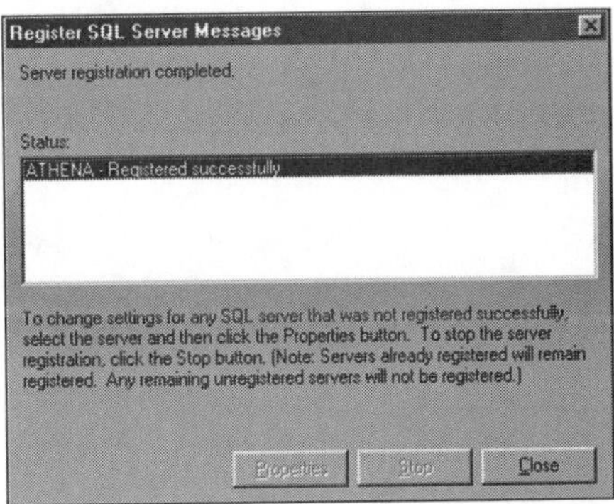

Figure 24-4: Placing the icon for the database server in the tree view

5. When you reach the end of the wizard, you will see a list of database servers you want to register. Pressing Finish will start a process to connect to each of the database servers you specified (see Figure 24-5). This process will report any errors that are encountered. When the process is finished, press Close to finish the wizard and return to Enterprise Manager.

Refer to Chapter 23 for a discussion on Windows NT Authentication vs. SQL Server Authentication.

Viewing database servers and their objects

Once you have registered your database server, you can expand the icon tree to show the database servers you can access and the server-level objects available (see Figure 24-6).

✦ **Databases** contains the collection of databases on the server you can access. You can create, browse, edit, modify and delete tables, indexes, stored procedures, users, roles, and other database objects.

✦ **Data Transformation** contains information about data transformation packages and the data repository. You can view and modify data transformation jobs, view and edit metadata, and search for information in the repository.

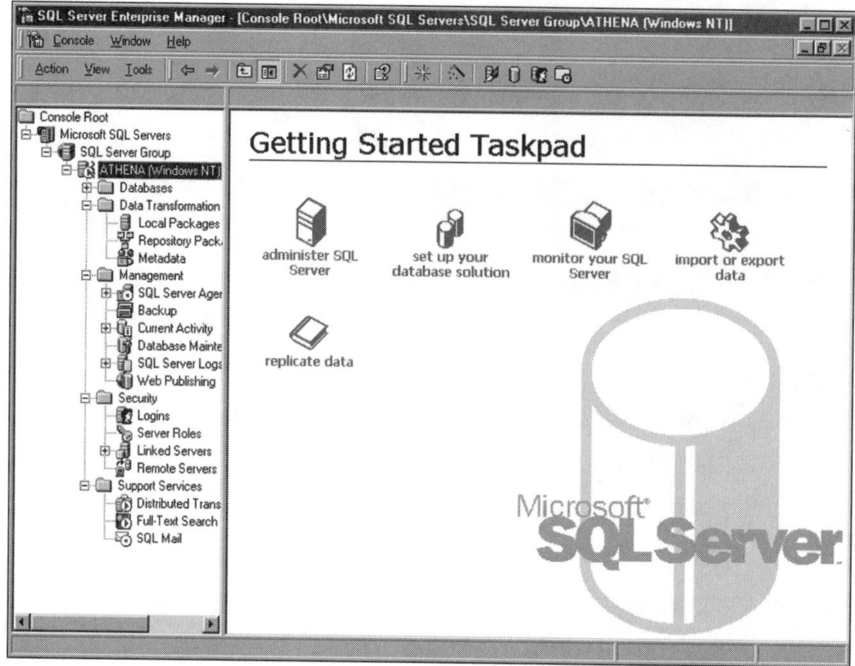

Figure 24-5: Registering the database servers

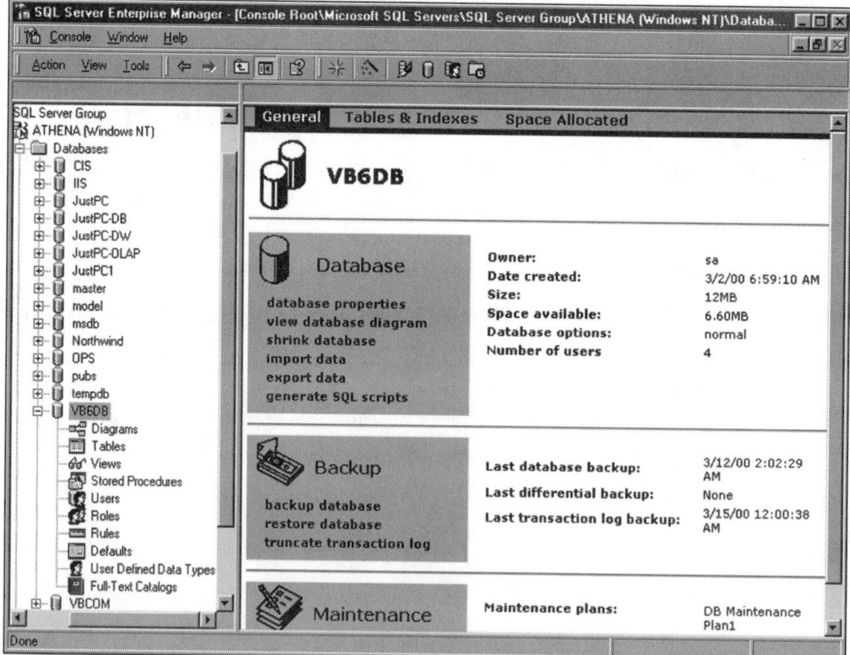

Figure 24-6: Browsing database servers and database objects

- ✦ **Management** contains information about operational activities performed by the database server. This includes things such as database backups, log files, maintenance jobs, and SQL Server Agent activities.
- ✦ **Security** contains information about login and server roles, plus information about how to access remote database servers and linked database servers.
- ✦ **Support Services** contains information about the Distributed Transaction Coordinator, the Full Text Search feature, and SQL Mail.

Expanding the icon associated with a database reveals the objects inside that can be managed by Enterprise Manager (see Figure 24-7). These objects exist only in the specified database, and not at the database server level. In order to access the database, your login must be mapped to a user in the database.

SQL Server Enterprise Manager - [2:Data in Table 'Customers']

Console Window Help

CustomerId	Name	Street	City	State	Zip	Phone	EMailAddress
0	Dexter Valentine	3250 Second Ave.	San Francisco	CA	94115	(800)555-5555	4/5/2000 9:31:5
1	Malik Hubert	7576 Redwood Driv	Waverly	OH	45690	(800)555-5555	MHubert@JustP
2	Lee Holt	3812 Junkyard Driv	Fredericksburg	VA	22407	(800)555-5555	LHolt@JustPC.n
3	Scotty Waltrip	9072 Main Street	Jefferson	LA	70121	(800)555-5555	SWaltrip@JustP
4	Hugh Hawkins	1292 Oakleigh Roa	Colton	WA	99113	(800)555-5555	HHawkins@Just
5	Stephen Donough	9769 Oak Road	Paterson	NJ	7503	(800)555-5555	SDonough@Just
6	Carlita O'Neal	3150 Main Street	Thorndale	PA	19372	(800)555-5555	CO'Neal@JustP
7	Brian Lewis	4470 Main Street	Loraine	TX	79532	(800)555-5555	BLewis@JustPC.
8	George Bishop	2839 Montgomery	Carpio	ND	58725	(800)555-5555	GBishop@JustP
9	Paul Williamson	3702 Main Street	Storden	MN	56174	(800)555-5555	PWilliam@JustP
10	Gary Labonte	8790 Queen Street	Taft	TN	38488	(800)555-5555	GLabonte@Just
11	Frederick Wallace	8341 Pikesville Pike	Gorham	KS	67640	(800)555-5555	FWallace@JustP
12	Marilyn Fitzgerald	4439 Main Street	Hot Springs	VA	24445	(800)555-5555	MFitzger@JustP
13	Raymond Epstein	4313 Third Street	Paint Bank	VA	24131	(800)555-5555	REpstein@JustP
14	Simone Kiley	376 Main Street	Hillside Manor	NY	11040	(800)555-5555	SKiley@JustPC.r
15	Ursala Fowler	7870 Main Street	Mishawaka	IN	46545	(800)555-5555	UFowler@JustP
16	Samuel Smith	7755 Plymouth Cou	North Salem	IN	46165	(800)555-5555	SSmith@JustPC.
17	Barbara Parson	2053 Jedi Court	Makawao	HI	96768	(800)555-5555	BParson@JustP
18	Bonita Bond	3374 Redwood Driv	Belvedere	CA	94920	(800)555-5555	BBond@JustPC.
19	Song Hansen	4882 Main Street	Blanca	CO	81123	(800)555-5555	SHansen@JustP
20	Betty Xu	3633 Main Street	Milford	UT	84751	(800)555-5555	BXu@JustPC.ne
21	Tina Perkins	3250 Queen Street	San Francisco	CA	94115	(800)555-5555	TPerkins@JustP
22	Bonnie Bell	2732 Main Street	Edmunds	ND	58476	(800)555-5555	BBell@JustPC.ne
23	Henry Goodman	2036 Chrisam Terra	New Stanton	PA	15672	(800)555-5555	HGoodman@Jus
24	Shannon Baxter	6220 Oakleigh Roa	Warrenville	SC	29851	(800)555-5555	SBaxter@JustP
25	Kat Ross	8317 Main Street	Stafford	KS	67578	(800)555-5555	KRoss@JustPC.
26	Paul Bond	6233 Loch Raven B	Smithville	TX	78957	(800)555-5555	PBond@JustPC.
27	Michelle Murphy	9554 Main Street	Woodbridge	CT	6525	(800)555-5555	MMurphy@JustF
28	Greg McLaughlin	1315 Baltimore Bvlc	Norwood	NY	13668	(800)555-5555	GMcLaugh@Just
29	Marie Spry	351 Main Street	Quincy	MA	2171	(800)555-5555	MSpry@JustPC.
30	Dexter Raskin	7135 Jaba Court	Akron	OH	44302	(800)555-5555	DRaskin@JustPC

Figure 24-7: Browsing the objects in a database

- ✦ **Diagrams** contains a set of database diagrams showing how the tables are related to each other.
- ✦ **Tables** contains the set of tables in your database.

✦ **Views** contains the collection of views in your database.

✦ **Stored Procedures** contains all of the stored procedure definitions for your database.

✦ **Users** contains information about all of the users that may access your database.

✦ **Roles** contains the description of the security roles used in the database.

✦ **Rules** is maintained for backwards compatibility with older versions of SQL Server. They have been superceded by **Check** constraints, which are maintained in the Design Table window.

✦ **Defaults** contains the collection of default values that may be referenced by name or associated with a particular column in a table.

✦ **User Defined Data Types** contains the set of user defined data types that may be used as the type for a particular column.

✦ **Full-Text Catalogs** contains the definitions associated for the full-text catalogs, which hold the set of full-text indexes in the database.

Browsing data

When you select a particular table or view, you can choose to browse its contents by right clicking on its icon and choosing Open Table or Open View from the pop-up menu. You can choose to return all rows in the table or specify the number of rows you wish to see starting from the top of the table. In either case, you'll see a display similar to that shown in Figure 24-8.

The information in the table is displayed using a grid, where each row in the grid corresponds to a row in the table, and each column corresponds to a column in the table. You can scroll through the values using the scroll bars and adjust the widths of each column to best display the information. The current row will be indicated with an arrow in the row prefix area, while the name of each column will be display in the column prefix area.

In addition to viewing the data from the table, you can also modify the data, assuming that you have the proper security permissions. To change a value in an existing row, simply edit the value in the cell. When you move to another row, the data in the table will be updated.

To add a new row, scroll to the end of the table and look for the last row. An asterisk (*) will be displayed in the row prefix area, indicating that this row has not been added to the table. As with updating a row, simply move to another row to commit the changes.

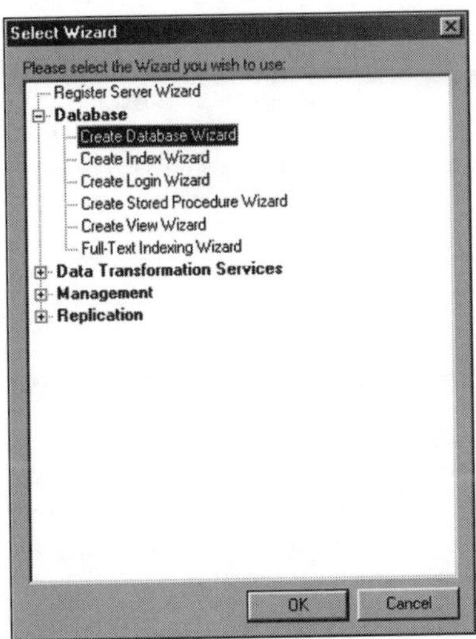

Figure 24-8: Browsing the contents of a table

Other operations, including delete, may be performed on a row by right clicking on the row and choosing one of the functions listed in the pop-up menu. Note you can use the pop-up menu to perform the same function on multiple rows by clicking on the row prefix area, holding the left mouse button down, and dragging the cursor to mark the rows as selected, then right clicking on the selected rows to display the pop-up menu.

A short term lock: When you browse rows in your table or view, you may be holding locks in the database. If there has been no activity for a while, the Enterprise Manager will ask you if you want to continue working with the results pane. If you respond No, or don't respond within a minute, Enterprise Manager will close the pane, and any uncommitted changes you have made will be discarded. You can refresh the data by right clicking anywhere on the pane and choosing Run from the pop-up menu.

There's more than meets the eye: Open Table and Open View functions exist on top of a table-oriented query facility. You can modify the underlying query to change the rows returned either by changing the SQL **Select** statement directly, or by using the grid and diagram graphical tools. You can view the panes that contain this information by right clicking on the results pane and selecting the panes you wish to view under the Select Panes pop-up menu item.

Databases and Tables

Databases exist in SQL Server to hold tables, and tables exist in the database to hold your data. Creating them with Enterprise Manager's wizards makes the job much easier than in earlier versions of SQL Server.

Creating a database

To create a new database, you must use a login that is assigned to either the sysadmin or dbcreater roles. Typically, you'll create your database using the `sa`, login, but depending on how your database security is organized, you may use another login.

Before you create a database

When you create a database, you should have the following information ready:

- The name of the database server where you want to create the database.
- The name of the database itself. While you can use nearly any combination of characters in the name, I suggest beginning the name with a letter, followed by any combination of letters, numbers, and special characters such as @, $, #, and _ up to a maximum of 123 characters. If you don't follow this suggestion, you may have to surround the name of the database with quotes or square brackets to ensure that the name is properly understood.
- The location of the database files. This is a reference to a directory somewhere on the database server where the files containing the objects inside the database will be held.
- The location of the log files. This is a reference to a directory somewhere on the database server where the file containing the information used to hold changes made to the database is kept.
- The initial size of the database files and how they should grow over time. You should choose initial values that are sufficient to cover the space you need in the beginning, and a growth method that allows your database over time.
- The initial size of the log files and how they should grow over time. The initial size determines how much space is originally allocated for the log, and the growth method determines how the log should be increased in case the server fills it up.

Creating your database

To create a database using Enterprise Manager, follow these steps:

1. Start Enterprise Manager (choose Start ➪ Program Files ➪ Microsoft SQL Server 7.0 ➪ Enterprise Manager) and select the database server where the new database will reside. Select Tools ➪ Wizards. This will display the Select Wizard dialog box. Expand the Database node, choose Create Database Wizard, and press OK (see Figure 24-9).

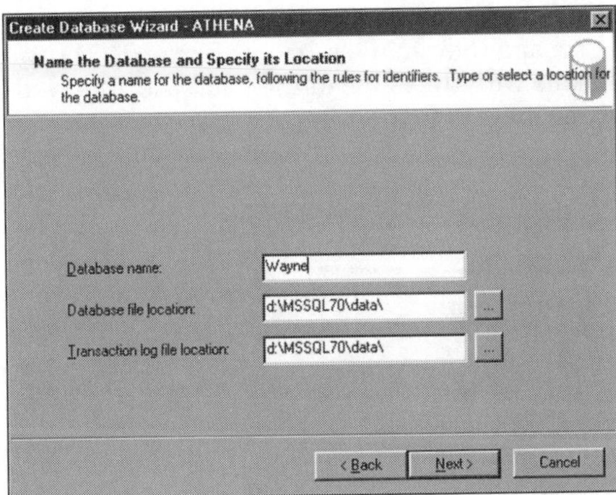

Figure 24-9: Choosing the Create Database wizard

2. When the wizard starts, press Next to go to the first step (see Figure 24-10). In this step, you'll have to provide a name for the database, plus the location of the files that hold the database.

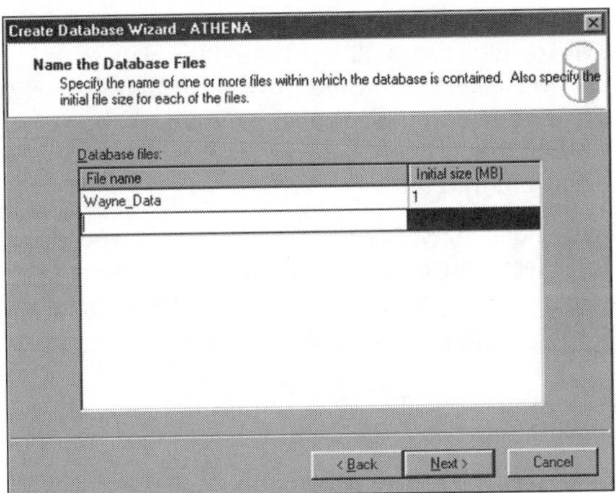

Figure 24-10: Naming your database and locating where its information will be stored

3. In the next step of the wizard, you'll be prompted to enter the name of the file or files you want to use, and their initial size (see Figure 24-11). By default, the wizard will create one file with the name of the database, followed by `_Data` and an initial size of one megabyte.

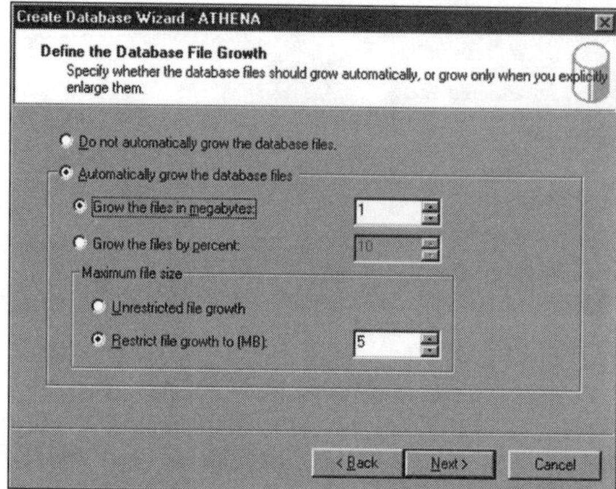

Figure 24-11: Specifying the files to hold your database

4. After specifying the file or files that will hold the database, you'll be prompted to choose how the database server should grow your files (see Figure 24-12). You can choose to grow your database file, in fixed sized chunks or by adding a fixed percentage of the currently allocated space. You can also place a maximum file size to prevent unlimited file growth.

Limits are good: When allocating space for a database file, you should place a limit on the file size. Unless you carefully monitor the amount of space your database uses, and periodically reorganize and compress the files, a ten-megabyte database may end up using ten gigabytes of disk space.

5. The wizard will repeat steps three and four, but for the transaction log files. The default file name is the name of the database followed by `_Log`.

6. In the last step of the wizard, all of the information collected will be displayed. If you want to change any of these parameters, press Back Otherwise, pressing Finish will begin the process to create the database. Because SQL Server physically writes binary zeros over every byte of space allocated for the database files and logs, the actual creation process may take a while if you are building a big database. A message box will be displayed letting you know if the database was successfully created. Press No to return to Enterprise Manager.

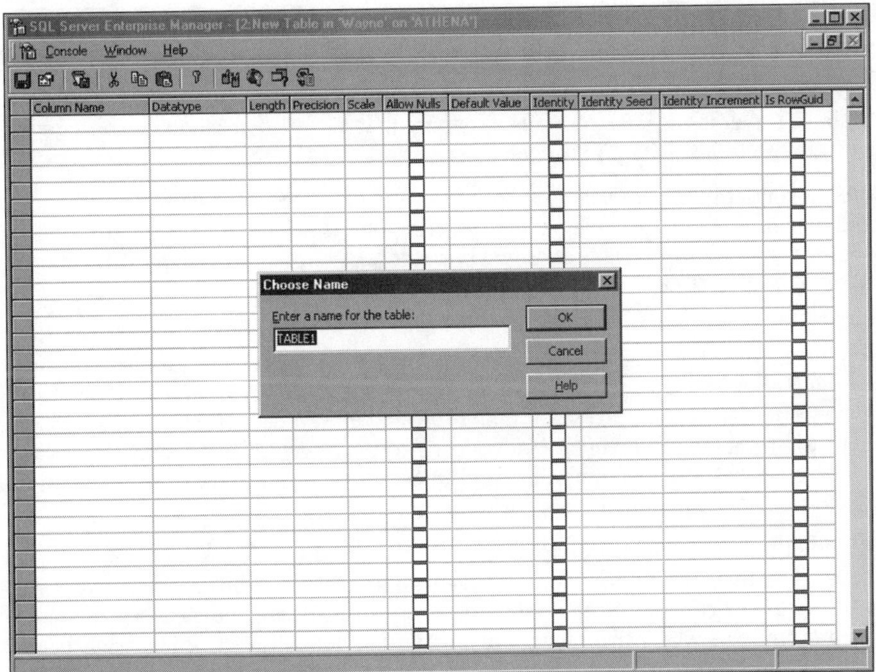

Figure 24-12: Choosing file limits

Covering your butt: If you don't have a maintenance plan for your database server that covers your new database, I strongly recommend that you create one when the Create Database Wizard finishes. See the *SQL Server 7 for Dummies* by Anthony T. Mann for details on how to create a maintenance plan.

Property pages: While this may be obvious, it's worth mentioning anyway. All of the information entered in the Create Database Wizard can also be entered using a database property page by right clicking on the Databases icon beneath the database server icon and choosing New Database from the pop-up menu. Once the database has been created, you can review and change this information by right clicking on the database and selecting Properties from the pop-up menu.

Creating a table

A database is pretty useless without any tables, so after creating your database, you'll probably want to create some tables. While the Enterprise Manager doesn't include a wizard to help you create a table, the Design Table window is very easy to use.

Database Performance

Believe it or not, having a faster CPU will not necessarily make your database server faster. A database server is very I/O intensive. Anything that allows your database to retrieve data faster from the disk will help the server's performance.

Before looking at hardware solutions to improve your database server's performance, you should ensure that the database server isn't competing with other processes on the server for memory and disk I/O. Dedicating a computer for the database server is highly recommended. If you can't dedicate a computer, you should at least try to place your database files on dedicated disk drives.

Adding memory to your server allows the database server to cache more data in memory; this is the biggest change you can make to improve database performance. After all, retrieving data from memory is much faster than retrieving it from disk. This is why Microsoft has gone to the trouble of making special versions of Windows NT to support more than the standard 2 gigabytes of main memory and to create the Data Center version of Windows 2000 which can support even more main memory.

After adding memory to your system, using SCSI disk drives is the next most important improvement. They not only allow you to manage up to 15 disk drives on a single card, but they also support concurrent operations on each drive. Thus, you can have multiple disk drives performing seeks, while others are transferring data. SCSI-III can transfer data faster than SCSI-II or SCSI-I and should be used for best performance.

Finally, using faster disk drives themselves will also improve performance. Disks that spin at 7,200 revolutions per minute (RPM) will transfer data faster than those that transfer data at 5,400 RPM, although two 5,400 RMP disk drives will probably perform better than one 7,200 RPM disk drive (assuming that you are using SCSI disk drives and that you can spread the I/O activity evenly between the two disk drives).

Before you create your table

Before you create your table, you should have a list of columns that the table will contain, along with values for the following attributes for each column:

- ✦ The name of each column. The name should begin with a letter and can be followed by any combination of letters, numbers, and special characters such as @, $, #, and _ up to a total length of 128 characters. While spaces and other special characters may be used, you may have to surround the column name with quotes or square brackets when coding SQL statements.
- ✦ The data type for each column. The data type should be one of the data types listed in Chapter 23. Depending on the exact data type, you may have to adjust values for Length, Precision, and Scale.
- ✦ Whether the column will accept **Null** values. Note that **Null** values should not be used in any column that is used as part of a primary or foreign key.

✦ The default value for the column. This is an optional attribute that allows you to specify a default value rather than assigning a value of **Null** when adding a new row to the table.

✦ Whether to make the column an identity column. An identity column contains a value that can uniquely identify a row in the table. Only one column per table may be an identity column. This value is an integer value, which increases with each new row. It can be used with **Int**, **Decimal(4,0)** and any other data type that represents a whole number. You can specify the initial value in Identity Seed, and the increment added after each value is used under Identity Increment.

✦ Whether to make the column a row GUID column. A row GUID column is similar to an identity column, but rather than storing an integer value, a GUID value is stored instead. As with identity columns, only one row GUID column is permitted per table. Typically, you would use a row GUID column only if you were planning to implement database replication.

Creating your table

Follow these steps to create a table:

1. Expand the icon tree to reveal the Tables icon in the database where you want to build the table. Then right click on the Tables icon and select New Table from the pop-up menu. This will display the Design Table window, plus a message box that prompts you for the name of the table (see Figure 24-13).
2. Enter the name of your table and press OK.
3. Fill out the grid by entering the information for each column in your table as a row in the form. You must enter values for Column Name and Datatype. Selecting a data type will automatically fill in values for the Length, Precision, and Scale columns. If the data type is a variable length data type such as **Char** or **Decimal**, then you should adjust these values as appropriate.
4. Insert additional columns if you need them.
5. To mark a column or group of columns as the primary key, select the rows containing the columns that make up the key, right click to display the pop-up menu, and choose Set Primary Key. Each column that is part of the primary key will have an icon of a key displayed in the row header. Also, remember to remove any check marks in the Allow Nulls column for each of the fields that are included with the primary key.
6. When you have finished entering all of the columns for the table, you can press the Save icon at the top of the form, or simply close the window to save your table definition. If you close the window, you'll be asked if you want to save your change. Press Yes if you do and No if you don't.

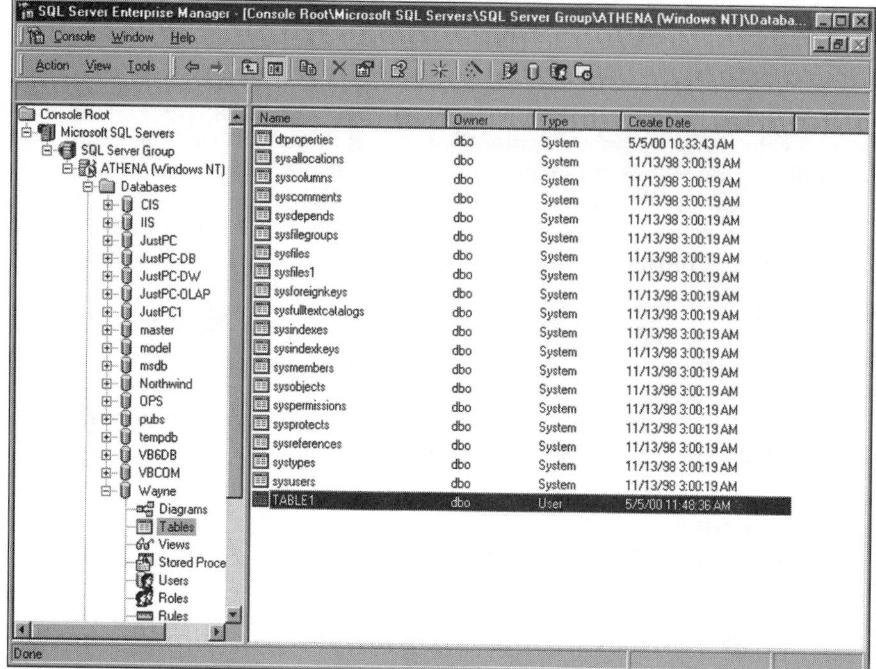

Figure 24-13: Creating a new table

Modifying your table

Once you've finished creating your table, you can always go back and modify it. Simply right click on the Tables icon under the appropriate database icon and choose Design Table (see Figure 24-14). The same window you used to create the table will be displayed containing your table's current definition. Other options on the same pop-up menu will allow you to rename and delete the table. Use these options with care because if your table participates in a foreign key or referenced by a stored procedure, the name change may not be propagated.

Don't do it: Do not change or delete any of the system tables or you will corrupt your database. If you do, the only way to recover your database will be to completely restore it from a database backup.

As long as your table is empty, you can make any changes you want to the table's definition. However, this isn't true if the table contains data. If you add a column to a table with data, the column's value will be set to **Null** unless you define a default value for the column, in which case the default value will be used. If you delete a column, all of the data stored in the column will be lost. However, you will be prevented from deleting the column if it is part of an index, used in a constraint, part of a **Default** definition, bound to a rule, or used as part of a full-text index.

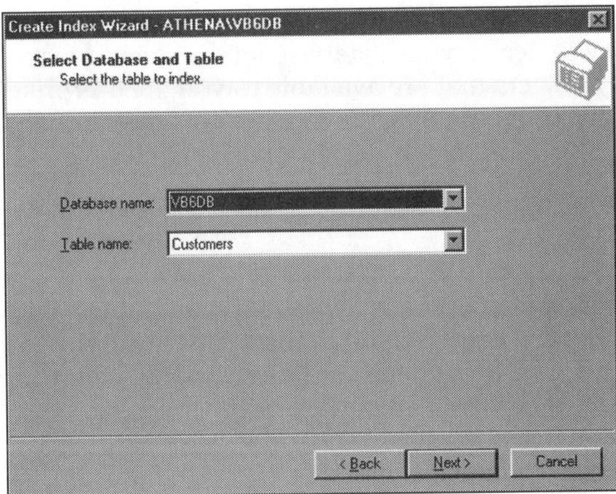

Figure 24-14: Selecting a table

You can change certain attributes of a column, such as making a column that previously rejected **Nulls** to accept **Null** values, without impacting the data already in the table. However, most changes will force Enterprise Manager to process each row physically and cause the table to apply the change. If you switch data types, Enterprise Manager will attempt to convert the value from the old data type to the new data type. Likewise, if you change the precision or length, Enterprise Manager will also have to perform the appropriate conversion.

Safety first: Before you make a change to a table, make sure that you have a good backup copy of your database before you begin. No matter how careful you are you can always recover your database to the point before you made your first change.

A better way to reformat a table: If you must change the data type for a column, and you're not comfortable with how Enterprise Manager will perform the function, consider using the Data Transformation Services. It allows you to code a VBScript macro to handle the actual conversion process.

See Chapter 23 for more information about DTS.

Indexes and Diagrams

The database server uses indexes to locate information in your database more quickly than they could be found without indexes. Whether indexes are present or not is irrelevant to the logical design of the database. They only affect the database's performance.

Not only do database diagrams provide a logical view of your database design, they provide you with the capability to design your database interactively. Most of the functions to create and modify objects that are available to you in Enterprise Manager are also available in the database diagram facility. This means that you don't have to learn yet another set of database design tools.

Creating an index

After creating your tables, the next step is to add indexes to your tables. Without indexes, SQL Server will have to scan every record in the table to find the rows you specify in a query. With an index, SQL Server can go directly to the rows you specify, assuming of course that your query took advantage of the index.

There are two main ways to create an index. The first is to create the index manually by using the Create Index wizard, while the second is to run the Index Tuning wizard that examines a typical set of queries to determine the optimal set of indexes.

Running the Create Index wizard

To run the Create Index wizard, follow these steps:

1. Expand the icon tree to expose the database where you want to add the index. Then select Wizards from the Tools menu. Choose Database ➪ Create Index Wizard to start the Create Index wizard.

2. Press Next to move from the introduction screen to the first step in the wizard, which asks you to select the database and table to be indexed (see Figure 24-15). By default, the currently selected database and the first user table in the database will be displayed.

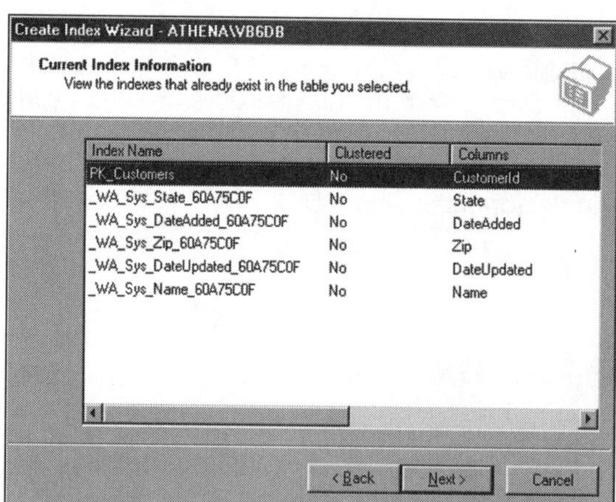

Figure 24-15: Selecting the database and table to be indexed.

3. In the next step of the wizard, all of the indexes associated with the table will be listed, along with the columns indexed (see Figure 24-16), Note that the primary key should always have an index and any foreign key constraints will also have an index. You should make sure that you don't duplicate an index that already exists.

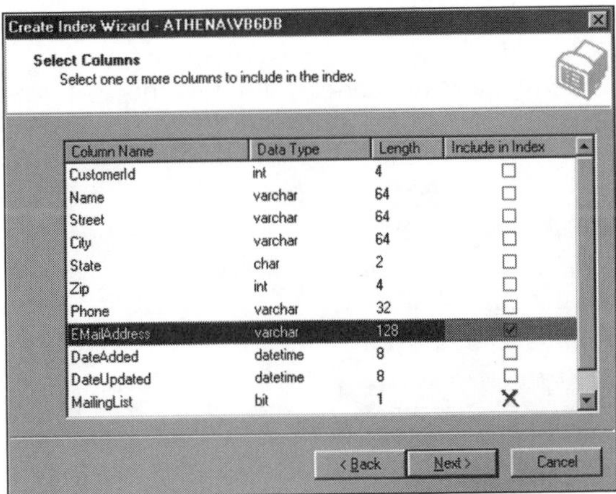

Figure 24-16: Viewing the existing indexes

4. After viewing the existing indexes, you need to choose the column or columns that will make up your new index by placing a check mark in the appropriate box (see Figure 24-17). Note that some columns may have data types that can't be indexed, in which case a big red X will be displayed in place of the check box.

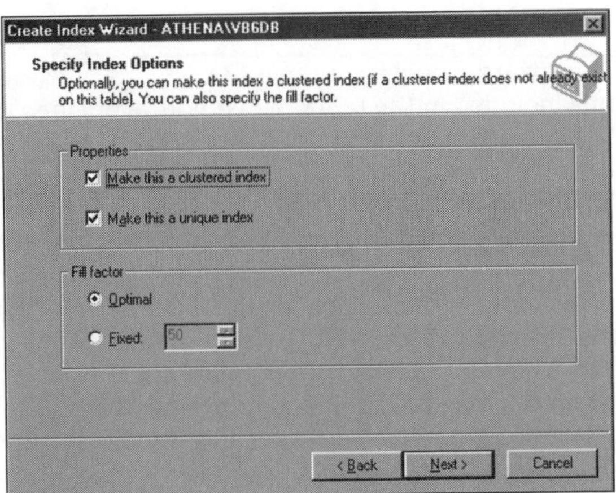

Figure 24-17: Selecting columns for the index

5. In the next to last step of the wizard, you can specify some options for the index (see Figure 24-18). By selecting Make this a clustered index, you can instruct SQL Server to keep the rows in the table in the same physical order as the index. This can improve performance dramatically when you retrieve a set of records that have a common key value. Only one clustered index is permitted per table however. You can ensure that only one row in the table can have a particular value in the key by selecting Make this a unique index. You can also influence the performance of the index by specifying how much space, or fill, SQL Server should leave in the individual index pages for adding new index values. Unless you really understand how this works, you should choose Optimal Fill Factor.

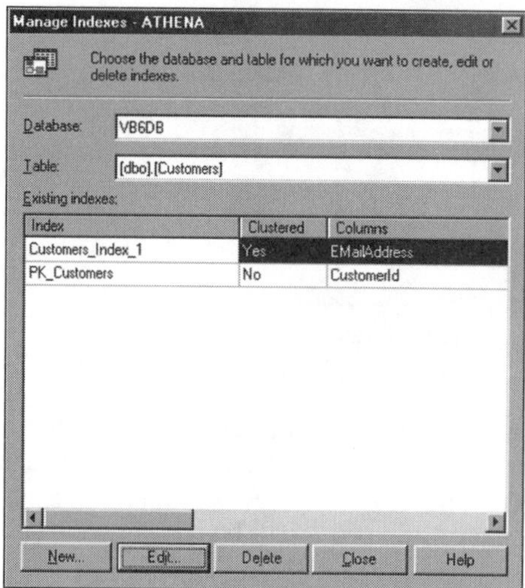

Figure 24-18: Specifying index options

6. In the last step of the wizard, you assign the index a name and adjust the order of the columns included in the table. When you're finished, press Finish to create the index. Since the index is created in real-time, you may have to wait a few minutes for this process to finish, depending on the size of your table and the speed of your database server. A message box will be displayed when the index has been created.

Order in the index: The order of the columns in the index is important, since an index on the columns A, B, and C can be searched three different ways: on column A by itself, on columns A and B, and on columns A, B and C. This index is useless if you want to search on columns B, C, or B and C together, since it is impossible to locate a particular value for B or C without searching through the entire index.

Managing your indexes

You can get a list of the indexes you created for a particular table by right clicking on a table in the Details window and choosing All Tasks ⇨ Manage Indexes from the pop-up menu. The Manage Indexes dialog box will be displayed, as shown in Figure 24-19. This window will display the set of the user created indexes. Using the buttons at the bottom of the dialog box, you can create a new index, edit, or delete an existing index.

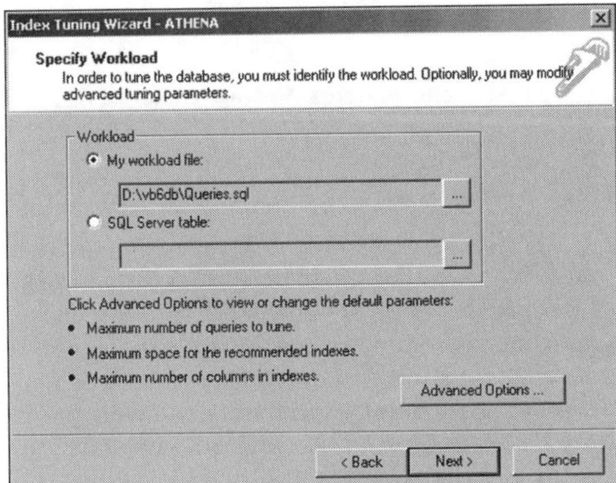

Figure 24-19: Displaying the Manage Indexes dialog box

Running the Index Tuning Wizard

Choosing the proper indexes for a database can be more of an art than a science. Trying to achieve a balance between too many indexes and too few is difficult. With too few indexes, you will waste time trying to retrieve rows from your table, while too many indexes increases the work needed to insert a new row.

The Index Tuning Wizard will analyze trace data collected by the SQL Server Profiler or a list of specific queries that you specify. It also takes into consideration the current set of indexes. Then, based on its analysis, the Index Tuning Wizard will make a list of recommendations that you can apply immediately or save to a disk file to be applied later with Query Analyzer.

To create the workload file, enter the SQL Queries you wish to optimize into a normal text file using Notepad. Make sure you save the file with a file type of `.SQL`.

To capture trace information, run the SQL Server Profiler utility and follow these steps:

1. Select New ⇨ Trace from the main menu to display the Trace Properties dialog box.

2. Enter a name for the trace in the Trace Name field and select the name of the database server where the trace information will be generated on the General tab. Then specify the name of a file or database table where the trace information will be stored.

3. On the Events tab, add the TSQL event to the list of selected events and press OK to start the trace.

Tracing can be hazardous to your database server's performance: Running a trace increases the amount of work for your database server to perform, and it may adversely affect your server's performance.

To analyze trace data or analyze a few specific queries, follow these steps:

1. In Enterprise Manager, select Wizards from the Tools menu, then select the Management ➪ Index Tuning Wizard and press OK. After the initial screen of the wizard is displayed, press Next to begin the tuning process.

2. On the Select Server and Database step of the wizard (see Figure 24-20), select the name of the database server and database you wish to analyze. Also, you need to choose whether you want to keep your existing indexes. If you're only analyzing a few problem queries, you should keep your current indexes, but if you are analyzing a large volume of trace data, then you may want to replace your current indexes. Choose Perform thorough analysis if you want to choose the optimal set of indexes. Note that this option will significantly increase the amount of time required to run the analysis.

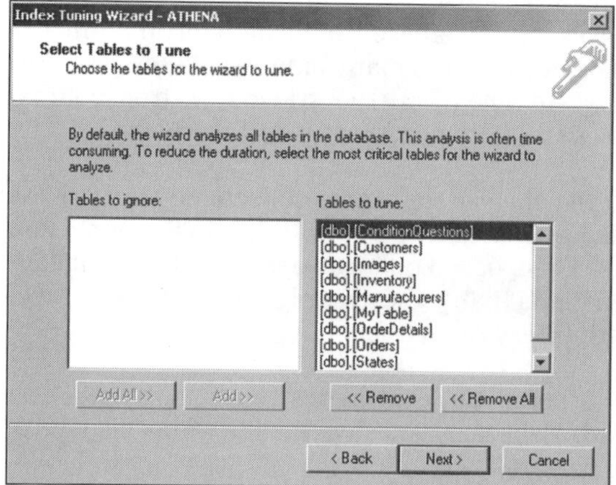

Figure 24-20: Select the database server and database you want to analyze

3. In the next step of the wizard, save a workload file and press Next. Then you will be prompted for the name of your workload file or the name of the database table where the trace information is stored (see Figure 24-21).

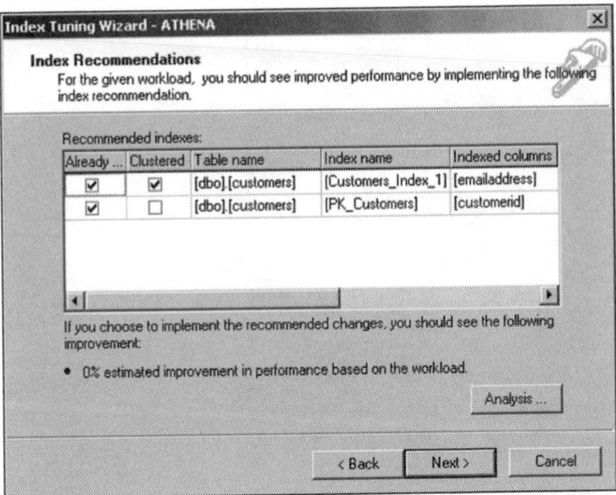

Figure 24-21: Specify the location of your workload

4. You can choose the tables you wish to tune in the next step of the wizard (see Figure 24-23). Unless you are worried about the amount of time to run the analysis or want to focus on a subset of the tables, you should select all of the tables in the database.

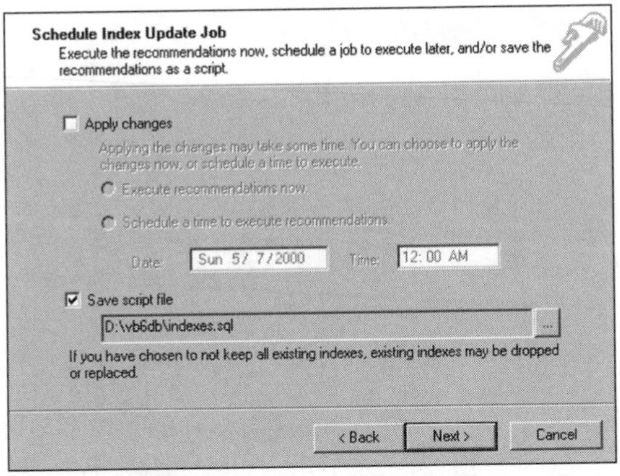

Figure 24-22: Selecting the tables to tune

5. Pressing Next will start the analysis process. A dialog box will be displayed that tracks the analysis process. When the analysis is complete, the results will be displayed in the Index Recommendations step shown in Figure 24-23. Pressing the Analysis button will show the detailed results of the analysis.

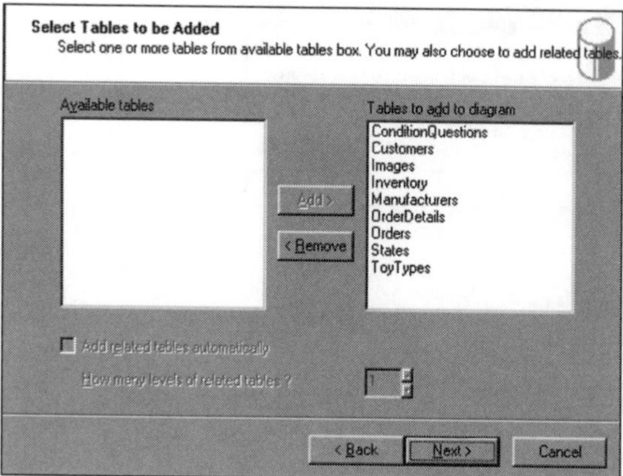

Figure 24-23: Reviewing the index recommendations

6. In the next to last step of the wizard, you can choose to apply the recommendations immediately, schedule them to be applied as a batch job, or save the recommendations as a script file that you can apply with Query Analyzer (see Figure 24-24). After making your choice, press Next to display the final step of the wizard, and Finish to complete the process.

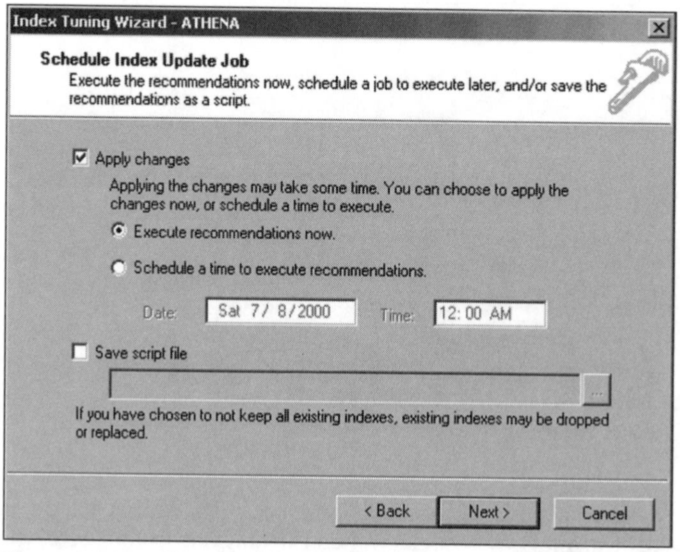

Index Tuning Wizard - ATHENA
Schedule Index Update Job
Execute the recommendations now, schedule a job to execute later, and/or save the recommendations as a script.
Apply changes
Applying the changes may take some time. You can choose to apply the changes now, or schedule a time to execute.
Execute recommendations now.
Schedule a time to execute recommendations.
Date: Sat 7/ 8/2000 Time: 12: 00 AM
Save script file
If you have chosen to not keep all existing indexes, existing indexes may be dropped or replaced.
< Back Next > Cancel

Figure 24-24: Choosing how to apply the recommendations

Creating a database diagram

Another useful database object you can create with Enterprise Manager is a *database diagram*. A database diagram contains a logical view of your database similar to an Entity/Relationship diagram. You can add new tables directly in the database diagram, as well as modify existing tables. You can also create relationships between tables by dragging and dropping column references. It is a powerful tool that makes it easy to design your database by allowing you to visualize your database and the relationships between its tables.

Refer to Chapter 3 for a discussion of Entity/Relationship diagrams.

Creating your database diagram

To create a database diagram, follow these steps:

1. Expand the icon tree to select the database server and database where you want to create the database diagram. Right click on the Diagrams icon and choose New Database Diagram from the pop-up menu. This will create a blank database diagram and start the Create Database Diagram Wizard. Press Next to begin creating your database diagram.
2. In the Select Tables to be Added step, you can choose which tables in the database will be included in your database diagram (see Figure 24-25). Sometimes it's useful to have a diagram that includes only a small subset of the tables in the database that focus on a particular function. Checking the Add related tables button, and then adding the table you want to focus on, will automatically add all of the tables that have a relationship to the original table. As tables are added to the Tables to add to diagram list, they will be removed from the Available tables list.
3. In the last step of the wizard, you see the list of tables you selected. Press Finish to add the tables to the diagram and automatically arrange them. Behind the wizard, you'll see your tables appear and then be arranged. When the diagram is complete, a message box will appear and you'll be left with a brand new database diagram to edit and save (see Figure 24-26).

Using the database diagram

Once your database diagram is complete, you should notice that each table is similar to the form you used to design a table discussed in the Creating a Table section earlier in this chapter. That's because it is the same, but only the first column from the form is shown in the diagram. You change the columns displayed by right clicking on the table and selecting one of the following views: Column Properties, Column Names, Keys, Name Only, and Custom View from the pop-up menu. To choose the information displayed in Custom View, choose Modify Custom View.

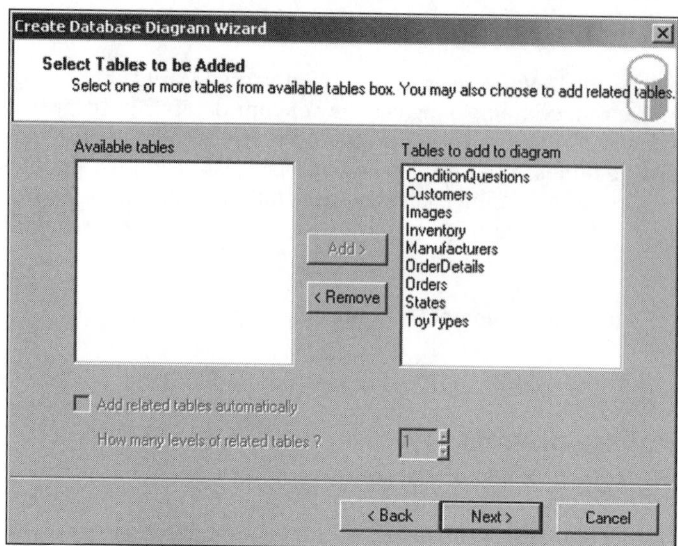

Figure 24-25: Selecting the tables for the database diagram

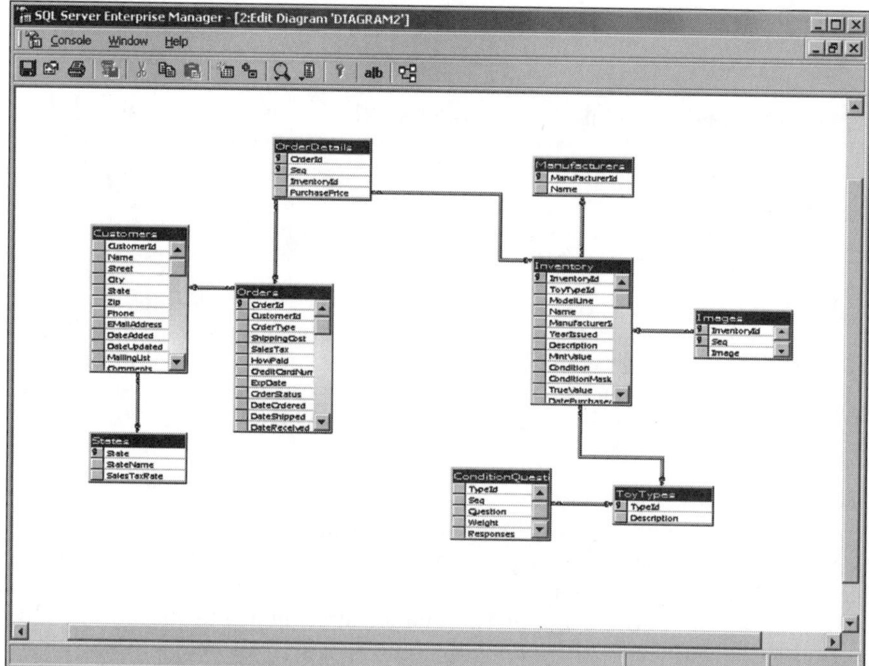

Figure 24-26: Viewing your new database diagram

The second thing you should notice about the diagram are the lines drawn between the tables. These lines represent foreign key constraints. To define a foreign key constraint, click on the prefix area in front of a column in one table, drag it to the other table, and drop it. A dialog box will be displayed that shows both the primary and foreign key tables and the columns that form the foreign key (see Figure 24-27). You can then choose the columns in each table that reflect the columns that comprise the foreign key.

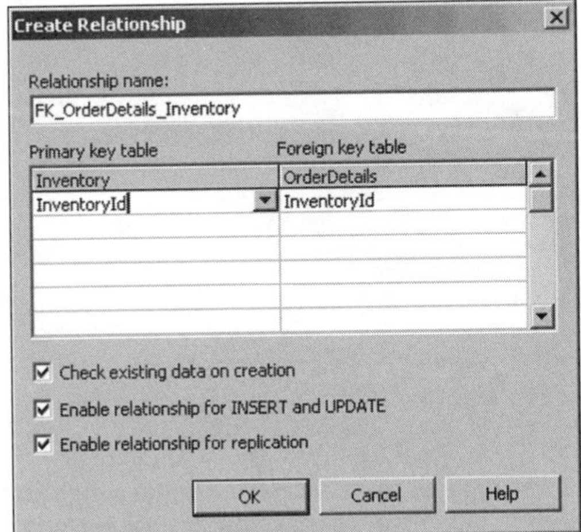

Figure 24-27: Creating a foreign key relationship

One nice thing about database diagrams is that you can print them. When programming, I usually have a printed copy of the database diagram handy to refer to table and column names and to identify relationships. Since a database diagram can get rather complicated, and may not fit on a single sheet of paper, you can zoom the diagram to create the best fit.

You can also drag the tables around on the diagram to arrange them the way you want. You should notice that the foreign key constraints will automatically follow the table. If you don't like where the constraints are placed, you can simply drag them around until you are happy with them.

As you make changes to your database diagram, you are not actually making any changes to the database. The diagram tool tracks the changes and applies them only when you save the changes or exit the diagram. In either case, a dialog box will be displayed listing the tables that you have changed (see Figure 24-28). You have the option to make the changes, discard the changes, or create an SQL script file containing the statements necessary to make the changes.

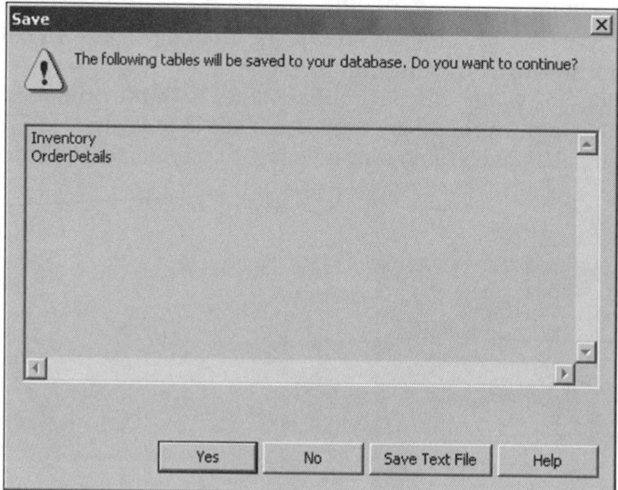

Figure 24-28: Saving the changes to the database diagram

Managing Security

Managing security is both easy and hard at the same time. Understanding the commands you use to apply security is easy. Making sure that you don't have any holes in your security is difficult.

Creating a login

As you might expect, Enterprise Manager includes wizards for creating logins. The Create Login Wizard not only creates a login id, but it also lets you pick database server roles and create a user with the same name in one or more databases.

To create a login, follow these steps:

1. Choose Tools ➪ Wizards and then select Database ➪ Create Login Wizard. Press OK to start the wizard. After skipping over the introduction to the wizard by pressing Next, you'll be prompted to choose the authentication mode for the user (see Figure 24-29). Select the desired authentication method and press Next.
2. If you chose Windows NT Authentication, you'll see the form shown in Figure 24-30. Specify the domain name and the account for the user and then either grant access to the database server or deny access. Press Next to continue.

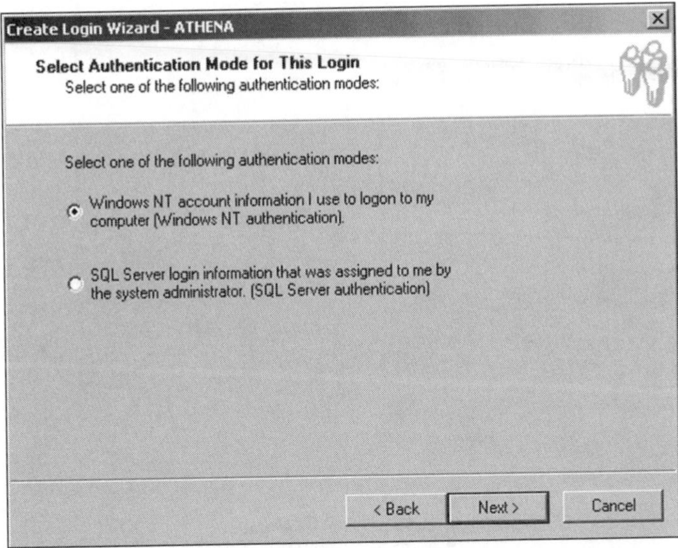

Figure 24-29: Choosing an authentication mode for your login

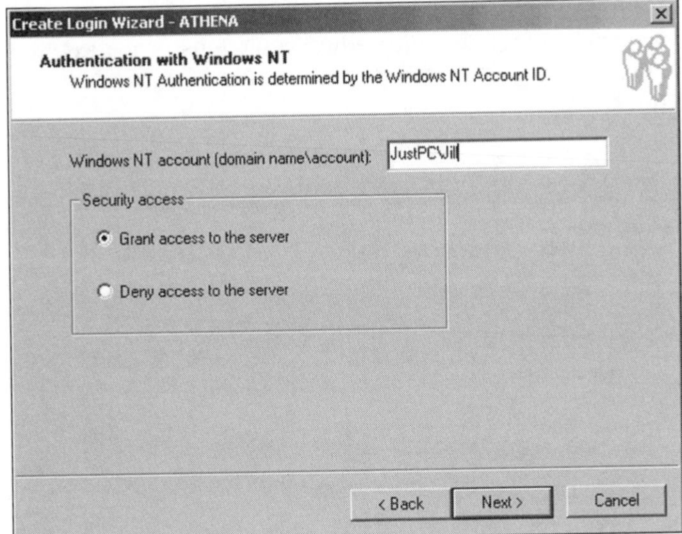

Figure 24-30: Entering information for a Windows NT Authentication login

3. If you chose SQL Server Authentication, the form shown in Figure 24-31 will be that you have to enter the password information twice to ensure that the password was entered properly.

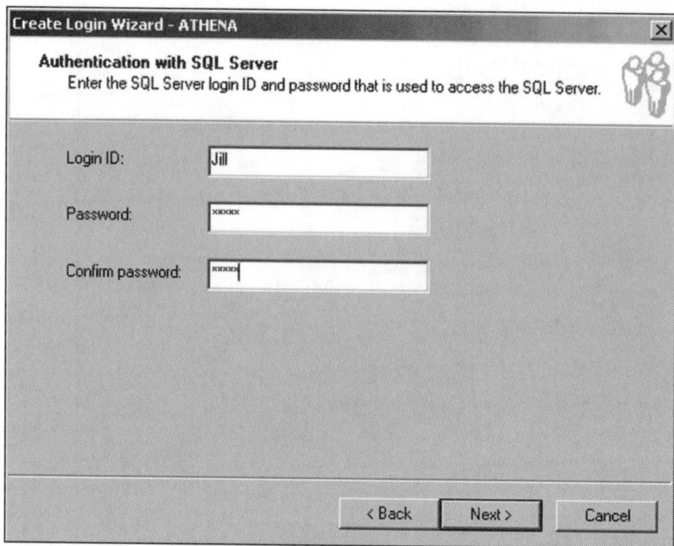

Figure 24-31: Entering information for an SQL Server Authentication login

4. No matter which authentication method you choose, the next step will ask you to choose which server security roles should be assigned to the login (see Figure 24-32).

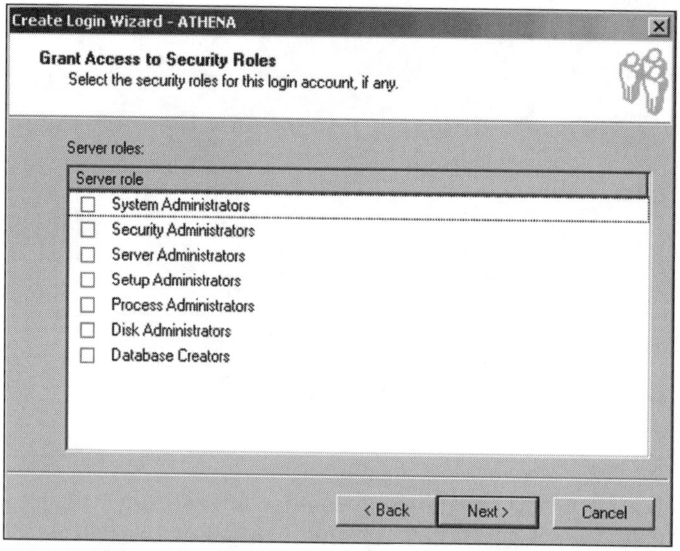

Figure 24-32: Choose server security roles for your new login

5. In the next to last step of the wizard, you'll be prompted to select the databases in which the new login should be granted access (see Figure 24-33). Press Next to review the information you entered and press Finish to create the login. Note that a user with the same name as the login will be created in each database you selected.

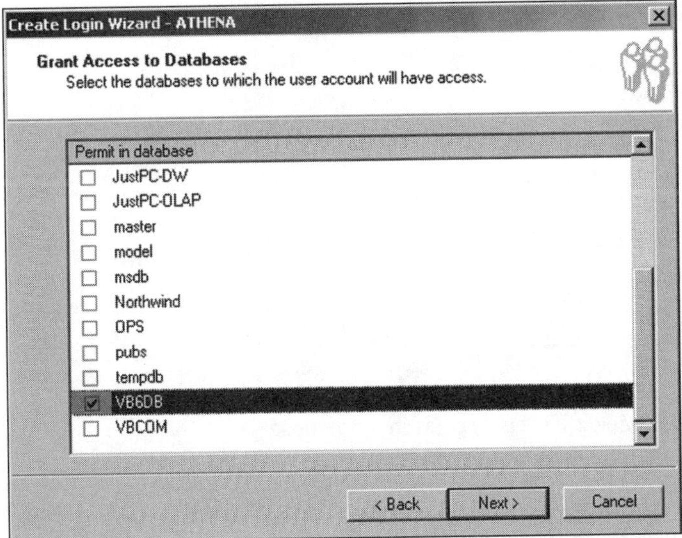

Figure 24-33: Grant your new login access to the databases on the server

What did I do?: You can see the list of logins on the database server by expanding the icon tree for the database server to show Logins, which is found under the Security icon. Selecting this icon will display all of the logins in the Details window. The list of users for a database can be displayed in the Details window by selecting the Users icon under the appropriate database icon.

Granting permissions in a database

Just because you have granted a user access to a database doesn't mean that they have complete access to your database. By default, they will be assigned to the public role, which means that any resources granted to the public will automatically be granted to the new user. You can review and change their assigned roles by expanding the icon tree to show the Users icon beneath the database you wish to manage. Then, by right clicking and choosing Properties from the pop-up menu, you can specify which roles they have been permitted (see Figure 24-34). On the General tab, you can add new roles by placing a check mark next to the desired role or revoke a role by removing the check mark. You can see the user's specific security permissions by pressing the Permissions button.

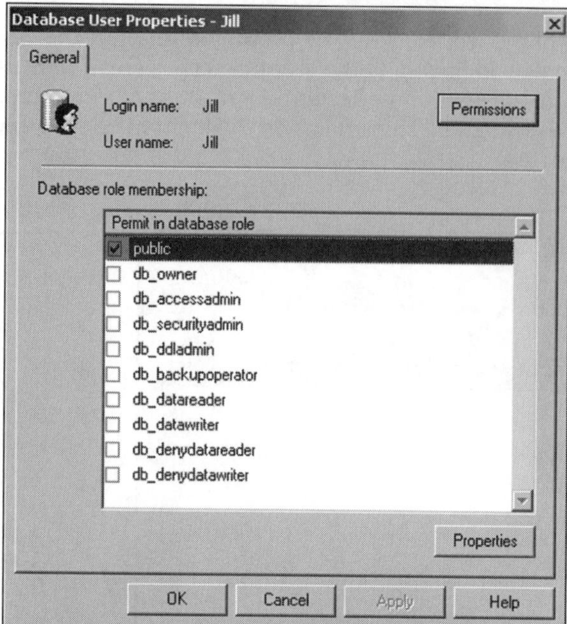

Figure 24-34: Reviewing security roles in a database

By clicking on the List only objects with permissions for this user on the Permissions tab, you can quickly determine which database objects, if any, this user has access to. The check marks indicate which commands the users may issue against which database objects.

You can modify the permissions associated with a role in the same way you modify them for a user. The only difference is that you have to select the role from the list of roles displayed in the Details window when you select the Roles icon for the desired database in the tree view area of Enterprise Manager.

A list of users assigned to that particular role will be displayed in the Role Properties dialog box (see Figure 24-36). You can then display the same detailed Security Permissions dialog box shown in Figure 24-35 by pressing the Permissions button. You can also get a list of users assigned to the role by selecting a role in the User Properties dialog box and pressing the Properties button.

Too much security can cause problems: While you can modify the permissions for each individual user, you will be much better off assigning the user to a role and modifying the permissions for the role. When you maintain security permissions at the user level, it is very easy to make a mistake and grant the user permission to something they should be denied. While it is still possible to do this with a role, double checking the roles will be a much easier job than double checking each user.

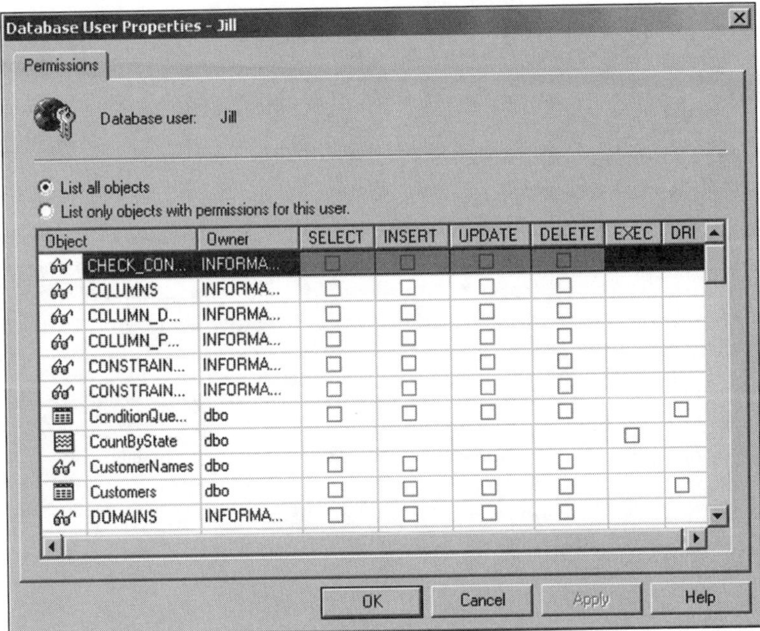

Figure 24-35: Reviewing the detailed security permissions for a user

Figure 24-36: Reviewing the properties of a role

Thoughts on Enterprise Manager

Enterprise Manager is a very powerful tool that simplifies the administration of an SQL Server database. In this chapter, I've barely begun to communicate what you can do with Enterprise Manager. I strongly recommend that you take the time to explore its capabilities, especially if you plan to do a lot of work with SQL Server.

If you look carefully, many of the tools that are used in Enterprise Manager look like those available in the Enterprise Edition of Visual Basic. This is no coincidence. The same code base is used for both. I feel that Enterprise Manager does a better job of implementing the tools than Visual Basic, but it is nice to be able to use some of the same tools with other databases also.

It's important to note that anything you can do with Enterprise Manager can also be done using the appropriate SQL statements. Enterprise Manager is nothing more than a very complex program that issues ADO requests to an SQL Server database, just like your application would.

Summary

In this chapter you learned:

- about the various features of SQL Server Enterprise Manager.
- how to browse data in your database.
- how to create a new table.
- how to add an index to a table.
- how to create a database diagram.
- how to create a login and assign security permissions.

✦ ✦ ✦

CHAPTER 25

Creating Stored Procedures with SQL Server

✦ ✦ ✦ ✦

In This Chapter

Introducing stored procedures

Using Transact-SQL to build stored procedures

Creating stored procedures with SQL Server

Debugging stored procedures in Query Analyzer

✦ ✦ ✦ ✦

In this chapter, I'm going to show you how to build and debug stored procedures using SQL Server. Stored procedures are basically subroutines that you can call from your program to perform a database task. They are written in a language called Transact-SQL, which is really just SQL with a few extra statements that help you test conditions and perform loops.

Introducing Stored Procedures

A *stored procedure* is a collection of SQL statements that are stored in the database server. These statements are stored in both text form and in compiled form for fast execution. They can be used in place of an SQL statement or called like a function or subroutine.

The concept of stored procedures is common to most database management systems on the market today, though the implementations are usually sufficiently different to make converting stored procedures from one vendor to another vendor a difficult task. Yet stored procedures can make a big difference in the performance of your application so many programmers rely on them for their applications.

Why use stored procedures?

Stored procedures allow you to create a block of code that can be called from any database application or database utility. This common block of code has three primary advantages: performance, convenience, and security. A stored procedure usually needs fewer resources to run when compared to a block of regular code, coupled with calls to the database server. A stored procedure is easy to use, since it typically represents a complicated programming object that can be used as easily as a normal SQL statement. Since a stored procedure is secured just like any other database object, you can also grant others the capability to perform a task that exceeds their normal security permissions.

Improving performance

The number one reason people use stored procedures is that they are usually more efficient than explicitly including the code in your application program. This is because when you submit an SQL statement to the database server, the following steps occur each time an application program attempts to perform a task:

1. The application program transmits the SQL statement to the database server over the network.
2. The database server parses the SQL statement and then compiles it for execution.
3. The database server executes the compiled statement.
4. The execution's results are returned over the network to the application program.
5. The application program receives the results and repeats steps 1 through 4 as needed to complete the task.

With a stored procedure, this process is much different. Before the program is run, the following steps occur:

1. The stored procedure is transmitted to the database server.
2. The stored procedure is parsed and compiled.
3. The compiled code is saved for later execution.

Then when the application program is ready to perform the same task:

1. The application program transmits a request to call the stored procedure over the network.
2. The database server retrieves the compiled copy of the stored procedure and executes it.
3. The results are returned to the application program.

Note that there is only one interaction between the application program and the database server. This reduces network traffic, which can make a big difference on heavily-loaded or low-speed networks. Also, the stored procedure is compiled before the application calls it. This saves a lot of work for the database server, since parsing and compiling SQL statements can be very CPU-intensive.

Increasing convenience

Stored procedures can be called by different application programs or called by any program that is capable of directly executing SQL statements. This means that you can develop standard stored procedures that perform a task that can be shared among all of your applications. Because the logic for the stored procedure is isolated to a single place (i.e., the database server), you can change the stored procedure without necessarily changing the application that calls it. Thus, you can change your underlying database structure, while leaving your applications untouched.

Providing security

Since a stored procedure is just another database object, it can be secured using the same techniques used to secure other database objects. Thus, you can create a stored procedure that allows your users to perform a particular task that they might not otherwise be able to perform. For instance, you might create a stored procedure to insert a row in a table that your users don't normally have access to.

Introducing Transact-SQL

Transact-SQL (also known as T-SQL) is the name of Microsoft's implementation of SQL on SQL Server. In addition to the SQL statements I've used throughout this book, there are a number of extensions that allow you to build complex stored procedures. Like any programming language, Transact-SQL consists of a number of syntax elements, such as identifiers, data types, variables, functions, expressions, and statements.

Comments

It's always a good idea to include comments in your code. There are two types of comment indicators you may use: double hyphen (--) and slash asterisk, asterisk slash (/* */).Double hyphen comments are usually used at the end of a line of code, though they can be placed on a line by themselves. Everything from the double hyphens to the end of the line is treated as a comment and is ignored by the parser. For example:

```
--
-- Procedure: GetCustomerByName
-- Written by: Wayne S. Freeze
-- Date written: 28 April 2000
-- Description: This procedure returns a customer's information
--              for a particular customer id.
--
CREATE PROCEDURE GetCustomerByName (@CustId Int)
AS
Select *
From Customers
Where CustomerId = @CustId
```

Slash asterisk, asterisk slash comments can be used anywhere a space can be used; thus, they can be embedded in your code. A slash asterisk (/*) marks the start of the comment, while an asterisk slash marks the end of a comment (*/). The comment may span multiple lines, as shown below:

```
/*
 ** Procedure: GetCustomerByName
 ** Written by: Wayne S. Freeze
 ** Date written: 28 April 2000
 ** Description: This procedure returns a customer's
 ** information for a particular customer id.
 */
CREATE PROCEDURE GetCustomerByName
   (@CustId Int /* customer id must be non-negative */ )
AS
Select *
From Customers
Where CustomerId = @CustId
```

Hiding code: Sometimes when you are debugging a stored procedure, it is useful to hide blocks of code from the server so they are not executed. One easy way to do this is to insert a line containing a slash asterisk before the code you want to hide and an asterisk slash after the code.

Identifiers

An *identifier* is simply the name of a database object, such as a database, table, or column. It can also be a Transact-SQL keyword or the name of a variable or label within a stored procedure.

There are two different types of identifiers: *delimited identifiers* and *regular identifiers.* Delimited identifiers can be any combination of characters up to 128 total. You may use letters, numbers, spaces, and any special symbol except for double quotes (") or square brackets ([ ]). This is because you must enclose the identifier in double quotes or inside a pair of square brackets. Some examples of delimited identifiers are:

```
"My Table"
[This identifier includes a comma, an asterisk * and a period.]
```

Regular identifiers must begin with a letter, an underscore (_), an at sign (@), or a number sign (#) and can also contain up to a maximum of 128 characters. The first character signifies how the identifier is used. System functions begin with two at signs (@@). Variables begin with an at sign, while a number sign identifies a temporary table. Some examples of regular identifiers are:

```
MyTable
@LocalVariable
```

Variables

Variables in T-SQL are basically the same as they are in Visual Basic. They hold information local to the stored procedure or represent parameters passed to the stored procedures. Variables begin with an at sign (@) and must be declared before they can be used. Before you can use a variable, you must declare it as a local variable using the **Declare** statement or as a parameter using the **Create Procedure** statement.

Each variable must be assigned a valid data type that is compatible with how you plan to use it. You can choose from the same data types that you would use in a **Create Table** statement, except for **Text**, **Ntext**, and **Image**. In the following example, I declare two variables, `@Counter` and `@Name`, which are assigned **Int** and **Varchar** data types respectively.

```
Declare @Counter Int
Declare @Name Varchar(64)
```

Functions

Functions in T-SQL are identical to those in Visual Basic. They take a series of zero or more parameters and return a value to the calling program. Table 25-1 contains some of the functions that are available for you to use in your stored procedure.

Table 25-1
Selected functions in T-SQL

Function	*Description*
@@CPU_Busy	Returns the number of milliseconds of CPU time SQL Server has consumed since it was started.
@@Cursor_Rows	Returns the number of qualifying rows for the most recently opened cursor.
@@DBTS	Returns the next timestamp for the database.
@@Error	Returns the error code for the more recently executed SQL statement.
@@Fetch_Status	Returns the status of the last **Fetch** operation.
@@IO_Busy	Returns the number of milliseconds SQL Server has spent performing I/O.
@@Nestlevel	Returns the nesting level of the current stored procedure. First level has a value of zero.

Continued

Table 25-1 *(continued)*

Function	*Description*
@@Servername	Returns the name of the database server.
@@Trancount	Returns the current nesting level of a set of nested transactions.
@@Version	Returns the date, version, and processor type for the database server.
App_Name	Returns the name of the current application.
ASCII	Returns the ASCII code of the left-most character of the specified character string.
Cast	Converts a value in one data type to another data type.
Ceiling	Returns the smallest integer value greater or equal to the specified value.
Char	Returns the character corresponding to the specified numeric ASCII code value.
Col_Length	Returns the length of the specified column.
Columnproperty	Returns the requested information about the specified column.
Convert	Returns the specified value using the specified data type using the specified style.
Current_User	Returns the name of the current user.
Cursor_Status	Returns the status of the specified cursor.
Datalength	Returns the number of bytes in the specified expression.
Floor	Returns the largest integer value less than or equal to the specified value.
Getdate	Returns the current date and time as a **Datetime** value.
Host_Name	Returns the name of the current computer. (Not the database server.)
Len	Returns the number of characters in a string, excluding trailing blanks.
Lower	Converts all uppercase characters to lowercase.
Ltrim	Removes leading blanks from a string.
IsDate	Returns **True** if the specified expression contains a valid date.
IsNumeric	Returns **True** if the specified expression is a valid number.
Is_Member	Returns **True** if the current user is a member of the specified role.
Object_Id	Converts the specified database object into a numeric object identification number.

Function	Description
Object_Name	Returns the name of the specified object identification number.
Patindex	Returns the location of a pattern in the specified string.
Rand	Returns a random value between 0 and 1.
Round	Rounds the specified value to the specified length or precision.
Rtrim	Removes trailing blanks from a string.
Substring	Returns the specified part of a string.
Suser_Sid	Returns the security identification number for the specified login name.
Suser_Sname	Returns the login name for the current user or the login name for the specified security identification number.
Typeproperty	Returns the requested information about a data type.
Upper	Converts all lowercase characters to uppercase.

Confusing, isn't it: To prevent confusion with system functions, you should never declare a variable with double at signs.

Expressions

Expressions are used to compute a single value based on a series of local variables, parameters, columns retrieved from a table, and functions. You can assign an expression to a variable by using the **Set** statement, as shown here.

```
Set @Counter = 0
Set @MyString = Upper(Rtrim(CustomerName))
```

You may also assign a value to a local variable using the **Select** statement. The only restriction is that the **Select** statement must return only one row. Otherwise, the variable will be assigned the last value retrieved by the **Select** statement. In front of each column, you must specify the local variable, followed by an equal sign (=), and then the column name. A simple example is shown below:

```
Select @Name = Name, @EMail = EMailAddress
From Customers
Where CustomerId = @CustId
```

Flow control

T-SQL includes flow controls statements, such as **If** and **While,** to help you build your stored procedures. You can even call other stored procedures using the **Execute** statement.

If statement

You construct an **If** statement using the following syntax:

```
If <boolean_expression>
    { <sql_statement> | Begin <sql_statement_list> End }
[Else
    { <sql_statement> | Begin <sql_statement_list> End }]
```

If `<boolean_expression>` is **True**, then the statement that immediately follows the expression will be executed. Otherwise, the statement that immediately follows the **Else** clause will be executed. You can substitute a **Begin End** pair that surrounds a list of SQL statements for the single statements if you want to execute one or more statements.

Beginnings and endings: Use **Begin** and **End** clauses even if you only have a single statement. This makes it easy to include additional statements in the future.

While statement

While statements are constructed with the following syntax:

```
While <boolean_expression>
    { <sql_statement> | Begin <sql_statement_list> End }
```

The statement or block of statements delimited by the **Begin End** pair are repeated until the `<boolean_expression>` is **False**. Inside a **Begin End** pair, you can end a **While** loop early by using the **Break** statement. The **Continue** statement ignores the rest of the statements in the **While** loop and restarts the loop.

Execute statement

The basic syntax for the **Execute** statement's syntax is shown below:

```
[Execute] [<return>=] <procedure_name>
[[<parm>=]{<value>|<var>}]...
```

The **Execute** statement is used to call another stored procedure. While the actual syntax is more complex, chances are you're not going to use much more than this. Note that the **Execute** part of the statement may be omitted. If the stored procedure returns a value, you must include a local variable for `<return>`. Otherwise, this clause should be omitted.

The name of a stored procedure follows normal database rules for the most part. However, if the name of a stored procedure begins with `sp_`, then the database server will search the master database for the stored procedure rather than the local database. If the name of the stored procedure isn't qualified and it isn't found under the current user name, the database server will search for the stored procedure using the `dbo` as the owner of the stored procedure.

For example, if you are accessing the database with the user name MyUser and specify the stored procedure name MyProc, SQL Server will look for the stored procedure named MyUser.MyProc in the current database. If it isn't found then it will look for the a stored procedure named dbo.MyProc also in the current database. If it still isn't found, then it will return an error message saying the stored procedure couldn't be found. This approach allows you to test a stored procedure with the same name and move it to under dbo only when you're satisfied it works properly.

Now if you call the stored procedure, sp_MyProc, SQL Server will look for the stored procedure dbo.sp_MyProc in the master database. If it isn't found there, then it will look for the stored procedure MyUser.sp_MyProc in the current database. If it still isn't found, then it will look for the stored procedure dbo.sp_MyProc in the current database. The reason it works this way is that you can't override how a system stored procedure works. Overriding a system stored procedure could compromise security.

There are two ways to specify parameters: you can simply list them in the order they were defined in the stored procedure, or you may assign a value explicitly to each parameter name. Note that if you list the parameters explicitly, you need not worry about the order you use.

The following calls are identical:

```
Execute MyProc @MyVar, 24
MyProc @MyVar, 24
Execute MyProc @Parm1 = @MyVar, @Parm2 = 24
MyProc @Parm2 = 24, @Parm1 = @MyVar
```

Exectly: You can also abbreviate **Execute** as **Exec.**

Cursors

Cursors are used to allow you to scroll through a set of rows identified by a **Select** statement. The cursor maintains the current record pointer and allows you to use other statements, such as **Fetch** to retrieve information from the current record into local variables, and **Update** to change the values in the current record.

Declare Cursor

This **Declare Cursor** statement defines a pointer and can be used to access one row of data returned by a **Select** statement:

```
Declare <cursor> Cursor
[Local|Global]
[Static | Keyset | Dynamic | Fast_Forward]
[Read_Only | Scroll_Locks | Optimistic]
For <select_statement>
```

The <cursor> is a normal SQL Server identifier that will be used by other statements to access the cursor. The **Local** keyword implies that the cursor can't be accessed outside this routine, while the **Global** keyword implies that the cursor can be accessed by other stored procedures as long as the current connection to the database is still active.

The **Static** keyword means that the database server will make a temporary copy of the data in tempdb to prevent modifications to the data while you are processing it. The **Keyset** keyword instructs the database server to keep a list of pointers to the rows, which means that your stored procedure will see the current values to the rows, but not rows that were added after the cursor was opened. The **Dynamic** keyword implies that any and all changes made to the selected rows will be visible to the stored procedure. However, this also implies that the order of rows may change as new rows are added and existing rows deleted. The **Fast_Forward** keyword implies that the rows can't be changed and that the cursor may only be moved in a forward direction (i.e., you can only use the **Fetch Next** statement).

The **Read_Only** keyword ensures that the rows can't be changed. **Scroll_Locks** implies that rows are locked when they are fetched, so that updates and deletes will always succeed. Specifying **Optimistic** means that the row isn't locked until you are ready to commit the changes. This also implies that there is the possibility that the changes may fail because the rows were changed by another program.

Where did I see that before: The keywords described here refer to the cursors and locking mechanisms that are available in ADO.

Open

In order to use the cursor, you have to use the **Open** statement. Its syntax is listed below:

```
Open <cursor>
```

The **Open** statement essentially executes the **Select** statement and creates the data structures necessary to access the rows you selected.

Fetch

The syntax for the **Fetch** statement follows:

```
Fetch [Next|Prior|First|Last|Absolute <location>|Relative
<offset>]
From <cursor> Into <variable_list>
```

The **Fetch** statement is used to retrieve information from a row. If **Next**, **Prior**, **First**, **Last**, **Absolute,** or **Relative** are specified, then the movement is performed before the information is returned. If the first call to **Fetch** after opening the cursor includes the **Next** keyword, the current record pointer is moved to the first row and **Fetch** returns the values from the first row. For **Fast_Forward** cursors, **Next** is the only allowable movement option.

The **Absolute** keyword allows you to move the current record pointer to the specified row, where the first row is **Absolute** 1 and the second row is **Absolute** 2. The last row would be known as **Absolute** –1, while the next to the last row would be found by using **Absolute** –2. The **Absolute** keyword is not legal when using a **Dynamic** cursor.

The **Relative** keyword allows you to move the current pointer relative to the current record pointer. If the current record pointer is pointing to row 7, **Relative** –2 will reposition the current record pointer to row 5, while **Relative** 3 will move the current record pointer to row 10.

The **Into** clause requires that you supply a series of local variables to receive the columns from the **Select** statement. The local variables must be compatible with the data types returned in the **Select** statement and must appear in the same order as those listed in the **Select** statement. A runtime error will occur if there are too few or too many variables listed in the **Into** clause.

Update

The syntax for using the **Update** statement with cursors is shown below:

```
Update <table> Set [<column> = <value>] ...
Where Current Of <cursor>
```

If you **Declare** a cursor that maps to a table, you can use the **Update** statement to update the row at the current record pointed to by the specified cursor by using the **Where Current Of** clause. In place of `<value>` you may use any expression of the appropriate data type, including functions and local variables.

Delete

Shown below is the syntax for using the **Delete** statement with a cursor:

```
Delete From <table>
Where Current of <cursor>
```

Substituting the table name of the table used in the **Declare Cursor** statement for `<table>` and the name of the cursor for `<cursor>` will allow you to delete the row that is pointed to by the cursor's current record pointer.

Where did my row go?: If you delete a row in a cursor's rowset and later try to read the row with a **Fetch** statement when you declared the cursor as **Static** or **Keyset**, the **@@Fetch_Status** function will return –2, meaning that the row has been deleted.

Close

The syntax for the **Close** statement is listed below:

```
Close <cursor>
```

The **Close** statement releases the results obtained when the specified cursor was opened. Any locks held also released.

Deallocate

The syntax for the **Deallocate** statement is listed below:

```
Deallocate <cursor>
```

Just because you have closed the cursor doesn't mean that the cursor is no longer available. You must **Deallocate** the cursor to free all of the resources owned by the cursor.

An example of how to use a cursor

Rather than try to build a small example for each of the above statements, I wrote a simple routine that demonstrates how to retrieve some information from your database (see Listing 25-1). This routine retrieves names from the Customers table and prints them (see Figure 25-1).

Listing 25-1: Using cursors in a simple stored procedure

```
Declare @CustName VarChar(64)
Declare @RecCount Int

Declare CustCursor Cursor
Local Fast_Forward Read_Only
For Select Name From Customers Where State = 'MD'

Open CustCursor

Set @RecCount = 0

Fetch Next From CustCursor Into @CustName
While @@Fetch_Status = 0
   Begin
   Print @CustName
   Set @RecCount = @RecCount + 1
   Fetch Next From CustCursor Into @CustName
   End
```

```
Print RTrim(Convert(VarChar(20), @RecCount)) + ' records
found.'
Close CustCursor

Deallocate CustCursor
```

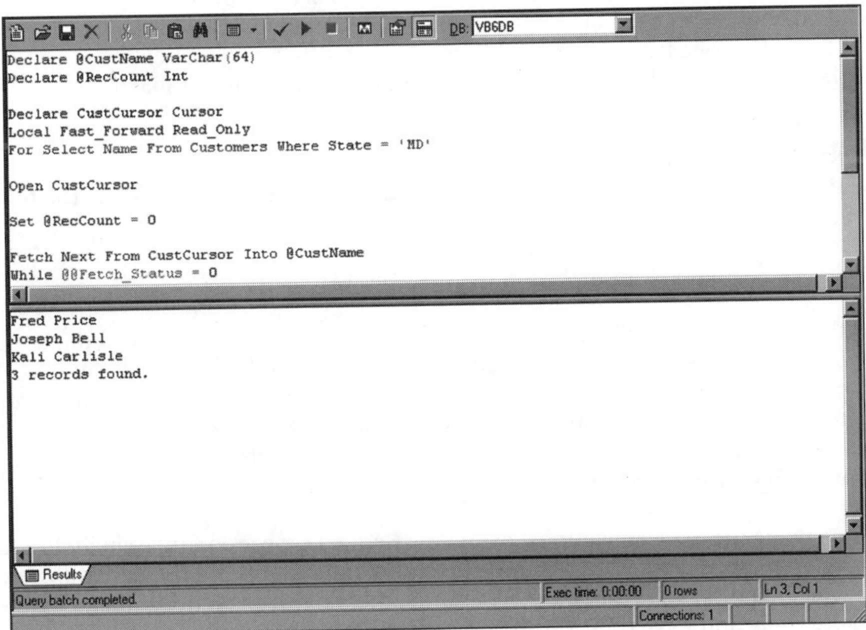

Figure 25-1: Running the sample routine

The routine begins by declaring variables to hold the customer's name and the number of records processed. Then it declares a cursor called `CustCursor` that will be used to access the information in the Customers table. To keep the amount of data to a minimum, I selected only those customers that live in Maryland. I also declare the cursor as local to this routine and choose to make it **Fast_Forward** and **Read_Only** since I'm just going to read the data in a single pass.

Next, I use the **Open** statement to open the cursor and retrieve the information from the database. After setting `@RecCount` to zero, I fetch the information from the first row into `@CustName` and start a **While** loop that will process the rest of the row in the cursor's rowset. For each row, I print the value saved in `@CustName` and use the **Fetch Next** statement to retrieve the next value. This process continues as long as the **Fetch** statement is successful (**@@Fetch_Status** =0).

At the end of the routine, I print the total number of records found, using the **Convert** function to convert the value in `@RecCount` to a string value. Then I **Close** the cursor and **Deallocate** it. This frees all of the resources associated with the cursor.

Processing transactions

Now that you know how to build simple T-SQL programs that can access individual rows in your database, I want to cover the facilities for transaction processing. As you might expect, these facilities parallel those found in ADO. Basically, you mark the beginning of a transaction and then you can either save the changes you made to the database or abort the changes without changing the database.

Begin Transaction

Begin Transaction marks the start of a transaction. This statement has the following syntax:

```
Begin Transaction [<transaction_name>]
```

You don't have to specify a value for `<transaction_name>`, but if you do, it must be a unique name following the standard rules for identifiers, though only the first 32 characters will be used. The names are only used for the outermost level of a set of nested transactions, though you may want to assign a name to any nested transactions as well to clarify which **Begin Transaction** is matched with which **Commit Transaction** or **Rollback Transaction**.

When using nested transactions, each new **Begin Transaction** increments the value in **@@Trancount**. This is important, since only the outer most transaction can commit the changes to the database. Of course, the inner transactions must complete successfully and have their results committed as well, but changes aren't actually posted to the database until the outermost transaction is committed.

Commit Transaction

The **Commit Transaction** statement saves the changes made by a transaction to the database. This statement has the following syntax:

```
Commit Transaction [<transaction_name>]
```

If the `<transaction_name>` parameter is specified, it must match the corresponding value in the **Begin Transaction** statement.

Rollback Transaction

The **Rollback Transaction** statement discards all of the changes made by a transaction to the database. This statement has the following syntax:

```
Rollback Transaction [<transaction_name>]
```

If the <transaction_name> parameter is specified, it must match the corresponding value in the **Begin Transaction** statement.

Other useful statements

There are a few other T-SQL statements that you may find useful when building a stored procedure that don't fit into any of the categories I've discussed so far.

Use

The **Use** statement specifies the database that will become the default database and has the following syntax:

```
Use <database>
```

You can use this statement at the beginning of a stored procedure to ensure that the stored procedure is running in the appropriate database. You can also use the **Use** statement to switch databases in the middle of a stored procedure.

User must exist in order to use Use: In order to switch databases, the person's login must map to a valid user, otherwise an error will occur.

Print

The **Print** statement is used to return a user-defined message to the calling program. The syntax of print is:

```
Print <string_expression>
```

where <string_expression> can be a string of text enclosed by quotes such as 'text', a local variable or function whose data type is either **Char** or **Varchar**, or an expression that evaluates to a **Char** or **Varchar** value, such as **Convert** or the string concatenation operator (+).

Some common uses of the **Print** statement are:

```
Print 'Hello Raymond'
Print Convert(Varchar(20), @@CPU_Busy)
Print 'CPU Busy is ' + Convert(Varchar(20), @@CPU_Busy)
```

Raiserror

Another way to return information to the calling program is to use the **Raiserror** statement.

```
Raiserror (<message>, <severity>, <state> [, <argument_list>])
```

Calling **Raiserror** simply sets a system flag to record that an error occurred. Your stored procedure will continue to run normally. The `<message>` parameter is either a numeric value that refers to a user-defined message in the sysmessages table or a string containing a custom error message. You can choose to allow values to be substituted into `<message>` by specifying a list of values in `<argument_list>` and including C style `printf` formatting commands in `<message>`.

You must also specify a severity code in `<severity>`. This value can range from 0 to 18 for normal users and 19 to 25 for users with the sysadmin fixed server role. Severity levels greater than 19 are considered fatal, and they will immediately terminate the connection to the database. Otherwise the exact meaning of `<severity>` is up to you.

But it's almost fatal: You should use a severity of 19 for non-fatal errors in stored procedures running under the sysadmin fixed server role.

The `<state>` value provides additional information about the particular error. It can range from 1 to 127. This value has no meaning outside the context of the error message.

Add your own errors: You can add errors to the sysmessages table by calling the `sp_addmessage` stored procedure. You may delete a message by calling the `sp_dropmessage` stored procedure.

Which way is right?: In Visual Basic, **RaiseError** is spelled with two E's, while in T-SQL **Raiserror** is spelled with one E.

Go

Technically, **Go** isn't a T-SQL statement, but a command that is used by Query Analyzer and some other query tools to execute the group of T-SQL statements that precede the **Go** command. **Go** must occupy a line by itself in order to be properly recognized.

For instance, the following statements are executed as a single batch:

```
Declare @MDCount Int

Select @MDCount = Count(*)
From Customers
Where State = 'MD'

Declare @SDCount Int

Select @SDCount = Count(*)
From Customers
Where State = 'SD'
```

```
Print 'MD Count = ' + Convert(Varchar(10),@MDCount)
Print 'SD Count = ' + Convert(varchar(10),@SDCount)
```

while these statements are executed as two independent groups:

```
Declare @MDCount Int
Select @MDCount = Count(*)
From Customers
Where State = 'MD'
Print "MD Count = " + Convert(Varchar(10),@MDCount)

Go

Declare @SDCount Int
Select @SDCount = Count(*)
From Customers
Where State = 'SD'
Print 'SD Count = ' + Convert(varchar(10),@SDCount)
```

Finally, these statements will generate an error in the first **Print** statement because the variable `@MDCount` will no longer be in scope.

```
Declare @MDCount Int
Select @MDCount = Count(*)
From Customers
Where State = 'MD'

Go

Declare @SDCount Int
Select @SDCount = Count(*)
From Customers
Where State = 'SD'

Print 'MD Count = ' + Convert(Varchar(10),@MDCount)
Print 'SD Count = ' + convert(varchar(10),@SDCount)
```

Creating and Testing Stored Procedures

While creating and testing a stored procedure isn't very difficult, it is very cumbersome. You have to develop the code using a tool like Query Analyzer, unless you're one of those perfect programmers whose code always runs correctly the first time. Then you have to save the code into the database as part of a **Create Procedure** or **Alter Procedure** statement using either Query Analyzer or Enterprise. Next, you have to build the Visual Basic program to access the stored procedure and verify that it works the way you expect it. Of course it won't, so you may have to revise the code using Query Analyzer and try it over again. Fortunately, Visual Basic includes a sophisticated T-SQL debugger to help you troubleshoot why your stored procedure didn't work as designed.

Creating stored procedures in SQL Server

Stored procedures created by using the **Create Procedure** statement are kept in system tables in your database. The **Create Procedure** statement supplies the name of the stored procedure and the list of parameters associated with it. Following the **As** clause is the list of SQL statements that comprise the stored procedure.

```
Create Procedure <procedure>
[<parameter> <data_type> [= <default>]] ...
As <sql_statement> [<sql_statement>] ...
```

You can use Enterprise Manager to create a stored procedure by following these steps:

1. Expand the icon tree to show the Stored Procedures icon beneath the database where you want to create the stored procedure. Right click on the Stored Procedures icon and select New Stored Procedure to show the Stored Procedure Properties window (see Figure 25-2).

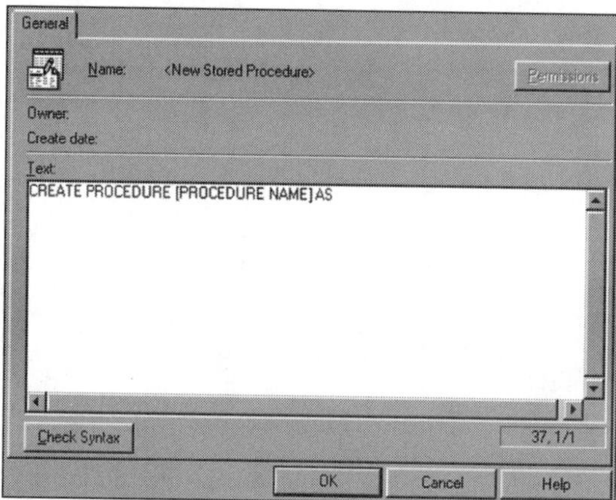

Figure 25-2: Creating a new stored procedure

2. Replace `[PROCEDURE NAME]` with the name you wish to call your stored procedures and include any parameters that belong to the procedure immediately after the name. Then add the body of your stored procedure (see Figure 25-3).
3. Press the Check Syntax button to verify that the syntax is correct. If there's an error, a message box will be displayed containing a short description of the error. Otherwise, a message box saying Syntax check successful! will be displayed.
4. Press OK to save your stored procedure.

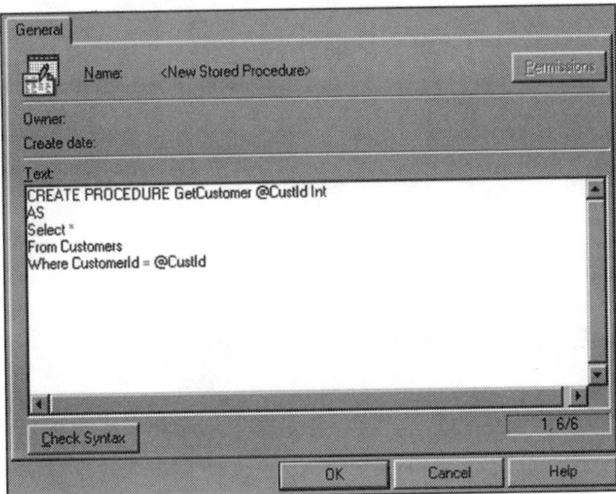

Figure 25-3: Typing your stored procedure into the Properties window

Changes anyone: You can change your stored procedure anytime by right clicking on the stored procedure name in the Details window and choosing Properties from the pop-up menu. The same Properties window you used to create your stored procedure will be displayed, though the **Create Procedure** statement will be changed to **Alter Procedure.**

Another way to do it: You can also execute the same **Create Procedure** statement in Query Analyzer to create a stored procedure.

Rename me twice: If you choose to rename your stored procedure by using the pop-up menu Rename command in Enterprise Manager, you must remember to open the Properties window for the stored procedure and correct its name in the **Alter Procedure** command.

Testing stored procedures in Query Analyzer

Query Analyzer is a general-purpose tool that allows you to run SQL statements interactively. This also includes stored procedures. There are two ways to test your procedure. First you can use the T-SQL debugger to your stored procedure. Second, you can test the block of code standalone Query Analyzer. This involves running the individual statements directly in Query Analyzer and verifying that they do what you want them to. Then you can create the stored procedure and call it using Query Analyzer.

For example, the stored procedure I just wrote can easily be run in Query Analyzer by typing its name followed by a CustomerId value (see Figure 25-4). This is a good way to make sure that you are getting the results you want before you build a Visual Basic program to use it.

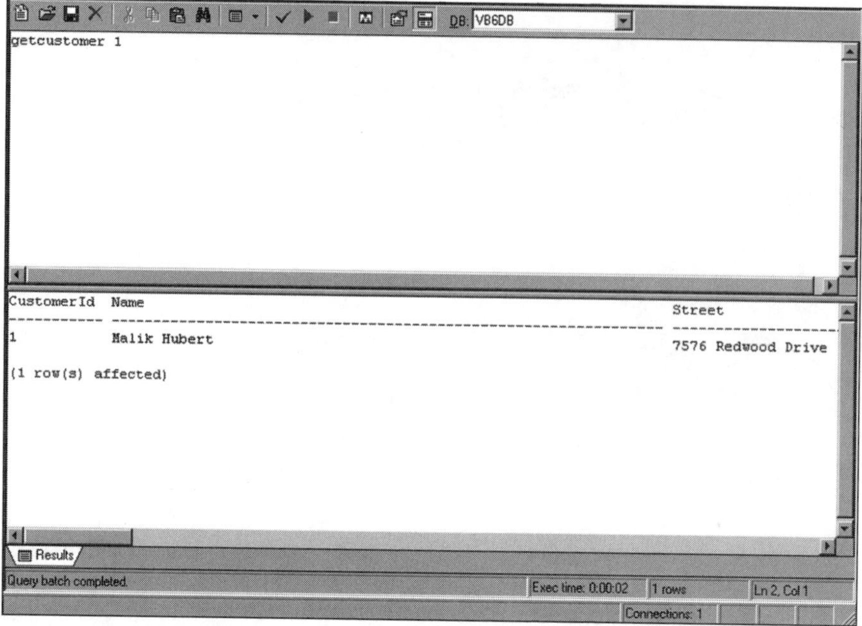

Figure 25-4: Running the stored procedure in Query Analyzer

But VB's better: Remember that Visual Basic includes a comprehensive stored procedure debugger, called the T-SQL Debugger. You can set breakpoints, examine variables and single step through the code. Refer to Chapter 13, "Using Commands and Stored Procedures," for details about how to use this powerful tool.

Thoughts on Stored Procedures in SQL Server

Stored procedures are a powerful tool in SQL Server that can make a big difference in how your application runs. They also are a way to isolate your application from the underlying database system, since you could create a series of stored procedures for each database management system you use.

However, in SQL Server, stored procedures to encapsulate simple SQL statements aren't as critical as they are in other database management systems. SQL Server 7 will remember the SQL statements you have used recently and reuse the compiled code if the query is the same. This makes parameterized queries nearly as efficient as stored procedures and somewhat easier to use.

Summary

In this chapter you learned:

- how stored procedures can improve performance, increase convenience and provide security.
- about the features of Transact-SQL.
- about the statements available in Transact-SQL that help you write stored procedures.
- how to use cursors in Transact-SQL.
- how to process transactions in Transact-SQL.
- hot to create and test stored procedures using Enterprise Manager and Query Analyzer.

✦ ✦ ✦

PART

VII

Oracle 8*i*

Oracle8*i* is one of the most widely used databases in the marketplace today. It offers high performance and is available for many different hardware platforms. In this Part, I'm going to discuss the key features of Oracle8*i*, including its architecture, the data types available for Visual Basic programmers, and an overview of Oracle8*i* security. I'll also cover how to use SQL*Plus, Enterprise Manager, and the DBA studio to create tables, index, and set security in your database. Finally, I'll show you how to create stored procedures using the PL/SQL language and test them using SQL*Plus.

✦ ✦ ✦ ✦

In This Part

✦ ✦ ✦ ✦

CHAPTER 26

Overview of Oracle8i

In this chapter, I'll introduce you to Oracle8*i*. I'll cover the key facilities included with the product, its architecture, and how security works. Then I'll cover how to use Visual Basic and ADO 2.5 with Oracle8*i*, including how to build a connection string and how Oracle's data types map into Visual Basic.

✦ ✦ ✦ ✦

In This Chapter

Introducing Oracle8*i* editions and utilities

Understanding the Database architecture

Explaining the Database data types

Connecting to Oracle8*i* with ADO

Reviewing the Security model

✦ ✦ ✦ ✦

Overview

Oracle8*i* is the most widely used relational database management system (RDBMS) in the world. It's well known for its high performance and stability. It runs on most computer systems, including most Unix variants such as Sun's Solaris, Hewlett-Packard's HP-UX, IBM's AIX and OS/390 (MVS/ESA/XA), and even Linux. Of course it will also run on Microsoft Windows 2000/NT Server operating systems.

Oracle8*i* includes these key features:

- High performance
- Integrated Internet capabilities
- High availability with automated standby database
- Extensive Java and XML support
- Support for OLE DB and ODBC
- Support for data warehousing and Very Large Databases (VLDB)
- Integration with Windows 2000 services and tools

Oracle8*i* editions

Oracle8*i* comes in four editions: Lite, Personal, Standard, and Enterprise. Since the same core database engine architecture is used for all of these editions, compatibility is assured throughout the product line.

The Lite Edition

Oracle8*i* Lite is targeted at environments where the smallest possible database system is needed, like mobile laptop computers, handheld computers, and information appliances. It includes built-in replication to Oracle8*i* Standard Edition and Oracle8*i* Enterprise Edition to facilitate easy exchange of information. While some features of the larger versions of Oracle8*i* are missing, you can run Oracle8*i* Lite Edition with as little as one megabyte of memory and five megabytes of disk space.

The Personal Edition

Oracle8*i* Personal Edition supplies a single user solution that is targeted at developers who want to develop and test their programs in a standalone situation and then deploy them against a Standard Edition server or an Enterprise Edition server. You can also use this Edition in situations where your application supports only a single user on a single computer.

You can run Oracle8*i* Personal Edition on Windows 98, Windows 2000, and Windows NT. It includes all of the same features and options found on Oracle8*i* Enterprise Edition, including Advanced Queuing and Oracle Partitioning. Note that some features may rely on facilities that aren't present in Windows 98.

Freebie copy of Oracle8*i* (at least for 30 days): You can download a demo version of the Personal Edition from Oracle's Web site at `technet.oracle.com`. You will be required to register before you can access this site, but there are no charges for registering. This Web site also has a wealth of information that you will find useful when working with Oracle databases.

The Standard Edition

Oracle8*i* Standard Edition includes all of the tools necessary to build robust multiuser applications. It represents an affordable alternative to the Enterprise Edition when you don't require all of the advanced features. Some of the key features of the Standard Edition include:

- ✦ **Extensive Java support**. While not important to most Visual Basic programmers, this feature is useful when developing multi-platform applications.
- ✦ **Windows specific support**. Includes native ODBC and OLE DB drivers, support for Microsoft Transaction Server, App Wizard for Visual Studio, and OLE Objects for Oracle.

The Enterprise Edition

Oracle8*i* Enterprise Edition is Oracle's high-end database management system. It is targeted at applications that experience high volumes of transactions and that require very high levels of availability. Some of the key features in the Enterprise Edition include:

✦ **Transparent Application Failover/Automated Standby Database**—a key tool for providing high availability. It allows you to have standby database server that is ready to take over in case of a database or application failure.

✦ **Oracle Parallel Server**—a high performance feature that allows you to divide your database into multiple chunks, where each chunk exists on a separate physical computer. This allows for higher performance, since multiple computers are actively processing data. The database servers are clustered together to form a single view of the system to make it easy to use.

✦ **Oracle Partitioning**—a feature that allows you to break large tables into smaller, individually-managed tables, which can be spread across multiple servers using Oracle Parallel Server. This feature is extremely useful when managing data warehouses.

✦ **Internet File System**—a feature that makes an Oracle8*i* database appear as a shared network drive. It supports a wide variety of standard protocols, including HTML, FTP, and IMAP4, which allows a large number of users to store and retrieve data using a platform that offers better reliability than a normal networked disk drive.

✦ **Oracle Time Series and Oracle Spatial**—tools that are useful when building a data warehouse. Oracle Time Series allows you to stored time stamped data efficiently in an Oracle database, while Oracle Spatial allows you to analyze data such as the proximity of a customer to a store location.

The best things in database aren't free: Some of the features available in the Enterprise Edition are extra cost items. Check the Oracle Web site for more information about which items aren't standard and how much they cost.

Oracle8*i* utilities

Oracle8*i* has the following utilities that you will use while developing your applications: SQL*Plus, Enterprise Manager, SVRMGR, PL/SQL, Net8, and Oracle Management Server. The key utility is called SQL*Plus and is used for a number of different tasks, from creating tables to testing stored procedures. Enterprise Manager is a tool similar to SQL Server's Enterprise Manager and is used to help you design databases and perform other system management-related functions.

SQL*Plus

SQL*Plus is a general-purpose query tool like Microsoft's Query Analyzer. This tool allows you to enter SQL statements and execute them. There are two versions of this tool. One operates in a DOS window, while the other runs in its own window (see Figure 26-1). Both versions are command-driven (i.e., you type commands rather than selecting menu items and/or pressing buttons).

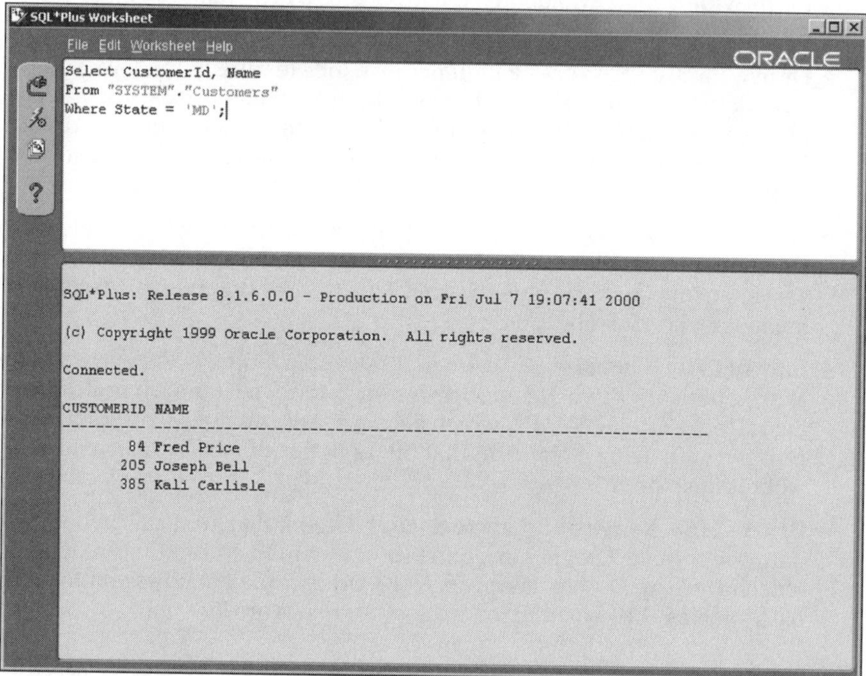

Figure 26-1: Running SQL*Plus Worksheet in a window.

Enterprise Manager

The Enterprise Manager utility assists you with functions typically performed by a database administrator, such as creating databases, creating users, and monitoring the activity of your databases (see Figure 26-2). It also includes a number of tools, such as SQL*Plus Worksheet, that allows you to enter, edit, and run SQL commands in a graphical environment, as well as DBA Studio, which can help you design your databases.

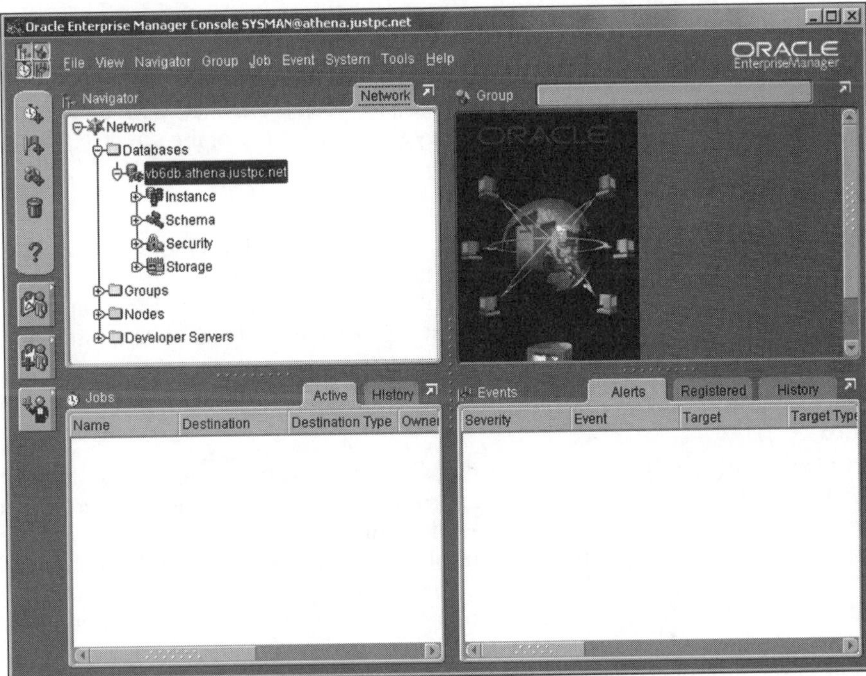

Figure 26-2: Running Enterprise Manager.

SVRMGR

The SVRMGR utility allows you to control the databases running on your server (see Figure 26-3). You can use this tool to start and stop your database, as well as run other SQL commands. Like SQL*Plus, it has both windowed and DOS-based versions.

```
Command Prompt - svrmgrl

C:\>svrmgrl

Oracle Server Manager Release 3.1.6.0.0 - Production

Copyright (c) 1997, 1999, Oracle Corporation.  All Rights Reserved.

Oracle8i Enterprise Edition Release 8.1.6.0.0 - Production
With the Partitioning option
JServer Release 8.1.6.0.0 - Production

SVRMGR> connect internal
Connected.
SVRMGR> shutdown
Database closed.
Database dismounted.
ORACLE instance shut down.
SVRMGR> _
```

Figure 26-3: Running SVRMGR in a command prompt.

Bigger is better: The normal DOS window displays only 25 lines. You can increase the number of lines displayed to 43 or 50 by right clicking on the icon in the upper-left corner of the window and choosing Properties and then the Screen tab. You can also enable the scrollbars to display even more lines. Both options make it easier to see your results before they scroll off the top of the screen.

PL/SQL

PL/SQL is Oracle's implementation of the SQL standard. It includes a number of extensions that make it a very powerful language for creating stored procedures. As you might expect, PL/SQL is not compatible with T-SQL in many areas, such as procedural statements and data definition statements. For the most part, statements like **Select** and **Update** will work the same as they do in other database systems.

Net8

Net8 isn't really a utility as much as it is a critical part of the network communications required to operate Oracle8*i*. It permits you to define various external communications protocols for different types of clients and translate them into an internal database protocol that is independent of the clients. On your database server, Net8 is also used to handle database-to-database communications for things like remote database access and replication. A copy of Net8 also runs on your local computer. The OLE DB provider passes your database requests to Net8, which in turn routes them to the appropriate database server.

By any other name: Net8 was known as SQL*Net in previous versions of the Oracle database server.

Oracle Management Server

Oracle Management Server is a utility process that allows you to manage the various components in an Oracle8*i* database system. It runs as its own process and maintains its own separate security system. It is tightly integrated with Enterprise Manager and provides facilities that allow Enterprise Manager to manage multiple database instances.

Understanding the Database Architecture

Like SQL Server, Oracle8*i* uses a true client/server architecture. This means that the database server runs in a different address space from the client program, and the client and server can be run on different computers. Unlike SQL Server, Oracle8*i* can run on a variety of hardware platforms. This means that some of the functions implemented on Windows will look and act a little differently than applications designed for non-Windows operating systems. However, the core Oracle8*i* database architecture is the same no matter which operating system is hosting the database server.

Key database objects

Oracle8*i* consists of one or more databases on the database server. Each database is known as an *instance*. Unlike SQL Server, which maintains a single database server with multiple databases beneath it, each Oracle8*i* database server is a unique instance and requires an independent software installation.

Tablespaces

Each database instance contains a series of objects known as *tablespaces*, which hold the data for your database. Each tablespace contains one or more physical files that are used to hold a collection of tables and indexes. One tablespace is reserved for system information, while other tablespaces are used to hold application data.

A table (or table partition if you partition the tables) can't span more than one tablespace. This means that there must be sufficient space in the tablespace for all of the tables in the tablespace. If you run out of disk space, you can either increase the space available in the existing physical files or add additional physical files to the tablespace.

Tables

By now, you are familiar with tables, so I won't go into all of the details about rows and columns, but there are a few unique aspects to Oracle's implementation. Each row in the database has a unique value known as a *rowid*. This value is used to locate the row in the database.

Tables that are often accessed together can be grouped together to share the same physical storage. This process physically places the rows close together for tables that are joined together using **Select** statements. This arrangement can make a big difference in performance, because when the data to be joined is in close proximity, fewer I/Os are required. This technique is known as *clustering*.

Schemas

The *schema* represents a view of the information in your database. It represents a set of tables and other database objects that can be accessed by a user. As such, a schema represents a good way to secure database objects. Only the database administrator is permitted to see the database objects in every schema in the database.

It is important to note that schemas are logical views of the database and are in no way coupled to tablespaces, unless of course the database administrator chooses to assign all of the tables for a particular schema to a particular tablespace.

Sequences

A *sequence* is an object that generates numbers according to a specified order. This allows you to generate unique values for things like counters and timestamps to guarantee that each row added to a table has a unique value.

Stored Procedures, functions, and packages

Recall that *stored procedures* are pre-compiled programs written in PL/SQL that are compiled and saved in the database server for quick execution. You have your choice of writing procedures that don't return a value or *functions* that return a single value. Stored procedures can also return a recordset containing a collection of rows selected from a table or a view.

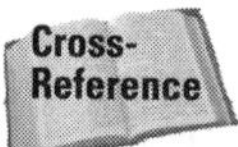

See Chapter 25, "Stored Procedures," for a detailed discussion of stored procedures.

A *package* is a way to group similar procedures, functions, and variables into a single Oracle8*i* object. This has two primary advantages: first, that because all of the objects are compiled into a single entity, calls between functions and procedures are faster, since there is no need to search for and load external routines; and second, that managing one package is easier than managing each of the individual routines.

Triggers

Triggers are one way you can enforce referential integrity. Each time you execute a **Delete**, **Insert**, or **Update** statement, a stored procedure will be called that can check the changes to ensure that they are being made properly. For instance, assume that you have two tables with a one-to-many relationship. You can create a trigger that will delete all of the associated rows in one table when you delete a record in the other table.

In the key of SQL: You can also use foreign keys to enforce referential integrity.

Synonyms

Synonyms are basically just another name for a database object. Suppose you want to change the name of a table, but you're not certain that you've updated all of the applications that use the old name. You can create a synonym for the table using the old table's name.

Memory architecture

One of the keys to Oracle's performance is its memory architecture. The key to database performance is being able to avoid disk I/O by proper buffering of information in memory.

A gig here and a gig there makes for good performance: One thing I can't stress enough is that you need lots of memory to run a database server. A perfect relational database would have enough memory to hold everything it stores on disk. In most cases, this isn't possible because you have too much data on disk – but it's nice to dream.

System Global Area

Each instance of an Oracle database has a block of memory called the System Global Area (SGA), which is used to hold shared resources. All users have access to this area. It is used for maintaining various types of buffers, including the library cache where the SQL cursors are maintained, and the data dictionary cache, where the structures that describe the objects in the database are kept. This information is extracted from system tables, including:

- **USER_OBJECTS**—contains information about the various objects in the database, plus a reference to other tables that contain more detailed information about a specific type of object.
- **USER_TABLES**—contains the definitions of the tables in the database.
- **USER_TAB_COLUMNS**—contains the definitions for the columns in the table.
- **USER_SOURCE**—contains the source code for stored procedures.
- **USER_SEQUENCES**—contains the definitions of the sequences in your database.
- **USER_INDEXES**—contains information about the indexes associated with each table.

Program Global Area

The Program Global Area (PGA) maintains information on the active processes running in the database. These processes either perform work on behalf of a client application or perform background processing and monitoring of the database server. For instance, when a client application requests a recordset, a server process will retrieve the necessary rows (hopefully from the SGA, otherwise from disk) and return them to the client. A background process, on the other hand, might collect performance statistics, which can be analyzed to determine bottlenecks.

Network architecture

While SQL Server is managed through a single server process, Oracle8*i* relies on a number of different server applications. Each database instance has its own server process, while there is another server application devoted to networking. The networking process uses a piece of software known as Net8 (described earlier in this chapter). Net8's function is to receive requests from client applications and pass them on to the appropriate database server for processing. It is also responsible for handling communications between the various database instances and for facilitating communications between various database instances on different computer systems.

Oracle8*i* data types

Oracle8*i* supports a wide variety of data types, as shown in Table 26-1.

Table 26-1
Oracle8*i* Data Types

Oracle8i Data Type	*Visual Basic Data Type*	*Comments*
`Bfile`	`Byte Array`	Contains a binary large object up to 4 gigabytes in length.
`Blob`	`Byte Array`	Contains a binary large object that can be up to 4 gigabytes in length.
`Char`	`String`	Since `Char` fields always have a fixed length, the length of the `String` value will be the same as the length of the field. A `Char` field may contain up to 2,000 characters.
`Clob`	`String`	A character-oriented large object up to 4 gigabytes in length.
`Date`	`Date`	A date and time value that is more accurate than the `Date` data type. The value will be rounded as needed.
`Decimal`	`Currency`	Contains a packed decimal number with up to 38 digits of precision.
`Float`	`Single, Double`	Uses the same storage format as `Number`.

Oracle8i Data Type	Visual Basic Data Type	Comments
`Long`	`String`	A character string whose maximum length can be up to 2 gigabytes.
`Long Raw`	`Byte Array`	A binary string whose maximum length can be up to 2 gigabytes.
`Nchar`	`String`	Contains a fixed-length Unicode string with up to 2,000 characters.
`Nclob`	`String`	A character-oriented large object containing Unicode characters.
`Number`	`Currency`	Contains a packed decimal number with up to 38 digits of precision.
`Nvarchar2`	`String`	Contains a variable length Unicode string with up to 4,000 characters.
`Raw`	`String`	A binary string up to 2,000 bytes long.
`Rowid`	`String`	The internal format is automatically converted to a `String` value.
`Varchar2`	`String`	Contains a variable length `String` with a maximum length of 4,000 characters.

Connecting to Oracle8*i*

Building an ADO connection string for an Oracle8*i* database involves specifying values for the provider and the database, as shown below:

```
Provider=MSDAORA.1; Data source=vb6db.Athena.justpc.net
```

You can also include the `User ID=` and `Password=` keywords if you want to add that information as part of the connection string, or you can supply them as arguments to the `Open` method.

You can also configure the Oracle OLE DB provider via the Data Link Properties window. The first step is to select the Microsoft OLE DB Provider for Oracle (see Figure 26-4). After pressing the Next button, you can enter the name of your Oracle database server and optionally specify your user name and password (see Figure 26-5). You can verify that the information you entered was correct by pressing the Test Connection button.

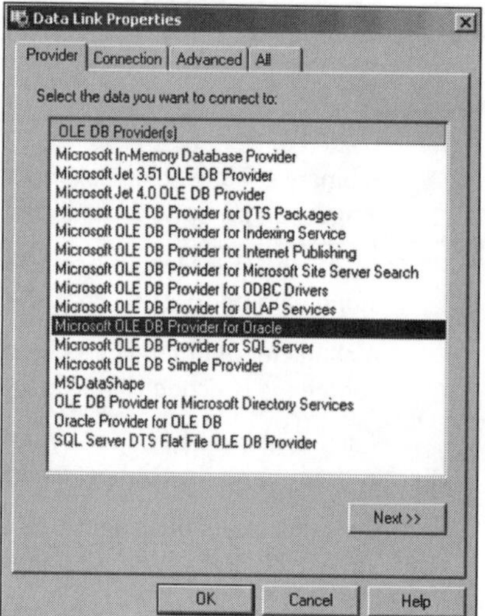

Figure 26-4: Choosing the Oracle provider.

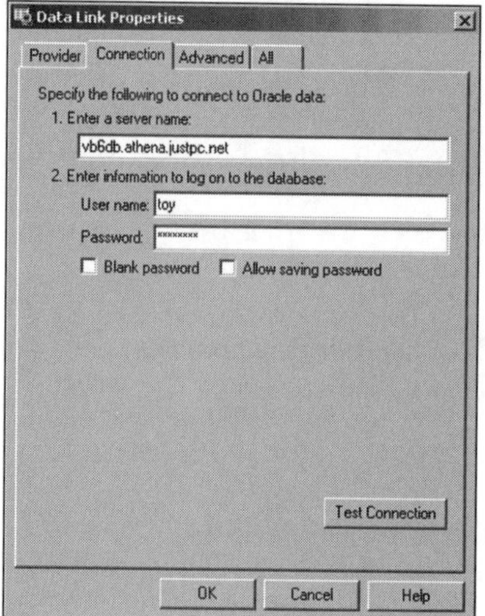

Figure 26-5: Specifying values for the key connection properties.

There's always a choice: Oracle also has a provider for OLE DB that you may wish to try, and there are third party OLE DB providers that may outperform both Microsoft's and Oracle's, though at a considerable cost in time and money.

Note

A provider is only provider: The Oracle provider supplied by Microsoft only translates the calls from your Visual Basic program into something that the Oracle8*i* client software on your computer will understand. You must install a copy of Net8 on your client computer for any program to communicate with an Oracle8*i* database.

Oracle8*i* Security

In order to access an Oracle8*i* database, you must be properly authenticated and authorized. Authentication ensures that the user name and password associated with an individual is valid before access is granted to the database server. Once the users have been granted access to the server, everything that the users can perform is based on the permissions they have been authorized.

Authentication

In order to access an Oracle database, every user must have a valid user ID and a valid password. This information is usually kept in the database, though Oracle does include hooks to use an external directory, such as the Windows 2000 Active Directory or Kerberos.

Authorization

Inside Oracle8, you must be granted the privilege to access a particular database object or command. In fact, without the proper privileges, you can't even connect to the database, even if you had a valid user ID and password. Privileges are managed using the **Grant** and **Revoke** SQL statements, or by using the Enterprise Manager utility's GUI interface. The two types of privileges, object privileges and system privileges, are discussed next. Object privileges dictate the user's access to a specific database object, while system privileges determine the user's ability to execute specific Oracle and SQL statements.

Object privileges

Object privileges specify which commands can be used against specific database objects. Depending on the object, you apply the privileges shown in Table 26-3. The syntax for the **Grant** statement to apply object privileges looks like this:

```
Grant <privileges> On <object> To <users> [With Grant Option]
```

where `<privileges>` contains a list of one or more privileges separated by commas selected from Table 26-2; `<object>` specifies the database object that the privileges are associated with;and `<users>` is a list of one or more user names separated by commas that will receive the privileges or the keyword **Public** indicating that any database user may have the privilege. The **With Grant Option** clause allows the user receiving the privilege to pass it along to other users by using the **Grant** statement.

With Grant Option security can really be compromised: Because you passed on the ability to control security to another user, they can pass it on to others. Thus, people that you may not want to have access to the object may get access from someone else. While using the **With Grant Option** is necessary to implement a distributed security management system, you must use it with care to ensure that only authorized users can access your database.

Table 26-2
Object Privileges

Statement	*Associated Privileges*
Alter	Tables, Sequences, Snapshots
Delete	Tables, Views
Execute	Procedures, Functions, Packages, Libraries, Types
Index	Tables
Insert	Tables, Views
Read	Directories
References	Tables
Select	Tables, Views, Sequences, Snapshots
Update	Tables, Views, Snapshots

For example, if you wanted to allow Jill to retrieve and update information in the Customers table, but not insert or delete rows, you would use this **Grant** statement:

```
Grant Select, Update On Customers To Jill
```

System privileges

System privileges control the ability to execute specific Oracle and SQL statements. Like object privileges, system privileges are based on the concept of allowing a user to use a specific command. Unlike object privileges, system privileges allow you to use that command on any object or against the database itself (see Table 26-4). Note that some of the privileges describe general capabilities within the database server, and not just the actual commands used to perform a task. These are also listed in Table 26-4.

```
Grant <privileges> To <user> [With Admin Option]
```

where `<privileges>` is a list of one or more system privileges, separated by commas, chosen from Table 26-3, and `<user>` is a list of one or more user names separated by commas.

The **With Admin Option** clause allows the user to pass the privilege to another user.

Table 26-3
System Privileges

Command	*Associated Privileges*
Alter	Any Cluster, Any Index, Any Procedure, Any Role, Any Sequence, Any Shapshot, Any Table, Any Trigger, Any Type, Database, Profile, Resource Cost, Rollback Segment, Session, System, Tablespace, User
Analyze	Any
Audit	Any, System
Backup	Any Table
Become	User
Comment	Any Table
Create	Any Cluster, Any Directory, Any Index, Any Library, Any Procedure, Any Sequence, Any Snapshot, Any Synonym, Any Table, Any Trigger, Any Type, Any View, Cluster, Database Link, Directory, Library, Procedure, Profile, Public Database Link, Public Synonym, Role, Rollback Segment, Session, Sequence, Snapshot, Synonym, Table, Tablespace, Trigger, Type, User, View
Delete	Any Table
Drop	Any Cluster, Any Directory, Any Index, Any Library, Any Procedure, Any Role, Any Sequence, Any Snapshot, Any Synonym, Any Table, Any Trigger, Any Type, Any View, Library, Profile, Public Database Link, Public Synonym, Rollback Segment, Tablespace, User
Execute	Any Procedure, Any Type
Force	Any Transaction, Transaction
Grant	Any Privilege, Any Role
Insert	Any Table
Lock	Any Table
Select	Any Sequence, Any Table
Update	Any Table
Non-command based privileges	Manage Tablespace, Readup, Restricted Session, Unlimited Tablespace, Writedown, Writeup

Roles

Managing permissions for individual users can be overwhelming on a database system with a large number of users. Thus, Oracle8*i* also uses the concept of roles to simplify database administration. A *role* represents a collection of privileges that can be assigned to a user. If you assign a role to a user, the user inherits all of the privileges in the role. Likewise, if you add a privilege to an existing role, all of the users that are assigned that role will automatically receive the new privilege.

When granting privileges to a role, you use the same **Grant** statement that you would use for an object privilege. You simply specify the name of the role in place of the user. For instance, you would use the following statement to grant the **Select** privilege to the Clerks role:

```
Grant Select To Clerks
```

When granting a role to a user, you use the form of the **Grant** statement used to associate system privileges to a user. In this case, the role is substituted for a system privilege. The following statement shows how to grant the Clerks role to the user Samantha. When executed after the previous **Grant** statement, Samantha will be able to use the **Select** statement.

```
Grant Clerks To Samantha
```

Thoughts on Oracle8*i*

Oracle8*i* is a high-performance database that runs on many different hardware and software platforms. It is also more difficult to install and maintain than SQL Server. If you need the biggest, fastest database management system in existence today, Oracle8*i* should be at the top of your list, since it runs on the biggest computer systems available. Companies like Amazon.com and eBay rely on Oracle database servers.

However, this power comes at a cost. You really need an experienced Oracle DBA to maintain your database. Unlike SQL Server, which contains a large number of wizards to perform routine tasks, Oracle8*i* doesn't. If you're not very familiar with Oracle databases in general, you need someone to help you set up the various processes and ensure that they work properly.

The other downside to Oracle8*i* is its cost. Oracle knows that Oracle8*i* is the highest performance database on the market today and charges accordingly. While it is hard to argue about the value of Oracle8*i*, it is important to note that solutions from other database vendors may be less expensive. Of course, if your application is large enough, then your only option may be Oracle, no matter how much the competition charges for their software.

I sometimes look at this issue from a mainframer's perspective. In the mainframe world, operating system software, including database management systems, are very complex products that are highly adjustable. You can't simply install a package and begin using it. It usually takes anywhere from a few days to a few months to install a piece of software. Some of this time is spent selecting options and setting various parameters in order to make the software work, while the rest of the time is spent ensuring that you have the right options set.

A person that is experienced in the software package can set the options much more quickly than a person learning the software. But in the long run, having lots of options to select and parameters to set allows an organization to make the software really fly by, eliminating the options not needed and tweaking the other settings so that each function performed by the database gets the resources it needs.

Summary

In this chapter you learned:

- about the Oracle8*i* database server and the various editions that are available.
- about the major utilities and key components.
- about the Oracle8*i* database architecture.
- about the data types available in Oracle8*i* and how they map into Visual Basic data types.
- how to connect to an Oracle8*i* database with ADO.
- about Oracle8*i* security.

✦ ✦ ✦

C H A P T E R

27

Creating Database Objects with Oracle8i

✦ ✦ ✦ ✦

In This Chapter

Introducing Oracle8*i* SQL*Plus

Introducing Oracle8*i* Enterprise Manager

Constructing tablespaces, tables, and indexes

Managing security

Creating roles and users

✦ ✦ ✦ ✦

In this chapter, I'm going to show you how to use the two most common utilities in Oracle8***i***, SQL*Plus and Enterprise Manager, to access your database. Then I'll talk about how to create tables and indexes using Enterprise Manager. Finally, I'll cover how to manage your security using Enterprise Manager.

Introducing SQL*Plus

SQL*Plus comes in two flavors: a command-line driven utility that runs under DOS and a window-oriented utility that provides a pane where you can enter SQL statements and a pane to show the results. Both tools accept the same set of SQL statements and will return the same results. The only difference between the two is how the data is presented to the user. I'll use the command-line variety in this section.

Command-Line SQL*Plus

The command-line version of SQL*Plus is started from a command prompt by entering `SQLPLUS`. You can enter commands directly from the keyboard or enter them into a file and execute the entire file. The results of the commands will be displayed immediately following the command you enter.

Note

DOS and commands: In trying to eradicate the concept of DOS from the user's mind, Microsoft engineers cleverly renamed the old DOS Window to Command Prompt in Windows 2000; however, it's the same old command interpreter you've come to love and hate.

Connecting to your database with SQL*Plus

These parameters include the user name, the password, and the database you plan to use. If you don't supply all of the information, you will be prompted for it. The format you must use is shown below:

```
<username>[/<password>][@<connectstring>]
```

where <username> is a valid user name for the database you wish to access, <password> is the password associated with the user name, and <connectstring> contains the name of the database you wish to access.

For example, if you want to have a user name of `toy` and `vb6db.athena.justpc.net` as the name of the database you wish to access, you can start SQL*Plus using the following command:

```
SQLPLUS toy@vb6db.athena.justpc.net
```

SQL*Plus will prompt you for the password, and assuming that you entered it correctly, you could be prompted with an `SQLPLUS>` prompt (see Figure 27-1).

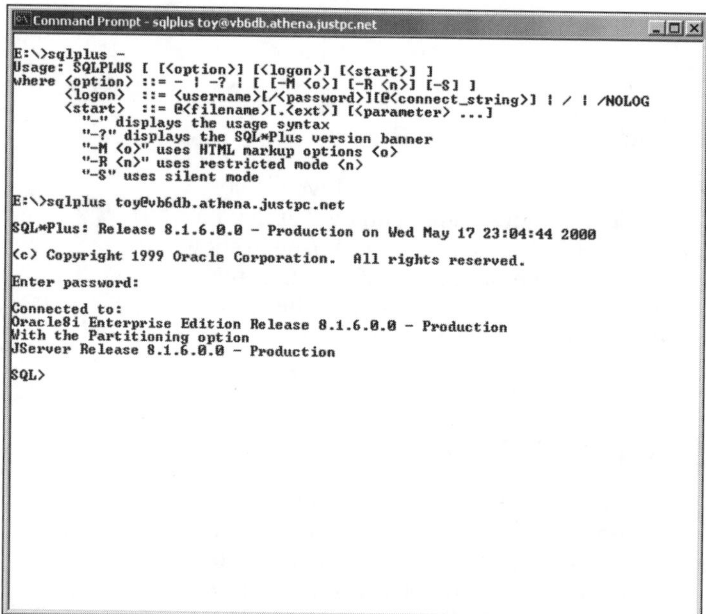

Figure 27-1: Logging onto a database with SQL*Plus.

There are other options also: SQL*Plus supports several other options on the command line. See *Oracle8i DBA Bible* by Jonathan Gennick, and published by IDG Books, for more information.

It's not very hidden: While you can enter your password on the command line, I don't recommend it. In Windows 2000, someone can simply press the up arrow until they see the command you executed to start SQL*Plus, even inside the SQL*Plus program. After quitting SQL*Plus, this information will remain in the command history of both Windows 2000/NT and Windows 98/95 systems with DOSKEY running. If it was the last command entered, it will be visible by simply hitting the F3 key.

Entering commands

Once SQL*Plus has been started, an `SQL>` prompt will be displayed. You can enter any command or SQL statement at the prompt. If the syntax is correct, the command or SQL statement will be immediately executed and the results displayed below what you typed.

If the display is too wide, it will automatically be wrapped to the next line. Note that the lines displayed in the DOS window will automatically scroll so that the most recent information is displayed. This can cause a problem if you are executing a **Select** statement, which returns a large number of rows. In this case, you should either use SQL*Plus Window or increase the screen buffer size under the DOS window's property settings.

Confusing, isn't it?: Commands and SQL statements are treated differently in SQL*Plus. Commands occupy only a single line, while SQL statements may occupy multiple lines. To indicate the end of an SQL statement, you must type a semicolon (;). Typing a semicolon at the end of a command will generate an error message. Also, if you don't supply sufficient information for a command, you may be prompted for the additional information, or you may receive a message describing how to use the command.

Useful commands

Table 27-1 lists some of the more useful commands you will find in SQL*Plus. While this is not a complete list, it should give you a feel for the types of commands available. You can use the **Help Index** command to find a complete list of the commands that are available.

Table 27-1
Useful Commands in SQL*Plus

Command	*Description*
Clear SQL	Clears the contents of the SQL buffer.
Connect	Logons to a different database server or the same database server as a different user.
Define _Editor	Specifies the name of your favorite editor program that will be run when you use the Edit command.
Describe	Provides a detailed description of a database object, such as a table or stored procedure.
Edit	Edits the contents of the SQL buffer in your favorite editor.
Get	Loads the contents of a file into the SQL buffer.
Help	Provides basic help on SQL*Plus commands.
Host	Runs the specified DOS command and returns to SQL*Plus.
List	Lists the statements in the SQL buffer.
Quit	Exits SQL*Plus and returns to DOS.
Run	Lists the statements in the SQL buffer and executes them.
Save	Saves the SQL buffer to a disk file.
Set Linesize	Determines the width of the line.
Set Newpage	Determines the number of lines displayed between pages.
Set Pagesize	Determines the number of lines in a page.
Set Pause	When On, means that the output will be displayed in pages.
Set Serveroutput	When On, means that output will be directed to the console when using the DBMS_OUTPUT package.
Spool	Directs output to an external file or to the system printer.
Start	Runs the SQL statements in a disk file.

One of the most useful commands in SQL*Plus is the **Describe** command. This allows you to quickly see the structure of a table or the statements in a stored procedure. I find this helpful if I don't have a piece of paper handy containing columns and tables in a database.

After running an SQL statement, it is stored in the SQL buffer. You can list the contents of this buffer, edit the statement, or run the statement over again using the commands shown in Table 27-1. The contents remain in the SQL buffer until another SQL statement is entered or the buffer is explicitly cleared using the **Clear SQL** command. You can list the contents of the SQL buffer with the **List** command. The **Save** and **Get** commands will write a copy of the buffer to a disk file and load it back again, respectively. Use the **Run** command to execute the statements in the SQL buffer.

The **Edit** command copies the SQL buffer to a file called `afiedt.buf` and loads it into uses whatever editor you specify in the **Define _Editor** command. You then edit your statements, save them and close the editor to return to SQL*Plus. By default on a Windows platform, you'll use `Notepad`. You could also use the **Save** command to save the SQL buffer into a file and then use the **Host** command to perform the same function. Note that your SQL*Plus session is suspended until the editor or host command is complete.

SQL*Plus contains commands that can make working with your SQL statements easier. The first thing you should do if you are testing **Select** statements is to use the **Set Pause On** command. This command will automatically break your output into pages and pause the output at the end of each page. The number of lines in each page is controlled by the **Set Pagesize** command. You can also control the number of lines displayed between page breaks by using the **Set Newpage** command.

If you choose, you can direct the output of the SQL statements to a disk file or a printer by using the **Spool** command. To redirect your output to a file, specify **Spool** followed by the name of the disk file. To redirect your output to the printer, issue the **Spool Out** command. Then you can issue any collection of SQL statements or commands that generate output. When you're finished, issue the **Spool Off** statement to close the output file or send your output to the printer.

Make it fit: Use the **Set Pagesize, Set Newpage,** and **Set Linesize** commands to adjust the characteristics of your printer.

Introducing Enterprise Manager

Enterprise Manager is a comprehensive tool designed to help you manage your database using graphical tools. It provides a central point from which you can manage all of your Oracle8*i* database servers, even if they are on multiple physical computers. It communicates with the Oracle Management Server, which in turn communicates with the database servers that you wish to access. While not as easy to use as SQL Server's Enterprise Manager, Oracle8*i* Enterprise Manager is a big improvement over issuing SQL statements in SQL*Plus to perform common tasks such as creating tasks and users.

The Enterprise Manager console

Rather than combine all of the tools into a single application, Enterprise Manager consists of the Enterprise Manager console, plus a number of other utilities that can be launched from the console or in a stand-alone fashion. Some of the more important tools include:

- **SQL*Plus Worksheet** — a graphical version of SQL*Plus.
- **DBA Studio** — provides a graphical way to create and maintain your database structures.
- **Enterprise Security Manager** — simplifies the processes needed to create users and map them onto the proper roles.
- **Net8 Assistant** — makes it easy to configure your communications network.

There's no substitute for page count: If you are working with a database like Oracle8*i* with lots of tools and utilities, you should invest in a good reference. I suggest the Oracle8*i* DBA Bible by Jonathan Gennick published by IDG Books.

Logging onto the Enterprise Manager console

When you initially start the Enterprise Manager console (choose Start ⇨ Oracle – OraHome81 ⇨ Enterprise Manager ⇨ Console), you will see the Enterprise Manager Login window (see Figure 27-2). In this window, you need to supply a valid administrator ID and password, as well as choose the location of the Oracle Management Server.

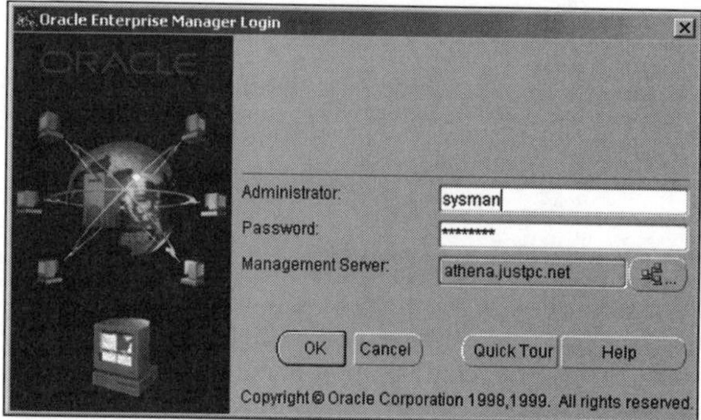

Figure 27-2: Logging onto the Enterprise Manager console.

Yet another ID: The administrative ID used to log in to the Oracle Management Server is not the same thing as the user name you specify when you log in to a database. The administrative ID is used to manage network resources, not database resources.

Using the Enterprise Console

The Enterprise Console presents a packed view of the resources and tools that are available for you to monitor and manage your collection of database servers (see Figure 27-3).

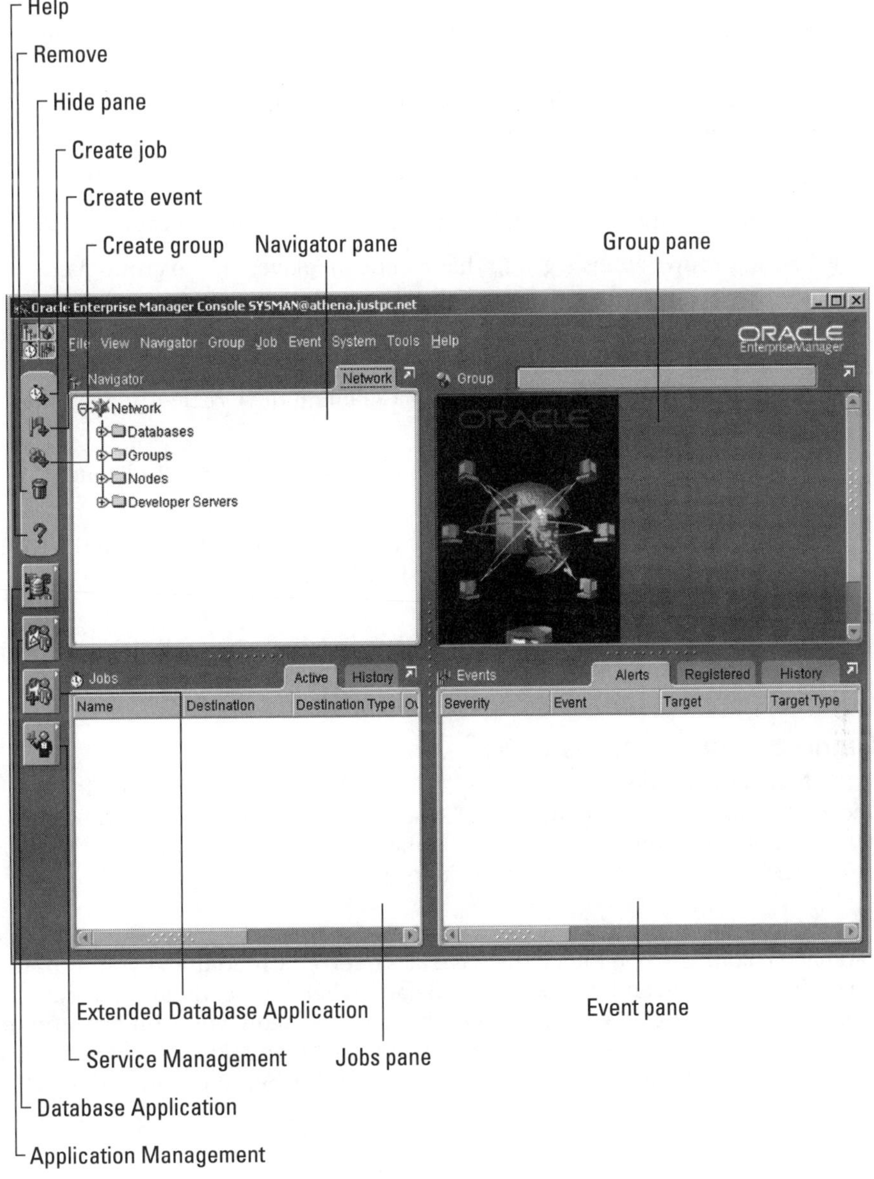

Figure 27-3: Running the Enterprise Console.

- **Navigator pane** contains information about the objects that can be managed through the Enterprise Manager console.
- **Group pane** is customized to display the information you wish from the Navigator pane.
- **Jobs pane** lists the jobs defined in the database that performs tasks like database backups and batch processing.
- **Event pane** contains information about the events you define in your database.
- **Hide pane** provides a quick way to hide any of the four main panes (Navigator, Group, Jobs and Events).
- **Create job** walks you through the process to add a job to the system.
- **Create event** displays a window that you use to define an event.
- **Create group** defines a group that can be displayed in the group pane.
- **Remove** allows you to delete an object in the console.
- **Help** invokes the help subsystem.
- **Application Management** allows you to launch the Oracle Applications Manager.
- **Database Applications** includes options to start the DBA Studio and the SQL*Plus Worksheet utilities.
- **Extended Database Applications** provides buttons that bring up the Oracle interMedia Text Manager, the Oracle Replication Manager, and the Oracle Spatial Index Advisor.
- **Service Management** launches the Net8 Assistant, the OSA Manager, or the Oracle Internet Directory Manager.

Connecting to databases

In the Navigator window, you can explicitly connect to a database to view the information about it. Just expand the Databases icon to show the databases that are available. Then right click on the database and choose Connect from the pop-up menu. This will display a connection form, as shown in Figure 27-4.

Fill in the user name and password that you wish to use to access that particular database instance. Then check the Save as Preferred Credential if you want to make the user name and password the default when connecting to this database. This means that whenever you expand the database icon, you won't be prompted for connection information. Since the Enterprise Manager knows which database you want to access, it supplies the information in the Service field and doesn't allow you to change it.

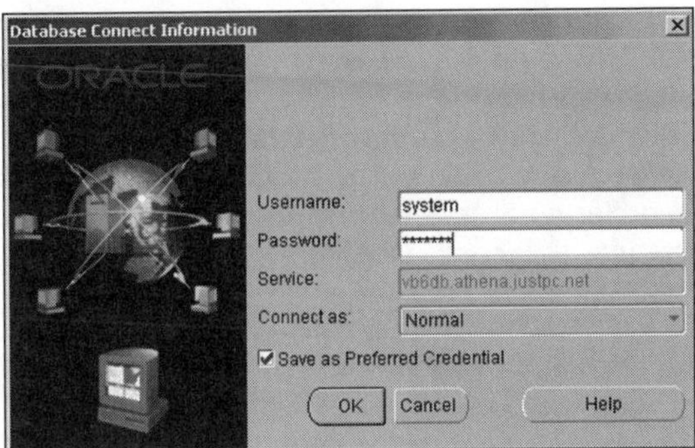

Figure 27-4: Connecting the Enterprise Manager to a database.

Application developers typically need many of the functions and resources available in the Oracle8*i* Enterprise Manager. However, the SQL*Plus Worksheet utility and the DBA Studio are two tools that are worth discussing in more detail.

SQL*Plus Worksheet

Running functions inside a DOS window isn't for everyone. Oracle8*i* includes an alternative to SQL*Plus, called SQL*Plus Worksheet. This utility is basically a graphical version of SQL*Plus. The main improvement is that the SQL buffer is displayed in one pane, while the results of its execution are displayed in another pane. You can start this utility directly from the Enterprise Manager or by choosing Start ➪ Oracle – OraHome81 ➪ Database Administration ➪ SQLPlus Worksheet.

SQL*Plus Window ain't SQL*Plus Worksheet: There's a third version of SQL*Plus, called SQL*Plus Window (Start ➪ Oracle – OraHome81 ➪ Application Development ➪ SQL Plus). This utility is merely SQL*Plus for DOS running in a window. You still enter commands at a prompt. Its primary advantage is the scrollbars that allow you to look back at the commands and SQL statements you execute and their results.

Connecting to your database

You start SQL*Plus Worksheet from the Enterprise Manager by right clicking on the database you wish to use and choosing Database Application ➪ SQL*Plus Worksheet from the pop-up menu. If you were already connected to the database, or have a preferred credential for this database, you will automatically be connected when SQL*Plus Worksheet starts. Otherwise, SQL*Plus Worksheet will be started without an active connection, and you will need to execute a **Connect** statement to connect to your database.

If you start SQL*Plus Worksheet using the Start button, you'll be prompted with the Enterprise Manager Login form. You have a choice of two ways to log in. You can log in through the Oracle Management Server using your administrator ID and password, or you can log in directly to the database using your normal database password (see Figure 27-5). If you wish, you can click on the Login to the Oracle Management Server and log in to the Oracle Management Server first. Then the preferred credentials will be automatically used for this particular database instance.

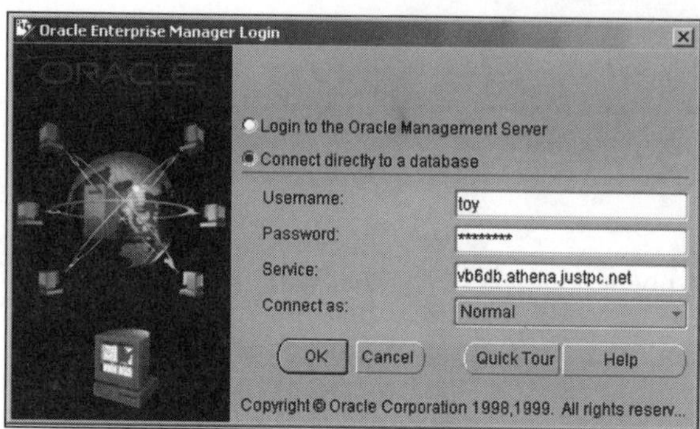

Figure 27-5: Login to SQL*Plus Worksheet using a normal database user name.

Running SQL*Plus Worksheet

After logging onto SQL*Plus Worksheet, you'll see a two-paned window with a set of icons along the left side, as shown in Figure 27-6. The top pane holds the SQL statements you wish to execute, while the bottom pane contains their results. When you initially log in, you'll see the results of the **Connect** command that was used to access the database.

- ✦ **Command pane** is the pane where you enter you SQL statements and/or commands for execution.
- ✦ **Results pane** is the pane where the results from executing a command are displayed.
- ✦ **Connection** allows you to log out from the database and back on as a different user.
- ✦ **Execute** starts processing the SQL statements listed in the command area.
- ✦ **History** maintains a list of the commands and SQL statements you have executed during this session.
- ✦ **Help** displays the Enterprise Manager Help System

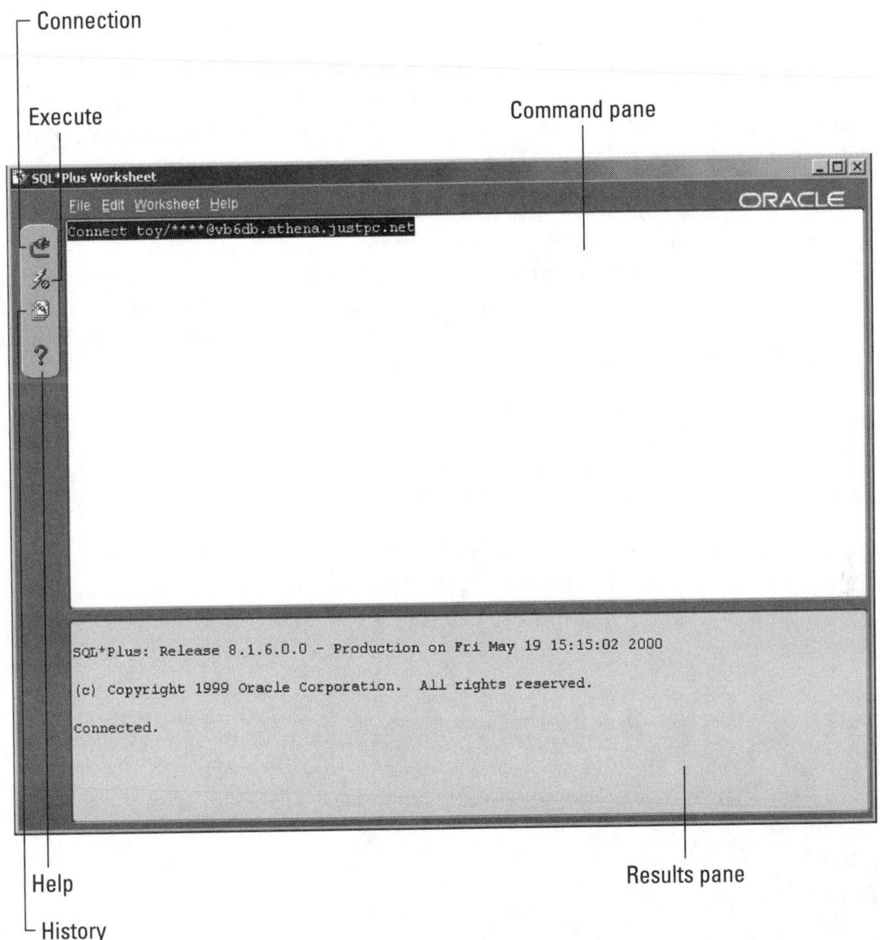

Figure 27-6: Running SQL*Plus Worksheet.

As you might expect, all you need to do to execute a command or SQL statement is to enter it into the Command pane and press the Execute button. One word of caution — once you start executing a command, you can't stop it. While this isn't a problem for most commands, consider the problem that might occur if you try to **Select** several thousand rows from a table.

DBA Studio

The DBA Studio utility is designed to make your life easier when you're designing an Oracle8*i* database. Many functions that previously required you to specify very complex SQL statements, like **Create Table** or **Create Schema**, are now implemented in a much easier to use GUI.

A real Oracle DBA uses ERWin: While DBA Studio is a powerful tool, you might want to consider using ERWin by Computer Associates. While this product is somewhat expensive, it can be worth its weight in gold when designing complex Oracle databases, and unlike database designer solutions from the database vendor, this tool allows you to design databases that can be implemented for nearly any database vendor.

Starting DBA Studio

You can start this utility directly from the Enterprise Manager, or by choosing Start ➪ Oracle – OraHome81 ➪ Database Administration ➪ DBA Studio. When you start the DBA Studio directly from Windows, you will be prompted to launch DBA Studio standalone or to log in to the Oracle Management Server. In either case, you will want to connect to the database as SYSDBA (see Figure 27-7). This will ensure that you have all of the appropriate capabilities you'll need while designing your database.

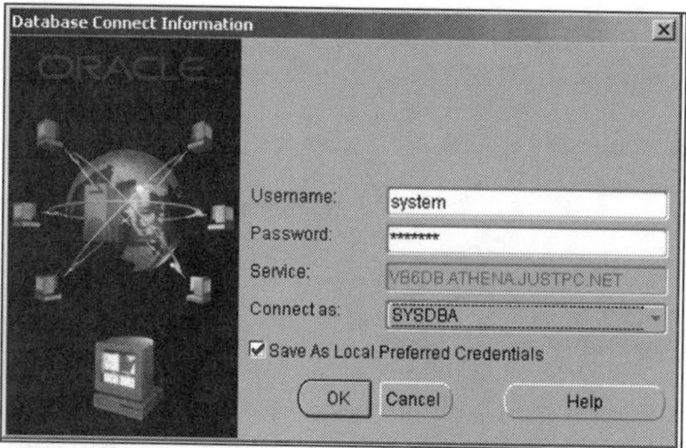

Figure 27-7: Logging onto DBA Studio in standalone mode.

But it's encrypted: If you choose to save your login information as the preferred credential when logging into DBA Studio in standalone mode, you should know that the password is stored on your local hard disk. Even though your password is encrypted, anyone who has physical access to your machine can access DBA Studio by using your default login information.

Running DBA Studio

DBA Studio presents a two-paned view similar to that used by SQL Server Enterprise Manager (see Figure 27-8). It also includes a column of icons down the left side of the window that you can use to perform commonly used functions.

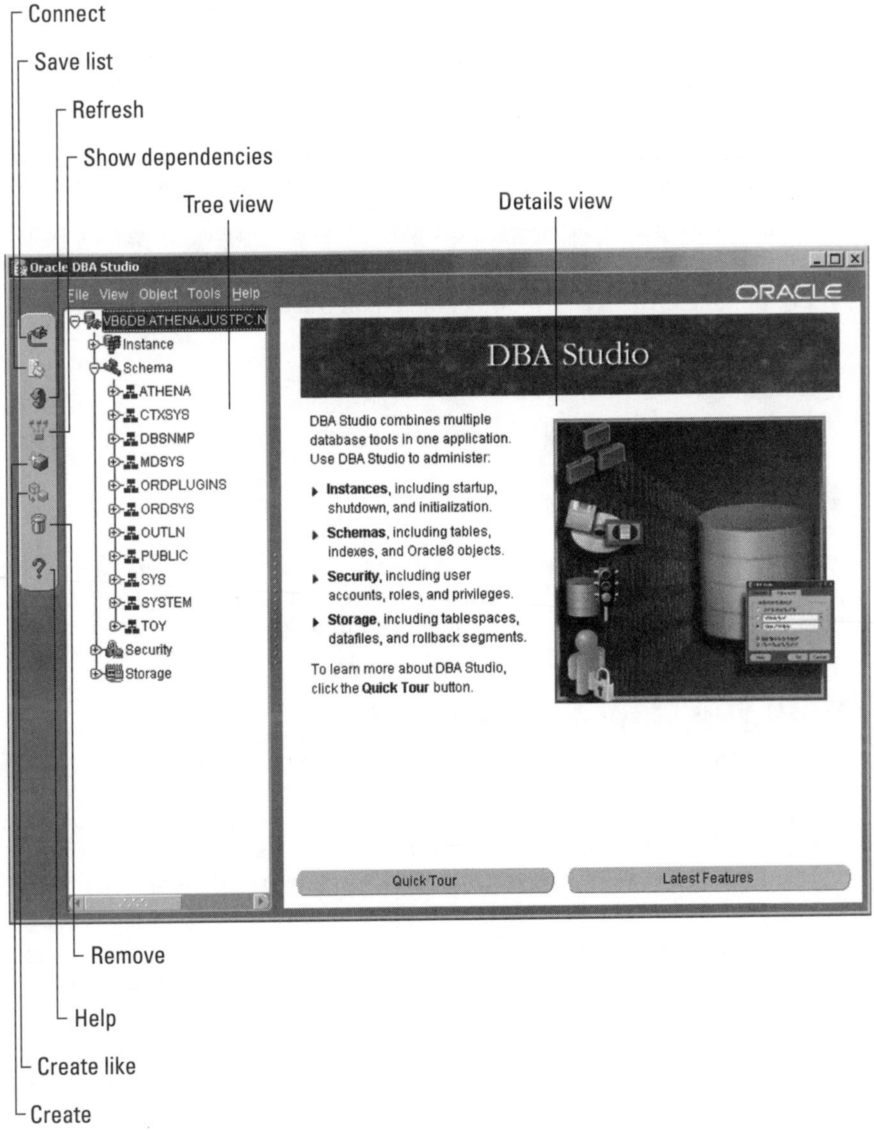

Figure 27-8: Running DBA Studio.

- **Tree view** contains a hierarchical list of icons that reference the database objects that you can manipulate with this utility.
- **Details view** provides additional information about the currently selected icon in the tree view.
- **Connect** allows you to establish a database connection to another database.
- **Save List** creates a file that contains the list of objects, such as the tables that are contained in a particular schema.
- **Refresh** gets a fresh copy of the information displayed in the details view and the icon view.
- **Show Dependencies** displays the objects that the selected object depends on, as well as those objects that depend on the selected object.
- **Create** creates a brand new object in the currently selected category in the icon view.
- **Create Like** creates a new object based on the currently selected object.
- **Remove** deletes the currently selected object.
- **Help** invokes the help subsystem.

Creating Tablespaces

Since creating databases is a task best suited to a database administrator, I want to begin by walking you through the process to create a tablespace. A *tablespace* represents a pool of disk storage that can be used to hold tables and indexes.

Before you create a tablespace

Before you create a tablespace, you should consider the following questions:

- Which database instance should hold the new tablespace? Most servers that run Oracle8*i* run multiple database instances. This allows the database administrator to allocate tablespace and tables to different database instances to optimize performance.
- What name do you want to give the new tablespace? Tablespace names can be from 1 to 30 characters in length and can't duplicate the name of another tablespace or an Oracle8*i* reserved word.
- Which disk location should hold the files for the tablespace? This information will vary depending on the operating system. On Windows-based systems, you'll have to provide the drive, directory path, and file name for each file that will hold the data in the tablespace.

✦ What should the initial size of each file be? If you need to grow your tablespace, you can add additional files or use the **Alter Tablespace** command to modify how the existing data files can grow.

Creating your tablespace

Start Oracle DBA Studio and follow these steps:

1. Verify that you are connected to the database where you wish to add a tablespace and click on the Create icon. This will display the Create On window, as shown in Figure 27-9.

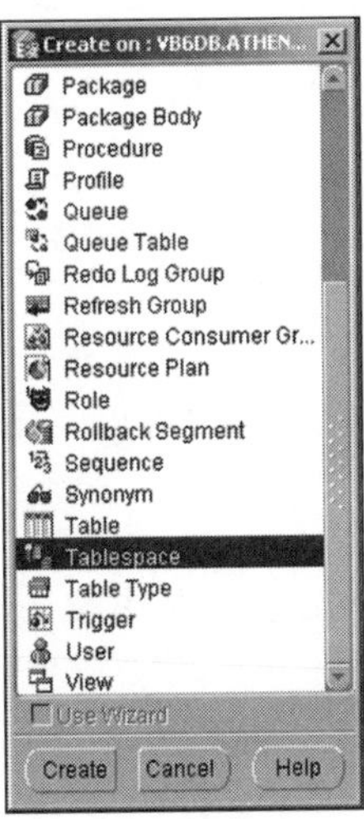

Figure 27-9: Select the tablespace icon to create a new tablespace.

2. Choose Tablespace and press the Create button. This will display the Create Tablespace property window, as shown in Figure 27-10. Then you just need to fill in the blanks. Enter a name for the tablespace. This will automatically fill in a value for the file name. If you wish, you can change the name of the file. If you plan to add additional files to this tablespace, you should include a `_01` to indicate that this is the first file. The File Directory will default to the one currently used by the database. You can also change it, if you wish to place the file on another disk drive. Finally, you need to fill in the size of the tablespace. If you click on the area next to the numeric value under Size, you can change the units from megabytes (`MB`) to kilobytes (`KB`).
3. Press the Create button to allocate the space for the tablespace. A message box will be displayed, letting you know when the tablespace has successfully been completed.

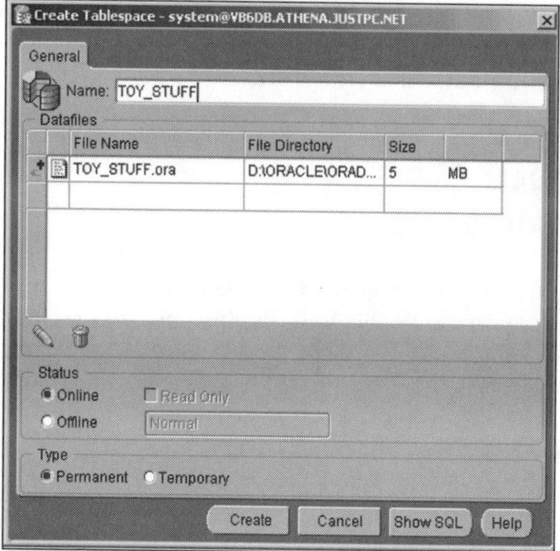

Figure 27-10: Provide the information for the tablespace.

Creating Tables and Indexes

Before you create the tables for your application, you should decide on a name for your database schema. A schema name will help you group all of the database objects you create into a single entity. While you don't explicitly create your schema in the DBA Studio, you reference its name each time you create a new database object.

Creating a table isn't much more than specifying a name for your table and the list of columns you want included. However, the more time you spend preparing to build your table, the better off you will be. Here are a few questions you may want to consider.

✦ What tablespace will hold your table?

✦ What is the name of your table? Your table name should be prefixed by the schema name that you want to use. If you don't specify a schema name, your user name will be used. Both identifiers can be up to 30 characters in length. While you can use spaces and other special characters as part of the table name, you will have to enclose the table name in quotation marks each time you use it. Also, this will make the table name case-sensitive. Also, remember that the table name must be unique within the schema you specify.

✦ What is the name of each column? The rules for naming a column are the same as naming the table.

✦ What is the data type for each column? The data type should be one of the data types listed in Chapter 26. You may have to choose the size of the field and the scale depending on the data type you select.

✦ Should the column accept **Null** values? Note that **Null** values should not be used in any column that is used as part of a primary or foreign key.

✦ Is there a default value for the column? This is an optional field that allows you to insert a specific value into the table instead of marking the column as **Null**.

✦ Should you perform a referential integrity check? This implies that each value entered in this field must exist in another table in this database.

Creating your table

Oracle DBA Studio allows you to create a table through a multi-step wizard or by displaying a worksheet-like form to fill out. I'm going to step you through the wizard since it simplifies much of the work. Then I'll show you how to modify the table using the form.

1. Start DBA Studio, select the appropriate database, and press the Create button to display the object list, as shown in Figure 27-11. Select Table from the list, make sure the Use Wizard check box is checked, and then press the Create button.

Figure 27-11: Starting the Create Table wizard.

2. In the first step of the Table Wizard (see Figure 27-12), you are asked to specify the name of the table, the schema, and the tablespace that should be used.

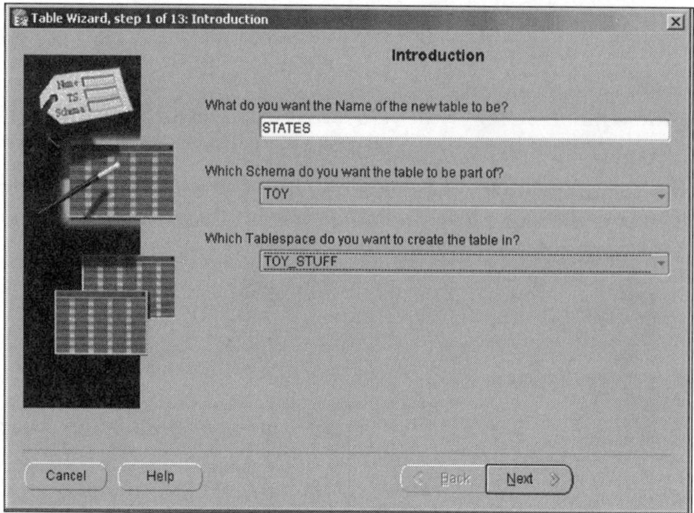

Figure 27-12: Entering basic information about the table.

3. In the next step of the wizard (see Figure 27-13), you will enter the columns you want to include and their data type. You can also specify a default value for each column as well. Simply enter the information in the Properties of Column section of the form and press the Add button. You can also remove a column that you have added by selecting it in the Columns defined area of the form and pressing Remove.

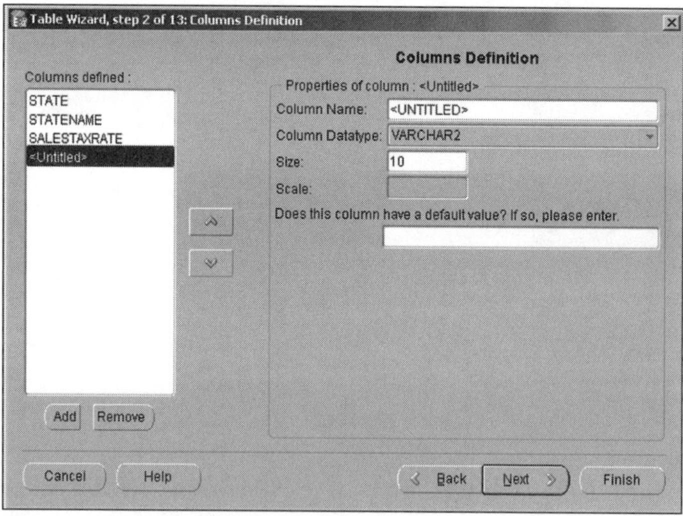

Figure 27-13: Entering column information.

4. In step 3 of the Table Wizard, you select the primary key (see Figure 27-14). While Oracle permits you to create the table without a primary key, I believe that every table you create should have a primary key. Choose the Yes, I Want To Create a Primary Key radio button to display the list of columns for the table, and then specify the order of the columns that comprise the primary key. If a column is not part of the primary key, leave the order field blank.

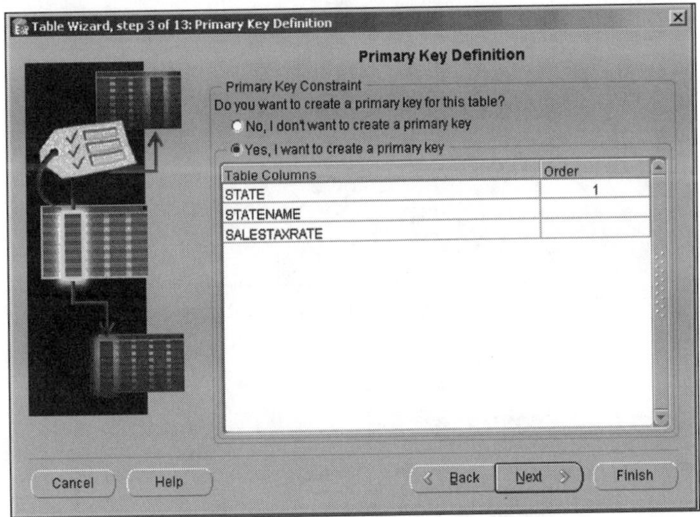

Figure 27-14: Selecting the primary key for your table.

5. Pressing Next allows you to specify **Null** and **Unique** constraints on each field in your new table (see Figure 27-15). To modify a column, select the column in the Columns Defined area of the form. You should always ensure that both constraints are selected for the primary key. However, you should only use **Unique** for the primary key if you have a very good reason for doing so because each **Unique** clause you add after the primary key imposes a lot of extra work each time you insert a new row.

6. Foreign key constraints are selected in step 5 of the Table Wizard (see Figure 27-16). For each column that references the primary key of another table, choose Yes, The Column is a Foreign Key and then specify the name of the Schema, Table, and Column that comprise the foreign key. If you have no foreign keys, then choose No, The Column is not a Foreign Key.

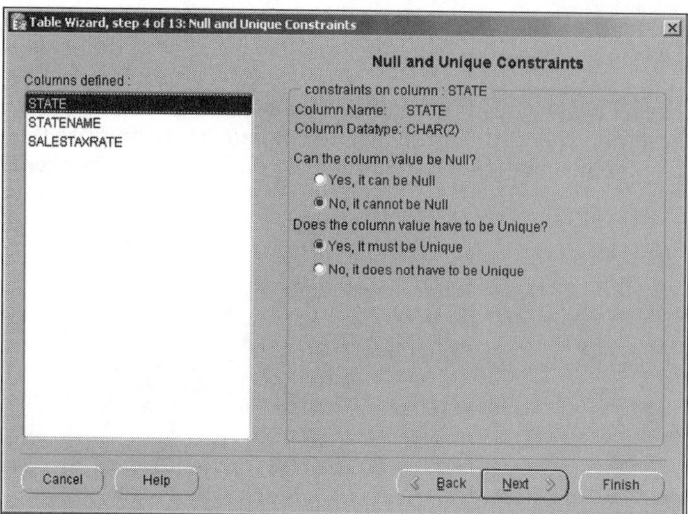

Figure 27-15: Choosing Null and Unique constraints for each column in your table.

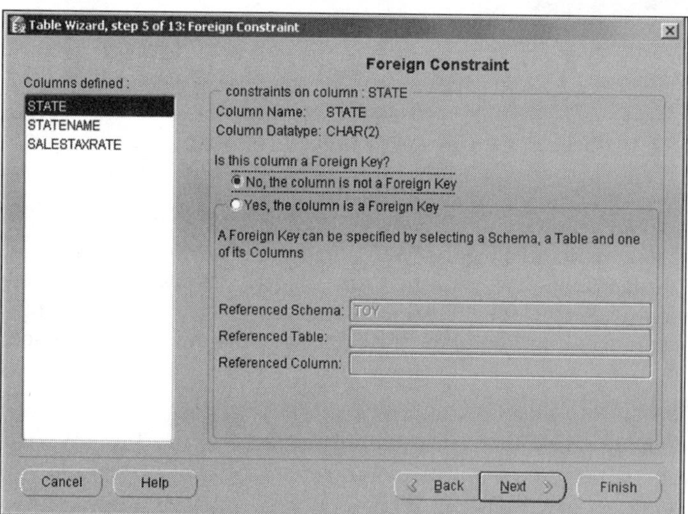

Figure 27-16: Defining foreign key relationships.

7. Step 6 allows you to define check constraints for each column (see Figure 27-17). These are tests that the value you insert into the column must meet before the row can be inserted or updated. Select the column in the Columns defined section of the form, and then add the constraint if desired.

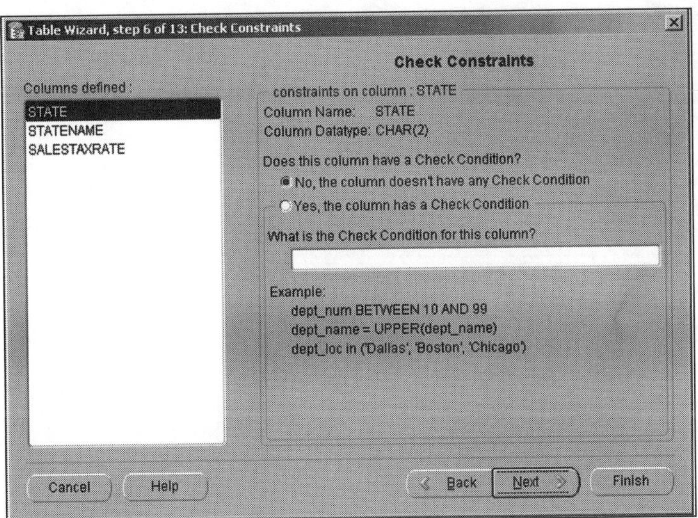

Figure 27-17: Creating check constraints.

8. The remaining steps of the wizard allow you to optimize how the table is stored. Unless you are a knowledgeable Oracle database administrator, I suggest that you skip these steps. Pressing the Finish button will create your table. When the wizard has finished, a message box will be displayed indicating that your table was successfully created.

Like Create Like, man: If you have to create a table that is similar to another table that is already in your database, consider clicking on the Create Like button, instead of the Create button. Select an existing table in tree view and press the Create Like button. Your new table will include all of the definitions that are in the table you previously selected. You may then make any modifications you want—add columns, delete columns, change names, data types, and so on. This can be much easier than you think.

Modifying a table

You can modify a table by right clicking on the table name from the tree view and choosing the Edit option from the pop-up menu. This will display the Edit Table property window, as shown in Figure 27-18. You may change any of the column's characteristics, including Datatype, Size, Scale, Foreign Key References (Ref), Nulls, and Default Value, all on this single form. Notice that you can't change any of the information at the top part of the form such as the name of the table, its schema or table space.

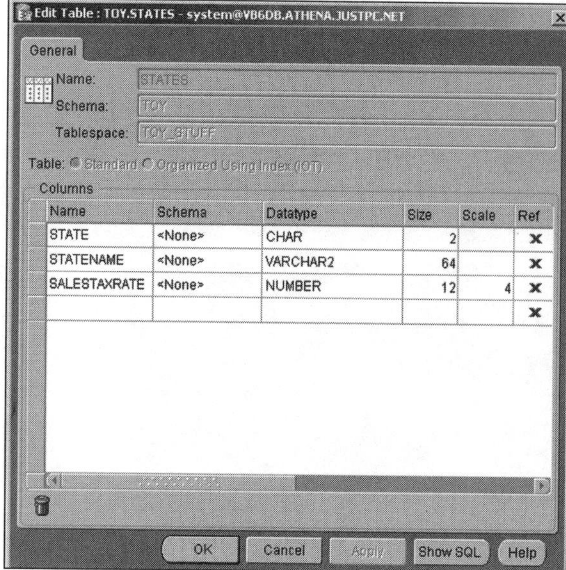

Figure 27-18: Modifying a table's characteristics.

You can make any changes you wish to a table as long as it doesn't have data in it. If your table does contain data, you can make changes as long as you follow these rules:

✦ A new column must accept **Null** values. If you wish to add a column that doesn't permit **Null** values, you add the column permitting **Null** values, then use an **Update** statement to assign a value to this column for every row in the table. Then you can modify the column to prohibit **Null** values.

✦ You always increase the size of a character-based column (**Char**, **Varchar2**, etc.). If you want to decrease the size, you must first change the value for each row in the table to **Null**, then make the change.

✦ You can always increase the number of digits or increase or decrease the number of decimal places in a **Number** column. To decrease the number of digits in the column, you must first ensure that each row contains a **Null** value for this column before making the change.

✦ You can change the data type assigned to a column only if the column's value for each row in the table is **Null**.

There's always a way if you really want to do something: One way to change the characteristics of a column is to add a temporary column to your table that accepts **Null** values, with all of the characteristics you want the changed column to have. Then use an **Update** statement and assign the value from the original column to the temporary column using whatever functions are necessary to convert the value properly. Then delete the old column from your table and give the original column's name to the temporary column.

Creating an index

You can always add an index to your table by clicking the Create button and choosing Index from the list of available database objects. This will display the Create Index property window (see Figure 27-19). Simply fill in the values for the name of the index, the schema it will be associated with, and the tablespace it will use for storage. Then choose the schema and table name for the table where the index will be applied. Next, choose the columns and the order they will appear in the index and and press Create to build the index.

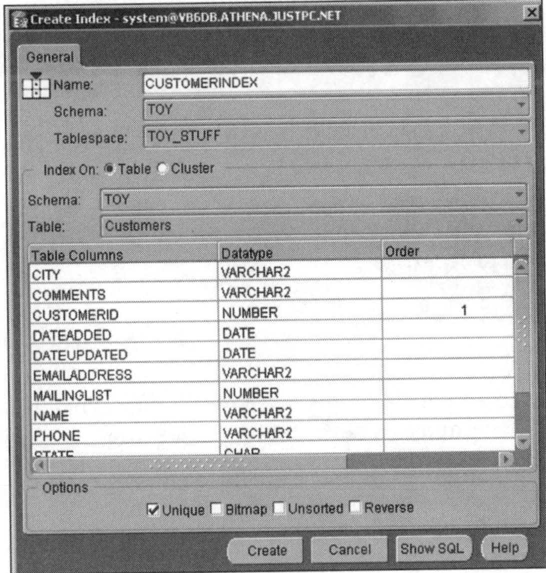

Figure 27-19: Creating an index.

Managing Security

Managing security is an important part of every database management system (DBMS). As you would expect, it involves three main processes: creating roles, creating users, and assigning permissions to both users and roles.

Creating roles

As you've seen before, a role is a way to bundle together permissions and other roles to form a single entity that can be associated with a user. Creating a role isn't very difficult. Simply press the Create button, and select Role from the list of database objects. This will display the Create Role property window (see Figure 27-20). You must enter a name for the role and choose whether you want additional authentication from the user in order to enable the role.

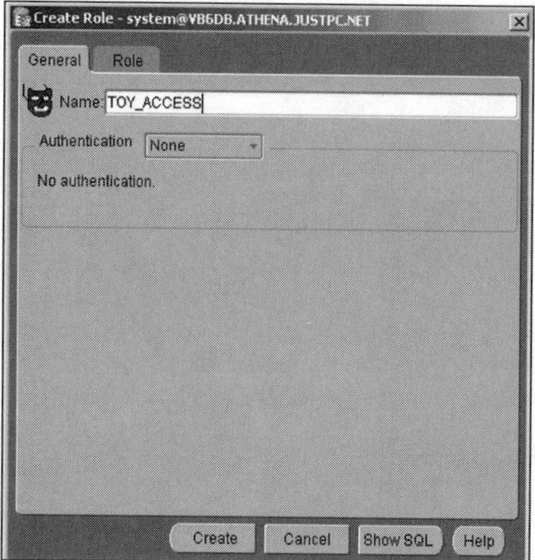

Figure 27-20: Creating a new role.

On the Role tab, you can choose to add any existing roles to this role. This means you can create a single role that encompasses several other roles, thus simplifying security management.

Creating users

Using DBA Studio, you can create a user very easily by pressing the Create button and selecting Users from the list of database objects. This will display the Create User property window. This property window has three tabs: General, Role, and System Privileges, each of which holds part of the information available about a user. After filling out the information in each tab, simply press the Create button to create the new user.

Create Like strikes again: Creating a new user is one of the most painful processes any computer center has to manage. One way to avoid some of the pain is to create a standard user and then use the Create Like process to duplicate it, including all of its security roles and privileges. While you should still review everything to make sure that it is appropriate for the user you are creating, Create Like will help you avoid making simple mistakes.

Entering general information for a user

Figure 27-21 shows the General tab of the Create User property window. To create a new user, simply fill out the user's name and specify the password information. Then associate the user with the appropriate Default and Temporary tablespaces. If you check the Expire Password Now check box, the user will be required to change their password the first time they log on to the system. Also, selecting Locked means that the user is prohibited from using the user name until you select the Unlocked radio button.

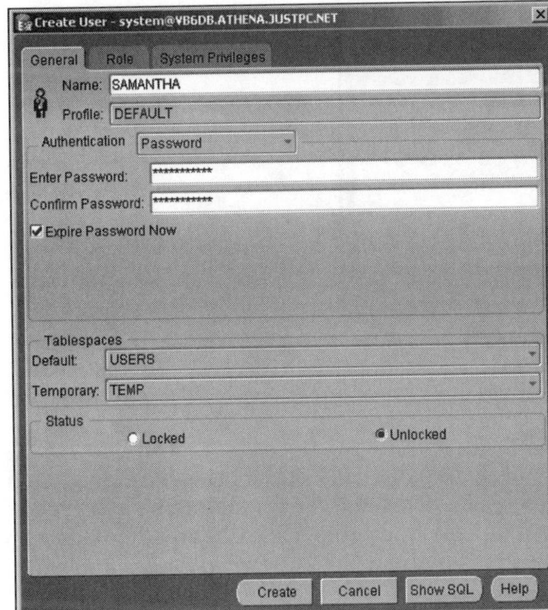

Figure 27-21: Entering general information about a user.

Three strikes and you're locked: You can enable a feature in your database that will lock a user out of the database if they specify an invalid password three times in a row.

Granting roles

In order for the user to perform any useful work, you must assign them to one or more roles (see Figure 27-22). At a minimum, they should be granted the `CONNECT` role, which will permit them to **Connect** to the database server. Simply select the roles you wish to grant to the user and press the arrow that is pointing down. The selected roles are copies to the Granted pane. When the user is created, the user will inherit the security permissions of each of the roles in the Granted pane.

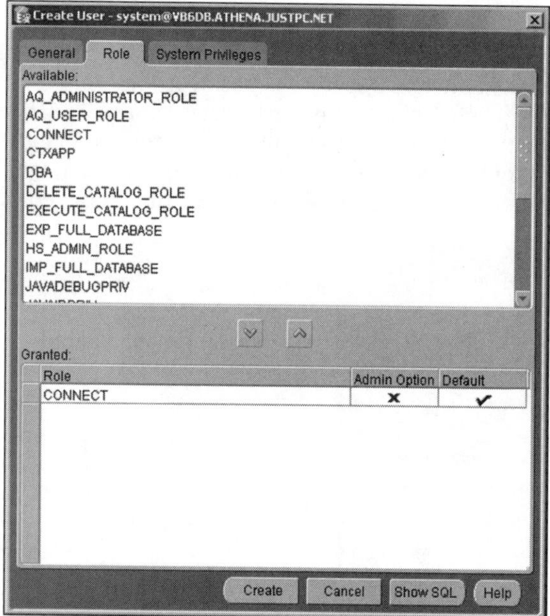

Figure 27-22: Selecting roles for a user.

Selecting system privileges

For the most part, a user shouldn't be assigned any of the privileges listed on the System Privileges tab (see Figure 27-23). These privileges should be reserved for database administrators and/or database operators. (See Chapter 26, "Overview of Oracle8*i*," for a more detailed discussion about the system privileges and what they permit the user to do).

Granting permissions

In order to secure your database, you must use one of the forms of SQL*Plus and enter the appropriate **Grant** and **Revoke** statements. You can't do this from DBA Studio. To simplify the permissions process, I suggest that you create separate roles for each type of access you want to provide for a table and grant the resources to the role. This means you might have a role for read access, one for update access, and another for administrative use. I would then repeat this process for each database object (view, stored procedure, etc.) that is part of the application.

I would then create another role for each access level for your application and assign each of the lower-level roles created earlier that are appropriate for the application. This simplifies the process of administration, since you would only have to associate one role for each application that the user has access to. Then if you change the application slightly, you need only manage the permissions associated with the lower-level roles.

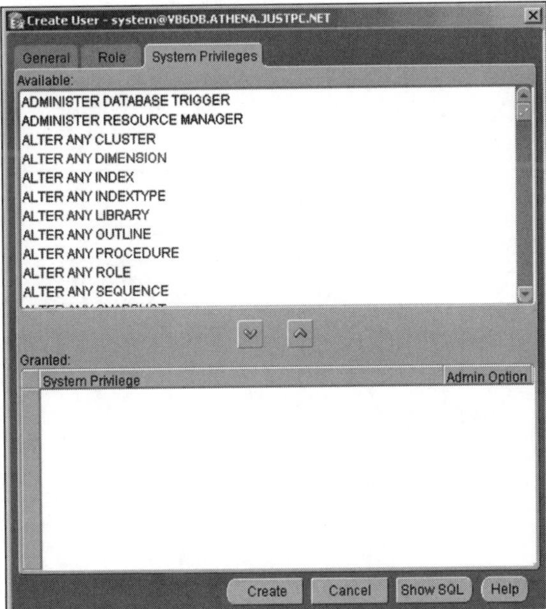

Figure 27-23: Selecting system privileges.

Thoughts on Creating Oracle8*i* Database Objects

Creating database objects in Oracle8*i* can be very simple or incredibly complex—it's your choice. Oracle8*i* includes many features that you can exploit when you build your database that I haven't discussed here. These features can make you database much more efficient. However using these features can be difficult. This is another reason that an experienced database administrator is worth their weight in memory chips.

Not all of the options available to you via SQL statements are available through the DBA Studio. If you need to be able to manage the details of how the data files are allocated in a table space or define more complex relationships between tables, you will need to use one of the SQL*Plus variants to execute the specific SQL commands that perform the desired function.

Summary

In this chapter you learned:

- ✦ about SQL*Plus and some useful commands you may want to use.
- ✦ about Enterprise Manager and how to use it to access multiple database instances.
- ✦ about SQL*Plus Worksheet and how it differs from SQL*Plus.
- ✦ how to create a tablespace.
- ✦ how to create tables and indexes.
- ✦ how to manage security by creating users and granting roles.

✦ ✦ ✦

CHAPTER 28

Creating Stored Procedures with Oracle8i

✦ ✦ ✦ ✦

In This Chapter

Introducing PL/SQL

Writing stored procedures in PL/SQL

Creating a package

✦ ✦ ✦ ✦

In this chapter, I'm going to discuss the details of how to create various procedural objects, such as stored procedures and functions. I'll also discuss Oracle's implementation of SQL and the extensions necessary to provide a rich programming environment.

Introducing PL/SQL

Every database vendor has its own variation of the SQL language, and Oracle is no exception. Procedural Language/SQL, also known as PL/SQL, contains a series of extensions that make it possible to build efficient programs which can perform complex database functions.

PL/SQL is used primarily to build stored procedures and functions. These routines essentially become an extension to the PL/SQL language. Thus, you can call your own stored procedure as easily as you would use a **Select** statement. In fact, it may be easier to call a stored procedure than use a **Select** statement, since stored procedures typically have fewer parameters.

Comments

Comments in PL/SQL are the same as SQL Server's T-SQL. Double hyphen comments (`--`) mark the start of a comment whose text continues to the end of the line. Slash asterisk, asterisk slash comments (`/* */`) can be used anywhere a space can be used, and may span multiple lines.

Constants

String values must be enclosed in single quotes ('), as shown below:

```
'This is a string constant.'
```

If you wish to embed a single quote in a string constant, simply use two single quotes together, like this:

```
'This is a ''string'' with embedded single quotes.'
```

This string constant would be understood by PL/SQL as:

```
This is a 'string' with embedded single quotes.
```

Quote'th the raven, never double: Double quotes (") are not the same thing as two single quotes (' '). Double quotes are used to indicate case-sensitive identifiers, while two single quotes inside a string constant indicate that a single single quote should be inserted at that position.

Numbers, as you might expect, may begin with a plus sign (+) or a minus sign (-), followed by a series of numeric digits, a decimal point, and more digits. Some examples of numbers are:

```
0          3.1415926    1000.0      -100.001     +512
```

Dates, which are stored internally in a special format, are written like strings, except theyare formatted as DD-MM-YY. For example,

```
'27-Jul-65'  '27-Jul-1965'   '1-May-2000'
```

are valid **Date** constants.

Identifiers

An identifier can be up to 30 characters in length. They must begin with a letter and may contain letters, numbers, and the underscore character (_). Identifiers are used as the name of a stored procedure or function, as a local variable, and as the name of various database objects. Double quotes (") surround identifiers that contain spaces or special characters.

Variables

PL/SQL allows you to define local variables that can be used in stored procedures and functions. They are declared in the **Declare** section of your procedure. You can declare a variable to be of any data type supported by Oracle8*i*. Unlike SQL Server, variables need not begin with a special character. Any identifier that doesn't conflict with an Oracle8*i* keyword may be used.

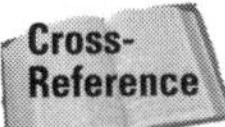

See the discussion of Oracle8*i* data types in Chapter 26 if you would like to become more familiar with them.

Functions

PL/SQL provides a number of functions that can be used to perform calculations or data conversions. Some of the more interesting functions are listed in Table 28-1.

Table 28-1
Selected Functions in PL/SQL

Function	*Description*
Add_months	Adds the specified number of months to the specified date.
ASCII	Returns the ASCII code of the left-most character of the specified character string.
Ceil	Returns the smallest integer value greater than or equal to the specified value.
Chr	Returns the character corresponding to the specified numeric ASCII code value.
Floor	Returns the largest integer value less than or equal to the specified value.
Initcap	Capitalizes the first character of each word in a string.
Instr	Returns the position of the specified search string in a specified data string.
Last_day	Returns the date of the last day of the month for the specified data value.
Length	Returns the size of a string, number, date, or expression.
Lower	Converts all uppercase characters to lowercase.
Ltrim	Removes leading blanks from a character string.
Mod	Computes the remainder after dividing the two values.

Continued

Table 28-1 *(continued)*

Function	***Description***
Months_between	Computes the number of months between two dates.
New_time	Converts a **Date** value to the specified time zone.
Next_day	Returns a **Date** value containing the day that follows the specified date.
Replace	Replaces the search string with a replacement string in the specified string.
Round	Rounds the specified **Number** or **Date** value to the specified accuracy.
Rtrim	Removes trailing blanks from a character string.
Substr	Returns a string of characters from the specified string with the specified starting location and length.
Sysdate	Returns the current date and time.
To_char	Converts the specified value to a character string.
To_date	Converts the specified value to a **Date** value.
To_number	Converts the specified value to a numeric value.
Trunc	Truncates the specified **Date** or **Number** value using the specified accuracy.
Upper	Converts all lowercase characters to uppercase.
User	Contains the user name of the current user.

If you don't like these, then build your own: If you need a function that isn't available in PL/SQL, you can easily build your own using the **Create Function** statement. Functions are a variation on stored procedures. The only difference is that a function returns a single value that can be used as part of an expression, while a stored procedure can't be used as part of an expression.

Block structure

The *block structure* is the fundamental way statements are organized into a stored procedure or function. A block structure is broken into three main sections, the **Declare** section, the main body and the **Exception** section. The **Declare** section is used to declare block-wide variables. These variables can be used in between the **Begin** and **End** statements. You may optionally assign an initial value for these variables.

The **Begin** statement marks the start of the executable commands section of the block. When the block is called, control will begin with the first statement following the **Begin** statement. Program flow will continue until it reaches either the **End** statement or the **Exception** statement. When either of these statements is reached, execution is complete and control will return to the calling program.

If an error occurs while running in the executable commands section of the block, control will be transferred to the first statement following the **Exception** statement. If the **Exception** section isn't present, an error message will be returned to the calling program. Once you transfer control the to **Exception** section, you can't return to the executable commands section.

Nesting: A block can be used anywhere a PL/SQL statement can be used. Thus, you can nest one block inside of another. In the innermost block, you can use any of the variables declared in the outer blocks. However, you can't use any of the variables declared in an inner block once you are outside that block. The syntax for a block is:

```
<< <block_name> >>
[Declare
   <variable> <datatype> [:= <initial_value>];
   [<variable> <datatype> [:= <initial_value>];] ...
]

Begin
   <statement>;
   [<statement>;]...
[Exception
   When <condition> Then <statement>; [<statement>;]...
   [When <condition> Then <statement>; [<statement>;]...]...
]
```

End [<block_name>]; where `<block_name>` is an identifier that is associated with the block; `<variable>` is an identifier that will be used to store information locally in the block; .`<datatype>` is any legal Oracle8*i* data type; `<initial_value>` is a constant that is appropriate for the data type; `<statement>` is any legal PL/SQL statement or command; and `<condition>` is an exception (see Table 28-2), a list of exceptions that are **Or**'ed together, or the keyword **Others**, which traps any remaining exceptions.

Table 28-2
Exceptions

Exception	*Description*
CURSOR_ALREADY_OPEN	An **Open** statement tried to open a cursor that was already open.
DUP_VAL_ON_INDEX	An **Insert** or **Update** statement created a duplicate value in a **Unique** index.
INVALID_CURSOR	An **Open** statement tried to open an undefined cursor; a **Close** statement tried to close a closed cursor; a **Fetch** statement tried to use an unopened cursor, and so on.
INVALID_NUMBER	An illegal numeric value was found when trying to convert a character string to a numeric value.
LOGIN_DENIED	The user name and password combination was invalid in a **Connect** statement.
NO_DATA_FOUND	A **Select** statement returned zero rows.
NOT_LOGGED_ON	An attempt was made to access database resources without being connected to the database.
PROGRAM_ERROR	A catchall error used by PL/SQL to trap its own errors.
STORAGE_ERROR	Insufficient memory was available to execute the function, or the available memory was corrupted (possible subscripting error).
TIMEOUT_ON_RESOURCE	A resource wasn't available when it should have been.
TOO_MANY_ROWS	A **Select** statement that should return a single row returned more than one row.
TRANSACTION_BACKED_OUT	A remote part of a transaction failed and was rolled back.
VALUE_ERROR	A conversion error, a truncation error, or a precision error affecting a variable or column value occurred
ZERO_DIVIDE	An attempt was made to divide by zero.

Blockhead: The name of a block is an optional feature that marks the beginning of a block. It is simply an identifier that is enclosed in double less than (<<) and double greater than (>>) signs, such as <<MyBlock>>. The same name that begins the block must also be specified in the **End** statement, like this:`End MyBlock`.

Procedures, functions, and packages

Procedures and functions contain code that can be treated as an extension to PL/SQL. A procedure can be used in much the same way as a command or SQL statement, while a function can be incorporated into any expression. Procedures and functions can be written as standalone routines or combined in a single unit called a *package*. (The **Create Package** statement is explained at the end of this chapter.)

Just a routine check: Procedures and functions are basically the same thing. The only difference is in how they are used. Functions can be used within an expression, while a procedure must be called as a separate statement I use the term "routine" to refer to something that can be either a procedure or a function. For instance, I might say that "Routines have parameters" rather than saying "Procedures and functions have parameters". Not only does this make things a little clearer, it also saves me a lot of typing.

Procedures and functions

Procedures and functions are just blocks with a header that defines the name of a particular routine and the list of parameters associated with it. A procedure is similar to a Visual Basic subroutine in how it is used. You pass a series of parameters to a procedure as a single statement. When it finishes, control is returned to the next statement in your program.

A PL/SQL function works like a Visual Basic function. It is used in an expression to compute a value based on a set of parameters. When the function returns its value, the rest of the expression is processed.

The syntax for a procedure definition is:

```
Procedure [<username>.]<procedure>
   [(<argument> [,<argument>]...)]
   {Is|As} <block>
```

The syntax for a function definition is:

```
Function [<username>.]<function>
   [(<argument> [,<argument>]...)]
   Return <datatype>
   {Is|As} <block>
```

where <username> is the name of the user associated with the procedure or function; <procedure> is the name of the procedure; <function> is the name of the function;<argument> is <parameter> [In|Out|In Out] <datatype>, where <parameter> is the name of the parameter; **In** means that the parameter is passed to the routine, but any changes in the parameter are not returned to the calling program, **Out** means that no value is passed to the routine, but the routine will return a value to the calling program, **In Out** means that a value is passed to the routine and any changes in the parameter will be returned to the calling program, and `<datatype>` is the data type associated with the parameter; and

`<block>` is a block declaration as I discussed in the Block structure section earlier in this chapter. It is separated from the rest of the statement by using the **Is** or **As** keywords.

Return statement

The **Return** statement is used to return a value to the calling program. It uses the following syntax:

```
Return(<value>);
```

where `<value>` is a variable or expression containing the information that will be returned as the value of the function.

Packages

A *package* is merely a single unit containing a collection of one or more procedures and functions (or routines), with some optional global variables. It corresponds to a Visual Basic module. The package consists of three parts: global declarations, which are optional, at least one routine, and a block of code that is executed each time a routine in the package is called. This block is executed first, which allows you to initialize global variables, open a cursor, or any other logic that is common to all of the routines.

I love packages: Besides the obvious benefit of creating a single installation unit that combines many different routines, packages are often more efficient than independent stored procedures and functions, since the code is compiled together as a single unit. Thus, you avoid the extra costs of locating the new routine, loading it, and preparing to run it. All of this work is done when the first routine in the package is called.

Expressions

You can compute a single value based on a collection of local variables, parameters, functions, and columns retrieved from a table, and then assign the value to a local variable or column. PL/SQL uses the assignment operator (:=) to perform the assignment, as shown below:

```
MyVariable := 'A string value';
MyNumber := 3.14159265;
MyNumber := MyNumber * 20;
```

Flow control

Oracle8*i* /SQL supports a wider range of flow control statements than Microsoft's SQL Server. You can use statements such as **If**, **For,** and **While** to control the flow through your stored procedure. You can also call procedures and functions directly without having to use a special statement.

If statement

The **If** statement has the following syntax:

```
If <boolean_expression>
   {<statement>|<block>}
[Elsif <Boolean_expression>
   {<statement>|<block>}]...
[Else
   {<statement>|<block }]
End If;
```

`<boolean_expression>` is a boolean expression that is either True or False. If the Boolean expression is **True**, then the statement or block that immediately follows the expression will be executed. Otherwise, the statement or block that immediately follows the **Else** clause will be executed.

`<statement>` is an SQL statement or PL/SQL command.

`<block>` is a PL/SQL block. While variables and exceptions can be included, typically all you would use is the **Begin** and **End** statements to enclose a group of statements to be executed if `<boolean_expression>` is **True**.

Exit statement

The **Exit** statement allows you to exit from a loop or from a block. Its syntax is:

```
Exit [<block_name>] [When <boolean_expression>];
```

`<block_name>` is the name of a block (such as, `<<myblock>>`). If `<block_name>` isn't specified, the processing will resume with the statement that immediately follows the next **End** statement. Otherwise, processing will resume with the **End** statement that matches the specified `<block_name>`.

`<boolean_expression>` is an expression that, when **True**, will exit a loop or block of code, Otherwise processing will continue normally.

Loop statement

The **Loop** statement has the following syntax:

```
Loop
   <statement>
   [<statement>]
End Loop;
```

where `<statement>` is a valid PL/SQL statement.

Note that this looping statement creates an infinite loop. The only way to leave the loop is to use an **Exit** statement.

While statement

While statements are constructed with the following syntax:

```
While <boolean_expression>
   Loop
   <statement>
   [<statement>]
End Loop;
```

`<boolean_expression>` is evaluated at the start of each loop. As long as this expression is **True**, the statements contained in the loop will be executed. If the expression is **False**, execution will resume with the statement after the **End Loop** statement.

`<statement>` is a valid PL/SQL statement.

For statement

The **For** statement should be familiar if you're a Visual Basic programmer. However, its syntax is a little different than that which Microsoft uses:

```
For <variable> In <start_expression> .. <end_expression>
   Loop
   <statement>
   [<statement>]...
End Loop;
```

where `<variable>` is the variable to be incremented; `<start_expression>` is the initial value for the **For** variable; and`<end_expression>` is the ending value for the **For** variable.

Unlike the Visual Basic **For** statement, the PL/SQL **For** statement allows you to increment only the **For** variable.

For cursors only: See the section on Cursors later in this chapter to see how to increment a cursor.

Cursors

Cursors are a special type of variable that allow you to access the contents of a **Select** statement one row at a time. You can move the cursor through the result set and perform various operations on the columns retrieved, including updating values, deleting rows, and inserting rows.

The Cursor statement

The **Cursor** statement defines a cursor. Its syntax is:

```
Cursor <cursor>
   [Is <select_statement>];
```

where `<cursor>` is the name of the cursor variable; and`<select_statement>` is a **Select** statement that returns rows to be accessed through the cursor.

Defining a cursor merely creates the data structures necessary to access information from the database. No rows are actually retrieved until the **Open** statement is executed. However, information about the columns retrieved is available and can be accessed by using the **%Rowtype** and **%Type** cursor attributes.

Cursor attributes

You can determine additional information about a cursor by using a cursor attribute. Cursor attributes are appended to a cursor variable, such as:

```
MyCursor%Found
```

which will return a value indicating whether the last operation that used it was successful. You can use the combination of cursor and attribute anywhere you can use a variable.

Table 28-3 lists the attributes available for each cursor. Note that you need not do anything to make these attributes available. They are automatically present once a cursor has been defined.

Table 28-3
Cursor Attributes

Attribute	*Description*
%Found	Is **True** when the last operation (**Select**, **Insert**, **Update**, or **Delete**) was successful.
%Isopen	Is **True** when the cursor is open.
%Notfound	Opposite of **%Found**.
%Rowtype	Returns a record variable containing the same structure as the entire row in the table.
%Type	Returns the data type of the selected column.

The **%Rowtype** and **%Type** attributes are used in the **Declare** section as a data type for other variables. This allows you to declare a variable for a column or for the entire row without necessarily knowing their data type. You reference a particular column by using `<rowtype_variable>.<column_name>`. Consider the following code fragment:

```
Declare
   Cursor MyCursor Is
      Select MyColumn, AnotherColumn From MyTable;
   MyRow MyCursor%Rowtype;

Begin
Open MyCursor;

If MyRow.MyColumn = 0
   /* insert processing statements here */

Else
   /* insert processing statements here */

End;

Close MyCursor;
End;
```

`MyRow.MyColumn` is used to retrieve information from the MyColumn column from the MyTable table in the database.

The **%Found** and **%Notfound** attributes are extremely useful when managing loops. You can retrieve rows of information from the database in a **While** loop using the **%Notfound** attribute, as in the following code fragment:

```
Open MyCursor
While MyCursor%Notfound
   Loop
   Fetch MyCursor Into MyVariable;

   /* insert processing statements here */

   End Loop;
```

As long as there are rows remaining to be fetched, this loop will process each row. If the cursor didn't return any rows, the processing loop would be skipped.

Open statement

Before you access a cursor, you must use the **Open** statement. The syntax follows:

```
Open <cursor>;
```

where `<cursor>` is the name of a cursor that has already been declared.

When the **Open** statement is executed, the **Select** statement associated with the cursor is executed and the information is made available. You can then use the **Fetch** statement to retrieve the information, and the **Delete** or **Update** statements to modify the information. (The **Fetch** statement is covered later in this chapter.)

But I did open it: Trying to access a cursor that hasn't been opened will generate an error. Also, trying to open a cursor that is already open will generate an error. You can use the **%IsOpen** attribute to verify that your cursor is in the proper state before trying to use it. This is extremely important if you are implementing code in the Exceptions section and you may not know the exact state of the cursor.

Close statement

The **Close** statement deallocates the resources associated with the cursor. Its syntax is simple:

```
Close <cursor>;
```

`<cursor>` is the name of a cursor that has already been declared.

Once a cursor has been closed, you need to open it again before you can use it.

Fetch statement

The **Fetch** statement is used to retrieve the next record into a variable for local access. It has the following syntax:

```
Fetch <cursor> Into {<record>|<variable> [,<variable>]...};
```

where

<cursor> is an open cursor; <record> is a variable declared using <cursor> **%Rowtype** as its data type; and<variable> is a variable whose data type is compatible with the data type of the corresponding column from the cursor. The list of variables must match the list of columns retrieved from the cursor in both number and data types.

For statement

Another variation of the **For** statement you saw earlier in "Flow Control" makes it easy to process all of the rows retrieved from the database. You should use the following syntax:

```
For <record> In <cursor>
```

where <record> is a variable declared using <cursor>**%Rowtype**,and <cursor> is an open cursor.

Consider the following code fragment:

```
Open MyCursor;
For MyRow In MyCursor
   Loop

   /* insert processing statements here */

   End Loop;
```

The statements in the **Loop** body will be processed for each row retrieved from the database. You don't need a **Fetch** statement to retrieve the row into a variable. The **For** statement handles that for you automatically. Using the record variable also simplifies your code, since you don't have to worry about ensuring that each individual column is specified correctly in the **Fetch** statement.

Update statement

You should use the following syntax when updating information retrieved by using a cursor:

```
Update <table>
   Set <column> = <value> [, <column>=<value>] ...
   Where Current Of <cursor>
```

where <table> is the name of the table you want to update; <column> is the name of the column you want to update; <value> is the value you want to assign to the column; and <cursor> is an open cursor containing the information you want to updated.

The **Update** statement affects only the information in the current row. No other rows are affected when the **Where Current Of** cursor clause is included. Note that in order to perform the update, you need to ensure that your cursor accesses an updateable view. This means that you may only access one table at a time when you declare the cursor.

Delete statement

Using the **Delete** statement, you can delete the current row pointed to by the cursor, with the following syntax:

```
Delete From <table>
   Where Current Of <cursor>
```

where `<table>` is the name of the table containing the row you want to delete, and `<cursor>` is an open cursor containing the information you want to delete.

Like the **Update** statement, the **Delete** statement may only reference a single table and the **Where Current Of** clause ensures that only the currently fetched row is affected by the statement.

Transactions

By now, you understand the importance of using transactions in your application where you need to ensure multiple changes are performed together as a single atomic unit. So it should come as no surprise that PL/SQL also includes support for transaction. As you would expect, there is a statement to mark the beginning of the transaction and another statement to mark the end of the transaction.

Set Transaction statement

The **Set Transaction** statement marks the beginning of a transaction and has the following syntax:

```
Set Transaction {Read Only|Use Rollback Segment &lt;segment&gt;}
```

where `<segment>` is the name of a rollback segment that is used by the transaction to hold undo information.

The **Set Transaction** statement must be the first statement in your transaction. You can ensure this by executing the **Commit** statement before executing the **Set Transaction** statement. (The **Commit** statement is covered later in this chapter.) The **Read Only** clause is used to ensure that records you read will always be consistent, though you will be prohibited from updating any of this data. If you want to update this data, you must specify the **Use Rollback Segment** clause and specify the rollback segment associated with your application. Each **Set Transaction** statement must be matched with the appropriate **Rollback** or **Commit** statement. (The **Rollback** statement is covered later in this chapter.)

Savepoint statement

The **Savepoint** statement allows you to mark a place in your transaction where you may choose to rollback your work. Its syntax follows:

```
Savepoint <savepoint>
```

where `<savepoint>` is an identifier that uniquely identifies the savepoint location.

Commit statement

The **Commit** statement saves all of the database changes made to the database since the **Set Transaction** statement was executed. It has the following syntax:

```
Commit [Work];
```

The **Work** keyword is optional and has no real meaning. It exists solely to comply with the ANSI SQL standard.

Rollback statement

The **Rollback** statement discards all of the changes made by a transaction to the database. This statement has the following syntax:

```
Rollback [Work] [To [Savepoint] <savepoint>]
```

If you rollback to the specified `<savepoint>`, all changes done after the **Savepoint** statement are discarded. All work done prior to the **Savepoint** remains uncommitted. You must use a **Commit** statement to save the changes or a **Rollback** statement without specifying a savepoint.

Other useful statements

Besides the statements and commands discussed so far, there are a few others that you may find useful.

DBMS_Output Package

PL/SQL includes a package to assist you with sending output to the console. This package is mostly useful when debugging your stored procedures using SQL*Plus. The package consists of three stored procedures with the following format:

```
DBMS_OUTPUT.PUT (<value>);
DBMS_OUTPUT.PUT_LINE (<value>);
DBMS_OUTPUT.NEW_LINE;
```

where `<value>` is a value to be printed on the console.

The **Put** routine displays a single value on the console. The output cursor remains on the same line, so that another call to **Put** will display another value next to the first. The **New_Line** routine advances the cursor to the first position in the next line. **Put_Line** is the equivalent of calling **Put**, immediately followed by **New_Line**.

These routines are controlled by the SERVEROUTPUT feature that you manage with the **Set** statement. Turning **On** this feature means that the output will be sent to the console, while **Off** means that the output will be discarded.

```
SET SERVEROUTPUT {ON|OFF}
```

Setting the **Serveroutput** feature outside your routines means that you can leave the debugging code in the routines. If you feel that you need to trace the routines execution, you can **Set Serveroutput On** and call the routine in SQL*Plus. If you don't want to view your debugging code, simply **Set Serveroutput Off**.

Raise statement

Handling errors is always interesting, especially when you have stored procedures calling other stored procedures. Sometimes you find an error condition where you want to kill the entire transaction or stored procedure. The **Raise** statement allows you to trigger an error condition.

The syntax for the **Raise** statement is:

```
Raise [<exception>]
```

where `<exception>` is an exception value selected from Table 28-2. If a value for `<exception>` is specified, the code in the current block's Exception section will be triggered. You can omit `<exception>` only when you are already processing an error in the Exception section and wish to pass the error onto the Exception section of the block that encloses the current block.

Creating Stored Procedures

Creating a stored procedure, function, or package in Oracle8*i* involves building a **Create Procedure**, **Create Function**, or **Create Package** statement and running it. While you can do this with DBA Studio, you can also use any of the SQL*Plus variations.

Creating a procedure or function

The **Create Procedure** statement is used to create a stored procedure, while the **Create Function** statement is used to create a stored function. The syntax for these are:

```
Create [Or Replace]
{<procedure_definition>|<function_definition>}
```

where <procedure_definition> is the syntax for a procedure as described above, beginning with **Procedure** and ending with **End**; and <function_definition> is the syntax for a function as described above, beginning with **Function** and ending with **End**;.

If you specify the **Or Replace** clause, the routine will be replaced with the new routine in <procedure_definition> or <function_definition>.

Creating a package

The **Create Package** statement is used to create a package. Its syntax is:

```
Create [Or Replace] Package Body <package> As
   [<variable> <datatype> [:= <initial_value>];] ...
   {<procedure_definition>|<function_definition>}
   [{<procedure_definition>|<function_definition>}]...
   [Begin
      <statement>
      [<statement>]...
      ]
   End [<package>];
```

where <variable> is an identifier that will be used to store information locally in the block; <datatype> is any legal Oracle8*i* data type; <initial_value> is a constant that is appropriate for the data type; <procedure_definition> is the syntax for a procedure as described above, beginning with **Procedure** and ending with **End**; <function_definition> is the syntax for a function as described above, beginning with **Function** and ending with **End**; and <statement> is any legal PL/SQL statement or command.

A happy ending: The last **End** statement in your routine should include the routine's name as the <block_name>, such as `End MyProcedure;`. This will prove extremely useful when trying to identify the beginning and end of a routine in the package.

Thoughts on Oracle8*i* Stored Procedures

I prefer to use three tools to create and test my stored procedures. I use a tool like Write to actually code the SQL statements. Then I use SQL*Plus for DOS to load the statements from the file and add them to my database. I leave the Write session active, so that I can correct syntax errors or add new functions while I have the SQL*Plus session. That way, all I have to do is save the file and reload it in SQL*Plus.

Once the stored procedure (or function or package) is loaded into my database, I execute the stored procedure directly in SQL*Plus. This lets me review the results interactively. I also like to use the **DBMS_OUTPUT** package to sprinkle my code with debugging statements. After all, executing the **Set Serveroutput** command allows me to quickly turn the information off or on, depending on how bad my luck is running.

After I'm satisfied that the procedure it doing what is should be doing, I create a simple Visual Basic program to verify it. Just because my procedure works with Oracle's tools doesn't mean that it will automatically work with Microsoft's tools. Once the program works, I'll move the procedure to my application and test it over again.

Now if you believe that I always follow this process, I've got a great deal for you on a bridge in San Francisco. But I do keep the tools lying around in case of problems, which occur more frequently than you might expect.

Summary

In this chapter you learned:

- ✦ about the language elements in PL/SQL language.
- ✦ about the key statements of the PL/SQL language.
- ✦ how to create transactions in PL/SQL.
- ✦ how to create stored procedures and functions in PL/SQL.
- ✦ how to create packages in PL/SQL.

✦ ✦ ✦

PART

VIII

Microsoft Jet

In this Part, I'm going to introduce you to the Microsoft Jet database engine. This engine is also known as the Access database engine. I'll cover the fundamentals, such as how to access the database from ADO, plus how the Visual Basic data types map into the data types that are available in Jet. Then, I'll discuss how to create databases, tables, and other database objects using the tools available in Visual Basic and Access. I'll also discuss how you can secure your Jet database.

✦ ✦ ✦ ✦

In This Part

✦ ✦ ✦ ✦

Overview of Microsoft Jet

✦ ✦ ✦ ✦

In This Chapter

Introducing Microsoft Jet

Understanding the Database architecture

Examining the security model

Connecting to Jet with ADO

✦ ✦ ✦ ✦

In this chapter, I'll discuss the Microsoft Jet database system. I'll explain its architecture, data types, and security model. I'll also cover how to use ADO with Jet, including how to build a connection string and use the special facilities built into Visual Basic to support designing Jet databases.

Overview of Jet

There are perhaps more copies of Microsoft Jet installed on PCs than any other database engine, due to the fact that Jet is a critical part of Microsoft Access, which is part of the Microsoft Office family. This is the ideal choice when you want to build a single-user database system or share your database on a file server with a small group of people.

Microsoft Jet contains the following key features:

- ✦ Standard part of Visual Basic Professional Edition and Enterprise Edition
- ✦ Limited version included in the Visual Basic Learning Edition.
- ✦ Can be included with your Visual Basic application at no charge
- ✦ Requires little or no maintenance to maintain
- ✦ Doesn't require a dedicated database server
- ✦ Compatible with Microsoft Access
- ✦ Supports both ADO and DAO object models

Jet and Access or Access and Jet: Since the Jet database is so tightly coupled to the Access application, many people use the terms interchangeably. For instance, the Visual Data Manager tool refers to Access databases rather than Jet databases. I will refer to the database itself as Jet and the application development tool as Access, unless I'm referring to a menu item or command that specifically refers to Access rather than Jet.

Microsoft Jet versions

Microsoft Jet is just the database engine component from the Microsoft Access database system. Jet became available for the first time in 1992, when Access 1.0 was released. When Visual Basic Version 3.0 was released in 1993, Jet version 1.1 was included. Each new version of Access resulted in a new version of the Jet database engine. When a new version of Visual Basic was ready for release, it would include the latest version of the Jet database, with a few minor improvements.

Because the same database engine is used for both Access and Visual Basic, you can build an application that includes components in Access and in Visual Basic. Of course, you will need to use compatible versions of the software. In other words, don't expect to use an Access 1.0 database with Visual Basic 6.

Visual Basic 6 includes version 3.51 of the Jet database engine, which is basically the same as the version 3.5 that was shipped with Access 97. Access 2000 includes version 4.0 of the Jet engine, which can also be used with Visual Basic. These are the two most common versions of the Jet engine you are likely to encounter as a Visual Basic programmer.

The tools don't work: The tools included with Visual Basic 6 only work on version 3.5 and earlier Jet databases. If you plan to use a version 4.0 database, you must have Access 2000 installed on your system or be prepared to write your own code using ADOX or DAO to administrator your database.Jet version 3.5

If you develop VB6 applications with Jet, you are most likely using version 3.51. This is a very stable release, and it works well with Access 97. It is significantly faster than previous versions of the Jet engine and designed to be a little bit more friendly when accessing a database stored on a file server.

Key features of Jet 3.5 include:

- Support for the most common SQL statements, such as **Select**
- Database kept in a single file
- Ability to secure information based on user name and security group

- Ability to link to remote tables and treat them as local tables
- Database replication with other database servers
- Page-level locking

Jet version 4.0

Access 2000 introduced a newly revised Jet database system. Most of the changes made to Jet between Version 3.5 and 4.0 are transparent to the typical user. These changes were made to improve Access's integration with other Office 2000 applications. However, some improvements were made in the database engine itself:

- Support for Unicode data
- Record-level locking
- Migration utility to convert version 3.5 and earlier databases to the version 4.0 format

Bigger is not always better: If you convert a database from Jet 3.5 to Jet 4.0 and the database contains a lot of character data, expect the size to double. This is due to the fact that the actual data in the database is stored using Unicode characters. So, even if you try to store simple ASCII characters, the Jet database will store them using their Unicode equivalents.

Jet and DAO

Jet was designed around using the *DAO* (Data Access Objects) to access the contents of the database. DAO is a highly-structured object model that has evolved alongside Jet since its beginnings. In many ways, it is difficult to view the Jet database engine without thinking of the DAO object library.

See Chapter 6, "Accessing Databases from Visual Basic," for explanations of the DAO, ADO, and RDO models.

There are more programs today that use DAO, rather than ADO, to access Jet databases. However, I recommend using ADO over DAO for two reasons. First the ADO object library offers a simpler interface to your database, which translates into less code needed to do the same work. Second, Microsoft has decided that ADO is the way everyone should access databases using Microsoft development tools such as Visual Basic. While this doesn't mean that DAO is DOA, it does mean that its days are numbered. Access 2000 already supports ADO access to the Jet database, which incidentally allows you to use Access 2000 as a development tool for SQL Server databases. Also, Microsoft has developed a client computer friendly version of SQL Server called the Microsoft Database Engine (MSDE), which is 100% upwards compatible with SQL Server — something that Jet is not.

Jet 4.0, DAO 3.6: Even though the Jet database engine has been upgraded to version 4.0, the Data Access Objects (DAO) most often associated with the Jet database have been enhanced to version 3.6.

Jet utilities

For the most part, there are very few utilities associated with the Jet database, other than Access of course. Visual Basic includes a tool called the Visual Data Manager. This is an add-in tool that allows you to design Jet databases. (I'll talk more about the Visual Data Manager in Chapter 30).

Understanding the Database Architecture

Microsoft Jet is designed to be an SQL-based database management system that supports a handful of concurrent users. It works especially well with only a single user. While it can easily be used with Visual Basic applications, much of the architecture revolves around supporting Access applications.

Unlike most database systems, Microsoft Jet relies on shared access to a single file to coordinate activities among multiple users. This means that the code that manages the database must run in each user's address space and that you can't buffer data in memory, because different programs can't share their memory. All sharing must be done at the file level, using file locking and other techniques. This really limits performance and means that you probably won't even get close to Jet's 255 concurrent user limit.

.MDB files

All of the information for the Jet database is stored in a single file, called the `.MDB` file. This file contains all of the data, including tables and indexes, that comprise the Jet database. In addition, facilities are included that permit Access to store information in the same file without storing it in regular database tables.

Data is stored in an `.MDB` file using different types of pages. The first page in the file is the database header page, which contains general information about the database, plus information that tracks user operations in a multi-user environment. Table pages are used to hold information stored in a table, while index pages hold index information. Long value pages keep long values such as Text and Memo fields, which can exceed the size of a normal page. Finally, system table information is stored in its own unique type of page.

There are four system tables:

✦ **MSysACES** holds security permissions.

✦ **MSysObjects** holds information about each database object, such as a table or index, plus information on Access objects, such as forms and reports.

✦ **MSysQueries** holds information about predefined queries in the database.

✦ **MSysRelationships** holds information about predefined relationships between tables in the databases.

In addition to these tables, other tables will store information about objects used only in Access applications.

You didn't hear this from me: Microsoft considers the system tables in Access to be undocumented. This basically means that Microsoft reserves the right to change the organization and number of system tables without notifying anyone. Therefore, you shouldn't attempt to use these tables as part of your application.

.LDB files

When someone opens an `.MDB` file for the first time, an `.LDB` file is created in the same directory as the `.MDB` file. After the last user closes the database, the `.LDB` file will automatically be deleted. This file contains locking information for the `.MDB` file. Each user that has a connection to the database has an entry in the `.LDB` file. This entry contains the user name and the name of the computer that is being used.

When the user locks a piece of data in the `.MDB` file, an extended byte range lock is placed on the `.LDB` file. With a little creativity, this type of lock provides both shared and exclusive access to data in the `.MDB` file without the overhead of using physical locks on the `.MDB` file itself.

.MDW Files

The security information for a Jet database is stored in an `.MDW` file, which is also known as a workgroup file. This file contains information about users and groups, including their login passwords. Once a user is validated, they will be assigned an internal security identifier (SID). The permissions that associate the SID with the various database objects are stored inside the `.MDB` file.

MDA or MDW: Depending on the version of Access you have installed, the `SYSTEM.MDA` file may also be known as `SYSTEM.MDW`.

Database objects

As you might expect, a Jet database can hold many of the same database objects that are found in other database management systems. However, due to the nature of the target audience, some of the database objects you wish to use may not be available. While tables and indexes are present in Jet, views and triggers are not.

Key database objects include:

- **Tables**, which store user data in fields.
- **Indexes**, which provide quick ways to locate information in a table.
- **Relationships**, which are used to define relationships between tables and to enforce referential integrity.
- **Queries**, which are used to define standard queries (similar to views) against the database.
- **Users and Groups**, which are used to associate individuals with database permissions.

Linked databases

One of the nicer facilities in Jet is the ability to create a link to a table in another database in such a way that the programmer thinks the table is local to the Jet database. Besides linking to other Jet databases, you can also link to these databases:

- dBase
- FoxPro
- Paradox
- Excel
- Exchange and Outlook data files (read access only)
- Some text file formats, including comma-separated value files
- Any ODBC-compliant database, such as SQL Server or Oracle8

Tip

Link-be-gone: In the past, the only way to access a remote database was to create a link using a Jet database. With Visual Basic 6, both DAO and ADO make this feature unnecessary. You can now access any ODBC-compatible database directly with DAO and the ODBCDirect interface, or you can use the more flexible OLE DB with ADO. (Of course, you can always use RDO, but ADO makes that tool even more obsolete than DAO).

Database capacities

Table 29-1 lists some of the key capacities and limitations of the Jet database.

Table 29-1
Database Capacities

Item	*Capacity*
Maximum database size	1 gigabyte
Maximum characters per object name	64
Maximum characters per user name	20
Maximum characters per user password	14
Maximum characters per database password	20
Maximum number of concurrent users	255
Maximum characters in a table name	64
Maximum characters in a field name	64
Maximum table size	1 gigabyte
Maximum number of fields per table	255
Maximum number of indexes per table	32
Maximum number of fields in an index	10
Maximum number of fields in an **Order By** clause	10

Jet data types

Jet supports a wide variety of data types, as shown in Table 29-2.

Connecting to Jet with ADO

In order to connect to a Jet database using ADO, you can use the following connection string:

```
Provider=MSDAORA.1; Data source=vb6db.Athena.justpc.net
```

Table 29-2
Jet Data Types

Jet Data Type	*Visual Basic Data Type*	*Comments*
`Boolean`	`Boolean`	**Null** values can't be used with a `Bit` field
`Byte`	`Byte`	Holds numbers from 0 to 255
`Currency`	`Currency`	Eight-byte scaled integer accurate to four decimal places
`Date`	`Date`	A date and time value ranging from 1 Jan 100 to 31 Dec 9999
`Double`	`Double`	A 64-bit floating-point number
`Integer`	`Integer`	Holds numbers from –32,768 to +32,767 (16-bit integer)
`Long`	`Long`	Holds numbers from –2,147,483,648 to +2,147,483,647 (32-bit integer)
`Memo`	`String`	A text field containing up to 1.2 billion characters
`OLE Object`	`Byte Array`	Holds pictures and other large, raw binary values up to 1.2 gigabytes in length
`Single`	`Single`	A 32-bit floating-point number
`Text`	`String`	Variable length string up to 255 characters in length

If you specified user-level security in your database, you can also include the `User ID=` and `Password=` keywords if you want to include that information as part of the connection string—or you can supply them as arguments to the `Open` method.

Of course, you can use the Data Link Properties window to configure the Jet Provider. Select the provider that corresponds to the version of Jet you are using (see Figure 29-1). After pressing the Next button, enter the name of your database, and the user name and password needed to access the database (see Figure 29-2). If you haven't implemented user-level security, you can leave the default values for user name (`Admin`) and password (Blank password). To test the connection, press the Test Connection button.

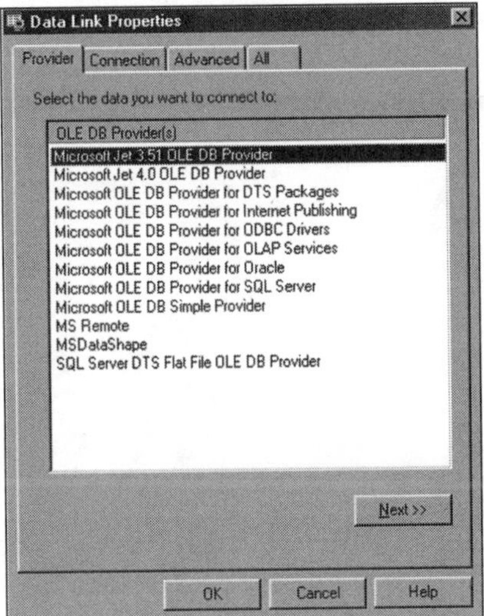

Figure 29-1: Choosing the proper OLE DB Jet provider.

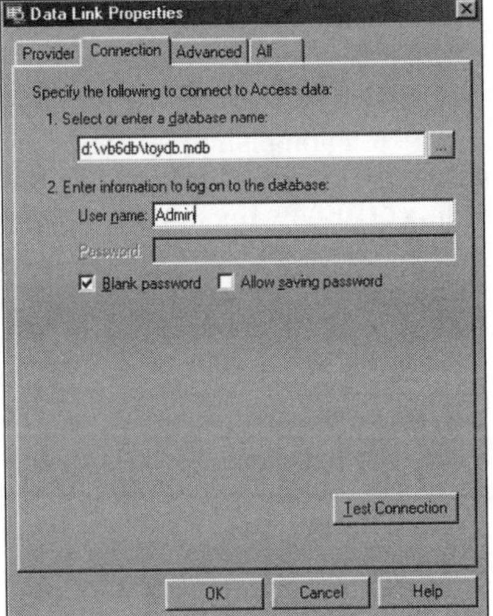

Figure 29-2: Specifying the name of the database, user name, and password information.

If you specified a database password, you can specify that value on the All tab of the Data Link Properties window. Simply select `Jet OLEDB: Database Password` field, press the Edit Value button, and enter the appropriate value (see Figure 29-3).

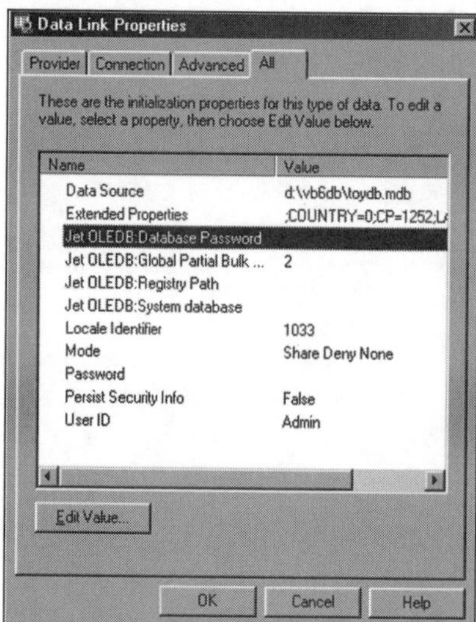

Figure 29-3: Specifying a database password.

Jet security

Like other database systems, Jet incorporates its own security subsystem. While you can choose to use it or ignore it, don't ignore it if you plan to let more than one person access your database. In fact, you should use it even if only one person will use your database. It just might stop them from corrupting the database by preventing them from opening the database with any other application.

Share-level security

In share-level security, the database is assigned a password. Anyone that knows the password can access the database. While this isn't as secure as user-level security (discussed next), it will prevent a user from accessing your database with Excel or Access. You can set the password using Access or by using the DAO `CreateDatabase` method in the Workspace object. Simply append the string `;pwd=MyPassword` to the end of the `Locale` parameter to set the database password to `MyPassword`. You then specify the password in the `Connect` parameter of the DAO `OpenDatabase` method. In ADO, you simply specify the password as part of the `Connection` string by using the `;pwd=MyPassword` keyword.

User-level security

User-level security works like the security systems in SQL Server and Oracle8i. A userID and password are created for each person who accesses the database. Then the userID is granted permission to access the various objects in the database. Groups can be used with user-level security to simplify administration. You can create a group and assign permissions to it, just as if it was another user. Then you can assign groups to various userIDs. When users log on to the database, they will inherit all of the permissions associated with the group or groups that have been assigned to them, plus any individual permissions they may have been granted.

Finding the workgroup file

Security information is kept in a workgroup file (.MDW). Only one workgroup file is required per system, and the following windows registry key will be used to locate it:

```
HKEY_LOCAL_SYSTEM\Software\Microsoft\Office\8.0\Access\Jet\3.5\
Engine\SystemDB
```

A typical value for this key is:

```
C:\WINDOWS\SYSTEM\system.mdw
```

Of course, if you are using a Jet 4.0 database with Access 2000 (Version 9.0), you will need to adjust the registry key to include the appropriate version numbers.

Security with Access: In order to use security with a Jet database, you must have installed Access 97 (or Access 2000 for a Jet 4.0 database). The file SYSTEM.MDW will automatically be installed.

SIDs, user ids, personal ids, and passwords

All information inside a database file is secured on the basis of a Security ID, or SID. A SID is derived by encrypting the user id and a special value known as a personal id. If you create a user id and don't bother to assign a personal id, it is possible for someone else to create another workgroup file with the same user id and their own password and user id to gain access to database resources for which they do not have permission.

The personal id is used to ensure that the SID is unique and can't be duplicated, so you should always choose a value that is hard to duplicate. Simply choosing someone's first name as the user id and their last name for the personal id is not a good idea.

By default, the user id Admin exists in all database systems with the same personal id. This means that Admin has the same SID no matter which computer they use. The same is true for the Users group. However, this is not true for the Admins group. The SID associated with the Admins group is always unique for each workgroup file.

Since anyone in the Admins group has access to the entire database, the first thing you want to do is create a new user id and assign it to the Admins group. Then you should remove the Admin user id from the Admins group to ensure that someone doesn't use their own workgroup file to override your database's security.

Permissions, SIDs, and ownership

The workgroup file exists simply to return a SID for a particular user and another SID for each group that the user is a member of. This value is used as a key into some of the system tables inside the database file to determine which permissions the user has.

If the user has overlapping permissions from multiple groups and/or explicit permission assignments, the least restrictive permission will apply. Thus, if a user has read and write permission to the Customers table via the Clerks group and has been explicitly granted read permission to the Customers table, the user will have read/write access to the Customers table.

Whenever an object is created in the database, the user id of the individual that created the object is used as the object's owner. The object's owner always has access to the object. You can and should change the ownership of the objects in your database to a user id other than Admin to prevent a security problem. I suggest that you use the Admins group as the object's owner, which means that anyone in the Admins group can always access the object.

Thoughts on Microsoft Jet

Microsoft Jet is a low-end database system designed primarily for use with Microsoft Access. Much of the design revolves around features that are important to Access users, while features that might be useful to Visual Basic programmers aren't present. Jet is not upwards-compatible with SQL Server and most other databases, due to these limitations.

Jet is also limited to a maximum of 255 concurrent users. However, its true maximum is far less, depending on how frequently the database is accessed. While many improvements have been made to make Jet more efficient, it is still limited by its file-oriented approach to synchronization for multiple users.

Just because Jet isn't perfect doesn't mean you should avoid using it. The Jet database engine is a standard part of the Visual Basic Professional Edition. This means that you don't have to purchase it separately. Also, there aren't any licensing charges associated with Jet.

This makes it ideal for those applications that are cost-sensitive, such as shareware, or part of a large distributed application where you want to cache data on the local computer.

Jet has also been around for a long time, though the ability to access it using ADO hasn't. Until recently, DAO included the ability to create database objects through its object model, while ADO could only create a database object by executing the appropriate SQL statement using the `Command` object. Since Visual Basic 6 was released, ADO has gone from version 2.0 to 2.1, and now to 2.5. The newer versions of ADO now include an independent object library known as ADOX, or ADO Extensions for Data Definition Language and Security. These objects improve on DAO's ability to create database objects while using an OLE DB interface to the database. So if you need to build database objects directly from your code, you no longer have to use DAO.

Summary

In this chapter you learned:

- about the various versions of the Jet database system.
- that the tools in Visual Basic do not support Jet 4.0.
- that you can use DAO 3.6 or ADO with the appropriate provider to write programs that work with Jet 4.0.
- about the architecture of the Jet database.
- how to connect to a Jet database.
- about the security capabilities for a Jet database.

✦ ✦ ✦

CHAPTER 30

Creating Database Objects with Microsoft Jet

✦ ✦ ✦ ✦

In This Chapter

Introducing Visual Data Manager

Constructing databases, tables, and indexes

Managing security for users and groups

✦ ✦ ✦ ✦

In this chapter, I'm going to show you how to use the Visual Data Manager add-in to Visual Basic to create a Microsoft Jet database and various objects, such as tables and indexes, inside it. I'll also cover how to create users and groups, and how to grant them permission to access database objects.

Introducing the Visual Data Manager

The Visual Data Manager (also called VisData) is a Visual Basic add-in that was written to make it easier to design a Jet database without building your own application or using Microsoft Access. To run the Visual Data Manager, choose Add-Ins ⇨ Visual Data Manager from the main menu. This will start the application.

You got it: The Visual Data Manager utility was written in Visual Basic 5 and shows what you can do with a little bit of work. The complete source code to the Visual Data Manager is included in the `Samples\VisData` directory of Visual Basic.

Since the Visual Data Manager is based on DAO, you can use it to open many other types of databases besides Jet databases. You can access dBase, FoxPro, and Paradox databases, as well as Excel worksheets and various types of text files. You can even open an ODBC connection to a remote database, such as

SQL Server or Oracle, though depending on your choice of database, some of the capabilities may not be supported.

Why doesn't it open the database I created with Access 2000?: Visual Data Manager uses DAO 3.5 to access databases. To access a Jet 4.0 database created with Access 2000, you must use DAO 3.6. While you could recompile the Visual Data Manager application using DAO 3.6, it's probably just easier to use Access to design your database.

Opening an existing database

To open an existing database, choose File ➪ Open DataBase ➪ Microsoft Access from the Visual Data Manager main menu. This will display a File Open dialog box. Simply choose the file containing your database and press the Open button. After you've opened your database, you'll see a form like the one shown in Figure 30-1. By default, the Visual Data Manager opens your database and displays two multiple document interface (MDI) windows. The first window (Database Window) displays your database's structure, while the second window (SQL Statement) allows you to enter and run an SQL statement.

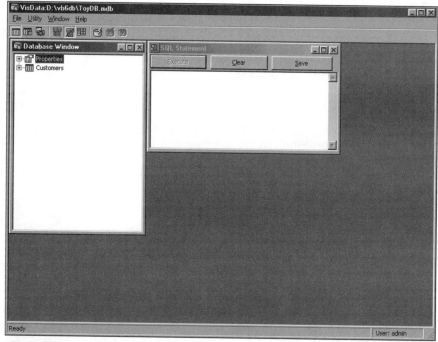

Figure 30-1: Viewing an open database.

Viewing Database Information

The Visual Data Manager allows you to see the structure of your database (see Figure 30-2). The tree view displays each table and its attributes, including columns and indexes. As you expand each entry in the table, you will eventually reach the details that would normally show up in the `Properties` collection associated with the object.

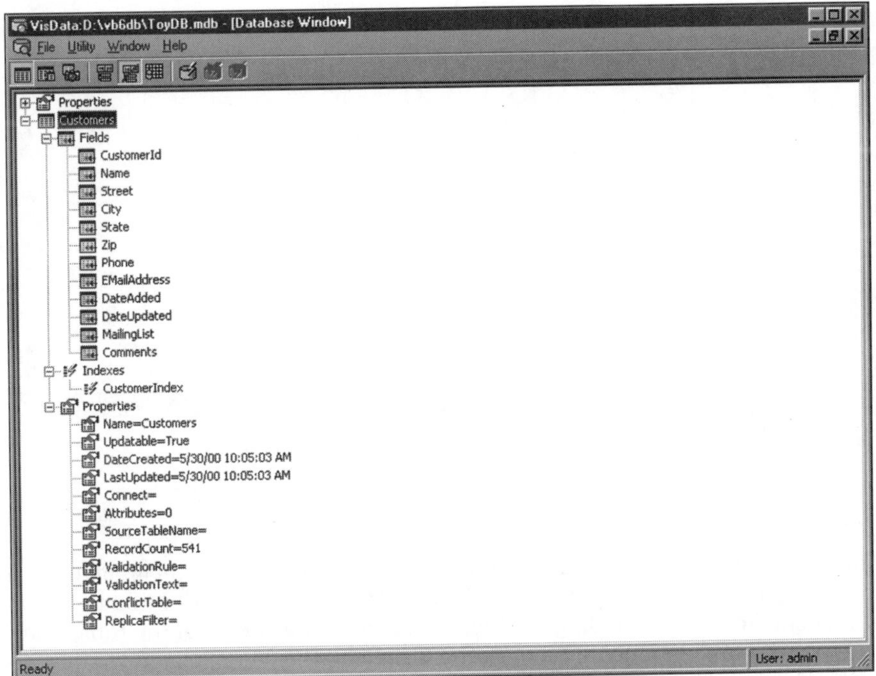

Figure 30-2: Viewing the structure of your database.

Running an SQL query

Another useful tool included in the Visual Data Manager is the ability to execute an SQL query against the current database. You can enter the query directly in the SQL Statement window (see Figure 30-3) or use the Query Builder to create the query (see Figure 30-4). Either way, when you run the query, your results will be displayed one row at a time in the Results window shown in Figure 30-5.

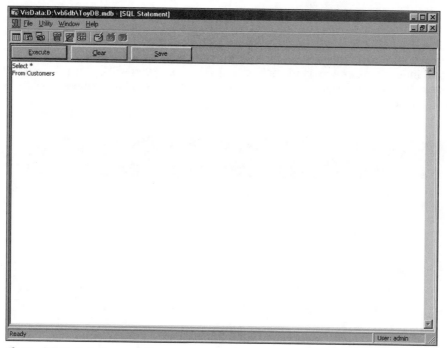

Figure 30-3: Entering an SQL statement in the SQL statement window.

Using the Query Builder

Choosing Utility ⇨ Query Builder from the Visual Data Manager main menu starts the Query Builder (see Figure 30-4). This utility assists you with building a **Select** statement. You begin building the **Select** statement by choosing the table you wish to start with in the Tables section of the form, and the columns you want to display in the Fields to Show section of the form. If you don't select any columns, all of the columns will be returned.

By default, all of the rows in the table will be returned. However, you can use the Field Name, Operator, and Value fields to select a value or range of values for a specific column. List Possible Values will populate the Value drop-down box with all of the values for that specific column in the table.

Once you've identified a field, operator, and value, you should press the And into Criteria button or the Or into Criteria button to include this expression in the Criteria section at the bottom of the form. Then you can select other criteria by selecting a new column, operator, and value combination. Pressing the And into Criteria button will insert an **And** operation between the two criteria, while pressing the Or into Criteria button will insert an **Or** operation.

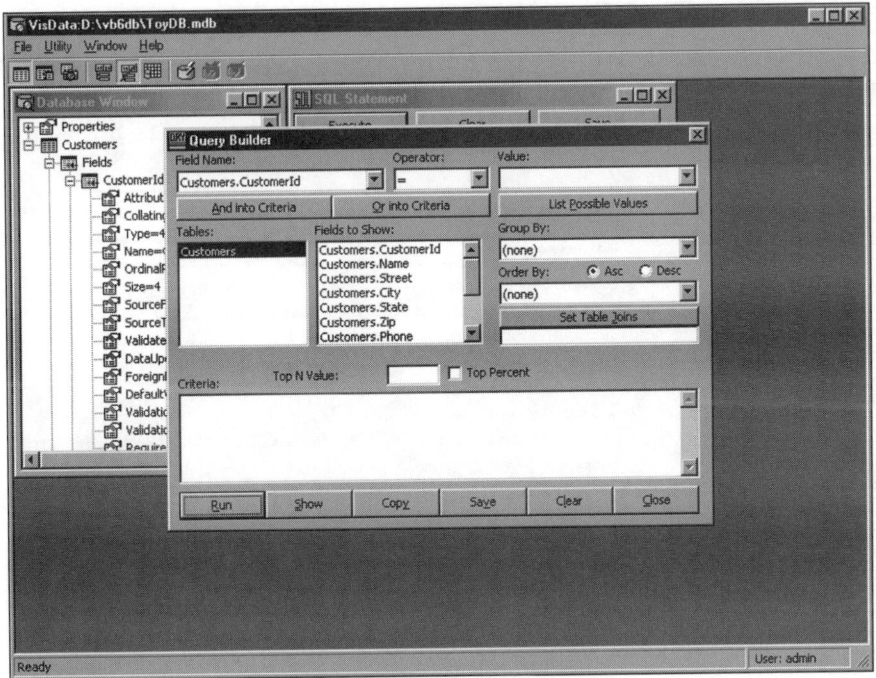

Figure 30-4: Building a query using the Query Builder.

You can choose to include **Group By** and **Order By** clauses by using the Group By and Order By drop-down boxes. If you have selected multiple tables, pressing the Set Table Joins button will display a dialog box that helps you select the join columns. The Top N Value field allows you to limit the number of rows retrieved by specifying an absolute number of rows or a relative percentage value.

When all of the information is entered into the form, you can press the Show button to see the **Select** statement you just built. Pressing Save will save the **Select** statement as a QueryDef in the database for use with Access, while pressing Copy will save a copy of the **Select** statement to the clipboard so that you may paste it into a different application. Pressing Close will close the Query Builder window and place the query you built in the SQL Statement window.

Getting your results

If you pressed the Enter key or clicked on the Execute button in the SQL Statement window, or clicked on the Run button in the Query Builder, the **Select** statement will be executed and the results will be returned in the Results window, as shown earlier in Figure 30-5.

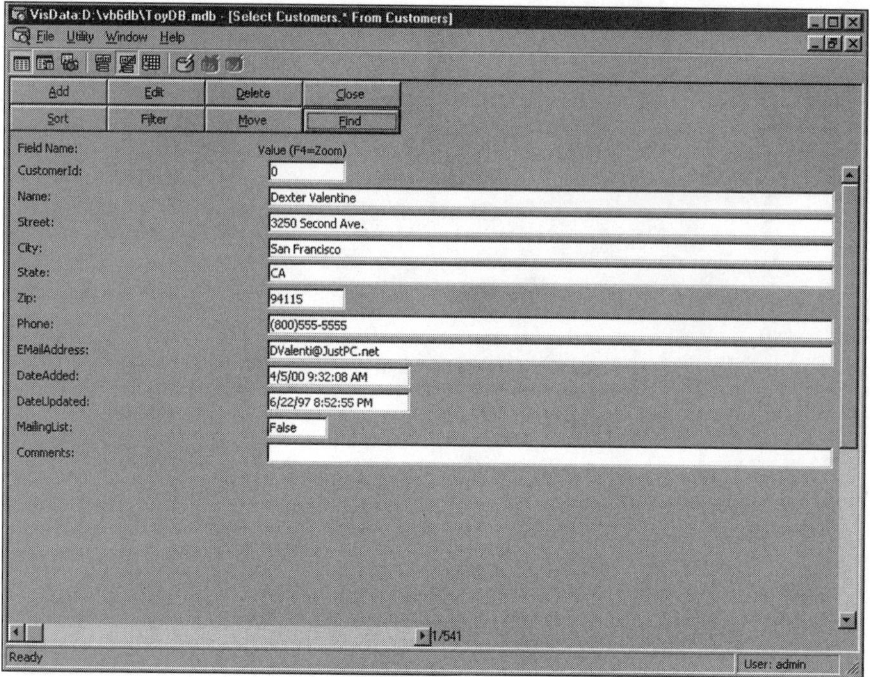

Figure 30-5: Seeing the results from running your query.

One row at a time will be displayed in the form. Clicking on the scroll bar at the bottom of the form will move you to another row that was retrieved from the database. The buttons at the top of the form perform the functions you would expect. Pressing the Add button will display an empty version of the Edit form in which you may enter the information you want to add to the database. Again, press Update to save your new row, or Cancel to discard it. Pressing the Edit button will change the configuration of the form slightly (see Figure 30-6). You can change any of the values and press the Update button to save the changes to the database, or press the Cancel button to discard the changes. The Delete button is used to delete the current row. Pressing the Close button will close the Results window and return you to the previous window where you created the query. Clicking on the Sort button will display a message box prompting you to enter the sort column, while clicking on the Filter button will display another message box prompting you to enter a filter expression. The Move button will allow you to specify the number of rows to be moved. The Find button displays a dialog box to help you find a particular row in the query. You must select a single field, a relational operator, enter a value and then choose whether you want to find the first value, next value, previous value or the last value in the table. Pressing the OK button will start the search and the record will be displayed in the main form.

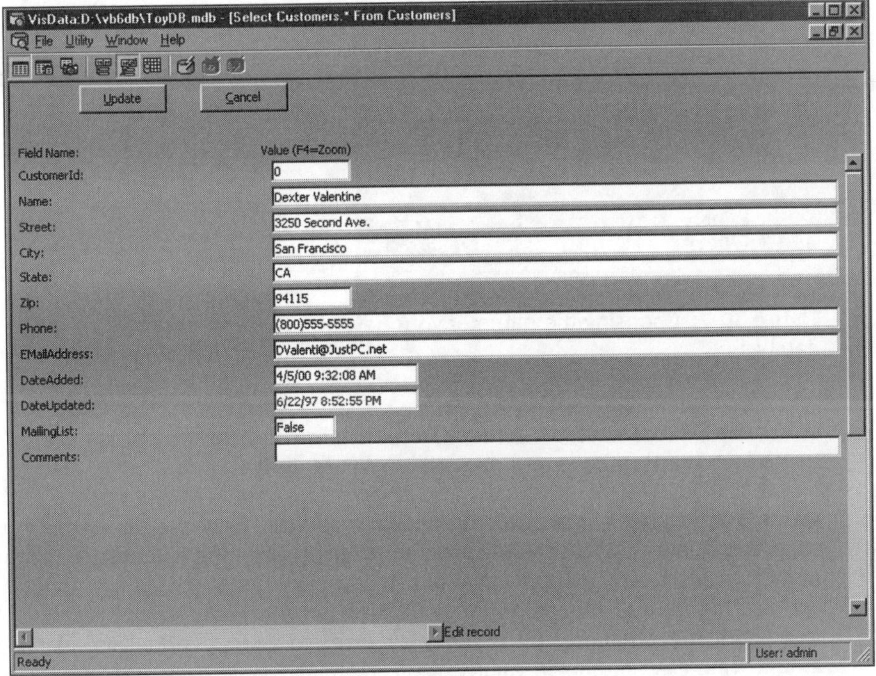

Figure 30-6: Editing a row in your database.

Constructing Databases, Tables, and Indexes

Probably the most common use for the Visual Data Manager utility is to create Jet database objects without using Access and without building your own application program.

Creating a new database

The following steps will show you how to use the Visual Data Manager to create a new database:

1. Start the Visual Data Manager and choose File ➪ New ➪ Microsoft Access ➪ Version 7.0 MDB from the main menu. This will display the Select Microsoft Access Database to Create dialog box (see Figure 30-7). Unless you have a specific need for an obsolete database, don't create a Version 2.0 MDB.

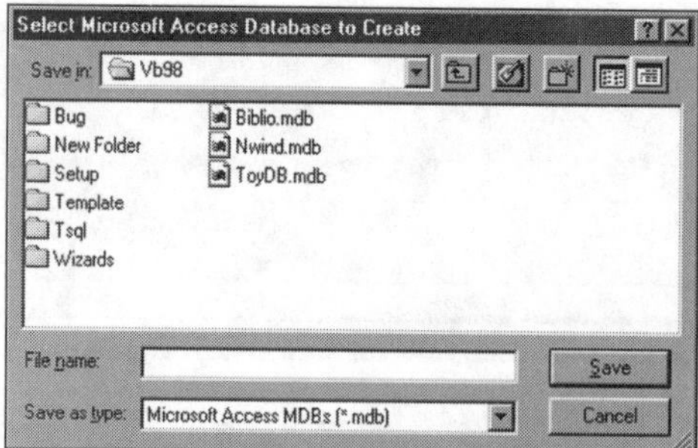

Figure 30-7: Choosing the name of your new database.

2. Using the Select Microsoft Access Database to Create dialog box, choose a name for your database and press Save to create it.

An empty database is a good thing: Because your database file is really just another disk file, I find it useful to keep an empty copy of the database file around when I'm developing an application. I can just copy the `.MDB` file to another file and use that to test my application, without having to go through the process of re-creating the database. Also, you may want to keep a populated database around with a set of known values. You can create a new copy of this file to test your application, while leaving the original populated file untouched for the next time you want to do some testing.

Creating a table

After creating a new database or opening an existing database, you can easily create a new table by following these steps:

1. While in the Visual Data Manager, select the Database window. Right click anywhere in the window and choose New Table. This will display the Table Structure window, as shown in Figure 30-8. Note that you can use the same window to display information about an existing table by right clicking on the table's name in the Database window and choosing Design from the pop-up menu.
2. Enter the name of the table in the Table Name field. Note that your table name should not duplicate any tables already defined in your database.

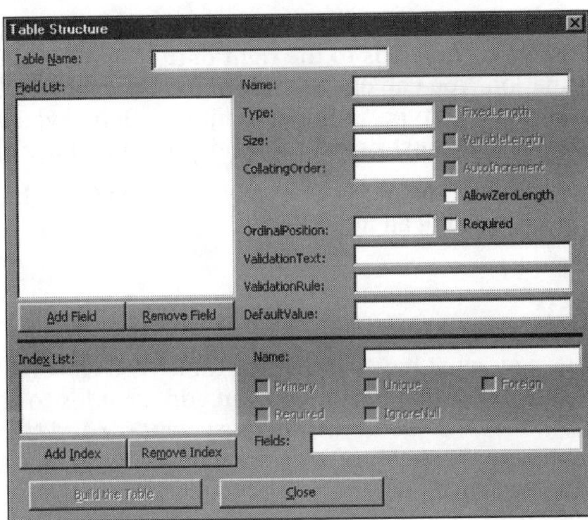

Figure 30-8: Creating a new table with the Table Structure window.

3. To add fields to the table, press the Add Field button. This will display the Add Field dialog box, as shown in Figure 30-9. Enter the name of the column in the Name field and select its data type in the Type drop-down box. You can ignore the OrdinalPosition box, since this value will be computed when the field is added. You may also specify a validation rule in the ValidationRule box. If you do so, you may also indicate the text that will be displayed when the validation rule fails in the ValidationText box. The value you enter in the DefaultValue text box will be used, instead of a **Null** value, whenever a new record is created. When you have entered the information for a field, press the OK button. The form will be cleared and you can enter the next field. When you have finished entering all of the fields, press the OK button to save the last field and then press the Close button to return to the Table Structure window.

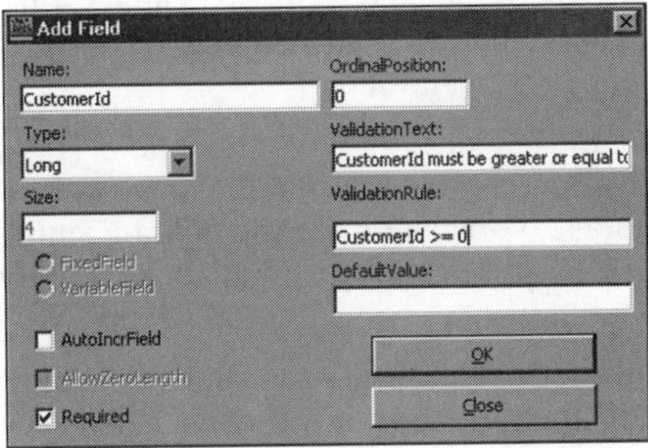

Figure 30-9: Adding a field to your table.

4. You can view the information associated with a field by clicking on the field's name in the Field List box. The fields to the right of the Field List will be populated with the information. You can change any of the information associated with a field, except for its data type and related information. If you wish to change this information, you must delete the field and add it back again.
5. When you have entered all of the fields, you may press the Close button, or continue this process by adding an index.

Creating an index

In order to create an index, you must have an existing table. You can create an index at the same time you create the table, or you can add an index to an existing table by right clicking on the table name in the Database window and selecting design from the pop-up menu to display the Table Structure window shown in Figure 30-9. Then follow these steps:

1. Press the Add Index button. This will display the Add Index dialog box, as shown in Figure 30-10.

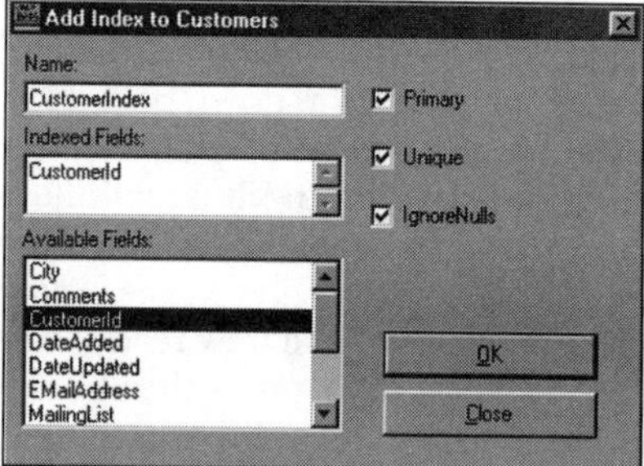

Figure 30-10: Adding an index to a table.

2. Enter the name of the index in the Name field. Choose Primary, Unique, and IgnoreNulls as appropriate. Just remember that you may have only one Primary index, and it should always be unique.
3. Add fields to the index by double-clicking on the field name in Available Fields. The field name will be added to the list of field names in the Indexed Fields field. If you make a mistake, you can delete the field by simply selecting the text in the Indexed Fields box and pressing the Delete key on the keyboard.
4. When you have finished adding your index, press the OK button. The form will be cleared so that you may add another index. If you are finished adding indexes to this table, press the Close button to return to the Table Structure window. Press the Close button on the Table Structure window to return to the Database Window.

Using the DAO and ADOX alternatives

You can also create database objects in a Jet database by using either DAO or ADOX (the ADO Extensions for Data Definition Language and Security). While the code to do this is very straightforward, it can be long and repetitive and not easily updated if your database design is still in a state of flux. However, having the ability to create a new, empty database from within your application can be useful in a single user application. This allows a user to easily create multiple, independent data files containing different sets of data.

See Chapters 6 and 11 for more information about the DAO and ADOX object models, respectively.

Managing Security

Every database system needs security, even if you plan to allow only one user to access it. If you have Access installed, managing security isn't very difficult, and this section discusses how to use Access 2000 to manage security for your Jet 4.0 database. Similar features exist in Access 97 in order to manage your Jet 3.5 database.

The security definition file

The first step in implementing security on a Jet database is to ensure that you have a workgroup database (`SYSTEM.MDW` file). This file contains information on the users and groups that secure a Jet database. By default, the `SYSTEM.MDW` file is created when you install Access 97 or Access 2000. Typically, this file is located in the `\Windows\System` directory; however, it can be located anywhere on your system, since a value in the Windows registry is used to locate the file.

If your application is running in a networked environment, where the database is shared among multiple users, you should make sure that the client systems point to a shared copy of the `SYSTEM.MDW` file. You can do this in DAO by specifying the `SystemDB` property in the `DBEngine` object, or by adjusting the windows registry key to point to the file.

Managing users and groups

Since the workgroup file is independent of any database file, you can manage the users and groups in Access without opening a database. You simply use the User and Group Accounts dialog box, which has the ability to view and change information about existing users and groups, as well as create new users and groups.

Managing users

To see the information about an existing user, start Access 2000 and choose Tools ➪ Security ➪ User and Group Accounts to display the User and Group Accounts dialog box (see Figure 30-11). Choose the user that you wish to view by selecting the user from the Name drop-down box.

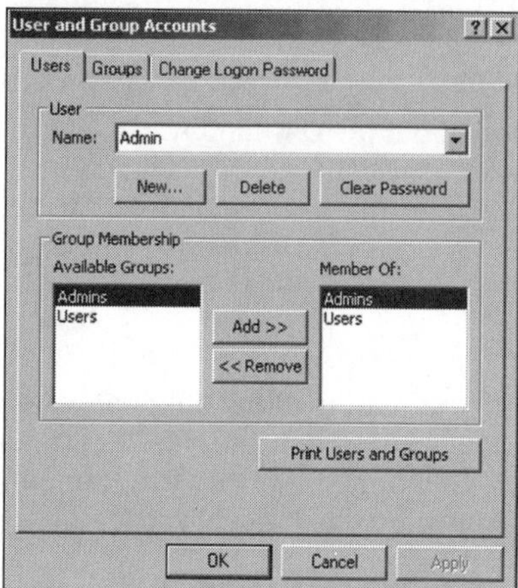

Figure 30-11: Displaying the User and Group Accounts dialog box.

Hidden secrets: While you can't see the password for a user, you can press the Clear Password button to remove the password from the user if you are a member of the Admins group, or you can switch to the Change Logon Password tab to change the password to a new value.

You can add a new user by pressing the New button in the User frame. This will display the New User/Group dialog box (see Figure 30-12). Enter the name of the user and a code phrase that will make the user name unique.

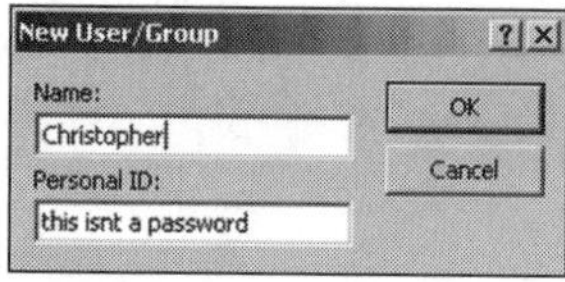

Figure 30-12: Creating a new user or group.

Ousting Admin

Removing Admin from power is one of the most important things you can do when you implement user-level security for your database. Unless you take the proper steps, it would be easy for a disgruntled employee to subvert your entire security system. Even if you trust everyone that uses your database, you should still take this precaution. Someone may take advantage of your open security and try to help you improve your database. Even with the best of intentions, and even if the individual has more knowledge about databases than you do, do you really want someone changing your application without your knowledge? A healthy paranoia about security is very important and helps to prevent problems in the long run.

Make personal ids personal: Given that you can easily substitute one workgroup file for another, it is important that user ids and groups be made universally unique. The key is supplying a value for the personal id that would not be easily guessed.

Managing groups

By switching to the Groups tab in the User and Group Accounts dialog box, you can see the list of security groups defined in the workgroup file (see Figure 30-13). You can create a new group by pressing the New button and entering the group and personal id as you did when you created a new user.

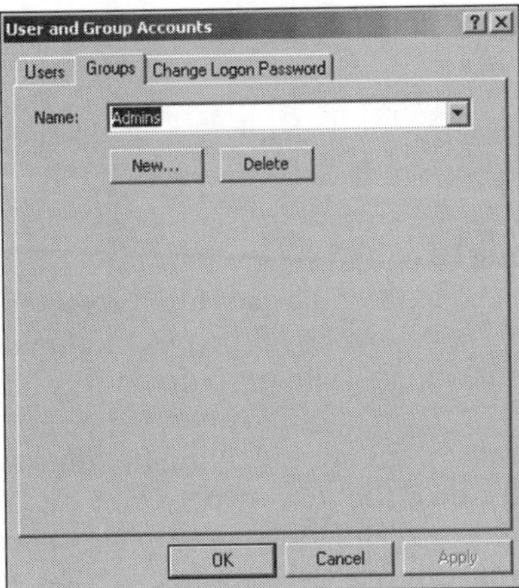

Figure 30-13: Viewing the groups in your workgroup file.

Managing permissions and ownership

Information about permissions to access a database object and the ownership of this object is stored in the system tables of your database. This information is really based on SIDs and not the actual user id or group name. Thus, your user id must have already been authenticated by using the workgroup file.

Managing permissions

Choose Tools ➪ Security ➪ User and Group Permissions from Access's main menu will display the User and Group Permissions dialog box shown in Figure 30-14.

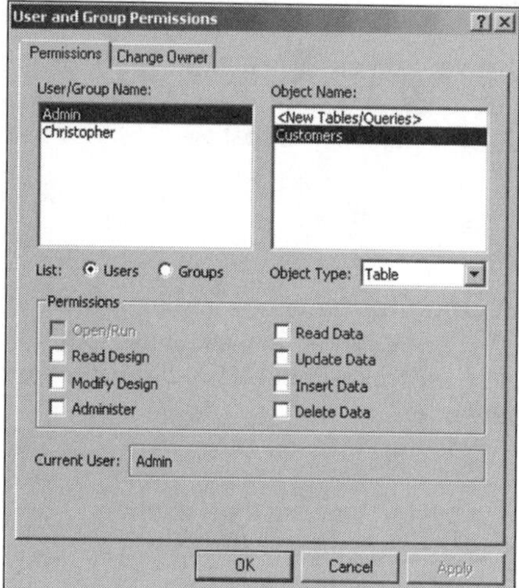

Figure 30-14: Editing a user or group's permissions.

Changing ownership

You can switch to the Change Owner tab of the User and Group Permissions dialog box to change the owner of a database object to a different user id or group (see Figure 30-15). The Object and Current Owner lists show all of the objects in your database that match the object selected in the Object Type drop-down box.

To change the ownership of the object, you must begin by selecting the database object you wish to change. Then you must decide if the new owner will be a group or a user and click on the appropriate radio button. The list of possible owners will be displayed in the New Owner drop-down box. Choose the user id or group and press the Change Owner button to make the change.

Don't forget the database: The database itself is an object that is owned by a user id or a group. By default, Admin owns the database. You should change this to the Admins group. Otherwise, the Admin user id is still all-powerful.

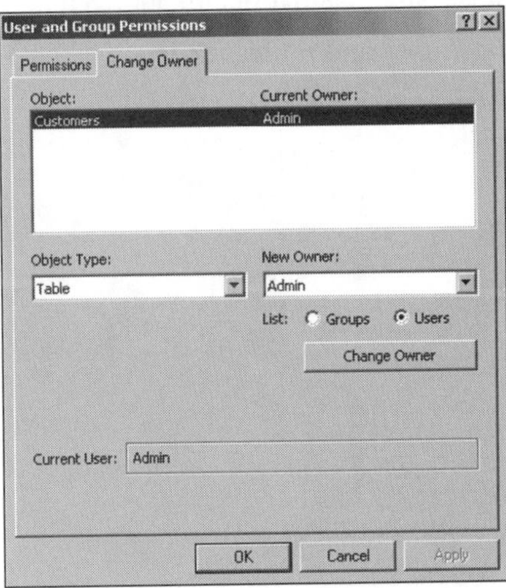

Figure 30-15: Changing the ownership of a database object.

Thoughts on Creating Jet Databases

Jet based Visual Basic applications are usually targeted at either individuals or small organizations with only a handful of users. This means that many of the approaches that I have discussed throughout the book may not apply. For instance, security in a small application is not nearly the problem it is in a larger application. For a single user application, the primary aim of security is to prevent the user from accidentally deleting information needed to run the application. Even with a handful of users, you are more concerned with identifying the actions of individual users rather than protecting the database from malicious actions.

Because of these differences, you might want to add some features that you wouldn't consider in larger applications. For instance, you may want to add a feature in your application to create a new copy of the database. This would let the user create multiple databases for different projects.

Another feature you might consider adding is a way to create a backup copy of the database. This means that the user has a way to make sure that their data is save in case of a system problem. Of course, creating a way to backup the database implies that a way to restore it will be necessary at some point.

Summary

In this chapter you learned:

✦ how to create databases, tables using Visual Basic tools for Jet 3.5 databases.

✦ how to use Access 2000 to create databases and tables for Jet 4.0.

✦ how to use Access 2000 to define security in a Jet 4.0 database.

✦ ✦ ✦

APPENDIX

What's on the CD-ROM?

✦ ✦ ✦ ✦

The CD-ROM that accompanies this book contains sample files that are designed to be used with Visual Basic, SQL Server 7, Oracle 8*i*, and Access 2000. These files do not require any special installation procedures, other than the sample database. Simply copy the files to a directory on your hard disk and load them using Visual Basic. The instructions for installing the sample databases appear on the last page of the book.

The CD-ROM also contains a full version of the book in electronic format, which can be read with Adobe Acrobat Reader.

Glossary

Access 2000 An easy-to-use tool to develop database applications. Part of the Microsoft Office 2000 suite.

ACID Stands for *atomic*, *consistent*, *isolation*, and *durable*, which describe the major characteristics of a *transaction*.

Active Directory A component of *Windows 2000 Server* that allows you to find information about various resources located across a network.

ActiveX A set of technologies that allows you to build and use *objects* using the *Component Object Model* (COM) and *Distributed Component Object Model* (DCOM).

ActiveX Controls Compiled software components developed with ActiveX technology that run on client computers.

ActiveX Data Objects (ADO) An object-oriented way to access a database such as Microsoft SQL Server, Access, and Oracle from an *application program*. This technology replaces older technologies such as *Data Access Objects (DAO)* and *Remote Data Objects (RDO)*. This is a high-level implementation of *OLE DB*, just like DAO and RDO are high-level implementations of *ODBC*.

ActiveX DLL A *COM* component residing in a *DLL* file that is loaded into the main program's address space at runtime. It is also known as an *in-process* object.

ActiveX EXE A *COM* component residing in an EXE file that is loaded into a separate *address space*.

Address Space The range of addresses that can be accessed by a program in virtual memory. Address space includes memory that can be used by an application and memory reserved for use by the operating system.

ADO See *ActiveX Data Objects*.

Administration Queue A *queue* that is used to hold system-generated acknowledgement messages, which indicate whether or not an *application message* reached its destination.

Aggregate The process of combining the values of a single column across a set of rows. Typical aggregation functions are: **Count**, **Max**, **Min**, and **Sum**.

Alias An alternate name for a column or table that exists only for the duration of a query.

ANSI SQL A standard for the *SQL* language from the American National Standards Institute (ANSI). The current version of the standard is referred to as SQL-92.

Apartment Model Threading A method that ensures that objects created in Visual Basic can be used by *multithreaded applications*. As each object is created, it is assigned to a single thread. All calls from code on different threads will need to be *marshaled* to access the object.

API See *Application Programming Interface*.

Application A collection of programs and *databases* that allows a *user* to solve a problem.

Application Log A file containing SQL Server status information in a Windows 2000/NT system.

Application Message A message generated by an application and sent using *COM+ Queued Components*. This is different from a *system message*, which is generated by the COM+ queued components, which stores copies of application messages after they are processed.

Application Programming Interface (API) A well-defined set of rules and calling conventions that describes how a programmer can invoke the services of another application or the operating system.

Application Queue A public or private *queue* that is used to send and receive application-specific messages.

Application Server A computer dedicated to running the *business rules* of an organization. These rules are often implemented using *transactions* running under the control of a *transaction server*.

Asynchronous Processing The type of processing that occurs when a program calls another program or component to perform a task and both programs continue to operate independently. See also *Synchronous Processing*.

Atomic A object that can't be subdivided. See *Atomic Field.* Also part of the *ACID* test for *transactions* when it refers to the concept that either all of the processing in a transaction must complete successfully or not if it completes. It ensures that there is no such thing as a partially-completed transaction.

Atomic Field A field whose contents can't be broken down any more. (For example, a date is not atomic since it can be broken down into day, month, and year, while a month is atomic since it can't be broken into smaller pieces.)

Authentication The process of establishing a *user's* identity. This usually involves providing a user name and a secret password to the operating system or to a *database server* to prove that you have access to the functions associated with the user name.

Authenticated User A person who has passed the *authentication* test.

Authorization The process of determining the access rights to functions and data that an *authenticated user* is allowed to perform.

Axis One dimension of an OLAP *cube*.

Backup A copy of the information in a database taken at a given point in time. It can be used to *recover* the information in the database.

Base Table A real table in the database that is referenced in a view.

Batch Job A process where a non-interactive program is executed, typically at a time when no one is around to control its execution.

Binary Large Object (BLOB) A *column* containing information such as an *image* that can exceed the size of a normal binary column. It often requires special handling when compared to a normal column.

Binding The process of locating an object and associating with your program. See also *early binding* and *late binding*.

BLOB See *Binary Large Object.*

BMP An *image* file format developed by Microsoft. It supports many different image formats (8-bit color, 24-bit color, and so on), but files are usually larger than with other image formats, such as *GIF* and *JPEG*.

Browser A program that is designed to translate *HTML* tags into a visible document.

Business Logic The set of *business rules* used to operate a business or other organization. The rules describe what an application program is supposed to do in a given situation. For example, a business rule may require a program to place an order for an item in inventory when its quantity on hand falls below a certain level.

Business Rule A set of instructions that implements a business procedure. For example, the steps that are taken to purchase a book by a business are considered a business rule. Business rules are often implemented as part of a *program* or set of programs that runs on a computer.

By Reference A type of parameter passing in which the address of a variable is passed to a routine. This allows the routine to directly change the contents of the variable. See also *By Value*.

By Value A type of parameter passing in which a copy of the variable is passed to the routine. If the routine changes the value of this parameter, the original variable remains unchanged. See also *By Reference*.

Cache A buffer that is used to hold frequently-used information. In a database system, a cache typically resides in the computer's memory and holds information from the database's disk storage.

Calculated Member A *member* of a *cube* that is computed on the fly based on data that already exists in the cube.

Cell The intersection of a *row* and a *column* in a *table*, containing a single value. In an OLAP *cube*, a cell represents the intersection of all of the *dimensions*.

Child A *member* in the next lower *level* in a *hierarchy*. This member represents a subset of the information of its *parent*.

Class Module A template from which an object is created. This template allows you to define *properties*, *methods,* and *events*, which can be used by other parts of your application. A *COM* component is built from one or more class modules in an *ActiveX DLL* or *ActiveX EXE*.

Client The user side of a multi-computer application. For example, Query Analyzer, Excel, and MapPoint can all be client programs for an SQL Server database.

Client/Server A programming technique where a *client* program makes requests of a *server* program. In the case of a *database server*, the *client* program running on the user's computer generates requests for information or supplies commands to the database server, which processes them and returns the results back to the calling application.

CLSID The class identifier for an object. All objects are assigned a CLSID, which is used as a key in the *Windows Registry* to locate the object's code. A CLSID is stored as a *GUID*, so that it will always be unique.

Clustered Index A special type of index that is used to determine the order of the rows in a table. A table can contain only one clustered index.

Codify A technique that replaces a field in a database with an encoded value that is used as a key to another table where the original field is extracted. This is typically used when dealing with "standard" text fields. For example, the text field JobTitle can be codified into an integer field called JobTitleCode. Using JobTitleCode in your database ensures that all employees have the same value for their job title. Since JobTitleCode is much smaller than JobTitle, you'll also save space in the database.

Column An attribute of a *table* that contains information. The concept of a column is similar to a *field* in a *record*. Also referred to as *data elements*.

COM See *Component Object Model*.

COM+ The next version of COM that includes many new services, some of which were previously independent of COM. These services include the *COM+ Transaction Server* (formerly known as the *Microsoft Transaction Server*) and *COM+ Queued Components*.

COM+ Application The primary unit of management by the *Component Services* tool. It consists of a single *DLL* or *EXE* file that contains a set of one or more *COM* components.

COM+ Queued Components An easy to incorporate *message queues* with COM+ components. This feature allows you to issue a method or access a property in an asynchronous fashion.

COM+ Transaction Server A software package that manages the execution of *transactions* under *Windows 2000 Server*. See also *Transaction server*.

Commit The act of saving a set of changes in a database. The changes can be abandoned by performing a *Roll Back*.

Compile-Time Refers to activities performed and events that occur while compiling a program.

Component An object that contains a set of *properties*, *methods,* and *events*. It is implemented in Visual Basic using a *class module* and represents a type that can be associated with a variable.

Component Object Model (COM) A technology used to create and access *objects* from a *Windows* program.

Component Services A utility included with *Windows 2000 Server* that is used to manage the *COM+ Transaction Server.*

Composite Field A field that can be broken into smaller parts. A date is an example of a composite field, since it can be broken into year, month, and day.

Composite Index An index that uses multiple columns as the key value.

Composite Key A *key* containing more than one *column*.

Concatenation The process of combining multiple *strings* into a single string by appending one string to the end of another.

Concurrency Occurs when multiple users share a resource; often requires *locks* to ensure that the sharing is done in an orderly fashion.

Connection A link between the client program and the *database server.*

Connection String A *string* containing the parameters necessary to connect to the *database server.* Typically used by ADO and RDO object models.

Consistent Part of the *ACID* definition of a *transaction*. It ensures that the work done by a *transaction* leaves the application in a consistent state.

Constituent Controls The set of controls that are used in an *ActiveX UserControl* object.

Constraint A restriction placed on a *column* or a set of columns that any value entered into the column must meet. Some examples of constraints are *foreign key*, *primary key*, and *unique*.

Container A *control* that can contain other controls.

Control An *object* that can be placed on a Visual Basic form or report to provide a specific function or to interact with the user. Some examples of controls are text boxes, where the user can enter and edit text *strings*, labels that display text values, and buttons that can be pushed by the user.

Cookie A set of data that is maintained by a user's *browser* and is available for processing by Web server based applications.

Cross-tabulation Report A report that aggregates every combination of two or more data fields.

Crosstab Report See *Cross-tabulation Report.*

Cube A set of data organized by *dimensions* and containing *measures*. The data is generally extracted from a *data warehouse* and is analyzed by tools like Excel *PivotTables*.

Cube Browser A tool included in the OLAP Manager that allows you to view the data in a cube.

Cube Editor A tool included with the OLAP Manager that allows you to view and change the structure of a cube.

Current Record The single row pointed to by the *cursor*. The current record can be changed by moving the cursor to a different row.

Cursor Used by an application program to point to a specific *row* in a *table* or *recordset*. This row is then considered the *current record.*

DAO See *Data Access Objects.*

Data Access Objects (DAO) An obsolete way to access a *database* from Visual Basic. *ActiveX Data Objects* have replaced this technology.

Data Bound Controls A way of linking a *control* in a Visual Basic program to a *column* in a *recordset*. Whenever the value in the column changes, it will automatically be updated in the control. Changing the value in the control will change the value in the *database*.

Data Consumer Receives data from a *data source* in the ADO object model.

Data Control A Visual Basic *control* that links other controls on a form to a *database*. This control supports scrolling through a *recordset* one record at a time and displaying the contents of the recordset on the *bound controls*. You can also use the data control to insert new records, update existing records, or delete existing records.

Data Dictionary A repository that contains detailed information about every field, table, and view in a database and how they are related to each other.

Data Element Another name for *column*.

Data Environment A tool in Visual Basic that simplifies database programming. It allows you to define and design your access methods to the *database*.

Data Mart A concept identical to a data warehouse, but smaller in scope. Rather than encompassing all of the data in an organization, a data mart may only contain information about a single department or application.

Data Scrubbing The process of analyzing data for consistency before data is loaded into a data warehouse.

Data Source The source of the data that is to be loaded into a *dimension* or *member* of a cube. A data source is also the source of data in the *ADO* model. It provides data to *data consumers* for processing.

Data Transformation Services (DTS) A tool in SQL Server that allows you to move and transform data from one database to another. This tool is extremely useful when you are extracting data from your production database to your data warehouse.

Data Type Defines the storage mechanism for a *column*. It also determines the set of basic operations that can be against the column. Some common data types include CHAR, which hold strings of characters, and INT, which hold numeric values.

Data Warehouse A central repository containing data that is made available to satisfy unstructured requests for information by end users. The data is generally extracted from production applications and summarized to minimize the amount of work needed to satisfy the request.

Database A collection of *tables*, *indexes*, and other *database objects* that are used by one or more *applications* stored inside a *database server*.

Database Administrator (DBA) A database administrator is the person responsible for the design and maintenance of a database. Besides creating and changing databases, this person is also responsible for such tasks as database backup and database recovery.

Database Client The computer that is used to access a *database server*. Typically, this computer will run either a tool such as Query Analyzer to perform *query* operations against the database or a custom application that allows the user to add, delete, and modify information in the database.

Database Diagram A graphical representation of a subset of the *database objects* contained in a database.

Database Management System (DBMS) A highly specialized piece of software that is used to store and retrieve data quickly and securely. It exists independently of an application program and allows concurrent access to the data it contains. See also *Database*.

Database Object A *table*, *column*, *index*, *trigger*, *view*, *constraint*, *rule*, *stored procedure*, or *key* in a database.

Database Owner (DBO) The *user name* of the individual who is responsible for the *database*. This individual is also known as the *database administrator*.

Database Query See *Query*.

Database Replication The process whereby the contents of one database are synchronized with another database.

Database Server The computer that contains the set of *databases* and the software that services requests from *database clients*.

Database Structure See *Database Object*.

DBA See *Database Administrator*.

DBMS See *Database Management System*.

DBO See *Database Owner*.

DCE See *Distributed Computing Environment*.

DCOM See *Distributed Component Object Model*.

DCOM Configuration Utility (DCOMCNGF) A utility program available in *Windows* that is used to maintain the additional information necessary to find *COM components* in a distributed environment.

Dead-Letter Queue A *system queue* that is used to hold *application messages* that can't be delivered.

Decision Support System An application designed to help people make better business decisions. Typically, a decision support system uses a data warehouse as the source of the data to be analyzed.

Delegation The impersonation of clients over a network when using DCOM or COM+. See also *Impersonation*.

Design-Time Refers to activities performed and events that occur while writing a program.

Dimension A part of the *cube* that is used to organize the *members* in the cube. A dimension may have one or more *levels,* which are used to group data values. For instance, a time dimension has the All level at the top, followed by a Years level containing the set of years, and a Months level containing the months in a particular year.

Distributed Component Object Model (DCOM) A superset of the *Component Object Model* (COM) that allows the distribution of objects over a local area and wide area network.

Distributed Computing Environment (DCE) The Open Software Foundation standards for distributed application services. These services include a distribute file system, a distributed security system, and *remote procedure calls*.

Dimension Table A table in a *data warehouse* that is used to index the values in a fact table.

DLL See *Dynamic Link Library.*

Drill Down The act of expanding the information displayed from a *cube* to see the next level of detail.

Domain A collection of computers in a Windows environment that share a common security database.

DTS See *Data Transformation Services.*

Dump See *Backup.*

Durable Part of the *ACID* definition of a transaction. It ensures that once a transaction has been completed, the operating system can always recover the work done by the transaction after a system failure.

Dynamic Link Library (DLL) A file containing compiled code that can be shared by multiple programs at *runtime.*

Early Binding Occurs when Visual Basic is able to determine the type of object you wish to access at development-time. To implement early binding, you must declare your variable as a specific object type, such as **Recordset** rather than **Object**. Early binding makes your program more efficient because less work is needed at *runtime* to determine the object's type. See also *Late Binding.*

Endpoints Represents each end of a TCP/IP connection. A specific TCP port number characterizes each endpoint.

English Query A tool included in Microsoft SQL Server 7 that allows you to enter queries using English-like questions and sentences.

Equijoin A join operation with two or more tables, where one field in one table must be equal to another field in the other table.

Event An external subroutine called by an *object* when a specific situation is encountered. This allows the program using the object to supply additional information to the object, or take a specific action based on information supplied by the object.

Excel 2000 A part of the Microsoft Office 2000 suite of programs that is used to analyze tabular data using worksheets and multi-dimensional data using PivotTables.

EXE See *Executable File.*

Executable File (EXE) Contains a compiled version of a program that can be loaded into memory and executed.

Export The process of moving data from a database to a file.

Expression An algebraic formula that can involve constants, columns, functions, and arithmetic operators. Often used in SQL statements.

External Transaction A *transaction* that includes units of work from more than one *resource manager.*

Fact Table A central table in a data warehouse whose primary key values link back to dimension tables. The remaining values typically describe a transaction within an organization such as a purchase. Sometimes these values are summarized according to the dimensions included in the table to reduce the amount of data stored.

Field An alternate name for *column* or *data element.*

Filter An expression that is used to identify a series of records in a query.

Friend Property A *property* that appears to be part of the public *interface* to a COM object, but can be accessed only by the other routines in the same project. Thus, you define a *friend property* in one *class module* and access it in another class module, just as if you had declared it as public. Friend properties can be used only in *ActiveX EXEs*, *ActiveX DLLs,* and *ActiveX Controls.*

Foreign Key A *column* or set of columns whose value must match the *primary key* of another *table.*

Full Backup A complete *backup* of a database. Can be used to restore the entire contents of a database without using any other backups.

Full-Text Query A *query* that searches for one or more words or phrases in a *column*.

Function A routine that returns a value based on zero or more parameters. Functions are typically used as part of an expression.

GIF See *Graphics Interchange Format.*

Graphics Interchange Format (GIF) A file format (which uses technology owned by Unisys Corporation) that is commonly used to store graphic *images* typically with 256 colors or fewer. Users whose *applications* use GIF images may have to pay a royalty fee to Unisys in order to use the technology.

Globally Unique Identifier (GUID) A 128-bit (16-byte) value that is generated by an algorithm that guarantees that the value will be unique. The algorithm that generates this value can be used at the rate of one new GUID per second for several centuries and never duplicate a value on your local computer or any other computer.

GUID See *Globally Unique Identifier.*

Hierarchy An arrangement of the *members* in a *dimension* into *levels* based on *parent child* relationships. For example, a time dimension is broken into years, years are broken into months, and so on.

Hierarchical Recordset A *recordset* in which a *column* in a particular *row* can contain another recordset.

HOPAP See *Hybrid OLAP Database.*

HTML See *Hypertext Markup Language.*

HTTP See *Hypertext Transport Protocol.*

HTTP User Agent A unique *string* that identifies the name and version of a Web browser. From this value, you can deduce its capabilities.

Hybrid OLAP Database (HOLAP) A Hybrid OLAP database uses techniques from both a MOLAP database and a ROLAP database to provide better performance than either approach.

Hypertext Markup Language (HTML) A simple language used to create a hypertext document consisting of tags to define formatting options and hypertext links.

Hypertext Transport Protocol (HTTP) A stateless object-oriented protocol used by Web clients and servers to communicate.

I/O See *Input/Output.*

Identifier A string of characters that is used to uniquely describe a database object, such as a *column* or *table.*

Identity Column A column in a table that contains a system-generated, monotonically-increasing value that is guaranteed to be unique within the table.

IID See *Interface Identifier.*

IIS See *Internet Information Server.*

Image A digital picture that can be stored on a computer. Many different image formats are available, such as *BMP*, *GIF,* and *JPEG.*

Import The process of copying data from a file to a *database*. This is the opposite of *export.*

Impersonation The ability to perform a task using the security permission of one user, while executing under the security permissions of another. See also *Delegation.*

In-process Object A *COM* object that is loaded into the same address space as the calling program. It is implemented in Visual Basic as an *ActiveX Control* or an *ActiveX DLL.*

Incremental Update The process whereby rows are added to a table, rather than replacing all of the rows in the table.

Index A database facility that stores details about the location of *rows* containing a specified *key* value. This *database object* allows the *database server* to retrieve rows from a *table* faster than without the index. Indexes are usually created based on typical searches performed by users to increase performance.

Input/Output (I/O) An operation whereby the computer either reads data from a device or writes data to a device. Some typical devices include disk drives, printers, keyboards, and modems.

Instance An object that has been allocated memory to hold information based on a template found in an *ActiveX DLL*, *ActiveX Control,* or *ActiveX EXE.*

Integrity Constraint See *Rule.*

Interactive User Refers to the user name associated with the keyboard and display on a *Windows* computer. While there is always an interactive user on a *Windows 98/95* computer, there may not always be an interactive user on a *Windows 2000/NT* machine. This is especially true of *Windows 2000/NT Server*.

Interface A way to access the services supplied by an *object*. A *COM* based object can contain zero or more *properties*, zero or more *methods*, or zero or more *events*. Standard interfaces are those defined by Microsoft. All *COM* objects are expected to implement IUnknown. IDispatch is required when you want to support late binding.

Interface Identifier (IID) The *GUID* that uniquely identifies an *interface*.

Internal Transaction A *transaction* where the *COM+ Queued Components* feature supplies the only resource manager.

Internet An international network that permits computers to communicate among one another using the TCP/IP suite of protocols.

Internet Information Server (IIS) Microsoft's high-performance Web server that runs on a *Windows 2000/NT Server* system.

Intranet An internal network for an organization that is based on the tools and protocols used by the Internet.

Intrinsic Controls *Controls* available in Visual Basic that are included with the runtime library. They are usually limited to performing relatively simple functions.

Isolation Part of the *ACID* definition of a *transaction*. It provides the viewpoint that each transaction operates independently of other transactions.

Job See *Batch Job*.

Journal Queue A *system queue* that is used to hold messages that have been processed and removed from a *transaction queue*.

Joint Photographic Experts Group (JPEG) An *image* file format optimized for 24-bit color images. It uses a compression scheme where data that may not be noticed by the user is thrown away and results in very small images.

JPEG See *Joint Photographic Experts Group*.

Junction Table The table in the middle of a *many-to-many relationship*.

Key A *column* or set of columns whose contents are used to identify one or more *rows*. See also *Primary Key*, *Foreign Key*, and *Index*.

Late Binding Occurs when Visual Basic is unable to determine the type of object you wish to access at development time. This happens when you declare your object variable as a general type, such as **Object** or **Variant**. Late binding slows your program at runtime because Visual Basic must determine the object's type each time it is accessed. See also *Early Binding*.

Level Describes the amount of detail displayed in a dimension. The lower the level, the more detail will be displayed.

License Key A way to prevent someone from redistributing an *ActiveX Control* you develop without your permission. The *license key* must be present either in the *Windows Registry* of the computer using the control or in the program using the control. Only controls whose license key is in the Registry can be used in the Visual Basic development environment.

Load Balancing The act of assigning new work or shifting existing work to the least-busy server in a defined group of computers. This helps to improve network performance by ensuring that all of the servers in the group of computers are equally busy.

Locking A process where a user is granted exclusive access to a particular *database object*. This prevents other users from changing the object until the first user has finished and released the lock.

Logical I/O An *I/O* request from the *database server* that may or may not be satisfied by information already in memory.

Login An identifier that gives an individual access to a *database server*. A *login* is mapped to a particular *user name* when accessing a specific *database*.

Many-to-Many Relationship A relationship between two *data elements* where a particular value for one field implies that the other field can have a particular range of values, while that field implies that the first field may also have a range of values. For example, an author may write many books, while a book may be written by many authors.

MapPoint 2000 An application that is a member of the Microsoft Office 2000 suite that is used to analyze geographic data.

MAPI See *Messaging Application Programming Interface*.

Marshaling The technique of sending interface message calls to an object on a different thread in the same address space or in a different address space.

Master Database The *database* used by the *database server* to manage all the other databases under its control.

MDX See *Multi-dimensional Expressions.*

Measure A numeric column that is included in a *fact table*. Typically contains information that can be analyzed.

Member An item in a *dimension* that represents one or more occurrences of data. The combination of a member and its parent values must be unique.

Message Information that is generated by an application or by the system and stored in a *message queue*.

Message Queue An application-generated queue that contains application-generated messages. Also used to refer to *Microsoft Message Queues*.

Messaging Application Programming Interface (MAPI) An interface developed by Microsoft to provide functions that developers could use to create e-mail enabled applications.

Metadata A collection of attributes that describes your database including, the data type of each column, the format that should be used to present the data, a description of the data, plus any other information that is useful in understanding how the data is created and how it should be used.

Method A way to access a subroutine or function to perform a specific task within an *object*.

Microsoft Message Queues (MSMQ) A feature that allows you to send asynchronous messages from one application program to another.

Microsoft Transaction Server (MTS) A server that manages distribute application *objects*. MTS has been superceded on Windows 2000 systems by COM+ Transaction Server.

Middle Tier The middle level of processing in an *n*-tier application system. Typically this tier consists of a *transaction server* such as the *COM+ Transaction Server*.

Model Database A *database* that contains all the default *tables* and supporting information that must exist in an empty database.

Module-Level Variable A variable defined at the start of a module. This variable can be accessed by any routine in the module, even if it is declared private. If it is declared public, it may be referenced by code outside the module. A *public variable* in a *class module* is treated as an object's property.

MTS See *Microsoft Transaction Server.*

Multi-dimensional Expressions (MDX) A language that is used for building queries that access a cube.

Multi-dimensional Database A multi-dimensional database stores information in a collection of large multi-dimensional arrays. This makes it easy to locate a specific piece of information quickly. However, this structure is extremely time consuming to load.

Multiprocessor A computer system with more than one CPU that is under *Window's* direct control. This allows two or more *threads* to be running at the same time.

Multithreaded A process that can have two or more active *threads* running at the same time.

N-Tier Application Indicates the number of computers where processing is performed as part of an application. A stand-alone computer is one-tier, and client/server computing is two-tier. DCOM and COM+ allow you to perform three-tier processing by adding another computer in between the client and server computers.

Nested Query A **Select** statement that contains one or more *subqueries*.

Nontransactional Message A *message* generated by an application that is not part of a *transaction*.

Nontransactional Queue A *queue* that is used to receive *nontransactional messages*.

Normalization The process of designing a database according to a set of well-defined rules that minimize duplication of information.

Null A condition that exists when a *column* doesn't have a value. This should not be confused with an empty string, whose value is a string of characters with a length of zero.

Object A software component that contains one or more *interfaces* that can be used to request information or perform functions.

Object Browser A function of the Visual Basic IDE that allows you to see the definitions of the *properties*, *methods,* and *events* of an object available to your program.

Object Code A collection of machine instructions and data that is loaded into memory for execution.

Object Pooling A facility in *COM+* that allows you to create a set of object instances that can be shared by the *transactions* running in the *COM+ Transaction Server.*

ObjectContext The object used to track the status of a transaction under *COM+*. It is created at the beginning of a *transaction*. At the end of the transaction, you can mark the transaction as successfully completed or abort all of the activities associated with the transaction.

OCX File A file that contains one or more *ActiveX Controls*. It is similar in structure to an *ActiveX DLL* file, but it must include extra *interfaces* that provide the graphical interface.

ODBC See *Open Database Connectivity.*

OLAP See *Online Analytical Processing.*

OLAP Manager A utility that allows you to manage an OLAP Server and contains tools that allow you to design and populate OLAP cubes.

OLAP Server A type of *server* that is designed to store *multi-dimensional databases* and to process queries against the data.

OLAP Services A facility in Microsoft SQL Server that includes tools like the *OLAP Manager* and a special server called OLAP Server that responds to requests to *Multi-dimensional OLAP databases.*

OLE DB An object-oriented programming interface to access a *database* or other data source that supports Microsoft's COM technology.

OLE DB Consumer A program that requests information from a data source using *OLE DB provider.*

OLE DB Provider A program that responds to requests for information from an *OLE DB consumer.*

One-to-Many Relationships A relationship between two *data elements* where a particular value for one *field* implies that the other field can have a particular range of values, while that field implies that the first field can have only one value. For example, there is a one-to-many relationship between a biological mother and her children. A mother may have many children, while a child has only one biological mother.

One-to-One Relationship A relationship between two *data elements* where a particular value for one *field* implies that the other field will have a particular value and vice versa. For example, there is a one-to-one relationship between a person and that person's social security number.

Online Analytical Processing (OLAP) A database technology that allows you to view multi-dimensional structures for data analysis.

Open Database Connectivity (ODBC) A technology developed by Microsoft that permits Windows programs to access different database systems. This technology has been superceded by *OLE DB*.

Operator A symbol that is used to perform computations, comparisons, and other tasks within an *expression*.

Out-of-Process Object A *COM* object that is loaded into its own address space. It is implemented in Visual Basic as an *ActiveX EXE* file.

Package The collection of information defined to Data Transformation Services that is used to *import* or *export* data from your database.

Page The fundamental unit of physical database storage. All *tables*, *indexes*, and other database information are mapped onto one or more pages, which are transferred as needed between disk and memory. In SQL Server 7.0, one page equals 8K bytes worth of data. 128 pages equals 1 megabyte of data.

Parameter A value or expression that is passed to a function.

Parent A *member* in the next higher *level* in a *hierarchy*. The parent represents the aggregation of the values of all of its *child* members.

Partition A storage container for data and aggregations of a cube. Every cube has at least one partition. Note that multiple partitions are only with some editions of SQL Server.

Partial Backup An incomplete *backup* of your database. A partial backup records the changes made since another backup was taken. Its primary advantage is that it runs much faster than a *full backup*. To completely recover your database, you will need a *full* backup and any other partial backups that were taken after the full backup was taken.

Pass-Through Query A query that is passed through the current server untouched onto another server for execution.

Pathname The fully qualified name of a queue. It is stored using the format machinename\queuename, where machinename is the name of the computer containing the queue and the queuename is the name of the queue.

Permission The ability to perform a specific function inside a *database*. Each user must have the proper *authorization* in order to use the resource specified by the permission.

Persistence The ability to save the information inside an object before it is destroyed and restore it after the object is recreated. An example of persistence is when Visual Basic saves the property values associated with an *ActiveX Control* from one development session to the next.

Personal Web Server (PWS) A lightweight Web server designed for use with *Windows 98/95*, *Windows 2000 Professional*, and *Windows NT Workstation*.

Physical I/O An *I/O* or output request that results in a physical transfer of data from or to a disk drive or other hardware device. This differs from a *logical I/O*, where the information may be buffered in memory and no physical transfer occurs.

Pivot The process of exchanging one dimension for another in a *cube* or *PivotTable*.

PivotTable A facility in *Excel* that allows you to analyze multi-dimensional data. The data can be extracted locally from a *worksheet* or remotely from a *database server* or an *OLAP Server*.

PivotTable Service A tool on a *client* computer that communicates with an *OLAP Server* to provide data for a *client application* such as *Excel*.

Precalculate The process of performing *aggregations* on *multi-dimensional* data in anticipation of future queries.

Primary Key The *column* or columns in a *table* that will uniquely identify a *row*.

Private Dimension A *dimension* that is used only by a single *cube*, as opposed to a *shared dimension*, which is common to multiple cubes.

Private Message A message that has been encrypted before being sent to a *queue*.

Private Queue A *message queue* that is registered only on the local machine. This queue is not published in the *Active Directory*, making it harder to find.

Private Variable A variable whose scope is limited to the routine or module in which it was declared. If the variable is declared inside a routine, it may not be accessible from outside the routine. If it was declared as a *module-level variable*, it cannot be accessed from outside the module.

Process The collection of an *address space*, *threads*, and other information that is associated with the running of a single program. See also *Refresh*.

Processing Processing is the act of loading data into a cube. This must be done each time a cube is created, when its structure has been changed, or when the data in the data warehouse has changed.

Production Application An application that implements *business logic* to help an organization perform its primary goals.

Property A way to access a data attribute stored inside an *object*. A property may be read/write, read-only, or write-only.

Property Bag An object associated with a Visual Basic *class module* that is used to provide persistent storage. Before the object is destroyed, you are allowed to save information in the *property bag*. When the object is created, you can restore this information from the property bag.

Property Page A *COM* object that allows a user to access the properties associated with an *ActiveX control* as design-time.

Protocol A set of rules that define how two or more computers communicate with each other.

Public Queue A *queue* registered in the *active directory*, which makes it easier to find.

Public Variable A variable that can be accessed from any module in your application program. If it is included as part of a *COM* object, it becomes a *property* available for any routine to read or write.

Publisher The source of data in the replication model.

PWS See *Personal Web Server*.

Query A request to retrieve, insert, update, or delete information in a *database*.

Query Optimizer A part of the *database server* that analyzes a database *query* to determine the most efficient way to execute the query.

Queue An object to hold messages between applications. Implemented by *Microsoft Message Queues*.

Queue Name The name of a *queue*. It may contain up to 124 characters, except for the backslash (\), semicolon (;), and dollar sign ($).

Rapid Application Development Tool A tool that allows you to build applications quickly, at the cost of execution efficiency.

RDBMS See *Relational Database Management System*.

RDO See *Remote Data Objects*.

Record A collection of fields containing related information that is treated as a single entity. Also known as a *row* in a *table*.

Recordset A collection of records retrieved from a database and made available to a Visual Basic program through a *COM* object. Recordsets are objects present in the *ADO*, *DAO*, and *RDO* object models.

Recovery The process of rebuilding a *database* based on database *backups* and *transaction logs*.

Referential Integrity A way to ensure that the information in the *database* is valid by only permitting values to be entered into a *table* if the value in the *foreign key* is found in the *primary key* of another table.

Registry The area in *Windows* that holds configuration information about the operating system and application programs.

Refresh The set of operations that deletes the data from a cube and loads the cube with a fresh set of data from the data warehouse. See also *Process*.

Relational Database A *database* that appears to the user as a simple collection of *tables*, where each table consists of a series of *columns* or *fields* across the top and a series of *rows* or records down the side. The underlying data structures used to hold the data are totally invisible to the user.

Relational Database Management System (RDBMS) A collection of *relational databases* on a single *database server*.

Relational OLAP Database (ROLAP) A Relational OLAP database stores its information in a relational database. This has the advantage of being easy to load, but can be time-consuming to search.

Relationship A situation whereby a *foreign key* in a table is linked to a *primary key* in another table. A relationship may be a *one-to-one relationship*, a *one-to-many relationship* or a *many-to-many relationship*.

Remote Data Objects (RDO) A technology that allows a program running on *Windows* to access a database using *ODBC* technology. This technology is much more efficient than *Data Access Objects* for accessing large databases. It has since been superceded by *ActiveX Data Objects*.

Remote Procedure Call (RPC) A technique used to allow a program on one computer to call a subroutine on another computer that is attached over a network.

Repeating Group A variable that contains multiple occurrences of information. This is similar to an array with dynamically-defined bounds. An example of a repeating group would be book authors, where book authors might have one, two, three or more authors depending on the particular book.

Replication A way of keeping two *databases* with the same information in sync.

Replication Model See *Database Replication.*

Report Queue A *queue* used to track the progress of *messages* as they move to the *Destination Queue*.

Repository See *Data Dictionary.*

Response Message An application-generated message that is returned to a *response queue* specified by the sending application.

Response Queue A *queue* used to receive a *response message* from the application that received a message.

ROLAP See *Relational OLAP Database*.

Role A predefined set of *permissions* in the *database*. When a *login* id is assigned to a role, it inherits all the permissions associated with the role.

Roll Back The process of undoing a set of changes to the database that have not yet been committed.

Row A collection of *columns* that are stored in a *table*.

RPC See *Remote Procedure Call.*

Rule A way to verify a value entered in a *column*. A rule is created by adding an *Integrity Constraint* to a table. You can specify a list of permitted values or place other limits on the particular values that are considered acceptable.

Run Time When the program is being executed as opposed to *design-time* (when the program is being written) or *compile-time* (when the program is being compiled).

SA See *System Administrator.*

Schema A description of the *database* using a language such as *SQL*.

Secondary Key A *column* or set of columns that can be used to identify a *row* in a *table*. Unlike the *primary key*, a secondary key need not be unique.

Server A server side of a client-server application. This program responds to requests from *client* applications.

Shared Dimension A dimension in an *OLAP database* is common to multiple cubes.

Single Threaded A block of code that can only be executed by one thread at a time. This typically includes functions where global data is in the process of being updated, such as a global counter or a complex database update that affects global data.

Slice and Dice The act of moving and combining dimensions while selecting one or more individual level values in a cube to see data from different viewpoints.

Snowflake Schema A database design where a fact table is surrounded by one or more dimensions and each dimension is represented by one or more tables. See also *Star Schema.*

Source File Contains the programming language statements that a compiler will translate into an *executable file*, which can be loaded into memory and run.

SQL See *Structured Query Language*.

SQL Server Microsoft's high performance database management system. Includes a number of tools, such as the Query Analyzer, Enterprise Manager, English Query, and OLAP Server.

SQL Statement A single *query* written in the *SQL* language.

Star Schema A database design where a fact table is surrounded by one or more dimensions and each dimension is represented by a single table. See also *Snowflake Schema.*

Stored Procedure A set of *SQL* statements that are executed on the *database server* and can optionally return a result to the database client program. Using stored procedures is usually more efficient than trying to perform the same function directly on the database client, because they are precompiled and may also be contained in the server's memory. Also, if multiple steps are included in the stored procedure, there is no need to transfer data between the database server and client, which also tends to improve performance.

Strategic Application Deals with the long range business goals of an organization. A *data warehouse* is an example of a strategic application. See also *Tactical Application.*

String A sequence of characters that can be stored in a *database* or manipulated by a program. Strings can contain ASCII characters or *Unicode* characters.

Structured Query Language (SQL) A language originally developed by IBM in the 1970s that has become the standard language for accessing relational *databases*.

Subquery A **Select** statement that is nested inside another *SQL statement*.

Subscriber The destination of data in a replication model.

Synchronous Processing The type of processing that occurs when a program calls a task and the calling program is blocked from performing any other work until the program it calls completes. See also *Asynchronous Processing*.

System Administrator (SA) The *login* associated with the individual responsible for an SQL Server database system. The system administrator is exempt from all security rules and is treated as the *database owner* of whatever *database* is being used.

System Catalog The *tables* found in the *Master Database*, which are used to store information on the other databases in the *database server* and also hold the database server's configuration information.

System Databases In SQL Server, the system databases include the *Master Database*, the *Temporary Database* (tempdb), and the *Model Database*. These *databases* are required to operate SQL Server.

System Queue A *queue* created by the *COM+ Queued Components* feature that is required to operate the queued components.

System Table A *table* required by a *database server* to hold information about itself. This includes such information as *user databases*, *tables*, *columns*, *indexes*, and so on.

Table The only database object that contains business data. It provides a view of this data by a series of *columns* and *rows*. Each column of data corresponds to a *field*, while a row is also known as a *record*.

Table Scan The process where the database server must read every row in a table in order to satisfy a *query*.

Tactical Application Deals with the day to day issues of running an organization. A payroll application is an example of a tactical application. See also *Strategic Application*.

Temporary Database A *database* in SQL Server that holds temporary information such as temporary tables and other temporary storage needs. All temporary tables are stored in this database, no matter which database the user is accessing. This database is known as "tempdb".

Thread An execution path through the same instance of a program.

Threading Model Describes how your application will use threads in an address space. A *single-threaded* application can take advantage of only one execution path through the program. A *multithreaded* application can have more than one execution path active at the same time.

Transact-SQL The name of the *SQL* language implemented in SQL Server. It consists of many extensions to the ANSI standard, including local variables, assignment statements, If statements, and other control flow statements that help you build *stored procedures*.

Transaction A logical unit of work that consists of one or more changes to a *database*. Either all of the steps in the transaction are completed or none of them. The classic example of a transaction is transferring money from one account to another, where the funds are subtracted from the source account and then added to the destination account. If only half of the transaction is completed, the database will be in error. In *COM+*, every transaction must meet the *ACID* test.

Transaction Log A file containing a list of changes made to the *database*. This information can be used to undo changes made to the database, or it can be combined with a *backup* file to recover *transactions* made after the backup was made.

Transaction Server A piece of operating system software that manages the execution of *transactions*. See also *COM+ Transaction Server*.

Transactional Message A message sent as part of a *transaction*.

Transactional Queue A *queue* that is used to hold *transactional messages*.

Trigger A special type of *stored procedure* that is called whenever a *row* is inserted in, deleted from, or updated in a *table*. If a severe error is encountered while running the trigger, the *transaction* will automatically be rolled back. It is used primarily for ensuring that new data is valid or to cascade changes from one table to another. For example, you may include a trigger on an order entry table that ensures that the customer ID exists in the customer table before an order is placed.

UDL File See *Data Link File*.

Underlying Table See *Base Table*.

Unicode A way to store international characters in a 16-bit character. This makes it easier for processing multilingual data.

Unique Index An index in which each row must have a unique *key* value.

Universal Data Link See *Data Link File.*

User Database A *database* where user information is kept.

User Name An *identifier* associated with a *login* that is used to determine an individual's *permissions* in a *database.*

View A virtual *table* that is created through the use of an *SQL* **Select** statement. A view appears to the user exactly as a table for all read operations and some write operations, depending on how the view was created.

Virtual Cube A logical cube that is created from existing dimensions and measures from one or more physical cubes. A virtual cube is similar in concept to a view.

Virtual Dimension A logical dimension that is created from an existing dimension in a cube.

Visual Basic A rapid application development tool that is often used to build database applications.

Visual Basic Script A version of Visual Basic that runs inside another application such as Data Transformation Services to provide the ability to customize a task.

Web Page A document typically written in *HTML* that is made available over the *Internet* for display on a *browser.*

Windows A family of operating systems from Microsoft.

Windows 98/95 An operating system designed to support interactive processing. Currently there are three versions of Windows 98/95: Windows 98 Second Edition, Windows 98, and Windows 95.

Windows 2000 Professional An operating system designed to support interactive processing. This operating system replaces Windows NT Workstation.

Windows 2000/NT Server An operating system designed to support various *servers*, such as a database server or a Web server.

Windows NT Workstation An operating system designed to support interactive processing. Typically used by power users.

Wizard A sequence of dialog boxes that are used to prompt a user for information that is used to perform a complex task.

Index

B

C

Continued

D

E

Continued

N

O

P

Continued

Q

R

Continued

T

Continued

U

Continued

IDG Books Worldwide, Inc. End-User License Agreement

READ THIS. You should carefully read these terms and conditions before opening the software packet(s) included with this book ("Book"). This is a license agreement ("Agreement") between you and IDG Books Worldwide, Inc. ("IDGB"). By opening the accompanying software packet(s), you acknowledge that you have read and accept the following terms and conditions. If you do not agree and do not want to be bound by such terms and conditions, promptly return the Book and the unopened software packet(s) to the place you obtained them for a full refund.

1. **License Grant.** IDGB grants to you (either an individual or entity) a nonexclusive license to use one copy of the enclosed software program(s) (collectively, the "Software") solely for your own personal or business purposes on a single computer (whether a standard computer or a workstation component of a multiuser network). The Software is in use on a computer when it is loaded into temporary memory (RAM) or installed into permanent memory (hard disk, CD-ROM, or other storage device). IDGB reserves all rights not expressly granted herein.

2. **Ownership.** IDGB is the owner of all right, title, and interest, including copyright, in and to the compilation of the Software recorded on the disk(s) or CD-ROM ("Software Media"). Copyright to the individual programs recorded on the Software Media is owned by the author or other authorized copyright owner of each program. Ownership of the Software and all proprietary rights relating thereto remain with IDGB and its licensers.

3. **Restrictions On Use and Transfer.**

   (a) You may only (i) make one copy of the Software for backup or archival purposes, or (ii) transfer the Software to a single hard disk, provided that you keep the original for backup or archival purposes. You may not (i) rent or lease the Software, (ii) copy or reproduce the Software through a LAN or other network system or through any computer subscriber system or bulletin-board system, or (iii) modify, adapt, or create derivative works based on the Software.

   (b) You may not reverse engineer, decompile, or disassemble the Software. You may transfer the Software and user documentation on a permanent basis, provided that the transferee agrees to accept the terms and conditions of this Agreement and you retain no copies. If the Software is an update or has been updated, any transfer must include the most recent update and all prior versions.

4. **Restrictions on Use of Individual Programs.** You must follow the individual requirements and restrictions detailed for each individual program in the Appendix of this Book. These limitations are also contained in the individual license agreements recorded on the Software Media. These limitations may include a requirement that after using the program for a specified period of time, the user must pay a registration fee or discontinue use. By opening the Software packet(s), you will be agreeing to abide by the licenses and restrictions for these individual programs that are detailed in the Appendix and on the Software Media. None of the material on this Software Media or listed in this Book may ever be redistributed, in original or modified form, for commercial purposes.

5. **Limited Warranty.**

   (a) IDGB warrants that the Software and Software Media are free from defects in materials and workmanship under normal use for a period of sixty (60) days from the date of purchase of this Book. If IDGB receives notification within the warranty period of defects in materials or workmanship, IDGB will replace the defective Software Media.

   (b) **IDGB AND THE AUTHOR OF THE BOOK DISCLAIM ALL OTHER WARRANTIES, EXPRESS OR IMPLIED, INCLUDING WITHOUT LIMITATION IMPLIED WARRANTIES OF MERCHANTABILITY AND FITNESS FOR A PARTICULAR PURPOSE, WITH RESPECT TO THE SOFTWARE, THE PROGRAMS, THE SOURCE CODE CONTAINED THEREIN, AND/OR THE TECHNIQUES DESCRIBED IN THIS BOOK. IDGB DOES NOT WARRANT THAT THE FUNCTIONS CONTAINED IN THE SOFTWARE WILL MEET YOUR REQUIREMENTS OR THAT THE OPERATION OF THE SOFTWARE WILL BE ERROR FREE.**

   (c) This limited warranty gives you specific legal rights, and you may have other rights that vary from jurisdiction to jurisdiction.

6. **Remedies.**

   (a) IDGB's entire liability and your exclusive remedy for defects in materials and workmanship shall be limited to replacement of the Software Media, which may be returned to IDGB with a copy of your receipt at the following address: Software Media Fulfillment Department, Attn.: *Visual Basic 6 Database Programming Bible*, IDG Books Worldwide, Inc., 10475 Crosspoint Blvd., Indianapolis, IN 46256, or call 1-800-762-2974. Please allow three to four weeks for delivery. This Limited Warranty is void if failure of the Software Media has resulted from accident, abuse, or misapplication. Any replacement Software Media will be warranted for the remainder of the original warranty period or thirty (30) days, whichever is longer.

(b) In no event shall IDGB or the author be liable for any damages whatsoever (including without limitation damages for loss of business profits, business interruption, loss of business information, or any other pecuniary loss) arising from the use of or inability to use the Book or the Software, even if IDGB has been advised of the possibility of such damages.

(c) Because some jurisdictions do not allow the exclusion or limitation of liability for consequential or incidental damages, the above limitation or exclusion may not apply to you.

7. **U.S. Government Restricted Rights.** Use, duplication, or disclosure of the Software by the U.S. Government is subject to restrictions stated in paragraph (c)(1)(ii) of the Rights in Technical Data and Computer Software clause of DFARS 252.227-7013, and in subparagraphs (a) through (d) of the Commercial Computer—Restricted Rights clause at FAR 52.227-19, and in similar clauses in the NASA FAR supplement, when applicable.

8. **General.** This Agreement constitutes the entire understanding of the parties and revokes and supersedes all prior agreements, oral or written, between them and may not be modified or amended except in a writing signed by both parties hereto that specifically refers to this Agreement. This Agreement shall take precedence over any other documents that may be in conflict herewith. If any one or more provisions contained in this Agreement are held by any court or tribunal to be invalid, illegal, or otherwise unenforceable, each and every other provision shall remain in full force and effect.

my2cents.idgbooks.com

Register This Book — And Win!

Visit **http://my2cents.idgbooks.com** to register this book and we'll automatically enter you in our fantastic monthly prize giveaway. It's also your opportunity to give us feedback: let us know what you thought of this book and how you would like to see other topics covered.

Discover IDG Books Online!

The IDG Books Online Web site is your online resource for tackling technology — at home and at the office. Frequently updated, the IDG Books Online Web site features exclusive software, insider information, online books, and live events!

10 Productive & Career-Enhancing Things You Can Do at www.idgbooks.com

- Nab source code for your own programming projects.
- Download software.
- Read Web exclusives: special articles and book excerpts by IDG Books Worldwide authors.
- Take advantage of resources to help you advance your career as a Novell or Microsoft professional.
- Buy IDG Books Worldwide titles or find a convenient bookstore that carries them.
- Register your book and win a prize.
- Chat live online with authors.
- Sign up for regular e-mail updates about our latest books.
- Suggest a book you'd like to read or write.
- Give us your 2¢ about our books and about our Web site.

You say you're not on the Web yet? It's easy to get started with IDG Books' *Discover the Internet,* available at local retailers everywhere.

CD-ROM Installation Instructions

The *Visual Basic 6 Database Programming Bible* contains sample files that are designed to be used with Visual Basic, SQL Server 7, Oracle 8*i*, and Access 2000. These files are stored in the \VB6DB directory and do not require any special installation procedures, other than the sample database. Simply copy the files to a directory on your hard disk and load them using Visual Basic. The instructions for installing the sample databases are listed below.

The CD-ROM also contains a full version of the book in electronic format, which can be read with Adobe Acrobat Reader.

\VB6DB

In the `\VB6DB` directory the following subdirectories are included:

- `Chapter07`: Codeless Database Programming
- `Chapter08`: More About Bound Controls
- `Chapter09`: Programming with Data Environments
- `Chapter10`: Building Reports with Microsoft Data Reporter
- `Chapter12`: Connecting to a Database
- `Chapter13`: Using Commands and Stored Procedures
- `Chapter14`: Working with Recordsets Part–I
- `Chapter15`: Working with Recordsets Part–II
- `Chapter16`: Working with Recordsets Part–III
- `Chapter17`: Building Your Own Bound Controls
- `Chapter18`: Creating COM+ Database Transactions
- `Chapter19`: Taking Advantage of Message Queues
- `Chapter20`: Introducing XML
- `Chapter21`: The Document Object Model
- `Chapter22`: Integrating XML with Internet Explorer 5
- `Chapter25`: Stored Procedures in SQL Server
- `Chapter26`: Overview of Oracle8*i*
- `Chapter29`: Overview of Microsoft Jet
- `SampleDB`: contains the information to build the sample database used in this book.

Each directory contains the sample code discussed in the corresponding chapter. The `SampleDB` directory contains the SQL statements and sample data that you can use to create the sample database introduced in this book.

Installing the Sample Databases

Follow these instructions for the specific database server to create the sample database.

Access

The file `ToyDB.MDB` contains the sample database in its entirety. Simply copy it to your hard disk and it is ready to use.

Oracle8*i*

Start SQL*Plus with a user that has DBA privileges and run the `Oracle.SQL` script to create the data structures.

SQL Server 7

Create a database using Enterprise Manager (see Chapter 24) and then run the `SQLServer.SQL` script in Query Analyzer to create the data structures.